AF213611

HISTORY OF WOMEN IN THE UNITED STATES

HISTORY OF WOMEN IN THE UNITED STATES

Historical Articles on Women's Lives and Activities

Edited by Nancy F. Cott

Series ISBN 3-598-41454-4

1. Theory and Method in Women's History
   ISBN 3-598-41455-2 Part 1
   ISBN 3-598-41477-3 Part 2

2. Household Constitution and Family Relationships
   ISBN 3-598-41456-0

3. Domestic Relations and Law
   ISBN 3-598-41457-9

4. Domestic Ideology and Domestic Work
   ISBN 3-598-41458-7 Part 1
   ISBN 3-598-41475-7 Part 2

5. The Intersection of Work and Family Life
   ISBN 3-598-41459-5 Part 1
   ISBN 3-598-41476-5 Part 2

6. Working on the Land
   ISBN 3-598-41460-9

7. Industrial Wage Work
   ISBN 3-598-41461-7 Part 1
   ISBN 3-598-41693-8 Part 2

8. Professional and White-Collar Employments
   ISBN 3-598-41462-5 Part 1
   ISBN 3-598-41694-6 Part 2

9. Prostitution
   ISBN 3-598-41463-3

10. Sexuality and Sexual Behavior
    ISBN 3-598-41464-1

11. Women's Bodies: Health and Childbirth
    ISBN 3-598-41465-X

12. Education
    ISBN 3-598-41466-8

13. Religion
    ISBN 3-598-41467-6

14. Intercultural and Interracial Relations
    ISBN 3-598-41468-4

15. Women and War
    ISBN 3-598-41469-2

16. Women Together: Organizational Life
    ISBN 3-598-41470-6

17. Social and Moral Reform
    ISBN 3-598-41471-4 Part 1
    ISBN 3-598-41695-4 Part 2

18. Women and Politics
    ISBN 3-598-41472-2 Part 1
    ISBN 3-598-41697-0 Part 2

19. Woman Suffrage
    ISBN 3-598-41473-0 Part 1
    ISBN 3-598-41696-2 Part 2

20. Feminist Struggles for Sex Equality
    ISBN 3-598-41474-9

HISTORY OF WOMEN IN THE UNITED STATES

Historical Articles on Women's Lives and Activities

3. Domestic Relations and Law

Edited with an Introduction by

Nancy F. Cott

Yale University

K · G · Saur

Munich · London · New York · Paris 1992

Publisher's Note

The articles and chapters which comprise this collection originally appeared in a wide variety of publications and are reproduced here in facsimile from the highest quality offprints and photocopies available. The reader will notice some occasional marginal shading and text-curl common to photocopying from tightly bound volumes. Every attempt has been made to correct or minimize this effect.

Copyright information for articles reproduced in this collection appears at the end of this volume.

Library of Congress Cataloging-in-Publication Data

History of women in the United States : historical articles on
women's lives and activities / edited with
an introduction by Nancy F. Cott.

p. cm.

Includes bibliographical references and indexes.

Contents: 1. Theory and method in women's history -- 2. Household constitution and family relationships -- 3. Domestic relations and law -- 4. Domestic ideology and domestic work -- 5. The intersection of work and family life -- 6. Working on the land -- 7. Industrial wage work -- 8. Professional and white-collar employments -- 9. Prostitution -- 10. Sexuality and sexual behavior -- 11. Women's bodies -- 12. Education -- 13. Religion -- 14. Intercultural and interracial relations -- 15. Women and war -- 16. Women together -- 17. Social and moral reform -- 18. Women and politics -- 19. Women suffrage -- 20. Feminist struggles for sex equality.

ISBN 3-598-41454-4 (set)

1. Women--United States--History. 2. Women--United States--Social conditions. I. Cott, Nancy F.

HQ1410.H57 1992

305.4'0973--dc20 92-16765

CIP

Die Deutsche Bibliothek - CIP - Einheitsaufnahme

History of women in the United States: historical articles
on women's lives and activities / ed. with an introd. by Nancy F. Cott.
- Munich ; London ; New York ; Paris : Saur.

ISBN 3-598-41454-4

NE: Cott, Nancy F. (Hrsg.)

Vol 3. Domestic relations and law. - 1992

ISBN 3-598-41457-9

∞
Printed on acid-free paper/Gedruckt auf säurefreiem Papier

All Rights Strictly Reserved/Alle Rechte vorbehalten
K.G.Saur Verlag GmbH & Co. KG, Munich 1992
A Reed Reference Publishing Company

Printed in the United States of America
Printed/Bound by Edwards Brothers Incorporated, Ann Arbor

ISBN 3-598-41457-9 (vol. 3)
ISBN 3-598-41454-4 (series)

Contents

Series Preface

In the space of one generation, women's history has become the fastest-growing area of scholarship in U.S. history. Since the resurgence of feminism in the late 1960s and 1970s, insistent questions about the historical meanings of "woman's place" have sowed and reaped a garden of scholarship. Where scholarly works used to be bare of mention of women, academic enterprise has now produced a vigorous growth of books and articles, bringing to light diverse women of every region, race, class and age. This research is marked by a renovating intent that refuses to accept as "human" history a history of men. Interest is lively and debate is stimulating and sought after: attendance at the Berkshire Conference on the History of Women rivals the size of the annual convention of the American Historical Association.

While books in women's history are daily increasing in numbers and strength, as in any fast-developing field the scholarly literature in the form of articles is most expansive and up-to-the-minute. All the history journals now publish articles on women's work, domestic settings, family relations, household matters, female politics and organizations and so forth, and new journals have sprung into being to concentrate on such topics. Women's historians publish in numerous regional and thematic history journals as well as in feminist outlets and in journals of other social science disciplines. This series brings together a collection of outstanding articles from the field, almost all written in the past twenty years and more than half published during the 1980s. It brings together, in volumes organized by topic, essays otherwise widely dispersed. These volumes reprint only articles that originally appeared in journals, not chapters of books; review articles are not included. Articles have been chosen for overall quality and for range. Each one was chosen for one or more of the following reasons: because it is the standard authority on its subject matter; represents an important statement on a topic by a recognized scholar; presages an important book to come; provides a first look at new evidence or new methods; or opens an untapped area or new controversy. Older articles have been reprinted if their data or interpretation have not been surpassed or if they marked an important stage in the historiography, even if since superseded.

The historical coverage of the series extends from the Revolutionary era to the 1960s. The articles themselves are dated from the 1940s through 1988. Volumes are organized by topic rather than time period. Within each volume, the articles are ordered chronologically (with respect to substance), so that the whole can be read as an historical overview. The only exception to this ordering principle is volume 1, on Theory and Method, in which the contents are arranged in order of publication. Within each volume there is an attempt to include articles on as diverse kinds of women as possible. None of the volume topics is regionally or racially defined; rather, all volumes are topically designed so as to afford views of women's work, family lives, and public activities which cut across races and regions. Any volume in the series stands on its own, supplying as full a treatment of a designated subject matter as the scholarly literature will provide. Several groupings of volumes also make sense; that is, volumes 2 through 5 all center around domestic and family matters; volumes 5 through 9 consider other varieties of women's work; volumes 9 through 11 concern uses and abuses of women's bodies; volumes 12 through 14 look at major aspects of socialization; and volumes 15 through 20 include organizational and political efforts of many sorts.

As a whole, the series displays in all its range the vitality of the field of women's history. Aside from imbuing U.S. history with new vision, scholarship in this area has informed, and should continue to inform, current public debate on issues from parental leave to the nuclear freeze. By bringing historical articles together under topical headings, these volumes both represent accurately the shape of historical controversy (or consensus) on given issues and make historians' findings most conveniently available for current reference.

Introduction

The laws of marriage, divorce, property transmission and child custody, made by men, have powerfully conditioned women's lives. In the tradition of the English common law--set down in print in a treatise by the English jurist William Blackstone just prior to the American Revolution--a woman, by marrying, buried her own legal individuality in the person of her husband: as she took on his name, he assumed legal responsibility for her economic welfare and rights to her property--including her earnings. The husband also had legal responsibility for and rights over the couple's children. In law a married woman could not own property in her own name; neither did she have the legal individuality to sue in court, make a contract, or write a will of her own (although she could do these things in alliance with her husband, under his name). A husband was legally responsible for any debts his wife might incur, and, traditionally, for crimes she might commit. Because of the husband's responsibility for his wife's economic survival and her inability to amass property for herself, the common law also provided widows with "dower" rights. Dower customarily meant that a widow was awarded use (not outright ownership) of one-third of her dead husband's property during her remaining years of life; after her death the inheritors would come into possession of the whole estate. Dower rights protected wives whose husbands died without having made wills, and wives with ungenerous husbands--for while a husband might by will leave his wife more (his entire estate, if he wished), he could not leave her less than her dower. These traditions of English common law were the basis for legal practice in the English colonies in America and in the new United States.

Modern scholars have generally assumed that husbands' legal right to control their wives' property and children--in an era when almost everyone married--was a central support to male domination of economic and political power in society. Therefore the study of married women's creation of "separate estates" for themselves under the common law system, through resort to equity courts and through the use of legal inventions such as ante-nuptial contracts and trusteeships has been of major interest to historians of women. The equation of property-owning with personal independence has been so essential to Anglo-American concepts of liberty and freedom that it has inevitably affected historians' views of women's power and autonomy. Married women's increasing ability to own and manipulate property through the legal system has been viewed as an unquestioned gain in economic freedom and status for women, although the concomitant decline in the custom of dower made widows' outlooks much less secure. Through the nineteenth century and into the twentieth the legal "disabilities" (so called by women who crusaded to remove them) imposed on wives by the common law gradually were eliminated, just as the common law more generally was superseded by statutory innovations and judicial decisions which attuned the American legal system to a modern commercial and industrial society. All of these changes took place piecemeal, at the state level: the laws and judicial decisions regarding marriage, divorce, child custody and property transmission were made in state legislatures and courts. Despite differences in pace and to some extent in substance, the direction of change in all states was the same, so that by the time a constitutional amendment in 1920 eliminated discrimination by sex in the right to vote, state laws generally regarded women, even married women, as individuals similar to men in the most significant marital and property rights.

The process of eliminating married women's legal handicaps--or, as it might alternatively be phrased, enabling wives to have economic and legal individuality in the eyes of the law--was a protracted one, in which many motives figured. Because advocates of "woman's rights" in nineteenth-century America campaigned to end the common-law treatment of wives, and state legislatures did pass married women's property acts establishing wives' rights to own property in their own names, to make contracts and appear in court to defend their estates, and to keep possession of their own earnings, it was often assumed, retrospectively (in the twentieth century), that woman's rights agitation was the *cause* of the new legal disposition. More recent scholars of women's history have discovered, as several articles in this volume indicate, that the process was more complicated. Besides the woman's rights agitation, the establishment of women's legal individuality began in a general move toward codification of American statutes from out of English common law, took part in a general reorientation of the legal system to deal with an era in which capital and wages rather than real estate principally defined property, and involved male legislators' willingness to protect husbands from debt prosecutions by insulating some of their property in their wives' names.

This volume includes important articles treating the complicated question of women's legal status over time and how it changed. Beyond property issues, some of the articles analyze change in the legal structure of marriage, especially by focusing on the increasing availability and changing implications of divorce. Painting the portrait of change in the legal system's treatment of women (namely wives) from roughly 1820 to 1920 in broad strokes, gain on several fronts seems prominent. New state legislation eliminated the tradition that a wife's property and earnings belonged to her husband, and enabled her to act in business and in the courts as an individual; moreover, other state legislation and judicial decision-making expanded the grounds for divorce, so that women were not necessarily tied for life to cruel or unstable husbands; and judges also overrode the common-law assumption that the father "owned" the offspring of a marriage by more and more frequently awarding custody of young children to the mother in cases of separation or divorce. Yet, as these articles inform us, the meaning of these changes was more complex and ambiguous than simply gain for women's power in the family as against men's, since the process of change involved a reorientation of all individuals' relation to the legal system and to the state.

Domestic Relations and Law

Women and Property in South Carolina: The Evidence from Marriage Settlements, 1730 to 1830

Marylynn Salmon

DURING the eighteenth and early nineteenth centuries two distinct sets of legal principles—those of the common law and equity law—governed the status of women in the British-American colonies and the American states. Complications arose when the rules contradicted each other, as they did, for example, with regard to property ownership. Under the common law, a married woman (feme covert) could not own property, either real or personal. All personalty a woman brought to marriage became her husband's. He could spend her money, sell her stocks or slaves, and appropriate her clothing and jewelry. He gained managerial rights to her lands, houses, and tenements and decided if land was to be farmed by the family or leased.[1] He also controlled the rents and profits from all real estate. With regard to conveyances, however, women held a single note of power. No husband could sell real property without the consent of his wife. The common law sanctioned conveyances only when wives freely agreed to them, although "free" consent was sometimes quite difficult to determine in court.[2]

Ms. Salmon is a member of the Department of History at the University of Maryland Baltimore County. She wishes to thank Mary Maples Dunn, Mary Beth Norton, and the members of the 1979-1980 seminar of the Philadelphia Center for Early American Studies for their critical comments on this and an earlier version of the article. The invaluable technical assistance of Joseph O'Rourke is also gratefully acknowledged.

[1] William Blackstone, *Commentaries on the Laws of England* . . ., 4 vols. (Oxford, 1765-1769), II, 132, 136, 255, 293, 355; Thomas Smith, *De Republica Anglorum: A Discourse on the Commonwealth of England*, ed. Leonard Alston (Cambridge, 1906), 127; William Holdsworth, *A History of English Law*, 16 vols. (London, 1903-1966), III (5th ed.), 193, 195-196, 249; *An Essay on the Nature and Operation of Fines and Recoveries* (London, 1728), 68-69; *The Laws Respecting Women* . . . (Dobbs Ferry, N.Y., 1974 [orig. publ. London, 1777]), 181; James Kent, *Commentaries on American Law*, 4 vols. (New York, 1826-1830), II, 151-154; Samuel Church, "Lectures on Law by Tapping Reeve, Esq." (1806) (unpubl. notebook, Cornell University Law Library, Ithaca, N.Y.).

[2] Tapping Reeve, *The Law of Baron and Femme, of Parent and Child, of Guardian and Ward, of Master and Servant, and of the Powers of Courts of Chancery* . . . (New Haven, Conn., 1816), 98; *Laws Respecting Women*, 70-72; Marylynn Salmon, "The Property Rights of Women in Early America: A Comparative Study" (Ph.D. diss., Bryn Mawr College, 1980), 27-84.

Since women could not own property under the common law, they could not exercise legal controls over it. A feme covert could not make a legally binding contract. She could not sell or mortgage property that she brought to the marriage or that she and her husband acquired. She possessed no power to execute a deed of gift or write a will unless her husband consented, and even then her power was restricted to personal property. During widowhood, the law allowed women only a life interest in one-third of the family's real property, no matter what proportion of that property had been hers before marriage. With regard to personal property, widows could claim absolute ownership of one-third, but only if the estate were free of debts. If a husband died heavily indebted or insolvent, his wife lost all her personal property (and in some jurisdictions her real property as well), even though she had exercised no control over the accumulation of her husband's debts. Regarding property, then, women were virtually powerless under the common law.[3]

Equity law as administered by the British and American courts of chancery was not similarly harsh. Through formal contracts called marriage settlements, femes covert owned and controlled property.[4] In their various forms, marriage settlements allowed women full or partial managerial rights over property. Separate clauses gave women the right to sell or mortgage property, give it away, or write wills. Some marriage settlements stated explicitly the traditional rights that men relinquished by signing them. Many settlements barred husbands from "intermeddling" with their wives' estates in any way and, perhaps most important, stated that settlement property could not be taken by creditors to pay a husband's debts. Separate estates for women also frequently included clauses guaranteeing the inheritances of children. Once women or their

[3] No comprehensive study of the legal status of early American women has yet been written. The best general discussion is still Reeve, *Baron and Femme. Laws Respecting Women* is a good survey of English law and is available in a reprint edition. Holdsworth's impressive overview of the history of English law is also helpful. The most commonly cited discussion of the legal rights of early American women is Richard B. Morris, *Studies in the History of American Law, with Special Reference to the Seventeenth and Eighteenth Centuries* (New York, 1930), chap. 3. This should be used with care, however, since it is only a cursory study and unreliable.

[4] Holdsworth cited *Avenant* v. *Kitchen* (1581) as the first case in which an equity court supported the right of a woman to hold property separately from her husband by the force of a prenuptial contract. Within a short period of time, the Chancery Court permitted women to exert active control over settlements. Decisions recognized the right of women to enter into binding contracts (1582), write wills (1594), make presents to their husbands (1614), and convey to strangers (1619). Holdsworth, *History of English Law*, I (7th rev. ed.), 494, V, 303, 310-315; Richard Francis, *Maxims of Equity* . . . (London, 1728), 5; Reeve, *Baron and Femme*, 222-223, 238; *Laws Respecting Women*, 179; Zephaniah Swift, *A System of the Laws of the State of Connecticut: In Six Books*, 2 vols. (New Haven, Conn., 1795-1796), I, 200-201.

relations protected property from the possible business misfortunes of a husband, it could safely be passed through the maternal line.

Marriage settlements were designed, then, to serve several functions. They gave women a measure of financial security during marriage and widowhood. They protected a portion of family property from creditors. They provided grandparents with the assurance that family fortunes would not be spent before grandchildren came of age. Historians of aristocratic society in seventeenth- and eighteenth-century England have tended to emphasize this last function of marriage settlements. They have found that beginning in the late sixteenth century, fathers created trust estates for their daughters in an effort to prevent sons-in-law from controlling, and perhaps squandering, family fortunes. For a man who wanted to guarantee the inheritances of his grandchildren, a trust presented an alternative to turning property over to an outsider—his daughter's husband. According to this interpretation, the primary purpose of English marriage settlements was to create and preserve large family estates.[5]

Historians of early America have tended to discount the importance of the British perspective on trust estates. Instead, scholars such as Richard B. Morris and Mary R. Beard stressed the utilitarian function of settlements for the feme covert. Pointing to the existence of equity law and trust estates, Beard and Morris claimed that in America (and Beard also applied the argument to England), women functioned virtually on a legal par with men. If a woman could own property, make contracts, and write wills under equity law, then common law restrictions on her activities lost meaning.[6] Thus the most generally accepted interpretation of equity law in America has emphasized its ability to elevate the legal status of women from subservience to relative independence.

Historians of women in early America have relied on this interpretation of equity law to help define the status of the feme covert. The hypothesis of equality has contributed to the assumption that colonial women enjoyed a legal and social status superior to that of both their English contemporaries and their nineteenth-century descendants.[7] For if, as

[5] Christopher Clay, "Marriage, Inheritance, and the Rise of Large Estates in England, 1660-1815," *Economic History Review*, 2d Ser., XXI (1968), 503-518; H.J. Habakkuk, "Marriage Settlements in the Eighteenth Century," Royal Historical Society, *Transactions*, 4th Ser., XXXII (1950), 15-31; Lawrence Stone. *The Crisis of the Aristocracy, 1558-1641* (Oxford, 1965).

[6] Morris, *History of American Law*, 126-155; Beard, *Woman as Force in History: A Study in Traditions and Realities* (New York, 1962 [orig. publ. 1946]).

[7] In fact, historians usually depict the colonial period as a golden age for women. In addition to Morris's legal study, books by Elisabeth Anthony Dexter (*Colonial Women of Affairs: Women in Business and the Professions in America before 1776* [Boston, 1924] and *Career Women of America, 1776-1840* [Francestown, N.H., 1950]) and Mary Sumner Benson (*Women in Eighteenth-Century America: A Study of Opinion and Social Usage* [New York, 1935]) helped to build the theory of a liberal legal and social climate for colonial women. More recently the theory has been supported by the work of John Demos in *A Little Commonwealth: Family Life in Plymouth Colony* (New York, 1970); Roger Thompson in *Women in Stuart*

Morris claimed, marriage settlements were "widely employed" in America, and if, as Beard believed, they were interpreted liberally, then women of all classes in the colonies enjoyed the rights of wealthy Englishwomen. In the view of these historians, the common use of settlements in the eighteenth century reflected a beneficial legal climate for American women. Similarly, the decline of equity law in the nineteenth century demonstrated the advantages enjoyed by eighteenth-century matrons.[8]

Neither Morris nor Beard studied marriage settlements in detail. They knew that equity law contained rules allowing women to own property and that some marriage settlements existed, but they did not know how frequently settlements were employed or what specific powers women exercised through them. Historical understanding of equity law and the use of marriage settlements has been based on scant research and impressionistic evidence. The current lively debate over the nature of women's legal and social status in the colonial and early national periods makes it important, however, to understand equity law more precisely.[9] We must learn who used marriage settlements, how often they were used, and for what purposes. Such information should reveal the degree to

---

England and America: A Comparative Study (London, 1974); Mary P. Ryan in *Womanhood in America: From Colonial Times to the Present* (New York, 1975); Ann D. Gordon and Mari Jo Buhle in "Sex and Class in Colonial and Nineteenth-Century America," in Berenice A. Carroll, ed., *Liberating Women's History: Theoretical and Critical Essays* (Urbana, Ill., 1976), 278-300; and Joan R. Gundersen and Gwen Victor Gampel, "Married Women's Legal Status in Eighteenth-Century New York and Virginia," *William and Mary Quarterly*, 3d Ser., XXXIX (1982), 114-134. In her pathbreaking study of American women between 1750 and 1800, Mary Beth Norton revises significantly the old interpretations, for she concludes that women possessed both a low status and a low self-image during the colonial period. The status of women changed as a result of the American Revolution, improving on some points such as self-esteem, but remaining ambiguous in the areas of politics and law (*Liberty's Daughters: The Revolutionary Experience of American Women, 1750-1800* [Boston, 1980]). Linda K. Kerber has also demonstrated that women's lives changed after the American Revolution, but she emphasizes points on which women lost rights, especially in the law (*Women of the Republic: Intellect and Ideology in Revolutionary America* [Chapel Hill, N.C., 1980]). Kerber's contention that the legal status of women deteriorated in the 19th century is not proved. For a revisionist study of the legal rights of women, see Salmon, "Property Rights."

[8] Morris, *History of American Law*, 138; Beard, *Woman as Force*, 151.

[9] There appears to be a growing split among women's historians concerning the changing status of women after 1800. Scholars such as Norton, and Kerber to a lesser degree, see a widening of the female sphere during the early national period away from the subservience and dependency of colonial women. Other historians still maintain that colonial women occupied a privileged position compared to 19th-century women, who lost status and economic power with the rise of industrialism. Most recently, Gerda Lerner has made the latter argument in a review of the Norton and Kerber books, "What the Revolution Meant for Women," *Washington Post Book World*, XV (Jan. 4, 1981), 9.

which settlements provided women with financial security and whether they were written to benefit women, or children and grandchildren, or all three groups.

Before the role of equity law in America can be understood, many separate studies of settlements must be conducted, because each colony and state handled principles of equity law differently.[10] Large numbers of settlement deeds must also be scrutinized, even though the informality of American recording practices frequently makes such analysis difficult. This article reports findings for South Carolina, for which a wealth of information is available. The extent of the documentation makes South Carolina a good place to begin an investigation into the nature of equity law. The legal record reveals remarkably liberal attitudes toward women's property rights—quite possibly the most liberal of all the colonies and states, although that supposition must be tested by comparative study.[11]

In 1720 the colony established a court of chancery that handled cases concerning marriage settlements in a sophisticated manner, imitating the English Chancery Court in style and decisions.[12] The court kept good records and remained active throughout the colonial and early national periods. The legislature did not require registration of marriage settlements until 1785, but before that date prudent persons frequently recorded their settlements with the secretary of state in Charleston. After 1785, all settlements had to be recorded within three months of their creation to be considered valid.[13] Altogether some 2000 settlements have survived from the colonial and early national periods.[14] For this study, an attempt was made to discover and analyze all recorded marriage settlements for the colonial and Revolutionary periods. For the period 1785-1830, when the law required settlements to be recorded and the number increased accordingly, a sample consisting of all deeds registered in Charleston in every fifth year has been analyzed, for a total of 638 (see

[10] Some colonies, such as Massachusetts, Connecticut, and Pennsylvania, did not have separate courts of equity in the English fashion. On the problem of equity law in early America, see Stanley N. Katz, "The Politics of Law in Colonial America: Controversies over Chancery Courts and Equity Law in the Eighteenth Century," *Perspectives in American History*, V (1971), 257, and Swift, *A System*, II, 419-460. For a full discussion of regional comparisons on the administration of marriage settlements, see Salmon, "Property Rights," 150-234.

[11] Salmon, "Property Rights," 150-256.

[12] Anne King Gregorie, ed., *Records of the Court of Chancery of South Carolina, 1671-1779* (Washington, D.C., 1950), 5-7.

[13] "An Act to oblige persons interested in Marriage Deeds and Contracts, to record the same in the Secretary's office of this state," in Thomas Cooper and David J. McCord, eds., *The Statutes at Large of South Carolina* (Columbia, S.C., 1836-1841), IV, 656-657.

[14] Marriage Settlements, Vols. 1-10 (1785-1830); Records of the Register of the Secretary of the Province, Vols. A-I (1721-1733); Miscellaneous Records of the Secretary of State, Charleston Series, Vols. AB, BB-XX (1735-1789). All manuscripts cited are located in the South Carolina State Archives, Columbia, unless noted otherwise.

TABLE I
MARRIAGE SETTLEMENT SAMPLE SIZE

Years	*N*	*% of Total*
1730-1740	23	4
1741-1750	35	5
1751-1760	55	9
1761-1770	107	17
1771-1780	107	17
1781-1790	88	14
1791-1800	51	8
1801-1810	54	8
1811-1820	49	8
1821-1830	69	11
1730-1780	327	51
1781-1830	311	49
1730-1830	638	100

Table I). Each settlement gives the names of the parties, the dates of creation and recording, the type of property settled, and the terms of the settlement. Also frequently noted are the occupations of the parties, their residence, their marital status, the name of the owner(s) of the property, and the location and amount of the property.

Proper marriage settlements were complicated documents, usually made in the form of trusts. Before the English case of *Rippon* v. *Dawding* (1769), all valid settlements were required to include trustees who nominally owned the property in the name of the feme covert (the *cestui qui trust*).[15] After 1769, in England and in some American jurisdictions, simple marriage settlements—contracts made directly between a man and a woman without the intervention of trustees—also sufficed to create separate estates.[16] In their handling of simple marriage settlements, equity courts initially referred to the husband as trustee for his wife. This language soon disappeared from most cases, however, perhaps as courts realized the irony of naming husbands trustees for their wives' separate estates. In South Carolina, judges disliked simple agreements, and trusts remained the most common form for separate estates. Trust estates composed 91 percent (582) of the deeds studied. Only 9 percent (56)

[15] *Rippon* v. *Dawding*, Ambler, 565 (1769).

[16] Reeve reported in 1816 that settlements without trustees had become "no uncommon thing" (*Baron and Femme*, 163). One of the earliest American cases dealing with a simple marriage settlement appeared on the docket of the Pennsylvania Supreme Court in 1793. See *Barnes Lessee* v. *Hart*, 1 Yeates 221 (1793). The case is analyzed in Marylynn Salmon, "Equality or Submersion? *Feme Covert* Status in Early Pennsylvania," in Carol Ruth Berkin and Mary Beth Norton, eds., *Women of America: A History* (Boston, 1979), 91-113.

were simple marriage settlements, indicating the reluctance of South Carolinians to abandon the formality of trusts.[17]

To create a trust estate in the normal fashion, the man, woman, and trustee(s) all joined in the execution of an "indenture tripartite," a contract stipulating the terms of the settlement. This form guaranteed the knowledge and consent of the parties, as required by law. In cases involving separate estates, equity standards demanded that men be fully apprised of the terms of their wives' settlements. Judges refused to support a woman who deceived her fiancé or husband into expecting property at marriage, only to secure it to herself through a trustee.[18] They viewed such action as a fraud against the husband's marital rights and held that "he [or she] that hath committed Iniquity, shall not have Equity."[19]

Settlements granting women separate estates could be written either before or after marriage, but most couples executed them prior to marriage. For the period under study, 87 percent (552) of the settlements were prenuptial. There was no significant change in this pattern over time, indicating the constancy of women's desire to secure separate property at the point when they exercised the greatest bargaining power over men.[20] Postnuptial settlements usually resulted when a wife inherited property unexpectedly, or when her husband encountered financial difficulties that made it necessary to secure some family property against creditors.

For understandable reasons, creditors disliked trust estates, particularly those made after marriage. They resented the ability of a feme covert to deny them access to her separate estate and argued that husbands as well as wives could find protection under the terms of marriage settlements. A man who lost his own estate through business misfortunes or extravagant living, they claimed, could fall back on the income from his wife's trust property. Indebted or insolvent husbands might even attempt to preserve a portion of their own fortunes by fraudulently settling property on their wives.[21]

[17] South Carolina courts preferred women to use formal trusts rather than direct agreements with their husbands. In *Barret* v. *Barret*, 4 S.C. Eq. (4 Des.) 491 (1814), and *Dupree* v. *McDonald*, 4 S.C. Eq. (4 Des.) 209 (1812), the judges noted their disapproval of settlements made without trustees. See also the arguments of counsel in *Executors of Smelie* v. *Executors of Smelie*, 2 S.C. Eq. (2 Des.) 72 (1802).

[18] Holdsworth, *History of English Law*, V, 313; George W. Keeton and L. A. Sheridan, *Equity* (London, 1969), 442-443; Reeve, *Baron and Femme*, 236. In the South Carolina case of *Cape* v. *Adams*, 1 S.C. Eq. (1 Des.) 567 (1797), a man tried to create a settlement of his wife's property for his own benefit without her knowledge or consent. The court disallowed his deed.

[19] Francis, *Maxims of Equity*, 5.

[20] Reeve noted the significant role of parents and guardians in bargaining with the suitors of young women (see *Baron and Femme*, 174).

[21] Some men did attempt to settle property on their families after contracting debts. Examples of cases involving fraudulent trusts include *Drayton* v. *Pritchard* (1816), Charleston District Equity Decrees, 3, 161; *Peigne* v. *Snowden*, 1 S.C. Eq. (1 Des.) 591 (1800); *Peace* v. *Spierin*, 2 S.C. Eq. (2 Des.) 500 (1807); and *Croft* v. *Townsend's Administrators*, 3 S.C. Eq. (3 Des.) 223 (1811).

Evidence from South Carolina undermines the argument that settlements commonly benefited husbands rather than wives. Women who wrote marriage settlements usually wanted to control the property they brought to their marriages, not their husbands' property. Eighty-two percent (523) of the settlements studied included only the wife's estate; 11 percent (68), only the estate of the husband; and 5 percent (35), property from both the husband and wife. (In 12 cases, 2 percent, it is unknown who owned the property.) No man put his entire estate into a trust for his wife. These figures demonstrate no general attempt by men to protect their property through marriage settlements. They benefited, of course, when women held property that could not be confiscated for family debts, but they did not usually safeguard their own estates. The need for credit in money-scarce economies gave men reasons to avoid trusts. In addition, by the end of the eighteenth century strict recording requirements made deceit difficult, for creditors could easily discover the status of a family's estate and refuse to extend credit on settled property.

Cases of fraudulent trusts demonstrate judicial solicitude for the rights of creditors. The recording statute of 1785 served primarily as a means of informing creditors about separate estates. In addition, chancellors refused to enforce trusts made to deny creditors their just claims.[22] But the South Carolina Court of Chancery also demonstrated sensitivity to the needs of debtors who wanted to create trust estates. A debtor could execute a valid settlement for the benefit of another person if he possessed assets to repay his debts above the value of the trust property.[23]

In the case of *Tunno* v. *Trezevant* (1804), to take a well-documented example, we find that a man consented to the marriage of his niece only after her fiancé agreed to create a settlement including all her property and some of his own.[24] The young man was a merchant whose credit appeared to be good at the time of his marriage (the uncle made inquiries), but within a year he became an insolvent debtor hounded by creditors who demanded payment out of both his business and his private property. From testimony the court found that he had not created his marriage settlement with any fraudulent purpose in mind. Both he and his bride-to-be had honestly believed that their financial position was secure when they executed the deed. In situations such as theirs, when a settlement was

[22] The preamble to the recording statute of South Carolina noted the problem. It read, "The practice prevailing in this State of keeping marriage contracts and deeds in the hands of those interested therein, hath been oftentimes injurious to creditors and others, who have been induced to credit and trust persons under a presumption of their being possessed of an estate subject and liable to the payment of their just debts" (Cooper and McCord, eds., *South Carolina Statutes*, IV, 656).

[23] Reeve, *Baron and Femme*, 176. In *Croft* v. *Townsend's Administrators*, Chancellor Desaussure ruled against a settlement that included too much of an indebted man's property. See especially his comments on p. 2. In *Taylor* v. *Heriot*, 4 S.C. Eq. (4 Des.) 227 (1812), a legal opinion noted that indebted men were fully justified in creating settlements of their future wives' estates before marriage.

[24] *Tunno* v. *Trezevant*, 2 S.C. Eq. (2 Des.) 264 (1804).

created for the "valuable consideration" of marriage, the court of chancery enforced it against the claims of creditors. In this instance the judges regarded the settlement as "a *bona fide* discharge of a moral duty" and refused to "weigh it too nicely." They did not attach the settlement property to discharge the husband's debts, acting on the fundamental principle that "marriage is not only a *bona fide* and valuable consideration, but the very highest consideration in law; this Court will therefore always support marriage settlements, if there is no particular evidence of fraud made out, showing an intention to deceive or defraud creditors."[25]

Tunno v. *Trezevant* clearly demonstrates the advantages of separate estates for women and their children. Through marriage settlements, families possessed a source of income that was free from obligations of the male head, either business or, if the estate were so designed, personal. Since separate estates could prove so beneficial, it is important to know how many women actually employed them. In this regard the documentation for colonial South Carolina is sadly limited. Before 1785, the absence of a recording statute makes it impossible to discover the total number of settlements. For the period 1785-1810, however, when virtually all marriage settlements were recorded in Charleston and when accurate census records are available for the state, it is possible to arrive at a rough estimate of the number of couples with settlements. During those years, approximately 1-2 percent of marrying couples created separate estates.[26] Settlements apparently were far from the common occurrence that some historians have believed, at least in South Carolina. Few women had either means or reason to utilize them.

Who, then, did create marriage settlements? Perhaps the small number of deeds indicates use of settlements only among the wealthy, landed families of South Carolina in the manner of the English aristocracy. Fortunately, the detailed information available in the deeds allows us to discover something about the status of couples who employed trust estates and marriage settlements. This can be done by analyzing the value of settled property and by noting the occupations of husbands. (We cannot consider the occupations of wives, because few identified themselves by

[25] *Ibid.*, 269-271.

[26] There are no accurate marriage rates for South Carolina in the period under study. Population figures are available, however, and by applying the earliest available marriage rate, that of 1860 (1/115), we can arrive at a rough percentage of marrying couples with settlements. Thus in 1790 when the white population was 140,000, the estimated number of marriages was 1610. Twenty-two settlements were written in that year and therefore the percentage of marrying couples with settlements was 1.4. The next federal census (1800) revealed a population figure of 196,000, making the estimated number of marriages 2254. Since 28 settlements were written in 1800, the percentage of marrying couples with settlements was 1.2. *The Statistical History of the United States: From Colonial Times to the Present* (New York, 1976), 1168; *Population of the United States in 1860* (Washington, D.C., 1869), xxxvi.

occupation.) The following discussion investigates property values first, and then turns to male occupations.

Analysis of property values presents some difficulty. Many settlements do not specify the amount or type of property, but refer to it as "everything" or "all her property both real and personal." When these deeds are excluded, 456 (71 percent) remain for analysis, but even these, while listing specific types of property such as slaves, cattle, or land, rarely give property values. Consequently, only broad, comparative categories will be considered here, and not specific property valuations.[27]

The upper ranks of South Carolina society relied on settlements more often than people of middling status. It appears that 69 percent (316/456) of the estates that specified types of property included property worth more than £500 sterling, or more than five slaves, or more than one town lot with appurtenances, or a plantation of more than three hundred acres.[28] Settlements of more than ten slaves and hundreds of pounds sterling were common. One settlement included one hundred slaves, another £50,000 sterling, and still another forty-four slaves and over four thousand acres of land. A number of settlements included more than ten slaves, land, and at least one town lot with appurtenances—the traditional estate of a wealthy South Carolina planter family.

Although the elite employed marriage settlements most often, persons with small amounts of property also used them. Settlements sometimes included only one or two slaves, a few articles of household furniture, or the woman's clothing and household goods. Approximately 9 percent (41/456) of the settlements included property estimated to be worth less than £150 sterling, or included only one slave, or a part of a house. Another 22 percent (99) included property estimated at £151-500 sterling, or contained two to five slaves, or one house, or 100 to 299 acres of land. The

[27] For determining the approximate values of property included in marriage settlements, the work of Alice Hanson Jones was indispensable. See *American Colonial Wealth: Documents and Methods*, 2d ed., 3 vols. (New York, 1977). Equally useful for determining exchange rates for South Carolina in the 18th century was John J. McCusker, *Money and Exchange in Europe and America, 1600-1775: A Handbook* (Chapel Hill, N.C., 1978), 223-224. Throughout the 18th century, approximately £7 South Carolina currency equaled £1 sterling.

[28] For the purpose of making comparative statements concerning settlement property, I assigned estimated values to certain types of property, based on information provided in Jones, *American Colonial Wealth*, III. A slave was valued at £85, one acre of improved land at £1, one head of cattle at £10, one riding horse at £75, one town lot with appurtenances at less than £500, and more than one town lot with appurtenances at more than £500. Settlements with a single slave were all classified as containing property of a value less than £150, as were settlements containing only part of a house. Settlements including only slaves, numbering two to five, were all classified in the £150-500 range. All pounds are pounds sterling. Although estimated valuations such as these are extremely unreliable for determining absolute wealth, they enable us to distinguish between individuals of great and middling wealth.

settlement of John Darrell and Elizabeth Legeaux is typical of contracts made by persons from the middling ranks of society:

> This is to certify to all whom it may concern that I John Smith Darrell of the city of Charleston and State aforesaid Mariner being now about to be joined in the holy Bond of Wedlock to Miss Elizabeth Browne Legeaux conceiving it just and right that she should continue after marriage to hold what property she might have at that time I do therefore by this Instrument Secure to her and the heirs of her body for ever all right and title to Two Negroes left to her by her Father (Vizt.) the Woman Named Constant and her son Caesar together with any other Issue that the said Constant may have. I do also secure to her her Bed Bedding and the household furniture that she now possesses reserving to myself the Services of the said Negroes during my Natural life.[29]

While Elizabeth Legeaux's estate of two slaves might have been enviable by eighteenth-century standards, it was hardly that of an heiress. The motivation for creating a trust estate of small value undoubtedly stemmed from more than a desire to protect the inheritances of future generations. A woman who went to the trouble and expense of creating a separate estate for her household furniture was concerned about herself and her own position in life at least as much as with the well-being of her children. Although the desire to protect family property for future generations may have motivated some of the wealthy couples with settlements, the preservation of family status was not the dominant consideration for all. Given the wide range of individuals with separate estates—from a woman with one slave, to an heiress with one hundred—we cannot rely on the traditional English interpretation of settlements.

Most women who made settlements owned personal rather than real property. Very few of the settlements included real estate to the exclusion of personalty (10/456), and only one-third (147) included some real estate. The other two-thirds (301) involved only personal property. In South Carolina, women's marriage settlements most often included slaves, money, cattle, and household goods, but not land. Such a pattern may indicate that fathers gave their land to sons, while daughters received slaves or money. In the absence of comparative probate materials, it is impossible to be sure. What is clear, however, is that settlements consisting entirely of personal property appeared twice as often in the sample as settlements including any real property. Given the fact that under the common law men acquired absolute ownership of their wives' personal estates at marriage, while they exercised only managerial rights over real property, this is not surprising. Settlements were more useful to women who owned personal property.

[29] Marriage Settlement between Elizabeth Legeaux and John Smith Darrell (1809), Marriage Settlements, 5, 522-523.

This consideration may explain why a substantial number of settlements involved slaves. Eighty-two percent (372) of the deeds that specify the nature of the property included at least some slaves, and 28 percent (129) included only slaves. No other type of property appears so frequently in the settlements. Moreover, settlements including only a few slaves appeared in the sample as often as those with many slaves. When settlements including only slaves are singled out, we learn that fully 32 percent (41/129) contained five slaves or fewer, and that an additional 19 percent contained six to ten slaves. Women with slaves appreciated the importance of protecting their property.

More may be learned about the function of settlements by studying the occupational status of the men who made them. Of the whole number of deeds analyzed, 68 percent (434) noted the husband's occupation (see Table II). Over half of these (228) involved planters (30 percent, N = 131) or gentlemen (22 percent, N = 97). From the settlements, we can learn no more about the status of these men than the words they used to describe themselves. We do not know, for example, how many of the planters were large landowners and therefore considered members of the social elite. The word planter stood for all farmers and landowners in South Carolina, large and small. The fact that 22 percent of the sample referred to themselves as "gentlemen," however, reveals the high social standing of a significant proportion of settlement holders.

Merchants composed the next largest group of men with settlements, 13 percent (58/434). Perhaps the volatile fortunes of merchant families gave them special incentives to protect their property from creditors. Indentures tripartite involving merchants frequently alluded to the financial risks of trade. The settlement of William Edwards and Elizabeth Moore in 1774, for example, gave the couple joint control over her property—seven slaves and a £6000 current money bond—"unless it shall happen that the said William Edwards shall become Bankrupt or meet with losses or misfortunes in Trade or Business so as to be unable to support himself and family."[30] In that case, Elizabeth Edwards would have full managerial rights, free from "interference" by her husband. In 1787 James Stephenson and Elizabeth Scott were equally careful. Their settlement stated that if James became insolvent "by losses in trade or otherwise by accumulation of debts by accident or misfortune," the trustees would give Elizabeth £350 current money for her separate use, "to the intent that the said Elizabeth may have a resource left."[31] The overseas expeditions of merchants could place wives and children in precarious financial situations. Before Josiah Smith left on a "sea voyage," he took out the 1789

[30] Marriage Settlement between Elizabeth Moore and William Edwards (1744), Miscellaneous Records, RR, 212-213.

[31] Marriage Settlement between Elizabeth Scott and James Stephenson (1787), Marriage Settlements, 1, 338.

TABLE II
MALE OCCUPATIONS

Title	*N*	*%*
Planter	131	30
Gentlemen and Professionals		
Gentleman, Esquire	97	22
Merchant	58	13
Physician	30	7
Lawyer, Judge	13	3
Minister	6	1
Schoolmaster	2	—
Shipmaster	1	—
Officials		
Military Officer	6	1
Government Official	3	1
Shopkeepers and Innholders		
Shopkeeper	5	1
Factor	5	1
Clerk	5	1
Innholder, Tavernkeeper	3	1
Trader	1	—
Indian Trader	1	—
Grocer	1	—
Artisans		
Carpenter	10	2
Cordwainer	9	2
Tailor	8	2
Blacksmith	4	1
Cabinetmaker	4	1
Baker	3	1
Bricklayer	3	1
Butcher	1	—
Cooper	1	—
Breechesmaker	1	—
Watchmaker	1	—
Frame Mole Knitter	1	—
Carver	1	—
Spinner	1	—
Saddler	1	—
Coachmaker	1	—
Wheelwright	1	—
Perriwigmaker	1	—
Shipwright	1	—
Painter	1	—
Distiller	1	—
Mariner	10	2
Free Black	1	—
Total	434	100

equivalent of flight insurance. He settled six slaves on his wife for her sole and separate use, free from his debts, if he never returned.[32] The case of *Tunno* v. *Trezevant*, discussed above, suggests that it was wise for a woman to be wary when entering marriage with a South Carolina merchant.

Almost as many artisans, innkeepers, and mariners made marriage settlements as gentlemen—20 percent (86/434). Although we cannot learn the economic standing of these men from the settlements (and some of them may have owned considerable amounts of property), the fact that they identified themselves by trade rather than by status indicates that they were not a part of the South Carolina elite. Even persons at the lowest social level could make use of equity law, as demonstrated by the appearance of a free black man in the sample. On the basis of male occupations, then, it is possible to state that marriage settlements were not made exclusively by the South Carolina aristocracy. Couples from the middling and even the lower ranks of society also sometimes took the precaution of establishing separate estates for wives.

It is easy to understand why the wife of a merchant or a mariner might want a separate estate, yet not all merchants' wives utilized equity provisions, and not all mariners followed in the footsteps of John Darrell, whose settlement appears above. Moreover, it is not as obvious why a planter's wife, or a physician's or a cordwainer's, might desire this special protection. Why did a particular gentleman and his fiancée step into the office of the secretary of state to register a settlement, given the fact that most genteel families did not? The motivations of individuals cannot be conclusively established; but by investigating the provisions for control and descent of settlement property and by analyzing the court cases concerning specific disputes over settlement terms, we may learn more about the use of separate estates.

Each marriage settlement contained various clauses for delineating control over settlement property. Couples could place property under the management of trustees, or they could give trustees no managerial powers at all, reducing them to figureheads. Some husbands retained control over their wives' estates, and in many cases, as will be shown below, femes covert managed their own property. The powers retained by women became significant for determining their level of independence. Some trusts gave women extensive authority over their own property, while others gave them none at all but instead directed trustees to pay them the rents and profits of their estates. Some settlements gave women one privilege of control while denying others. For example, if a deed granted a feme covert the right to devise, she could not also sell or mortgage her estate; those powers had to be granted in a separate clause. In the same vein, a woman whose settlement gave her rights to the rents and profits of

[32] Marriage Settlement between Mary Smith and Josiah Smith (1789), *ibid.*, I, 446-447.

her property could not regulate the principal, which remained in the hands of trustees who made all investment decisions.[33]

Although most South Carolina settlements were trust estates, trustees rarely managed property. Only 3 percent (16) of the deeds gave trustees sole powers of control. In 93 percent (591) trustees were vested with minimal powers, such as the right to approve a property sale initiated by the feme covert, or were not employed at all. In 5 percent of the settlements (31), control was shared by the trustee and the couple, or the arrangement is unknown. Settlement terms demonstrate that many creators of separate estates, whether parents, relatives, or the women themselves, wanted women rather than trustees—or husbands—to manage their own property. Over the entire period studied, 40 percent (254) of the women administered their estates alone. In 28 percent (180) of the deeds, husbands and wives managed settlement property together, and in 25 percent (157), men possessed exclusive managerial rights (see Table III).

Some change in this division of authority occurred over time (see Figure 1). There was a small but steady decline in the number of women who managed their own estates, offset by an increase in the number of husbands and wives who shared control. With the exception of a slight rise between 1780 and 1800, the number of men who managed settlement property alone remained fairly constant, at about 22 percent. What we see then, is a shifting pattern, away from exclusive privileges for women and toward joint privileges for couples.

A plausible explanation for this pattern may be found in Mary Beth Norton's study of marital relationships in the eighteenth and early nineteenth centuries. Norton discovered that before the Revolution wives rarely played an active role in family business beyond their sphere of domestic concerns. They deferred to their husbands on most questions and relied on men to manage family finances. By the end of the century, however, this deferential relationship was changing. Marriages became more egalitarian, as wives abandoned passivity to participate in broader decisions concerning family affairs. The need for female autonomy in regulating separate estates would decrease as relationships between spouses became more equal over time. Femes covert might no longer desire total independence in managing their own estates precisely because they exercised more authority over the general fund of family property.

For the 180 settlements involving coadministration, we cannot know who actually managed the property. Perhaps men dominated in all cases, and the figure should be combined with that for sole male control. Total freedom for all husbands in this category is unlikely, however, for many of the joint control settlements restricted husbands in various ways. Some

[33] Reeve, *Baron and Femme*, 162-163, 170-173; *Price* v. *Michel* (1821), Charleston District Equity Decrees, 3, 377; Kent, *Commentaries on American Law*, II, 164-165.

TABLE III
CONTROL OF SETTLEMENT PROPERTY

Years	Woman		Man		Couple		Trustee		Mixed/Unknown		No. Deeds
	N	%	N	%	N	%	N	%	N	%	
1730-1740	12	52	7	30	4	17	0	0	0	0	23
1741-1750	20	57	6	17	6	17	0	0	3	9	35
1751-1760	29	53	12	22	9	16	3	5	2	4	55
1761-1770	44	41	25	23	32	30	2	2	4	4	107
1771-1780	44	41	25	23	31	29	4	4	3	3	107
1781-1790	34	39	28	32	22	25	1	1	3	3	88
1791-1800	14	27	18	35	16	31	2	4	2	4	51
1801-1810	19	35	13	24	18	33	2	4	2	4	54
1811-1820	17	35	8	16	16	33	1	2	7	14	49
1821-1830	21	30	15	22	26	38	1	1	6	9	69
Total	254	40	157	25	180	28	16	3	31	5	638

FIGURE 1

CONTROL OF SETTLEMENT PROPERTY

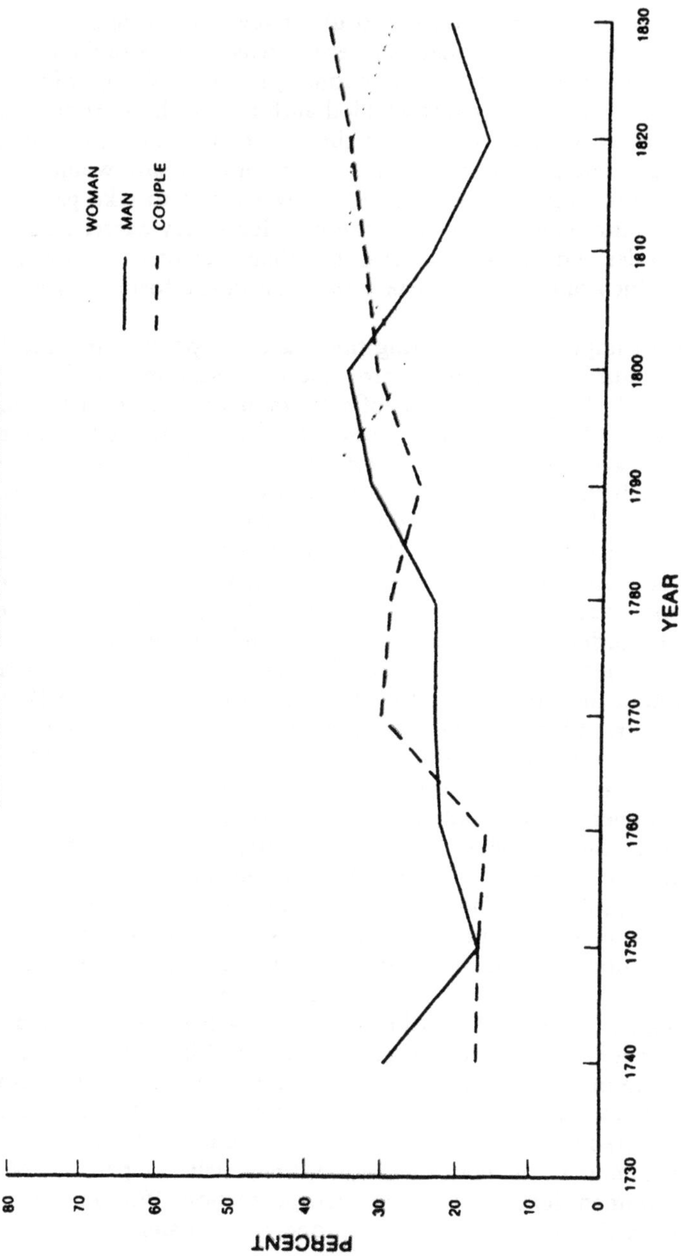

required that the wife consent to all conveyances made by her husband (16 percent, N = 29). In others, either the trustee or both the trustee and the wife had to consent to all transactions (5 percent, N = 9). More important, the fact that a feme covert wielded authority with her spouse says a great deal about the way she wanted the property handled, that is, under her management as well as her husband's. Since many women did possess managerial rights, we can assume they wanted to take part in decisions concerning their property. At the very least they exercised a veto power over sales and investments stronger than that provided by the common law, which offered only weak protection in the form of private examinations.

Most important for limiting the degree of power exercised by men in joint-control settlements were clauses restricting creditors' interests. Although the principal sums of settlements could never be taken to pay husbands' debts, rents and profits could be so applied if the settlement terms gave men access to them. To avoid this danger, yet still allow husbands the use of separate estates, many couples relied on clauses that explicitly denied creditors' rights. Martha Baker and Allen Bolton wrote such a settlement in 1765. They agreed that Allen, a planter, could "have Receive and take the use enjoyment profits and interest" of Martha's £5000 estate as long as he continued "in good Circumstances." If his affairs suffered, however, Martha would be permitted to take over management of her own estate. The settlement specified her right to act "without the Controul or Intermeddling of the said Allen Bolton or any Creditors of his in the same manner as if she were sole and unmarried and no part [of her estate] thereof or the interest thereof shall be thereafter liable to any Debts Contracts or engagements of the said Allen Bolton."[34]

Another woman and her fiancé took similar precautions. Although Thomas Bee considered himself a "gentleman," he and Susanna Holmes thought it wise to place £1000 of her money in a trust as protection against future insolvency. The settlement terms allowed the couple full use of the money, unless "by misfortunes or losses (which God avert) the present occupation calling or business of him the said Thomas Bee as a Planter or otherwise, shall fail or decline very considerably, and there shall be manifest danger, or probability, that he will be reduced and obliged to surrender quit or deliver up his Estate and Effects for the Satisfaction of his Creditors."[35] In that case, the money went into the hands of the couple's trustees, who were directed to pay them the annual interest, safe from creditors' demands. Similar stipulations commonly appeared in settlements throughout the period. Over half (51 percent, N = 326) of the women demanded this explicit protection. Without clauses denying creditors' claims on settlement property, husbands' debts, poor business

[34] Marriage Settlement between Martha Baker and Allen Bolton (1765), Marriage Settlements, 1, 110.

[35] Marriage Settlement between Susanna Holmes and Thomas Bee (1761), *ibid.*, 1, 170.

decisions, fraud, or, simply, financial misfortunes could destroy the utility of a separate estate.

Carefully constructed settlements specified each restriction or power of control separately and included sections allowing or disallowing certain basic changes in the settled property. For example, when creating trusts for the benefit of daughters or other female relatives, some individuals perceived a need to forbid future changes in the settlements. They feared the power of their beneficiaries to annul the protective function of their trusts by conveying them to their husbands or making use of the principal.[36] To protect women from male coercion or prevent them from making damaging business decisions, creators of settlements sometimes employed clauses forbidding changes or certain kinds of potentially harmful dispositions. A deed of settlement might state that it could not be altered in any way, or it might include provisions allowing a feme covert control over the rents and profits but not the principal of her estate.

When settlements did not include provisions restricting the right of a woman to control her own property, she could change or even dissolve her marriage settlement at any time.[37] Although some women wanted to alter settlement terms for the benefit of their husbands, more often wives acted to transfer controls from husbands to themselves. At the time of marriage it might seem appropriate for a woman to give her husband powers of active control over her property, without any reference to contingency arrangements in the event he encountered difficulties. Many women, unlike Martha Baker and Susanna Holmes, did not express

[36] In any case in which it appeared conclusively that a man forced his wife to transact a certain agreement against her will, she was not held liable for the agreement. Reeve, *Baron and Femme*, 165; *Bethune* v. *Beresford*, 1 S.C. Eq. (1 Des.) 174 (1790). The evidence had to be positive, however, for once a woman possessed separate property jurists defined her as a feme sole rather than a feme covert and did not regard her as susceptible to coercion. In the mid-19th century a debate arose in Maryland and South Carolina over the need for women with trust estates to undergo private examinations when conveying their property. Maryland decided that women did not need private examinations because they were legally femes sole. South Carolina decided just the opposite. See *Tiernan* v. *Poor*, 1 G. & J. 216 (1829); *Brundige* v. *Poor*, 2 G. & J. 1 (1829); *Ewing* v. *Smith*, 3 S.C. Eq. (3 Des.) 467 (1811). The South Carolina stance indicates concern with protecting women from male coercion. See Marylynn Salmon, " 'Life, Liberty, and Dower': The Legal Status of Women after the American Revolution," in Carol R. Berkin and Clara M. Lovett, eds., *Women, War, and Revolution* (New York, 1980), 85-106.

[37] Reeve, *Baron and Femme*, 162-163; *Curtis* v. *Duncan* (1821), Charleston District Equity Decrees, 3, 468; *Price* v. *Michel* (1821), *ibid.*, 3, 377; *Garner* v. *Garner's Executors*, 1 S.C. Eq. (1 Des.) 477 (1795); *Dupree* v. *McDonald*, 4 S.C. Eq. (4 Des.) 209 (1812). In *Garner*, the court corrected nonsensical words in a deed of settlement that had the effect of denying a woman all rights to her property until after her own death. The court opinion noted that it was the duty of a chancellor to correct such errors. In *Dupree*, the court interpreted a poorly worded settlement to benefit the feme covert and her son against the claims of the woman's second husband, who attempted to seize all of her property after her death.

publicly their fears for the future. But if a husband later suffered financial setbacks threatening his wife's estate, she might want to rescind his powers. By inserting a clause in her settlement allowing unspecified changes in her trust, a woman who initially wanted to leave property in her husband's hands could do so, confident that at a future date she could use her power to restrict his managerial capacity.

Such was the case for Charlotte Poaug, whose prenuptial settlement gave her husband control over the rents and profits of her real property.[38] John Poaug was a merchant who became indebted several years after his marriage. In 1771, to prevent John's creditors from seizing their estate, the Poaugs changed the terms of their settlement. In the new document, Charlotte retained all powers of control for herself. Clearly, a safety valve of this nature was invaluable for families with uncertain fortunes.

Unfortunately, some individuals did not understand the importance of precision. They wrote loose documents, failing to delineate specific powers of control. Occasionally, friends or relatives failed to clarify the fact that they were creating a separate estate for a feme covert through a deed of gift or a devise. They gave a woman property, meant for her separate use, but failed to say so explicitly. In South Carolina, when settlements were vague and disputes brought couples into court, judges in equity did everything in their power to protect women. The intent of settlements, gifts, or wills, however haphazardly designed, governed judicial decisions.

Court records indicate that by the early nineteenth century, South Carolina jurists interpreted unclear words in a deed of gift or marriage settlement consistently for the benefit of women. For example, following the English Chancery case of *Tyrrel* v. *Hope* (1743), the South Carolina court ceased requiring the specific words "to her sole and separate use" for the creation of a separate estate.[39] Instead, chancellors began to assume that any conveyance to a married woman was meant for her own use, whether the donor said so explicitly or not. If it appeared from other evidence, either parol evidence concerning the donor's intent or the wording of the document in question, that the property was intended for the sole use of a woman, the standard phrase could be omitted.

The South Carolina case of *Johnson* v. *Thompson* (1814) exemplifies judicial practice in this regard.[40] Here a father made a bequest of personal property to his married daughter. Her husband claimed the property and disposed of it. After the woman's death, her children contested his disposition. They stated that their grandfather intended the property to descend to his daughter as a separate estate, free from the control of her husband. In deciding favorably for the children, the court of appeals noted

[38] Marriage Settlement between Charlotte Poaug and John Poaug (1771), Marriage Settlements, 1, 78.

[39] *Tyrrel* v. *Hope*, 2 Atkyns 561 (1743); Reeve, *Baron and Femme*, 164; *Lowndes' Trustee* v. *Champneys' Executors* (1821), Charleston District Equity Decrees, 3, 354.

[40] *Johnson* v. *Thompson*, 4 S.C. Eq. (4 Des.) 498 (1814).

that since the devise was made to a feme covert, its wording had to be examined closely to determine intent. Here the words "fairly inferred" that the estate was designed to be a separate one, and therefore the woman's husband possessed no right to dispose of it. The implementation of this liberal policy in South Carolina indicates strong support for marriage settlements as a legal form.

South Carolina chancellors also interpreted unclear words in settlements for the benefit of married women. When coercion was not an issue, judges assumed that the absence of restrictive clauses meant freedom to exercise control.[41] In *Lowndes' Trustee* v. *Champneys' Executors* (1821), the chancellor declared that it was "immaterial in what form or phrase a trust of this nature creating a seperate [*sic*] estate for the Wife is described—technical language is not necessary—All that is requisite is that the intention of the gift should appear manifestly to be for the wife's seperate enjoyment."[42] An inference, or the circumstances of a gift or devise, could induce the court to rule in favor of separate estates.

The favorable perspective on marriage settlements in South Carolina equity courts is also demonstrated by acceptance of the doctrine called "equity to a settlement." Settlements became so respectable, and chancellors supported them so wholeheartedly, that by the mid-eighteenth century in England and by 1762 in South Carolina, equity courts regarded them as a positive right for all married women.[43] Under certain circumstances, chancellors ordered men to give their wives separate estates. Most often chancellors made such orders when the executor of an estate refused to give a woman her proper inheritance under a will, thereby forcing her and her husband to sue in Chancery for possession. Before awarding them the property, the chancellor would order the husband to settle all or part of it on his wife. The amount of the settlement depended on the man's financial situation. In this way, chancellors knew that they were not giving property to men who could take it for themselves, providing their wives—the rightful owners—no benefits from it.

South Carolina equity courts closely followed English law on the wife's equity to a settlement. Chancellors maintained that any man who sued in an equity court for the property of his wife assumed a moral obligation to settle at least a part of it on her as a separate estate. Thus in *Mathewes and others* v. *The Executors of Mathewes et al.* (1762), the court ordered the

[41] During the period under study, only one case indicated a judicial reluctance to support female powers of control, and there the controversial subject of divorce clouded the issue. See *Barret* v. *Barret*, 4 S.C. Eq. (4 Des.) 491 (1814).

[42] *Lowndes' Trustee* v. *Champneys' Executors* (1821), Charleston District Equity Decrees, 3, 354.

[43] Reeve, *Baron and Femme*, 9, 178-179. Favorable decisions include *McPike* v. *Hughes and Rumph* (1816), Charleston District Equity Court Decrees, 3, 175; *Tatnell* v. *Fenwick's Executors*, 1 S.C. Eq. (1 Des.) 147 (1786); *Greenland* v. *Brown*, 1 S.C. Eq. (1 Des.) 196 (1791); and *Postell and Smith* v. *Skirving's Executors*, 1 S.C. Eq. (1 Des.) 158 (1789).

creation of a trust for Mary Lloyd.[44] Her husband, Thomas, had refused to appear in court for hearings concerning the execution of his father-in-law's estate. What other transgressions Thomas may have committed are unclear, but the court refused to give him Mary's inheritance. The chancellor ordered division of the deceased's estate and distribution among the heirs, "except the Share and proportion claimed by the Defendant Thomas Lloyd in right of his said Wife Mary." His share was ordered invested, and the proceeds paid to Mary "for her own and separate use, and after her Death the said Money to go to and become the property of the said Thomas Lloyd the Son, if he be then living, if not, then the Interest of said Money shall be paid to the said Thomas Lloyd the Defendant during his Natural life."[45]

Chancellors ordered the creation of a separate estate when the financial situation of a husband caused them concern for his wife's well being. Men of good standing in the community were not usually handled as harshly as Thomas Lloyd. When William Henry Drayton, a prosperous planter, member of the Governor's Council, and subsequently chief justice of South Carolina, won a chancery suit against his father-in-law's executors, he did not have to place the property into a trust.[46] Undoubtedly the court believed that his respectable position, added to the fact that his wife already possessed a settlement, made the order unnecessary.

In another similar case, the court ordered no settlement for Mrs. Postell, a plaintiff with her husband in the suit of *Postell and wife, and Smith and wife* v. *The Executors of James Skirving* (1789).[47] The chancellor explained his omission carefully for the record. "The court having in private examined Mrs. Postell, who has attained twenty-one years of age, and the said Mrs. Postell being very desirous that no settlement should be made on her; and it appearing to the court that Mr. and Mrs. Postell have constantly lived together in the greatest harmony; and he being a gentleman of fortune in his own right, it is not requisite that he should make any settlement on his said wife."[48] With regard to the other plaintiff, Mrs. Smith, the court was not so trusting of the husband. She received a settlement, and the words of the chancellor demonstrate his opinion about the importance of female separate estates. "With regard to Mr. O. B. Smith," he wrote, "his wife is not of age to make such request as Mrs. Postell has done, (although the court entertains a similar opinion of him as of Mr. Postell), they find themselves bound to order that the said O. B. Smith do make the usual settlement on his wife, of the fortune she is entitled to from her father."[49] The "usual" settlement gave the Smiths

[44] Gregorie, ed., *Chancery Records*, 507-511.

[45] *Ibid.*, 510.

[46] *Ibid.*, 551-552; Marriage Settlement between Dorothy Golightly and William Henry Drayton (1764), Marriage Settlements, 2, 185-192.

[47] *Postell and Smith* v. *Skirving's Executors*, 1 S.C. Eq. (1 Des.) 158.

[48] *Ibid.*, 158.

[49] *Ibid.*, 158-159.

joint control over her property, with descent to the survivor and then to their children. Presumably in a case of this nature, Mrs. Smith could void her own trust upon reaching her majority. As previously noted, such action could be taken under the law and occasionally was.

On one point South Carolina chancellors were not willing to make liberal interpretations. Unless a settlement explicitly gave a feme covert power to write a will, she could not do so.[50] Women and their benefactors were careful, therefore, to include this right as a clause in settlements. It appeared frequently, particularly during the first two decades under study, when 62 percent (36/58) of the women specified the power to make a will. The figure rises to 71 percent if we include those women who possessed the right to bequeath in the event they outlived their husbands. Over the course of the eighteenth century, this figure fell, but until 1800 more than half of the women with settlements possessed testamentary powers. After the turn of the century the figure declined until fewer than one-third of all femes covert could write wills under the stated terms of their settlements. From 1801 to 1830, 26 percent (45/172) of the settlements sampled gave women this privilege, while 29 percent (50/170) gave it to either the feme covert or the survivor of the marriage (see Table IV). As the number of settlements allowing women to write wills declined, those arranging for automatic descent to children increased (see Figure 2).

The reasons for this decline are not clear. One explanation may lie in the increasing standardization of settlements. As the chancellor noted when ordering creation of a trust for Mrs. Smith, there was a "usual" settlement. It consisted of joint control for husband and wife, with descent to their children. Over the period studied, we have seen an increase in settlements allowing for joint control, as well as descent to children. Chancellors ordered this kind of settlement in most cases coming under their jurisdiction, and the increasing use of automatic descent provisions may demonstrate female acceptance of a standard form on this point. Moreover, as marriages became less patriarchal over the period, women may have regarded the right to make wills as less vital to their financial autonomy. The desire to exert control after death dwindled as more women possessed authority during life. Most mothers undoubtedly divided their estates equally among children, even when they did write wills. The change to automatic descent probably represents little difference in the way estates were administered but does demonstrate a weakening of women's desires for explicit protection and control.

[50] Women without the right to make wills through marriage settlements could bequeath personal property if their husbands consented. See *Grimke* v. *Grimke*, 1 S.C. Eq. (1 Des.) 366-382 (1794), and *Smelie* v. *Smelie*, 2 S.C. Eq. (2 Des.) 66-79 (1802). The law on this point is discussed in Blackstone, *Commentaries*, II, 498, and *Laws Respecting Women*, 178-179. Without valid marriage settlements, however, women could never devise real property. Smith, *De Republica Anglorum*, ed. Alston, 127; *Laws Respecting Women*, 149; Holdsworth, *History of English Law*, III, 185; Kent, *Commentaries on American Law*, II, 130-131.

TABLE IV
DESCENT OF SETTLEMENT PROPERTY

	Woman Controls		*Survivor Controls*		*Combined**		*Automatic to Children*		*Mixed/Unknown*		
Years	*N*	*%*	*N*	*%*	*N*	*%*	*N*	*%*	*N*	*%*	*No. Deeds*
1730-1740	12	52	4	17	16	70	3	13	4	17	23
1741-1750	24	69	1	3	25	71	10	29	0	0	35
1751-1760	26	47	3	5	29	53	24	44	2	4	55
1761-1770	37	35	9	8	46	43	52	49	9	8	107
1771-1780	50	47	6	6	56	52	45	42	6	6	107
1781-1790	39	44	6	7	45	51	43	49	0	0	88
1791-1800	20	39	1	2	21	41	29	57	1	2	51
1801-1810	15	28	2	4	17	31	30	56	7	13	54
1811-1820	14	29	1	2	15	31	27	55	7	14	49
1821-1830	16	23	2	3	18	26	47	68	4	6	69
Total	253	40	35	5	288	45	310	49	40	6	638

* Woman Controls and Survivor Controls

FIGURE 2

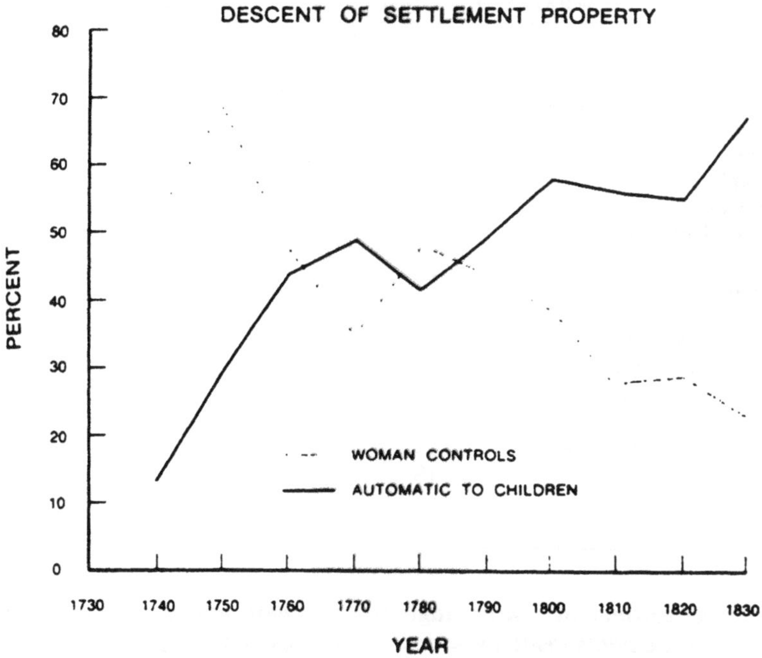

Some mothers were fully aware of the potential power of testamentary rights. Mary Ladson, marrying for the first time in 1760, included a clause in her settlement allowing her to write a will. She wanted her estate to be divided among her children "in such shares and proportions and at such times as the said Mary by her last Will and Testament shall give Limit." The widow Jane Wilkie was equally explicit about her desire to decide what property should go to her children. In 1774 she wrote in her settlement, "All such Child or Children shall possess & enjoy all such part & proportion in the manner & form as she the said Jane Wilkie shall point out & direct." Even after the turn of the century, when fewer women possessed the legal ability to write wills, some women still realized the power they held. Elizabeth Legare wrote in 1825 that she intended to use her estate during her lifetime for the provision of her children "at her own discretion," and not otherwise.[51]

Women who had already experienced married life, such as Jane Wilkie and Elizabeth Legare, took special care to protect their property rights in

[51] Marriage Settlements between Mary Ladson and Thomas Poole (1760), Miscellaneous Records, MM, 41-44; Jane Wilkie and Charles Cogdell (1774), Miscellaneous Records, RR, 314-316; Elizabeth Legare and William B. Legare (1825), Marriage Settlements, 9, 185-187.

TABLE V
WIDOWS AND SINGLE WOMEN COMPARED

	Widows		*Single Women*	
Control	N	%	N	%
Woman	133	52	59	21
Man	50	19	90	33
Couple	55	21	107	39
Trustee	3	1	10	4
Mixed/Unknown	16	6	9	3
Total	257	100	275	100
Descent				
Woman Controls	150	58	53	19
Survivor Controls	10	4	19	7
(Combined)	160	62	72	26
Automatic to Children	79	31	185	67
Mixed/Unknown	18	7	18	7
Total	257	100	275	100

marriage settlements. Most single women were not so careful. Comparison of settlements made by widows and single women proves valuable for understanding some individuals' needs for separate estates. A woman's marital status frequently acted as a motivating force for the creation of a settlement and for the inclusion of female managerial and testamentary powers.[52]

Of the 638 settlements sampled, 532 recorded a marital status for the woman. During the period 1730 to 1780, widows appeared in over half of the settlements giving status, 56 percent (159/286), while single women constituted 44 percent (127) of the sample. Even if we take into account the high mortality rate in colonial South Carolina and the use of the state as a Revolutionary battlefield, the high percentage of widows is surprising. After 1780, the number of widows declined, but they still made settlements in 40 percent (98/246) of the sample.

When we compare the powers of control exercised by widows with those held by single women, it becomes clear that experienced matrons were more emphatic about managing their own property than were women marrying for the first time (see Table V). Widows held complete

[52] For a discussion of one enterprising widow's experience, see Mary Beth Norton, "A Cherished Spirit of Independence: The Life of an Eighteenth-Century Boston Businesswoman," in Berkin and Norton, eds., *Women of America*, 48-67. Although the woman Norton describes was a Bostonian, the same influences governed her actions in creating a marriage settlement as governed the actions of many South Carolina women.

FIGURE 3

DESCENT OF SETTLEMENT PROPERTY

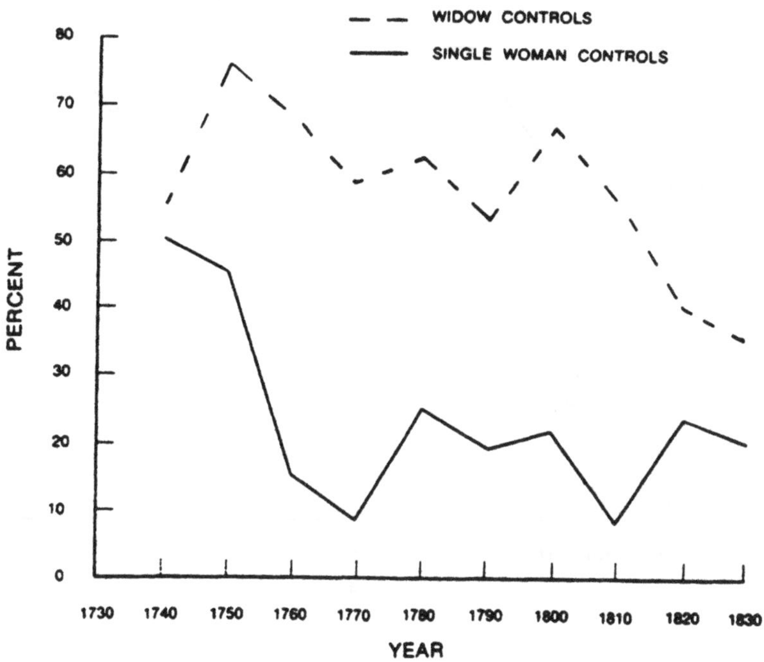

managerial powers and specified the right to make wills at more than double the rate of first brides. Rather than directing settlement property by themselves, most single women divided between giving their husbands authority and arranging for coadministration. They also provided for automatic descent of settlement property in fully two thirds of their deeds, whereas widows did so less than one-third of the time. The settlements of first brides thus demonstrate a less protective attitude than those of experienced matrons. Moreover, after 1740 there was remarkably little change in this pattern either for control or descent (see Figures 3 and 4).

Clearly, the experience of marriage affected the attitudes of women toward property control and management. Before entering a second union, many women demanded the right to administer their own property. Widows' desire for active control may have reflected the fact that their estates were no longer simply gifts from parents and friends but property they had worked for themselves, either alone or with their former husbands. Parents who initiated the settlements of new brides concerned themselves primarily with protecting property from husbands' creditors. They did not seek to provide daughters with the power to control and

FIGURE 4

SETTLEMENTS WITH PROVISIONS FOR CHILDREN

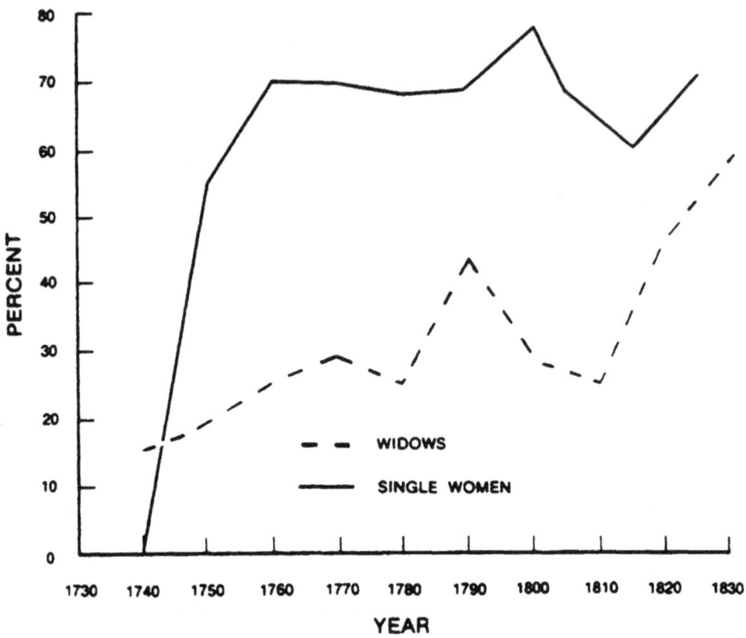

devise property as much as they created a fund for family income. Widows, however, frequently demanded the right to manage the property that they had obtained themselves. Elizabeth Meshaw's settlement in 1736 observed, "The said Elizabeth Meshaw since the Death of her said Husband hath by her great pains care Labour and Industry acquired a considerable addition to the Estate and Interest so left her. . . . [P]articularly [she] hath purchased a Tract of Land containing Two Hundred and Fifty Acres." Elizabeth retained the right to devise her estate as she saw fit, without the interference of her new husband. When Christiana Hoff purchased a slave through her own labor, she wrote a settlement in 1772 explicitly denying her husband any rights to it. The case of Elizabeth Baxter may be most revealing. Before Elizabeth, a "merchant," consented to marry Thomas Robinson, a "mariner," in 1771, she executed a settlement of all her personal estate and business property. She reserved absolute control over the property for herself "in order the better to enable her to support & maintain her & her children & which the said Thomas Robinson is at present rendered incapable of doing."[53] Elizabeth

[53] Marriage Settlements between Elizabeth Meshaw and Thomas Snipes (1736), HH, 27-28; Christiana Hoff and John Hoff (1772), PP, 254; Elizabeth Baxter and Thomas Robinson (1771), PP, 6-8, Miscellaneous Records.

was taking no chances. If Thomas could not support her, she would arrange to do so herself. Women such as Elizabeth, who knew the dangers of marriage and widowhood, took special care for their own and their childrens' futures.

Although the number of widows who provided for children in their settlements increased throughout the period, widows remained less likely than young brides to arrange for automatic descent. Widows such as Elizabeth Baxter had the responsibility of caring for the children of their previous marriages and undoubtedly felt pressure to include protective clauses for children in their settlements, yet did so at half the rate of single women. Thus Mrs. Baxter retained the right to devise her estate. Although she clearly was concerned with providing for her children, she did not think it necessary to arrange for their inheritances when she wrote her settlement. Such dispositions could be made later, when she was closer to death. For the moment she worried primarily about living in a male-dominated world with a new husband who could not support her. The failure to arrange for automatic descent implies that many widows did not view settlements primarily as a means of guaranteeing the inheritances of their children. More than anything else, they wanted absolute control over management decisions and the right to bequeath to whomever they pleased. When they chose to remarry, they did so with strings attached.

Although the comparative powers of widows and single women remained largely the same throughout the eighteenth and early nineteenth centuries, one development in the settlements of single women may indicate an increasing desire on their part to exercise authority. There was a gradual but steady increase in the number of settlements allowing couples joint powers of administration. Single women did not feel the need to exercise sole control to the same degree as widows, but they did become less willing to give husbands absolute managerial rights. From 1730 to 1780, only 32 percent (41/127) of their settlements gave couples joint powers of administration, whereas 45 percent (66/148) did so from 1781 to 1830. The number of men with sole powers fell from 39 percent (49/127) to 28 percent (41/148). With regard to the management of property, therefore, the settlements of widows and single women became slightly more uniform over time, with both groups favoring partnerships in managing separate estates.

Widows, heiresses, merchants' wives, the wives of debtors, and women whose parents warned them about the dangers of married life—these were the South Carolina matrons with trust estates. They were frequently women of wealth with a great deal to lose if their husbands proved wasteful or unfortunate in business. Sometimes they were women of small fortunes intent on protecting what little they had. They were intelligent, or experienced, or protected by concerned parents. Above all, given the legal status of women under the common law, they were fortunate.

Courts of chancery in South Carolina offered liberal support for marriage settlements. Judges regarded separate estates as the right of every feme covert, necessary for women's security in many cases and helpful to society in providing some families with economic support. Judges consistently ruled in favor of the creation of separate estates and enforced liberal precedents for administering them. Realizing the delicate position of married women under the common law, chancellors acted to mitigate legal hardships by wholeheartedly supporting women's rights to separate estates. Judicial acceptance of settlements increased in the period studied, demonstrating expansion of women's property rights under equity law. As seen in the cases of *Postell and Smith* v. *Skirving's Executors, Johnson* v. *Thompson,* and *Lowndes' Trustee* v. *Champneys' Executors*, equity law promoted the legal rights of South Carolina women. Historians of colonial American law may have been overly optimistic in positing wide use of settlements among femes covert, but they were correct in stressing the legal importance of equity law. Women with separate estates in eighteenth and early nineteenth-century South Carolina enjoyed many of the legal rights of men. It remains to be seen if other jurisdictions duplicated this pattern.

Although chancellors supported the use of separate estates, settlements were rare, used either by wealthy women with valuable family interests to protect or by women with an uncommon perspective on their legal status. Equity proved invaluable to women such as the widow Elizabeth Holson, who wanted to enjoy her own estate without "the Least or Smallest Controul or intermeddling" of her husband, but Elizabeth was one of only a small number of women with marriage settlements.[54] We still do not know why so few women relied on separate estates. Either they were satisfied with their common law status, or they did not regard equity law as a viable alternative. In South Carolina, it may be important that settlements were not necessary to confer feme sole trader status. Independent businesswomen functioned under the common law as long as their husbands demonstrated tacit consent to their activities. But more important, the majority of women apparently regarded equity law protections as superfluous to their needs. For women without much property or for women who perceived their legal status as secure, separate estates served no purpose.

We must learn more about the application of common law principles before we will fully understand the meaning of equity law. Perhaps the harshness of common law rules were mitigated in practice, making separate estates largely unnecessary. If most women did not feel a need to use equity law, then we must reevaluate the effect of common law restrictions on women's lives. We must also consider an alternative possibility: that social custom so oppressed women, they did not consider the possibility of employing separate estates. Community scorn or family opposition may have prevented women from acting on their desire for separate estates. There is some evidence to show that the fear and distrust women exhibited by creating settlements antagonized men. The wording

[54] Marriage Settlement between Elizabeth Holson and John Harth (1779), Marriage Settlements, 1, 152.

of settlements, for example, occasionally reveals attempts to appease men's feelings. Some women wrote that their desire for separate estates arose from a fear of the system, not the individual. Such public statements relieved men of responsibility for the anxiety experienced by women and thus saved them face in the community. Otherwise, the mere existence of a settlement attested to the insecurity of a particular woman.

At this point it is impossible to be sure whether male antipathy to settlements prevented most women from making them. Final conclusions await further research on the social customs of families in the South and on the use of common law rules pertaining to the rights of women. Perhaps the words of Sarah Ann Binnikes demonstrate, as well as anything we now have, the attitude of women who wrote settlements. Sarah's settlement stated that its object was to protect her separate interests so that she would not be "defeated or defrauded" out of her property "by the collusive act or device" of her husband. The job of Sarah's trustees was to sue her husband in case he "bargained, sold, or inveigled away" her lands and to demand damages from the court "for any waste which he may commit upon the said lands or injury he may commit upon the said personal or any of the said personal property."[55] There can be no doubt that Sarah Ann did not trust her husband-to-be. It is unlikely that most couples began married life with such distrust. Undoubtedly women as well as men preferred to demonstrate hope, rather than fear, on the day of their marriage. But if experience proved women naive, then we can understand why so many widows insisted on the creation of settlements, and we can also comprehend why they carefully reserved managerial rights for themselves.

[55] Marriage Settlement between Sarah Ann Baxter and Joseph Binnikes (1825), *ibid.*, 9, 159.

"Smiling Through Her Tears": Ante-Bellum Southern Women and Divorce

by Jane Turner Censer*

During the recent upsurge of interest in all aspects of family life, studies of American divorce law have proliferated,[1] but only perfunctory attention has been paid the ante-bellum South's legislation.[2] Old stereotypes of the South as hostile to divorce and possessing extremely restrictive laws have been perpetuated even in the most recent literature.[3] To explore these views, this study surveys briefly early nineteenth century Southern divorce law, and more important, scrutinizes the Southern state supreme courts' interpretations of those laws.[4] These opinions are especially valuable since

---

* The Frederick Law Olmstead Papers, Department of History, American University, Washington, D.C. The author would like to thank Jack R. Censer, Daniel Flanigan, William Harris, Peter Karsten, Willie Lee Rose, James C. Turner, and Bertram Wyatt-Brown for their helpful comments on and suggestions for earlier versions of this paper.

1. Among the historical studies detailing attitudes toward divorce and reforms and changes in divorce law are Nelson M. Blake, *The Road to Reno: A History of Divorce in the United States* (New York, 1962); Richard Wires, *The Divorce Issue and Reform in Nineteenth Century Indiana* (Muncie, 1967), William O'Neill, *Divorce in the Progressive Era* (New Haven, 1967); Christopher Lasch, "Divorce and the 'Decline of the Family'" in *The World of Nations* (New York, 1973); Henry S. Cohen, "Connecticut's Divorce Mechanism 1636-1969," *American Journal of Legal History* 14 (1970): 35-54.

2. "Early Statutory and Common Law of Divorce in North Carolina," 41 *North Carolina Law Review* 604 (1963), and Guion G. Johnson, *Ante-bellum North Carolina: A Social History* (Chapel Hill, 1937), pp. 217-33, show the genesis and early application of one Southern state's divorce laws.

3. Arthur C. Calhoun's dated but unreplaced *Social History of the American Family*, 3 Vols., (New York, 1917) helped further the erroneous notion that divorce was almost impossible in the South. Lawrence Friedman, *A History of American Law* (New York, 1973), pp. 181-84, also implies that Southern divorce law was unusually harsh. Even Michael Hindus and Lynne E. Withey's fine survey of domestic law in Virginia, South Carolina, and Massachusetts, "The Law of Husband and Wife in Nineteenth Century America: Changing Views of Divorce," (unpublished paper presented at the 1978 meeting of the American Society for Legal History), uses Virginia (next to South Carolina the most conservative Southern state in divorce) as representative of all the South. Thus their comments reinforce the vision of the South as an area of unusually restrictive divorce legislation. I would like to thank Hindus and Withey for making their paper available to me.

4. This study is based primarily on 109 divorce cases adjudicated in Southern supreme courts between 1800 and 1860 but also utilized 60 other cases dealing with alimony, property settlements, custody of children and other matters relating to

supreme courts, as appellate bodies, laid down rules serving as guidelines for lower courts adjudicating divorce.

Examining interpretations of Southern divorce laws can also illuminate two other topics of interest to historians. Attitudes toward women expressed in court cases can provide important evidence about how educated, middle and upper class men viewed women. Scholars who have studied Southern male attitudes primarily from literature and polemical writings have found extremely conservative beliefs. For example, Ronald Hogeland and John Ruoff argue that many middle class or wealthy Southern men saw women as merely ornamental and peripheral to society. In another study, Anne F. Scott posits that Southern men's attitudes toward women stressed feminine submissiveness, weakness, and dependence.[5] Judicial decisions offer an alternative view by providing opinions of real men, not distorted either to entertain readers or to promote a particular viewpoint. Although the judges' rulings relate to specific legal disputes and thus are not unchecked expressions of personal opinion,[6] they still offer a valuable counterpoint to literary images of women.

Second, Southern supreme court cases also form a testing ground for Christopher Lasch's assertions about the origins of modern divorce law. Lasch, in an influential article, has linked expansion and liberalization of divorce legislation to sympathy for victimized women, especially those of the lower classes. Although he ties nineteenth century reforms in divorce to a more idealized vision of women, this vision only pictures women as suffering inferiors.[7] Judicial decisions can reveal whether judges saw their task as the protection of lowerclass subordinates. Thus, this study will examine Southern divorce laws and their interpretation at the appellate level, the attitudes manifested in them toward women, and the applicability of Lasch's theories to Southern divorce law.

Modern judicial divorce was a nineteenth century innovation that both North and South embraced. Following English precedent, legislative bodies often decreed divorces during the colonial and

---

divorce. I somewhat arbitrarily defined the South as the eleven states later forming the Confederacy. Since Virginia, Florida, and South Carolina supreme court records reveal no divorce cases adjudicated during this period, I removed them from consideration, but their divorce laws will be discussed. See the appendix for the outcome of these cases.

5. Ronald W. Hogeland, "'The Feminine Appendage': Feminine Life Styles in America, 1820-1860," *Civil War History* 17 (1971): 101-14; John C. Ruoff, "Frivolity to Consumption: Or, Southern Womanhood in Ante-bellum Literature," *Civil War History* 18 (1972): 213-29; Anne F. Scott, *The Southern Lady from Pedestal to Politics, 1830-1930* (Chicago, 1970), *pp. 4-21*. See also William R. Taylor, *Cavalier and Yankee: The Old South and American Character* (New York, 1961); and Barbara Welter, "The Cult of True Womanhood," *American Quarterly* 18 (1966): 151-74.

6. For a discussion of the methodological drawbacks to be faced in using appellate decisions as sources, see G. Edward White, "The Appellate Opinion as Historical Source Material," *Journal of Interdisciplinary History* 1 (1971): 491-509.

7. Christopher Lasch, "Divorce and 'Decline,'" p. 39.

revolutionary periods. By 1800 the Northeastern states possessed divorce statutes and the Southern states had begun to enact them.[8] Much borrowing back and forth of laws took place between the states and territories, but generally Southern territories and newer states tended to pass more liberal divorce laws. During the antebellum period, the Southern seaboard states (with the exception of intractable South Carolina which possessed no divorce law until Reconstruction) slowly liberalized their laws, and the frontier states often further expanded their statutes' scope.[9]

Southern states generally included among the grounds for divorce consanguinity, insanity or impotence at the time of marriage, and bigamy—in other words, conditions that in English law had been grounds for annulment of the marriage. All ten states also decreed adultery, cruelty, and desertion as causes for divorce. The evolution of the cruelty clauses indicates the direction divorce law took.

Nineteenth century lawmakers significantly altered the conception of cruelty and its role in divorce cases. In English law, cruelty endangering life or limb justified a legal separation but not a di-

---

8. Divorce laws were passed in Tennessee (1800), Georgia (1802), Alabama Territory (including both Alabama and Mississippi, 1803), Arkansas (1807), North Carolina (1814), Florida, Louisiana and Virginia (1827), and Texas (1841). Tenn., *Acts* (1799), ch. 19; Ga., *Compilation of General and Public Statutes* (Cobb, 1859), 300-01; Ala., *Digest of the Laws* (Toulmin, 1823), Title 19, ch. 1; Ark., *Laws of the Arkansas Territory* (Steele and M'Campbell, 1835), 218-20; N.C., *Revised Statutes* (1837), ch. 39; La., *Acts* (1826), 130-35; Va., *Acts* (1826-27), ch. 31; Fla., *Compilation of the Public Acts* (Duval, 1839), 81-82; Tex., *Digest of the Laws* (Dallas, 1845), 80-81. In both Southern and Northern states, the legislatures sometimes retained some jurisdiction over divorce after it had been granted to the judiciary. New constitutions or constitutional amendments in Tennessee (1834), North Carolina (1835), Arkansas (1836), Florida (1838), Louisiana (1845), Texas (1845), and Virginia (1850) prohibited the legislature from passing private divorce bills. Alabama retained legislative sanction until the Civil War but after 1819 that power was limited to final action on divorces first granted in chancery courts. Virginia's legislature granted divorces until 1850, but after 1827 a trial by jury of the alleged facts of the suit was required.

9. This liberalization of divorce laws during the period 1830 to 1860 occurred throughout the United States. Although Lawrence Friedman, *History of American Law*, p. 473, dates these changes as occurring between 1850 and 1870, two of his examples, Connecticut and Maine, adopted their liberal laws in 1849 and 1847 respectively. Except a short-lived divorce statute in South Carolina during Reconstruction, divorce law in the South showed little change after the ante-bellum period until the twentieth century. Among the liberalizations in divorce law nationwide was a tendency to broaden the grounds allowing divorce (*a vinculo matrimonii*) by including causes that earlier had justified only legal separation, then called "bed and board" divorces. Florida (1835), Arkansas (1837), Tennessee (1842), and Mississippi (1842) legislated that all causes for bed and board divorces would be causes for total divorce. In Louisiana bed and board divorces could become total divorces after a separation period of two years (later reduced to one year). Fla., *Comp.* (1839), ch. 849, pp. 83-84; Ark., *Digest of the Statutes* (Gould, 1856), ch. 59; Miss., *Code* (Hutchinson, 1848), 397; Tenn., *Statute Laws* (Nicholson, 1846), ch. 133, p. 149; La., *Acts* (1826), 130-33; La., *Acts* (1857), 137.

vorce.[10] In much of the nineteenth century South, cruelty not only became a cause for divorce, but the conception of cruelty was considerably enlarged. Alabama's statute of 1820 requiring cruelty to endanger life was softened by 1832 to "cruel, barbarous and inhuman treatment." Other laws were so worded as to embrace a potentially broader definition of cruelty. North Carolina, Tennessee, Arkansas, Louisiana, and Texas all legislated "excesses" or "personal indignities" rendering cohabitation "intolerable" as well as physical cruelty as cause for divorce.[11] Since these statutes could greatly modify the kind of cruel action required for a divorce, they gave the high courts problems of interpretation.

Many of the changes in Southern divorce laws should be viewed as remedies for "wronged wives," the group most likely to benefit. Cruelty statutes were sometimes framed in feminine terms as Alabama's law decreeing a divorce to the wife when "his treatment to her is cruel, barbarous and inhuman," or Tennessee's statute covering a husband's conduct "which would make her living with him unsafe or improper." Probably shortening the time period constituting legal desertion most aided women. Other less widely adopted statutes primarily applicable to husbands' deficiencies included conviction of a felony, habitual drunkenness, nonsupport, and property wastage.[12]

Southern judges responded to the liberalized laws both in a symbolic rhetorical manner and with a sometimes contradictory willingness to use their discretion to aid or impede women in certain divorce cases. Jurists on almost every Southern supreme court felt compelled to detail their beliefs in the sanctity of marriage and their hesitancy to grant divorces without a clear legal imperative fortified

---

10. George E. Howard, *History of Matrimonial Institutions* (Chicago, 1907), Vol. 3, pp. 52-54, 93-97.

11. Ala., *Digest* (1823), ch. 5, p. 255; Ala., *Digest of Laws* (Clay, 1843), 170; N.C., *Revised Code* (Moore, 1857), ch. 39, p. 251; Tenn., *Compilation of the Statutes* (Caruthers and Nicholson, 1836), ch. 26, sec. 18, pp. 257-58; Ark. *Digest* (1856), ch. 59, sec. 1, p. 447; La., *Acts* (1826), 130; Tex., *Digest* (1845), 80.

12. Ala., *Digest* (1843), 170; Tenn., *Comp.* (1836), ch. 26, sec. 18, p. 261. Desertion in the South involved time periods varying from 5 years in Virginia and Louisiana to 1 year in Arkansas and Florida. Arkansas reduced its time period from 4 years (1807) to 2 (1817) to 1 year (1832), Mississippi from 5 (1822) to 3 years (1840), and Florida from 3 years (1820) to 1 year (1835). Only Alabama lengthened its requirement from 2 (1820) to 3 years (1832). Arkansas, Florida, Georgia, Louisiana, and Mississippi legislated drunkenness as a cause for divorce, and Arkansas, Georgia, Louisiana, Mississippi, Tennessee, and Virginia held that conviction of a felony justified divorce. Tennessee and Mississippi called nonsupport cause for divorce and North Carolina decreed alimony to the wife of a spendthrift. Ala., *Digest* (1823), sec. 1, p. 255; Ala., *Digest* (1843), 170; Ark., *Laws* (1835), sec. 1, 8, pp. 218, 221; Ark., *Digest* (1856), ch. 59, sec. 1, p. 447; Fla., *Comp.* (1839), ch. 843, sec. 1, pp. 81, 83; Ga., *Comp.* (1859), 302-03; La., *Acts* (1826), 130-31; La., *Acts* (1832), 152-53; La., *Acts* (1855), 376-77; Miss., *Code* (1848), 495-97; Miss., *Code* (1857), sec. 4, art. 11, 13, pp. 333-34; N.C., *Statutes* (1837), ch. 39, sec. 4, p. 239; Tenn., *Comp.* (1836), ch. 26, sec. 2, 18, pp. 258, 261; Va., *Acts* (1847-48), 165; Va., *Acts* (1852-53), 47.

by strong proof. Included in many opinions were lengthy digressions on the relationship of laws of marriage and divorce to the well-being of society. Judges bewailed in their decisions the problems of interpreting what they considered to be broad, indefinite laws.[13]

Yet these guardians of public morality actually differed in their willingness to use the powers legislatures had granted them. At one extreme stood North Carolina Supreme Court justice Thomas Ruffin who expressed misgivings about the divorce bill of 1827 that included an omnibus clause authorizing courts to grant divorces "for any other just cause." Faced with almost absolute discretion, Ruffin chose to incorporate the omnibus clause into the existing grounds for divorce and justified his position: "I can not suppose, however, that the discretion conferred is a mere personal one, whether wild or sober, but must from the nature of things be confined to those cases for which provision was before made by law, or for those of a like nature." Thus Ruffin virtually nullified a clause of the new divorce law.[14]

The cruelty and indignities clauses presented the judges with their greatest challenges in construction and their greatest opportunities to use their judicial discretion. By the end of the ante-bellum period, North Carolina, Tennessee, Arkansas, and Texas all had granted divorces on grounds of cruelty without physical violence. The definition of "mental cruelty," then called personal indignities, varied among the states and justices.[15]

The Arkansas Supreme Court probably most expanded the scope of any indignities clause. Although Justice Christopher Scott declared that the clause obviously enlarged the concept of cruelty, he expressed a resolution to retain a strict construction of the law, an attempt that appears belied by his exhaustive list of acts constituting a "personal indignity" including: "rudeness, vulgarity, unmerited reproach, contumely, studied neglect, intentional incivility, injury, manifest disdain, abusive language, malignant ridicule and every other plain manifestation of settled hate, alienation and estrangement, both of word and action. . . ." Such indignities must also be "habitual, continuous and permanent." With such requirements, it is not surprising that Nancy Rose, the plaintiff in that case, obtained a divorce from her irritable and surly husband who encouraged disobedience to her orders among her slaves, labeled her a liar and a "lazy white woman," and slept in an outbuilding during the

---

13. See *Rutledge* v. *Rutledge*, 37 Tenn. (5 Sneed) 554 (1858); *Whittington* v. *Whittington*, 19 N.C. (2 Dev. & B.) 64 (1836); *Moyler* v. *Moyler*, 11 Ala. 620 (1847); *Jones* v. *Jones*, 13 Ala. 145 (1848); *Head* v. *Head*, 2 Ga. 191 (1847); *Rose* v. *Rose*, 9 Ark. 507 (1849); *Hare* v. *Hare*, 10 Tex. 355 (1853).

14. *Scroggins* v. *Scroggins*, 14 N.C. (3 Dev.) 535 (1832).

15. These discussions of the judges' interpretations of law will not only indicate the legal rationale for the opinion but will also include *dicta* about how similar cases should be decided and what would justify a divorce.

last five months of their relationship.[16]

Although other high courts did not admit such a wide array of offenses within the definition of cruelty, Texas, Tennessee, and North Carolina all agreed that some kinds of verbal abuse constituted an indignity. The Texas Supreme Court's interpretation of cruelty most resembled that of Arkansas in the variety of abuses falling under the indignities clause. In 1848 Chief Justice John Hemphill declared, "It can not be doubted that a series of studied vexations and deliberate insults would under our statute be sufficient cause for divorce without apprehension of personal violence or bodily hurt."[17] His interpretation is best illustrated by the 1857 case of *Taylor* v. *Taylor* in which the most violent act had been the throwing of a hat. Chief Justice Hemphill disapprovingly described Charles Taylor's actions:

> after persisting some months in this deliberate course of unkindness . . . he finally assaulted her, and after being guilty of the unmanly and cruel act of throwing his hat in her face, he left the house . . . and has ever since wholly deserted his wife, . . .

Thus Taylor was guilty of such "studied vexations" as would entitle his wife to a divorce.[18]

The Texas cases involving a husband charging his wife with infidelity did not completely clarify whether those accusations constituted legal cruelty. In *Sheffield* v. *Sheffield*, Hemphill found Mr. Sheffield's charges of his wife's adultery and cruelty unproven and commented, "The imputation [of adultery] . . . falls unhonored to the ground, and I can not forbear the observation that there is more cruelty in this blighted charge, unsustained as it was by proof than all the sulkiness and short words proved against [Lydia Sheffield]. . . ."[19] Although Hemphill overturned the divorce that a lower court had granted Mr. Sheffield, his wife had not countersued; and thus the question of whether false accusations of adultery could entitle a litigant to a divorce was not directly addressed. In another Texas case, Elizabeth Simons countersued her husband, Paul, for cruelty in response to his suit charging her with adultery. Justice Abner Lipscomb overturned the lower court's verdict decreeing a divorce to Paul Simons and remanded the case but also ruled that the filing of

16. *Rose* v. *Rose*, 9 Ark. 507 (1849). Pennsylvania also possessed an indignities clause and in 1848, in *Elmes* v. *Elmes*, 9 Pa. 166 (1848), upheld a divorce granted by a lower court and devoid of physical violence, saying, "To render the condition of a wife intolerable and her life burdensome, it is not necessary that there should be blows or cruel and barbarous infliction of batteries that endanger her life."

17. *Sheffield* v. *Sheffield*, 3 Tex. 79 (1848).

18. *Taylor* v. *Taylor*, 18 Tex. 574 (1857). Although Chief Justice Hemphill used the term "assaulted, he did not appear to believe that the husband's actions were menacing or gave the wife any reason to fear bodily harm. Despite the mention of desertion, the time period involved did not attain the legal minimum and could not form a cause.

19. *Sheffield* v. *Sheffield*, 3 Tex. 79 (1848).

a divorce petition alleging adultery did not give Elizabeth Simons cause to cross file on grounds of cruelty. Lipscomb also commented, "If the husband should fail in his suit for the divorce and should continue to asperse her character, publicly denouncing her as an adulteress, how far such facts would sustain the wife's application for a divorce would require some consideration."[20]

Another Texas judge more directly stated that accusations of adultery constituted personal indignities. Berthania Camp who sought to divorce her husband on grounds of drunkenness and cruelty was not successful in her 1853 suit. But in his decision, Chief Justice Hemphill strongly suggested that accusations of adultery would entitle a wife to a divorce when he reproved Mrs. Camp for not specifying whether her husband's abusive language was "mere rudeness" or charges of infidelity justifying a divorce.[21] Although the Texas court granted no divorces based upon charges of adultery as cruelty, the judges' remarks indicated a belief that groundless accusations made outside judicial proceedings constituted an indignity to a wife.

The Texas court probably also considered that charges other than adultery could be cruelty. Although Elizabeth Nogees's case against her husband, Jacques, could rest upon charges of physical brutality, Justice Hemphill also indicated that Nogees's allegations of his wife's thievery were a form of cruelty. Hemphill blasted Nogees's actions in a series of rhetorical questions, "But was there no cruelty in the public accusation that the wife had stolen his money? Did he not intend to blacken her character, destroy her reputation, inflict upon her lasting disgrace and thus poison the sources of her happiness?" Whether such accusations alone could justify a divorce was not in issue.[22]

Both Tennessee and North Carolina supreme courts decided that mental cruelty, usually repeated accusations of a wife's infidelity, constituted an indignity. In *Sharp* v. *Sharp*, the Tennessee Supreme Court granted Mrs. Sharp a divorce from her husband who had publicly charged her with unchastity. Sharp averred his willingness for a reconciliation, but Justice A. W. O. Totten discounted such expressions as motivated by a desire to retain property fraudulently obtained from Mrs. Sharp.[23] Although an earlier Tennessee case, *Payne* v. *Payne*, could rest upon physical cruelty, Justice Nathan Green emphasized the verbal abuse W. L. Payne directed toward his wife, Eliza, "He is in the habit of using language to her, which a

---

20. *Simons* v. *Simons*, 13 Tex. 468 (1855). Despite the reversal of the lower court verdict, Mr. Simons eventually obtained a divorce from his wife. See *Simons* v. *Simons*, 23 Tex. 344 (1859) for the appeal he lodged against the property settlement granting his wife one-half of the property. The Supreme Court upheld the division.

21. *Camp* v. *Camp*, 18 Tex. 528 (1857).

22. *Nogees* v. *Nogees*, 7 Tex. 538 (1852).

23. *Sharp* v. *Sharp*, 34 Tenn. (2 Sneed) 496 (1855).

gentleman will not employ to his slaves; he threatens to drive her from his house; he slaps and chokes her; and . . . he prays to God to deliver him from her." Green avowed himself particularly shocked by Payne's "prayers," declaring that were such a wish heartfelt, Eliza Payne's life might be endangered, but were it merely intended to upset her, "language is wanting to express the indignant reprobation which every virtuous mind must feel, at the brutality, the hypocrisy, and the profanity of the act."[24]

Justice William H. Battle of the North Carolina Supreme Court ruled in the 1856 case of *Coble* v. *Coble* that personal indignities did not require physical violence. Using the Webster's Dictionary definition of indignity, Battle held, "Contumelious words, especially when accompanied with a contemptuous demeanor towards a person may amount to an indignity which would be felt by a sensitive mind with far keener anguish than would be inflicted by a blow."[25] Although Battle's interpretation could include a wide array of vindictive acts and utterances, actual decisions interpreted indignities only as unfounded charges of adultery. And, according to Judge Richmond Pearson in *Erwin* v. *Erwin*, a wife should receive a divorce whether or not her husband actually believed his allegations:

> When a husband charges his wife with infidelity . . . if he does not believe the charge to be true he is a brute . . . and the only motive that can be imputed to him is a desire to be rid of her, and a determination to break her heart or to force her to leave him. If he believes the charge to be true he is dangerous and the wife's safety requires her to leave him.[26]

In either cases, whether the accusation be made in good or bad faith, Justice Pearson ruled that the innocent wife would be entitled to a divorce.

A divorce not upheld by Justice Battle in 1857 reveals the limits the North Carolina court observed in ruling upon indignities. Matilda Everton charged her husband with a host of misdeeds; he mistreated her children from a previous marriage, verbally abused and accused her of adultery, shot a valuable slave belonging to her children, and whipped two slaves near her sickroom window so that their shrieks and moans aggravated her illness. Dismissing the complaint that her husband accused her of adultery as too vague on time and place, Battle also ruled that brutality to her children could not

---

24. *Payne* v. *Payne*, 23 Tenn. (1 Humph.) 500 (1844).

25. *Coble* v. *Coble*, 55 N.C. (2 Jones Eq.) 392 (1856).

26. *Erwin* v. *Erwin* 57 N.C. (4 Jones Eq.) 82 (1858). The Erwin divorce was not completely decided by the high court. North Carolina law allowed appeal to the Supreme Court against a grant of alimony pending litigation to decide upon the sufficiency of the petition. A petition was declared sufficient and alimony upheld when its allegations fell under the grounds for divorce; such charges, however, must be proven in the lower court to obtain the divorce. See also *Harrison* v. *Harrison* 29 N.C. (7 Ired.) 484 (1847).

constitute cruelty to her. He cited the *Coble* case to illustrate how the concept of cruelty had been enlarged but declared that any other indignity devoid of violence "must have as an essential ingredient, a willful and malicious intent to offer insult and do injury, and such intent must be alleged and proved."[27] Thus Mrs. Everton's allegation about the shooting and whipping of the slaves was insufficient because she did not show that her husband's actions sprang from a desire to harm her or to worsen her illness. Battle further defended the husband's position:

> But so far as appears from the petition, he may have had good cause for inflicting punishment upon the slaves and the only error he committed was in using an improper instrument [gun] with which to punish the first and to have selected an improper time and place for chastising the others.[28]

Other Southern state courts also indicated that an expanded view of cruelty was appropriate although they did not specifically decide how far such enlargement would extend. Louisiana law allowed divorces for "excesses, cruel treatment, or outrages," and Justice Henry Bullard ruled in 1836 in *Tourne* v. *Tourne* that "A series of studied vexations and provocations on the part of the husband, without ever resorting to personal violence might constitute that degree of cruel treatment and outrages, . . ."[29] In that case, however, Bullard held that Mrs. Tourne, who had proved that her husband neglected her and allowed their children to speak insultingly of her, had not shown sufficient cruelty to sustain her case. No other Louisiana cases posed the question of what nonviolent acts comprised cruelty.

The Alabama court's position on cruelty was more ambiguous. Although the state supreme court judges granted a large number of divorces involving cruelty, the cases included some physical abuse.[30] The Alabama court did not consider legal cruelty to cover false accusations of adultery. In *Hardin* v. *Hardin*, in which a husband was denied a divorce for his wife's desertion because he had accused her of infidelity, Justice Silas Parsons carefully noted that those charges would not have entitled the wife to a divorce, "We are far from saying that this accusation is a ground upon which the defendant could have obtained a divorce from her husband. However groundless and cruel, it was not sufficient for that opinion."[31] Justice Samuel Rice, however, in a case alleging nonsupport as well as physical violence indicated that a husband's deliberate failure to

---

27. *Everton* v. *Everton*, 50 N.C. (5 Jones Law) 202 (1857).

28. Ibid.

29. *Tourne* v. *Tourne*, 9 La. 452 (1836).

30. See, for example, *Moyler* v. *Moyler*, 11 Ala. 620 (1847); *Hughes* v. *Hughes*, 19 Ala. 307 (1851); *Reese* v. *Reese*, 23 Ala. 785 (1853); *King* v. *King*, 28 Ala. 315 (1856); *Mims* v. *Mims*, 33 Ala. 98 (1858).

31. *Hardin* v. *Hardin*, 17 Ala. 250 (1850).

perform his legal duty of adequately maintaining his wife also constituted cruelty.[32] Despite Rice's remarks, it remains problematic whether the Alabama court, which so often cited British court decisions as precedents, would have departed from the standard British interpretation of cruelty as violence by admitting as grounds nonsupport unbolstered by physical brutality.[33]

The Georgia Supreme Court, despite the standard cruelty clause of its statute, which had no provision for "indignities," "excesses," or "outrages," also lent support to an enlarged view of cruelty. Although the court did not define cruelty until 1867 when the British concept was affirmed,[34] it upheld in 1860 a charge to a jury in which the lower court judge declared:

> whipping or cowhiding . . . is not all that constitutes cruel treatment. The commission of acts that outrage the feelings of modesty and decency, such as threatening to commit, or attempting to commit adultery, or cursing, abusing or using insulting and approbrious language . . . these also, if persisted in and unatoned for, constitute cruel treatment.[35]

Although Mr. Ghoulston, the defendant, specifically contested that charge in his appeal, the Supreme Court seconded without comment that expanded notion of cruelty. Thus neither the Alabama nor Georgia high courts read an enlarged interpretation of cruelty into law, but isolated decisions illustrated a belief that cruelty need not be confined to physical brutality.

Only the ante-bellum Mississippi court strictly adhered to the traditional view of cruelty. Eliza Waskam's suit against her husband for habitual drunkenness, "vicious demoralizing conduct" around their children, and his "violent, abusive and cruel manner" toward her, failed because in the court's view: "mere intemperance in a man's habits, harshness of manner and . . . indecency of conduct are not sufficient. The cruelty must be something more than mere injuries to a person's sensibility or sense of delicacy."[36]

Thus only one of the Southern supreme courts ruling upon cruelty had not favored an enlarged conception. Even those states

32. *Smedley* v. *Smedley*, 30 Ala. 714 (1857). According to Hindus and Withey, "The Law of Husband and Wife," the Massachusetts court in 3 Mass. 321 (1807), ruled that a husband's refusal to support his wife did not constitute cruelty, but in the divorce statute of 1857 nonsupport was included under the desertion clause.

33. The Alabama court cited British ecclesiastical court precedents more frequently than did any other Southern court. See *Richardson* v. *Richardson*, 4 Port. (Ala.) 467 (1837); *Moyler* v. *Moyler*, 11 Ala. 620 (1847); *Jones* v. *Jones*, 13 Ala. 145 (1848); *Gray* v. *Gray*, 15 Ala. 779 (1849); *Hardin* v. *Hardin*, 17 Ala. 250 (1850); *Hughes* v. *Hughes*, 19 Ala. 307 (1851) for some examples.

34. *Odom* v. *Odom*, 36 Ga. 286 (1867). "Legal cruelty may be defined to be, such conduct on the part of the husband, as will endanger the life, limb or health of the wife or create a reasonable apprehension of bodily hurt. . . ."

35. *Ghoulston* v. *Ghoulston*, 31 Ga. 625 (1860).

36. *Waskam* v. *Waskam*, 31 Miss. 154 (1856).

without indignities statutes declared in their rulings that cruelty need not be physical harassment. Not only had these statutes been worded expressly to help women, the cases involving a liberalized interpretation of cruelty almost invariably had been filed by women who sought release from their husbands.

Southern judges not only extended the scope of cruelty clauses, they also interpreted cases relativistically. Intrinsically cruelty was not the act, but its motives and effects. As we have seen in divorce suits instigated by women like Nancy Rose of Arkansas, Mary Taylor of Texas, and Martha Sharp of Tennessee, this relativism could aid women.[37] But, it was also capable of narrowing the interpretation of cruelty since some jurists conjectured that physical abuse might not constitute cruelty among all social groups. Chief Justice Hemphill of Texas had defined indignities to include non-physical cruelty, but he also speculated that physical violence might not constitute cruelty in other cases:

> no exact definition of legal cruelty can be given, for there may be cases in which mere blows should not be so considered. These may be given, but there still may be strong affection in the party. Among persons of coarse habits they may pass for little more than rudeness of language or manner. They might occasion no apprehension and be productive of but slight unhappiness.[38]

Justice George Goldthwaite of the Alabama Supreme Court advanced a similar argument in 1855:

> Between persons of education, refinement, and delicacy, the slightest blow in anger might be cruelty; while between persons of a different character and walk in life, blows might occasionally pass without marring to any great extent their conjugal relations or materially interfering with their happiness. We can lay down no certain rule, as to what violence will amount to cruelty, when it does not affect life, limb or health. Each case must depend on its own particular circumstances.[39]

This two-edged argument could result in class bias. Divorce could be used only to protect the Southern lady rather than the lower class woman who, in the judges' opinion, might expect rough treatment. More important, the relativity of cruelty meant an increase in judges' discretion and could result in close scrutiny of all female petitioners to ascertain if they possessed the tender delicacy of feeling that would be severely injured by verbal or mild physical abuse.

Southern judges not only aided women by expanding the scope of cruelty, but some also followed British precedents and granted

---

37. *Rose* v. *Rose*, 9 Ark. 507 (1849); *Taylor* v. *Taylor*, 18 Tex. 574 (1857); *Sharp* v. *Sharp*, 34 Tenn. (2 Sneed) 496 (1855).

38. *Nogees* v. *Nogees*, 7 Tex. 538 (1852).

39. *David* v. *David*, 27 Ala. 222 (1855).

alimony pending litigation so that a wife might procure the funds necessary to prosecute a case against her husband. Justice William Gaston found no justification for such alimony in North Carolina law but added that common law would hold the husband liable for his wife's necessities during the separation and she could sue *in forma pauperis*, as a pauper, with court-appointed counsel.[40] Justice E. A. Nisbet of the Georgia Supreme Court ruled the power to award temporary alimony to be incidental to the power to grant divorces:

> The right to be divorced would be a bitter mockery, if to obtain it an injured wife is obliged to endure, not only violence to a womanly delicacy, but penury and destitution. Equally revolting is to a proud albeit wounded spirit, to be constrained to sue (as Judge Gaston suggested she may) *in forma pauperis* and beg the whilst for food and raiment.[41]

Nisbet's decision emphasized a woman's right to counsel and a hearing, "And what if she be not innocent—what if her suit be unfounded or her defence impossible. Surely, even then, she is entitled to the privilege of the vilest of felons, that of being heard. To be heard, she must have the means."[42] In a society where a woman's property vested in her husband at marriage, Nisbet's decision more accurately reflected the realities of woman's situation than Gaston's. Nisbet and other members of the Georgia Supreme Court consistently upheld the wife's right to alimony prior to her suit's adjudication and allowed the courts only the right to inquire into whether the parties were married.[43]

Although Southern judges' enlarged interpretation of cruelty aided women in divorce cases, judicial concern, as intimated by their relativism toward cruelty, lay most with ladies, not poorer women. Southern divorce decisions usually involved middle or upper class women. Most divorce appeals stemmed from those, who if not well-to-do, were in comfortable circumstances. Indeed it seems unlikely that many poor people ever used the judicial machinery for divorce. The liberalization of divorce law applied to the propertied groups in society, and possibly their well-being inspired

---

40. *Wilson* v. *Wilson*, 19 N. C. (2 Dev. & B.) 377 (1837). In 1852 the North Carolina legislature granted women the right to alimony pending litigation. N. C., *Code* (1855), ch. 39, no. 15.

41. *McGee* v. *McGee*, 10 Ga. 477 (1852). Gaston's decision should also be contrasted with that of Justice Jeremiah Black of the Pennsylvania Supreme Court who ruled in 1856 to grant alimony pending litigation to Catherine Breinig. Black declared, "She cannot sue *in forma pauperis* for she is not a pauper if she is the wife of a man who has property. To deny her the means of paying for process and professional aid is to deny her justice." *Breinig* v. *Breinig*, 26 Pa. 161 (1856).

42. *McGee* v. *McGee*, 10 Ga. 477 (1852).

43. *Roseberry* v. *Roseberry*, 17 Ga. 29 (1855). Justice Henry Benning questioned whether the court had gone too far in allowing that question in *Frith* v. *Frith*, 18 Ga. 26 (1855).

such broadening.[44]

The expansion of causes for divorce and the granting of alimony pending litigation of the suit aided women seeking divorces, but the peculiar nature of divorce meant that women in divorce suits would be carefully scrutinized. Divorce in the nineteenth century—and into the twentieth century—was above all an adversary proceeding. To obtain a divorce, the plaintiff not only had to prove the spouse's "guilt" but also show his or her own "innocence." In some cases the British doctrine of recrimination in which both parties were judged to be guilty of mutual wrongs was invoked to refuse a divorce.[45] In short, one party must be "worthy" or deserving of the divorce. A man had only to prove that his wife had committed an action justifying divorce and that he had not encouraged her to do so. But a woman had to show her own essential virtue in the face of provocation. Therefore, the attitudes expressed in judicial suits were not incidental but were linked to the outcome of the process.

Respectability and propriety—or the appearance of them—played an important role in determining whether a divorce would be granted to a woman. Certainly charges and the evidence brought forward to support them were most crucial to the disposition of the case. But the courts intended divorce to relieve women who possessed the requisite virtues as well as the lawful case. Unless a woman showed she met contemporary standards of decorum as well as morality, she could not be sure of a sympathetic audience by the courts. This interest in finding the "innocent" as well as the "guilty" party in divorce suits gives us important insights into judicial perceptions of ideal, acceptable, and unacceptable conduct and character in women.

Domesticity with its corollaries of industriousness and good management were admiringly cited by judges as sterling traits belonging to some "wronged" wives. Nancy Rose was "industrious, managing and attentive to her domestic duties." Jane Robinson possessed "economical, prudent and industrious habits."[46]

Many of the women most favored by the judges were consid-

---

44. Although only further research in lower court records can fully reveal the proportion that poorer groups formed among those seeking divorces, the lower classes are little in evidence in suits being appealed. A rough survey of the appellate cases revealed only one North Carolina pair described as poor. Undoubtedly others had little property—probably the two Texas and two Tennessee couples in which the husband was confined to prison for a violation of property laws had small incomes. At least 22 of the couples owned property—often considerable amounts—or were distinguished in their community. Another 24 couples were slaveowners, a position that economically placed them in the upper one-third of Southern families. For a discussion of slaveholding, see Otto Olsen, "Historians and the Extent of Slave Ownership in the Southern United States," *Civil War History* 18 (1972): 101-16.

45. See M. M. Moore, "Critique of the Recrimination Doctrine," 68 *Dickinson Law Review* 157 (1963-64), for a discussion of the doctrine's history.

46. *Rose* v. *Rose*, 9 Ark. 507 (1849); *Robinson* v. *Robinson*, 26 Tenn. (7 Humph.) 440 (1846).

ered particularly well-bred and ladylike. Justice Turley of Tennessee described Catherine Chunn, who not only received a divorce but most of the property she took into the marriage, as "one who seems to be esteemed and loved by all who know her except her husband."[47] Eliza Payne, also of Tennessee, held a "most exemplary character" in her community and was an "educated, sensitive, and polished lady."[48] Mary L. Taylor, successful in her Texas divorce suit, was "delicately" reared, and Chief Justice Hemphill called her conduct "exemplary."[49] Not all "respectable ladies" received divorces; in some cases the judges either believed that those cases were too weak or that a possibility of reconciliation existed.[50] But ladylike conduct strongly disposed many judges to consider divorce in the wife's favor justified.

Submissiveness, however, seems to have been an essential virtue. Justice John Ormand found Mrs. Moyler, whom he granted a divorce for her husband's cruelty, to be "kind, dutiful and obedient."[51] Justice Scott conceded that Nancy Rose had faults; but, more important, for four years she had "submitted in meekness, smiling through her tears, to an almost continued (*sic*) flow of insult and unmerited contumely."[52]

The state courts' use of the British rule of condonation further illustrates their admiration for docile women. Under condonation, the continued cohabitation of husband and wife after the "innocent" party knew the "guilty" party's action condoned or accepted the fault and removed it as a cause for divorce. Southern supreme courts often ruled that condonation should be less binding upon women than men. Chief Justice Hemphill of Texas declared that an abused wife might still hold hopes of her husband's rehabilitation.[53] The Alabama Supreme Court decided in *Hughes* v. *Hughes* that new offenses removed any condonation of earlier ones.[54] Later that court fully upheld a chancellor's decision that condonation did not apply to a woman's enduring violence before seeking a divorce. Chancellor Ligon had argued that a "timid fearful" woman who wished to avoid the stigma of a separation might first become a "patient martyr" before filing for divorce. He sketched the scene:

> The wife of a dissipated and drunken husband, who has become the mother of his children and the subject of his cruelty and inhumanity, will patiently bear her wrongs, under the hope, sometimes well founded but often delusive, of being able to

47. *Chunn* v. *Chunn*, 19 Tenn. (1 Meigs) 131 (1838).

48. *Payne* v. *Payne*, 23 Tenn. (4 Humph.) 500 (1844).

49. *Taylor* v. *Taylor*, 18 Tex. 574 (1857).

50. See, for example, *Harrison* v. *Harrison*, 29 N.C. (7 Ired.) 484 (1847); *Rutledge* v. *Rutledge*, 37 Tenn. (5 Sneed) 554 (1858); *Tourne* v. *Tourne*, 9 La. 452 (1836).

51. *Moyler* v. *Moyler*, 11 Ala. 620 (1847).

52. *Rose* v. *Rose*, 9 Ark. 507 (1849).

53. *Wright* v. *Wright*, 6 Tex. 2 (1851).

54. *Hughes* v. *Hughes*, 19 Ala. 307 (1851).

> reform him. Her forbearance in this respect, influenced as it is by the most praiseworthy of all motives, should not be construed into condonation of the brutal wrongs inflicted upon her, . . .[55]

Thus submissive women were not to be penalized for their "praiseworthy" conduct.

More important, lack of docility hampered other women in their attempts to secure divorces. In *Gray* v. *Gray*, Judge Chilton of Alabama censured the lack of "manly forebearance" shown by Mr. Gray, but significantly concluded in denying the divorce, "the wife has not left him without apology in her *want of conformity to his wishes*, her peevish, fretful disposition, and occasional use of epithets calculated to wound him."[56] Henrietta Carlin of Louisiana was no more successful in her attempt to gain a divorce. C. T. Carlin, irritated by his young wife's interference in the plantation management, her complaints about his business trips, and her "improper language" before the overseer, had used corporal punishment to chastise her. The Louisiana Supreme Court refused to grant the divorce and only mildly rebuked her husband's conduct.[57] That court also unfavorably characterized another Louisiana woman for taking over administration of the family financial affairs and making "incessant demands for money" upon her husband.[58] Women with such managing, assertive manners met with a hostile reception in the high courts.

The Mississippi High Court of Errors and Appeals assumed the most extreme position requiring wifely obedience. Chief Justice Cotesworth D. Smith not only rebuked but also punished Rebecca Fulton's stubbornness and insubordination by granting her husband, David, the divorce he sought. While Mrs. Fulton lay ill at her doctor's home, Mr. Fulton survived an assault; and the county grand jury later indicted Samuel Montgomery, Rebecca's son by a previous marriage, for attempted murder. When Fulton informed his wife that he would no longer allow her son to visit their home, she refused to return. Although a reconciliation was attempted, a stalemate ensued, ending in Mr. Fulton's suit for divorce upon grounds of desertion. Avowing it had been Mrs. Fulton's wifely duty to return home immediately upon recovery, Chief Justice Smith fully upheld David Fulton's actions, "No question can be raised as to the perfect legal right of Colonel Fulton as master of the house, and as husband, to exclude any person from his door, and to determine as to whom

55. *Reese* v. *Reese*, 21 Ala. 785 (1853). Hindus and Withey, "The Law of Husband and Wife," argue that in Massachusetts, condonation was also not strictly applied to women in cruelty cases but was in adultery cases. My researches, however, reveal no Southern cases in which the wife's charges of adultery were affected by condonation.

56. *Gray* v. *Gray*, 15 Ala. 779 (1849). Emphasis added.

57. *Trowbridge* v. *Carlin*, 12 La. Ann. 882 (1857).

58. *Naulet* v. *Dubois*, 6 La. Ann. 403 (1851).

should be received as a visitor. . . ."[59] Smith also dismissed the attempts at reconciliation as not showing sufficient willingness on Mrs. Fulton's part since "it is impossible to consider the offer to live with . . . [her husband] as made in good faith, and free from conditions, *upon which the appellee, as a wife, had no right to insist.*"[60]

Thus Southern courts displayed ambiguity about what women's proper behavior should be. They applauded feminine capability in domestic matters, but in Louisiana and Alabama they frowned upon assertive behavior and censured those actions by refusing to grant forward females the divorces they sought.[61] The *Fulton* case provides a dramatic example of the severity of the Mississippi High Court toward a woman who challenged her husband's authority. Yet that submissiveness and docility other judges so often admired were a quieter but no less telling testimony of their confidence in the rightness of the husband's place as "lord and master."

In disputes over alimony and property settlements, the supreme courts usually favored women's claims but showed some of the same ambivalence about women's capabilities. Believing that the divorced woman should receive some property, Southern judges often supported a right to alimony for wives whose husbands had divorced them as well as for the women who sought an end to their marriages. The property grants sometimes were based upon the women's dependence, sometimes upon their competence.

Community property statutes in Louisiana and Texas granted divorced wives a share of that property regardless of who instituted the suit,[62] but elsewhere other judges also believed that women should receive a property settlement. In fact Justice Ormand of the Alabama court interpreted a statute giving the courts power to order a division of property upon conferral of divorce as decreeing that every wife should receive a "maintenance" from her husband's estate. Ormand further expounded:

> We use the term maintenance in preference to subsistence because we think the statute evidently contemplated something beyond a mere support. She should be able if her husband's estate was such to justify it, to live in such a manner, as if possible to enable her to regain her lost standing in society.[63]

Ormand conceded that distinctions of amount should be made in awards of alimony depending upon the wife's "innocence" or

59. *Fulton* v. *Fulton*, 31 Miss. 154 (1858).

60. Ibid. Emphasis added.

61. See *Gray* v. *Gray*, 15 Ala. 779 (1849); *Crow* v. *Crow*, 23 Ala. 583 (1853); *Naulet* v. *Dubois*, 6 La. Ann. 403 (1851); *Trowbridge* v. *Carlin*, 12 La. Ann. 882 (1857).

62. For some cases dividing community property see *Taylor* v. *Felps*, 10 La. 114 (1836); *Headen* v. *Headen*, 15 La. 61 (1840); *Rowley* v. *Rowley*, 19 La. 557 (1841); *Ledoux* v. *Boyd*, 10 La. Ann. 66 (1855); *Wright* v. *Wright*, 6 Tex. 2 (1851); *Trimble* v. *Trimble*, 15 Tex. 18 (1855); *Simons* v. *Simons*, 23 Tex. 344 (1859).

63. *Lovett* v. *Lovett*, 11 Ala. 763 (1847).

"guilt" but a division of property or provision for the wife should take place in every case.[64]

Justices sometimes linked a woman's right to alimony or a property settlement to her legal disabilities. Chief Justice John Catron of Tennessee declared that every divorced wife must be supported because:

> The husband, of course, has taken all the goods by marriage, and is entitled to the lands, if there be children of the wife, as tenant by the courtesy, and she must not be permitted to perish with hunger and cold, because frail.[65]

In Alabama, Justice Ormand linked his decision to grant property to a woman, divorced for abandoning her husband, to good public policy and indirectly to the difficulties women faced, "the public at large has such an interest, that the offender should not become an outcast upon society, cut off from the common charities of life, without the means of support and thus tempted to continue in the commission of vice."[66] Thus part of Ormand's concern focused upon women's economic disabilities that could leave prostitution or crime the only means of support.

State high courts granted support for a "wrongdoer" out of the spouse's estate only to females.[67] Although the Tennessee Supreme Court had ruled that even "guilty" women were entitled to alimony, it was unwilling to extend that ruling to men found to be at fault. When Mr. Chunn contested the amount of property granted to his wife, Justice William Turley indignantly rejected the claim to a part of Mrs. Chunn's estate:

> Shall a man, who has violated his matrimonial vows in every disgusting form, and by harsh and unkind treatment, forced his wife to seek protection in a recission of her nuptial contract, be heard when he asks support out of her estate? It is mockery, worse than mockery.[68]

Thus women's disabilities placed them in a different category from men whose claims to a part of their wives' property were rejected.

Although special treatment for women in property settlements seemed to arise from their dependent status, the courts also used grants of alimony or property to uphold the idea of women's competence. Mrs. Jeter, whose husband had denied paternity of their only child, received twenty-six thousand dollars from an estate valued at

---

64. Ibid.

65. *Richardson* v. *Wilson*, 16 Tenn. (8 Yerg.) 67 (1835).

66. *Lovett* v. *Lovett*, 11 Ala. 763 (1847).

67. The only exception to this rule, *Fitts* v. *Fitts*, 14 Tex. 443 (1855), involved a man who had earlier conveyed all his property to his wife and children and was granted a part of the income from his wife's slaves. Even this decision reaffirmed that such support would generally go to wives.

68. *Chunn* v. *Chunn*, 19 Tenn. (1 Meigs) 131 (1838).

forty-six thousand. The Alabama court ruled that her award should be generous since the child had been wrongly disowned. Tacitly rejecting the defense attorney's contention that a lump sum decree was erroneous and the wife might waste the money, Justice A. J. Walker outlined the extent of Mrs. Jeter's duties, "The wife's expenses and responsibility . . . will be increased and the duty must devolve on her alone of bringing the child forward when he attains his majority; and the child can never receive any of his father's estate, save through its (*sic*) mother."[69] Thus a Southern supreme court acknowledged that women could be competent in planning a child's future and handling its money.

Alimony and property settlements illustrate the ambivalence Southern judges felt about women. Most agreed that females faced difficult economic hurdles, and they sought to ensure that divorced wives would receive an adequate income. In this respect they accepted a notion of women as victims, if not of their husbands, then of society. Yet the jurists also indicated that women, who after all were often competent household managers, could also carefully dispense money and make long-range plans even though they could not earn money.

This ambivalence over women's competence and the importance of their role as moral paragon also affected the judges' decisions about the custody of children in divorce suits. Ante-bellum Southern jurists modified the traditional disposition of children. According to English common law, a father possessed his children. Legal custody was his, and he could award it to anyone regardless of the wishes of the children's mother.[70] Although these rules were not completely discarded, state supreme courts in Tennessee, Louisiana, Alabama, and Texas sometimes awarded custody of children to mothers.[71]

In a legal battle over the children, however, the courts hesitated to give the woman custody unless both her fitness and her husband's

69. *Jeter* v. *Jeter*, 36 Ala. 391 (1860).

70. See Matilda Fenberg, "Blame Coke and Blackstone," *Women Lawyers Journal* 34 (1948): 7-10, for a discussion of women's custody rights (or lack thereof) in English law. Unfortunately some historians have simply assumed that nineteenth century American women suffered similar disabilities. See, for example, Carroll Smith Rosenberg, "Beauty, Beast and the Militant Woman: A Case Study in Sex Roles and Social Stress in Jacksonian America," *American Quarterly* 23 (1971): 563; Andrew Sinclair, *The Better Half: The Emancipation of the American Woman* (New York, 1965), pp. 83-89.

71. For cases in which women received custody of children, see *Trimble* v. *Trimble*, 15 Tex. 18 (1855); *Rice* v. *Rice*, 21 Tex. 58 (1858): *Taylor* v. *Felps*, 10 La. 114 (1836); *Ledoux* v. *Boyd*, 10 La. Ann. 663 (1855). Internal evidence in *Thomas* v. *Tailleu*, 13 La. Ann 127 (1858) and *Jackson* v. *Stewart*, 20 Ga. 120 (1856) indicates that the women in those divorce suits retained custody. Although Maxwell Bloomfield, *American Lawyers in a Changing Society, 1776-1876* (Cambridge, Mass., 1976), pp. 118-20, recognizes that women sometimes received custody of children, he cites only Southern cases which awarded custody to the father—a tiny minority of the appellate cases.

incapacity were pronounced.[72] The same Tennessee judge who so scathingly repudiated a wayward husband's claim to any of the wife's property allowed another husband, divorced for physical abuse of his wife and excessive drinking, to retain custody of the elder two of their four children.[73]

The Louisiana Supreme Court, which had awarded custody of children to the wife in several divorces, revealed its prejudices about "special fitness" in a case so notorious that initials rather than names were used in the report. JFC initiated divorce proceedings by charging his wife ME with adultery, and she countersued alleging that he had been cruel and was a fugitive from justice. The judges overturned the divorce that a lower court had awarded the wife, ruling, "All the circumstances taken together leave no room for reasonable doubt that the defendant and [JM]G were surprised by the husband in his own house *in flagranti delicto (sic)*."[74] Although Justice Henry Bullard conceded that JFC had abused his wife and had murdered JMG "in cold blood and in a manner both cruel and unmanly" while the wife's previous conduct had been "ladylike and above reproach," he granted custody of the only child, E, to the murderer rather than to the adulteress.[75]

Alabama jurists' ambivalence about custody appeared in two cases decided at the end of the ante-bellum period. In 1858 the Supreme Court affirmed a lower court's decision that Emily Cornelius rather than her drunken husband should have custody of their three-year-old son. Justice George Stone carefully qualified the precedent his ruling established:

> We do not wish to be understood as laying down a rule, that intemperance will justify a court of chancery in depriving him of his children. The testimony shows . . . that Mr. Cornelius, in his frequent fits of intoxication, becomes a boisterous madman; that these fits last for days, and when under their influence, the care and control of friends has to be called into requisition.[76]

Unwilling to grant permanent custody to Mrs. Cornelius, Stone pointed out that should Mr. Cornelius reform, "there certainly should be no insurmountable barrier to the recovery of his child."[77] The jurist also believed that a young child needed the special care its mother provided, but he intimated that a boy should remain with his father:

72. An exception seems to be *Trimble* v. *Trimble*, 15 Tex. 18 (1855) in which Moffatt Trimble in his appeal challenged his wife's custody of their four children. The court denied his appeal on the grounds that since he had not originally asked for custody, he could not request it on appeal.

73. *Robinson* v. *Robinson*, 26 Tenn. (7 Humph.) 440 (1846).

74. *JFC* v. *ME*. 6 Rob. (La.) 135 (1843).

75. Ibid.

76. *Cornelius* v. *Cornelius*, 31 Ala. 479 (1858).

77. Ibid.

> There would be much difficulty in laying down an absolute rule, fixing a period when custody of a male child should be taken away from the mother and given to the father . . . evidently the child should remain with her until he has reached an age when he can dispense with those tender offices only a mother can bestow.[78]

Thus even an especially fit mother might retain custody of her sons for only a few years.

Frances Bryan was less successful in her 1859 attempt to gain custody of her two children. Her divorce case against her husband failed; and her charges of drunkenness also did not convince the Supreme Court judges. Justice Walker ruled that the testimony of fifty witnesses on Leonidas Bryan's habits indicated that he drank "freely and in some instances to inebriation" but that his drinking did not "materially interfere with his business habits or . . . make his association dangerous to his wife or children. . . ."[79] Since Leonidas desired that his wife and children return home, Walker believed stronger proof than in usual cases should be exacted. Although Leonidas was "often rude, harsh and indecorous," witnesses testified that Frances sometimes flew into fits of anger.[80] Furthermore, although the children were aged only four and two, Walker deemed them old enough to be parted from their mother. He summed up the important aspects of the case:

> the defendant is not shown to be of such character, or to have such habits as would necessarily contaminate the children, or render them unsafe in his custody, and the *strong favor with which the law regards the father's prior right to the custody of his children* and the unauthorized state of separation from her husband . . . and *her want of peculiar fitness for the custody and care of the children*, and also that the children have passed the age when the mother's care though valuable and desirable, is not indispensable.[81]

Thus, in a case where the father had not proved himself incapacitated and the mother had not demonstrated "peculiar fitness," his rights would take precedence over hers.

The Southern courts, although far from turning custody over to women, had chipped away at the common law interpretation of custody rights. True, in contested cases, a woman had to prove her superiority over her husband. But even that ruling was a significant alteration of the common law. And given the notion of women's

78. Ibid. This decision in its "child-centerness" closely resembles the New York case of *Mercein* v. *People ex rel. Barry* (1840) described in Bloomfield, *American Lawyers*, pp. 118-19.

79. *Bryan* v. *Bryan*, 34 Ala. 516 (1859).

80. Ibid.

81. Ibid. Emphasis added

inherent special capacity to care for children that had gained ground during the nineteenth century, one can discern in the ante-bellum cases a fore-shadowing of twentieth century decisions that usually awarded custody to women.[82] Although the ante-bellum courts protected men's custody rights, the judges were not rigidly patriarchal.

Divorce was neither prohibited nor impossible in most of the ante-bellum South. Divorce laws there also expanded to benefit "wronged" wives during that era. In the cases reviewed, judges often further amplified the scope of existing laws in ways that helped women. Although the greater use of discretion could hinder as well as aid women in divorce suits, the enlargement of the concept of cruelty, decisions decreeing alimony and property settlements necessary, and changes in custody all were modifications favoring women.

Christopher Lasch's contention that modern divorce law arose from the desire to protect suffering lower class women does not explain the liberalization of Southern ante-bellum divorce. To be sure, Lasch is correct that sympathy for women played a part. Southern judges, however, believed an enlarged view of divorce necessary to aid refined ladies, not lower class women. And, in fact, few cases involving poor people came before supreme courts there. Moreover, not only Lasch's notion of woman as victim, but her combined position as moral superior, physical inferior, and subordinate in the husband-wife relationship inspired divorce liberalization by the judiciary. Indeed, woman's supposedly inherent virtue compelled her removal from a morally callous or degenerate husband. The judges' grants of divorce, their awards of property and of custody of children also sometimes implied that women's abilities extended beyond marriage. But women had to prove at least their moral superiority in order to be allowed to divorce and use other capabilities.

Southern attitudes toward women were also considerably more complex than scholars have indicated. Like other conservative men of their day, Southern judges did not question the subordination of women in marriage. Although the jurists looked with distaste upon assertive, managing females who were neither long-suffering nor submissive, they admired women who could competently dispatch responsibilities. With their beliefs about women as both inferior and superior to men, Southern judges never found even upper class women to be only ornamental or peripheral members of society.

---

82. For the notion of women's inherent capabilities in child rearing, see Anne L. Kuhn, *The Mother's Role in Childhood Education: New England Concepts 1830-1860* (New Haven, 1947), *passim*.

These attitudes differed significantly from contemporary literary stereotypes of women.

All of these findings should caution us against simplistic views of ante-bellum Southern society. The judges believed in their social order, but did not mindlessly uphold the tenets of patriarchalism; and they significantly modified legal concepts and expanded women's abilities to gain divorces, alimony and property, and custody of children. Their attempts to juggle increased aid for females in divorce suits with the traditional subordination of women in marriage illustrate both the efforts and limitations of that society in dealing with women's problems.

APPENDIX
DIVORCES DECIDED BY SOUTHERN HIGH COURTS 1800-1860

State	Number of Suits	Begun by Wife	Granted Wife	Begun by Husband	Granted Husband	Remanded (New Trial)	Other
Ala.	28	21	11	7	2	2	1[a]
Ark.	2	2	1	0	0	1	—
Ga.	7	3	0	4	1	4	—
La.	22	16	7[b]	6	1	1	—
Miss.	5	3	2	2	1	—	1[a]
N. C.	15	9	1	6	2[c]	2	2[d]
Tenn.	15	13	9[c]	2	0	—	—
Tex.	15	10	4	5	1	4	—

[a] case dismissed without prejudice.

[b] Five of these were bed and board divorces which could become total divorces in Louisiana after two years of separation without reconciliation. In 1857 the separation period was reduced to one year.

[c] In each state, one of the divorces was a bed and board divorce.

[d] A divorce petition instituted by a woman was found to be sufficient in its allegations and would justify a divorce if the allegations were proven. A divorce was also to be granted to a man, Jesse Barden, if a man of reasonable prudence would have misled in similar circumstances.

THE POLITICAL AND CIVIL STATUS OF WOMEN IN GEORGIA, 1783-1860

BY ELEANOR M. BOATWRIGHT

The philosophies, facts, practices and sentiments governing the political and civil rights of white women in Georgia between the Revolution and the Civil War were confused, fickle, contradictory, and paradoxical. The Constitution would have allowed full political equality, but theory and practice granted none; whereas the statutes denied the civil existence of a married woman, yet permitted her to establish it if she chose and protected it if she did. It seems to have been a system of letting the right hand know not what the left hand did, but public opinion approved the conspiracy and guarded its secrets.

Georgia women were denied the suffrage between 1777 and 1789 otherwise they might have voted from the founding of the colony until the Civil War. The facts were that the original charter had no disqualifying clause, the Constitution of 1777 limited the franchise to males, those of 1789 and 1798 were silent on the subject, and the Constitution of 1861 barred women from the suffrage.[1] This does not mean that women voted nor that Georgia intended that they should. Neither were Negroes explicitly disqualified until 1861. The Constitution of 1789 and 1798 neither say that women may vote nor that they may not. Women are not mentioned. This failure of the framers

1. Walter McElreath, ed., *A Treatise on the Constitution of Georgia* (Atlanta, 1912), Charter of the Province, 212-237; Constitution of 1777, Art. IX, 232; Constitution of 1789, Art. IV, sec. I, 247; Constitution of 1798, Art. IV, sec. I, 264; Constitution of 1861, Art. V, sec. I, 296.

was not due to masculine liberality but to feminine insignificance. If a woman had taken advantage of the loophole and attempted to vote it is safe to wager public opinion would have left her in no condition to contest the point.

It appears that Georgia men heard, or thought they heard, the rustle of petticoats in the vogue for democracy that came with the Revolution and fortified their prerogative with the Constitution of 1777. The flutterings were so stilled by 1789 that precautions were abandoned.

Nevertheless Georgia women were not wholly negative in politics. They rarely entered into political discussions, in part because they were uninformed, or found it socially expedient to pretend so; in part, perhaps, because the same code which demanded that a gentleman never contradict a lady, expected that a lady should never embarrass a gentleman with a controversial issue. When there was uniformity of public opinion, however, women who enjoyed politics had their innings. James Buckingham, an Englishman who visited the slave states and wrote of his observations, noticed that in "the struggle between the nullifiers of South Carolina and the General Government of the United States" women "took a very important part," and, according to him, long afterwards retained "more of the enthusiastic feeling of that period than the men."[2] This was not surprising. Life was drab for ante-bellum Georgia women unless they were unmarried and young.

Sometimes a woman held political power. Nancy Rumsey did. "This white female," according to her contemporary Garnett Andrews, "levied blackmail on all office-seekers in Elbert county for half a century." She began her career with a traveling restaurant which she made from an ox cart. When court was in cession

2. J. S. Buckingham, *The Slave States of America* (London, 1842), II, 182-183.

she drove her team into Elberton, hitched at the court house, and opened up for business. Nancy must have been a good cook for her profits enabled her to build a comfortable house called "Goshen" in the Chinquapin settlement near Elberton. There she established her "throne." Her talents were such that politicians sought her support. "Each got her promise of favor and she got money from each." Her practices became well known but her opposition was so feared that office seekers continued to pay their tax. During the last twenty years of her power it was said, "lawyers who were looking up business took care to say pleasant things to her as they passed, and the Judge, as he went by paid his respects."[3]

Feminine good will was considered important enough for women to be "flattered and appealed to by political orators, and by newspapers, whenever the occasion presented itself for so doing with effect."[4] It was common to see the ladies in the gallery of the legislature. A good murder trial was sure to find them present.[5] At one it was reported the ladies "filled the gallery and even took possession of the floor of the Senate."[6] Wives, daughters, and sweethearts were frequently taken to political celebrations, toasted at political dinners, and danced with at political balls,[7] but that was about the limit of their public activities. What political influence Georgia women had was usually individual and was exercised socially. The men of their state rarely acknowledged that any existed.

The political status of women was ignored but the civil received the most unfavorable attention. Both married and single women shared some civil disabili-

3. Garnett Andrews, *Reminiscences of an Old Georgia Lawyer* (Atlanta, 1870), 37.
4. Buckingham, *Slave States*, II, 182-183.
5. I. S. Bradwell to Adam Alexander, May 31, 1820, in mss. Letters and Papers of Adam Leopold Alexander, Washington, Georgia, in Duke University Library.
6. Milledgeville *Daily Federal Union*, Nov. 17, 1859.
7. Buckingham, *Slave States*, II, 182-183.

ties. Neither performed jury service and the testimony of both, except in criminal cases, was taken out of court.[8] There the likeness stopped. The law allowed unmarried women to contract; to sue and to be sued; to act as administrators of estates and as guardians of children; to hold bequeath, inherit, or purchase property; and to work, keep their earnings, or to spend them as they pleased. All of which they did as bountiful court evidence proves.

The ceremonial pledge of a man to his bride "with all my worldly goods I thee endow" did not have the legal significance of a valentine. For the civil law saw to it that the new-made husband lost nothing of his own at the altar and took away from it all his bride possessed—perhaps even the ring with which he made his vow. For the common law of England gave a man unconditional title to his wife's personal property[9] while the Georgia Act of 1789 guaranteed him her real property on the same terms.[10]

In 1784 Georgia legally adopted all the English common law not repugnant to the State of Federal Constitution.[11] This common law gave a wife no legal civil status. It recognized the husband and wife as one person, suspended the legal existence of the woman, and put her under the protection of "her husband, her baron, or lord." Under the common law a husband could neither grant anything to his wife nor enter into an agreement with her for "the grant would suppose her separate existence, and to covenant with her would be to covenant with himself."[12]

8. *Acts of the General Assembly of the State of Georgia, 1829*, p. 94 (Hereafter referred to as *Acts of Georgia*); Foster Blodgett, Jr. to David L. Roath, Jan. 18, 1860, in mss. Letters of David L. Roath, Augusta, Georgia, in Office of the Ordinary of Richmond County.
9. William Blackstone, *Commentaries on the Laws of England*, with Analysis of Contents by Thomas M. Cooley, ed. by James DeWitt Andrews (Chicago, 1899), Book II, sec. 434-436.
10. Oliver H. Prince, comp., *A Digest of the Laws of the State of Georgia* (Athens, 1837), Act of 1789, p. 225; Royston *vs.* Royston, 21 Georgia 161.
11. Prince, comp., *Digest*, Act of 1784, p. 570.
12. Blackstone, *Commentaries*, Book I, sec. 442.

Georgians, following the English common law, wrote into their statutes:

"In this State the husband is the head of the family, and the wife is subject to him; her civil legal existence is merged in the husband except so far as the law recognizes her separately, either for her own protection or for her benefit, or for the preservation of public order."[13]

The estates of husband and wife were mutually responsible for debts existing at the time of marriage until the Act of 1856.[14] It left the husband responsible for his wife's debts only to the extent of the property she brought him and relieved her estate of all claims of his creditors.[15]

After marriage a man's financial obligations were reduced to a legal minimum. He was required to provide his wife with the "necessities suitable to her habits and conditions of life," but for "anything besides necessaries" he was not "chargeable."[16] After his death she was entitled to dower rights in his estate[17] or to her part, under the law, in its distribution if he died intestate;[18] and to a year's support for herself and their children, even though the estate was insolvent.[19] Otherwise what a wife had was her husband's, free from all rights of survivorship, to sell, dispose of, or bequeath as he wished, regardless of whether his wife's property was derived from parents, relatives, friends,[20]

---

13. R. H. Clark, T. R. R. Cobb, D. Irwin, comps., *The Code of the State of Georgia* (Atlanta, 1861), sec. 1700. (Hereafter referred to as Clark, Cobb, and Irwin, comps., *Code of 1861*.)
14. *Acts of Georgia*, 1856, p. 229.
15. Clark, Cobb, and Irwin, comps., *Code of 1861*, sec. 1705.
16. Blackstone, *Commentaries*, Book I, sec. 443.
17. Thomas R. R. Cobb, comp., *A Digest of the Statute Laws of Georgia* (Athens, 1851), Acts of: 1768, p. 163; 1807, p. 228; 1824, p. 228; 1826, p. 171; 1839, p. 230; 1850, p. 231.
18. Prince, comp., *Digest*, Acts of: 1804, p. 233; 1829, p. 253.
19. Cobb, comp., *Digest*, Act of 1838, p. 296; John Silcox and others *vs.* John Nelson and others, Richmond County Superior Court, 1842 Term, in *Decisions of the Superior Courts of the State of Georgia*, Part I (Augusta, 1843), 24-25. In De Renne Collection, University of Georgia Library. (Hereafter referred to as *Georgia Superior Court Decisions*.)
20. Penalton & Co. *vs.* Mills & *al.*, Cobb County Superior Court, 1843 Term, *ibid.*, Part II (Augusta, 1844), 116-117; Royston *vs.* Royston, 21 Georgia 161.

her former husband,[21] the child of a previous marriage,[22] or the profits of her own labor.[23] Even if a husband deserted his wife prior to 1851 he might appear periodically and collect her earnings, those of their minor children, or anything else the family which he had abandoned might have accumulated.[24]

The following wills from Wilkes County are typical of the period. John Bowen left: "to wife Rachel all that her father gave her, a slave boy Adam, the dun mare, and her bed and furniture."[25] And Samuel Jack's will reads: "Whereas at the time of our marriage my wife owned a house and lot at Chambersburg and three hundred acres . . . willed to her by her former husband Alex. Stewart, she shall hold it."[26]

A striking case that came up in the Cobb County Superior Court was that of Penalton & Co. *vs.* Mills & *al.* It is concerned with the ownership of a slave girl. She had been kept by the daughter of a widowed mother for some time. The two women had no clear understanding as to whether the negro was a gift or a loan. All went well until both of them were married. Then the mother's husband sued the daughter's husband for the return of the slave, not because she was his wife's property but because she was his own. Both mother and daughter were left out of the case. It was a question of whose husband owned the slave.[27]

The story of Fanny Kemble, the beautiful and successful English actress who married Pierce Mease Butler during her brilliant season in Philadelphia, is

---

21. A. Edwards and wife *vs.* B. Leigh and W. Leigh, Richmond County, Superior Court Records: Minute Book, 1805-1811, April Term, 1818, p. 246. Mss in Richmond County Superior Court Office.
22. Cobb, comp., *Digest*, Acts of: 1804, p. 291; 1845, p. 294; Uriah B. Holden and wife *vs.* David Harrell, 6 Georgia 126.
23. Gorman *et al.* *vs.* Wood, 68 Georgia 524, 73 Georgia 307; Wilson *vs.* Wilson Sewing Machine Company, 76 Georgia 104.
24. *Acts of Georgia*, 1851, p. 237.
25. Grace G. Davidson, comp., *Early Records of Georgia, Wilkes County* (Macon, 1932), I, 47. (Hereafter referred to as Davidson, comp., *Wilkes County Records*.)
26. *Ibid.*, 85.
27. Penalton & Co. *vs.* Mills & *al.*, in *Georgia Superior Court Decisions*, Part II, 116-117.

the story of a rebel against the code of her day. Theirs was a clash to two cultures which soon led to unhappiness, separation, and divorce. This niece of Mrs. Siddons with a background of Drury Lane and Covent Garden, with generation of distinguished actors behind her, who was held in adoration by two continents, and who had been married in the Unitarian Church which omitted "obey" from its ceremony, was ill designed for ante-bellum domesticity. Butler may have been bigoted but he was charming, educated, and wealthy. During their whirlwind courtship Fanny Kemble apparently never inquired the source of his wealth—slave labor on Butler's Island at the mouth of the Altamaha.[28]

Fanny Kemble had always disliked slavery. Her disapproval of it blazed into a burning hatred the winter she and her husband visited his plantation. The system which she so violently attacked he as jealously defended.[29] Slavery came to serve as a battle ground for all the differences that lay between them.[30]

Fanny Kemble was English, she spent only one unhappy winter in Georgia, she was an odd pattern for the mistress of a remote rice plantation, and most of her legal controversies were in Philadelphia; still she was the wife of one of Georgia's richest planters. The problem of her rights to earn, to dispose of her earnings, and to retain the custody of her children were the products of the English common law which she would have found as binding in Georgia as it was in Pennsylvania.[31]

One of their early quarrels was over Fanny Kemble's *Journal of a Residence in America*. It was an account of her first tour in this country. She had contracted for

28. Leota S. Driver, *Fanny Kemble* (Chapel Hill, 1933).
29. Frances Anne Kemble, *Journal of a Residence on a Georgian Plantation* (New York, 1863), *passim*.
30. Driver, *Fanny Kemble*, 92-114.
31. Pierce M. Butler, *Mr. Butler's Statement, Originally prepared with the aid of his Professional Council* (Philadelphia, 1850).

its publication soon after she landed here but was married before the proof was ready. When it came from the press her young husband edited and altered it in spite of her violent protest. This was his marital right and Pierce Butler knew his rights. The *Journal* appeared with the marks of his censorship still on it.[32]

It seemed to Fanny Kemble "too beneficient a provision of the law for the protection of male superiority" that "the man whose wits could not keep him half a week from starving" should be entitled to his wife's earnings.[33] But that was possible.

A case heard three times in the Georgia Supreme Court was that of a woman who had made a little money keeping boarders and from renting property belonging to her. Her husband collected her earnings, invested in land, took the title to it in his own name, and subsequently lost the property. The wife protested against the seizure but the courts ruled in favor of her husband's creditors.[34]

In establishing a husband's claim to his wife's property there was one important qualification. He must "reduce it to possession" during coverture[35] for the wife had the right to her "choses in action."[36] This had its origin in common law. It meant that debts due her—such as rents, legacies, residuary personal estate, money in funds, or shares—which at the time of her marriage were in the possession of a third person, remained there unless her husband took steps to "reduce them to possession"—gain control. To do this he had to show his intentions together with some overt act to give them force—such as receiving payment on a debt

32. Butler, *Statement*, 22-24.
33. Dorothie Bobbé, *Fanny Kemble* (New York, 1931), 170, citing letter to Harriet Martineau (n. d., n. p.).
34. Gorman *et. al.* *vs.* Wood, 68 Georgia 524, 73 Georgia 370; Wilson *vs.* the Wilson Sewing Machine Company, 76 Georgia 104.
35. Sayre & Sayre *vs.* Flournoy, adm'r and others, 3 Georgia 541.
36. Blackstone, *Commentaries*, Book II, secs. 389, 397.

due his wife, having stock belonging to her transferred to him, or bringing action for an offence against her property in his name.

In the case of the woman with the boarding house the court held that her earnings had been reduced to possession by her husband's action. He had received and invested the money as though it were his own and had not recognized the title as being his wife's until it was attached. He had then attempted to set up her equity in the property. The decision was that a wife's earnings became her husband's if he invested them, whether he took the money with or without her consent, and "whether such earnings were made from keeping a boarding house or from washing, ironing, or cooking."[87]

In another Georgia Supreme Court case, Oglesby and wife *vs.* Hall, Oglesby had permitted his wife to sell cakes and to put her earnings in the bank in Athens. She added to them with money which she borrowed from her brother and bought a negro woman and her four children. Mrs. Oglesby took the title in her own name, held the slaves as separate property, met the taxes, and paid her debt to her brother with the profits of her baking. Oglesby neither objected to her actions nor attempted to establish his claim. Nevertheless he secretly deeded the slaves away retaining for himself and his wife a life interest only. His action became known, Mrs. Oglesby contested his rights, and brought suit for the return of the slaves. At the trial Oglesby admitted he was ignorant at all times and drunk when he executed the deed, but he said he was prompted by "love and affection." The court held that since he had neither reduced his wife's earnings nor the slaves to possession that the property was hers and the deed void.[88]

---

87. Gorman *et. al. vs.* Wood, 68 Georgia 524.
88. Oglesby and wife *vs.* Hall, 80 Georgia 386.

The laws governing a married woman's property were harsh. George Paschal found during the panic of 1837 they took a grim toll in Georgia and produced "moral and social" disorders which were impossible for later generations to understand.[39] Yet a Philadelphia lawyer's remark, that the presumption of the law which gave a husband complete control over his wife's actions "in nine cases out of ten . . . resolved itself into fiction,"[40] had some foundation.

The law allowed a woman to establish a separate estate.[41] The object of this, Judge Bleckley said from the Supreme Bench of Georgia, was to guard a wife from the " 'kicks and kisses' especially the kisses of her husband."[42] The separate estate originated in the common law and did not appear on the statute books of Georgia until 1847.[43] It might be created in several ways: by conveyance to a trustee before marriage;[44] by prenuptial agreement between the parties;[45] by postnuptial settlement—under which a husband conveyed property to a third person to hold for his wife;[46] and by gift or legacy especially establishing a woman's sole ownership and disavowing her husband's claim.[47]

The common law gave a wife "without aid of statute" control over her separate estate and permitted her husband none "except as he may be trustee by implication." It bound him, even then, to follow her directions and required that he be removed if he failed to do so.[48] In Georgia an agreement creating a woman's separate estate, whether or not in writing could be enforced in the courts of equity. Both judge

39. George Paschal, *Ninety-Four Years, or Agnes Paschal* (n. p., 1871), 97.
40. Augusta *Georgia Constitutionalist*, June 8, 1846.
41. Clark, Cobb, and Irwin, comps., *Code of 1861*, secs. 1724-1729.
42. Humphrey *vs.* Copeland, 54 Georgia 543.
43. Cobb, comp., *Digest*, Act of 1847, p. 180.
44. Lydia C. Pepper and Alexander Fawnes, Chatham County Superior Court Records: Minute Book "2F," Folio 107. Mss. in Chatham County Court Office.
45. Joseph Welcher and Ann Miller, *ibid.*, Book "Z," Folio 507.
46. Clark, Cobb, and Irwin, comps., *Code of 1861*, sec. 1730.
47. Will of William Lowden, Chatham County, Inferior Court Records: Will no. 50. Mss. Chatham County Court Office.
48. Blackstone, *Commentaries*, Book I, sec. 444 (note).

and jury were inclined to be friendly to the wife's interest, and, in legal controversies, they might be expected to construe the agreement liberally.[49]

Throughout the ante-bellum period the laws to protect a married woman's property were adequate if she had safeguarded her rights in time. The weakness of the system was that it offered no shelter to those who had not. Yet, as Harriet Martineau pointed out, weak and ignorant women were the ones most likely to need legal protection and the least likely to have sought it.[50]

Little by little women in Georgia gained control of their earnings. Beginning in 1851 certain wives who applied to the legislature for "reliefs" were allowed to carry on an independent business. They were called "free traders." During 1851 and 1852 there were four women so recognized, from 1853 to 1854 there were ten, and from 1855 to 1856 the number rose to fourteen.[51] After that a woman who had gained the consent of her husband was allowed to become a free trader by publishing a notice of her intentions in the paper for a month before beginning business.[52] She was then liable for her contracts and entitled to her profits.

Even when the Married Woman's Act of 1866[53] and the Constitution of 1868 insured a wife's unqualified control of her possession the courts did not relax their guardianship. In 1875 Supreme Court of Georgia decided this legislation had not modified those sections of the Code which prevented a wife from selling her estate to her husband without a court order and which prohibited his creditors buying it under any conditions.[54]

49. McBride *vs.* Greenwood and others, 11 Georgia 379; Kempton *et al. vs.* Hallowell and Co., 24 Georgia 52; Hicks *vs.* Johnson, 24 Georgia 194.

50. Harriet Martineau, *Society in America* (New York, 1837), II, 238.

51. *Acts of Georgia*, 1851-1852, pp. 515-518; 1853-1854, pp. 527-529; 1855-1856, pp. 512-514.

52. Clark, Cobb, and Irwin, comps., *Code of 1861*, sec. 1708.

53. *Acts of Georgia*, 1866, p. 146.

54. Humphrey *vs.* Copeland, 54 Georgia 543; Clark, Cobb, and Irwin, comps., *Code of 1861*, secs. 1783, 1785.

Fanny Kemble saw in the increasing liberality of the law a "possible advantage to the magnanimous sex." For according to her, it enabled dishonest men to settle extensive property on their wives and then to "baffle the claims of the creditors."[55]

In general a woman's share in her husband's estate was for life only. The laws of inheritance favored the male line and the majority of wills seem to have followed the same trend.[56] The laws regulating intestate estates made the husband the sole heir of his wife and excluded her children,[57] but only allowed a widow to choose between a child's portion and her dower. Before 1829 if a husband left no children his widow was entitled to half of his estate. The remainder went to his next of kin.[58] In that year, however, the law was altered and where there were no lineal descendants the wife became sole heir of her intestate husband.[59]

The best legal protection a woman had for a share in her husband's estate was her dower. The courts defined it as the "favorite of the law" and stipulated "neither the husband nor the courts, nor any other human power can compel a wife to relinquish this right."[60] The law restricted a husband's disposal of his property during his lifetime so as to protect the wife's dower rights.[61] It established her claim to "all he died possessed of."[62] This the Supreme Court of Georgia interpreted to mean free of all mortgages that might be on the estate at the time of the husband's death—as though no encumbrances existed.[63] The law

55. Frances Anne Kemble, *Records of Later Life* (London, 1882), I, 28.
56. Davidson, comp., *Wilkes County Records*, I, II, *passim*.
57. Prince, comp., *Digest*, Act of: 1789, p. 225; 1827, p. 251.
58. *Ibid.*, Act of 1804, p. 233.
59. *Ibid.*, Act of 1829, p. 253; Clark, Cobb, and Irwin, comps., *Code of 1861*, sec. 2452.
60. Royston *vs.* Royston, 21 Georgia 161; Blackstone, *Commentaries*, Book II, sec. 129; Clark, Cobb, and Irwin, comps., *Code of 1861*, sec. 1714.
61. Cobb, comp., *Digest*, Acts of: 1760, p. 161; 1768, p. 163; 1785, p. 165; 1842, p. 179.
62. *Ibid.*, Act of 1826, p. 171.
63. Green *vs.* Causey, 10 Georgia 485; Dennis *et. al.* *vs.* Green, 20 Georgia 386.

permitted a wife to choose her dower property.[64] And it allowed her a year's support for herself and her children even though the estate was insolvent.[65]

The status of a wife under the law was, in part that of a minor whose husband was her guardian. In general public opinion accepted this theory although it was not always practiced. Like a minor her contracts were void;[66] her husband was answerable for her words and her misdemeanors;[67] if through commands, threats, coersion or persuasion he induced her to commit a crime not punishable by death or life imprisonment he must pay the penalty in her stead;[68] and, if she disobeyed he was entitled to administer punishment.[69]

It was explained that inasmuch as the husband was made responsible for his wife's misdemeanors the "law thought it reasonable to intrust him with the power of restraining her by domestic chastisement in the same manner that a man is allowed to correct his apprentice or children." There was a time when, for some offences, a man was permitted to "beat his wife severely with scourges and sticks," but in England the "politer reign of Charles II" brought this power of correction into "doubt,"[70] and in Georgia the law required that the stick be no larger than a man's thumb.[71]

Husbands of the upper class in Georgia did not use the lash but women were expected to obey. Something of a code of honor reinforced a husband's discipline. Probably the young ladies of LaGrange College had been reminded of their responsibilities many times before Robert Charlton told them "a woman ought not to

64. Cobb, comp., *Digest*, Acts of: 1830, p. 230; 1850, p. 231.
65. *Ibid.*, Acts of: 1838, p. 296; 1850, pp. 297-299; Hopkins *vs.* Long, 9 Georgia 261.
66. Blackstone, *Commentaries*, Book I, sec. 443-445.
67. Smith *vs.* Taylor and wife, Louise Lynch *vs.* same, 11 Georgia 20.
68. Blackstone, *Commentaries*, Book I, sec. 445.
69. Cobb, comp., *Digest*, Penal Code of 1833, Div. I, sec. VIII, 779.
70. Blackstone, *Commentaries*, Book I, sec. 445.
71. Orville A. Park, comp., *History of Georgia in the Eighteenth Century as Recorded in the Reports of the Georgia Bar Association*, reprint from the Annual Report of the Georgia Bar Association (Macon, 1921), June, 1921, 90.

speak what she pleased," because her husband must answer for her words "either by fight or by law—the first threatening his person, and the last invading his purse."[72]

Yet Georgians could say with their English ancestors "the lower ranks of people . . . still claim and exert their ancient privileges"[73] for here too husbands continued to give disobedient wives corporal punishment. Public opinion was increasingly hostile, however, and sometimes it intruded. Only a broken rail and cool headed intervention prevented a lynching when the husband of one of the mill girls in Columbus attempted to beat her.[74]

In 1857 the law made beating or mistreating a wife a penal offense. It carried a possible six months sentence and allowed the wife to testify in her own behalf.[75] But public opinion still found cause for complaint. When a husband in the factory region of Augusta was fined only "$5.00 for whipping his wife" the *Evening Dispatch* strongly protested against the "cheapness of the luxury."[76]

A wife was the property of her husband to this extent: he had the right of action against another for abducting, harboring, seducing or beating her. These were actions at common law for which the husband might collect damages.[77] Many husbands advertised their fugative wives, and warned against "dealing with, harboring, or concealing" the runaways undeı the penalty of the law.[78]

Women were expected to accept their lot as part of the punishment visited upon Eve, to continue the "even

72. Robert M. Charlton, *Address*, delivered at the commencement of LaGrange Female College, July, 1853 (Savannah, 1853).
73. Blackstone, *Commentaries*, Book I, sec. 445.
74. Augusta *Daily Constitutionalist*, July 14, 1847 citing *Muscogee Democrat*, 1st inst.
75. *Acts of Georgia*, 1857, p. 126.
76. Augusta *Evening Dispatch*, Feb. 1, 1859.
77. Blackstone, *Commentaries*, Book III, sec. 139-140; Clark, Cobb, and Irwin, comps., *Code of 1861*, sec. 2949.
78. Augusta *Chronicle and Gazette of the State*, Oct. 14, 1797.

as Sarah obeyed Abraham" teachings of the Jews, and to "reverence their husbands" in accordance with the theology of Paul.[79]

When Pierce Butler was preparing for his divorce he, with the aid of his lawyers, drew up his *Statement* to be used as testimony. In it he cited as "perhaps the fundamental" reason for the failure of his marriage the "peculiar views which were entertained by Mrs. Butler . . . she held that marriage should be a companionship on equal terms—partnership, in which if both partners agreed all is well—but at no time has one partner a right to control the other."[80] He claimed the things to which his wife objected were "the customary and pledged acquiescence of a wife to marital control—nothing more."[81] Pierce Butler asserted that "nothing is required to show the error of this principal of equal rights in marriage. . . . No one who is not morally astray can fail to see the heedlessness of the pretension."[82]

A man was the head of his family. His wife and his minor children were his wards. The common law provided that "a mother as such is entitled to no power but only to reverence and respect," but that "the Empire of the father continues even after his death."[83] Both the statute law[84] and public opinion supported the father's authority. And this authority, Fanny Kemble discovered, "endowed" the father with the power of "supreme torture."[85] Yet she accepted her husband's right to the custody of their children.

Her ecceptance is significant of the code under which she lived. Fanny Kemble was not lacking in daring.

79. Mary S. Benson, *Women of the Eighteenth-Century America* (New York, 1935), 184-185, citing David Ramsey, *Memoirs of the Life of Martha Laurens Ramsey*, 41-42.
80. Butler, *Statement*, 9.
81. *Ibid.*, 9-10.
82. Bobbé, *Fanny Kemble*, 247.
83. Blackstone, *Commentaries*, Book I, sec. 454.
84. *Ibid.*, secs. 447-452, Clark, Cobb, and Irwin, comps., *Code of 1861*, sec. 1744.
85. Fanny Kemble to Harriet Martineau, Sept. 22, 1846, in Kemble, *Records of Later Life*, III, 137.

There was no doubt of her devotion to her children. Her personal conduct was unquestioned. Yet she possessed adequate proof of her husband's infidelity and made no use of it. He divorced her in 1849 and got the custody of the children.[86]

Butler himself admitted "her care and management of our children was admirable we have never disagreed once about them."[87] But both he and his wife regarded the children as a species of the father's undisputed personal property and behaved accordingly.

Fanny Kemble was planning a separation when their second child was expected. She wrote her husband that she could reach England in time for it to be born there and "if you will appoint the means for your child being brought over to you, I shall of course observe them."[88] In considering his wife's determination to leave him Butler questioned the welfare of the children without her, his own ability to care for them, and her happiness if separated from them, but not the possibility of the mother being given the guardianship of the children.[89]

The father had the right to will away the custody of his children. He might, and frequently did, name their mother as their guardian. This was the only way in which she ever gained complete control over legitimate children. If the father died without providing for their guardianship the mother was eligible for appointment by the courts, but on remarriage her authority terminated. She might be reappointed or dismissed at the discretion of the court and the father's next of kin, the new step-father, or someone else named by the court replace her.[90]

A widowed mother's estate was divided among her children but under the Act of 1804 she was entitled

86. Driver, *Fanny Kemble*, 114-156; Butler, *Statement*, *passim*.
87. Pierce Butler to Mrs. Sedgwick, May 31, 1839, *ibid.*, 33.
88. Fanny Kemble to Pierce Butler, 1838, in Butler, *Statement*, 27.
89. Pierce Butler to Mrs. Sedgwick, May 31, 1839, *ibid.*, 38.
90. Cobb, comp., *Digest*, Acts of: 1792, p. 309; 1828, p. 327; 1842, p. 335.

to nothing from an intestate legitimate child whom she might have survived. If such a child had no descendants, father, brother, and sisters shared his estate. Whole or half blood on the paternal side inherited equally. If the father was dead and the mother had remained a widow she was entitled to her husband's part of the estate, but if she had remarried the father's next kin inherited his share.[91]

The Act of 1843 was less harsh. Remarriage still barred a mother from participation in the estates of all children except her last or only one. This she might inherit unconditionally.[92]

This law took an odd turn in the settlement of the estate of William Harrell, a posthumous child who died before he was three years old. His mother had married again and by that marriage had had a daughter, Mary. When the girl was two days old the boy died. Since he had inherited considerable property from his father the disposition of it became a matter for the courts. The case finally reached the Supreme Bench. It defined the "last child" as being the last surviving child of the mother and named Mary as the sole heir. Thus she inherited the estate of her mother's first husband, through a half brother, who never saw his father and who was probably never aware that his sister had been born.[93]

Illegitimate children had "no blood except that given them by the law."[94] Under it they belonged to the mother and, unless the father legally adopted them,[95] it was as though he were dead and his relatives had never existed. An illegitimate child shared equally in the estate of its mother with a legitimate one. If it died intestate, provided there were neither wife nor

91. Prince, comp., *Digest*, Act of 1804, p. 233.

92. Cobb, comp., *Digest*, Act of 1843, p. 297; Clark, Cobb, and Irwin, comps., *Code of 1861*, sec. 2452.

93. Uriah B. Holden and wife *vs.* David Harrell, 6 Georgia 126.

94. Clark, Cobb, and Irwin, comps., *Code of 1861*, sec. 1751.

95. *Ibid.*, sec. 1750.

lineal descendants, its estate was divided alike between mother, brothers, and sisters. If none of these existed the property went to the mother's legitimate children.[96]

The law of 1793 provided that both man and woman accused of misconduct should be indicted but the Supreme Court of Georgia left no room for doubt that the "primary object of the act . . . was to protect the county from the charge of bastard children."[97]

The mother of an illegitimate child might choose between naming the father and giving security for its support. If the father were known he was forced to provide for the expenses of the child's birth and its maintenance. Whomsoever the mother accused was held guilty unless proven innocent. The father's offence was not his paternity but his failure to pay the bills. This was held to be a misdemeanor.[98]

The fate of such children was always sad but the taxpayers were determined to protect their pocket books if possible. Most of the Bastard Bonds seem to cover the care of the child until it was fourteen years of age,[99] but among the court records are items such as: "Lucy Sheet, illegitimate child of Anna Shorter, four years old bound to Joseph Barker,"[100] which tell their own story.

With Protestanism both Church and State accepted marriage as a civil contract and divorces became permissible. They were avoided, however, if possible for there had lingered a fondness for the sacramental marriage doctrines of the Catholic Church and the causes for which divorces were allowed placed a stigma on them for either sex. And for a woman a divorce might prove socially and economically disastrous.

96. Clark, Cobb, and Irwin, comps., *Code of 1861*, secs. 1751-1752; Cobb, comp., *Digest*, Acts of: 1816, p. 293; 1850, p. 299.
97. Locke *vs.* the State, 3 Georgia 534.
98. Cobb, comp., *Digest*, Act of 1793, pp. 148-149; Penal Code of 1833, Div. X, sec. XXIX, 1818; Clark, Cobb, and Irwin, comps., *Code of 1861*, secs. 4640-4643.
99. Richmond County, *Inferior Court Records*: Bastard Bonds.
100. Davidson, comp., *Wilkes County Records*, I, 145.

The Georgia divorce code was brought from England and, in theory at least, was severe for it still bore the marks of the canon law which did not recognize divorce. The Catholic Church prohibited marriage under certain conditions. If these were not observed Rome declared the marriage void, but if both parties were qualified only death could dissolve the bond. This plan the English incorporated in their civil law—even though the recorder of the common law was "led to wonder that the same authority which enjoined the strictest celebacy to the priesthood should think itself proper judge in causes between man and wife."[101]

The English code classified divorces as complete and partial. Complete divorces were given only to parties who had not made a legal contract. They were not allowed for any causes which arose after a legal marriage—not even when "it became impossible for the parties to live together; as in the case of intollerable ill temper or adultery." Partial divorces were granted for infidelity and cruel treatment. They permitted separation from "bed and board" only and prohibited remarriage.[102]

In Georgia the same distinction existed[103] but as the State Constitution of 1798 provided that divorces should be granted on "legal principles" and these were not defined by the Supreme Court for almost fifty years there was a lack of uniformity in the degree and the causes for which divorces were given. Judge Floyd, in the case of Head *vs.* Head, put a stop to the "flagrant facility" with which divorces were being granted and restricted them to the grounds recognized in the laws which the colonies had brought from England.[104]

---

101. Blackstone, *Commentaries*, Book III, sec. 93.
102. *Ibid.*, Book I, sec. 440-441.
103. Prince, comp., *Digest*, Act of 1806, p. 188.
104. Head *vs.* Head, 2 Georgia 191.

The decision necessitated a revision of the divorce code. The amendment of 1849 gave the General Assembly the right to determine the grounds for divorce.[105] The Act of 1849 recognized all divorces allowed before the decision and relieved the parties who had remarried of any possible charge of bigamy.[106] And the Act of 1850 assigned inability of the parties to contract as defined by law, incontinence, and desertion as reasons for total divorce; in cases of cruel treatment or habitual drunkenness the jury was empowered to determine whether the decree should be final or separation from bed and board only; and all other grounds permitted partial divorce only.[107]

Nevertheless the divorce code remained in confusion. The first divorce procedure in Georgia required action by both courts and legislature,[108] but in 1833 the General Assembly amended the Constitution and vested sole authority in the courts.[109] Georgians, however, did not seem to be fully aware of the change for the Legislature continued to receive frequent applications for divorce and sometimes acted upon them. Governor Brown said only one such petition had been granted since the amendment and that was to complete action begun before the alteration of the Constitution. Yet he was called upon to veto a divorce bill in 1859.[110]

The law prohibited the guilty party to a divorce suit from remarrying,[111] but the Legislature by granting a "relief" could remove the disability. It was said on the floor of the House that no petition of this character had ever been denied. In 1859 came a call for a repeal of the restriction. The discussions of the bill show that Georgians had become more charitable toward divorce.

105. McElreath, *Constitution of Georgia*, Constitution of 1798, amendment to Art. III, sec. IX, 278.
106. Cobb, comp., *Digest*, Act of 1849, p. 227.
107. *Acts of Georgia*, 1850, pp. 151-152.
108. McElreath, *Constitution of Georgia*, Constitution of 1798, Art. III, sec. IX, 263.
109. *Ibid.*, amendment to Art. III, sec. IX, 274.
110. Milledgeville *Daily Federal Union*, Dec. 15, 1859.
111. Prince, comp., *Digest*, Act of 1806, p. 188.

One representative dared say, "God does not put his eternal sanction on everything done by preachers and justices of the peace," and to pronounce, "continued cohabitation under the coercion of law, where there is no affection legalized adultery."[112]

As the years went by the divorce rate increased in Georgia. Oliver H. Prince counted 291 divorces granted between 1798 and the close of the legislative session of 1835. He found they averaged about four a year from 1800 to 1810. The next ten years the rate doubled —eight a year. Between 1820 and 1830 it more than doubled again—eighteen a year. And from 1830 to 1835 Georgia granted an average of twenty-eight divorces a year.[113]

By 1833 the weight of divorce legislation had become so great that the General Assembly stepped out from under the load and added a constitutional amendment which included their grievance in its preamble.[114] And by 1859 Representative Wallace of Taylor estimated the state had spent $200,000 on special divorce legislation.[115]

The divorce laws placed the same value on the character of the husband as they did on that of the wife, but public opinion differed. As Judge Floyd pointed out, in his Head *vs.* Head decision, society accepted the delinquency of the husband with greater grace than it was willing to allow his wife. He found this was being justified by presuming the failings of the wife to be more injurious to the home than those of the husband. Judge Floyd denied this theory and refused to believe it was "illustrative of the high esteem placed on feminine virtue." He held that the double standard was owing to the "prevelence of vice among men." And, though he deplored it, he charged that

112. Augusta *Daily Constitutionalist*, Dec. 11 1859.
113. Prince, comp., *Digest*, 187.
114. Cobb, comp., *Digest*, Preamble to the amendment of 1833, Constitution of 1798, Art. III, sec. IX, 1123.
115. Augusta *Daily Constitutionalist*, Dec. 11, 1859.

wives were required to "meekly endure" what husbands were "justified in making good cause for loathing, contempt, and repudiation."[116]

In an unhappy marriage the unsurbordinate status of women was likely to prove tragic. It is true the law granted alimony. The amount was conditioned on the wealth of the husband and the separate estate of the wife.[117] Any part of her property which he might have lost or squandered previously was forgotten by the law. There was the forlorn Elizabeth Harper, for example. She wrote of her husband to the Brothers and Sisters of Mars Hill Church, "he have taken my property and gave it to another and now is sporeting with my carecttor." But she could only be "sory" she had been driven out of her home with nothing but "a little flower and a small piece of meat" and forced to seek "sheltor" with the neighbors. There seems to have been no comfort for her destitution.[118]

Elizabeth Harper's social position was not responsible for her unhappy situation. Women of the aristocracy played with loaded dice too. There is a Charleston gentleman's own record. It appears he had killed his wife's reputed lover, probably in a duel in Georgia. Later with the full connivance of Georgia gentlemen of equal rank he attempted to secure letters which his wife had written to the dead man and which would incriminate her. He wanted them not only as testimony should he decide to sue for divorce and to exhonorate himself should he be extradited for trial, but also because there was a possibility of his "unfortunate" wife inheriting "seventy thousand pounds sterling" from her father's estate. If she did, he made no secret of

116. Head *vs.* Head, 2 Georgia 191.

117. Cobb, comp., *Digest*, Act of 1810, p. 225; Clark, Cobb, and Irwin, comps., *Code of 1861*, secs. 1676, 1688-1699.

118. Elizabeth Harper to the Brothers and Sisters of Mars Hill Church, Nov. 12, 1818, in mss. Letters and Papers of Edward Harden, Athens, Georgia in Duke University Library.

his plan to use the proof her letters contained of "her behavior and feelings" toward him to "so impress the Court of Chancery with her unworthiness as to induce them to settle the entire fortune on her children."[119]

It was common to find a husband who advertised that his wife had "left his bed and board without the least shadow of provocation,"[120] and to "forewarn all others from trading with or trusting her" as he was no longer responsible for her debts.[121] It is possible these husbands were frequently as poor risks as the wives they advertised. At least the Southern Banner seems to have been suspicious. Beginning in 1842 and continuing for years it charged for "announcing candidates for office $5.00—payable in advance," and for "husbands advertising their wives . . . $5.00 *invariably* payable in advance." All other patrons got twelve lines of advertising for $1.00—on credit.[122]

Taken all-in-all the political status of women in Georgia from 1783 to 1860 was of microscopic importance and their civil status was capricious. That of the unmarried woman was secure but, in theory at least, a husband spoke from a burning bush and a married woman had no legal civil status. In fact, however, the law was flexible. It never intruded but if solicited it could give substantial protection to married women.

The statutes governing the relations between husband and wife were based on a mixed concept. In regard to property they were feudal—she, the vassal, surrendered all she possessed to her overlord in return for protection; in regard to a wife's conduct her relations with her husband were those of guardian and ward; and, if a wife was stolen, damaged, or abused,

119. John Rutledge to Robert MacKay, Feb. 11, 1804, in mss. Letters and Papers of Robert MacKay and W. H. H. Stiles, Savannah, Georgia, in University of North Carolina Library.

120. *Athens Gazette*, June 16, 1814.

121. Milledgeville *Georgia Patriot*, July 11, 1826.

122. Athens *Southern Banner*, June 13, 1842.

the law regarded the husband's loss as though his wife were his personal property and allowed him to collect damages.

A married woman's greatest legal liability was her lack of property rights. But here again she played hide-and-seek with the law. The law permitted her marriage vow to confiscate her possessions but did not hesitate to shut one eye, help her establish a separate estate, and maintain it during her husband's life. After her husband's death she was entitled to a year's support and to her dower. In case of divorce there was alimony. The courts were inclined to be friendly to a wife's financial interest, but expected her to keep her marriage contract and were not inclined to show mercy if she failed.

Due to the English heritage and American custom, the tendency was to keep estates in the male line. So women were in the red there. But during the antebelum period public opinion was slowly crystalizing into laws more beneficial to women. While children were the property of the father, here too a slight change in favor of the mother was in progress.

A married woman's position in Georgia before 1860 was always hazardous, frequently humiliating, and often tragic. Her true status, nevertheless, was far more commonly determined by her character, that of the man she married, their personal relations to each other, the use they made of the laws, and even by public opinion, than by the statutes alone.

"An Act for the Relief of Females . . .": Divorce and the Changing Legal Status of Women in Tennessee, 1796-1860, Part I

By Lawrence B. Goodheart, Neil Hanks, and Elizabeth Johnson

In August 1861 Mary Chesnut recorded the following conversation in her diary:

> But you know, our women all speak in that low plaintive way because they are always excusing themselves for something they never did.
>
> And the Yankee women are loud and shrill because they fight it out—fair field and no favor—and when incompatibility comes in, they go for divorce.[1]

Using a timely military metaphor this upper class South Carolinian depicted the battle of the sexes as one in which southern women passively acquiesced to male domination, while their northern sisters boldly asserted themselves, even to the point of dissolving unsatisfactory marriages. Mrs. Chesnut's characterization of divorce as alien to southern mores, a foreign thought to the long-suffering but ever deferential wife, represents a ringing affirmation of well established wisdom which a number of scholars have endorsed.[2]

Certainly there is an important element of truth in Chesnut's sectional stereotype. National statistics on divorce, first collected in 1867, show that for the last half of the nineteenth-century the rate of divorce was lowest in the South compared to any other region until 1880 and that in the percentage of divorces granted to the wife the

This paper began as a joint effort in a research seminar directed by Lawrence B. Goodheart, then visiting assistant professor of history at Vanderbilt University. The authors wish to thank Bertram Wyatt-Brown for his insightful comments on this study.

[1]C. Van Woodward, ed., *Mary Chesnut's Civil War* (New Haven, 1981), 181.

[2]Arthur C. Calhoun, *Social History of the American Family*, 3 vols. (N.Y., 1917), v. II, 49-50, purported that divorce was virtually nonexistent in the South. William R. Taylor, *Cavalier and Yankee: The Old South and American National Character* (N.Y., 1961), 166, declared that "divorce was almost impossible." Anne F. Scott, *The Southern Lady: From Pedestal to Politics, 1830-1930* (Chicago, 1970) implied that since ante-bellum women were so hopelessly trapped in claustrophobic sex roles that divorce was not an option. Bertram Wyatt-Brown, *Southern Honor: Ethics and Behavior in the Old South* (N.Y., 1982) 244-46, 283-92, 300-06, stressed that a dominant code of male honor greatly restricted female options for divorce. And Catherine Clinton, *Plantation Mistresses, Woman's World in the Old South* (N.Y., 1982), 79, concluded that divorces "were difficult to obtain throughout the antebellum period."

South held the bottom position well into the twentieth century.[3] Yet the evidence from this case study of divorce in Tennessee raises substantial questions about the accuracy of conventional thinking regarding the status of women and divorce in the Old South, at least for the Volunteer State.

Because no systematic national, regional, and state information on divorce exists for the ante-bellum period,[4] four sets of legal data on divorce in Tennessee—the statutes, supreme court rulings, divorce petitions to the legislature, and circuit court decisions for three selected counties—have been examined. Although the vast majority of husbands and wives in Tennessee remained married, incidents of divorce serve as a social barometer. Divorce measures the expectations that women and men have toward marriage, family, sexual roles, and morality; it establishes boundaries for what is legally and culturally sanctioned. Moreover, the major problem in investigating the history of most southern women before the Civil War is in the paucity of traditional literary evidence.[5] The availability of divorce records is, however, a means to compensate for this lack of material.

The divorce laws throughout the United States from the end of the eighteenth-century through the Civil War clearly demonstrate the imbalance of legal power in the relationship between husband and

---

[3]Alexander Plateris, "One Hundred Years of Marriage and Divorce Statistics, United States, 1867-1967," Department of Vital and Health Statistics, Series 21, No. 24, National Center of Health Statistics (Washington, 1973), 50-51.

[4]There have been, however, a number of specialized studies on divorce. A comprehensive study of state supreme court decisions throughout the South is found in Jane T. Censer, " 'Smiling Through Her Tears': Ante-Bellum Southern Women and Divorce," *American Journal of Legal History*, 25 (1981), 24-47. Guion G. Johnson, *Ante-Bellum North Carolina: A Social History* (Chapel Hill, 1937), 217-23, and James H. Johnston, *Race Relations in Virginia and Miscegnation in the South* (Amherst, 1970; orig., 1937), 237-68, pioneered in the examination of legislative divorce petitions. Two early studies that are still valuable are Joel P. Bishop, *Commentaries on the Law of Marriage and Divorce and Evidence in Matrimonial Suits* (Boston, 1852) and George E. Howard, *A History of Matriomonial Institutions*, 3 vols. (Chicago, 1904).

Studies on the Northeast dominate the literature and include Henry S. Cohn, "Connecticut's Divorce Mechanism, 1636-1969," *American Journal of Legal History*, 14 (1970), 35-54; Nancy F. Cott, "Divorce and the Changing Status of Women in Eighteenth-Century Massachusetts," *William and Mary Quarterly*, 33 (1976), 586-614; Cott, "Eighteenth-Century Family and Social Life Revealed in Massachusetts Divorce Records," *Journal of Social History*, 10 (1976), 20-43; Thomas Meehan, " 'Not Made Out of Levity': Evolution of Divorce in Early Pennsylvania," *Pennsylvania Magazine of History and Biography*, 92 (1968), 441-64; and Matteo Spalletta, "Divorce in Colonial New York," *New York Historical Society Quarterly*, 39 (1955), 422-40.

[5]Anne F. Scott has noted, "In ante bellum times the wives of small farmers and the slave women lived, bore children, worked hard, and died leaving little trace for the historians coming after"—*The Southern Lady*, xi. Indeed, the two major recent works on southern women, Scott's and Clinton's *Plantation Mistresses* relay heavily on the written records of upper class women.

wife. This disability of women caused Sarah M. Grimké, an alienated member of one of Charleston's best families who became an early abolitionist and feminist, to observe in 1838 that "the very being of a woman, like that of a slave, is absorbed in her masters."[6] Although a wife did not fall into the category of chattel as did a slave, Grimké was right in suggesting that the act of matrimony in terms of the common law transformed a single women (a *femme sole*) into a wife (a *femme covert*) whose legal existence with few exceptions was assumed by her husband.[7] The institution of patriarchal marriage involved a definite hierarchy of power between the sexes. But male dominance, if abused in a manner that questioned the legitimacy of the husband's sway over a faithful spouse, could be checked through two forms of divorce. A bed and board divorce (*divortium a mensa et thoro*) was similar to a modern day marital separation; the couple remained married but lived apart. An absolute or complete divorce (*divortium a vinculo*) returned the wife to a non-married state, to a *femme sole.* There was a notable double standard in the divorce process favoring the husband, but the striking feature of Tennessee's divorce history from 1796 to 1860 was the assertion and expansion of the wife's legal prerogatives against an unfit husband, especially given the patriarchal bias.

Only three years after statehood, Tennessee's first divorce statute of 1799 allowed a relatively wide latitude in the grounds for absolute divorce that included impotence, bigamy, adultery, and desertion. Tennessee's law contrasts with its parent state of North Carolina which did not enact similar legislation until 1814, with South Carolina, which had no divorce statutes until 1868, and with New York which before the Civil War permitted divorce only because of adultery. It is not a north-south sectionalism, therefore, that explains the liberality of Tennessee's divorce law but an east-west polarity. Tennessee's divorce law was similar to that of other trans-Appalachian states such as Ohio and Kentucky which achieved statehood around the turn of the century. In the case of Tennessee in the late eighteenth-century, Frederick Jackson Turner's thesis that the frontier had a democratizing effect on the culture was true in

---

[6]Sarah M. Grimké, *Letters on the Equality of the Sexes and the Condition of Woman* (Boston, 1838), 74. The analogy of the wife as slave was also made by Mary Chesnut, in Woodward, ed., *Chesnut's Civil War*, 59, and Stephen P. Andrews in Henry James, Horace Greely, and Stephen P. Andrews, *Love, Marriage, and Divorce and the Sovereignty of the Individual* (N.Y., 1972; orig., 1853), 120.

[7]See Richard B. Morris, *Studies in the History of American Law with Special Reference to the Seventeenth-Century and Eighteenth-Century* (N.Y., 1930), 173, and Maxwell Bloomfield, *American Lawyers in a Changing Society, 1776-1876* (Cambridge, 1976), 96-97.

regard to divorce laws. Influenced by the Revolutionary ideals of personal freedom and the social flux of their own pioneer conditions, the newly settled states west of the Appalachians adopted progressive divorce laws. Tennessee is a southern state but its divorce laws are western in origin.[8]

The divorce statute of 1799 is also a benchmark to measure the statute of women in Tennessee. Although the provision for absolute divorce was gender blind, other sections singled out women, either penalizing the unfaithful wife or protecting the wronged wife. Neither divorced spouse could marry their partner in adultery but a divorced woman who openly cohabitated with her lover was declared incapable to dispose of her real estate whether during her life or by a will. In effect, the Hester Prynes of Tennessee bore a sex specific economic liability, their own scarlet A, that punished them more severely for adultery than it did their husbands.[9]

The law purposely punished female vice but it also rewarded the virtuous woman. In order to protect a dutiful wife from a brutish husband, a court could grant a bed and board divorce to a woman whose husband "shall maliciously abandon or turn his wife out of doors, or by cruel or barbarous treatment endanger her life, or offer such indignities to her person as to render her condition intolerable, and thereby force her to withdraw."[10] Because under the system of female coverture, the wife lacked independent financial status (although in some cases through ante-nuptial agreements brides kept their property in their own name), the court could grant the wife alimony in a bed and board divorce up to one-third of her husband's annual income. Court directed alimony affected unhappily married couples in two important ways: it allowed a virtuous wife and often her children the financial wherewithal to escape from an intolerable living situation, and it levied a financial burden on the husband in the hope that such a pecuniary penalty would force him to alter his unsatisfactory behavior. Moreover, the provision for a bed and board divorce transformed the court into an institutionalized marriage counselor which sought a mutual "reconciliation" of the couple or a reunion in which the "husband shall by his petition offer to

---

[8] *Tn. Acts* (1799), chap. 19, sec. 1, 645; Howard, Matrimonial Institutions, v. 3, 58; Nelson M. Blake, *Road to Reno* (N.Y., 1962), 50-51; Mary Beth Norton, *Liberty's Daughters: The Revolutionary Experience of American Women* (Boston, 1980), 234; Linda K. Kerber, *Women of the Republic: Intellect and Ideology in Revolutionary America* (Chapel Hill, 1980), 159-84; and Julie R. Jeffrey, *Frontier Women: The Trans-Mississippi West, 1840-1880* (N.Y., 1979), 144.

[9] *Tn. Acts* (1799), chap. 19, sec. 6, 647.

[10] *Tn. Acts* (1799), chap. 19, sec. 9, 647-48.

cohabit with her again, and use her as a good husband ought to do."[11] Thus the state hoped to maintain the permanence of marriage, the protection of a victimized wife, and the stability of the family by mitigating the excesses of patriarchy through court intervention.

The progressive quality of the 1799 law must, however, be viewed in terms of its intended conservative purpose. This legislation set the standard for subsequent reforms of the divorce process that sought to ensure the spontaneous acceptance of patriarchal marriage by eliminating its worst abuses just as the southern master class would analogously eliminate gratuitous cruelties in the slave system during the ante-bellum period.[12] The relatively broad grounds for absolute divorce established in 1799 and subsequently expanded recognized that the institution of patriarchal marriage was better protected by admitting the reality of impotence, bigamy, adultery, and desertion rather than creating a divorceless state, such as South Carolina, modeled after an illusionary religious ideal of life-long union for all married couples. After all, blatant discrepancy between official law and unofficial behavior mocked the sanctity of patriarchal marriage. Tennessee did, in fact, experiment with a repeal of the entire 1799 law from 1807 to 1809 but common sense soon prevailed and the complete law was reinstated in 1809.[13]

Moreover, the provision for a bed and board divorce in the 1799 law sought to compensate for an inherent contradiction in patriarchal marriage: the unchecked power of the husband might not result in a benevolent rule but could well lead to a noxious tyranny over the weaker sex. Historian Christopher Lasch's observation that "It was not the image of women as equals that inspired the reform of divorce laws but the image of women as victims" applies exactly to ante-bellum Tennessee.[14] Court supervision to protect the wife from extreme abuse was an essential safety value that prevented the worst excesses of patriarchal marriage from becoming an obvious social outrage and thus underminding the validity of the husband's dominance itself. Ironically the effort to preserve patriarchal marriage through reform of the divorce laws broadened the wife's rights and provided the opportunity for increasing numbers of women to seek legal redress from unsatisfactory marriages.

With the exception of the divorce statutes of 1819 and 1822 with

[11] *Ibid.*, 648.

[12] See Eugene D. Genovese, *Roll, Jordan, Roll: The World the Slaves Made* (N.Y., 1974), 25-49, on "The Hegemonic Function of the Law."

[13] *Tn. Acts* (1807), chap. 97, sec. 1, 1077, and *Tn. Acts* (1809), chap. 98, sec. 1, 1189.

[14] Christopher Lasch, "Divorce and the Decline of the Family," in his *The World of Nations: Reflections on American History, Politics and Culture* (N.Y., 1973), 39.

their special racial concerns,[15] legislation from 1825 to 1860 progressively expanded the wife's legal prerogatives and facilitated the divorce procedures. A legislative act of 1825 was significantly worded to be for "the benefit of married women whose husbands have either left them, or driven them from their homes."[16] The law aided the abandoned wife by barring any property she had accrued after the separation from being attached to pay for her husband's debts. The burden of the law was to prevent a situation where the wealth of a hard-working and virtuous wife would inadvertently subsidize a spendthrift and negligent husband.

Similarly, in 1831 the General Assembly came to the financial relief of wronged wives with "an act to authorize females to obtain divorces in court without cost." Women had to procure a bond for the prosecution of their divorce petition, but if the applicant won the case, court costs could in "no event" be "chargeable upon a female."[17] Court costs then took on a moral cost which the 1799 law had left ambiguious—female virtue was now clearly recompensed.[18] Presumably the male legislators were repelled by the prospect of a decent woman having to pay court costs after having secured a divorce from a proven scoundrel. In addition, the same law dispensed in the case of women only with the stipulation of the 1799 law which required the newspaper publication of the divorce suit for four successive weeks—a small procedural concession but one indicative of the chivalry of a legislature concerned with protecting female virture from male vice.[19]

A procedural shift barring private divorce bills from the legislature and giving the equity courts original jurisdiction over "all petitions and suits for divorce" led to the consolidation and clarification in 1836 of nearly four decades of experience with such litigation.[20] The

---

[15]The imperative for the planter class to fix a clear racial caste system upon the state led to legislation in 1819 and 1822 that in part sought to regulate the sexual behavior of white women. The 1799 law was amended in 1819 so that a court could grant a divorce if a "woman was in a state of pregnancy with a child of color" at the time of marriage. Although a narrowly focused piece of legislation, its larger import was to call attention to the emotion laden issue of sexual relations between white women and black men, a subject that directly challenged the power of white male slaveholders over women and blacks. Although there was no equivalent law regarding white men and black women, an 1822 statute declared interracial marriages null and void and levied a $500 fine on both participants. See *Tn. Acts* (1819), chap. 20, sec. 2, 477; *Tn. Acts* (1822), chap. 19, 22-23; and Lawrence B. Goodheart, "Tennessee's Antislavery Movement Reconsidered: The Example of Elihu Embree," *Tennessee Historical Quarterly*, 41 (1982), 224-38.

[16]*Tn. Acts* (1825), chap. 10, 8.

[17]*Tn. Acts* (1831), chap. 20, sec. 1, 35-36.

[18]*Tn. Acts* (1799), chap. 19, sec. 8, 647.

[19]*Tn. Acts* (1799), chap. 19, sec. 2, 646.

[20]*Tn. Acts* (1836), chap. 19, sec. 4, 90.

systematic legislation of that year extended the grounds for absolute divorce, enumerated judicial procedures, and significantly expanded state protection offered to abused women and their children. Prior to 1836, a married woman could petition for divorce only through the representation of a "friend" since she lacked legal standing as a *femme covert;* the law of that year, however, allowed her to sue in her own name, a telling modification of common law because it meant increased recognition of the individual status of the wife. In a further break with the tradition of the woman's identity being subsumed onto the husband's, the wife's residency in a divorce petition was defined in terms of her own place of domicile, not her husband's. Yet,. as in the 1799 law, the overall dominance of the husband remained paramount, most notably in terms of a double standard on adultery and property ownership. In addition, a new gender-specific grounds for absolute divorce was codified against a wife who had refused without reasonable cause for over a two-year period to accompany her husband to establish residency in Tennessee—a pragmatic albeit biased way to cope with marital problems caused by the geographic mobility of the trans-Appalachian West.[21]

The 1836 statute also drew the distinction between the "good" and "bad" divorcée more sharply. Female vice was punished more severely than equivalent male wrong-doing, while female virtue warranted paternalistic state protection. Not only did an adulteress who lived with her lover lose the ability to dispose of her property, but a male complainant who won a divorce maintained a legal right to his wife's property. In contrast, a female plantiff who successfully divorced her husband did retain her own property but she did not gain any access to her husband's.[22]

Given the financial dependence of female coverture and the economic hardship facing most divorced women, court intervention was essential in order to relieve the probable destitution of the wronged wife in absolute divorce cases. An important addition to the 1836 law provided that a successful female plantiff in a suit for absolute divorce could compel her husband "to provide for the maintenance of the children of the marriage, if any there shall be, and to provide a suitable allowance to the complainant" as the court deemed suitable. Moreover, the court could sequester the husband's property and place it in receivership if he failed to pay the stipulated maintenance payments.[23]

---

[21] *Tn. Acts* (1836), chap. 26, sec. 2,3,7,11,12,14, 117-21.
[22] *Tn. Acts* (1836), chap. 26, sec. 7,11,12, 119-20.
[23] *Tn. Acts* (1836), chap. 26, sec. 10, 199-120.

The expansion of the grounds for a bed and board divorce in the 1836 law gave the dutiful wife significant new latitude in order to secure court protection against an unfit husband. A married Tennessee woman was empowered to petition any equity court for action against her husband for "cruel and inhuman treatment" or any conduct which may "render it unsafe and improper for her to cohabit with him, and be under his dominion and control, or of such indignities offered to her person as to render her condition intolerable, and thereby forcing her to withdraw, or that he has abandoned her, or turned her out of doors, and refuses or neglects to provide for her. . . ." She could also indicate in her petition the specific "relief as she may think herself entitled to," and thus force her husband to appear before the court.[24] If the court found the defendant guilty, a bed and board divorce could be granted for a limited time or "forever thereafter," an innovation that allowed for permanent marital separation. Again because of the wife's economic dependence, the court could order "suitable support and maintenance of the complainant and her children" out of the husband's property, which the court could sequester and place in receivership if necessary.[25]

The law of 1836 marked the recognition that a more liberal divorce law with greater protection for victimized women and children was essential if patriarchal marriage was to survive with a veneer of justice. Two ad hoc divorce laws passed in 1840 and 1842 embodied this principle. The 1840 act "for the relief of females" allowed any married woman who had been a resident of Tennessee for at least two years and who was of "good character" to petition for divorce on any legal grounds even if they had occurred in another state.[26] In this case the wife's divorce prerogatives outstripped her husband's, an unusual example of a female double standard that the legislators quickly rectified by a gender blind amendment in 1846.[27] A section of the 1842 law, however, lessened women's liability in matters of property settlement in all divorce cases, not just ones in which the wife was a successful complaintant. The court was instructed to allow to any divorceé "such a part of the real and personal property of the husband as they shall think proper" with special reference to any of her property that her husband had acquired through marriage.[28] The discretion of the court might well still favor

---

[24] *Tn. Acts* (1836), chap. 26, sec. 18, 121.
[25] *Tn. Acts* (1836), chap. 26, sec. 19, 122.
[26] *Tn. Acts* (1840), chap. 54, sec. 1, 90.
[27] *Tn. Acts* (1846), chap. 67, 135.
[28] *Tn. Acts* (1842), chap. 133, sec. 2, 155.

Tennessee Supreme Court

Judge William B. Turley
(Justice 1835-53)

Tennessee Historical Society Collection

Judge John Overton
(1766-1833)

Tennessee State Library & Archives

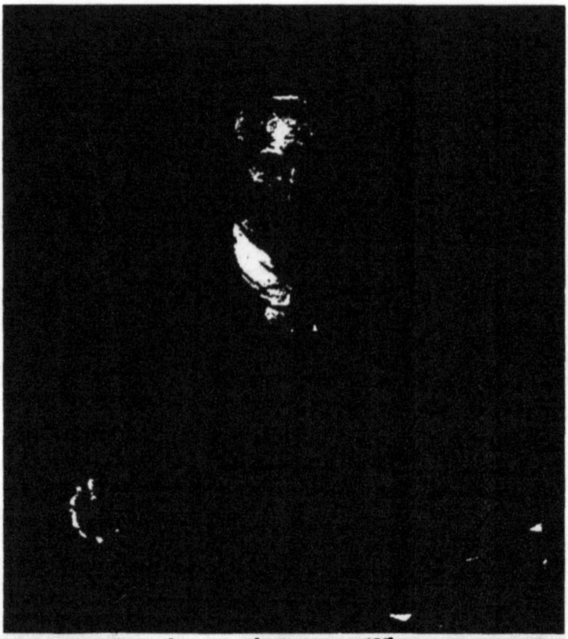

Judge Hugh Lawson White
(1773-1840)

Tennessee State Library & Archives

Judge Robert Looney Caruthers
(1800-1882)

TABLE 1

Divorce Appeals Heard by the Supreme Court according to Who and When Filed

Date	Wife	Husband
Before 1800	0	0
1800-1809	0	1
1810-1819	0	1
1820-1829	0	2
1830-1834	1	0
1835-1839	0	3
1840-1844	1	0
1845-1849	1	3
1850-1854	1	1
1855-1859	6a	5a
1860	0	0
Total	10	16

a-One jointly filed appeal has been counted in each column
Source: Tennessee State Supreme Court Reports

TABLE 2

Disposition of Divorce Appeals Heard by the Supreme Court

Number of Suits	Begun by Wife	Begun by Husband
25	10a	16a
Won by Wife	Won by Husband	Dismissed (no grounds)
15	9	1

a-one jointly filed appeal has been counted in each column.
Source: Tennessee State Supreme Court Reports

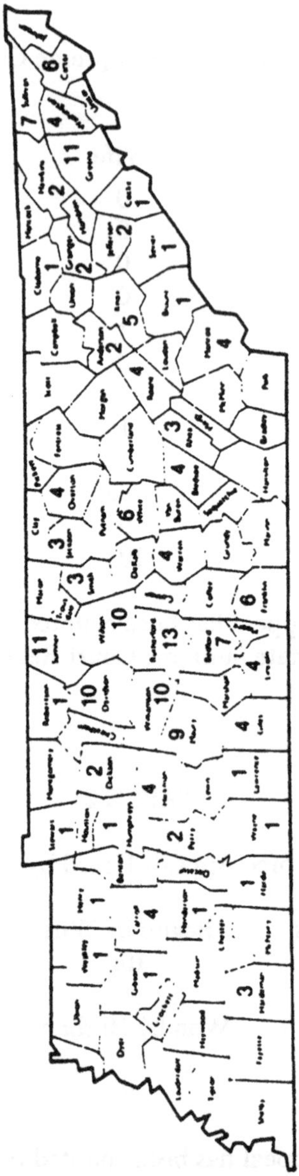

MAP 1
County of Origin of Petitions for Legislative Divorce

Source: Tennessee Legislative Manuscripts, Tennessee State Archives

the vitimized wife over the undutiful wife in arriving at settlements, but the law no longer mandated a linkage between virtuous behavior and property rights.

Additional divorce laws further expanded the grounds for absolute divorce making Tennessee one of the most liberal states in the nation. In the words of Justice Robert L. Caruthers of the state supreme court, "In one if not more of our sister states it is said that a divorce has never been granted, either by the courts, or by the legislature, in others only for adultery, but in most of them the causes have been multiplied, and perhaps in none more largely than in our own state."[29] A section of the 1842 statute extended absolute divorce to all causes that had previously pertained to bed and board divorces, including the loosely defined grounds of "intolerable condition," "cruel and inhuman treatment," and "willful and malicious desertion," and thus considerably increased the wife's prerogative as complainant.[30] In addition, the conviction for a felony or the attempt of either spouse to murder the other were deemed divorceable situations. With the exception of a minor procedural amendment in 1860, Tennessee's progressive laws that sanctioned at least a dozen grounds for divorce remained unaltered from 1846 to the Civil War.[31]

The Tennessee legislature passed thirteen divorce bills between 1799 and 1860 but the actual implementation of the law was a judicial process ultimately dependent on the interpretations of the state supreme court in its appellate function. In twenty-five decisions between statehood and the Civil War, the supreme court set the guidelines for the circuit and chancellory courts in adjudicating divorce. Moreover, because the commentary in the legislative proceedings is sparse, the opinions of the supreme court justices furnish invaluable legal and cultural perceptions on divorce and the status of women.

After the passage of the systematic divorce law of 1836 and the liberal amendment of 1842, the number of appeals brought to the supreme court increased sharply. As Table 1 shows, only six cases were heard between 1799 and 1836, but there were nineteen cases between 1836 and 1860 with seventeen of those cases between 1842 and 1860. Thus over 50 percent of the appeals occurred in the last third of the years between 1799 and 1860. A major factor that increased the total number of appeals after 1835 was the statutory

[29]Caruthers is quoted in *Shell v. Shell*, 34 Tn. 719 (1855).

[30]*Tn. Acts* (1842), chap. 133, sec. 1, 155.

[31]*Tn. Acts* (1842), chap. 133, sec. 3, 135; *Tn. Acts* (1844), chap. 176, sec. 1, 200-201; and *Tn. Acts* (1860), chap. 88, 86.

abrogation of private legislative divorce bills, but the greater frequency of divorce cases before the high court also emphatically documents the effects of reforms in the divorce law that extended new prerogatives and greater protection to wives. Before 1839, only one appeal out of eight was initiated by a woman; after 1843, there were nine out of seventeen and between 1855 to 1860 six out of eleven. Moreover, in the adversary relationship of divorce, the court ruled in favor of the wife, affirming its designated legal role as protector of the "weaker sex," on fifteen occasions compared to only nine for the husband (see Table 2). With expanded legal standing, women more actively engaged in divorce litigation and did so with notable success at the appellate level.

Except for technical violations of procedures or lack of jurisdiction, the court sided unequivocally with the victimized wife.[32] The adulterous husband gained no favor if his wife embodied what historian Barbara Welter has termed the four cardinal virtues of ante-bellum womanhood—piety, purity, submissiveness, and domesticity.[33] The very first divorce case that the court heard in 1804 raised Justice John Overton's righteous ire when Darling Jones appealed that the principle of *ex post facto* invalidated his divorce because he had committed adultery before the 1799 statute was enacted. Overton sharply rebutted, "Adultery by the law of nature is an offense. It was so before the passage of this act, and an evil in any possible view of the subject." With greater moral feeling than legal reasoning, Overton declared that retrospective laws applied solely to marriage contracts, and he further directed commissioners to apportion Darling's property to his wronged wife.[34] In another adultery case, the high court sustained a lower court's ruling that granted a woman a divorce from her husband who openly cohabited with his slave Polly in Nashville. The supreme court found a jury's conclusion that miscegnation had occurred difficult to resist when among other incriminating evidence a witness testified that he "saw them near each other in the house in town, he buttoning up his pantaloons, and she brushing down her disordered and rumpled dress."[35] The supreme court held no brief for philandering husbands.

[32] *Pillow v. Pillow*, 13 Tn. 420-22 (1826) and *Klutts v. Klutts*, 36 Tn. 423-26 (1858) constitute two cases in which the supreme court ruled against a virtuous wife, but only in order to sustain a writ of error and an admitted flaw in the 1842 law that did not extend the grounds for divorce to imprisonment for a felony committed outside of the state.

[33] Barbara Welter, "The Cult of True Womanhood, 1820-1860," *American Quarterly*, 18 (1966), 151-74.

[34] *Jones v. Jones*, 7 Tn. 5-7 (1804).

[35] *Richmond v. Richmond*, 18 Tn. 349 (1838).

The supreme court also acted to alleviate economic victimization that was rife under female coverture. In his decision favoring Margaret Fickel, Justice Nathan Green emphasized her financial duress: "The petitioner was helpless, abandoned by her husband; she sought the house of a relation as an asylum from want and penury."[36] In 1856 the court broadened the provision of the 1836 law in an interpretation which allowed a wife to petition for divorce in her own name to include the right to file *in forma pauperis*—in other words, an indigent wife did not have to post bond for court costs. Justice Robert L. Caruthers observed, "A *femme covert* having wrongs to redress, above all others needs the benefit of such a provision, because by the marital right of the husband, her property goes, with herself, under his dominion and control."[37] Justice Robert L. McKinney concurred in a subsequent case that "the wife, destitute of means of her own, would be denied justice" if she were unable to file for divorce because she lacked the economic wherewithal. A wife without independent means who pursued a divorce bill in good faith could expect that her husband would be required to bear the court costs.[38]

Alimony was a financial assessment based on the husband's wealth used to sustain the woman and to punish the man. As the supreme court interpreted the alimony provision of the 1799 law, "The act of the legislature intended to subject him to instantaneous compensation both to keep him in order and for the effectual protection and preservation of the *femme*, which object could not otherwise be attained." The court ruled that alimony must occur even during the husband's appeal least his wife "starve in the mean time," and the bench also came to the relief of Evaline Brooks whose husband purposely conveyed his property to a third party in order to defeat her right to alimony.[39]

Although the court consistently assured the wife's right to alimony,[40] it did set limits as to when and how much maintenance the husband must pay. Justice William B. Turley recognized that "the wife is entitled to a fair portion of her husband's estate for her support," but he ruled in *Robinson v. Robinson* (1846) that given the husband's resources the settlement of half interest to his wife, Jane, in 250 acres and complete ownership of the "negro Kate" and her

[36] *Fickle v. Fickle*, 5 Tn. 204 (1834).
[37] *Hawkins v. Hawkins*, 36 Tn. 107 (1856).
[38] *Thompson v. Thompson*, 40 Tn. 529 (1859).
[39] *Pearson v. Pearson*, 7 Tn. 28 (1823), and *Brooks v. Caughran*, 40 Tn. 464-68 (1859).
[40] See also *Sloan v. Cox*, 4 Tn. 323-325 (1817), and *Richardson v. Wilson*, 8 Tn. 67-83 (1835).

children was "too much." Therefore he awarded only the slaves to Jane despite her "fair fame and reputation."[41] Another case restricted alimony pending the decision of the court of original jurisdiction. Justice Nathan Green lamented, however, the distress of the wife denied maintenance—"With every disposition to afford the complainant relief, forlorn and wretched as her condition has become, we cannot perceive any legal ground upon which it can be done."[42]

In the matter of alimony, the court acted paternalistically to relieve, if possible, the utter economic degradation of the woman. Yet, regardless of judicial charity, patriarchal marriage made the wife's financial position subservient to that of her husband's. Woman's lot could be harsh, as the court fatalistically recognized: "And if, upon the divorce, nothing can be given to her, or less than may be suitable to her rank, and condition in life, by reason of the husband's poverty, it is her misfortune, to which she must submit."[43]

The wife's right to property, like alimony, was hotly contested. Over one-half of the husbands' fifteen appeals dealt with such issues, but the high court consistently restored women's ante-nuptial property except when the legitimate claims of creditors took precedent. Justice William B. Turley, who had found Jane Robinson's alimony settlement excessive, gave no ground in another case to Joseph S. Chunn, an adulterer, who claimed the extensive wealth that his wife had brought to the marriage. The judge thundered at the covetous husband: "Shall a man, who was violated his matriomonial vows, in every disgusting form, and by harsh and unkind treatment, force his wife to seek protection in a recission of her nuptial contract, be heard when he asks support out of her estate? It is mockery, worse than mockery."[44] In two other cases the court restored property to divorceés Margaret Hackney and Martha E. Sharp whose husbands had failed to honor agreements respecting their separate realty rights during marriage.[45] Unfortunately for Nancy McGhee and Anna Ames, however, Justice Robert J. McKinney ruled that a creditor's bona fide claims on marital property prevailed over rights of the wife.[46]

In addition to alimony and property settlements, the court modified the common law practice that a father was automatically

[41] *Robinson v. Robinson*, 26 Tn. 443 (1846).
[42] *Persons v. Persons*, 26 Tn. 183 (1846).
[43] *Chenault v. Chenault*, 36 Tn. 252 (1857).
[44] *Chunn v. Chunn*, 19 Tn. 136 (1838).
[45] *Hackney v. Hackney*, 28 Tn. 450-454 (1848), and *Sharp v. Sharp*, 34 Tn. 496-500 (1855).
[46] *McGhee v. McGhee*, 34 Tn. 221-224 (1854), and *Ames v. Norman*, 36 Tn. 683-98 (1857).

entitled to custody of his children.[47] The fate of children of divorced parents was first mentioned in the statute of 1836 in regard to the father's responsibility for their financial maintenance, a legal recognition of ante-bellum concern with child nuture.[48] Justice William B. Turley in the high court's initial ruling on custody rights contrasted the "feudal tradition" of paternal autocracy with the "refined idea" of the day that the wife and children had "equal rights to all the enjoyments of life, and as safe and adequate protection for them, as the husband and father." Through a *habeas corpus* proceeding, the court could divest the father of his exclusive right to the children under common law. Turley acted with "pain and regret" in interfering with the "sacred" relationship of parent and child, but he regarded the supreme court's role as essential in contested cases, especially when the child was not old enough to decide which parent it preferred to live with.[49].

Turley, however, was not as generous to the wife as a lower court which had awarded Eliza Paine all three of her children. Nevertheless the Justice granted complainant William L. Paine the custody only to his seven year old son and left the care of the two younger children to the mother. Turley rationalized his partial reversal of the lower court's decision because neither parent had perfect behavior—William was "peevish" and Eliza "high-spirited"—and thus neither deserved exclusive custody.[50] Yet, in another decision Turley sanctioned Joseph Robertson's appeal that a chancery court had awarded his wife Jane too much alimony without commenting on the child custody award which violated the Justice's precepts in the Paine case: Joseph gained control of his two oldest children, and Jane the two youngest despite the husband's violent behavior and the wife's exemplary character.[51] The lesson of these two cases is that although women made some headway, especially in regard to gaining the custody of young children where the argument for maternal care held sway, a common law bias favoring the husband, notably in the award of older children, still continued.

The unhappy marriage of the Paines also served as a precedent for granting the wife an absolute divorce under the liberalized laws of

[47]Carroll Smith-Rosenberg, "Beauty, Beast and the Militant Woman: A Case Study in Sex Roles and Social Stress in Jacksonian America," *American Quarterly*, 23 (1971), 563, wrongly states that ante-bellum women lacked child custody rights.

[48]*Tn. Acts* (1836), chap. 26, sec. 10, 19, 120, 122.

[49]"The State on the Relation of *Paine v. Paine*," 23 Tn. 534 (1844). Paine is also spelled Payne in the records; we have used both spellings as they appear in the documents but the people referred to are the same couple, William L. and Eliza.

[50]Ibid., 534.

[51]*Robinson v. Robinson*, 26 Tn. 440-43 (1846).

1836 and 1842. Justice Nathan Green granted Eliza's appeal for a complete divorce and alimony on the grounds of the "intolerable condition" of her marriage. Despite Eliza's "high temper," her minister testified to her "Christian character" as did a number of other "ladies and gentlemen" of the Methodist church. Her husband's behavior was more reprehensible than the "peevish" sort that Justice Turley had described in the Paines' child custody suit, for Justice Green noted that William had slapped, choked, and cursed Eliza in language that was "not usual to be addressed to slaves."[52] Despite Turley's understatement of William's behavior and his award of the eldest son to the father, Green's ruling for Eliza made *Payne v. Payne* [sic] (1844) a landmark decision for mistreated wives under the "intolerable condition" cause.

During the 1850s a ground swell of divorce applications based on the liberalized laws inundated the lower courts and caused the high court to man the dikes. Justice A.W.O. Totten had more general concerns in mind than the specific denial of a divorce to complainant John Stewart in 1853 when he exhorted, "It is a duty which the parties owe to themselves, their children and society to be reconciled, and to live together."[53] The case of the bickering newlyweds Margaret L. and Lewis C. Shell in 1855 gave Justice Robert L. Caruthers the occasion to expostulate on what he thought were permissive inferior court rulings as he refused Margaret an absolute divorce because Lewis had used abusive language and threatened to beat her during one of their frequent spats, behavior for which he later apologized. Caruthers lectured that large numbers of divorces granted by the inferior courts were "unwarranted" and "productive of very great mischief to families, the cause of morality and religion, and the best interest of the public."[54] Frustrated by the definitional vagueness inherent in section 19 of the 1836 law that stipulated that "intolerable conditions" were sufficient grounds for a wife to file a divorce suit, Caruthers warned that the institution of patriarchal marriage itself was challenged:

> upon the least discontent, a case can be made out for divorce without any difficulty. The wife may not make any effort to adapt herself to the feelings, interest and habits of her husband, but in order to make her situation happy and tolerable, he must adapt himself to her peculiar temper and habits, and at all times keep so

[52] *Payne v. Payne*, 23 Tn. 501 (1844).
[53] *Stewart v. Stewart*, 32 Tn. 593-94 (1853).
[54] *Shell v. Shell*, 34 Tn. 719 (1855).
[55] Ibid., 720-21.

> strict a guard upon his tongue and conduct, as to give her no offense because this would be a personal "indignity" that would "render her situation intolerable, and force her to withdraw."[55]

In sum, Caruthers feared that the permissive rulings of the inferior courts would stand the hierarchical relationship of man and wife on its head, curtailing masculine privilege, encouraging feminine whims and threatening social order.

It would be an error, however, to see Caruthers as a reactionary on divorce. He favored the liberalization of the divorce laws, supporting the victimized wife and endorsing *Payne v. Payne* [sic] (1844), but like his peers on the bench he did not envision women as equals. Reform has boundaries, and Caruthers imposed them. "We have endeavored," he wrote in one decision, "to confine within proper limits, the action of the Courts under these statutes, so as to save families and society from the direful consequences of indiscriminate dissolution of the bonds of matrimony."[56] Patriarchal marriage imposed definite sexual roles which, for better or for worse, man and wife contracted to play. To the squabbling Shells, Caruthers avuncularly advised, "We can see no sufficient reason why they should not again come together, forgetting the past, except so far as it may afford lessons for the future, and yet enjoy a long life of peace and happiness."[57] And to another couple, Sarah nursing a badly bitten finger and John mending a broken leg suffered during a connubial altercation, the Justice denied an absolute divorce but decreed a temporary separation until these "good" but "high tempered" Rutledges were reconciled. In order to guide Lewis Shell and John Rutledge to proper husbandship, Caruthers ordered Lewis to pay court costs and John alimony.

The state supreme court had inadvertently become an institutionalized marriage counselor with a judicial concern for aiding the wronged wife and reconciling alienated spouses. The justices contended with brutish husbands, alimony, property rights, child custody, and even "intolerable conditions" with the paternalistic belief that a legal relationship based on male dominance and female subservience was just. A friend to female virtue and foe to male vice, they knew that masculine power meant responsibility for the well being of the "weaker sex" and that true womanhood embodied dutiful obedience to their protective husbands—a beneficent reciprocity if

---

[56]*Rutledge v. Rutledge*, 36 Tn. 558 (1858).
[57]*Shell v. Shell*, 34 Tn. 728 (1855).

both genders played their roles correctly, so it was assumed. By the 1850s, however, the justices acted to check what they perceived as an alarming rash of divorces based on a permissive reading of the state's expanded divorce laws that challenged husbandly hegemony itself. With Justice Caruther's words—". . .we would be derelict in duty to sanction the loose administration of divorces, which has obtained in some of the courts"[58]—ringing in their ears, the justices of the high court sought to restore a balance that would ensure the well being of patriarchal marriage and still allow divorce as an escape hatch for a truly victimized spouse.

In addition to state laws and supreme court decisions, legislative divorces are a third important source of information. Divorce by a legislative act was an adaptation by American colonists of English tradition to new world conditions that persisted through the mid-nineteenth-century in some southern states until it was superceded by judicial divorce.[59] The assessment of George Elliott Howard, the twentieth-century's most thorough historian of divorce law, that "conservative as southern sentiment is supposed to have been regarding dissolution of the marriage bond, it is precisely in the South that legislative divorce was tried on the widest scale and where it bore its most evil fruit" is highly applicable to Tennessee.[60]

Howard's prescriptive reference to the "evil fruit" of legislative divorce is not unwarranted. Divorce petitions were presented to the state assembly where an oversight committee made recommendations to the whole house. Like any other special interest legislation, those petitioners who were financially able, socially prominent, and politically connected were most likely to gain their way. Joel Prentiss Bishop, who wrote the first systematic study of divorce in 1852, noted that legislative divorce was a "luxury quite beyond the reach of the mass of the people."[61] Residency proximate to the state capitol at Nashville was also advantageous: of petitioners who identified their county of residency, those in or near Davidson County were disportionately numerous (see Map 1). In addition, Justice H.L. White of the state supreme court complained as early as 1804 that "it is well known that the legislature had been frequently incommoded by numerous applications for divorces each session, and it was con-

---

[58]*Rutledge v. Rutledge*, 36 Tn. 559 (1858).
[59]See Howard, *Matrimonial Institutions*, v. 3, 366-76; Friedman, *American Law*, 179.
[60]Howard, *Matrimonial Institutions*, v. 3, 31.
[61]Bishop, Commentaries, 633. See also Johnson, *North Carolina*, 217-18, on the inequities of private divorce bills.

ceived that much of the time of that body was injuriously exhausted by inquiries of this kind."[62]

Moreover, historian Bertram Wyatt-Brown has recently pointed out that some divorce petitions to the Tennessee legislature reveal gross inequities in which women were denied divorce despite their husband's flagrant adultery, desertion, and cruelty.[63] The impunity of brutish husbands and the degradation of virtuous wives called into question the legitimacy of legislative divorce, an issue the supreme court addressed in *Richardson v. Wilson* (1835). After a brief and unhappy marriage, Mary Ann Wilson (later remarried as Richardson) left her husband because of "intolerable conditions." Some eight months after the separation of this well-to-do Nashville couple, Colonel Wilson successfully petitioned the legislature for an absolute divorce that denied Mary Ann alimony; he had filed without notifying her and without any attempt at reconciliation. Outraged, Mary Ann took the Colonel to a Davidson County Court, proved herself of good character and was awarded $325 per year in alimony, a verdict which her ex-husband appealed to the high court.[64]

Justice Jacob Peck, of the supreme court, denied the complainant's suit, condemned Wilson's behavior, and damned the legislative divorce process. Speaking of male duty, Peck instructed that because "*his* will was a law to *her*" in the case of abandonment the husband should not "exact subjection with savage force; but by a bland, persuasive and soothing deportment, call back the wanderer, and restore the peace which had departed for a time from the domestic circle." The Justice observed that Mary Ann acted capriciously in leaving, but the Colonel had been highly irresponsible in not initiating an effort at reunion given his husbandly pregoratives. Peck addressed the fait accompli of the legislative divorce with anger at the injustice done to the wife: "By the divorce Wilson places himself in a condition to marry again, or, if you please, to shut his door against his late wife, while he may have, and actually does have, advantages by the act, which, otherwise, he could not claim. Still, the question recurs, are all her rights gone?"[65] No, ruled the high court, sustaining the decision of the lower court that benefited the wife.

---

[62] *Jones v. Jones*, 2 Tn. 3 (1804).
[63] Wyatt-Brown, *Southern Honor*, 285-301,303,305-306.
[64] *Richardson v. Wilson*, 8 Tn. 79 (1835).
[65] Ibid., 80.

"An Act for the Relief of Females. . .": Divorce and the Changing Legal Status of Women in Tennessee Part II

By LAWRENCE B. GOODHEART, NEIL HANKS, AND ELIZABETH JOHNSON

The supreme court's qualms with legislative divorce reflected wider sentiment that led to its statutory abolition in 1836. The abrogation of legislative divorce coupled with the concurrent divorce law of 1836 marked a democratization, a limitation on special privilege including that of husbands. Legal scholars Lawrence M. Friedman and Maxwell Bloomfield have rightly compared the replacement of legislative with judicial divorce with that of bills for private charters with general incorporation laws as analogous reforms during the Age of Jackson. Popular demand for liberalized divorce laws, which in Friedman's words reflected a "desire to stabilize and legitimize relationships, to settle doubts about ownership of family property," doomed the anachronistic and ill functioning system of private divorce bills.[66] Not only would the legislature's time be better spent but favoritism to the wealthy and well appointed would be lessened. The rationalization of judicial divorce and the systematic reform of the divorce laws meant greater equity for more women simply in a procedural sense.

Yet, despite the fact that legislative divorce was subject to bias based on class and sex, Wyatt-Brown's contention that "for women abused, the outcome of a petition to court or legislature (laws varied) was very problematic" was not the overall experience in Tennessee as measured by the appellate process or even legislative divorce.[67] Four hundred and twenty-six divorce petitions to the legislature from 1799 to 1855 have been identified. The vast majority of petitions flooded the General Assembly within the last fifteen years before legislative divorce was abolished in 1836, documenting not only the growing popular demand but the practical necessity of getting the legislature out of the time-consuming divorce business (see Table 3).

Of the 426 petitions, the legislature completed action on 260 in one of three ways: it granted an absolute divorce, awarded a bed and board to women petitioners, or referred the case to the circuit court of the petitioner's home county. Table 4 shows that from 1797 to 1833 the General Assembly granted 111 absolute divorces, 66 decisions (59 percent) to male petitioners and 45 (41 percent) to female petition-

[66]Friedman, *American Law*, 182-183, and Bloomfield, *American Lawyers*, 121-122.
[67]Wyatt-Brown, *Southern Honor*, 283.

ers. The legislature awarded the first bed and board divorce in 1823 and female petitioners gained 80 legal separations, a not inconsiderable measure that the legislators sustained the woman's initiative to seek relief from "intolerable conditions" stipulated in the 1799 law. The remaining 69 petitions were referred to circuit courts: twice as many wives (46) had their petitions delegated to the bench as husbands (23), indicating that probably more of the women's suits were contested and subject to a jury trial according to the 1799 statute. Only 56 legislative divorces listed specific causes for the suit. The largest single cause, constituting 61 percent of all grounds, was abandonment, with 24 wives and 10 husbands claiming desertion.[68] In sum, among husbands and wives whose petitions the General Assembly acted on nearly twice as many women (171) filed as men (89). And women were granted 69 percent of all legislative divorces (counting absolute and bed and board together) compared to 31 percent for men. Dissatisfied wives actively and rather successfully pursued divorce through private legislative bills despite the liabilities and abuses of the system.[69]

The last set of documents examined were divorce cases decided in the circuit courts of Washington, Davidson, and Tipton Counties. The circuit courts located within Tennessee's nearly 100 counties provide a means to gauge the rate of divorce, judicial attitudes toward women and the activity of female petitioners on a local level. Washington, Davidson, and Tipton Counties are respectively located in Tennessee's three major geographic areas—East, Middle, and West. Because the sample includes only about 3 percent of the circuit courts, it is not definitive, but the evidence from Davidson and Washington Counties emphatically supports the thesis that women energetically and effectively utilized the divorce laws, especially during the 1840s and 1850s.[70]

---

[68]In North Carolina, Johnson found that desertion constituted one-third of all causes for divorce among 266 legislative divorce petitions filed from 1800 to 1835—*North Caroliona*, 220-221.

[69]In *Southern Honor*, Wyatt-Brown has relief heavily on private divorce bills to the Tennessee legislature, especially for the year 1821, to draw his conclusion that women were denied what would appear to be prima facie legal grounds for divorce even in extreme cases of adultery, beatings, and desertions. As he puts it on p. 286, "In fact, there was little of an aggressive nature that a man could do that might win sympathy for a wife's suit. The problem was not just the protection of women, but of male self-image and reputation before the world: honor." Wyatt-Brown's conclusions are, however, flawed for Tennessee. His evidence is highly selective, based on less than a dozen Tennessee petitions out of a total of 426 filed. And his thesis is contradicted by the fact that women were granted 69% of all legislative divorces (counting absolute and bed and board divorces together).

[70]Wyatt-Brown's assessment of divorce for the South as a whole again does not apply to Tennessee: "First of all, divorce for any cause was seldom granted, either by state legislatures or by equity or chancery courts"—*Southern Honor*, 301.

Judicial procedures regulating divorce petitions to the county circuit courts were significantly simplified over time. Not until 1809 were county circuit courts invested with the power to decide divorce cases of petitioners residing within their jurisdiction; previously, according to the 1799 law, the superior court had purview over such matters. While the 1809 law transferred the authority to hear divorce petitions, it did not change the filing procedure. The 1799 law established a long and cumbersome process; it was not uncommon for a divorce suit to be on the court docket for several sessions before a final decision was reached. After a petition and affidavit had been filed, a subpoena had to be issued ordering the defendant to appear at the next court session.[71] If the defendant could not be found, a second "alias subpoena" was issued "returnable the first day of the next term."[72]

Depending upon when the plantiff filed, a year's time could elapse between initiating action and having a second subpoena returned to the court. Additionally, if the defendant did not appear, during this process the law required that public proclamations be made at the courthouse and that notice be given in several newspapers for four weeks before the case could be considered for a hearing at the second term. The law further stated that the petitions not be "made out of levity or collusion between husband and wife, and for the mere purpose of being freed and separated from each other."[73] This time-consuming process allowed ample opportunity for reconciliation between spouses. In Davidson County roughly 11 percent of all petitions filed between 1809 and 1860 were dropped; the onerous legal procedure reflected a general social attitude that frowned on divorce.

As the negative attitude toward divorce lessened, the laws changed and it became easier to obtain a divorce. In 1831 a female petitioner's notice no longer had to be placed in local newspapers; as the law stated, "filing of the petition in the clerk's office and the issuance of a subpoena . . . shall be deemed to answer all the purposes of publication as now required by law."[74] In 1840 and 1846 the law extended the grounds for divorce to include causes that "may have occurred in another State."[75] Less cumbersome divorce procedures at the county circuit court level especially worked for the benefit of women legally impaired by female coverture.

In Davidson County, the seat of the state capitol, Table 5 shows that 220 petitions were filed with the local circuit court from 1809 to

[71] *Tn. Acts* (1799), chap. 19, sec. 2, p. 646, and *Tn. Acts* (1809), chap. 98, sec. 2,3, p. 1189.
[72] *Tn. Acts* (1799), chap. 19, sec. 2, 646.
[73] *Ibid.*, p. 646
[74] *Tn. Acts* (1831), chap. 20, sec. 1, pp. 35-36.
[75] *Tn Acts* (1840), chap. 54, sec. 1, p. 90, and *Tn. Acts* (1846), chap. 67, p. 135.

1860 with 166 divorces granted, the disposition of 26 cases remains unknown.[76] From 1809 to 1819 two-thirds of the divorce petitions were filed by men. Beginning in the next decade, however, female petitioners increasingly outnumbered their male counterparts, which can be attributed to the expansion of women's legal rights within patriarchal marriage. During the entire 51 year period, women filed twice as many suits as did men (147 to 73). After the passage of the reform divorce laws of 1836 and the early 1840s, there were 2.4 times as many suits begun by women from 1840 to 1860 than from 1809 to 1839. Female petitioners gained divorces at the rate of 80 percent (118 divorces our of 147 petitions) compared to 66 percent for males (48 divorces out of 73 petitions)—a statistic that overwhelmingly contradicts the contention that divorce was rare and hard to get, especially for women, in the South.

The number of cases begun by men remained fairly constant until the decade of the 1850s when their petitions greatly increased. In fact, there were more divorce cases begun by men during this decade than during the entire preceeding forty years. As more wives asserted their statutory rights, so did more husbands. An increasing unwillingness to abide a repugnant spouse led more wives and husbands to petition for divorce at mid-century, which suggests a rising level of individual expectations about marriage and less social opprobrium attached to divorce.[77]

In Davidson County women filed for divorce most often on grounds of abandonment, which after 1841 was a statutory cause for absolute as well as bed and board divorces.[78] Case records indicate that the accused husbands often deserted their homes to settle in other areas, often outside Tennessee where they could remain untouched by the law.[79] With each successive decade the number of cases filed and won by women on grounds of adultery increased. No longer charging their spouses solely of desertion, women became willing publicly to accuse their husbands of adultery, often naming the defendant's partner as well. By the 1850s, when 28 such cases were filed, women

[76]References to the circuit court records in Washington, Davidson, and Tipton Counties are from the minute books of the clerk of the county circuit court which are on microfilm at the Tennessee State Library, Nashville. Divorce petitions are listed chronologically in the minute books.

[77]For example, the first American novel with an emphasis on divorce—*The Hand But Not the Heart* by T.S. Arthur—appeared in 1858 with a theme that the ideal of romantic love led an unhappy women to gain a divorce from a loveless marriage. See James H. Barnett, "Divorce and the American Divorce Novel, 1858-1937" (Ph.D., University of Pennsylvania, 1939), 70-75.

[78]Of all divorce petitions filed in the Davidson County Circuit Court, 54 cases were either dropped or their outcomes were not described in the minute books. Therefore, the data pertaining to why petitioners filed are based on a total of 166 cases.

[79]See, for example, *Scholl v. Millon* (1822), Davidson County Circuit Court.

were explicitly describing their victimization in order to ensure their case's success. One petitioner disclosed that her husband was in the "habit of frequenting houses of ill fame and of associating with lewd women," and that "he communicated to [the] complainant a venereal disease which he had contracted from some such lewd women."[80]

While abandonment and adultery could be readily defined and decided upon by the courts, "intolerable conditions" were a cause of divorce that led to subjective judicial interpretation. During the 1850s there were more petitions filed by women on grounds of "intolerable conditions" than abandonment or adultery. Supreme Court Justice Caruthers charged (rather accurately) that the "crowding of the courts with applications" was a result of the increasing permissive attitude taken by the lower courts.[81] Offensive language, inhuman treatment, frequent beatings, and repeated intoxication were some examples of "intolerable conditions" upon which Davidson County judges granted absolute divorces to female petitioners. In 1855 Sarah Ashley was granted a divorce on grounds that her husband "was in the habit of using language to her which a Gentleman would not use to his slave." Several cases were won because the husband was often inebriated and "when so became a terror."[82] More women were openly speaking out against drunkenness and cruelty, believing that these vices should not be tolerated and hidden within the home. The courts, as well as female plaintiffs, were increasingly unwilling to tolerate male excess. Expressions such as "cannot safely or happily live longer with defendant as his wife" became a common complaint among Davidson County female petitioners at mid-century.[83]

A growing assertiveness was not exclusive to alienated wives. While the number of cases males filed was one-half the number of female applicants, they were also becoming more outspoken. The number of men who judicially accused their spouses of adultery and abandonment grew throughout the 1800s. Husbands filed 45 petitions on grounds of abandonment and adultery from 1809 to 1860 but 32 were lodged during the 1850s alone. More husbands were willing to breech tabooed subjects and admit the failure of their marriage, charging their wives with promiscuity and as not being "a proper person to have custody [of their children.]"[84] In brief, the courts as well as the

---

[80]*Owen v. Owen* (1856), Davidson County Circuit Court.

[81]*Shell v. Shell*, 34 Tn. 718 (1856).

[82]*Ashley v. Ashley* (1855), *Courron v. Courron* (1856), *Picaud v. Picaud* (1856), *McLauden v. McLauden* (1857), *Hefferman v. Hefferman* (1858), Davidson County Circuit Court.

[83]*Conley v. Conley* (1853), Davidson County Circuit Court.

[84]*Hearn v. Hearn* (1853), Davidson County Circuit Court.

public believed that while the family unit was the foundation of society, a marriage in which one partner was continually mistreated could no longer be accepted or ignored.

The divorce statistics for the circuit courts of Washington and Tipton Counties are not as dramatic as Davidson County, but they indicate that women gained divorces in other regions of the state as well. Washington County in the extreme northeast corner of the state with its seat at Jonesboro, is an upland area bordering the Appalachian Mountains. Table 6 shows that from 1809 to 1860 55 petitions were filed, 37 were granted, and the disposition of 13 remains unknown. Although men petitioned more actively than women (34 suits to 21), women were awarded a higher percentage (72 percent) of divorces than men (65 percent). The increasing rate of petitions during the 1850s is particularly notable with 56 percent of all suits filed during that decade and with all 10 female plantiffs winning their cases.

From 1840 to 1860 in Washington County women increasingly won child custody suits from drunken and dangerous husbands. Because John Hinit's violence toward his wife, Sarah, rendered her life "intolereable," the court awarded her custody of the children, a property settlement, and alimony.[85] Women and men gained divorces if abandonment or adultery were proven, such as the divorce decreed to the cuckolded Adolphus Chandler who discovered his "incontinent" wife *in flagrante delicto* with a stage driver with whom she absconded.[86] The court favored victimized spouses of either gender rather even handedly in divorce decisions.

Historian Jane Censer's conclusion that "indeed it seems unlikely that many poorer people ever used the judicial machinery for divorce" accurately describes the appellate process in Tennessee, but, as she suggests, the generalization needs qualification for the inferior courts.[87] Although the sparse commentary in the minute books of the county circuit courts prevents an accurate assessment of the social and economic status of the petitioners, some people on the margins of society did sue for divorce in the local courts. In Washington County, for example, four of the litigants, two women and two men, were identified as illiterate, unable even to sign their name. Martha Ruble, though only able to "x" her mark, gained a divorce and alimony from a wife-beater for whom she had "labored like a slave."[88] And

---

[85]*Hinit v. Hinit* (1859), Washington County Circuit Court. See also *Bailey v. Bailey* (1847), *Rogers v. Rogers* (1848), *Good v. Good* (1858), *Brown v. Brown* (1858), and *Adams v. Adams (1859), Washington County Circuit Court.*

[86]*Chandler v. Chandler* (1844), Washington County Circuit Court.

[87]Censer, " 'Smiling Through Her Tears,' " 37.

[88]*Ruble v. Ruble* (1816), Washington County Circuit Court.

David Brown, an illiterate plaintiff, successfully divorced his wife, who was in "the habit of prostituting herself to the lusts of men of various colors and characters."[89] It was, however, married couples who owned property or had at least some economic stake in society that benefitted most from divorce adjudication. Maxwell Bloomfield's thesis that the lower middle class provided the major constituency for divorce liberalization during the Age of Jackson appears credible for Tennessee.[90]

In contrast to Davidson and Washington Counties, Table 7 shows the low occurrence of divorce in Tipton County, which mirrors the traditional perception of southern divorce with the exception that equal numbers of women and men secured divorces. Even computed on the per capita basis of the average white population between 1850 and 1860 (see Table 8), Tipton County had a rate of only one divorce per 1,689 people compared to 1 per 273 for Davidson County and 1 per 892 for Washington County. Several factors explain the low rate of divorce in Tipton County: the lack of significant population centers, isolated agrarian life, and the conservative attitudes further generated by a predominantly cotton based economy in which the slave population nearly equaled the white in 1850. Until more study in local court records in done, the correlation between Tipton County's heightened black belt characteristics and its low rate of divorce remains a tentative hypothesis. Yet therein may lie the truth in the regional stereotype about the southern divorce and the ever deferential wife.

The county circuit court records reinforce the fact of the geographic, economic, and social diversity of the latitudinally long Volunteer State. Such variety helps to explain the differences in the divorce statistics of the three counties studied. Unlike the reign of king cotton in Tipton County, Washington County was a mixed agrarian economy that included some iron works, a significant town, and a slave population that constituted only 7 percent of the total in 1850. Although 37 percent of Davidson County's population in 1850 were slaves, the capitol city of Nashville contrasted sharply with the black belt provincialism of Tipton County and the upcountry simplicity of Washington County. While the other areas remained rural in outlook, attitudes in Davidson County were influenced by the changing patterns of

---

[89]*Brown v. Brown* (1846), Washington County Circuit Court. See also *Rose v. Rose* (1838) and *Mitchell v. Mitchell* (1820), Washington County Circuit Court.

[90]Bloomfield, American Lawyers, 138. See also Friedman, *American Law*, 183.

[91]Margaret J. Hapgood, *Mothers of the South: Portraiture of the White Tenant Farm Women* (Chapel Hill, 1939), 56-57, 168, states that there were fewer divorced women in rural than in urban areas because of the wife's economic dependence on a husband in an agricultural area, a fact lamented by widows.

urban life. Being at the seat of the legislature and the state courts, residents of Nashville and environs were more willing and able to accept the liberal ideas of the day on divorce. Everything else being equal, the complex effects of urban life on thought and behavior explain Davidson County's high rate of divorce compared to that of Washington and Tipton Counties. Davidson County may well have been exceptional, but its divorce statistics, as well as those of Washington County, belie facile generalizations about the rarity and difficulty of divorce throughout the South.

The evidence from statutes, supreme court rulings, legislative petitions and a sample of county circuit court decisions overwhelmingly documents not only that divorce was available and possible in Tennessee but that women actively and successfully used established legal procedures, especially during the 1840s and 1850s, to secure divorces. Mary Chesnut's characterization of antebellum southern women as "always excusing themselves for something they never did" does not explain the actions of hundreds of Tennessee women who refused to excuse their husband's behavior and gained divorces.[92] Yet, if Mrs. Chesnut and a number of historians have underplayed the existence of divorce in the Old South, their stress on a male dominated ethos of gender relationships was very much a reality in Tennessee.

Judge Caruthers feared that Tennessee's liberal laws might be abused by some wives, but the divorce procedure itself was intentionally designed to frustrate any significant alteration in conventional marital roles. Given the cultural expectation of women's subservience and the patriarchal tradition of the common law, a surprising number of women nonetheless sought divorces. More needs to be known about the motivation, hopes and lifes of southern divorcées. It is clear, however, that in order to gain a divorce a woman had to demonstrate to a male judiciary that she was a model wife, compliant and dutiful, not "high-spirited" or independent minded, and that she had been grieviously mistreated by her spouse. The irony is that Tennessee's reformed divorce laws were designed to buttress patriarchal marriage, not to eliminate female subordination.

Tennessee legislators and judges, male guardians of the family hearth, made a concerted effort to protect virtuous wives from vile husbands. Christopher Lasch's thesis that a concern with the victimization of women, and not with sexual egalitarianism, led to divorce reform describes accurately what happened in the Volunteer State.[93]

---

[92]Woodward. *Mary Chesnut*, 181.
[93]Lasch. *World of Nations*, 39.

Female coverture made wives potential recipients of gratuitous husbandly abuse—physically, psychologically and pecuniarly—which the state sought to mitigate. The degenerate husband not only brutalized his own spouse but degrated female virture, debased motherhood and challenged the wisdom of patriarchal marriage itself. Progressive divorce laws, especially those of 1836 and the early 1840s, were a safety value by which women, whose predestination was marriage and motherhood, could seek a modicum of relief from the "intolerable conditions" of a socially assigned fate gone awry. Liberalized laws expanded the grounds for divorce and simplified judicial procedures, while the courts at all levels censored morally hardened husbands, awarded alimony, safeguarded women's property rights and even granted mothers child custody. Judicial chivalry succored the wronged wife, but at the same time it affirmed the legitimacy of male hegemony over the "weaker sex." Honorable men were duty bound to rescue victimized wives from villainous husbands, and thus a system based on female subordination was shown to be just, magnanimous and part of the natural order of things. Divorce in Tennessee before 1860 was a paternalistic concession to aggrieved wives who embodied the virtues of southern womanhood.

TABLE 3

Number of Divorce Petitions to the Legislature

1797	(one passed but no petition in records)
1799	1
1809	3
1812	6
1813	6
1817	3
1819	12
1820	15
1821	54
1822	25
1823	12
1824	3
1825	26
1826	16
1827	44
1829	37
1831	62
1832	15
1833	69
1835	3
1841	3
1845	3
1848	1
1849	3
1851	1
1853	1
1855	1
	426 Total

TABLE 4

Disposition of Divorce Petitions by the Legislature

Year	Complete Divorce		Bed & Board Divorce		Referred to Circuit Court	
	men	women	men	women	men	women
1796						
1797	1					
1798						
1799	4					
1800						
1801						
1802						
1803						
1804						
1805						
1806						
1807	8	1				
1808						
1809	6					
1810						
1811	1					
1812	11					
1813						
1814						
1815						
1816						
1817						
1818						
1819 a	2	5				
1820	3	5				
1821	1	1				
1822	1	1			1	
1823				11		
1824				1	2	3
1825	1	1		4	3	5
1826				10	5	4
1827				7	9	13
1828						
1829	1			13	8	
1830	1	1		4		7
1831	3	2		17		2
1832	2	2		5	2	2
1833	20	26		8	1	2
1834						
1835						
1836 b						
Totals	66	45		80	23	46

a - Until 1819 the wording of the divorce acts does indicate the gender of the petitioner. Only one case was clearly filed by a woman; the others we have counted as filed by men.

b - No cased decided after the 1836 law abolished legislative divorce.

89 men filed 171 women filed 260 total of all petitions acted on by the legislature

Source: Session Laws of Tennessee General Assembly, 1796-1834, Tennessee State Library

TABLE 5

Divorce Petitions Filed at Davidson County Circuit Court, 1809-1860

	Begun by Wife	Granted	Unknown	Dropped	Abandonment	Intolerable Conditions	Adultery	Other	Begun by Husband	Granted	Unknown	Dropped	Abandonment	Adultery	Other
1809-1819	4	4	0	0	3	0	1	0	8	4	4	0	3	1	0
1820-1829	16	7	8	1	5	0	2	0	10	0	3	7	1	2	0
1830-1839	23	17	1	5	11	2	3	1	4	0	3	1	3	0	0
1840-1849	22	19	1	2	10	0	6	3	13	5	6	2	3	2	1
1850-1860	82	71	5	6	25	28	18	0	38	2	32	4	12	20	0
Totals	147	118	15	14	54	30	30	4	73	11	48	14	22	25	1

Source: County Circuit Court Records, Tennessee State Library

TABLE 6

Divorce Petitions Filed at Washington County Circuit Court, 1809-1860

	Begun by Wife	Granted	Unknown	Abandonment	Adultery	Other	Begun by Husband	Granted	Unknown	Abandonment	Adultery	Other
1809-1819	4	1	3	0	0	1	3	2	1	2	1	0
1820-1829	3	1	2	0	0	0	2	0	2	0	0	0
1830-1839	0	0	0	0	0	0	1	1	0	1	0	0
1840-1849	4	4	0	0	1	1	6	4	0	2	5	0
1850-1860	10	10	0	6	3	2	21	15	0	6	8	1
Totals	21	15	5	6	4	4	34	22	3	12	14	1

Source: County Circuit Court Records, Tennessee State Library

TABLE 7

Divorce Petitions Filed at Tipton County Circuit Court, 1809-1860

Year	Who Filed	Cause	Dismissal	Granted
1829	husband	abandonment	1832	
1830	husband	abandonment	1832	
1831	husband	abandonment		1831
1845	wife	abandonment		1845
1846	wife	(no cause cited)		1846
1848	husband	abandonment/adultery		1848
1849	husband	abandonment		1850
1850	wife	abandonment	1851	
1851	wife	abandonment		1852
1853	wife	intolerable conditions		1854
1853	husband	abandonment		1854

Total cases	11	
Granted	8	6 male petitioners—4 divorces granted
Dismissed	3	5 female petitioners—4 divorces granted

Source: County Circuit Court Records, Tennessee State Library

TABLE 8

Census of Davidson, Tipton, and Washington Counties, 1850 and 1860

1850 Census

	Davidson		Tipton		Washington	
White Male	12,643		2,417		6,247	
		23,853		4,673		12,671
White Female	11,210		2,256		6,424	
Free Black Male	422		16		123	
		854		22		260
Free Black Female	432		6		137	
Slave—Male	7,211		2,118		463	
		14,175		4,192		930
Slave—Female	6,964		2,074		467	
Totals		38,882		8,887		13,861

Source: *The Seventh Census of the United States—1850*, J.D.B. DeBow (Superintendent of the U.S. Census), Washington: Robert Armstrong, 1853, pp. 573-574.

1860 Census

	Davidson		Tipton		Washington	
White Male	16,597		2,860		6,760	
		31,056		5,408		13,580
White Female	14,459		2,548		6,820	
Free Black Male	544		8		132	
		1,209		9		297
Free Black Female	665		1		165	
Slave—Male	7,214		2,706		456	
		14,790		5,288		952
Slave—Female	7,576		2,582		496	
Totals		47,055		10,705		14,829

Source: *Population of the United States in 1860, Compiled from the Original Returns of the Eighth Census*. Joseph C.G. Kennedy, (Superintendent of the Census), Washington: Government Printing Office, 1864, pp. 456-465.

THE MISSISSIPPI MARRIED WOMEN'S PROPERTY ACT OF 1839

By Sandra Moncrief

Mississippi was the first state in the nation to grant married women the right to hold property in their own names. Two little known but important events in the 1830s led to this reform in women's rights. These events and the laws that resulted have been virtually overlooked by historians — possibly because the circumstances surrounding the reform were, and continue to be, a mystery.

As early as 1823, Maine granted property ownership rights to women deserted by their husbands, and Massachusetts followed with a similar law in 1835.[1] But in no state were married women, living with their husbands, allowed ownership of property, either willed to them or earned by them. When a woman married, her property was placed under the absolute control of her husband. This practice was based on the belief that the wife's personality merged with that of the husband at the time of marriage. After marriage, the wife's property could be attached and sold to pay her husband's debts. Many women, especially daughters of large plantation owners, lost all of their property and thus financial security when their husbands fell on hard times. Mary Chesnut, a native of South Carolina, wrote in her diary as late as 1863, "We had our share of my father's estate. It came into our possession so long after we were married, and it was spent for debts already contracted."[2] In Mrs. Chesnut's case, her father-in-law had died and left his estate to her husband, James Chesnut, along with all of the debts incurred, which were more than the assets. Thus, Mrs. Chesnut's property, left to her by her father, Stephen Miller, was lost. It was long after the Civil War that South Carolina granted property rights to women.

In the 1830s, Mississippi was experiencing rapid growth and radical change. Until this time the river counties controlled politics in state government, but with the advent of the Jacksonian Democracy in the late 1820s and the opening of new lands

Ms. Moncrief is a graduate student in history at the University of Southern Mississippi.

[1]Eugene A. Hecker, *History of Women's Suffrage* (New York, 1910), 200.
[2]*Mary Chesnut's Civil War*, ed. C. Vann Woodward (New Haven, 1981), 284.

through the Indian Cessions of 1820, 1830, 1832, and 1837, life began to take on a different tone. Jacksonian Democracy flourished as the masses of immigrants poured into the state and populated the newly acquired Indian lands. Mississippi now was experiencing "flush times." Land speculators using easy credit and diverse banking entities operated unsupervised. Joseph G. Baldwin wrote in his account of *The Flush Times of Alabama and Mississippi:*

> The country was just settling up. Marvellous accounts had gone forth of the fertility of its virgin lands; and the productions of the soil were commanding a price remunerating to slave labor as it had never been remunerated before. Emigrants came flocking in from all quarters of the Union, especially from the slave holding states. The new country seemed to be a reservoir, and every road leading to a vagrant stream of enterprise and adventure. Money, or what passed for money, was the only cheap thing to be had. Every crossroad and every avocation presented an opening, through which a fortune was seen by the adventurer in near perspective. Credit was a thing of course. To refuse it — if the thing was ever done — were an insult for which a bowie-knife were not a too summary or exemplary a means of redress. The state banks were issuing their bills by the sheet, like a patent steam printing press *its* issues; and no other showing was asked for of the applicant for the loan than an authentication of his great distress for money. Finance even in *its* most exclusive quarter, had thus already got, in this wonderful revolution, to work upon the principles of the charity hospital. If an overseer grew tired of supervising a plantation and felt a call to the mercantile life, even if he omitted the compendious method of buying out a merchant wholesale, stock, house and good will, and laying down, at once, his bull-whip for the yardstick — all he had to do was to go on to New York, and present himself in Pearl Street with a letter avouching his citizenship, and a clean shirt, and he was regularly given a through ticket to speedy bankruptcy . . . Under this stimulating process, prices rose like smoke. Lots in obscure villages were held at city prices; lands, bought at the minimum cost of government, were sold at from thirty to forty dollars per acre and considerd dirt cheap at that . . . Banks, chartered on a specie basis, did a very flourishing business on the promissory notes of the individual stockholders ingeniously substituted in lieu of cash. They issued ten for one, the *one* being fictitious. They generously loaned all the directors could not use themselves, and were not choice whether Bardolph was the endorser for Falstaff, or Falstaff borrowed on his own proper credit, or the funds advanced him by Shallow. The stampede towards the golden temple became general; the delusion prevailed far and wide that this thing was not a burlesque on commerce and finance . . . The condition of society may be imagined; — vulgarity — ignorance — fussy — and arrogant pretention — unmitigated

> rowdyism — bullying insolence, if they did not rule the hour, seemed to wield unchecked dominion. The workings of these choice spirits were patent upon the fact of society; and the modest, unobtrusive, retiring men of worth and character (for there were many, perhaps a large majority pf such) were almost lost sight of in the hurly-burly of those strange and shifting scenes.[3]

As the ability of get-rich-quick schemes increased, so did the possibility to fail increase. Many speculative landowners found themselves ruined when, in 1836, specie payments were required of receivers of public money. Payment of public lands and the Distributive Act of 1836, which provided that each state receive a share proportional to its representation in Congress, proved to be a drain on the Mississippi banks. The banks thus had to call in loans to make the transfer of funds to the state government; land owners, whose financing was mostly on paper, were forced into bankruptcy.[4] Like the rest of the country, Mississippi was now experiencing the Panic of 1837, but she was especially hard-hit by the turmoil in the state.

The lives of two Mississippi women intertwined into all of this turmoil. They were very different from each other, but both had the same goal in mind: to preserve what was rightfully their own. Their husbands also had a stake in the proceedings, but one would assume that both spouses were concerned with protection of their joint property.

Who were these women and what personal interest did they have in seeking protection for their property? Did they want control of the estates left to them by their fathers? Did they want the revenue from the businesses they operated, hand in hand with their husbands? Were they feminists, influenced by Jacksonian Democracy and the writings of the Grimké Sisters and other feminists in the North? Or possibly, was this all a strategy on the part of each husband to protect his property from confiscation for debts?

The first of these women to counter the English common law was Betsy Love Allen. She was the daughter of one of the Colberts, a half-breed Chickasaw chief. Upon his death, Colbert had left his daughter a very wealthy woman, in possession of many

[3]Joseph G. Baldwin, *The Flush Times of Alabama and Mississippi: A Series of Sketches* (New York: Hill and Wang, 1967, c 1957), 82-9.

[4]John Edmond Gonzales, "Flush Times, Depression, War and Compromise," in *A History of Mississippi*, 2 vols. (Jackson, 1973), I, 292

slaves and land. Betsy Allen was the wife of James Allen, a white man. He and his wife operated a trading post on the Natchez Trace.

Betsy Love married John Allen before 1830, according to the tribal customs and laws of the Chickasaw tribe. In January, 1830, the laws of the State of Mississippi were extended over the Indians. The legislature stated at time of the passage of these laws that all marriages and matrimonial connections entered into by virtue of any custom or usage of the Indians, and by them deemed valid, shall be held as valid and obligatory as if the same had been solemnized by the laws of the State of Mississippi. By the customs of the Chickasaws the husband acquired no right to the wife's property that she possessed at the time of marriage. It remained to her separate use and subject alone to her disposition and constraint. She was perfectly independent of the husband, so far as regards the obligation of contracts and the acquisition and rights of property.[5]

On November 14, 1829, Betsy Allen deeded the slave Toney, who had been left to her by her father, over to her infant daughter Susan. In August, 1830, John Allen became indebted to a Mr. Fisher. The deed of gift was recorded in Monroe County on November 2, 1830. Allen later defaulted and Fisher sued him for the slave Toney. The case went to the Mississippi Supreme Court, where the justices had two questions to resolve: first, did Allen acquire legally protected interest in Betsy Love's property at the time of their marriage, and, second, was the gift of property to his daughter, Susan Allen, void as to his creditors?

In January, 1837, the Mississippi Supreme Court handed down a decision written by Judge William L. Sharkey, who ruled in favor of the Indian woman, Betsy Love Allen, who was allowed to retain control of the property left her by her father.[6] The court ruled that the slave was proved to be the separate property of Betsy Allen at the time of the donation, and since the marriage of Betsy and John Allen was a valid union under tribal law, it was considered as equally valid at their commencement as at the passage of the state laws. The terms of the marriage contract between Allen and Betsy Love, as modified by the customs of the Chickasaws, conferred no right on him to the separate property of his wife. Also, no just construction could be given to the act by

[5]Fisher v. Allen, 2 Howard (Miss.) 611 (1837).

[6]*Ibid.*

the customs of the Chickasaws, conferred no right on him to the separate property of his wife. Also, no just construction could be given to the act validating their marriage, which would alter their condition or extend the marital rights on the husband. Such a construction would be in conflict with the constitution and would work a divestiture of her rights. The property of Betsy Love Allen was therefore not subject to the demands of John Allen's creditors. As the court ruled in favor of Betsy Allen, the second question as to the validity of the gift to Susan Allen was moot.

Mrs. Allen never saw her initial effort come to fruition in 1839 through the efforts of another woman, Piety Smith Hadley, and the passage in the legislature of the Married Women's Property Act. Betsy Allen died the same year the court decision was handed down. It is believed that her remains were removed from the old Indian Burial Ground that had become a pasture in the early 1960s and ceremoniously re-interred in a new grave on the campus of the Toccopola High School at Toccopola, Mississippi. It is said that a piece of concrete from an old sidewalk marks the grave of Betsy Allen.[7]

Two years after the Allen decision, a bill was introduced into the Mississippi legislature entitled "An act for the protection and preservation of the rights and property of Married Women."[8] This bill was introduced by State Senator Thomas B.J. Hadley of Hinds County, husband of Piety Smith Hadley. Colonel Hadley and his wife Piety owned and operated a boarding house in Jackson, approximately two blocks from the newly constructed State Capitol. The boarding house was located on a plot of land comprising the block of George Street, North State Street, and North Street. In Jackson's earliest days as a town and seat of state government, early state officials, legislators, and travelers boarded with private families while tending to their official duties. Out of this the need for and popularity of boarding houses grew. Although the new Capitol was still unfinished in 1839, the legislature moved in and held its first session in the new building. Jackson was now a hustling, bustling city that had grown from six families in the 1820s to approximately 900 residents in 1839.[9]

[7] *Clarion Ledger*, December 26, 1961.
[8] *Journal of the Senate of the State of Mississippi* (1839).
[9] W.F. Powell, *Jackson's Early History* (Jackson, Miss., 1945).

Mr. and Mrs. Hadley's boarding house became a social center for the legislators when the legislature was in session. Because of lack of documented evidence from this period, one can only imagine the excitement generated and the content of the conversations that occurred around Mrs. Hadley's dining room table. She served three meals a day to the influential gentlemen, but tradition has it that during the legislative session she would suggest to these gentlemen bills that she was interested in having passed. It is said that, if they refused to agree, she would serve short rations and traditional hash and give no comfort until they came around to her way of thinking.[10] It was in this climate that Mrs. Hadley began to lobby for the rights of married women to retain control of their property, left to them or earned by them. Traditionally upon marriage a woman's property became her husband's property, and any revenue generated by her labors was also legally his.

An examination of Mrs. Hadley's background and that of her husband partially explains their desire to change the law. Piety Smith Hadley was born on April 2, 1807, in Christian County, Kentucky. She was the daughter of Major David Smith and his wife, Obedience Fort Smith. Major Smith had ridden the Wilderness Trail with Andrew Jackson and Jackson's wife from Natchez, Mississippi, to Nashville, Tennessee. Smith had also formed a military unit from his own kin — nephews, uncles, brothers and sons — and fought with Jackson at Horseshoe Bend.[11] In 1820, the Indian cessions in Mississippi were beginning to open, and Major Smith purchased a large section of land near present-day Raymond. He carved his home out of the wilderness and named it "Soldiers Rest." Here, Piety Smith, who was then fifteen, grew up. Major Smith became a leader in politics and an important figure in the new frontier of Mississippi. Eventually he would have a Mississippi county dedicated to him and named for him. His children numbered eleven, Piety being the seventh child. She had an older sister, Obedience, who married Hiram G. Runnels the year after their move from Kentucky. Runnels, a prominent state leader at the time, would later be elected governor of Mississippi.

[10] *Jackson Jewels*, political drawings compiled by Neppie R. Lockwood (Jackson, Miss., n.d.).
[11] Mae Wilson McBee, *The Life and Times of David Smith* (Greenwood, Miss., 1958).

In June of 1831, Piety Smith became the wife of Thomas B.J. Hadley in Hinds County, Mississippi. The same month, Major Smith, Piety's father, added a codicil to his will, leaving to his two sons, Benjamin Fort Smith and Jackson Smith, two Negro female slaves, one named Rose and the other Caroline, both about fourteen or fifteen years of age, "to have and hold to themselves and to the survivor of them and his heirs, to and for the use and benefit of said daughter, Piety Smith Hadley and her heirs forever."[12] He also bequeathed to Piety one quarter section of land to be laid off of lands as directed.[13] Major Smith either sensed a need to protect his daughter's property from the bad judgment of her husband or was determined to keep the property in his own family's control.

From all indications, Colonel Hadley was a successful businessman and politician; but some newspaper articles lead one to believe that at times he was experiencing difficulty in his public and private life, any of which could have led to his interest in protection of his property.

In the 1839 legislative term, Thomas Hadley asked and obtained leave to the introduction of a bill to be entitled "An act to incoporate the Mississippi Importing and Exporting Company."[14] A deed in the Raymond courthouse during this time names Thomas Hadley as president of Mississippi Importing Company. In this same term of the legislature, Henry Stuart Foote, in a grand oration to the House of Representatives, stated that the firm of Messrs. Richter, Hadley, Davis and Company was in collusion with the Mississippi Union Bank in misuse of bank funds to finance this cotton agency.[15] Just prior, in 1835, Governor Hiram G. Runnels resigned his post as governor one month early and immediately accepted the position as president of the newly formed Mississippi Union Bank. Were Runnels and Hadley involved in dubious dealings? Was Mr. Hadley using his political clout to feather his own nest?

Thomas Hadley was evidently experiencing financial difficulties of some sort. In the same term of the legislature a bill

[12]Mississippi Court Records from the files of the High Court of Errors and Appeals, 1799-1859, compiled by M.L.F. Hendrix, 351-55.

[13]*Ibid.*

[14]*Journal of the Senate of the State of Mississippi* (1839), 231.

[15]*Journal of the House of Representatives of the State of Mississippi*, January, 1839, p. 233.

was introduced in the Senate "for the relief of T.B.J. Hadley and Samuel M. Puckett, his security."[16] Hadley and Puckett each had executed three joint promissory notes for $401.33 to the governor for the use of the state of Mississippi, and they had received no consideration. The auditor of public accounts was authorized to release them from payment of these notes. This money was probably used for the completion of the governor's mansion, which (although funds were appropriated in 1833) was not completed until 1841, at a cost of several times the original amount. Hadley's brother-in-law and governor at the time, H.G. Runnels, had to borrow money in his own name for the completion.

Thomas Hadley was also in trouble with members of his political party. The newspaper *Southern Sun* in February of 1839 lambasted Hadley and others for joining ranks of a "party against whose manifold abuses they battled manfully for many years — a party diametrically opposed to them in every political opinion. Professing to be genuine states-rights men, those apostate nullifiers have deserted their proud and enviable stations and are now familiarly 'sipping tea' in the camps of the 'party' — a party that openly proclaimed in the Proclamation that States have no rights. They are therefore nullifiers by name, but federalists in practice."[17] Hadley's name is encircled in a bold, black square, in "order that the people may more readily place their eyes upon those who were deaf to the cry of their distresses."[18] The article concluded, "We do not say or believe, that those Senators were influenced by improper motives. No doubt they were *Honest* in their position, but with all due deference, we humbly consider them most egregiously *mistaken*."[19] At this time, Colonel Hadley was requested by some of his constituents to resign from office. A petition was to be circulated throughout the county for signatures. It stated that shortly after taking office, Colonel Hadley "gave manifest signs that he was not what the people considered him to be."[20] He stood for the side of the Locofocos, a radical group, and their advocacy of the sub-treasury bill, a measure calculated to place the national purse in the hands of the federal executives.

[16]*Journal of the Senate of the State of Mississippi* (1839).
[17]*Southern Sun* (Jackson, Miss.), February 5, 1839.
[18]*Ibid.*
[19]*Ibid.*
[20]*Ibid.*

Aside from Thomas Hadley's problems, an additional influence on the Hadleys' thinking might have been the close proximity to Louisiana and the influence of its civil laws. Thomas Hadley's family had moved to Wilkinson County, Mississippi, from South Carolina in the early 1820s.[21] About ten years later, some of the family migrated farther west into Rapides Parish, Louisiana. It is thought that at this time Piety and T.B.J. Hadley moved to Louisiana for a short time.[22] Elizabeth Gaspar Brown suggests that while living there, Mrs. Hadley might have become impressed with the Louisiana Civil Code, which allowed married women control of their own property.[23]

Whatever the influence, the fact remains that on Monday, January 21, 1839, the bill "for the protection and preservation of the rights and property of married women"[24] was introduced. The *Journal of the Senate* reported that the bill was read for the first time, two hundred copies ordered printed, and the bill was laid on the table. On Saturday, January 26, Thomas Hadley moved to call the bill from the table. The bill was ordered to be placed upon the orders of the day. The Senate resolved itself into a committee for debate of the bill.[25]

Mississippi newspapers reported the proceedings, as the bill immediately provoked strong feelings on both sides. Brown summarizes the progression of the debate that preceded the bill's passage.[26] Mr. Grayson, a state senator, predicted that within "six months all the married women would have all the property and it would thus be exempt from their husband's creditors." Hadley answered Grayson, saying that the bill was not intended for fraud, but "to secure to man's dearest idol the possession of the property which they have required */sic/* by their own exertion or the liberty of a fond father." Hadley continued,

[21]Bess Varnado, Jackson, Mississippi, personal correspondence, February 24, 1984.

[22]*Ibid.*

[23]Elizabeth Gaspar Brown, "Husband and Wife — Memorandum on the Mississippi Woman's Law of 1839," *Michigan Law Review* 42 (1944): 1110.

[24]*Journal of the Senate of the State of Mississippi* (1839), 99-100.

[25]*Ibid.*

[26]Since the bill was debated in committee, the proceedings are not reported in the *Senate Journal.* The following summary of the debate was excerpted from Brown, 1114-16.

> Is there a wish of such gross injustice in the mind of any man, that he would withhold from women the shield of protection which this bill proposes. Does man delight in woman's happiness. Then give them the plighted faith over legislation that they shall possess and enjoy the means of their own pleasure. I would, sir, secure to them the product of their own labor — I would secure to them the possession of the property given them by fond parents or relatives. Secure this, sir, — 'tis all I ask.

Senator Tucker, in agreement with Senator Grayson, stated that "'female delicacy forbids their participation in the turmoils and strife of business' and moreover 'the bill proposes a total and radical change in the settled law of the country.'" Senator Matthews agreed with these gentlemen and stated that

> a man would have it "in his power to defraud his creditors by selling his property and putting the money into the hands of a friend to buy a plantation and negroes to be given to his wife. The injury to be inflicted by this bill upon creditors is incalculable and the credit of Mississippi is, in all conscience, low enough already."

Grayson concluded,

> If you degrade and disgrace all that is lovely in woman, pass this bill; but if you would sustain them firmly in the high and exhaulted eminence which they now occupy in the eyes of the world and of men, spurn and reject this bill, as one of the most unholy and fraudulent devices ever presented.

According to the *Journal of the Senate*, the committee rose February 11 and approved said bill with an amendment thereto, "that any married woman may become seized or possessed of any property, real or personal, by direct bequest, demise, gift, purchase, or distribution in her own name, and as of her own property, provided the same does not come from her husband after coverture."[27] Another amendment submitted by Grayson was rejected:

> That the names of all slaves under the provisions of this act, that become the property of the wife during her coverture or which she may be entitled to at the time of her marriage, shall be recorded and the slaves designated as her property, in the registrar's office of the county of her residence, within twelve months after she shall become entitled to the same, and on failure to record the same said

[27] *Journal of the Senate of the State of Mississippi* (1839), 260-61.

> property, shall be liable to the debts of her husband contracted thereafter.[28]

Grayson, adamant in his beliefs, moved to postpone the bill indefinitely, but before the question was taken, the Senate adjourned for the day. The bill was ordered read for the third time the next day. Grayson tried again to propose another amendment that would shorten the period of possible registration to three months and eliminate the restraint on the time of contraction of the husband's debts by striking out the words, "contracted thereafter."[29] This amendment was also rejected and the bill then came up for a final vote. Nineteen voted in favor of the bill; nine against. On February 15, four days after passage of the bill by the Senate, a message was received from the state House of Representatives, stating that they had passed the bill, but not without opposition.[30]

In the House, the Honorable Robert Josselyn pointed out the obnoxious features of the bill and urged its rejection. "Pass the bill," he said, "and what will be the result? Where there should be union, there will be division. Confidence will be impaired — jealousy will arise — matrimonial quarrels will occur — domestic happiness will be lost. The maxim *[sic]* of the law, that the husband and wife are one, will be no longer true. There will be two heads of the family — two separate interests."[31] He also opposed the bill because it afforded great facilities to dishonest people for cheating their creditors. According to Josselyn, "the ladies of Mississippi are unanimously opposed to the passage of the bill, a fact which should cause it to be voted down, without division."[32]

It is an indisputable fact that in Mississippi, a slave state with a paternalistic society, radical reform had been set in motion with the passage of this bill. But it also seems certain that "powerful personal and economic forces must have been present to have overcome the great opposition to its passage."[33] There

[28] *Ibid.*
[29] Brown, "Husband and Wife," 1116.
[30] *Journal of the Senate of the State of Mississippi;* Brown, "Husband and Wife," 1116.
[31] *The Mississippian* (Jackson, Mississippi), April 26, 1839.
[32] *Ibid.*
[33] Brown, "Husband and Wife," 1118.

should be no doubt about Mrs. Hadley's influence in the passage of this law. First, her theory that "the way to a man's heart is through his stomach," was implemented by the meals she served to the legislators at her boarding house. Second, she exerted a strong influence upon her husband. It would seem that Mr. and Mrs. Hadley were of the same mind and spirit in securing rights for married women and in the protection of their property.

Colonel Hadley was given accolades in several state newspapers for his efforts to secure passage of the bill. The *Southern Sun*, on February 5, stated that "Colonel Hadley was entitled to much credit for having originated so salutary an enactment and should this bill become law its good effects will soon manifest themselves in society."[34] It continued,

> There should certainly be some legislative enactment to prevent some unscrupulous husbands, from wantonly squandering the estate vested in them by marriage and bring virtuous wives and helpless children to want and wretchedness. There are also such people in the world as "fortune hunters" — men without morality — without hearts, who are ever prone to deceive and divest women of wealth, that their prodigal hands may be furnished with the pecuniary means of continuing a life of splendid dissipation and degrading indolence. The licentiousness of such men should be checked. They not only disgrace the name of man — they not only sport with the holiest feelings of a women's heart — but they prey upon their victim and their children, the countless miseries of poverty.[35]

In a different article, the same newspaper suggested that Colonel Hadley may have had an ulterior motive for promoting women's rights:

> The Colonel has avowed himself an advocate of the "rights of women," and we being devoted to the gentle sex, (God Bless Them), are especially pleased with this gallant demeanor — (So soon as the ladies are permitted to vote), we have no doubt our Senator will attain another and a higher office than the one he now holds."[36]

But this great divergence from the common law would have to

[34]*Southern Sun* (Jackson, Miss.), February 5, 1839.
[35]*Ibid.*
[36]*Ibid.*

suffice for the time; women's suffrage would not come for another eighty years.

There is a possibility that Colonel and Mrs. Hadley wanted this law passed to gain control of her estate from her brothers, as the census rolls show the Hadleys no longer living in Hinds County after 1841. In the Hinds County Deeds, at the Raymond Courthouse, a deed shows that T.B.J. Hadley sold to Harriet Wooster of Louisiana all personal property: thirty-five Negroes, all mules, cattle, hogs and furniture, implements, and farming utensils attached to the farm in Hinds County, and located about two miles from Jackson, executed on February 17, 1839, two days after final passage of the Married Women's Property Act. Also listed in the same deed book, but probably with a discrepant date of December 30, 1837, T.B.J. Hadley and wife, Piety L. Hadley, sold to Joel Hardwick for $1,500, one-half of Lot #3, North, one acre, in the City of Jackson. This was probably the land where their boarding house stood. The deed was signed by both parties.

A family historian reports that between 1840 and 1841, Colonel and Mrs. Hadley migrated to Texas, as did many Mississippians at that time, looking for cheap and fertile land and a new frontier. In 1842, Mrs. Hadley's sister and brother-in-law, Hiram and Obedience Runnels, also moved to Texas. They followed their mother, Mrs. Obedience Smith, who had sold all of her property in 1835 when Major Smith died and moved to the Brazos River Area, somewhere close to present-day Houston. Mr. and Mrs. Hadley purchased property on the north side of the San Felipe Stage Route in Houston, and in 1844, they sold this property and on the same day purchased twenty-five acres including the site of the San Felipe Cottage from Mrs. Hadley's mother. It seems they all lived in close proximity in a settlement known as the "Smith Compound," along with the Runnels and were evidently a close family.[37] Mrs. Hadley's brother-in-law, H.G. Runnels, became a planter in the Brazos River Area and eventually represented Brazoria County in the Texas Convention of

[37]Mary Jane Lyle, Louisville, Miss., personal correspondence, February 7, 1984.

1845, while Texas was still a republic.[38] It is interesting to note that in this convention a provision was made allowing married women property rights.

Thomas Hadley continued to be active politically, serving his county as chief justice and the city of Houston as recorder. Colonel Hadley died September 25, 1869, in Houston, and Mrs. Hadley lived a long life, finally succumbing at age ninety-one, on August 23, 1889. Both are buried in Houston, Texas.[39]

While we may never know all the details and all the reasons that prompted the passage of the Married Women's Property Act, nonetheless, the fact remains that Mississippi was the first state to radically depart from the common law. This fact is not given its proper prominence in the history of women's emancipation, which traditionally begins with the passage of the New York Statue of 1848. In Mississippi, major revisions were seen in the law in 1846 and 1857.

After initial passage of the Married Women's Property Act, the law was expanded several times to give women such ancillary privileges as the right to keep the profits derived from their property, the right to sign contracts or deeds relating to their property, and the right to operate alone without the joint consent of their husbands. The Reconstruction constitution of the state included a provision for married women's property rights; the J.A.P. Campbell Code of 1880 abolished all the disabilities of coverture; and the Constitution of 1890 raised that protection to the constitutional, rather than the statutory level.

In *Radical Reconstruction and the Property Rights of Southern Women*, Susan Lebstock makes the following observations:

> In hard times a married women's property act became a significant new form of debtor relief. The general demand for debtor relief probably did much to promote the approval of laws, specifically for the protection of the property of married women. A married women's law shielded the husband, while it also shielded the wife; a man who

[38] Jeanette Runnels Espy, San Antonio, Texas, personal correspondence, February 22, 1984.

[39] *The Baptist Encyclopedia, A Dictionary*, ed. Wm. Cathcart (Philadelphia, 1883).

> was about to lose his own holdings could rest in the knowledge that in the future his wife's property would be secure.[40]

It is ironic that in shielding themselves economically, Mississippi men were advancing women's rights.

Five years would pass before two other states, Michigan and Maine, would give married women control over their property. The Maine law is strikingly similar in content, except for the slavery clauses, to the Mississippi law. Since the Mississippi law was printed in 1840, it may be that newspaper accounts or personal correspondence found its way into some interested legislators' hands.[41]

The drive of two strong-willed women — one the daughter of an Indian Chief, the other the daughter of an Indian fighter — coalesced with the practical concerns of men to secure the passage of the first law in the nation regarding women's property rights.

[40]Suzanne D. Lebsock, "Radical Reconstruction and the Property Rights of Southern Women," *Journal of Southern History* 43 (May 1977), 195-216.

[41]Brown, "Husband and Wife," 1120.

INVISIBLE WOMEN: THE LEGAL FICTION OF MARITAL UNITY IN NINETEENTH-CENTURY AMERICA

NORMA BASCH

In *Thaler* v. *Thaler*, a 1977 New York divorce case awarding alimony to the husband, the judge had occasion to summarize the nineteenth-century shift in the legal status of married women. At common law, he asserted, "the husband and wife were one and the husband was the one.... But with the advent of the married woman's property acts . . . any previous justification for this one-way support duty faded."[1] In the same year, however, an unemployed Brooklyn construction worker aired his reservations about his wife's employment by evoking the old common law image of marriage. "When you get married," he said, "you figure it's gonna be like one. Only it's always the husband's one."[2] The first of these comments suggests the focus of this essay: challenges to the common law doctrine of marital unity during a pivotal era of American law, roughly 1820-1860.[3] The second comment reflects its emphasis: the uncanny persistence of that doctrine far beyond its Christian and common law origins.

The judge in *Thaler* v. *Thaler* based his decision, in part, on an 1848 statute extending to married women the right to own their own property. He interpreted the statute as a significant legal alteration in the patriarchal family and implied that like the many other statutes passed in common law jurisdictions during this period, it marked the beginning of legal equality between wives and husbands.[4] By contrast, this essay contends that the married women's property acts failed to make such a significant alteration. Admittedly, if one defines patriarchy in the husband-wife relationship as the reduction of the wife to the status of property owned and controlled by the husband, one could argue that it never existed in its purest form in the Anglo-American legal tradition.[5] Yet, basic elements of that patriarchal construct underpinned all of Anglo-American domestic relations law, and they continued to exist long after the enactment of the married women property acts of the mid-nineteenth century.

Feminist Studies 5, no. 2 (Summer 1979). ©1979 by Feminist Studies, Inc.

One reason for the failure of the statutes was the power, comprehensiveness, and resilience of the common law doctrine of marital unity. The legal doctrine of marital unity, which was the starting point for spelling out the spacious powers of the husband over his wife at common law, was in and of itself an important patriarchal concept; and its impress on jurists, legislators, and judges was so profound as to make statutory reform difficult. This explanation approaches law as a "partially autonomous force" capable of affecting modes of thinking about the legal relationship between wives and husbands, and inherently resistant to radical changes.[6] Law, of course, is also a derivative phenomenon reflecting widespread social and economic changes. Yet, it was precisely the ability of the old common law doctrine to adapt to some changes that enabled it to blunt the nineteenth-century drive for married women's property rights.

Any explanation of the legislation has to take into account how marital unity functioned in a legal context. It was a legal fiction, a metaphor creating specific legal results. Over a period of centuries, English jurists gradually evolved a complex body of theory based on the simple presumption that "in the eyes of the law" the husband and wife were one person—the husband. Common law jurisprudence perpetuated this legal fiction as a convenient device for ordering the relationship of a married couple to the outside world, to their kin, to their children, and to each other. As a direct result of this metaphor, a wife came under her husband's wing or protective cover in a legal status designated as *coverture.* She could neither sue nor be sued in her own name. Theoretically, all of her personal property belonged to her husband; the management of her real property came under his control; and she was restricted in making contracts and wills. If the legal oneness of the husband and wife was a common law axiom, the legal invisibility of the wife was its corollary.

The concept of marital unity functioned in a diversity of historical contexts. Although its religious origins were in the one-flesh doctrine of Christianity, its empirical roots were in the customs of medieval Normandy; accordingly its formal vocabulary was feudal and French.[7] Its introduction into English law after the Norman Conquest signaled a decline in the status of English wives that reached a nadir in the early capitalism of the sixteenth and seventeenth centuries. What is striking about the long course of the legal fiction was its ability to serve the legal needs of three shifting social structures: the kin-oriented family of the late Middle Ages, the patriarchal nuclear family of early capitalism, and even the more companionate nuclear family of the late eighteenth century.[8] But by the nineteenth century it was controversial.

Despite its vaunted flexibility, it could not be incorporated into a new marital prototype in which the wife and husband were fully equal partners.

In nineteenth-century America, the legal solution was to riddle the old prototype with exceptions instead of creating a new one. Many exceptions existed already. The legal fiction of marital unity defined a legal situation with great simplicity when the legal reality was infinitely more complex. As Mary Beard pointed out in *Woman as Force in History*, this crude common law metaphor was not an accurate description of the legal condition of wives in any period of either English or American history.[9] In England the ecclesiastical courts, which adjudicated marriage, separation, and the few divorces that were granted, and which controlled the law relating to the sexual morals of spouses, had to recognize the wife as a separate legal entity in some cases. Furthermore, the common law courts afforded a certain amount of leeway in the wife's contractual capacities and allowed her to act as her husband's agent. Married women living in centers of trade participated in commerce either as a matter of local custom or through sole-trader statutes.

The most important exceptions developed in the courts of equity, a jurisdiction separate from the common law courts that gave relief when no remedy was available at law. Originating in the concept of fairness as opposed to legal strictness, equity grew into an ancillary system of law with its own forms, pleadings, and precedents. By the end of the seventeenth century the chancery courts, which administered equity, recognized the married woman's trust and the antenuptial agreement, two devices that forged an important breach in the doctrine of marital unity.[10]

In colonial America a shortage of women and labor necessitated lenient application of some common law principles.[11] In most American jurisdictions an enterprising woman with assets, initiative, and access to legal advice could free herself from many of her common law disabilities by means of a trust or antenuptial agreement, or both. By placing nominal ownership of her property in the hands of a third party or by contracting with her husband in advance of marriage for special terms under which her property was to be separate, a wife could keep her property beyond the reach of her husband's creditors. In some cases she could manage, sell, and devise it as if she were single.[12] Husbands engaged in high-risk speculation or fathers distrustful of future sons-in-law obviously favored such legal options.

Trusts and antenuptial agreements, however, the mechanisms for creating a married woman's separate estate, created two legal views of marriage—one for the wealthy and legally sophisticated, and one for everybody else. While equity precedents recognized marriage as an individual bargain in which the contracting parties set their own financial terms, the common law depicted marriage as a monolithic institution in which the state imposed uniform rules for marital property. Resentment to this two-level system took shape in the Jacksonian era and coalesced in the codification movement. Criticism took the form of attacks on the common law in general and the law of husband and wife in particular.[13] Thus part of the drive for married women's property rights was political and represented a tendency to offer to the many by statute what had been available to the few by custom and judicial precedent.

The impulse for legal change was economic as well. A readjustment between the married couple and the commercial world seemed essential to the flow of commerce. Coverture, after all, was designed to meet the needs of a medieval agricultural monarchy whose economic focus had been descending scales of tenancy in land; its emphasis was on the rights and duties associated with real property. It was a striking anachronism in an economy in which land was a salable commodity and personal property was growing in significance. The development of life insurance, the growth of savings banks, the increase in corporate stock, and the presence of a female wage-earning class all compelled a redefinition of the legal position of the wife. Severe economic dips like the Panic of 1837 and the ensuing depression encouraged legislatures to pass statutes insulating the wife's property from the husband's creditors. Consequently by the middle decades of the nineteenth century, states began passing piecemeal legislation ameliorating the legal disabilities of married women.[14]

Although the antebellum drive to alter marital property laws was primarily a part of the drive to simplify law and expedite commerce, it was also an attack on the legal outlines of the patriarchal family. Statutory reform was the juncture at which some of the legal and economic requisites of nineteenth-century America confronted patriarchal values. By maintaining the meticulous definition of gender roles and by mandating the complete dependence of wives on husbands, the old common law fiction of marital unity meshed neatly with the cult of domesticity. The wife's legal invisibility in coverture was a potent cultural symbol and the object of feminist and antifeminist polemics. Nineteenth-century American feminists attacked the common law fiction of marital unity because they believed it was prescriptive and embodied a classic example of patriarchal values.[15] Antifeminists defended it for the very same reason.[16] Thus the tensions accompanying the challenge to patriarchy and the continuities associated with the preservation of the legal fiction appeared in both legal and nonlegal literature. A representative sampling of the way jurists, laypeople, and feminists utilized the doctrine of marital unity between the years 1820 and 1860 and an investigation of the doctrine's impact on the legislation and adjudication of married women's property rights in New York through 1880 illustrates these tensions and continuities.[17]

We begin with Blackstone's *Commentaries*, not because he is the preeminent authority on the history of the common law, but because he was its most popular theoretician. It was Blackstone, the eighteenth-century codifier and classifier, who fashioned the disarmingly simple map of the common law on which most nineteenth-century Americans relied.[18] Variations, exceptions, and technicalities were not his concern; broad principles such as marital unity were.[19] Because he perceived marital unity as a kind of shorthand for a whole bundle of specific rights and duties, his presentation of it was straightforward and expository. He was not, however, without an underlying rationale for English marriage laws, which he believed best served the one critical function of marriage—the creation of lawful heirs. His rationale was essentially economic. According to Blackstone, marriage was an arrangement of property for the propertied and their children, who were the conduits for family wealth.[20]

In Blackstone's rendition of marital unity, women and men approached marriage as theoretical equals to a civil contract. After marriage, nothing remained of that equality because of the very nature of the contract:

> [T]he very being or legal existence of the woman is suspended during marriage, or at least is incorporated and consolidated into that of the husband; under whose wing, protection and *cover*, she performs everything; and is therefore called in our law-french a *feme covert, faemina viro co-operta*; and it is said to be *covert-baron*, or under the protection and influence of her husband, her *baron*, or lord; and her condition during her marriage is called her *coverture.*[21]

The Anglo-Norman language eloquently points up the change created by marriage. The two former equals have become baron and feme, the male of lordly status and the female without status, the protector and the protected. Blackstone did not create this version of coverture incorporating the power and protection inherent in feudal statuses. It was as integral a part of the legacy of English law as the rights of English men. Nevertheless, Blackstone's concise depiction of coverture belied the legal and social changes that were taking place in his own time. Equity, which he treated perfunctorily, was ameliorating the rigidity of the marriage contract he described. The patriarchal, nuclear family he championed was giving way to a more modern, companionate ideal. He endowed American jurisprudence with a view of English domestic relations law that was dated. Still it was a highly influential view, and it reduced the wife to complete economic dependence and legal invisibility.

The legal inferiority of the wife, moreover, was built into the organization of the *Commentaries.* Although sections of the *Commentaries* treated life, liberty, and property, the trichotomy of inalienable, natural rights, domestic relations appeared in a subsystem of private, relative rights including other relationships of "natural" superiors and inferiors, such as parent-child, master-servant, and guardian-ward.[22] This organization structured the curricula of newly forming American law schools as well as the composition of new legal treatises.

Yet, Blackstone's treatment of women and marriage engendered a certain amount of controversy among his editors on both sides of the Atlantic. Edward Christian, for example, an English editor of several late eighteenth- and early nineteenth-century editions took strenuous exception to Blackstone's assertion that "even the disabilities which the wife lies under are for the most part intended for her protection and benefit. So great a favorite is the female sex of the laws of England." Not only did Christian expose the inequities in marital property laws, but he pointed out that in the case of women's property in general, "there is taxation without representation."[23] John F. Hargrave, editor of an 1847 edition, expressed characteristic American ambivalence to married women's common law disabilities by citing the need to free wives "from the harsh unending rules of the common law" without inverting gender roles. Too much change, he warned, could lead to "women on juries, in the militia," and "serving on posses."[24]

Recoiling from Blackstone's stridently patriarchal approach and struggling against his feudal vocabulary, American editors filled in the gaps left by his failure to deal fully with equity jurisprudence. They underscored American statutes relating to dower, bankruptcy, and abandonment. As they updated the *Commentaries* year after year, they ultimately created a series of glosses through which one can trace the slowly diverging path of American domestic relations law. Still it was Blackstone who set the terms. Like the medieval canonists before him, he created a seemingly static model of the family around which antebellum discussion revolved. Even jurists writing new treatises seemed locked in an explicit or implicit dialogue with Blackstone.

The work of Tapping Reeve, founder of the first national law school and author of the first American domestic relations treatise, exemplifies the strain American jurists experienced with respect to the married woman's common law status.[25] Always practical, always contending with the commercial intricacies of marital property, Reeve stressed the need for the wife to be able to contract freely when her husband was away for long periods of time. In Reeve, moreover, there are glimpses of a sanctification of marriage and motherhood in direct conflict with the wife's childlike common law status. He was particularly embarrassed by the wife's inability to make a will because it suggested marriage caused a loss of her understanding and volition. Why, he asked, should she "die intestate when all others of the community may devise their property?"[26] Consumed with practical considerations requiring a wife to act separately, and buttressed by a long tradition of equity precedents, Reeve flatly denied the entire doctrine of the unity of spouses.

This denial enabled him to justify a wider range of economic activity for the wife, but he arrived at equally patriarchal results by reversing the fiction of marital unity, a process Blackstone undoubtedly facilitated with the circularity of his own logic. Where Blackstone claimed the wife came under the husband's power and protection because they became one person in the eyes of the law, Reeve insisted they were two people in a relationship in which the wife was inevitably the weaker of the two. Reeve made the results of coverture his premise and significantly changed the rationalization for the wife's inferior legal status. He saw physical coercion and psychological dependence as an ineluctable reality in relations between the sexes. A woman "in the moments of her warm confidence in the honorable and generous intentions of her suitor," was incapable of protecting her own rights.[27] For good or ill, the wife was in the husband's power. Marriage, therefore, was not a contract between equals, but a relationship between the stronger sex and the weaker sex, which the common law in its wisdom recognized.

Another American variation on the common law theme entailed emphasizing marital unity as an historical fiction, a symbol of Anglo-American legal continuity and social stability. This view accommodated moderate change while preserving the legal fiction as a buffer against profound readjustments in gender roles. Both James Kent and Joseph Story, two towering figures in antebellum jurisprudence, took this position.[28] Although each played a significant role in educating American lawyers in equity jurisprudence, they played an equally significant role in retaining the old common law marital prototype.

Story's dissent in *Dartmouth College* v. *Woodward*, the historic

1819 Supreme Court case in which debate over the constitutional limits of state divorce laws arose tangentially, illustrates the way judges consistently reiterated the husband's right to his wife's property and person. Reviewing marriage as a contract, Story unequivocally asserted, "A man has as good a right to his wife as to *the property* acquired under a marriage contract. He has a legal right to her society and her fortune. . . ."[29] Few American jurists, however, had a better technical grasp of equitable options or a greater familiarity with community property systems. Story did not believe the wife was or should be literally the property of the husband, but neither did he favor statutory changes in the marriage contract. Equity was available to ease the rigidity of the common law. Even in his rigorous, authoritative 1836 treatise on equity in which he examined the liberating exceptions to the common law slighted by Blackstone, Story continued to stress the historical legitimacy and social value of the husband's legal and economic control over his wife.[30]

Similarly, in his *Commentaries on American Law*, Kent, who as Chancellor of New York had applied English equity precedents liberally on behalf of married women's estates, supported marital unity as a matter of legal continuity and public policy. Idealizing the institution of marriage and elevating it to heights far beyond Blackstone's simple civil contract, Kent construed any deep, irrevocable incursions on the husband's legal powers as anarchic threats to the whole social organism. "We may justly place to the credit of the institution of marriage," said Kent, "a great share of the blessings which flow from the refinement of manners, the education of children, the sense of justice, and the cultivation of the liberal arts."[31] Kent recognized those situations in which the husband abused his powers or was unable to meet his responsibilities, but he considered them exceptions and was confident that trusts and marriage settlements could prevent the wife from "being overwhelmed by the misfortunes or unkindness, or vices of her husband."[32] Because the husband is the natural guardian of the wife, he reasoned, "the law has given him a reasonable superiority and control over her person, and he may even put gentle restraints upon her liberty."[33] Under the haze of Romantic rhetoric, Kent invested marriage with dimensions that were as patriarchal as Blackstone's.

For the most part erudite American jurists envisioned marital unity as a flexible legal principle, not to be interpreted too literally, from which gradual change could safely evolve. They tended to compartmentalize the legal consequences of the marriage contract and thereby avoided connections between private law and public law, between the wife's legal status within the family and her status as a citizen of the state. Conversely amateurs, along with those professionals whose legal education consisted of Blackstone, quoted the strictures of coverture as if they constituted the eternal letter of the law. Nonlawyers, moreover, considered the private and public domains inseparable. Their discussions of married women's property rights invariably included discussions of women's suffrage.

Nonlawyers construed the legal fiction not as a specific legal device, but as a broad metaphor for relations between the sexes. The sexual politics resonating from the metaphor of the husband submerging the wife were exploited most dynamically by antifeminists and feminists. In *The American Democrat*, for example, James Fenimore Cooper drew on the old common law fiction as a paradigm for the naturally hierarchical structure of all human relationships. He used the model of familial authority to justify political authority. Equality of civil rights, claimed Cooper, can never be absolute. "Thus women nowhere possess precisely the same rights as men; or men the same rights as women. The wife, usually, can neither sue nor be sued, while the husband, except in particular cases, is made liable to the legal claims on account of the wife."[34] In citing the disabilities of coverture and their religious antecedents, Cooper was evoking reverence for the political principle of the superior dominating, representing, and protecting the inferior.

Nineteenth-century American feminists seized upon the emotive power of the metaphor in the same comprehensive manner, only they counted on eliciting rage. In their view, any equation in which one plus one equaled one by virtue of the woman's invisibility was a vivid symbol of male dominion in a cultural as well as a legal context. Thus the demand for married women's property rights became a focal point of the women's movement. The 1848 Declaration of Sentiments at Seneca Falls stated in its allegations against man: "He has made her, if married, in the eye of the law, civilly dead. He has taken from her all right in property even to the wages she earns."[35] Petitions to legislatures protested against women being classified with other legal incompetents. One impassioned petition read:

> Your laws, after depriving us of property, of the means of acquiring it, and even of individuality, require the same obedience from us as from free citizens. We therefore think common justice and humanity would dictate that when you classify us and our privileges with those of *idiots* and *lunatics*, you should do the same with regard to our responsibilities. . . .[36]

Feminist challenges to the common law depicted marital unity in its harshest and most unremitting form, and as Beard insisted, perpetuated an image that was legally imprecise and historically inaccurate. But these challenges, appearing first in the 1830s, forced public debate beyond the barriers of Blackstone's common law classifications. Logically, effective opposition necessitated removing wives from Blackstone's subsystem of private, relative rights, which mandated inferior status by its very organization, and placing them instead in the national mainstream of fundamental, inalienable rights. Feminists argued, for example, that the husband's ownership of the wife's services and earnings, the fruits of her labor, was tantamount to the husband owning the wife. Marriage, therefore, was a form of slavery. They also argued that because coverture deprived the wife of due process by divesting her of rights she had held when she was single—and marriage was itself an inalienable right—it was incompatible with the Bill of Rights.[37]

Liberal feminist opposition to the principle of marital unity was ideologically significant. It applied the political rhetoric of natural rights to the private relationship of husband and wife.[38] It reversed the traditional pattern of using the family as a model for the authoritarian state and used the state as a model for the democratic family. Only by merging the public and domestic spheres which Enlightenment jurists, such as Blackstone, had so carefully segregated could feminists carry popular natural law doctrines to nonsexist conclusions.

The demand for married women's property rights created a bridge between the private sphere of domesticity and the public arena of political power. While Sarah Hale, editor of *Godey's Lady's Book*, supported a married women's statute on the basis of the moral superiority of American wives and mothers, Ernestine Rose, a prominent New York feminist, found the absence of such a statute symptomatic of female exclusion from the political and judicial process.[39] Suffrage and property rights, she insisted were inseparable. As Ellen DuBois has pointed out, suffragism challenged the male monopoly of public power.[40] By embracing the goals of a larger audience which demanded some statutory changes in domestic relations laws and by linking those goals to the more radical demand for suffrage, antebellum feminists insured themselves a public forum.

In some ways the emergence of a forum for the development of feminist ideology remains the most significant legacy of the drive for married women's property rights. Those statutes that were passed gave feminists a sense of success and contributed to the rising expectations that animated the early movement, but the statutes did not deliver "the death-blow to the old Blackstone code for married women" that the participants in the movement first believed they had.[41] If the New York pattern of legislating and adjudicating married women's property rights was at all representative of other jurisdictions, it demonstrates the limitations of the statutes relative to the power of the old legal fiction.[42]

From 1836 until 1848, the twelve years it took New York to pass a major statute, successive legislatures floundered in the cross-currents of marital property reform. Thus in 1840 the legislature passed a married women's insurance act which gave considerable impetus to the newly emerging life insurance business and enabled a wife to be the beneficiary of her husband's insurance free from the claims of his creditors.[43] In 1844, however, an assembly judiciary committee, pressed by petitions, reaffirmed the old marital prototype in words closer to its Christian origins: "It has been ascertained to be necessary that man and wife should have but one interest, one feeling, one existence; that they should be as one, and become for all civil purposes, 'one flesh.' "[44]

Public support for marital property reform grew in this period and coalesced in New York at the Constitutional Convention of 1846.[45] The ideological spectrum of support ranged from those favoring lenient debtor laws, to those advocating a correction of the legal imbalances in marriage, to those urging complete legal and political equality for women. The general legislative intent, however, seems to have been to place the options available at equity into statutory form. A report of an 1846 judiciary committee advised that statutes "may have the effect to familiarize the public" with the provisions of equity.[46] The goal of the New York legislature, then, was not to forge new legal outlines for marriage, but rather to offer the advantages of equity to everyone.

This was a difficult task at best. In fact, none of the statutes in this period empowered a wife as effectively or securely as a carefully worded antenuptial contract could.[47] In sharp contrast to equity principles, a much-heralded 1848 statute making the wife's property part of her separate estate failed to give her the contractual powers needed to bind her estate. This omission was partially corrected the following year.[48] Economic developments, however, continued to spur legal innovations. In 1850 the New York legislature passed a statute protecting the deposits of married women in savings banks.[49] Designed originally to encourage thrift in the poor, savings banks by this time included depositors of substance; and the growth of savings institutions in New York was particularly significant.[50] In 1851 and with little fanfare New York passed a statute allowing married women who owned stock to vote in person or by proxy for corporate officers.[51] No act, however, went so far in readjusting the relationship between the husband and wife as the earnings act of 1860.[52] Yet this act which included the wife's earnings as part of her separate estate and which enabled her to sue and be sued in her own name was substantially vitiated by judicial conservatism.

Judicial opposition emanated, in part, from confusion caused by poor drafting and ambiguous legislative intent. Court tests, moreover, took place when judicial jealousy of growing legislative power was rampant.[53] More importantly, judges reared on the old common law principle of the wife's invisibility and dependence were conditioned to interpret the statutes as narrowly as possible. Some judges, to be sure, welcomed the statutes as an important improvement in the legal status of American women,[54] but most displayed covert or overt hostility. One judge, for example, predicted that the earnings act "very likely will prove to be very mischievous and pregnant with much evil."[55] In their decisions, judges invariably cited the common law first, and then examined the extent to which the statutes abrogated it. To many the married women's acts were deviations from the clear, hard logic of the common law, deviations with which they had to come to terms. Their role was to prevent legislative tinkering from completely subverting that logic.[56]

Judges limited the impress of the first statutes to property acquired after 1848, declaring any larger application unconstitutional.[57] They excluded interest, rents, and profits accruing after 1848 on property acquired before 1848. But even wives who married or acquired property after that date gained little in the way of property rights. Although husbands and wives together took advantage of the new laws to try to defeat creditors, wives fared poorly in terms of approaching legal equality with their husbands. One persistent problem was what constituted a wife's "separate estate." The entire concept of the separate estate was an outgrowth of equity jurisprudence, which required the separation of marital property to be specific and unambiguous. It was not difficult, therefore, for the courts to construe most property as belonging to the husband. Enterprises such as farms or boardinghouses that wives were likely to run while their husbands worked elsewhere were almost uniformly regarded as the husband's property regardless of who the original purchaser was.

The case of Caroline Switzer, whose name is notably absent from the parties in litigation, exemplifies the limitations of the 1848-1849 acts. As the wife of a New York carpenter, Mrs. Switzer operated boardinghouses in the city during the 1850s. She leased houses in her own name, placed her brass nameplate reading "Mrs. A. Switzer" on each door, contracted independently with the boarders, cooked and cleaned for them with the help of her daughter Harriet, and collected the rents. In the course of her business, she signed a note borrowing money and secured it with a chattel mortgage on furniture. When she failed to pay at the specified time, her creditor foreclosed and took the furniture. Her husband sued the creditor, claiming his wife had no authority to execute the mortgage. The court decided that the boarding-house was the husband's business because it was used for the support and well-being of the whole family and that the statutes in no way impinged on this situation. Do the statutes, asked the court, "authorize a married woman . . . to become a general trader and make valid contracts in respect to any business which she may be disposed to undertake, or in respect to any speculations in which she may choose to engage?" The answer was they did not.[58]

As an example of the tenacity of the old marital prototype, eighteen years after the earnings act the Court of Appeals allowed a husband to sue singly for his wife's earnings because the couple had habitually intermingled their money. Because the wife had not specifically "elected" to labor on her own account, the court decided she labored on her husband's account and that her husband could recover a judgment for her wages in a woolen mill. In this case, said the court, "the husband's common law right to her earnings remains unaffected."[59]

Furthermore, because the statutes did not relieve the husband of his support duties regardless of the size of the wife's estate, judges inured to the common law equipoise of rights and duties refused to strip the husband of his common law rights. One basic tenet of common law relationships was that the individual with large obligations was the individual with large powers. The husband's obligations continued. As one judge put it, "The husband is bound to provide for her and them whatever is necessary for their suitable clothing and maintenance according to his and their situation and condition in life."[60] If the husband had to continue to pay for his wife's necessaries, then he had to retain his right to enjoy her services and earnings, control her behavior, and select their place of domicile.[61] Clearly, quintessential principles of coverture survived statutory reform.

Further investigation of the adjudication of statutes on a state-by-state basis is needed. Yet the evidence presented here and drawn from nationally prominent legal treatises and from the legislation and adjudication in one of the nation's most influential jurisdictions suggests that the legal fiction of marital unity inhibited the reform of marital property laws. In one context, individuals consciously selected this richly suggestive and readily available metaphor for their own purposes. This was a matter of thought dominating language. But in another context, especially a legal one, it was also a matter of language dominating thought. The evidence suggests that the legal fiction of marital unity was so pervasive in the language and literature of the law that it affected as well as reflected attitudes towards women and marriage. The adaptability and flexibility of the legal fiction, attributes for which the common law tradition is famous, helped it to survive. Thus while the doctrine of marital unity underwent superficial alterations in the antebellum period, it simultaneously tempered substantial changes. This is one explanation of why the statutes do not constitute a significant historical discontinuity.[62]

The evidence suggests that the inherently conservative processes of law embodied in the power and legitimacy of the ancient legal fiction blunted the inherently radical possibilities of dismantling the legal foundations of the patriarchal family. When nineteenth-century American feminists attacked common law categories, they at least dimly perceived that language orders and classifies, and contains the existing conceptual apparatus for creating new law. When they registered their shared rage and humiliation at being lumped together with infants and lunatics, they were groping towards a fundamental restructuring of power and readjustment of gender roles that those in power–jurists, legislators, and judges–would not and could not permit as long as they utilized the fiction of marital unity.

These conclusions raise questions about the relationship of women's legal status to broader economic, social, and cultural changes. An alternate view of the law as a purely derivative phenomenon might conclude that the legal inferiority of nineteenth-century American wives reflected their real economic dependence on the male head of the household, their position in a family structure that was still more patriarchal than companionate, and the domestic role to which the dominant culture assigned them. Fundamental change in domestic relations law, therefore, awaited larger changes.

This essay has reversed the traditional view of law as a derivative phenomenon to suggest that "the law" in all of its manifestations, including jurisprudence and judicial precedents, was capable of retarding change. This approach supplements the derivative explanation, and it takes into account the special character of the Anglo-American legal tradition. The common law was particularly resistant to statutory change. A statute creating legal equality between spouses had to be comprehensive in scope and gender-neutral in language. Because no such statute was passed, the married women's acts were small islands in the vast ocean of the common law. Furthermore, in a precedent-oriented legal tradition legislatures were able to create the illusion of radical change by passing loosely drafted statutes that left the ultimate disposition of change to the judiciary. Subsequently the legal fiction of marital unity, part of every nineteenth-century lawyer's education, informed the judicial resistance to those changes that were made. Not only did it function as a legal maxim put into service by a conservative judiciary, but it was also a device of persuasive power extending beyond the confines of the courts to the public. "Eliminate metaphor from the law," one modern jurist has asserted, "and you have reduced its power to convince and convert."[63]

Because the last vestiges of the legal fiction of marital unity remain in the statutes and recent precedents of many jurisdictions, these conclusions carry contemporary feminist implications. The language of the law is important; only sex-free language can create legal equality between the sexes. Such equality need not destroy the special legal position of the spouse who remains at home to attend to domestic duties. As the United States Supreme Court noted, the protective, compensatory aspects of marriage law can be served by gender-neutral language, but marriage law that gender-classifies "carries with it the baggage of sexual stereotypes."[64] The removal of sexual stereotypes from the law is not a panacea. It cannot compensate American women for their larger economic and social disabilities, but it can remove the sanctions of the law from their disabilities. And if the law has the power to retard changes, as suggested here, should we not assume that it has the power to accelerate them as well?

NOTES

This article was delivered as a paper in a slightly different version at the Berkshire Conference on the History of Women at Mount Holyoke College, August 25, 1978. Research, which is part of a larger study on married women's property rights in nineteenth-century New York, was funded by a Woodrow Wilson Grant in Women's Studies.

1 Thaler v. Thaler, *New York Law Journal*, 21 January 1977, p. 14.

2 Anna Quindlen, "Relationships vs. Intimacy," *New York Times*, 28 November 1977, p. 36.

3 Some significant assessments of the period by legal historians include: Roscoe Pound, *The Formative Era of American Law* (New York: Peter Smith, 1950); George M. Haar, ed., *The Golden Age of American Law* (New York: George Braziller, 1965); Maxwell Bloomfield, *American Lawyers in a Changing Society 1776-1876* (Cambridge: Harvard University Press, 1976); Lawrence Friedman, *A History of American Law* (New York: Simon & Schuster, 1973); and Morton J. Horwitz, *The Transformation of American*

Law 1780-1860 (Cambridge: Harvard University Press, 1977). Perry Miller placed the jurisprudence of the era into the context of American intellectual history in *The Life of the Mind in America from the Revolution ot the Civil War* (New York: Harcourt Brace & World, 1965). For important scholarship on legislative activity in the period, see Louis Hartz, *Economic Policy and Democratic Thought: Pennsylvania 1776-1880* (Cambridge: Harvard University Press, 1948); and J. Willard Hurst, *Law and the Conditions of Freedom in the Nineteenth Century United States* (Madison: University of Wisconsin Press, 1956).

[4]My focus, which is on the prevailing common law tradition in the United States, excludes consideration of states like Louisiana and California which structured marital property law on French and Spanish codes.

[5]Lawrence Stone, "The Rise of the Nuclear Family in Early Modern England: The Patriarchal Stage," in *The Family in History*, ed. Charles E. Rosenberg (Philadelphia: University of Pennsylvania Press, 1975), p. 34. On the desire of men to own women, see Keith Thomas, "The Double Standard," *Journal of the History of Ideas* 20 (1959): 216.

[6]For law as an autonomous and derivative phenomenon, see Eugene Genovese, *Roll Jordan Roll: The World the Slaves Made* (New York: Random House, 1974), pp. 25-49.

[7]See St. Paul's opinions on marriage, Ephesians 5: 22-24, 31; for the links between canon law and English law, see Julius Goebel, Jr., *Cases and Materials on the Development of Legal Institutions* (Brattleboro: Vermont Printing Co., 1946), pp. 446-47.

[8]Considerable controversy exists over the precise chronology of these shifts. I have relied on Stone, "The Rise of the Nuclear Family." For the decline in the legal status of English wives, see Florence Griswold Buckstaff, "Married Women's Property in Anglo-Saxon and Anglo-Norman Law and the Origin of the Common-Law Dower," *Annals of the American Academy of Political and Social Science* 4 (1893-94): 233-64.

[9]Mary Beard, *Woman as Force in History: A Study in Traditions and Realities* (New York: Macmillan, 1946).

[10]South Carolina, New York, New Jersey, Maryland, and Delaware had separate equity jurisdictions. Those states which did not have them, incorporated English and American equity precedents into their common law courts. American access to equity, however, on a state-by-state basis needs further historical exploration for the early national and Jacksonian periods. For the development of exceptions to the common law, see Sir Frederick Pollack and Frederic William Maitland, *The History of English Law*, 2d ed., 2 vols. (1898; reprint ed., London: Cambridge University Press, 1968), 2: 99; John D. Johnston, "Sex and Property: The Common Law Tradition, The Law School Curriculum, and Developments Towards Equality," *New York University Law Review* 47 (1972): 1057, 1069-70; Frederic William Maitland, *Equity* (Cambridge: Cambridge University Press, 1926), pp. 2-5; Elizabeth Bowles Warbasse, "The Changing Legal Rights of Married Women 1800-1861" (Ph.D. diss., Radcliffe, 1960), p. 39; Beard, *Woman as Force*, p. 135.

[11]Richard Morris stresses the improved legal status of colonial wives in his pioneering *Studies in the History of American Law with Special References to the Seventeenth and Eighteenth Centuries* (New York: Columbia University Press, 1930). Also see Julia Cherry Spruill, *Women's Life and Work in the Southern Colonies* (1938; reprint ed., New York: Norton, 1972); John Demos, *A Little Commonwealth: Family Life in Plymouth Colony* (London: Oxford University Press, 1970); Elizabeth W. Anthony Dexter, *Colonial Women of Affairs: A Study of Women in Business and the Professions in America Before 1776* (Boston: Houghton Mifflin, 1924); George Lee Haskins, *Law and Authority in Early Massachusetts: A Study in Tradition and Design* (New York: Macmillan, 1960). For a comparative approach, see Roger Thompson, *Women in Stuart England and America: A Comparative Study* (London: Routledge & Kegan Paul, 1974). For a comparison between the colonial and early national periods, see Joan Hoff Wilson, "The Illusion of Change: Women and the American Revolution," in *The American Revolution: Explorations in the History of American Radicalism*, ed. Alfred F. Young (DeKalb: Northern Illinois University Press, 1976), pp. 383-445.

[12]Technical discussions of trusts and antenuptial agreements appeared regularly in contemporary law journals. See "Recent Revisions etc. of Statute Laws," *American Jurist* 18 (October 1837): 244-47; "Trust for the Separate Use," *New York Legal Observer* 1 (November 1842): 113-15; "Marriage Settlements," *American Law Magazine* 3 (April 1844): 16-22: "Property of Married Women," *New York Legal Observer* 2 (October 1843): 284; "The Validity of Marriage Settlements in Exclusion of the Marital Rights of a Future Husband," *American Law Magazine* 3 (July 1844): 273-97; "Accumulation from Property Settled to Separate Use," *New York Legal Observer* 3 (March 1844): 3-4; "Uses and Trusts as Affected by the Revised Statutes of the State of New York." *American Law Magazine* 6 (January 1846): 268-81. Forms for such devices appeared in do-it-yourself legal manuals. See John S. Jenkins, *The New Clerk's Assistant or Book of Practical Forms* (Auburn: Miller, Orton, and Mulligan, 1853); David Wright, *Executor's, Administrator's and Guardian's Guide*, 3d ed. (Auburn: Derby and Miller, 1852); and George Bishop, *Every Woman Her Own Lawyer* (New York: Dick and Fitzgerald, 1858).

[13]See, for example, Caleb Cushing, "The Legal Condition of Women," *North American Review* 26 (April 1828): 316-19. Other articles in the *North American Review* favoring codification include C. S. Daveis, "Common Law Jurisdiction," 21 (July 1825): 104-41; Henry D. Sedgwick, "Correspondence on the History of the Law," 23 (July 1826): 197-201. Criticism of the common law and the law of husband and wife was also one of the hallmarks of Jacksonian democracy and appeared regularly in the *United States Magazine and Democratic Review*. See "Edward Livingston and his Code," 9 (July 1841): 11, and 9 (September 1841): 213; "The Legal Wrongs of Women," 14 (May 1844): 477-83; "The Abuses of Law Courts," 21 (October 1848): 309. For professional criticism of the law of husband and wife, see "Facetiousness of the Law: Husband and Wife," *New York Legal Observer* 3 (March 1845): 155-56; Timothy Walker, "Legal Condition of Women," *Western Law Journal* 1 (1849): 145-50. See also the debate over married women's property statutes between John Neal and Eliza Farnham in Neal's short-lived *Brother Jonathan* 5 (June 1843): 183-85; 5 (June 1843): 236-38; 5 (July 1843): 266-68; and 5 (July 1843): 304-09.

[14]Maine, Missouri, Mississippi, and New York were in the vanguard of married women's statutes, but by 1865 twenty-nine states had passed some form of married women's property law. Kay Ellen Thurman, "The Married Women's Property Acts" (LL.M. diss., University of Wisconsin Law School, 1966), p. 4.

In addition to the work of Beard, Johnston, Warbasse, and Thurman cited above, for scholarship on the married women's acts see Leo Kanowitz, *Women and the Law: The Unfinished Revolution*, 2d ed. (Albuquerque: University of New Mexico Press, 1975), pp. 35-99; Peggy Rabkin, "The Origins of Law Reform: The Social Significance of the Nineteenth-Century Codification Movement and its Contribution to the Passage of the Early Married Women's Property Acts," *Buffalo Law Review* 24 (1974-75): 683-760: and Joseph Warren, "Husband's Right to Wife's Services," *Harvard Law Review* 38 (1925): 421-39. For the influence of the statutes on the women's movement, see Keith Melder, "The Beginnings of the Women's Rights Movement in the United States 1800-1848" (Ph.D. diss., Yale University, 1963), pp. 28-30. A similar trend toward modernization and democratization appears to have impelled reform of English marital property laws. See Lee Holcombe, "Victorian Wives and Property: Reform of the Married Women's Property Law, 1857-1882," in *A Widening Sphere: Changing Roles of Victorian Women*, ed. Martha Vicinus (Bloomington: Indiana University Press, 1977), pp. 3-28.

[15]All of the printed proceedings of women's rights conventions as well as the voluminous pamphlet literature of the movement document emphasis on the legal fiction of marital unity. See, for example, Sarah M. Grimké, *Letters on the Equality of the Sexes and the Condition of Woman* (Boston: Isaac Knapp, 1838), pp. 70-74, 86-87; Elisha P.

Hurlbut *Essays on Human Rights and Their Political Guarantees* (New York: Fowlers and Wells, 1850), pp. 148-52; Elizabeth Oakes Smith, *Woman and Her Needs* (New York: Fowlers and Wells, 1851), pp. 43-53; Elizabeth Cady Stanton, *Address to the Legislature of New York* (Albany: Weed, Parson & Co., 1854), p. 9; *The Woman's Almanac for 1858* (Worcester: Z. Baker, 1858), p. 4; Caroline Dall, *Woman's Rights Under the Law* (Boston: Walker, Wise & Co., 1861), pp. 134-36. For a famous English attack on the common law status of married women, see *The Subjection of Women* in John Stuart Mill and Harriet Taylor Mill, *Essays on Sex Equality*, ed. Alice S. Rossi (Chicago: University of Chicago Press, 1970), pp. 158-61.

[16] See, for example, R. W. Foster, *Women's Rights and Servants' Rights According to the Bible* (Corning: n.p., 1854); William A. Alcott, *The Young Wife or Duties of Woman in Marriage* (Boston: George W. Light, 1836), pp. 29-30; Timothy Titcomb, *Letters to Young People*, 21st ed. (New York: Charles Scribner, 1861), p. 55.

[17] My specific analysis of the way the legal fiction of marital unity was utilized relies on a penetrating general analysis of legal fictions by Lon L. Fuller. See *Legal Fictions* (Stanford: Stanford University Press, 1967), pp. 51-57.

[18] A partial list of the innumerable editions and abridgments of the *Commentaries* can be found in Catherine Spicer Eller, *The William Blackstone Collection in the Yale Law Library: A Bibliographic Catalogue* (New Haven: Yale University Press, 1938). For an excellent analysis of Blackstone's Enlightenment framework, see Daniel Boorstin, *The Mysterious Science of the Law: An Essay on Blackstone's Commentaries* (Cambridge: Harvard University Press, 1941).

[19] Blackstone envisioned himself as a legal cartographer, "marking out the shape of the country, its connections and boundaries, its greater divisions and principal cities." Sir William Blackstone, *Commentaries on the Laws of England in Four Books*, 4th ed., ed. Thomas Cooley (Chicago: Callahan & Co., 1899), 1: 31.

[20] Ibid., pp. 358, 402.

[21] Ibid., p. 387. Because Blackstone set out to place marriage squarely within the province of secular law and separate from ecclesiastical law, he underscored the fact that marriage was a civil contract. In the nineteenth century, however, differences between marriage and other contracts were stressed and marriage increasingly was called "a status." David E. Engdahl, "Proposal for a Benign Revolution in Marriage Law and Marriage Conflicts Law," *Iowa Law Review* 55 (1960): 57.

[22] This organization followed Hale's *Analysis of the Civil Part of the Law*. Law is divided into the rights of persons and things and private and public wrongs.

[23] Christian's notes were published as a fifth volume to an 1801 Boston edition and were incorporated into many American editions. *Commentaries on the Laws of England*, 15th ed., ed. Edward Christian (London: A. Strahan, 1809), 1: 444-46;

[24] *Commentaries on the Laws of England*, ed. John F. Hargrave (New York: Harper & Brothers, 1847), 1: 452.

[25] Tapping Reeve, *The Law of Baron and Femme*, 3d ed. (Albany: William Gould, 1862). Reeve's treatise, first published in 1816, marked the American trend of giving French spellings to Anglo-Norman terms like *feme*.

[26] Ibid., p. 232.

[27] Ibid., p. 64.

[28] In the Harvard Law School catalogue of 1834, Kent's *Commentaries*, first published in 1826-30, and Blackstone's *Commentaries* were required reading for all students. Kent, who had been a New York Supreme Court judge and Chancellor of the state, and Story, a Supreme Court justice and first Dane Professor of Law at Harvard, were probably the two most influential figures in American legal education. Later treatises such as Joel Prentice Bishop's *Commentaries on the Law of Marriage and Divorce* (1852) relied heavily on Kent and Story. Haar, *Golden Age*, pp. 67-70; Friedman, *A History of American Law*, p. 288; Bloomfield, *American Lawyers*, p. 107.

[29] Dartmouth College v. Woodward, 17 U.S. 518, 596-97 (1819). Story's remarks were cited in cases involving marital property three and four decades later. See, for example, White v. White, 5 Barb. (N.Y.) 474, 478 (1849); and Yale v. Dederer, 18 N.Y. 265, 277-78 (1858).

[30] Story pointed out that equity did not alter common law classifications; it ministered to difficulties created by common law classifications. Accordingly, he altered Blackstone's bold pronouncement on the principle of marital unity to state that "in most cases" the wife's legal identity was merged with that of her husband. Joseph Story, *Commentaries on Equity Jurisprudence*, 2 vols. (Boston: Little Brown, 1839), 2: 581-85, 621.

[31] James Kent, *Commentaries on American Law*, 4 vols., 11th ed., ed. George F. Comstock (Boston: Little Brown, 1867), 2: 39. Kent was influenced by the "theological utilitarianism" of William Paley's *The Principles of Moral and Political Philosophy*. Bloomfield, *American Lawyers*, pp. 105-6.

[32] Kent, *Commentaries*, 2: 157-58.

[33] Ibid., p. 180.

[34] James Fenimore Cooper, *The American Democrat* (1838: reprint ed., New York: Minerva Press, 1959), pp. 37-38.

[35] Elizabeth Cady Stanton et al., *History of Woman Suffrage*, 6 vols. (1881-1922; reprint ed., New York: Arno, 1972), 1: 70.

[36] *New York Assembly Documents*, 15 March 1848, vol. 5, no. 129, p. 1. This was a petition "of fourty-four ladies of Genesee and Wyoming [counties], praying for the repeal of certain laws."

[37] New York legislator Thomas Herttell, who first introduced a married women's bill in 1836, developed a particularly effective liberal feminist position with respect to due process. *Argument in the House of Assembly of the State of New York . . . in Support of the Bill to Restore to Married Women "The Rights of Property" as Guaranteed by the Constitution of This State* (New York: Henry Durell, 1839), especially pp. 8-9.

[38] Two perceptive discussions of the advantages and pitfalls of relating natural law theory to the status of women are: Elizabeth Fox-Genovese, "Property and Patriarchy in Classical Bourgeois Political Theory," *Radical History Review* 4 (1977): 36-59; and Christine Pierce, "Natural Law Language and Women," in *Women in Sexist Society: Studies in Power and Powerlessness*, eds. Vivian Gornick and Barbara K. Moran (New York: New American Library, 1972), pp. 242-58.

[39] "Editor's Table," *Godey's Lady's Book* 14 (May 1837): 212-14; and 34 (May 1847): 269; Ernestine Rose, Letter to the Editor, *New York Daily Times*, 2 July 1858, p. 5. For a discussion of the function of moral superiority arguments, see Nancy Cott, *The Bonds of Womanhood: "Woman's Sphere" in New England, 1780-1835* (New Haven: Yale University Press, 1977); and "Passionlessness: An Interpretation of Victorian Sexual Ideology, 1790-1850," *Signs* 4 (1978): 219-36.

[40] Ellen Carol DuBois, "The Radicalism of the Woman Suffrage Movement: Notes Toward the Reconstruction of Nineteenth Century Feminism," *Feminist Studies* 3 (1975): 63-71; and *Feminism and Suffrage: The Emergence of an Independent Women's Movement in America 1848-1869* (Ithaca: Cornell University Press, 1978).

[41] Stanton et al., *History of Woman Suffrage*, 1: 64.

[42] New York, to be sure, was anomalous in some ways. Statutory revisions in 1828 had narrowed the use of trusts. The state's extremely sophisticated development of equity was blunted to some extent because of high costs and long delays that engendered attacks on both the administration and substance of equity. Also, the boldest of its married women's statutes were chronologically slightly ahead of other jurisdictions. Nevertheless, its economic diversity, commercial preeminence, and large population make it a valuable laboratory for the study of nineteenth-century legal change.

Support for the conclusion that the statutes in general were unable to obliterate basic common law principles appears in Kanowitz, *Women and the Law*, pp. 35-99;

Warren, "Husband's Right," pp. 421-39; Johnston, "Sex and Property," pp. 1090-91; Blanche Crozier, "Marital Support," *Boston University Law Review* 15 (1935): 25-58; Robert C. Brown, "The Duty of the Husband to Support the Wife," *Virginia Law Review* 18 (1932): 823-24; Paul Sayre, "A Reconsideration of Husband's Duty to Support and Wife's Duty to Render Services," *Virginia Law Review* 29 (1943): 857-75; Monrad G. Paulson, "Support Rights and Duties Between Husband and Wife," *Vanderbilt Law Review* 9 (1955-56): 709, 719-42.

[43] *Laws of New York*, 1840, chap. 80.

[44] *New York Assembly Documents*, 26 February 1844, vol. 3, no. 96, p. 5.

[45] See the speeches of Ansel Bascom, Conrad Swackhamer, Benjamin Brundage, George Simmons, and Ira Harris at the Constitutional Convention. This convention passed a resolution to insert a married women's clause in the new constitution and subsequently rescinded it. William J. Bishop and William H. Attree, *Report of the Convention for the Revision of the Constitution of the State of New York* (Albany: Evening Atlas, 1846), pp. 1038-42, 1056-61.

[46] *New York Assembly Documents*, 9 May 1846, vol. 6, no. 219, pp. 1-2.

[47] This estimate is based on a survey of all the married women's property cases that appear in printed chancery reports between 1814 and 1848 (subsequently equity was merged with the common law courts); all of the printed reports of the New York Supreme Court and the Court of Appeals, the two highest appellate courts in the state, between 1848 and 1880; and a sampling of printed reports in lower courts. Judicial acceptance before 1848 of marriage settlements freeing the wife from common law disabilities appears in Methodist Episcopal Church v. Jaques, 1 Johns. Ch. 450 (1815); Bradish v. Gibbs, 8 Johns. Ch. 523 (1818); North American Coal v. Dyett, 7 Paige Ch. 9 (1937); Searing v. Searing, 9 Paige Ch. 283 (1841); Shirley v. Shirley, 9 Paige Ch. 363 (1841); and Danforth v. Wood, 11 Paige Ch. 9 (1844).

[48] *Laws of New York*, 1848, chap. 200; *Laws of New York*, 1849, chap. 375.

[49] *Laws of New York*, 1850, chap. 91.

[50] George Rogers Taylor, *The Transportation Revolution 1815-1860* (New York: Rinehart, 1951), pp. 321-22.

[51] *Laws of New York*, 1851, chap. 321.

[52] *Laws of New York*, 1860, chap. 90.

[53] Warren, "Husband's Right," pp. 21-33; Thurman, "Married Women's Property Acts," pp. 48-49.

[54] See the opinions of Judges Morgan and Leonard in Gage v. Dauchy, 34 N.Y., 293, 296, 298 (1866). Leonard admonished the bench, "It has become the duty of the courts to execute the law, both in letter and spirit, and they are not to see how not to do it." Morgan said of the married women's statutes, that "The principal object of these statutes was, doubtless, to obliterate all those common law doctrines by which the husband was enabled to acquire any of his wife's estate through his marital relations."

[55] Barton v. Beer, 35 Barb. 78, 80 (1861), cited in Thurman, "Married Women's Property Acts," p. 82, note 126.

[56] Some important narrow constructions of married women's property rights include: Holmes v. Holmes, 4 Barb. 295 (1848); Snyder v. Snyder, 3 Barb. 621 (1848); White v. White, 5 Barb. 474 (1849); Perkins v. Cottrell, 15 Barb. 446 (1851); Glan v. Younglove, 27 Barb. 480 (1858); Ryder v. Hulse, 24 N.Y. 372 (1862); Briggs v. Mitchell, 60 Barb. 288 (1873).

[57] The constitutionality of the 1848-1849 statutes was discussed in Perkins v. Cottrell, 15 Barb. 446 (1851); Smith v. Colvin, 17 Barb. 157 (1853); Blood v. Humphrey, 17 Barb. 660 (1854); Sleight v. Read, 18 Barb. 159 (1854); Thurber v. Townsend, 22 N.Y. 517 (1860); In the Matter of Reciprocity Bank, 22 N.Y. 9 (1860); Ryder v. Hulse, 24 N.Y. 372 (1862); Knapp v. Smith, 27 N.Y. 277 (1863); Buckley et al. v. Wells, 33 N.Y. 518 (1865).

[58] Switzer v. Valentine, 10 How. 109, 116 (1854).

[59] Birbeck v. Ackroyd, 74 N.Y. 356, 358 (1878).

[60] Keller v. Phillips, 39 N.Y. 351, 354 (1868). It was difficult, however, for a wife still living with her husband to compel support because "necessaries" were not spelled out. Crozier, "Marital Support," p. 40.

[61] In common parlance the principle was known as "he who dances pays the piper." Bewailing what they believed was the wife's new freedom from her husband's control, critics asserted that the husband was paying while the wife was dancing. See "Men's Rights," *Putnam's Monthly Magazine* 7 (February 1856): 208-13.

[62] The popular perception was somewhat different. One writer called the New York earnings act "the most sweeping innovation ever made upon any established usage. . . ." "Leo," *New York Daily Times*, 21 March 1860, p. 5.

[63] Fuller, *Legal Fictions*, p. 24.

[64] Orr v. Orr, U.S. Supreme Court, 5 March 1979 (77-1119), *New York Law Journal*, 7 March 1979, p. 6

Married Women's Property Law: 1800-1850*

RICHARD H. CHUSED**

In the middle of the nineteenth century, numerous jurisdictions passed acts for the protection of married women's property. Many commentators hold the view that these acts were part of a concerted attack on the institution of coverture and the prevailing societal view of married women. Professor Chused takes a fresh look at this conception, tracing the development of the property rights of women in the early 1800s. In Part I, he presents archival material that reflects an increase in wives' control of family property prior to the enactment of married women's property laws. Part II presents an analysis of the legal arena in this pre-enactment period, illuminating reforms that represented a growing trend to ameliorate some of the more extreme features of coverture law. In Part III, the author uses recent literature on women in the early 1800s to show that this trend was accompanied by growth in the responsibility women had for their families. Professor Chused concludes that it is likely that the enactment of married women's property laws reflected an increase in women's family responsibilities, more than their emergence into the larger commercial and political world.

INTRODUCTION

1848 is commonly thought of as the year the women's rights movement began. That year witnessed both the Seneca Falls Convention and the adoption of the well-known New York married women's act. The dearth of literature on women's law in the 1800-1850 period[1] has made it all too easy for the legal community and the modern feminist movement to label 1848 as the pivotal year. The confluence of events in 1848 has created a mythology that the married women's acts adopted in the 1840's were a frontal attack on both the institution of coverture established by the common law and the prevailing cultural view of women as repositories of domestic virtue. Because a public women's movement and married women's legislation appeared in the same decade, it is

---

* © 1983 by Richard H. Chused, Washington, D.C.

** Associate Professor of Law, Georgetown University Law Center. A number of people have worked with me intensely on this and related projects during the last two years. My colleague Wendy Williams, with whom I teach Women's Legal History, has spent so much time talking with me I have lost all ability to state the extent of her contributions to this article. My gratitude rather than a precise credit will have to suffice. Marjorie Brown, David Zolensky, Robert Stack, Elizabeth Ungar, and Robin Fradkin have provided terrific research assistance. I could not have completed this project without their help. Thanks are also due to Jim Oldham, another colleague newly immersed in legal history, for his guided tour through research into English law.

1. While the literature on women is now growing very rapidly, there is still a remarkable shortage of material on the early 19th century. The best of the general histories is E. FLEXNER, CENTURY OF STRUGGLE (rev. ed. 1975). Flexner's section on the Seneca Falls Convention describes some of the early experiences of those women who organized the meeting, particularly their exclusion from the 1840 World Anti-Slavery Convention in London which barred all women. *Id.* at 71-77. The recent release of N. BASCH, IN THE EYES OF THE LAW: WOMEN, MARRIAGE, AND PROPERTY IN NINETEENTH-CENTURY NEW YORK (1982) provides a major improvement in the state of the literature.

thought that women petitioning for change must have "caused" the state legislatures to act. As with many areas of women's history, such speculation may be flawed.

This article takes a fresh look at the development of married women's property acts by making use of three different sets of materials: Archival records, case law and legislative sources, and recent historical literature. Courthouses and archives have records of potentially enormous importance. Property ownership and trends in the disposal of property should reveal a great deal about the pressures leading to the adoption of married women's property acts. My archival work was originally structured to establish an agenda for further research rather than to be a comprehensive study, but this tentative look produced so much useful information that it is appropriate to reveal it now. Results of this work are discussed in Part I.

Part II of this article delves into the vast case law and legislative record of legal events occurring before the married women's acts were adopted. This material includes not only the married women's property acts and related cases, but also an array of legislative and judicial documents in other areas of importance to women. Inheritance standards, probate codes, and divorce law, for example, tell a great deal about developments in married women's property law. In reviewing this material I placed particular emphasis on investigating the importance of English law as a model for American development, the degree to which norms existing in 1840 were actually altered by the new legislation, property law reform trends before 1840, and the relationship between the property acts and other areas of women's law in the first half of the nineteenth century.

All of this material should be viewed against the backdrop of current literature on women in the first half of the nineteenth century. Recent books present a large amount of new and useful information.[2] By and large historians have concluded that role changes for most early nineteenth-century married women involved increased family responsibilities, not greater participation in the larger commercial and political world. Such a conclusion is consistent with

---

2. Five works have provided much of the background for my own research in early reform of women's property law. Mary Beth Norton and Linda Kerber have each written a wonderful book on the changing status of women at the turn of the 19th century. M. NORTON, LIBERTY'S DAUGHTERS: THE REVOLUTIONARY EXPERIENCE OF AMERICAN WOMEN, 1750-1800 (1980); L. KERBER, WOMEN OF THE REPUBLIC: INTELLECT AND IDEOLOGY IN REVOLUTIONARY AMERICA (1980). C. DEGLER, AT ODDS: WOMEN AND THE FAMILY IN AMERICA FROM THE REVOLUTION TO THE PRESENT (1980) describes substantial developments in the history of the family during the first part of the 19th century. N. COTT, THE BONDS OF WOMANHOOD: "WOMAN'S SPHERE" IN NEW ENGLAND, 1780-1835 (1977) weaves together many of the threads of women's special sphere in the early 19th century. And Keith Melder's thesis charts the vast array of social, cultural, and political enterprises of women in the first decades of the 19th century. K. Melder, The Beginnings of the Women's Rights Movement in the United States, 1800-1840 (1965) (unpublished thesis). Other books of importance for this period include E. FLEXNER, *supra* note 1, at 1-77; B. BERG, THE REMEMBERED GATE: ORIGINS OF AMERICAN FEMINISM, THE WOMAN AND THE CITY, 1800-1860 (1978); N. BLAKE, THE ROAD TO RENO: A HISTORY OF DIVORCE IN THE UNITED STATES (1962); E. Warbasse, The Changing Legal Rights of Married Women, 1800-1861 (February 1960) (unpublished thesis); P. RABKIN, FATHERS TO DAUGHTERS: THE LEGAL FOUNDATIONS OF FEMALE EMANCIPATION (1980); M. Salmon, The Property Rights of Women in Early America (1980) (unpublished thesis); J. MOHR, ABORTION IN AMERICA: THE ORIGINS AND EVOLUTION OF NATIONAL POLICY, 1800-1900 (1978); C. DIENES, LAW, POLITICS AND BIRTH CONTROL (1972). *See also* Zainaldin, *The Emergence of a Modern American Family Law: Child Custody, Adoption and the Courts, 1796-1851*, 73 NW. U.L. REV. 1038 (1979).

the results of my own archival and legal research which suggests that the early married women's acts made only modest adjustments in coverture law, and that these adjustments generally confirmed rather than confronted prevailing domestic roles of married women. The recent literature is discussed in Part III.

As the nineteenth century began, real property owned by a married woman in a legal estate was subject to the management and control of her husband. Personal property of a wife became the property of her husband as soon as he reduced it to possession. Where equity courts existed, separate equitable estates could be created for married women's property, but the protections to be provided a wife by the equitable forum had to be specifically delineated in the document creating the estate. Although married women's property acts significantly altered the old rules by the end of the nineteenth century, the early wave of reform statutes appearing before 1850 have been given credit for accomplishing too much in the reform of married women's legal status.

In combination, the three parts of this study produce a coherent picture of the developments leading to the adoption of the early acts. The archival work suggests that use of equitable separate estates for married women increased before 1850. Analysis of legislative materials and judicial opinions shows that a number of legal norms having an economic impact on married women were modified before married women's acts appeared. Several reforms, including the liberalization of inheritance rules and divorce laws and the enlargement of benefits for widows and abandoned women, appeared in the early decades of the nineteenth century. Meanwhile, developments in the culture at large created a milieu sympathetic to changes in coverture law. Romantic notions of family formation and maintenance, introduction of industrial production, and increases in literacy and educational goals for children gave women significant family roles. When distressed economic times appeared after 1839, the moment was right for legislatures to codify a portion of the equitable separate estate tradition by insulating wives' property from their spouses' creditors. The acts, usually adopted with little lobbying from women, created a special set of assets available for family use when husbands found themselves in trouble with creditors. Only after this initial wave of debtor protection measures appeared did the women's movement get deeply and successfully involved in substantial reform of coverture law.

I. A Study of Wills and Trust Deeds

A. Introduction

While it is generally (and erroneously) supposed that the first married women's property act appeared in 1839,[3] little is known about the changes in property ownership patterns and the economic status of women in the decades prior to the appearance of the new legislation. Important questions about whether the mid-century legislation "codified" existing practice, whether mar-

3. In reality the acts began to appear in 1835. *See infra* note 205 and accompanying text (Arkansas act passed in 1835). The use of 1839 or 1840 as an approximation of the beginning of a transition period, however, is appropriate. Most of the early married women's acts appeared in the 1840's. *See infra* notes 207-11 (listing acts).

ried women gained financial influence within the family before 1840 and whether married women benefitted from the separate equitable estate, are answerable only by doing a great deal of sleuthing in courthouse records.[4] For two reasons, this study was designed to search for changes in participation rates of women in the property system and in the dispositional patterns of family property, rather than for alterations in women's wealth. First, wealth studies suggest that married women's economic status did not change much relative to men's during the nineteenth century. Second, the married women's acts themselves did not legitimate any radical shifts in the economic status of women. One therefore should not expect changes in the patterns of women's wills and deeds during the early decades of the nineteenth century to display dramatic movements of money or other assets. Rather one would hypothesize that the mild changes made by the married women's acts would be preceded by some shifts in the ways families disposed of or controlled their assets. This study suggests that such shifts occurred.

What little is known about women and the economy before 1850 confirms the need to be cautious about claiming that married women's acts caused or resulted from significant shifts in wealth between men and women. During the late eighteenth century subsistence farming was giving way to commercial production and home industry, particularly spinning, needlework, and weaving.[5] Trade was becoming more pronounced and some men began to leave home to go to work. Increasing agricultural efficiency[6] and expanding markets began to separate household from work. It became possible for some women, and

---

4. Two other studies of courthouse documents are available. They are Salmon, *Women and Property in South Carolina: The Evidence From Marriage Settlements, 1730-1830*, 39 WM. & MARY Q. 655 (1982) [hereinafter Salmon, *South Carolina*], and N. BASCH, *supra* note 1, at 100-12. Salmon's study asks some of the same questions posed here and uses somewhat similar research techniques.

5. N. COTT, *supra* note 2, at 21-30. Women played a significant role in these areas, particularly in the provision of cloth for home use. An 1810 government report estimated that two-thirds of all clothing, hosiery, and linen was produced at home. *See* Summer, *History of Women in Industry in the United States*, in 9 REPORT ON CONDITION OF WOMEN AND CHILD WAGE-EARNERS IN THE UNITED STATES 37-50 (1810 & photo. reprint 1974).

6. *See* N. COTT, *supra* note 2, at 23-24. During the 19th century, yields per acre for wheat and corn stayed fairly constant. But the man-hours required to produce this yield declined substantially. Data from U.S. BUREAU OF THE CENSUS, THE STATISTICAL HISTORY OF THE UNITED STATES FROM COLONIAL TIMES TO THE PRESENT 500 (1976) [hereinafter STATISTICAL HISTORY], was used in producing this table:

	Wheat		Corn	
Year	Yield/acre	Man hrs./ 100 bushels	Yield/acre	Man hrs./ 100 bushels
1800	15*	373	25*	344
1840	15*	233	25*	276
1880	13.2	152	25.6	180
1900	13.9	108	25.9	147

* These figures are estimates.

Similar changes in the raising of cotton occurred. Some of this improvement in efficiency probably arose because of improvements in tools such as the cotton gin, scythe, and plow. *See* Rasmussen, *The Mechanization of Agriculture*, 247 SCI. AM. 76 (1982). There is much debate over the rate of increase in agricultural output in the early United States. The traditional view is that output increased moderately before 1840. Parker & Whartenby, *The Growth of Output Before 1840*, in TRENDS IN THE AMERICAN ECONOMY IN THE NINETEENTH CENTURY 191 (National Bureau of Economic Research ed. 1960). Others have argued that there was a more substantial growth in output. Gallman, *The Agricultural Sector and the Pace of Economic Growth: U.S. Experience in the Nineteenth Century*, in ESSAYS IN

necessary for others, to undertake chores in addition to those crucial for the operation of a subsistence farm. While the location of activity for most was still the home or a business attached to the home,[7] sending children off to work in others' homes, in schools, or in the towns became a possibility in some cases.[8] Although home industry diminished in importance during the first decades of the nineteenth century, teaching, domestic service, and mill work by unmarried women became commonplace by the 1830's.[9] Wages for single women rose rapidly between 1820 and 1850 when they reached fifty percent of the male level, a plateau which has remained almost unchanged to this day.[10]

But the impact of these changes on the economic standing of married women was not great. Women who did work were usually single and tended to obtain low-paying jobs. By 1840, many who had worked as young women were married and without paying jobs, carrying with them only memories of their prior work.[11] Historians have provided us vivid anecdotal descriptions of the differences between the lives of married and unmarried women to demonstrate that by 1840 many women considered marriage to be a large step from relative freedom into an important, but confining, social role.[12] Even as late as 1890 less than five percent of all married women worked,[13] and women's share of the nation's wealth did not rise during the nineteenth century. Wealth studies suggest that white women constituted less than ten percent of wealth holders and that wealth holders constituted less than two percent of the total

---

NINETEENTH CENTURY ECONOMIC HISTORY: THE OLD NORTHEAST 35 (D. Klingaman & R. Vedder eds. 1975).

7. For example, shops and boarding houses both drew women's attention. N. COTT, *supra* note 2, at 42-43.

8. *Id.* at 31-36.

9. *Id.* at 36-37; S. LEBERGOTT, MANPOWER IN ECONOMIC GROWTH: THE AMERICAN RECORD SINCE 1800 520 (1964). By 1830, women and children comprised a large percentage of the industrial labor force, which they maintained despite a relative decline in the textile industry after 1830. A. GOLDIN & N. SOKOLOFF, WOMEN, CHILDREN, AND INDUSTRIALIZATION IN THE EARLY REPUBLIC: EVIDENCE FROM THE MANUFACTURING CENSUS (NBER Working Paper No. 795, 1981). Even on the frontier, working single women comprised a significant segment of the community. *See* J. JEFFREY, FRONTIER WOMEN: THE TRANS-MISSISSIPPI WEST 1840-1880 87-94 (1979). Dramatic increases in teaching employment also appeared as a result of the development of universal elementary education. *See* W. ELSBREE, THE AMERICAN TEACHER: EVOLUTION OF A PROFESSION IN A DEMOCRACY 199 (1970); 1 T. WOODY, A HISTORY OF WOMEN'S EDUCATION IN THE UNITED STATES 460-83 (1929); Bernard & Vinovskis, *The Female School Teacher in Ante-bellum Massachusetts*, 10 J. SOC. HIST. 332 (1977). Bernard and Vinovskis conclude that one out of every five antebellum Massachusetts women taught school during her lifetime, even if the total percentage of women in the entire workforce at any one time was small. Bernard & Vinovskis, *supra*, at 338.

10. A. GOLDIN & N. SOKOLOFF, THE RELATIVE PRODUCTIVITY HYPOTHESIS OF INDUSTRIALIZATION: THE AMERICAN CASE, 1820-1850 (NBER Working Paper No. 795, 1981). As of 1970, full-time white women workers earned about 59% of a male worker's wage. STATISTICAL HISTORY, *supra* note 6, at 305.

11. In fact, the proportion of working married women remained very low until recently. *See* A. GOLDIN & N. SOKOLOFF, *supra* note 10. It is unlikely that women's labor produced much wealth for most women. Wages were too low. *See id.*

12. *See* N. COTT, *supra* note 2, at 80-83.

13. STATISTICAL HISTORY, *supra* note 6, at 133. Data from STATISTICAL HISTORY at 129-34 provides additional material for this table:

population in the Revolutionary War years,[14] and that in 1860, women's and children's wealth still constituted less than ten percent of men's wealth.[15] Average men's wealth was much higher than women's.[16]

Thus, one would not expect a study of intestate and testate estates to display dramatic increases in women's wealth. Rather, discussion of the evolution of women's property law during the first half of the nineteenth century must focus on the mechanisms by which wealth was controlled. While some tentative effort is made here to look for wealth indicia in the archival data, the primary focus is on changes in the dispositional patterns for women's property.

B. METHODOLOGY

Document studies were undertaken in Dukes County, Massachusetts, and Baltimore City and County, Maryland, for the period 1800 to 1850.[17] The different sizes of the document banks available necessitated somewhat differ-

Year	% of labor force that is female	% of female labor force that is: single	widowed/ divorced	married
1870	14.8	—	—	—
1880	15.2	—	—	—
1890	17.2	68.2	17.9	13.9
1900	18.3	66.2	18.4	15.4
1910	19.9	60.2	15.7	24.7
1920	20.4	77.0*	—	23.0
1930	22.0	53.9	17.2	28.9

* For this entry, single also includes widowed and divorced women.

By 1979, the situation was quite different, with 60% of the female labor force married and 50% of the married women working. U.S. BUREAU OF THE CENSUS, STATISTICAL ABSTRACT OF THE UNITED STATES: 1980 402 (101st ed. 1980) [hereinafter STATISTICAL ABSTRACT].

It is possible that the five percent married women working data is misleading. Even though few unmarried women were working at any one time early in the 19th century, a large number of women worked at some time before marriage. *See supra* note 9. Perhaps by 1890, a large number of married women had worked at some point (probably before starting a family), even if only five percent of married women worked at any particular point in time.

14. A. JONES, WEALTH OF A NATION TO BE 39 (1980).

15. L. SOTLOW, MEN AND WEALTH IN THE UNITED STATES, 1850-1870 200, n.12 (1975).

16. *Compare* L. SOLTOW, THE RISE OF LITERACY AND THE COMMON SCHOOL IN THE UNITED STATES 156 (1981) *with* L. SOLTOW, *supra* note 15, at 23, 64-65, 156. This outcome is confirmed by the very tentative data available from the Dukes County wills study which show that the men's estates tended to be much larger than the women's. The average size of the nine male inventories reviewed was over $6000 (These wills were not randomly selected. Rather, they were picked because they involved petitions by women for widow's allowances). The female inventories averaged a bit less than $950. *See infra* Table 8.

17. Given the original exploratory purposes of this research, the locations were chosen for reasons of convenience. There are, however, important characteristics of these two locations which make them very useful. The Baltimore area provides both urban and rural areas for study. The lack of significant differences between the two areas is itself interesting. *See infra* note 63 (comparing Baltimore city and county results). The two areas also provide different legal milieus, with Maryland probably having a stronger equity tradition. *Compare* M. SALMON, *supra* note 2, at 162-82 (discussing Maryland's equitable enforcement of marriage settlements) *with* E. Warbasse, *supra* note 2, at 44-45 (discussing Massachusetts' refusal to create equity courts or grant equity powers to its law courts). Consistent results between the two areas give some basis for suggesting that future replicative work will reveal similar trends.

The Dukes County study was made at the Courthouse in Edgartown, Massachusetts, on Martha's Vineyard. For the years in question, the clerk took the handwritten indices and recorded document books out of her safe. There is no cataloging system. The indices are basically in chronological order. Next to each name in the index is a list of documents recorded in the case, and next to each document is

ent research techniques in the two locations. In Dukes County the Register of Probate Index provided a list of volume and page entries for matters in which documents were recorded. Prior to 1820 about one-third of the indexed matters gave only the name of the person involved in court action followed by an entry like "records not recorded." After 1820 the index was much more complete. A "no record" entry might not even involve a deceased person, because the index also included other probate matters such as guardianships and incompetencies. The total number of entries was not very large. Meaningful data therefore are useful only for periods of a decade or longer. The number of men's and women's estates (both with and without wills) and the number of "no record" entries for each decade is displayed in Table 1.

TABLE 1: DUKES COUNTY RECORDS

Years	Male Estates	Female Estates	Male No Record	Female No Record
1801-1810	44	1	21	0
1811-1820	39	3	28	2
1821-1830	88	14	5	1
1831-1840	88	17	5	1
1841-1850	92	16	0	0

All the recorded women's wills in Dukes County from 1801-1850 were read. A number of the women's estates (both testate and intestate) contained inventories; they were also read. Some men's wills involving disputes over spousal estate shares were reviewed as well.

The Baltimore study was done from a significantly larger document base. Sampling was necessary. Index data on estates with wills were taken for the years 1800, 1805, 1810, 1815, 1820, 1825, 1830, 1835, 1840, and 1846.[18] All women's wills were read for the years 1810, 1825, 1840, and 1846. A few men's wills were read for 1810, 1825, 1840, and 1846 as well.[19] Finally, a search was made in the deed index for trust documents establishing separate estates for married women. Documents discovered in the index were read for the years 1810, 1825, and 1840.

C. THE LEGAL STAGE IN 1800

As the nineteenth century opened, the status of women's property was in the

a book and page number where it may be found in the volumes of recorded documents. I simply recorded the names, documents, books, and page numbers that I was interested in and looked them up.

The same basic system operates at the Maryland Hall of Records in Annapolis, except that the volume of records was much larger, and the recorded documents were on microfilm. Indices to the Register of Wills and the land records for Baltimore were checked first. Relevant volume and page numbers were listed and the materials were read.

18. 1846, rather than 1845, was selected to provide an additional year of breathing space from the married woman's acts adopted by Maryland in 1842 and 1843.

19. The men's wills were sampled by turning the microfilm crank 10 times and reading the first male will to appear thereafter.

midst of a lengthy period of transformation. While land transfer systems had been streamlined and married women's dower rights had been modified to permit easier transfer of titles,[20] substantial reform of the testate and intestate roles of women had just begun. Reforms of the post-Revolutionary War era enhanced the ability of women and children to be beneficiaries of intestate estates. Even before primogeniture was abolished in England, many of the American colonies had rejected it. A deluge of reform statutes finished the job after the Revolutionary War.[21] New laws covering intestate succession in New England provided for descent to widows and children of both sexes.[22] These statutes were of considerable importance because the vast bulk of people never wrote wills.[23] The changes in intestacy rules, therefore, operated to provide a minimum level of economic security for some surviving widows and children.[24] Thus, well before 1800, married female children and widows could inherit property. And even though wealthier men of the early nineteenth century tended to will assets to women in life estates or other forms that insulated the property from the creditors of present or future husbands,[25] it was not uncommon for married women to own assets long before women's property acts were adopted.

Most jurisdictions, however, did not pass statutes granting married women contractual or testamentary control over property held at law until well into the nineteenth century.[26] The power to dispose of property by will was granted in a few places early in the nineteenth century, but statutory reform most commonly occurred after 1850.[27] Will studies suggest that women did

20. *See infra* notes 157-82 and accompanying text (discussing reforms affecting ease of transfer).

21. R. MORRIS, STUDIES IN THE HISTORY OF AMERICAN LAW 72-81 (1930). England did not abolish primogeniture until 1926. *Id.* at 77. Fee tails met the same fate as primogeniture in the colonies. *Id.* at 82-103.

22. L. FRIEDMAN, A HISTORY OF AMERICAN LAW 57-60 (1973).

23. *Id.* at 220.

24. The intestate succession reforms also had some of the same effects as dower reform—land was less likely to be encumbered by future interests that would lower its marketability. Primogeniture mandated takers for a significant period of time. The new intestate succession statutes provided for estates to be divided into shares and distributed. While some assets would be distributed to tenants in common, partition was available to settle ownership disputes and, if necessary, to force sales of the disputed assets. *See* L. FRIEDMAN, *supra* note 22, at 57-58.

25. *Id.* at 220-21. This trend may have begun to disintegrate by mid-century. *See infra* Table 13.

26. Connecticut is an interesting exception, providing for wills in 1809. This is particularly puzzling because the Connecticut colony is thought to have been most restrictive of women's property rights. *See* M. SALMON, *supra* note 2, at 324-39. What, then, were women being permitted to transfer by will? A study of estate records in Connecticut should be fascinating.

27. In general, women lost their interest in personal property upon marriage and therefore had nothing to will before 1800. As to real property, instruments in the nature of wills for the disposition of equitable estates were sometimes enforced, but they were seldom written. Women could dispose of personal property with the consent of their husbands. *See* 2 J. BISHOP, COMMENTARIES ON THE LAW OF MARRIED WOMEN 421-36 (1875); M. SALMON, *supra* note 2, at 119-25. Salmon found records of decisions from the 1790's permitting women to devise their own property in Pennsylvania and Maryland. M. SALMON, *supra* note 2, at 119 n.49. In my study of Maryland wills, women began to write wills with greater frequency as the 19th century unfolded. But most of the will writers were either widows or unmarried women, and most of the property being willed was personal, not real. In general, legislation providing women with the power to write wills came slowly. While some states acted during the early decades of the 19th century, there is no clear time period in which this reform arrived. Some states had fairly well-developed equitable rules permitting married women to write wills if their deeds permitted it. *See infra* note 29. Statutes appeared in a few states at very early dates. Connecticut: Act of May, 1809, ch. VII, 1809 Conn. Pub. Acts 15 (May Sess. 1809); Florida: Act of June 29, 1823, 1825 Florida Territorial Legis. Council Acts 101 (2d Sess. 1823); Ohio: Act of Feb. 18, 1808, ch. XVIII, § 1.

not make wills in significant numbers until after 1800.[28] For the most part, a married woman's property was disposed of at death either by the operation of intestate succession laws or by the constraints contained in the equitable instrument establishing her title to the property.[29] These inheritance rules followed the more general structure of coverture law under which a married woman's real estate was subject to the management and control of her husband, and her personal property, once in the possession of her spouse, was permanently lost by the wife. While a number of exceptions to these rules arose in various areas of the United States, especially in jurisdictions with

---

1807 Ohio Acts 64 (1808). The Ohio statute was re-enacted in slightly revised versions in 1810, 1840, and 1852. While the roots of the Ohio legislation presumably were in the Northwest Ordinance, more study of this statute is needed. It is also a bit of a mystery why Connecticut moved so early. Warbasse suggests that judicial changes of heart over the old common law rules made legislative action necessary. E. Warbasse, *supra* note 2, at 15-16. Florida's statute probably resulted from its Spanish civil law heritage. A few states also adopted statutes that basically codified the common law rule that wives could write wills with their husband's consent. Maryland: Act of Mar. 10, 1843, ch. 293, § 6, 1842 Md. Laws (1843); Massachusetts: Act of Mar. 3, 1842, ch. 74, 1842 Mass. Acts 527; Pennsylvania: Act of Apr. 8, 1833, No. 128, § 2, 1833 Pa. Laws 249. Other states adopted statutes permitting women to write wills in pursuit of powers. New York: N.Y. Rev. Stat., art. 3, §§ 80, 87, 110, 1829 N.Y. Rev. Stat. 731; Pennsylvania: Act of Apr. 8, 1833, No. 128, § 2, 1833 Pa. Laws 249. A few states adopted limited wills acts in the 1840's. Alabama: Act of Feb. 4, 1846, No. 19, §§ 1-3, 1845 Ala. Acts 23, 24 (1846) (abandoned or mistreated wives only); Indiana: Act of Jan. 26, 1847, ch. LXXIX, 1846 Ind. Acts 108 (1847) (real property only); New Hampshire: Act of July 2, 1841, ch. 157, 1841 N.H. Laws 533 (deserted wives) and Act of June 27, 1845, ch. 236, 1845 N.H. Laws 235 (real property). Most states adopted general wills-enabling statutes after 1850. The exceptions include Michigan: MICH. CONST. of 1850, art. XVI, § 5; Pennsylvania: Act of Apr. 11, 1848, No. 372, §§ 5-6, 1848 Pa. Laws 536, 537; New York: Act of Apr. 11, 1849, ch. 375, 1849 N.Y. Laws 528. The later enactments include Arkansas: ARK. CONST. of 1868, art. XII, § 6; Georgia: REV. CODE § 2375 (1867); Indiana: Act of Mar. 3, 1859, ch. CXLI, 1859 Ind. Acts 245; Kansas: Act of Feb. 11, 1858, ch. 2, 1858 Kan. Territorial Sess. Laws 327; Massachusetts: Act of May 5, 1855, ch. 304, 1855 Mass. Acts 710; New Jersey: Act of Apr. 12, 1864, ch. CCCXCVI, 1864 N.J. Laws 442; New Hampshire: Act of July 8, 1854, ch. 1522, 1854 N.H. Laws 1418; Act of July 4, 1860, ch. 2342, § 3, 1860 N.H. Laws 2248; North Carolina: N.C. CONST. of 1868, art. X, § 6; Rhode Island: 1856 R.I. Pub. Laws 68 (Jan. Sess. 1856); South Carolina: Act of Dec. 12, 1866, 1866 S.C. Acts 473; Tennessee: Act of Feb. 21, 1852, ch. CLXX, § 4, 1851 Tenn. Pub. Acts 259. In some states, late enactments still prohibited married women from writing wills. *See* Kentucky: Gen. Stats., ch. 113, § 2 (1873).

28. K. LOCKRIDGE, LITERACY IN COLONIAL NEW ENGLAND 38 (1974); A. JONES, *supra* note 14, at 39. A. JONES, AMERICAN COLONIAL WEALTH: DOCUMENTS AND METHODS (1977) (3 volumes) reproduces all the inventories used in Jones' WEALTH OF A NATION TO BE. There were 82 women's estates. Forty-two wrote wills, 39 died intestate and for one woman, testacy status is not known. This 52% rate of testacy is a bit lower than that found in Dukes County. *See infra* Table 7.

29. In a number of states, early equity cases provided that married women could write wills to dispose of real property if the instrument giving title permitted it. *See* Beach v. Manchester, 56 Mass. (2 Cush.) 72 (1848); Wilkinson v. Wright, 45 Ky. (6 B. Mon.) 576 (1846); Yates Will, 32 Ky. (2 Dana) 215 (1834); Lewis v. Hudson, 6 Ala. 463 (1848); Shaw v. Dawsey, 26 S.C.L. (1 McMul.) 247 (1841); Ewing v. Smith, 3 S.C. Eq. (3 Des.) 417 (1813); Rogers v. Smith, 4 Barr 93 (Pa. 1840); Lowery v. Tiernan, 2 H. & G. 34 (Md. 1827); West v. West's Executor, 24 Va. (3 Rand.) 373 (1825); Jaques v. Methodist Episcopal Church, 17 Johns. 548 (N.Y. 1820). A will devising personal property required the husband's consent, unless an instrument under which property was held provided a right to dispose of property by will. *See, e.g.*, Lewis v. Hudson, 6 Ala. 463 (1844); Reed v. Blaisdell, 16 N.H. 194 (1844); Marston v. Norton, 5 N.H. 105 (1830); Yates Will, 32 Ky. (2 Dana) 215 (1834). *See also* 2 J. BISHOP, *supra* note 27, at 412-36.

A few states applied the equity rules very liberally, holding that general statements creating a separate estate implied the right to dispose of the property by will. Lamb v. Wregg, 8 Port. 73 (Ala. 1838); Lewis v. Hudson, 6 Ala. 463 (1844); Jaques v. Methodist Episcopal Church, 17 Johns. 548 (N.Y. 1820). Kentucky appeared to be such a jurisdiction, Yates Will, 32 Ky. 215 (1834), but a narrow rule emerged later, Wilkinson v. Wright, 45 Ky. (6 B. Mon.) 576 (1846). Maryland took the opposite trend. *Compare* Tarr v. Williams, 4 Md. 68 (1853), *with* Cooke v. Husbands, 11 Md. 486 (1857).

strong equity traditions supporting the creation of separate estates for married women, wives were treated as civilly dead persons in many situations.

Massachusetts and Maryland common law followed these general trends. In Massachusetts, case law placed severe constraints on married women's right to will property at law, prohibiting the devising of real estate and requiring the husband's consent for the devising of personal assets.[30] Both of the married women's wills found in Dukes County were written in 1810, though they were not probated until 1815 and 1821. The scarcity of married women's wills probably reflects the common law rules. A statute permitting married women to write wills with their husband's consent was adopted on March 3, 1842, but the act was construed to prohibit devises to husbands.[31] This result was overruled by statute on April 15, 1850. In 1842, Maryland adopted a statute permitting married women to write wills with their husband's consent. Married women's property acts were passed in 1842 and 1843. In both Maryland and Massachusetts the power of a wife to dispose of equitable property at death was limited to the rights granted by the instrument under which she took title.[32]

The development of inheritance rights of women and children during the late eighteenth and early nineteenth centuries required some method for legitimating the holding of property by married women. Finding the methods used before 1840 is sometimes difficult. Although the Baltimore document study suggests the separate equitable estate was the logical choice in most jurisdictions, America's varied reception of equity forces legal historians to search state-by-state for the ways in which women typically held property. While English chancery had both developed rules for a wife's separate estate and declared dower inapplicable to equitable estates by the end of the eighteenth century, the colonies did not uniformly adopt chancery.[33] While the Southern colonies generally had equity courts, New England practice was spotty.[34] The Northwest Ordinance specifically called for reception of the common law, but was silent as to equity.[35] Although this omission was probably not meant to prohibit creation of equity courts,[36] not all the territories so understood it, leading to different results in the various jurisdictions.[37]

Not until well into the nineteenth century did most American states and

---

30. Osgood v. Breed, 12 Mass. 525 (1815).

31. Morse v. Thompson, 58 Mass. (4 Cush.) 562 (1849).

32. Beach v. Manchester, 56 Mass. (2 Cush.) 72 (1848); Lowery v. Tiernan, 2 H. & G. 34 (Md. 1827); Miller v. Williamson, 5 Md. 219 (1853).

33. Katz, *The Politics of Law in Colonial America: Controversies Over Chancery Courts and Equity Law in the Eighteenth Century*, in LAW IN AMERICAN HISTORY 257 (D. Fleming & B. Bailyn eds. 1971); L. FRIEDMAN, *supra* note 22, at 47-48; E. Warbasse, *supra* note 2, at 38-42; Wilson, *Courts of Chancery in the American Colonies*, in 2 SELECT ESSAYS IN ANGLO-AMERICAN LEGAL HISTORY 779 (1908); M. SALMON, *supra* note 2, at 150-233.

34. 1 J. STORY, COMMENTARIES ON EQUITY JURISPRUDENCE 62 n.1 (1836); E. Warbasse, *supra* note 2, at 39-48. M. SALMON, *supra* note 2, at 150-233, catalogues in great detail the differences in equity traditions in four states, concluding that the Southern jurisdiction she studied maintained stronger traditions than the Northern areas.

35. *See generally* Blume, *Chancery on the American Frontier*, 59 MICH. L. REV. 49 (1960).

36. *Id.* at 54.

37. Despite the terms of the Northwest Ordinance, Michigan gave its supreme territorial court equity jurisdiction as early as 1805. *Id.* at 55-56. But the early history of chancery in the territories varied, and Congress frequently had to step in later to resolve any lingering ambiguities. *See* Blume & Brown, *Territorial Courts and Law: Unifying Factors in the Development of American Legal Institutions*, 61 MICH. L. REV. 39, 54-59 (1962).

territories have chancery courts. While Story argues that equity, once adopted, was accepted with much less variation than the common law,[38] there is little modern commentary analyzing his arguments. Thus, during much of the formative period of English chancery rules on coverture,[39] America was in a state of "equitable disarray." Although some have attributed the cool reception given equity courts to antipathy to the English crown,[40] a more sophisticated explanation suggests that the desire of colonial legislatures to control chancery courts rather than leave them to the prerogatives of the crown led some areas to resist the adoption of equity. There was less opposition to the principle of equitable relief itself than to the institutions supporting it.[41] Furthermore, there is evidence that substitutes for equity, such as private bills and courts of law serving equity traditions, existed in some jurisdictions.[42]

Colonial and early American reception of equitable coverture rules reflect the variety in reception of equity law generally. Despite the contentions of Kent and Story that equity generally provided a release from the more egregious common law coverture norms,[43] there is a growing body of recent work confirming that the vagaries of local precedential and procedural settings created significant variety among the colonies and newly independent states.[44] While the resistance to equity in parts of the Northeast during the late eighteenth and early nineteenth centuries[45] is one of the causes of the variety, there are also intriguing indications that private legislative bills were used in some jurisdictions to alter more traditional coverture rules,[46] and that some common

---

38. 1 J. STORY, *supra* note 34, at 62-65.

39. *See infra* notes 100-96 and accompanying text (discussing English developments).

40. *See* E. Warbasse, *supra* note 2, at 42-45.

41. *See* Katz, *supra* note 33, at 271-72 (resistance to equity recognized the need for such an institution but feared its abuse in the hands of the executive). Warbasse recognized that alteration of New York's equity practice arose because of complaints about the complexity of equitable procedure, not the notion of equity itself. E. Warbasse, *supra* note 2, at 217-18.

42. *See* Katz, *supra* note 33, at 283; Salmon, *Equality or Submersion?: Feme Covert Status in Early Pennsylvania*, in WOMEN OF AMERICA: A HISTORY 92 (C. Berkin & M. Norton eds. 1979).

43. J. KENT, COMMENTARIES ON AMERICAN LAW 136-49 (1826); 2 J. STORY, *supra* note 34, at 596-655. Both Kent and Story wrote without close attention to actual practice at the time in the various jurisdictions. Morris later wrote in a similar vein that equity was a general release valve from the restrictions of the coverture rules at law. R. MORRIS, *supra* note 21, at 135.

44. *Compare* M. SALMON, *supra* note 2, at 162-81; Salmon, *supra* note 42, at 92-113; *and* L. KERBER, *supra* note 2, at 139-55 *with* E. Warbasse, *supra* note 2, at 42-48; *and* J. SPRUILL, WOMEN'S LIFE AND WORK IN THE SOUTHERN COLONIES 361-64 (1938). For material on reception of equity, *see generally* Blume, *supra* note 35; L. FRIEDMAN, *supra* note 22, at 185-86; 1 R. POWELL, THE LAW OF REAL PROPERTY 447-52 (rev. ed. 1981); 1 J. STORY, *supra* note 34, at 62-64. Some of the carefully written commentary in 19th-century treatises confirms that equitable coverture rules were received in a variety of ways. *See* 1 J. BISHOP, *supra* note 27, at 16-22 (1873); J. SCHOULER, A TREATISE ON THE LAW OF DOMESTIC RELATIONS 167-69 (3d ed. 1882) [hereinafter SCHOULER, DOMESTIC RELATIONS]; 1 J. SCHOULER, TREATISE ON THE LAW OF MARRIAGE, DIVORCE, SEPARATION AND DOMESTIC RELATIONS 264-66 (rev. ed. 1921). This last work is the sixth edition, as revised by Blakemore, of a work originally written in 1870.

45. *See supra* notes 33-34 and accompanying text (discussing resistance to equity in Northeast).

46. Until the mid-19th century, private bills were sometimes passed in traditional equitable coverture areas. L. KERBER, *supra* note 2, at 150-51 (petitions for feme-sole status); J. SPRUILL, *supra* note 44, at 361-62 (petitions for feme-sole status); Zainaldin, *supra* note 2, at 1043-44 (petitions for divorce, legitimacy of birth, change of name, and adoption); E. Warbasse, *supra* note 2, at 75, 169 (petitions for feme-sole status). For an unsatisfactory history of special bills, *see* Cloe & Marcus, *Special and Local Legislation*, 24 KY. L.J. 351, 355-58 (1936). Cooley wrote at length about special bills in his famous treatise, but only those bills dealing with granting new trials, conferring power on guardians to sell

law courts acted as surrogate equity courts.[47] The use of the separate estate as a model in many of the married women's acts indicates that equity's influence grew as the nineteenth century unfolded.[48] In fact, there is some evidence that reception occurred in reverse—American treatises were being "received" in England during this period.[49]

While it is fair to suggest that the chancery picture varied in the era before the adoption of married women's acts, the lack of scholarship on private bills[50] and common law forms of equity in the coverture law makes it difficult to evaluate the situation. Furthermore, the increased use of equity precedents in the nineteenth century occurred shortly before the emergence of movements to merge law and equity,[51] to restrict legislative authority to enact private bills,[52]

---

lands, validating irregular judicial proceedings, and divorces. *See* T. COOLEY, A TREATISE ON THE CONSTITUTIONAL LIMITATIONS 103-35 (5th ed. 1883).

From my own research, the state of Alabama is an interesting example. On March 3, 1848, the state legislature enacted a law providing that abandoned married women could apply to chancery for a decree permitting them to act as feme soles. Act of Mar. 3, 1848, No. 40, 1847 Ala. Acts 100 (1848). During that same session of the legislature, private bills granted feme-sole status to 35 women. Among them were acts for the relief of Mary Sitton, Act of Jan. 15, 1848, No. 368, 1847 Ala. Acts 411 (1848); Mary H. Clopton, Act of Feb. 29, 1848, No. 370, 1847 Ala. Acts 412 (1848); Margaret Craig, Act of Mar. 4, 1848, No. 372, 1847 Ala. Acts 413 (1848); Martha C. Towles, Act of Mar. 2, 1848, No. 373, 1847 Ala. Acts 414 (1848); Christian Linington Child, Act of Mar. 3, 1848, No. 374, 1847 Ala. Acts 415 (1848); Susannah C. Waldron and Kitsey Ann Stephens, Act of Feb. 22, 1848, No. 375, 1847 Ala. Acts 415 (1848); Aurelia Mary Carpenter, Act of Mar. 3, 1848, No. 377, 1847 Ala. Acts 416 (1848); Obedience Ledlow, Act of Feb. 25, 1848, No. 377, 1847 Ala. Acts 416 (1848); Mary Brame, Act of Feb. 11, 1848, No. 378, 1847 Ala. Acts 417 (1848); Susan B. Gee, Act of Feb. 28, 1848, No. 379, 1847 Ala. Acts 417 (1848); Sylvia Fowler, Act of Mar. 4, 1848, No. 380, 1847 Ala. Acts 417 (1848); Mary Peoples, Act of Mar. 6, 1848, No. 381, 1847 Ala. Acts 418 (1848); Bethaney Grimes, Act of Mar. 3, 1848, No. 383, 1847 Ala. Acts 418 (1848); Mourning Hanelson, Act of Mar. 4, 1848, No. 384, 1847 Ala. Acts 419 (1848); Elizabeth Rickard, Act of Mar. 6, 1848, No. 387, 1847 Ala. Acts 420 (1848); Olivia Lanier, Act of Feb. 21, 1848, No. 391, 1847 Ala. Acts 421 (1848); and Eliza N. Randall, Act of Feb. 4, 1848, No. 392, 1847 Ala. Acts 422 (1848). The practice of enacting private bills for abandoned wives was a longstanding habit. A review of Alabama state session laws (I did not look at territorial enactments) reveals that such private bills were enacted very frequently after 1840 and with lesser frequency as far back as 1826. The legislature did not meet in 1846. Alabama switched to biannual sessions after 1845. I found that 4 women were granted feme-sole status by such acts in the 1845 session, 35 in 1844, 10 in 1843, 10 in 1842, 5 in 1841, 2 in 1840, 2 in 1839, 2 in 1838, 6 in 1837, 3 in 1836, 3 in 1835, 4 in 1834, 4 in 1833, 2 in 1832, and 1 each in 1831, 1828, and 1826. There also was a scattering of other private acts dealing with the power of married women to sell slaves and dispose of property as guardians or administrators.

47. See the tempting generalizations by Katz, *supra* note 33, at 283, and the tidbits on Pennsylvania. Liverant & Hitchler, *A History of Equity in Pennsylvania*, 37 DICK. L. REV. 156 (1933); 1 J. BISHOP, *supra* note 27, at 9-12; and Fisher, *The Administration of Equity Through Common Law Forms in Pennsylvania*, in 2 SELECT ESSAYS IN ANGLO-AMERICAN LEGAL HISTORY 810 (1908). *See generally* M. SALMON, *supra* note 2 (discussing common law courts and equity).

48. Kent's COMMENTARIES appeared in 1827, Story's in 1836. That equity and the notion of the wife's separate equitable estate were "in the air" by the 1820's seems clear. Illustrations of its use appear in this era, even in New England. *See* Porter v. Bank of Rutland, 19 Vt. 410 (1847) (dispute over 1824 trust); Ayer v. Ayer, 33 Mass. (16 Pick.) 327 (1835) (dispute over 1824 trust involving transfer of asset from mother to daughter). *See also* Conway v. Hale, 5 Tenn. (4 Hayw.) 1 (1817).

49. *See* Simpson, *The Rise and Fall of the Legal Treatise: Legal Principles and the Forms of Legal Literature*, 48 U. CHI. L. REV. 632, 671 (1981).

50. For starters, I undertook a study of Ohio's private bills in the 19th century. Although divorce and other expected subjects were treated by private bills, there was nothing to suggest that the legislature of Ohio was a forum used to loosen the boundries of coverture. This may be because Ohio had an early and strong equity tradition, or because dower was protected. *See infra* note 173 (discussing extent of dower rights in Ohio). In any case, the dearth of bills on the subject suggests that there is vast state-by-state variation in this area.

51. M. HORWITZ, THE TRANSFORMATION OF AMERICAN LAW 265-66 (1977), suggests that the merger of law and equity in the second half of the 19th century was an effective limit on equity. To the extent this is true in coverture law it significantly complicates analysis of both equity and the role of

and to codify the law generally. The equitable separate estate, therefore, was not only a precursor to the married women's acts,[53] but was also enmeshed in the more general package of reform movements in the first half of the nineteenth century. For example, New York's enactment of substantial reforms in trust law, which made the establishment of married women's estates more difficult, is an intriguing sign of the links between married women's law reform and the early nineteenth-century movement to merge law and equity and reform pleading practices.[54] More research must now be done to link codification of coverture rules to the equitable and legislative situations extant in states other than New York.[55]

The great variety in early American chancery practice is particularly important for analysis of married women's acts. The language of separate estates became an important part of much of the legislation. The chancery model, which permitted the use of special trust instruments to provide for married women's assets, was formalized, and the complexity of early formats was abandoned in favor of simple conveyancing language. Whatever the differences between American and English chancery law may have been, there can be little doubt that the idea of a separate estate was well-known in America long before married women's acts were adopted. It also seems certain that the slow growth in the use of the married women's separate estate eventually compelled

---

married women's property acts. In New York, for example, the married woman's act of 1848 was adopted in the same legislative session that adopted the Field Code, two years after equity courts had been abolished and three years after the state Chancery Court had held that an active trustee was necessary in separate equitable estates. *See* L'Amoureaux v. Van Rensselaer, 1 Barb. Ch. 34, 5 N.Y. Ch. 288 (1845); E. Warbasse, *supra* note 2, at 205-29. While Horwitz's theory that equity in New York was limited may be true, it is not clear that his theory may be extended to other states. In addition, the New York equity changes were apparently not duplicated elsewhere before married women's acts were adopted. The New York setting is particularly interesting because of the clear interplay between law, equity, procedure, judicial decisions, and the reshaping of women's roles. *See generally* P. Rabkin, *supra* note 2, at 61-90 (discussing the New York setting); N. Basch, *supra* note 1 (same).

52. C. Binney, Restrictions Upon Local and Special Legislation in State Constitutions 6-7 (1894). It is interesting to note that far-reaching constraints were imposed on the enactment of private bills by the New York Constitution adopted in 1846, only two years before passage of New York's first married women's act. *Id.* at 7.

53. E. Warbasse, *supra* note 2, at 289, notes that states with strong equity traditions tended to lag behind other states in adopting married women's acts, thus casting doubt on any theory that equity led to enactment of the statutes. Although Warbasse's theory may be true for acts adopted after the initial wave of debt statutes, *see infra* notes 263 (listing separate-estate statutes of the 1850's) and 361 (listing earnings statutes of the 1870's), she appears to be partially in error as to the early acts. The lag may simply confirm the idea that the early acts were not very far-reaching and that the later statutes found tougher sledding in the more traditional Southern legal milieu.

54. P. Rabkin, *supra* note 2, at 52-90. Rabkin's work on the relationship between the codification movement and the New York married women's act is very useful. Not only is it consistent with Horwitz's general description of the rise of codification in the first half of the 19th century, M. Horwitz, *supra* note 51, at 17-18, but it also begins the task of linking coverture rules to other general trends in the legal arena.

55. One of the interesting questions not answered by Rabkin's work is the relationship outside of New York between changes in rules of civil procedure and the emergence of married women's acts. New York was among the first states to revamp its procedural system. To the extent that equity and law were merged, legislation might have been necessary to preserve existing equitable rights of married women. Examining equity practice prior to the adoption of married women's acts might prove a useful line of inquiry in states that adopted reforms in court practice about the same time they passed married women's legislation. At first glance, it does not appear that significant procedural reform occurred before married women's property acts were passed in other jurisdictions.

a simplification of the process by which a separate estate was created and maintained.

But just as with disposition of women's property at death, there was probably not enough married women's property held at equity in 1800 to command the attention of late eighteenth-century reformers.[56] Nor was there yet a general cultural desire to permit a married woman, rather than the person creating an equitable separate estate, to control the disposition of a separately held asset.[57] Not until separate equitable estates were routinely used by both men and women to control family wealth, rather than simply by wealthy fathers to protect their daughters from creditors of untrustworthy husbands, would the law likely respond with significant alterations in form. Therefore, one of the most important tasks for any archival study of married women's property is to investigate the changing rates at which equity was used to protect such property.[58]

D. FINDINGS

The proportion of recorded wills in Massachusetts and Maryland written by women rose significantly between 1800 and 1850.[59] At first glance, the data on wills in Tables 2 and 3 supports the thesis that women began to exercise more control over property as the nineteenth century developed.

TABLE 2: DUKES COUNTY[60]

Years	Number of Male Wills	Number of Female Wills	Percent of Wills Written By Females
1801-1810	40	1	2%
1811-1820	26	2	7%
1821-1830	46	10	18%
1831-1840	35	12	26%
1841-1850	45	13	22%

56. Note that women generally did not write wills before 1800, *see supra* note 28 and accompanying text, and that women held very little property before 1800. *See supra* notes 13-16 and accompanying text.

57. Even after 1800, married women's ability to dispose of their separate property was generally limited by the contents of the trust deed under which they took title. *See supra* notes 29-32 and accompanying text (discussing constraints on women's ability to dispose of their separate property).

58. A trust deed search in Dukes County is yet to be done. In addition, a large sample of male wills needs to be read. If the female wills are indicative of trends, separate estate language does begin to appear in some wills after 1830. The data is much too tentative at this point to be useful.

59. Data in both tables are from the indices for Dukes County and Baltimore. These results are fairly consistent with earlier studies suggesting that women's wills did not appear in significant numbers until after 1800. K. LOCKRIDGE, *supra* note 28, at 38, 128 (noting dearth of samples of women's handwriting); A. JONES, *supra* note 14, at 39 (showing that few women were "wealth holders" in the Thirteen Colonies in 1774).

60. This data, of course, does not include the "no record" cases. *See supra* Table 1. The reliability of the pre-1820 data is therefore more dubious, especially for men. The low number of "no record" entries for women suggests that their data are more useful.

TABLE 3: BALTIMORE CITY AND COUNTY

Year	Number of Male Wills	Number of Female Wills	Percent of Wills Written by Females
1800	68	7	9%
1805	63	13	17%
1810	75	13	15%
1815	72	27	27%
1820	68	26	28%
1825	95	19	17%
1830	96	30	24%
1835	82	28	25%
1840	71	47	40%
1846	86	53	38%

It would be improper to argue, however, that the appearance of more women's wills indicates that women were behaving in remarkably different ways in 1850 than they were in 1800. There were differences, but they were subtle. Though the proportion of probated wills written by women rose, it does not follow automatically that the proportion of women writing wills rose. In fact, as Table 4 indicates,[61] the proportion of women's wills in relation to the adult death rate[62] in Baltimore did not rise during this period.

TABLE 4: WOMEN'S WILL-WRITING RATE—BALTIMORE

Time Period	Avg. Number of Female Wills/Yr. for Baltimore City and County	Avg. Adult Death Rate/Yr. for Baltimore City	Female Wills as Percent of Death Rate
1815-1819	24.2	613.8	3.9%
1820-1824	25.0	948.4	2.6%
1825-1829	26.8	796.2	3.4%
1830-1834	34.4	1189.4	2.9%
1835-1839	44.2	979.2	4.5%
1840-1844	38.2	995.4	3.8%
1845-1849	50.4	1441.2	3.5%

These figures do not give true will-writing rates because the will data cover a larger geographic area[63] than the death rate data, and the death rates include

61. Death rate data for all Baltimore tables are taken from W. HOWARD, PUBLIC HEALTH ADMINISTRATION AND THE NATURAL HISTORY OF DISEASE IN BALTIMORE, MARYLAND, 1797-1920 521-23 (1924).

62. "Adult" is defined as those persons age 20 and above.

63. Will data are for both city and county. Where data was available in the wills actually read, there appeared to be no significant difference between the will-writing rates of the city and county. Since

both men and women. Nonetheless, Table 4 is very valuable as a trend indicator since the same data bases are used as measuring devices for both genders. The women's will-writing rate only kept pace with population trends. The proportion of wills written by women increased in Baltimore only because, as Table 5 suggests, men wrote fewer wills as the nineteenth century progressed.[64]

TABLE 5: MEN'S AND WOMEN'S WILL RATES FOR SELECTED YEARS—BALTIMORE

Selected Years	Number of Male Wills City & County	Number of Female Wills City & County	Baltimore City Adult Deaths	Male Wills as Percent of Deaths	Female Wills as Percent of Deaths
1815 and 1820	140	53	1267	11.8	4.2
1825 and 1830	191	49	1691	11.3	2.9
1835 and 1840	153	75	1872	8.2	4.0
1846	86	53	1234	7.0	4.3

The data for Dukes County are not as easily used to determine trends in will-writing rates because of the large number of male "no record" entries for the 1800-1820 period. Death rate data are also not easily available. A crude estimate may be made by tabulating a will-writing rate based on population rather than death rates. The results of such a tabulation, as can be seen in Table 6, produce much less clear data than for Baltimore. Even so, it does appear that women began writing wills at a greater rate after 1820.

---

locale was not available in the death rate data and will indices used to compile this data. I had to fudge a bit and use the wills themselves to find locale and the census to find population trends. Nonetheless, the data are quite useful as a means of discussing rate change over time, especially since there does not appear to be any significant difference in will writing rates between city and county when population is used as a rate base.

City Versus County Will-Writing Rates

Year	% of Population in City*	% Female Wills From City
1800	46%	—
1810	63%	100% (2/2)
1820	66%	—
1825	—	71% (12/17)
1830	69%	—
1840	77%	72% (26/36)
1846	—	74% (31/42)
1850	80%	—

* This figure represents the percent of the combined populations of the city and county that resided in the city. The population data is taken from the decennial census. The percent data on residence is derived from statements made in the wills about the residence of the testator.

64. The index was combed for male wills in selected years only. Nonetheless, the trends are quite clear when compared to the female data for the same selected years. As with Table 4, *infra*, Table 5 does not give true will-writing rates since the will base is city and county, the death base is city only, and will-writing rates are figured from total adult deaths, not just male or female deaths.

TABLE 6: WILL-WRITING RATES—DUKES COUNTY[65]

Years	Number of Male Wills	Number of Female Wills	Population as of Last Yr. of Decade	Male Wills as Percent of Population	Female Wills as Percent of Population
1801-1810	40	1	3118	1.3%	—
1811-1820	26	2	3290	0.8%	—
1821-1830	46	10	3517	1.3%	.3%
1831-1840	35	12	3958	0.9%	.3%
1841-1850	45	13	4540	1.0%	.3%

Just as women may have bucked the male trend to lower will-writing rates, those women with property may have died testate more frequently than their male counterparts. The Dukes County index produced some data on the proportion of probated estates that were intestate. These data certainly overstate the use of wills since many estates were not probated.[66] Table 7 gives the proportion of probated estates that were testate.

TABLE 7: TESTACY RATE—DUKES COUNTY

Years	Male Recorded Estates Testate (%)	Female Recorded Estates Testate (%)	Number of "No Record" Entries	
			Male	Female
1801-1810	91% (40/44)	— (1/1)	21	0
1811-1820	67% (26/39)	— (2/3)	28	2
1821-1830	52% (46/88)	71% (10/14)	5	1
1831-1840	40% (35/88)	71% (12/17)	5	1
1841-1850	49% (45/92)	81% (13/16)	0	0

After 1830, twenty-four percent (25/105) of the testate estates were female, but only seven percent (8/108) of the intestate estates were female.

There are at least two possible explanations for the tendency of the women's will-writing rate to stay constant while the men's declined, and for women with assets to write wills at a higher rate than men. First, it is possible that women were making a subtle statement of goals by attempting to control the disposition of their assets in the face of countervailing male trends. And second, it may be that constraints on the ability of women to hold property were being

65. Population data is taken from 2 C.E. BANKS, HISTORY OF MARTHA'S VINEYARD (1911). The population figures in Table 6 are the sums of data for each of the three non-Indian towns on the island at the relevant times. These data are in the Annals for each town contained in volume 2 of Banks' work at pages 15-16 of the Annals of Edgartown, pages 5-6 of the Annals of Tisbury, and pages 5-7 of the Annals of Chilmark.

66. Certainly the vast bulk of people never wrote wills. *See* L. FRIEDMAN, *supra* note 22, at 220 (estimating that less than five percent of the persons who died each year left wills that passed through probate). Similar data for Baltimore was not gathered for this study.

released so that the opportunities for taking dispositional control were more frequently available. Some support for both theories is present in the data.

There is something intriguing about women writing wills when the size of even their probated estates was probably smaller than that of their male counterparts. While the data is too tentative to rely upon with great confidence, there is certainly a possibility that women with small estates were taking extra care to guide the disposition of their possessions at death. The Massachusetts study revealed a number of detailed inventories, though not enough to create a large sample. The average size of the inventories of women's estates suggests some income growth among women writing wills in the nineteenth century.

TABLE 8: SIZE OF FEMALE ESTATES—DUKES COUNTY

Time	Number of Wills with Inventories	Average Size	Number of Intestate Estates with Inventories	Average Size
1840-1850	7	$1364	4	$540
1800-1839	3	871	4	637[67]

Nonetheless, it appears that these estates were significantly smaller than men's estates. Among the ten men's estate files examined in which widows requested an allowance out of their husband's personal estates, eight were intestate. Of these eight, six were appraised at a value over $1,000. One was appraised at almost $20,000. Both of the testate estates were very large. While this is certainly not a random sampling of men's estates, the vastness of the difference between the values of these estates and their female counterparts gives rise to the thesis that women were writing wills in situations where men would not have done so. The detailed disposition of small items such as clothing, furniture, and housewares in a large number of the women's wills in both Dukes County and Baltimore also supports the thesis that women were taking special care with the disposition of their assets.

An array of other data confirms that even if women were not consciously exercising control more frequently as the century progressed, men were becoming more willing to let them. Evidence of two sorts is available. First, data on the gender of beneficiaries demonstrate that both male and female wills tended to favor women as primary beneficiaries. Second, use of the equitable estate for married women grew over time and changed in form to permit married women greater dispositional authority.

One of the more fascinating findings of the study, as illustrated by Tables 9 and 10, is that both men and women tended to dispose of property to women rather than to men. The data gathered preclude the argument that women's preference to repose assets with women was more pronounced than men's preference to do the same thing. The primary beneficiary of each will was usually very clear. When there was doubt about a particular will, but all the possibili-

67. Two other partial inventories existed suggesting administered estates in the range of $30 and $300, respectively.

ties were of one sex, the primary beneficiary was tabulated in the "other" category for that gender. When it was not clear whether one sex or another was the primary beneficiary, the will was labeled as "mixed."[68] The years represent the year of probate, which was not always the year in which the will was written. These two tables show that both men and women favored women as primary beneficiaries in their wills and that this trend, at least in Baltimore, increased over time.

TABLE 9: PRIMARY BENEFICIARIES OF WOMEN'S WILLS

Primary Beneficiaries		Dukes County (all years)	Baltimore: 1810 and 1825	1840	1846
Females:	Daughter	7	5	11	8
	Mother	2	0	1	3
	Sister	3	3	3	6
	Other	3	4	4	8
	Total	15(50%)	12(43%)	19(49%)	25(53%)
Males:	Son	4	2	6	2
	Nephew	3	1	0	3
	Other	3	4	3	4
	Total	10(33%)	7(25%)	9(23%)	9(19%)
Mixed:	Children	2	6	4	5
	Other	3	3	7	9[69]
	Total	5(17%)	9(32%)	11(28%)	13(28%)
	Total Wills	30(100%)	28(100%)	39(100%)	47(100%)

68. The few cases where it was not possible to make any conclusion or the cases where the will could not be found have not been included in the tables.
69. One of these wills involved charity as the primary beneficiary.

TABLE 10: PRIMARY BENEFICIARIES OF MEN'S WILLS (BALTIMORE)[70]

Primary Beneficiaries		Total Male Wills	1810 and 1825 Wills	1840 and 1846 Wills
Female:	Wife	6	0	6
	Wife, then daughters	5	0	5
	Daughter	3	2	1
	Other female	5	4	1
	Total	19(58%)	6(46%)	13(65%)
Male:	Other male	2	2	0
	Total	2(6%)	2(15%)	0(0%)
Mixed:	Wife, then children	4	2	2
	Children	3	1	2
	Other mixed	5	2	3
	Total	12(36%)	5(38%)	7(35%)
	Total Wills	33(100%)	13(100%)	20(100%)

Of even greater importance than beneficiary trends, the wills demonstrate that testators of both genders began to grant female beneficiaries, and more importantly, married female beneficiaries, greater control over the ultimate disposition of their assets. While studies of wills have suggested that wealthy men of the early nineteenth century tended to will assets to women in life estates or other forms that would insulate the property from creditors or from present or future husbands,[71] the Baltimore data demonstrates that trend may have diminished by mid-century. None of the thirteen men's wills probated in 1810 or 1825 named a wife as the sole primary beneficiary. Of the twenty 1840 and 1846 wills, six named a wife as primary beneficiary[72] and four more provided for interests in a wife, followed by grants to daughters. Furthermore, the wills confirm that the equitable estate became an increasingly preferred device as the century progressed. This was true for both men's and women's wills, although the male sample is small. Table 11 shows the percentage of wills that either created a trust with a woman as a beneficiary, or used sole and separate estate language in a grant to a woman, or combined both devices.

70. The Baltimore male sample included 3 wills from 1810, and 10 each from 1825, 1840, and 1846. The sample was gathered by turning the microfilm crank 10 times and stopping at the next male will.

71. L. FRIEDMAN, *supra* note 22, at 220-21.

72. Five of the six were straightforward grants to wives. The other had a restriction if the widow remarried.

TABLE 11: USE OF SEPARATE ESTATE—BALTIMORE

Year of Probate	Female Wills With Separate Estate	Male Wills With Separate Estates
1810 and 1825	14% (4/29)	8% (1/13)
1840	15% (6/41)	
1846	25% (12/48)	25% (5/20)[73]

This trend is further confirmed by data on use of deeds creating separate equitable estates in Baltimore. A search of deed indices was made for January to June, 1810, 1825, and 1840. This search, as seen in Table 12, revealed that the appearance of separate estate trust deeds increased at a rate just a bit lower than women's wills.

TABLE 12: WILLS & TRUST DEEDS FOR SELECTED YEARS—BALTIMORE

Year	Number of Women's Wills	Number of Separate Estate Deeds
1810	13	8
1825	19	11
1840	46	17

Analysis of these deeds also reveals that the later instruments gave married women more dispositional authority more frequently (see Table 13).

TABLE 13: TRUST DEED DISPOSITIONAL AUTHORITY—BALTIMORE

Year of Instrument	Full Disposal Authority	Limited Disposal Authority	Life Estate With Designated Remainders
1810	4	1	3
1825	4	2	5
1840	11	4	2

The limitations on dispositional authority varied substantially from instrument to instrument. Among the limitations were a spousal consent requirement, designation of a class from whom grantees must be selected, and grant of either sale or will capacity but not both. If the 1810 and 1825 instruments are combined, fifty-eight percent (11/19) of the women obtained some disposi-

73. This entry covers both 1840 and 1846.

tional authority. Eighty-eight percent (15/17) of the 1840 instruments provided some powers of disposal to women.

Because married women rarely wrote wills in the early nineteenth century, use of will data alone to tabulate the rates at which women disposed of property at death is artificially low if nontestamentary methods of transfer were available to wives. Trust instruments granting disposal authority were just such a substitute for testation. Combining the trust deed data for 1825 and 1840 with the will data produces the intriguing, but tentative, conclusion that by 1840 the effective will-writing rate for women rose to the same level as for men. If we assume that the number of trust deeds found for the January to June periods of 1825 and 1840 represents exactly half of the rate for each year, then the following table results:

TABLE 14: WILL/TRUST DEED RATES[74]

Year	Male Wills Per Year	Female Wills Per Year	Trust Deeds Per Year	Baltimore City Adult Deaths	Male Wills as % of Deaths	Female Wills And Trust Deeds as % of Deaths
1825	95	19	12	772	12.3	4.0
1840	71	46	30	932	7.6	8.2

The column for Trust Deeds Per Year includes only deeds giving women some dispositional authority; the other deeds involve no substitute for testamentary capacity. Similarly, the final column adds wills to trust deeds granting some dispositional authority. Use of death rates is an artificial device for measuring trust deed rates, and the use of only a two-year sample renders the results tentative at best. At a minimum it is fair to suggest that by 1840 married women in Baltimore had obtained significantly more authority to dispose of assets at death than had previously been the case. It may be that the will-writing rate for men fell in part because women were being substituted as testamentary actors.

The Baltimore trust deed data also confirms the availability of equity as a means of limiting the impact of common law restrictions on married women. While virtually no married women's wills were found in either Dukes County or Baltimore (see Tables 15 and 16),[75] the testamentary capacity of married women did not necessarily remain unchanged between 1800 and 1850.

74. Remember that the will rates in this table are not real since the death base includes all adults in the city and the will and trust deed rates include both the city and the county. Death rates are taken from the same source as Table 4, *supra*.

75. In Tables 15 and 16 the columns labelled "probably widow or single" involve wills where the circumstances strongly suggested the woman's status, but the status was not stated explicitly. For example, a woman who willed property to her mother, and had the same last name as her mother was almost surely a single woman.

TABLE 15: MARITAL STATUS OF FEMALE TESTATORS—DUKES COUNTY

Decade of Probate	Widow or Single	Probably Widow or Single	Married	Unclear
1801-1810	1	0	0	0
1811-1820	0	0	1	1
1821-1830	7	1	1	1
1831-1840	7	2	0	3
1841-1850	9	3	0	1

TABLE 16: MARITAL STATUS OF FEMALE TESTATORS—BALTIMORE

Year of Probate	Widow or Single	Probably Widow or Single	Married	Unclear
1810	6	2	1	4
1825	8	7	0	4
1840	15	14	2	15
1846	21	18	2	7

E. CONCLUSION

The post-1820 appearance of women's wills, the growth in use of the equitable separate estate in wills by both male and female testators, and the increase in use of trust deeds with disposal powers indicates that some growth occurred in the ability or propensity of Maryland's women to dispose of property. This growth, however, occurred within very narrow bounds. The rate at which women's will-writing increased only kept pace with population growth; the proportion of wills written by women increased only because Baltimore men wrote fewer wills as the nineteenth century progressed. Married women's dispositional authority was constrained by the wishes of their grantors. The use of trust deeds with dispositional powers, if thought of as substitutes for wills, may push the women's "will-writing" rate to the level of the men's rate, but these instruments were inherently creatures of male draftsmen. All this suggests that small changes were occurring. Because women were probably not wealthier in relation to men in 1850 than they were in 1800,[76] there may have been a slow trend toward giving women dispositional authority over property at the expense of some fathers, husbands, and trustees.

76. General historical information suggests that women's proportion of wealth did not rise in the first half of the 19th century. *Compare* A. JONES, *supra* note 14, at 39 *with* L. SOLTOW, *supra* note 15, at 200 n.12. A complete investigation of the reasons for the different will-writing rates of Baltimore men and women is necessary, but is beyond the scope of the present study. If men of lesser wealth tended to stop writing wills over time and women of similar or growing wealth began appearing as will-writers, perhaps some rewriting of known history would be possible. If the numbers in Table 8, *supra*, hold up with larger samples, some interesting conclusions could be drawn, especially since the 1840's was a time of deflation. *See generally* A. COLE, WHOLESALE COMMODITY PRICES IN THE UNITED STATES: 1700-1861 (1938). On the other hand, whaling produced a great deal of wealth in Dukes County during this period. The increase in women's wealth, if any, may simply reflect community trends.

The results of this study confirm that research into the actual use of wills, trusts, and other forms of control over property will reveal a great deal about social patterns and customs prior to the adoption of married women's acts. But the varied reception given equity in America requires caution in drawing general conclusions from any single piece of research. Two other studies of early nineteenth-century documents, which reached somewhat different conclusions than this study, suggest an agenda for further work.

Marylynn Salmon, in her study of marriage settlements in South Carolina,[77] found that between 1730 and 1830 control of marriage settlement property by men remained fairly constant, control by women fell, and control by couples rose.[78] Authority, she found, moved from women alone toward joint management by husbands and wives. Salmon, pointing to Mary Beth Norton's conclusion that women's participation in family governance increased in the decades surrounding the turn of the nineteenth century,[79] suggested that the changes in control arose because women needed less autonomy as they "exercised more authority over the general fund of family property."[80] Salmon also found that descent of settlement property to children increased over time, while control of descent by women declined.[81] She tentatively concluded that marriage settlement form became more standardized by the nineteenth century, and that the standardized children descent provisions were accepted because wives had become more secure about their financial autonomy while alive and generally desired their children to have their property at death.[82]

Both Salmon's overall finding that control of marriage settlement property in South Carolina became more egalitarian by 1830 and my conclusion that women may have gained authority over property at the expense of some men are consistent with Norton's thesis that women's role in family decisionmaking grew in importance between 1750 and 1830. But Salmon's twist that control by couples replaced control by women is different from my suggestion that control by women replaced control by men. In part this may be due to the different ways the data were gathered. Salmon looked at changes in the form of marriage settlements over time. I was interested as much in the rates at which women participated in the property transaction process as in the authority of women to dispose of trust assets. Insofar as our reviews of trust instruments alone are concerned, our results may turn out to be consistent. A larger Maryland sample of trusts may change my results. Salmon's look at a century of documents may have caught a long trend, while my look at half a century may mirror the last half of Salmon's data. Looking only at the South Carolina marriage settlements from 1800 to 1830, Salmon does appear to have found a slight increase in control by women and couples, and a slight decline in control by men.[83] In addition, my tentative conclusion that women may have replaced some men as actors in the property system arises from a look at combined

77. Salmon, *South Carolina*, *supra* note 4, at 668.
78. *Id.* at 668-72
79. M. NORTON, *supra* note 2.
80. Salmon, *South Carolina*, *supra* note 4, at 669.
81. *Id.* at 677-79.
82. *Id.* at 677.
83. *Id.* at 672.

patterns in both wills and equity instruments, rather than equity instruments alone. Further research on the rates in which women participated in all sorts of transactions, in addition to the forms of these transaction, is needed before solid conclusions may be reached about the status of women just prior to the adoption of married women's acts.

It is also possible that the studies display significant differences in the use of equity between the Deep South and the more industrialized border areas. It is logical to hypothesize that further research into Southern and border state equity documents will provide clues about why Southern states tended to adopt the first wave of married women's acts insulating wives' property from husbands' creditors, but spurned many other reforms adopted in the North after 1850, while some border jurisdictions moved quickly to revamp most major common law coverture rules.[84] If Southern equity documents show that the role of women was reduced prior to the era of married women's acts, and that married women's acts were adopted in bad economic times to solidify a fairly narrow role of married women in equitable separate estates, one would expect that further legislation to enlarge married women's autonomous role in the family would not readily be adopted. If border state documents confirm that women were seen more as autonomous persons in a marriage than as subservient financial partners, one would expect a somewhat different legislative response.

The only published study of Northeastern documents from the early nineteenth century raises as many questions as it answers. Norma Basch, in her study of New York married women's legislation,[85] undertook a small study of wills in Westchester County. Although she sampled only two years of documents, Basch found that there was little change in the content of wills between 1825 and 1850,[86] that sons were favored over daughters,[87] and that women were usually denied power over the disposition of trust assets or granted only interests for life.[88] These results conflict somewhat with my Massachusetts results, where women seemed to fare somewhat better. Basch's work, like mine, needs to be replicated with much larger samples. In addition, Basch did not focus on the possibility that women fared better in *inter vivos* trust instruments or that participation rates of women in various aspects of property decision-making may have increased, even if the contents of wills did not change.

Trust deeds were certainly used in New York, but the lack of comprehensive recording statutes led Basch not to study them except through judicial decisions.[89] Nonetheless, Basch's work confirms that the equity jurisprudence in New York[90] was underlaid with use of trusts in wills at least as early as 1825. While there is certainly the possibility, affirmed by other work,[91] that North-

84. *See infra* notes 204-11 and accompanying text (discussing the first wave of acts insulating wives' property); *see also infra* notes 260-73 and accompanying text (discussing reason for and extent of reforms).
85. N. Basch, *supra* note 1, at 100-12.
86. *Id.* at 101-03.
87. *Id.* at 101, 105.
88. *Id.* at 108.
89. *Id.* at 73.
90. *See id.* at 70-100 (reviewing cases).
91. Salmon, *South Carolina*, *supra* note 4.

eastern jurisdictions with equity traditions operated more conservatively before 1850 than Southern or border states, there is now little doubt that once the reforming impulses of the abolitionist era struck with full force, many of the more rigid impulses of Northern coverture law fell.[92] If more complete explorations of the terms of Northern trusts confirm Basch's findings, it may be that the great dissonance between the reality of day-to-day property usage and the aspirations of women in a quickly industrializing region provided significant strength to the Northeastern women's movement after 1850.

II. The Adoption of Married Women's Property Acts

The Baltimore data confirm that the equitable separate estate underwent significant development from 1800 to 1850, and that the availability of equity to protect married women's property was known well before married women's acts were adopted. But equity was not the only impetus for reform of married women's property law. Like equity, many of the sources for coverture law reform had both English and American roots. The obvious relevance of English law makes it easy to underestimate the importance of American legal developments. In this section, I place English law in its proper perspective and expose the multiplicity of American legal developments during the first half of the nineteenth century that shaped the married women's acts.

A. The English Roots

While Blackstone's famous 1765 commentaries were the focus of much of the nineteenth-century public debate on women's law, there is remarkably little legal history scholarship on the influence of Blackstone, or even of English law generally, on nineteenth-century American coverture law. There is literature suggesting that English legal materials were more influential in the 1820's and 1830's than before,[93] that along with moral revivals and Jacksonian idealization of the strong male farmer came legal Anglicism, treatise writing, and codification movements.[94] Legal education, which along with education generally, developed and grew from the 1790's through 1830, was heavily influenced by the treatise writers, English law, and Blackstone.[95] Yet these very facts make it unlikely that Blackstone became the subject for public debate in the 1840's because contemporary law reflected his eighteenth-century ideas. Rather, it is likely that conservative segments of the legal and academic communities were searching British treatises for precision in an era of multiplying sources for legal rules.[96] Blackstone's writings were easily understood both by

---

92. *See infra* notes 204-11, 260-73 and accompanying text (detailing reforms).

93. Zainaldin traces the reemergence of conservative English child custody cases in the 1830's, perhaps encouraged by the heavy use of English cites in the treatises of Kent and Story. Zainaldin, *supra* note 2, at 1059-68. *See also* Nolan, *Sir William Blackstone and the New American Republic: A Study of Intellectual Impact*, 51 N.Y.U. L. Rev. 731, 759-767 (1976) (discussing the growing influence of Blackstone on legal education in the period).

94. *See* P. Rabkin, *supra* note 2, at 40-60; Bloomfield, *William Sampson and the Codifiers: The Roots of American Legal Reform, 1820-1830*, 11 Am. J. Leg. Hist. 234 (1967); C. Cook, The American Codification Movement: Study of Antebellum Legal Reform (1981).

95. *See* Nolan, *supra* note 93, at 759-67 (discussing Blackstone's impact on legal education in early America).

96. *See* C. Cook, *supra* note 94, at 46-48 (noting that by 1815 sources for American law were quickly

men reading to become lawyers in a culture loosening the constraints on entry into the legal profession[97] and by women publicly criticizing the extant order.

For a number of reasons, Blackstone's vision of reality[98] is a less than satisfactory basis for measuring the influence of English coverture law. First, English law changed between the time Blackstone wrote and the opening decades of the nineteenth century. Second, by 1800 important differences between American and English law existed in conveyancing, dower, intestate succession, equity, and divorce.[99] Third, the overall impact of English law on coverture developments was diffuse. So many other influences were at work during the early nineteenth century that English law was only one of numerous factors. Well before married women's legislation appeared, American law witnessed the arrival of the codification and treatise movements, the rise and incipient decline of legislative private bills, and the appearance of efforts to merge law and equity. To ignore these and other legal developments by focusing on Blackstone's version of our English heritage is to miss the peculiarly American context of married women's property legislation.

1. Change in English Coverture Law

Blackstone wrote his Commentaries while the separate equitable estate of a married woman was reaching maturity in English chancery courts.[100] Decisions rendered in the late eighteenth century both subjected a wife's separate property to her debts, and narrowly construed dispositional powers in trust instruments to avoid overreaching by husbands.[101] The failure of much modern scholarship to note the changes in English law during the very era in which America began seriously to reconsider the legal status of women is quite remarkable.[102] Many have written of English law as if it were monolithic and

proliferating). Case reports, statutes, and books were emerging in a nation with more than twenty states. Doctrinal and theoretical diversity was becoming commonplace. Uncertainty over legal norms was becoming a real concern for many.

97. *Id.* at 158-60, 172-73. *See also* L. FRIEDMAN, *supra* note 22, at 276-78.

98. The 1803 St. George Tucker edition of BLACKSTONE'S COMMENTARIES was the most prominent of the early American editions of the 1765 English treatise. Chapter XV, part III, on the law of husband and wife, at 441-45, is the section most often chastised. There Blackstone writes that "the very being or legal existence of the woman is suspended during the marriage, or at least is incorporated and consolidated into that of the husband; under whose wing, protection and cover, she performs everything."

99. Divorce is an enormous area all by itself. I have chosen largely to pass by this area for now because so little good work has been done and the task is so enormous. Blake, *supra* note 2, does make it clear that divorce was an early and important area where the colonies differed notably from England. But the lack of work on the economics of divorce—the relative positions of men and women before, during, and after marriage—makes it very difficult to evaluate the importance of the growth of divorce between 1780 and 1840. If the major thesis of this article is correct, one should find reforms between 1800 and 1850 that provided divorced women slightly greater rights to property or money upon divorce. This would occur not because of any modern notions about protecting women, but to protect increasing numbers of children coming into the custody of women and to prevent women on the edge of poverty from becoming public charges.

100. Holdsworth writes that by 1750 property could be set aside in a separate estate or disposed of by a married woman by will or gift without a husband's consent. 12 W. HOLDSWORTH, A HISTORY OF ENGLISH LAW 275-76 (1938 & photo. reprint 1966).

101. 12 W. HOLDSWORTH, *supra* note 100, at 325-26.

102. There is a fairly large body of literature on the reception of English law. Among the more interesting items suggesting the diffuse nature of America's reception of English law are G. HASKINS, LAW & AUTHORITY IN EARLY MASSACHUSETTS 113-40 (1960); M. HORWITZ, *supra* note 51, at 3-30; D. KONIG, LAW AND SOCIETY IN PURITAN MASSCHUSETTS: ESSEX COUNTY 1629-1692 3-63 (1979); W.

unchanging.[103] Holdsworth notes that English law on married women changed substantially during the seventeenth and eighteenth centuries. The general outlines of common law coverture rules emerged in the thirteenth century.[104] Upon marriage, the husband gained power and control over his wife's freehold estate for the term of the marriage, or, upon the birth of a child, for the husband's life, and obtained ownership of his wife's personal property. A woman's ability to contract was suspended upon marriage. Equitable exceptions to these rules did not emerge until the late sixteenth century,[105] when antenuptial contracts and trusts for the separate use of the wife appeared.[106] The chancery cases also gave wives power to will their separate estates, donate them to their husbands, sell them to strangers, and perhaps deal with them by contract.[107] Though consent of the husband for the establishment of the separate equitable estate was still necessary,[108] equity courts of the late seventeenth century began to require an "equity to a settlement" to insure some financial safeguards for wives whose husbands sought to make use of assets in a separate estate.[109] This period also saw the emergence of enforceable separation agreements, support decrees for wives leaving their marital home due to the fault of the husband,[110] and cases confirming the ability of married women to execute powers.[111] Not until the mid-eighteenth century did chancery courts take the crucial step of recognizing a separate estate created without the husband's consent.[112] In a related development, the courts began to examine dispositions of a separate estate more carefully to avoid coercion by husbands.[113] The separate estate became subject to the debts of married women by the end of the eighteenth century.[114]

Dower also changed dramatically from its fifteenth-century roots.[115] By the fifteenth century the one-third share was established, and it was clear that dower could be avoided if land was sold by means of a fine and the wife was

---

NELSON, AMERICANIZATION OF THE COMMON LAW: THE IMPACT OF LEGAL CHANGE ON MASSACHUSETTS SOCIETY, 1760-1830 1-64 (1975); E. Warbasse, *supra* note 2, at 3-6; Blume & Brown, *supra* note 37; DePauw, *Women and the Law: The Colonial Period*, 6 HUMAN RIGHTS 107 (1977); Nolan, *supra* note 93; Note, *The Tennessee County Courts Under the North Carolina and Territorial Governments: The Davidson County Court of Pleas and Quarter Sessions, 1783-1796, as a Case Study*, 32 VAND. L. REV. 349 (1979) [hereinafter Note, *Tennessee County Courts*]; Goebel, *Ex Parte Clio*, 54 COLUM. L. REV. 450-59 (1954) (reviewing O. CROSSKEY, POLITICS AND THE CONSTITUTION IN THE HISTORY OF THE UNITED STATES (1953)).

103. Authors often speak of the common law without reference to its modification over time. *See, e.g.*, R. MORRIS, *supra* note 21, at 128, 155, 164, 166, 173, 185, 195, 197; P. RABKIN, *supra* note 2, at 19-22; L. KERBER, *supra* note 2, at 139-41.

104. 3 W. HOLDSWORTH, A HISTORY OF ENGLISH LAW 520-33, 541-43 (1908 & photo. reprint 1966).

105. 4 W. HOLDSWORTH, A HISTORY OF ENGLISH LAW 428-29 (2d ed. 1937).

106. 5 W. HOLDSWORTH, A HISTORY OF ENGLISH LAW 310-15 (1924).

107. *Id.* at 315.

108. 6 W. HOLDSWORTH, A HISTORY OF ENGLISH LAW 645 (2d ed. 1937 & photo. reprint 1966).

109. *Id.*

110. *Id.* at 646.

111. 7 W. HOLDSWORTH, *supra* note 108, at 180-81.

112. 12 W. HOLDSWORTH, *supra* note 100, at 275-76. *See also* P. RABKIN, *supra* note 2, at 81. Rabkin notes that chancery development gradually permitted fathers to guarantee that the property they passed on to their daughters would be free from the clutches of untrustworthy husbands. It was to protect daughters, Rabkin argues, more than to free wives that the chancery acted. *Id.*

113. 12 W. HOLDSWORTH, *supra* note 100, at 276, 324-26.

114. *Id.* at 325.

115. 3 W. HOLDSWORTH, *supra* note 104, at 193.

examined separately by the court.[116] Even at this early date, other devices for avoiding dower had emerged, including the use of jointures and premarital settlements providing for life estates in the husband's lands at his death.[117] The development of jointure led to the already mentioned development of ante-nuptial contracts and trusts for the separate use of the wife. By the middle of the eighteenth century, it was clear that equitable estates were free of dower.[118] While the lack of dower at equity was reversed by statute in 1833, the same act provided for dower only in lands actually held at death by the husband.[119] Thus, the English rules governing both dower and coverture at equity underwent significant changes from the time America was first colonized in the early seventeenth century through the turn of the nineteenth century.

Coverture doctrines at law were also under stress in the same period. For some time before the turn of the eighteenth century, it was clear that married women divorced from bed and board, abandoned by their husbands, or left behind after their husband's banishment from the realm could act as single women.[120] During the eighteenth century, cases arose where women, living apart on separate maintenance provided by their husbands after a marital separation, pled coverture as a defense to actions by their creditors.[121] Lord Mansfield, confronted with such a dispute in *Corbett v. Poelnitz*[122] in 1785, took the opportunity gently to criticize the extant coverture rules at law, and to bind the separately maintained wife to her contract as if she were a feme-sole.[123] Though the case was overruled after Mansfield left the King's Bench,[124] it is clear from the judicial turmoil and the commentary of the day that the less central portions of the coverture rules were under attack even at law.[125] Mansfield's opinion in *Corbett* spoke of "new customs and new manners"[126] and noted the growing prevalence of deeds under which a married woman assumed the appearance of a feme-sole.[127] Mansfield's general penchant for liberalizing rules of commercial transactions meshed neatly with his attempt to reform coverture rules as they applied to married women acting independently in the business world.[128]

---

116. *Id.* at 193.
117. *Id.* at 196.
118. *Id.* at 196-97.
119. *Id.* at 197.
120. 1 J. POWELL, ESSAY UPON THE LAW OF CONTRACTS AND AGREEMENTS 75-77 (1790).
121. *See id.* at 77-93; C. FIFOOT, LORD MANSFIELD 217-18 (1936); 1 W. EVANS, A GENERAL VIEW OF THE DECISIONS OF LORD MANSFIELD 99-110 (1803); Ringstead v. Lady Lanesborough, 99 Eng. Rep. 610, 3 Douglas 197 (1783); Corbett v. Poelnitz, 99 Eng. Rep. 940, 1 Term Rep. 5 (1785); Marshall v. Rutton, 101 Eng. Rep. 1538, 8 Term Rep. 545 (1800).
122. 99 Eng. Rep. 940, 1 Term Rep. 5 (1785).
123. *Id.* at 945, 1 Term Rep. at 8.
124. Marshall v. Rutton, 101 Eng. Rep. 1538, 8 Term Rep. 545 (1800).
125. *See* J. POWELL, *supra* note 120, at 77-93. In the most widely-circulated American edition of BLACKSTONE'S COMMENTARIES, that of St. George Tucker issued in 1803, there are a number of notes critical of the Blackstone version of coverture. BLACKSTONE'S COMMENTARIES 441-45 (S.G. Tucker ed. 1803). Some of these notes are reprints of those penned by Edward Christian, who had edited an earlier English edition of the Commentaries. Tucker added a few references, including one to *Corbett v. Poelnitz*. *Id.* at 943. *See also* Nolan, *supra* note 93, at 736-37.
126. 99 Eng. Rep. at 942, 1 Term Rep. at 8.
127. *Id.* at 943, 1 Term Rep. at 9.
128. Though Mansfield apparently was not well-received in America after the Revolutionary War,

Another indication of the pressure Mansfield must have felt is revealed by cases on the custom of London, confirmed by the courts of law beginning at the end of the sixteenth century and continuing through the eighteenth century.[129] According to the custom, women could sue and be sued on debts arising out of trade in which their husbands did not intermeddle. While the cases do not reveal whether the custom was more heavily used in Mansfield's time than in prior centuries, one would certainly hypothesize that it, or some substitute, was.[130] The growth, if any, in the wealth and commercial activity of the wives of London[131] may have imposed pressures on both the coverture rules at law and on the equitable notion of the separate estate. It is quite possible that use of the custom declined rapidly in the late eighteenth century once equity had affirmed the ability of women to use separate estates free of their husbands' control.

Changes in English law were well-known in America before 1840. The most widely used edition of Blackstone, that edited by Tucker in 1803,[132] had some significant debunking notes and commentary. Even suffrage for unmarried women was implicitly approved in a note saying that women "pay taxes without having the liberty of voting for representatives; and indeed there seems at present no substantial reason why single women should be denied this privilege."[133] "I fear," the note goes on, "there is little reason to pay compliment to our laws for their respect and favour to the female sex."[134] In addition, the early American treatises by Kent and Story[135] noted many developments, especially at equity, which had flowered in England since Blackstone's time. My archival work certainly confirms this. Furthermore, studies of court and other records in frontier areas indicate that some frontier lawyers and judges paid lavish attention to English and American precedents in the early nineteenth century, and that they had access to a wide array of case reports and treatises

---

see Goebel, *supra* note 102, at 455-56; M. HORWITZ, *supra* note 51, at 18, his work was better known and perhaps more influential by the time of Kent and the beginnings of the treatise movement in the United States. *See* 2 J. KENT, *supra* note 43, at 133-36; M. HORWITZ, *supra* note 51, at 257-58; L. FRIEDMAN, *supra* note 22, at 95.

129. Chamberlain v. Throp, 74 Eng. Rep. 121, 1 Leonard 130 (31 Eliz., 1589-1590); Bowett v. Langham, 124 Eng. Rep. 299, Hetley 9 (3 Car., 1628-1629); Langham against the wife of John Bewett, 79 Eng. Rep. 661, Croke Car. 68 (3 Car., 1628-1629); Barns v. Barns, 90 Eng. Rep. 32, Skinner 66 (34 Car. 2, 1683-1684); Fabian v. Plant, 89 Eng. Rep. 525, 1 Shower, K.B. 183 (3 W. & M., 1690-1691); Anonymous, 88 Eng. Rep. 1549, 12 Modern 603 (13 Will. 3, 1702-1703); Mrs. Pool's Case, 88 Eng. Rep. 1021, 11 Modern 253 (8 Anne, 1710-1711); Caudell v. Shaw, 100 Eng. Rep. 1065, 4 Term Rep. 361 (1791).

130. The frequency of reported cases in Viner's Abridgement goes down in the eighteenth century as compared with the seventeenth century. Perhaps this is because of the increasing utility of trusts, powers, and other devices to avoid the restrictions of the coverture rules at law. There may have been less need to dispute the legitimacy of the custom if other tools were available to women to protect their commercial interests.

131. That wives were involved in trade is fairly clear. *See* M. GEORGE, LONDON LIFE IN THE XVIIITH CENTURY 168-73, 175, 181-85, 195, 198, 202, 207-08, 427-29 (1925). It is not at all clear that the same may be said of married women in the United States, since little scholarship exists on the commercial role of married women in the early part of the century. Two works by E. Dexter, COLONIAL WOMEN OF AFFAIRS: WOMEN IN BUSINESS AND PROFESSIONS IN AMERICA BEFORE 1776 (1924) [hereinafter E. DEXTER, COLONIAL WOMEN OF AFFAIRS] and CAREER WOMEN OF AMERICA 1776-1840 (1950), pay no attention to marital status.

132. *See* Nolan, *supra* note 93, at 737 n.38.

133. 2 BLACKSTONE'S COMMENTARIES 445 (S.G. Tucker ed. 1803). The note was written by Edward Christian, an Englishman, not Tucker, shortly before Tucker did his work.

134. *Id.*

135. J. KENT, *supra* note 43; J. STORY, *supra* note 34.

within a very short time after the areas were opened for settlement.[136] Available treatises included not only the expected volumes, such as Blackstone and Kent, but also a number of now obscure American and English books.[137] There is every reason to believe that the influence in America of Blackstone's conservative commentary on coverture law was equally balanced by general knowledge of the more liberal equity concepts emerging after the Revolutionary War. As Nolan has concluded about Blackstone generally, "The Commentaries did significantly influence the evolution of American institutions, but their influence on each differed in kind and degree. In every case, however, Blackstone's influence was more oblique and more diffuse than his biographers have claimed."[138]

2. Early Differences Between English and American Coverture Law

Although our legal system was based in very substantial part on English models,[139] there were enough differences between English and American coverture law to suggest that the United States was marching to a significantly different drummer by 1800. The earliest settlers were confronted with many problems not routinely dealt with by English law. There is evidence that women, sometimes even married women, received land grants in some of the Colonies.[140] While this practice may have been designed to attract women to the new Colonies,[141] it is also possible that the exigencies of colonial life sometimes forced relaxation of the strict roles of husbands and wives.[142] There is some literature suggesting that early colonial married women did not labor under legal restrictions to the extent Blackstone's commentaries would sug-

---

136. Brown, *Frontier Justice: Wayne County 1796-1836*, 16 AM. J. LEG. HIST. 126 (1972); Blume, *supra* note 35, at 88-95; Note, *Tennessee County Courts*, *supra* note 102, at 377-82. These studies looked at cases not generally reported by the digest system. But even in early reported opinions, the knowledge of chancery developments seems quite up-to-date. *See, e.g.*, Trustees of Methodist Episcopal Church v. Jaques, 3 Johns. Ch. 77 (N.Y. 1817); Franklin v. Creyon, 1 Harp. Eq. 243 (S.C. 1824); Trenton Banking Co. v. Woodruff, 2 N.J. Eq. (1 H.W. Green) 117 (1838); Porter v. Bank of Rutland, 19 Vt. 410 (1847).

137. Nolan's thesis that Blackstone's influence was somewhat diffuse is lent credence by Brown's work on the Michigan territorial records. *See* Brown, *supra* note 136 (suggesting that frontier lawyers possessed and used same sources of law as their metropolitan contemporaries).

138. Nolan, *supra* note 93, at 732.

139. *See* C. COOK, *supra* note 94, at 3-45. But even as to the general influence of English law, there does appear to be some agreement that legislative differences arose in great profusion. The Northwest Ordinance, for example, required the new territory's Governor and judges to adopt statutes previously enacted by one or another state "as might be necessary and best suited to the circumstances of the district." Blume & Brown, *supra* note 37, at 523. *See generally* BROWN, BRITISH STATUTES IN AMERICAN LAW: 1776-1836 (1964); Blume, *Legislation on the American Frontier*, 60 MICH. L. REV. 317 (1962). This provision governed much of the territorial development of the United States, since the Northwest Ordinance was extended from time to time to other territories. As a result, territorial statutes tended to be eclectic in origin. The tendency for legislatures to copy other statutes has appararently been a constant in American legal history. *See* L. FRIEDMAN, *supra* note 22, at 78-81. Even in 17th-century Massachusetts the practice occurred, and it was continued in the other Colonies. *See* Riesenfeld, *Law-Making and Legislative Precedent in American Legal History*, 33 MINN. L. REV. 103 (1949); Haskins, *Codification of the Law in Colonial Massachusetts: A Study in Comparative Law*, 30 IND. L.J. 1 (1954).

140. J. SPRUILL, *supra* note 44, at 9-12, 340; R. MORRIS, *supra* note 21, at 131; M. RYAN, WOMANHOOD IN AMERICA 6-7, 13 (1979). See also the numerous anecdotes of women landowners in E. DEXTER, COLONIAL WOMEN OF AFFAIRS, *supra* note 131, at 98-125. Unfortunately, Dexter did not focus on the marital status of her subjects or the impact of coverture rules.

141. J. SPRUILL, *supra* note 44, at 9-12.

142. *See* M. RYAN, *supra* note 140, at 1-40 (discussing roles of women in colonial society).

gest.[143] However significant the initial colonial land grants to women and the somewhat looser rules of the earlier colonial era, there is little disagreement that the practices were altered and that English law became more influential as the Colonies developed. The more traditional English pattern of the husband's dominance certainly governed in most places during the late seventeenth and the greater part of the eighteenth century.[144] Nonetheless, early variations in colonial practice and different traditions in colonial administration left opportunities open for novel American practices to develop.

These generalizations about married women's law coincide with the conclusions drawn in the general literature on pre-Revolutionary War use of English law in the colonies. As the colonies matured, English legal models became more important.[145] Nonetheless, substantial room was left for independent development of American legal institutions.[146] Even though American legal developments were subjected to appellate review by the Privy Council during much of the colonial era,[147] it is likely that such review was used only to protect the Crown's power to direct colonial legal institutions and to promote the economic interests of Great Britain.[148] As Goebel notes,[149] the Colonies, lacking the centralized institutions of the English chancery system, adopted particularized procedural formats from their earliest days.[150] The diffuse system gave significantly more control to judges than in England.[151] Furthermore, the diverse needs of the Colonies, and the ability of the settlers to adopt their own legislation, naturally led to deviations from English common law practice. Much of the new law avoided Privy Council censure.[152] Finally, Goebel notes that the colonists generally acted as if they had the authority to decide which English statutes were applicable to their territory.[153]

By the end of the colonial era, therefore, the American legal system was peppered with localized procedural systems and variegated lines of cases and statutes. Judges and legislators alike considered themselves to be repositories

143. R. MORRIS, *supra* note 21, at 126-200; Gundersen & Gampel, *Married Women's Legal Status in Eighteenth Century New York and Virginia*, 39 WM. & MARY Q. 114 (1982).

144. J. SPRUILL, *supra* note 44, at 340-66; L. KERBER, *supra* note 2, at 119-84.

145. L. FRIEDMAN, *supra* note 22, at 42-49.

146. *See, e.g.*, Reinsch, *The English Common Law in the Early American Colonies*, in 1 SELECT ESSAYS IN ANGLO-AMERICAN LEGAL HISTORY 367 (1970); L. FRIEDMAN, *supra* note 22, at 15-16, 30-32. *See generally* G. HASKINS, *supra* note 102 (suggesting diffuse nature of America's acceptance of English law); M. KAMMEN, COLONIAL NEW YORK: A HISTORY 91-94 (1975) (same); Gundersen & Gampel, *supra* note 143 (same).

147. During the earliest years of the colonies, direct English control of American legal development was weak at best. 1 R. POWELL, *supra* note 44, at 99-102; *see* Goebel, *King's Law and Local Custom in Seventeenth Century New England*, 31 COLUM. L. REV. 416 (1931). Only after the Restoration in 1660 did the Crown begin to exercise more control over its colonial domain. This early period of relative freedom in the colonies planted the seed for much of the power exercised by the judicial and legislative authorities in the 18th century. *See* L. FRIEDMAN, *supra* note 22, at 43-45. Of course, some colonies developed legal systems from non-English roots because of the early exploration patterns of the European powers. M. KAMMEN, *supra* note 146, at 91-94.

148. Goebel, *supra* note 102, at 466.

149. Goebel's piece is a severe critique of O. CROSSKEY, POLITICS AND THE CONSTITUTION IN THE HISTORY OF THE UNITED STATES (1953).

150. *See also* G. HASKINS, *supra* note 102, at 113-40.

151. Goebel, *supra* note 102, at 464.

152. *Id.* at 464; L. FRIEDMAN, *supra* note 22, at 43. *See also* M. HORWITZ, *supra* note 51, at 1-30; W. NELSON, *supra* note 102, at 9-10.

153. Goebel, *supra* note 102, at 465; *see also* L. FRIEDMAN, *supra* note 22, at 78-81.

of substantial legal authority. Similarly, the post-war process of deciding which segments of colonial legal institutions were to be left intact gave a great deal of discretion to judges, and statutes were received if local demands warranted. The problem for revolutionary era courts was to keep legal systems operating, rather than to simply reject, or accept, English law.[154]

Modern legal historians studying coverture are now recognizing that post-war judicial and legislative decisions on the applicability of English law in the state, territorial, and federal systems were not uniform.[155] An array of recep-

154. Goebel, *supra* note 102, at 467-68. Although Horwitz is more sympathetic than Goebel to the idea that natural law concepts motivated much of the legal community's actions in the 18th century, the factual predicate for his theory is similar to Goebel's. *Compare* Goebel, *supra* note 102, at 456-57, *with* M. HORWITZ, *supra* note 51, at 7-9. *See also* W. NELSON, *supra* note 102, at 13-35. Horwitz, like Morris, *supra* note 21, is subject to the criticism that he makes very broad generalizations from scattered evidence. Nonetheless, his generalizations are useful categories even if only as a starting point for measurement. Horwitz argues that Revolutionary War era lawyers had great respect for the common law system, despite colonial deviations from English rules of law. *See also* L. FRIEDMAN, *supra* note 22, at 95-96. Precedent was important in the formation of norms that generally governed the human condition. M. HORWITZ, *supra* note 51, at 4-5. While common law was equated with the divination of customary practice and natural law, *id.* at 7-8, statutes were perceived as man-made instruments of the Crown. While the colonists felt entitled to the common law system, if not its results, *id.* at 8, they felt free to alter English statutes. As a result, both judges pronouncing the common law and legislators enacting statutes ignored English solutions when necessary. Not until well after the Revolution did reactions set in decrying the diversity of judge-made law, *id.* at 18, and seeking the general unification and codification of legal norms, *id.* at 9-30, 253-56. The treatise tradition, which grew vigorously in the United States after 1820, also undertook to rationalize the diverse case law. The trend began with Kent's COMMENTARIES in 1827 and Story's COMMENTARIES ON EQUITY in 1836. But before the reaction, judges were emboldened to decide cases by reference to perceived public policy needs, M. HORWITZ, *supra* note 51, at 30, and legislatures felt free to adopt far-ranging alterations in English law. L. FRIEDMAN, *supra* note 22, at 97-100. By the turn of the 19th century, Horwitz argues, legal thought had moved from natural law to law as an instrument of social policy.

155. The best of the recent articles on variations during the colonial era is Salmon, *The Legal Status of Women in Early America: A Reappraisal*, 1 LAW & HIST. REV. 1 (1983). Salmon argues that modern legal historians may not with confidence rely on the general conclusions of an earlier generation of historians, including Morris, Beard, Dexter, and Bensen. Johnston opened the recent law journal debates on many of the questions taken up in this paper. Johnston, *Sex and Property: The Common Law Tradition, the Law School Curriculum and Developments Toward Equality*, 47 N.Y.U. L. REV. 1033 (1972). His cites to R. MORRIS *supra* note 21, suggest the difficulty Johnston had in deciphering the reception of English law in a culture as diverse as early America's. Even though chapter III of Morris' book has been aptly applauded as a path-breaking work, it is most certainly flawed. *See* M. SALMON, *supra* note 2, at 18-21. Morris drew a generally optimistic conclusion about the improved colonial status of women by noting a number of scattered examples of exceptions to the general English practice. Although these examples are very useful and interesting, they do not arise out of the intense cultural analysis necessary to support Morris' overall conclusion. *See* Goebel, *supra* note 147, at 416 n.3. Indeed, Morris was at times wrong in suggesting that his examples were exceptional and different from English practice. For example, Morris notes that a Mistress Margarett Brent acted as Maryland Governor Calvert's executor beginning in 1647. R. MORRIS, *supra* note 21, at 132-33. This is said to be an example of a woman acting as an attorney. But women were acting as executors of estates in England for some time before 1647. 3 W. HOLDSWORTH, *supra* note 104, at 528, 544; 7 W. HOLDSWORTH, *supra* note 108, at 180. Similarly, in an effort to make American commercial practice seem more open to women, Morris dismisses the English feme-sole trader status "merely as a local custom in some of the commercial boroughs," citing 3 W. HOLDSWORTH, *supra* note 104, at 525. But the period Holdsworth described was much earlier than the 17th century. Morris also ignores other available material on feme-sole trader status in England. *See infra* notes 183-96 and accompanying text. The custom of London can hardly be so easily dismissed. It is also not clear that Dexter's books, COLONIAL WOMEN OF AFFAIRS: WOMEN IN BUSINESS AND PROFESSIONS IN AMERICA BEFORE 1776 (1924) and CAREER WOMEN OF AMERICA 1776-1840 (1950) portray any different picture than that of London given by M. George in chapter IV of LONDON LIFE IN THE XVII CENTURY (1925). The colonies may have been more open to businesswomen than England, but Morris fails to make a case for that view. Morris also suggests that ante-nuptial contracts calling for husbands to dispose of assets by will to their wives were not clearly enforceable in England in the 17th century, while they were in the Colonies. R. MORRIS,

tion statutes was passed in the late eighteenth and early nineteenth centuries, and they differed in the era of English common law to be followed, the acceptance of equity, and the binding force of statutes.[156] Reception statutes frequently gave courts some discretion to decide which English precedents or statutes to apply. In addition, legislatures took upon themselves the task of resolving many disputes by passing private bills. In this milieu, pre-war changes in coverture-related legal norms were unlikely to be impeded by English interests. After the war, there was room for legal institutions to reexamine coverture law.

Development of Conveyance Reforms. From early in the eighteenth century, simplified documentary systems of land transfer emerged in most, but not all, of the Colonies.[157] The vast number of land transfers occurring in the eighteenth and nineteenth centuries required simple conveyancing methods. Warranty and quit claim deeds emerged in easily useable forms early in the eighteenth century.[158] The Northwest Ordinance provided for transfer of property by deed, free of the technical constraints of English common law.[159]

---

supra note 21, at 135-36. Morris ignores, however, the contemporaneous development of trusts in England that served the same purposes. 5 W. HOLDSWORTH, *supra* note 106, at 312-15. Finally, Morris' examples are localized. There is no way to know the depth or breadth of the colonial practice from his discussion.

156. Although some American reception statutes referred to specific dates for determination of the English common law to be received, almost all the reception statutes allowed local judges discretion in deciding when to declare the law to be "received." Even in areas where reception statutes designated a specific date, judges were left with discretion to adopt later English case law. L. FRIEDMAN, *supra* note 22, at 97-100. It is therefore predictable that the American legal system absorbed some segments of English law and rejected others.

The most comprehensive summary of reception provisions appears to be 1 R. POWELL, *supra* note 44, at 72-363. Every state's situation is discussed. A number of states had time-specific provisions. In 1776, for example, Virginia adopted a statute providing for reception of "the common law of England, and statutes or acts of parliament made in aid of the common law prior to the fourth year of the reign of King James the First 1607, and which are of a general nature, not local to that Kingdom." 1 REVISED CODE OF THE LAWS OF VIRGINIA 135 (1819). The statutory segment of this provision was significantly narrowed in 1792 after Jefferson completed a general statutory revision project for the state. Blume & Brown, *supra* note 37, at 480. Massachusetts provided in its first constitution that "All the laws which have heretofore been adopted, used, and approved . . . and usually practised on the courts of law shall still remain and be in full force until altered or repealed by the legislature; such parts only excepted as are repugnant to the rights and liberties contained in this constitution." MASS. CONST. ch. VI, art. VI (1780). While this was later construed broadly to permit discretionary adoption of English law, Commonwealth v. Churchill, 2 Metc. 118 (Mass. 1840), it obviously lacked the certitude of Virginia's code. The Virginia Ordinance of 1776 was adopted by the territorial government of the Northwest Territories in 1795. Blume & Brown, *supra* note 37, at 39. The Northwest Ordinance itself provided simply that the territory's inhabitants should have the "benefits of . . . judicial proceedings according to the courts of the common law." *Id.*

The statutes frequently left much discretion with courts. In Vermont a fairly typical statute was passed providing for reception of common law "not repugnant to the Constitution, or to any acts of the legislature of this state." 1 Vt. 118 (1793). A contemporaneous commentary on this act by the Chief Justice of the Vermont Supreme Court noted that circumstances were different in America from England, that monarchy and aristocracy had been overthrown, and concluded that the reception statute should not be read to accept principles "which from the peculiar circumstances of that government, exist only in England." Chipman, *A Dissertation on the Act Adopting the Common and Statute Laws of England*, 1 Vt. 117, 138 (1793).

157. R. MORRIS, *supra* note 21, at 69-72; L. FRIEDMAN, *supra* note 22, at 54-57; G. HASKINS, *supra* note 102, at 171-73. New York, interestingly enough, was among the later states to alter its conveyance rules. *See* Gundersen & Gampel, *supra* note 143, at 125-27 (1982); M. SALMON, *supra* note 2, at 31-37.

158. L. FRIEDMAN, *supra* note 22, at 207-09.

159. Blume, *supra* note 139, at 326-27.

While these provisions were probably inserted in the Ordinance to benefit the Ohio Company, which was seeking rights to develop Ohio,[160] they had effects on coverture rules as well. The use of a fine and recovery to convey a married woman's interest in her husband's land gave way to joint conveyance accomplished by signature.[161] Even though many Colonies, states, and territories retained the English practice of approving a land sale only after a married woman was separately examined before a judge or magistrate,[162] the general liberalizing of conveyancing practices had substantial impact.[163] While in hindsight the ease with which a wife's dower or other interest in real property could be transferred may be viewed as a double-edged sword,[164] there is little doubt of its importance in early American women's law.[165]

Development of Dower. Among the active debates in women's legal history, that involving reception of English dower may be the most lusty. The notion that dower was imported untouched from England is universally viewed as untenable.[166] The debate concerns whether the American changes were more[167] or less[168] favorable for women than the English law. Scholars on both sides of the controversy may be correct. Nineteenth-century scholarship indicates that dower was treated more favorably in some parts of the country than in others.[169] Some Colonies and states awarded dower in equitable estates; others did not.[170] Some states awarded dower in land held during coverture, others only in land held at death.[171] Although Pennsylvania law has recently been strongly criticized,[172] evidence suggests that neighboring Ohio

---

160. *Id.*

161. R. MORRIS, *supra* note 21, at 147-55; L. KERBER, *supra* note 2, at 145; 1 J. BISHOP, *supra* note 27, at 406-10.

162. 1 C. SCRIBNER, A TREATISE ON THE LAW OF DOWER 29-31, 37 (1867) (practice retained in Connecticut, New York, and North Carolina); 1 J. BISHOP, *supra* note 27, at 410-15; M. SALMON, *supra* note 2, at 37-83.

163. Dower, for example, was easier to defeat by conveyance than in England, at least at law. *See* 1 J. BISHOP, *supra* note 27, at 312-15; 2 C. SCRIBNER, *supra* note 162, at 268-78.

164. The use of separate examinations to protect women from overreaching husbands could act beneficially. It could also be an unnecessary hurdle, or could lapse unfairly into informality. *See* L. KERBER, *supra* note 2, at 145; Salmon, *supra* note 42, at 101-06.

165. Despite the easing of transfer restrictions, the general content of the husband-dominating coverture rules certainly continued. Married women's contracts were still not generally enforced, so promises to convey or warranties to guarantee title were frequently unenforceable. Immediate conveyances without contractual preliminaries were easier.

166. J. SPRUILL, *supra* note 44, at 359-60; L. FRIEDMAN, *supra* note 22, at 59, 375-76; L. KERBER, *supra* note 2, at 123-32, 146-48; M. HORWITZ, *supra* note 51, at 56-58; R. MORRIS, *supra* note 21, at 155-64; Salmon, *supra* note 42, at 106-08. Though not cited by the recent authors, the only significant 19th-century American treatise on dower confirms the recent work. *See* 1 C. SCRIBNER, *supra* note 162, at 23-57 (state-by-state review of dower law describing numerous state-by-state differences from English law).

167. *See generally* R. MORRIS, *supra* note 21, *and* J. SPRUILL, *supra* note 44 (arguing American changes in dower were more favorable to women).

168. *See generally* L. KERBER, *supra* note 2; M. HORWITZ, *supra* note 51; L. FRIEDMAN, *supra* note 22; and Salmon, *supra* note 42 (arguing American changes in dower were less favorable to women).

169. *See* 1 C. SCRIBNER, *supra* note 162, at 23-57; M. SALMON, *supra* note 2, at 264-98.

170. 1 C. SCRIBNER, *supra* note 162, at 382-90, 396-417.

171. *Id.* at 589-601.

172. *See* Salmon, *supra* note 42, at 108. Salmon's judgment that dower was placed in jeopardy by 18th-century Pennsylvania law may not tell the entire story. Scribner writes:

> But the courts of Pennsylvania have not left the widow to the uncertain and precarious provision contemplated by the above statute. That enactment being limited to the estate

had a lengthy tradition of protecting married women's dower interests.[173] In addition, England was limiting the impact of dower during the eighteenth century. The substantial use of equity practice in England led to very general avoidance of dower rules during the reception eras.[174] When dower reform came before Parliament in 1833, dower was extended to equitable estates, but only those actually held by the husband at death.[175] Thus, whether American law was more or less favorable to women may be impossible to assess with certainty.

The early dower statutes exhibit several interesting characteristics. They were sometimes passed in acts containing more general conveyancing reforms permitting transfer by deed,[176] or with provisions for the separate examination of married women.[177] The link between conveyance reform and dower is also illustrated by those statutes that provided widows a right to reject either dower or the provisions of their husbands' legitimate wills in favor of a statutorily prescribed share of their deceased husbands' estates.[178] Such statutes were passed in some states shortly after the Revolutionary War, and the practice existed well before the war in some areas.[179] This elective share scheme did

---

> which the husband held at his death, and in respect of which he died intestate, the courts have determined that as to lands which were aliened by him during the coverture without the concurrence of the wife, or which he attempts to dispose of by will to her prejudice, she may take her dower as by common law.[3] This doctrine is the result of judicial construction, solely, and appears to be unsupported by any express law upon the subject. It is now too well established, however, by an unbroken current of authority, to admit of serious question or doubt.
>
> While adopting the rule of the common law to the extent just stated as a part of the law of Pennsylvania, the courts have gone one step further in behalf of the widow. They have so far modified that rule as to give dower in equitable as well as legal estates. In Kelly v. Mahan, it was held that dower may be had of a mere improvement claim, and in Shoemaker v. Walker, the right of dower in equitable estates was expressly determined. "In Pennsylvania," said Tilghman, Chief Justice, after remarking upon the doctrine of common law, "the usage has been more reasonable, and more analogous to the general principles of dower."

1 C. SCRIBNER, *supra* note 162, at 410. Scribner's footnote 3 refers to a line of decisions starting with Borland v. Nichols, 12 Pa. (2 Jones) 42 (1849). The intriguing question is whether this case was a shot out of the blue or a reflection of more long-standing practice. If the latter turns out to be true, the 18th-century dower statutes in Pennsylvania may not be read to be as harsh to women as Salmon suggests. Statutes providing widows a right to elect a share of their husbands' estate were passed on Apr. 8, 1833 (1833 Pa. Laws 250, § 11) and Apr. 11, 1848 (1848 Pa. Laws 537, § 11).

173. The Northwest Ordinance provided for dower as did later territorial and Ohio state statutes. There, in contrast with Pennsylvania, dower was not subject to a husband's debts. Jointure could be waived under a Jan. 19, 1804, statute. Ch. XIV, § 2, 1804 Ohio Acts 34-35. Equitable assets held at death became subject to dower under a Feb. 12, 1805, statute. Ch. X, 1805 Ohio Acts § 1. Dower at law was not restricted to lands held at death, nor did a wife lose the benefit of the increase in value of the land from the date of its sale to the date of assignment to her. Allen v. McCoy, 8 Ohio 418, 466-67 (1838). For a more complete review of Ohio dower cases see M. Brown, *Reception of English Common Law and Chancery in Ohio* 14-22 (1981) (unpublished paper) (copy on file at *Georgetown Law Journal*).

174. 1 C. SCRIBNER, *supra* note 162, at 367-68.

175. 3 W. HOLDSWORTH, *supra* note 104, at 197.

176. 1 C. SCRIBNER, *supra* note 162, at 31, 38, 44 (New York, Georgia, and New Hampshire).

177. *Id.* at 31, 40-41 (New York, Rhode Island, and Maryland).

178. *See id.* at 27, 33, 36-42, 46, 49-50 (Massachusetts, Delaware, North Carolina, Tennessee, Georgia, Mississippi, Alabama, Maryland, Vermont, Ohio, and Illinois). *See also* 2 C. SCRIBNER, *supra* note 162, at 413-17, 464-97.

179. Many states passed such statutes in the 1820's and 1830's. *See infra* note 239. But earlier examples of the practice also exist. Kentucky passed a statute in 1797 giving widows the right to elect the share of their deceased husbands' estates they would have received under intestacy. Act of Feb. 24, 1797, § 24, 1797 Ky. Acts 162. But it is apparent that the practice described in this general enactment on wills was in existence well before that. *See* Trigg's Administrator v. Daniel, 5 Ky. (2 Bibb) 301 (1811). Similarly, Maryland's general codification of the law of wills passed in 1798 provided that a

not always give widows the right to take a share of the personal estate of their husbands prior to the payment of debts. It did, however, provide some increased access to wealth while the institution of dower was fading in significance. In cases where a woman elected to take her statutory share, she usually had to waive her dower rights. Thus these statutes also had the effect of removing dower as an encumbrance upon lands distributed to persons other than widows.[180] The same trend is displayed by the late eighteenth- and early nineteenth-century growth of statutes permitting or requiring dower to be awarded in a single cash sum upon the death of the husband.[181] Such release of dower rights freed the underlying fee simple of constraints impeding alienation. The perceived need, at least in some Colonies and states, to make land transfer as simple and as free of encumbrances as possible sometimes had the effect of reducing the scope of protection afforded married women.[182]

Feme-Sole Trading. An interesting contrast to the early developments in conveyancing and dower law is presented by the general lack of feme-sole trader acts in the Colonies. One might hypothesize that any historical trend to protect commercial dealing would carry over to permit women to act and be held accountable for business contracts. The general colonial acceptance of the law merchant[183] in the seventeenth and eighteenth centuries suggests that the colonies were not oblivious to the needs of trade. It is also clear that some women were traders in America.[184] How then can the presence of a broad feme-sole trader statute in only one colony[185] and the delay in development of trading rights for married women until late in the nineteenth century be explained?

Several hypotheses are plausible. Perhaps married businesswomen used trusts or separate estates, especially in the South.[186] Northern examples of

---

widow could reject her husband's will in favor of dower and a third of the personal estate. Act of Jan. 20, 1798, ch. 101, 1798 Md. Laws § 15. Here, too, case law suggests that the practice existed long before the statute. *See* Coomes v. Clements, 8 Md. 382, 385 (1821). *See also* North Carolina: Ch. XXXII, April 1784 Session; Virginia: Ch. LX, October 1785 Session.

180. M. HORWITZ, *supra* note 51, at 56-58, suggests that commercial pressures in early America sometimes led to significant changes in dower rules, effectively denying widows access to the increased capital values of unimproved land. *See also* L. FRIEDMAN, *supra* note 22, at 375-76.

181. *See* 2 C. SCRIBNER, *supra* note 162, at 612-55. Scribner gives a fairly detailed description of developments in Maryland and South Carolina. *See id.* at 637-46, 646-50.

182. Kerber's fascinating study of the relation between dower and the treason confiscation acts of the Revolutionary War era makes an analogous point. To the extent that the threat of losing dower upon going over to enemy territory was used as a device to influence married women's political loyalities, dower was being used for social purposes deemed more important than the economic well-being of married women. *See* L. KERBER, *supra* note 2, at 123-36.

183. L. FRIEDMAN, *supra* note 22, at 69.

184. Spruill, *supra* note 44, at 276-313; E. DEXTER, COLONIAL WOMEN OF AFFAIRS, *supra* note 131; E. DEXTER, CAREER WOMEN OF AMERICA 1776-1840 (1950); Gundersen & Gampel, *supra* note 143, at 129-33. *See also* Norton, *A Cherished Spirit of Independence: The Life of an Eighteenth Century Boston Businesswoman*, in WOMEN OF AMERICA: A HISTORY 49 (C. Berkin & M. Norton eds. 1979).

185. South Carolina was the single colony. It is described in J. SPRUILL, *supra* note 44, at 362 n.80; L. KERBER, *supra* note 2, at 148-49; 2 J. BISHOP, *supra* note 27, at 418-20. Pennsylvania also had an early (1718) feme-sole trader statute, but it was limited to wives of mariners at sea. *See* 2 J. BISHOP, *supra* note 27, at 420; J. KELLY, A TREATISE ON THE LAW OF CONTRACTS OF MARRIED WOMEN 504-05 (1881).

186. *See* J. SPRUILL, *supra* note 44, at 362-65. Equity was received more warmly in the South than in the North. *See supra* notes 33-42 and accompanying text (discussing practice of equity in the states).

feme-covert trader trusts may have existed which have not yet been uncovered.[187] Legislative private bills were used in some jurisdictions to grant women the power to trade, but extensive studies of this activity have not been done.[188] Other areas that may reveal explanations for the lack of trader statutes include the law of agency,[189] the use of arbitration,[190] and the use of specialized business tribunals for which reported decisions were not generally published.[191] The most likely explanation, however, is that many of the women operating businesses outside their homes were not married,[192] and that the few married businesswomen worked with their husbands or subjected themselves to the general rule that a wife's income belonged to her husband.[193] In contrast to the development of the custom of London in England, American law simply may not have reflected commercial reality for the few married women involved in business.[194]

Thus, by 1800 American law had freed land from some of the constraints of technical conveyance and dower rules while apparently leaving married women's business rights constrained by coverture doctrines. The reduction of home industry and the rise of a wage system for employed women may have meant that there was little need to free them from commercial constraints. And certainly trading by a married woman separate from her husband and her home was likely to be subject to some public disapproval.[195] While the begin-

---

187. Some feme-sole trader trust cases do exist in the northeast. *See* North Am. Coal Co. v. Dyett, 7 Paige Ch. 9 (N.Y. Ch. 1837); Stammers v. Macomb, 10 N.Y. Common L. Rep. (2 Wend.) 454 (1829).

188. *See* J. Spruill, *supra* note 44, at 361-62; 2 J. Bishop, *supra* note 27, at 475-76 (Alabama); M. Benson, Women in Eighteenth Century America 241 (1935) (Virginia); L. Kerber, *supra* note 2, at 150-52 (Connecticut). It is intriguing that many states later imposed specific restrictions on passage of bills dealing with land transfers of persons under civil disabilities. *See* C. Binney, *supra* note 52, at 143-44.

189. Old American treatises suggest that married women may have been treated as agents of their husbands even when the relationship was established by practice and behavior rather than by express documents. *See* J. Story, Commentaries on the Law of Agency 8 (1844); 1 F. Livermore, Treatise on the Law of Principal and Agent 28-34 (1818); J. Dunlap, Treatise on the Law of Principal and Agent 163-64 (1847). *See also* M. Benson, *supra* note 188, at 240.

190. J. Morse, The Law of Arbitration and Award 26-29 (1872) has a fascinating suggestion that businessmen could voluntarily agree to arbitrate with a married woman in the early 19th century.

191. This was certainly a common practice in mercantile England, but there has been no investigation of the phenomenon here.

192. The presence of large numbers of married women in the labor force is a 20th-century phenomenon. At the end of the 19th century, less than 20% of women were in the labor force. About 40% of unmarried women, but only five percent of married women, were in the labor force. The number of married women in the labor force increased significantly during World War II, fell a bit after the war, and then began a sustained climb. Statistical History, *supra* note 6, at 133 (table of women's employment). Today, over half of married women are in the labor force. Statistical Abstract, *supra* note 13, at 402 (table of women's employment).

193. *See* 1 J. Bishop, *supra* note 27, at 140-42.

194. *See* L. Kerber, *supra* note 2, at 152; Gundersen & Gampel, *supra* note 143, at 131. An early Massachusetts case certainly suggests that absent use of a trust or other device, feme-sole traders operated at some risk. In Russell v. Brooks, 24 Mass. (7 Pick.) 65 (1828), Eleanor Swan operated a fur manufacturing business while her husband Joshua visited her on Sundays and lived in adultery with another woman. The case apparently arose because the husband's business had become insolvent in 1819, leaving his estate heavily indebted. The couple had separated in 1815, but had not divorced. The court held that money received and notes taken by the wife in her separately operated business prior to the 1821 death of her husband were owned by his estate. *Id.* at 67.

195. Even the most famous of 19th-century women tended to withdraw from public life upon marriage and risk censure upon reentry before divorce or widowhood. Biographers are now beginning to be quite sensitive to the problems such constraints caused. *See generally* J. Furnas, Fanny Kemble: Leading Lady of the Nineteenth Century Stage (1982). Furnas devotes considerable attention

nings of reform of land transfer and inheritance rules in order to insure the economic viability of surviving widows in the face of dower's decline was perfectly compatible with the late eighteenth-century emergence of concern for family well-being,[196] feme-sole trading by married women may have been seen as quite another matter.

3. Summary

This review of reception resolves a few issues and opens up many more. While English law and equity provided substantial impetus to the development of coverture law in this country, each American jurisdiction developed variations from the general pattern. English influence, however, was not the most significant barrier to the reform of American coverture law. The more liberal aspects of English equity were also influential during the early nineteenth century. In addition, too many important differences between English and American law had appeared by 1800 to conclude that the later reform movement was simply a throwing off of colonial remnants. Rather, it appears that by 1800 American legal institutions were beginning to grapple with changing family patterns and growing commercial interests. Divorce was growing just as romantic companionate marriage emerged. New methods of providing surviving spouses and children with means of support were emerging at the same time that substantial impediments to transfer of property were being removed. The vast difference between married men and women in their job patterns and wealth made it easy to legislate separately about their property, and to create different systems of control. The very notion of a separate estate for married women, which was reaching maturity at the time historians tell us that the modern family was emerging, could be expected to grow and take on characteristics consistent with the still limited but expanding role of most early nineteenth-century married women. The unfolding of these developments is the next part of the tale.

B. THE MARRIED WOMEN'S ACTS

During the 1700's women rarely publicly expressed dissatisfaction with the legal institution of coverture.[197] Alterations in legal rules before 1800 were

---

to the marital controversies of Fanny Kemble, including property disputes, problems with her English property trust, and loss of contact with her daughters from the time of her divorce until the daughters reached the age of majority.

196. *See infra* notes 336-39 and accompanying text (discussing Degler's work on the emergence of the American family).

197. There certainly were some early examples of women pressing their male contemporaries for significant alterations in gender roles. Among the most famous of these early exchanges is that between Abigail and John Adams, Abigail writing to John that "If particular care and attention is not paid to the ladies, we are determined to foment a rebellion, and will not hold ourselves bound by any laws in which we have no voice or representation." Abigail Adams to John Adams, Mar. 31, 1777, in FAMILIAR LETTERS OF JOHN ADAMS AND HIS WIFE, ABIGAIL ADAMS, DURING THE REVOLUTION 149-50 (C. Adams ed. 1876). The correspondence is reprinted in a readily available documentary history, THE FEMINIST PAPERS 7-15 (A.S. Rossi ed. 1973). Like most women in her day, however, Abigail Adams largely kept her ideas private, in letters to her husband and to her friends. *See* L. KERBER, *supra* note 2, at 73-85. Some English materials were beginning to find their way to these shores, such as Mary Wollstonecraft's VINDICATION OF THE RIGHTS OF WOMEN (1792) and the lectures and pioneering work in education of Scotswoman Frances Wright. *See* E. FLEXNER, *supra* note 1, at 27-28. It really was not

generated more by economic needs than by any widely articulated desires to redefine the role of American women.[198] By the late 1840's the nature of the debate changed. Legal rules became subjects of public debate, statutes were adopted in a number of jurisdictions, movements arose, and controversy boiled. What happened? The roots for this change are certainly not limited to the need for simplified means of exchanging land. The married women's acts themselves reflect the complexity of developments in the first half of the nineteenth century.

According to conventional historical views,[199] Mississippi adopted the first married women's property act in 1839.[200] In fact, the acts were passed in at least three waves, beginning in 1835, and each wave arose for somewhat different reasons. The first group of statutes, passed almost entirely in the 1840's, dealt primarily with freeing married women's estates from the debts of their husbands.[201] By and large these statutes left untouched the traditional marital estate and coverture rules. The second wave of legislation, the most frequently discussed, established separate estates for married women. These statutes appeared over a long period of time beginning in the 1840's and ending after the Civil War.[202] The third set of statutes took the important step of protecting women's earnings from the institution of coverture. These laws generally did not appear until after the Civil War, although Massachusetts enacted an early statute in 1855.[203]

The first wave of legislation protecting the property of married women from the debts of their husbands emerged in a deluge. Almost every state and territory then in existence adopted such legislation.[204] While there were a few general patterns to the enactments, their terminology differed and remarkably little verbatim copying occurred. The earliest statute I have found that deals

---

until the 1830's, when the Grimke Sisters surfaced, that women's issues became subjects of widespread public debate. *See infra* note 346 and accompanying text (discussing Grimke Sisters).

198. Though individual petitions were filed with legislatures, *see* L. KERBER, *supra* note 2, at 85-99, it would be a generation before more organized and overt activity would emerge.

199. The only work noting the existence of the 1835 Arkansas statute is E. Warbasse, *supra* note 2, at 159.

200. L. FRIEDMAN, *supra* note 22, at 185. *See* Brown, *Memorandum on the Mississippi Women's Law of 1839*, 42 MICH. L. REV. 1110 (1944) (discussing the origin of the Mississippi statute and the debate surrounding its passage). In fact, Florida moved well before Mississippi, and as this article later suggests, there were a number of other legislative actions which were precursors to the later women's acts. Florida's statute appears to have been the result of a desire to protect marriage arrangements made under civil law before the territory became American, since only pre-1824 married women were protected by the legislation. W. CORD, A TREATISE ON THE LEGAL AND EQUITABLE RIGHTS OF MARRIED WOMEN 719 (1861); E. Warbasse, *supra* note 2, at 77, 163.

201. *See infra* notes 204-11 and accompanying text (discussing first phase).

202. This legislative phase overlapped with the debt statutes. But the early statutes inevitably needed refinement to account for ambiguity, enlarged goals, or hostile judicial reception. For some of the separate estate statutes, see *infra* notes 207, 209, and 263.

203. Massachusetts' act was adopted on May 5, 1855. For other earnings statutes, *see infra* note 361.

204. Finding this statutory material is difficult unless one has access to the session laws and codes of all the states and territories. The session laws are now available on microfiche, but for the benefit of readers who are not fortunate enough to have access to such material, I have included in the notes that follow citations to some of the major 19th century treatises that discuss married women's acts. The treatises used are J. BISHOP, *supra* note 27; W. CORD, *supra* note 200; J. KELLY, *supra* note 185; J. ROBINSON, THE LAW OF HUSBAND AND WIFE (1890); R. TYLER, COMMENTARIES ON THE LAW OF INFANCY AND THE LAW OF COVERTURE (1873). In addition, references to these statutes by E. Warbasse, *supra* note 2, have also been included. On the New York acts, *see* P. RABKIN, *supra* note 2; N. BASCH, *supra* note 1.

directly with marital property and husband's debts was adopted by the territorial legislature in Arkansas in 1835.[205] This largely undiscussed piece of legislation protected a wife's property from debts incurred by her husband prior to marriage. Only Alabama appears to have borrowed this legal formula.[206] Following Mississippi's lead in 1839, three other states protected married women's slaves from their husband's creditors.[207] A number of jurisdictions protected only the real property of married women from debts of their husbands.[208] Most statutes, however, went further and included both real and personal property under the umbrella of protection.[209] About half of the legis-

---

205. Act of Nov. 2, 1835, 1835 Ark. Terr. Laws 34-35; E. Warbasse, *supra* note 2, at 159.

206. In 1846, after a long period of acting by private bill, Alabama adopted an act granting feme-sole status to abandoned married women. Act of Jan. 31, 1846, 1845 Ala. Acts 24 (1846). Jurisdiction to handle such cases was given to the equity courts in March 1848. The last section of the 1846 act protected the property of married women from ante-nuptial debts of the husband. This scheme lasted only two years. On March 1, 1848, Alabama adopted a separate estate married women's act. Act of Mar. 1, 1848, 1847 Ala. Acts 79 (1848).

207. Mississippi: Act of Feb. 15, 1839, ch. 46, 1839 Miss. Laws 72; 2 J. BISHOP, *supra* note 27, at 535; W. CORD, *supra* note 200, at 722-23; J. KELLY, *supra* note 185, at 427; E. Warbasse, *supra* note 2, at 138-60. Maryland: Act of Mar. 10, 1843, ch. 293, 1842 Md. Laws 33 (1843); E. Warbasse, *supra* note 2, at 155-59. Kentucky: Act of Feb. 23, 1846, ch. 368, 1845 Ky. Acts 42 (1846); 2 J. BISHOP, *supra* note 27, at 515-16; W. CORD, *supra* note 200, at 603-06; E. Warbasse, *supra* note 2, at 173. Arkansas: Act of Dec. 8, 1846, 1844 Ark. Acts 38 (1846); 2 J. BISHOP, *supra* note 27, at 478-79; W. CORD, *supra* note 200, at 731-32; E. Warbasse, *supra* note 2, at 159-60. The Maryland statute is very similar to Mississippi's. It added, however, sections giving married women the right to make a will and to retain up to $1,000 as separate property. Arkansas' statute is also much like Mississippi's. Kentucky took a separate path, merging its slave provisions with others protecting the real property of married women from the debts of husbands. The Mississippi, Maryland, and Arkansas statutes also have very general provisions apparently creating a separate estate in married women.

208. The earliest of these statutes was that of Maryland: Act of Mar. 1, 1842, ch. 161, 1841 Md. Laws (1842); 2 J. BISHOP, *supra* note 27, at 100. Statutes followed in Connecticut: Act of June 10, 1845, ch. XXXIX, 1845 Conn. Acts 36; 2 J. BISHOP, *supra* note 27, at 7; W. CORD, *supra* note 200, at 736; J. KELLY, *supra* note 185, at 336; E. Warbasse, *supra* note 2, at 191. Iowa: Act of Jan. 2, 1846, ch. 5, 1845 Iowa Terr. Acts 40 (1846); E. Warbasse, *supra* note 2, at 204-05. Kentucky: Act of Feb. 23, 1846, ch. 368, 1845 Ky. Acts 42 (1846); *see supra* note 207. Indiana: Act of Jan. 23, 1847, ch. VI, 1846 Ind. Acts 45 (1847); E. Warbasse, *supra* note 2, at 205. Vermont: Act of Nov. 15, 1845, No. 37, 1847 Vt. Acts 26 (1845); J. KELLY, *supra* note 185, at 526; E. Warbasse, *supra* note 2, at 192. North Carolina: Act of Jan. 29, 1849, ch. XLI, 1848 N.C. Sess. Laws 12 (1849); 2 J. BISHOP, *supra* note 27, at 555-56; J. KELLY, *supra* note 185, at 463. Tennessee: Act of Jan. 10, 1850, ch. XXXVI, 1849 Tenn. Pub. Acts 111 (1850); 2 J. BISHOP, *supra* note 27, at 569; J. KELLY, *supra* note 185, at 517-18. Maryland's statute was a very simple, one sentence enactment. In fact, Maryland adopted a more detailed statute modeled after Mississippi's about a year later. *See supra* note 207. The statutes in Connecticut, Iowa, Indiana, Vermont, North Carolina, and Tennessee are similar in content, but the language in each varies from the prior enactments.

209. Michigan: Act of Mar. 11, 1844, No. 66, 1844 Mich. Pub. Acts 77; 2 J. BISHOP, *supra* note 27, at 532-33; J. KELLY, *supra* note 185, at 416; E. Warbasse, *supra* note 2, at 202-03. Maine: Act of Mar. 22, 1844, ch. 117, 1844 Me. Acts 104; 2 J. BISHOP, *supra* note 27, at 518; R. TYLER, *supra* note 204, at 675; E. Warbasse, *supra* note 2, at 200-01. Massachusetts: Act of Mar. 25, 1845, ch. 208, 1845 Mass. Acts 531; 2 J. BISHOP, *supra* note 27, at 525; J. KELLY, *supra* note 185, at 411; E. Warbasse, *supra* note 2, at 190-91. Alabama: Act of Jan. 31, 1846, No. 20, 1845 Ala. Acts 24 (1846); W. CORD, *supra* note 200, at 725; J. KELLY, *supra* note 185, at 291; E. Warbasse, *supra* note 2, at 170 (ante-nupital debts only), and Act of Mar. 1, 1848, No. 43, 1847 Ala. Acts 79 (1848) (real and personal property generally); Florida: Act of Mar. 6, 1845, No. IX, 1845 Fla. Terr. Laws 24; Ohio: Act of Feb. 28, 1846, 1845 Ohio Laws 75 (1846); W. CORD, *supra* note 200, at 709-10; J. KELLY, *supra* note 185, at 467; E. Warbasse, *supra* note 2, at 205. New Hampshire: Act of July 10, 1846, ch. 327, 1846 N.H. Laws 307; 2 J. BISHOP, *supra* note 27, at 544; J. KELLY, *supra* note 185, at 444; R. TYLER, *supra* note 204, at 681-82; E. Warbasse, *supra* note 2, at 191. New York: Act of Apr. 7, 1848, ch. 200, 1848 N.Y. Laws 307; 2 J. BISHOP, *supra* note 27, at 545-47; W. CORD, *supra* note 200, at 649; J. KELLY, *supra* note 185, at 455; R. TYLER, *supra* note 204, at 635-36; E. Warbasse, *supra* note 2, at 205-40. Pennsylvania: Act of Apr. 11, 1848, No. 372, 1848 Pa. Laws 536; 2 J. BISHOP, *supra* note 27, at 560-61; W. CORD, *supra* note 200, at 660-63; J. KELLY, *supra* note 185, at 486-87; E. Warbasse, *supra* note 2, at 236. Missouri: Act of Mar. 5, 1849, 1848 Mo. Laws

lation also included general statements that married women could hold property separate and apart from their husbands.[210] These generalized attempts to permit married women to control their own property were frequently construed narrowly by the courts.[211] This judicial hostility made it apparent that later legislative efforts would be required to complete the married women's property reform movement.

There are a number of explanations for the appearance of the first wave of married women's acts in the 1840's. First, widespread economic problems prompted numerous changes in debtor's law and made exemptions of property from attachment by creditors a pressing concern. Second, legislation chipping away at a number of the harsher consequences of coverture law had been enacted in earlier parts of the century. Abandoned women and widows were the objects of much attention; divorce laws changed; imprisonment of women for debt disappeared; and family law developed. If further reform was to occur, the institution of coverture had to become the focus of attention. Third, the fact that public debate about the role of women in society and legislation protecting the property of married women appeared in the same decade is not mere coincidence. Although it is difficult to argue that lobbying or petitioning by women or their supporters led directly to the passage of most of the debt statutes, the legal and cultural developments of the first third of the century certainly created a more sympathetic environment for their enactment.

1. The Economy of the 1840's and Debtor Legislation

The economic climate of the 1840's was established by the Panic of 1837. Some have called the depression that followed one of the worst in our history, describing devastation in virtually every phase of the economy.[212] Others argue that the economic problems were concentrated in trade and commercial

---

67 (1849); J. KELLY, *supra* note 185, at 433. Connecticut: Act of June 22, 1849, ch. XX, 1849 Conn. Acts 16; 2 J. BISHOP, *supra* note 27, at 7; W. CORD, *supra* note 200, at 737; J. KELLY, *supra* note 185, at 336; E. Warbasse, *supra* note 2, at 190. Wisconsin: Act of Feb. 1, 1850, ch. 44, 1850 Wis. Laws 29; 2 J. BISHOP, *supra* note 27, at 572; W. CORD, *supra* note 200, at 715. New Jersey: Act of Mar. 25, 1852, ch. CLXXI, 1852 N.J. Laws 407; 2 J. BISHOP, *supra* note 27, at 545. These statutes are remarkably varied in content. Those of Alabama (second act), Michigan, Maine, Massachusets, Iowa, New York, Pennsylvania, and Wisconsin each have clauses providing that a married woman's property should be hers as if she were unmarried, or in her own name. The acts of Alabama (first act), Ohio, Missouri, and Connecticut lacked such phraseology. In addition, some of the acts dealt with other subjects such as abandoned wives (Alabama's first act); intestate shares (Alabama's second act); conveyancing (Ohio); husband's trusteeship in the property of his wife (Connecticut); ante-nupital contracts, conveyancing, intestacy, wills, and trusteeships (Massachusetts and New Hamshire); conveyancing, wills, and intestacy (Pennsylvania), and wills (Wisconsin). Rhode Island, in its codification of 1844, also adopted a general debt statute. E. Warbasse, *supra* note 2, at 197.

210. *See supra* notes 204-09.

211. The hostile reception given the New York act has been told by others. *See* P. RABKIN, *supra* note 2, at 125-38; E. Warbasse, *supra* note 2, at 237-40. Warbasse also tells of similar hostility in Maine, Rhode Island, and Pennsylvania. E. Warbasse, *supra* note 2, at 201, 237, 241-44. Courts in other states may have been more favorably disposed to married women's acts. *See* M. Brown, Reception of English Common Law and Chancery in Ohio, 67-75 (1981) (unpublished paper) (copy on file with author). The state courts in Oregon also construed their acts broadly. *See* Brummet v. Weaver, 2 Or. 168 (1866). As with much of the legal history in this area, the possibility of a mixed picture is high. But there is little doubt that the narrow contents of most of the first wave of married women's acts, together with judicial hostility, necessitated the passage of more legislation in following years.

212. R. MCGRANE, THE PANIC OF 1837 1 (1965).

sectors of the economy, not in industrial and agricultural production.[213] In any case, a number of strains in the economy of the young United States appeared about this time. Extensive land speculation in the Western states and territories occurred during the 1830's. Revenues from land sales skyrocketed in the middle of the decade.[214] Government investigations of widespread land office abuses also occurred.[215] In 1836 Congress considered legislation to return to the states a budget surplus generated in significant part by land sales. In 1837, however, following a precipitous decline in land revenues, Congress found itself confronting a budget deficit.[216] Large-scale borrowing by states and territories for the construction of internal improvements occurred in the 1830's. After the panic, states heavily obligated to pay off internal improvement bonds found themselves at or near bankruptcy.[217] Textile and other manufacturing industries grew dramatically in the Northeast in the 1830's.[218] After the panic, however, industry was in general decline. Cotton sales overseas boomed in the 1830's, but by the following decade the world's cotton trade was in disarray due to falling prices.[219] Prices for slaves also fell dramatically.[220] The cause of the economic collapse is the subject of some debate, but most explanations focus on some or all of the following factors: Excessive land speculation, enormous balance of trade deficits, heavy borrowing for internal improvements by states and territories, concentration of bank ownership, decline in European demand for cotton, and President Jackson's dismantling of the national bank and issuance of the *Specie Circular* in 1836.[221] Whatever the cause or causes of the panic, the resulting economic stress was the impetus for the enactment of numerous pieces of legislation on bankruptcy, banking, and debtor's rights at both the federal and state levels. A look at some of this legislative activity makes the first wave of married women's property acts a logical part of a much larger movement of economic reform.

Proposals for bankruptcy legislation at both the federal and state levels appeared frequently during the first half of the nineteenth century. Prior to 1841, Congress had enacted bankruptcy legislation only once. This early act, passed in 1800, was designed as a five-year measure, but was repealed after only three years.[222] After the onset of distressed economic times in 1839, new demands

---

213. P. TEMIN, THE JACKSONIAN ECONOMY 148-77 (1969).

214. Revenues from land sales rose from four million dollars in 1833 to almost $25 million by 1836. That extraordinarily rapid rise was followed by an even more precipitous decline to just under $7 million in 1837. Sales fell further to about $2 million a year in the mid-1840's. P. TEMIN, *supra* note 213, at 168; HAMMOND, BANKS AND POLITICS IN AMERICA 451 (1957). For a general review of land speculation see R. MCGRANE, *supra* note 212, at 43-69; HAMMOND, *supra* note 214, at 452-53; P. GATES, HISTORY OF PUBLIC LAND LAW DEVELOPMENT 177-78 (1968).

215. R. MCGRANE, *supra* note 212, at 58-61; P. GATES, *supra* note 214, at 173-75.

216. HAMMOND, *supra* note 214, at 451-52; S. REZNECK, BUSINESS DEPRESSIONS AND FINANCIAL PANICS 92-93 (1968).

217. R. MCGRANE, *supra* note 212, at 9-13, 19-24, 30-35, 112-14, 128-30.

218. *Id.* at 96-112; B. BERG, *supra* note 2, at 40-42.

219. HAMMOND, *supra* note 214, at 467-77. Cotton prices fell steadily from the late 1830's to the middle of the 1840's. G. WRIGHT, THE POLITICAL ECONOMY OF THE COTTON SOUTH 96 (1978). P. GATES, *supra* note 214, at 177-78.

220. R. MCGRANE, *supra* note 212, at 116-18.

221. *See supra* notes 212-20 (literature discussing the Panic of 1837).

222. For a short but information-laden summary of the history of federal bankruptcy legislation, see P. COLEMAN, DEBTORS AND CREDITORS IN AMERICA: INSOLVENCY, IMPRISONMENT FOR DEBT, AND BANKRUPTCY, 1607-1900 16-30 (1974). Coleman is also a rich bibliographic source.

arose for federal bankruptcy legislation. An act was adopted in 1841, and thousands of debtors found relief under its terms.[223] Though the act was quickly repealed, it did serve to relieve some of the immediate pressures on debtors. Not until the Panic of 1857, and the economic dislocations caused by the Civil War, did pressure again build for the adoption of national bankruptcy legislation.[224] Although the short-lived federal provisions of 1841 had relieved much of the need for state bankruptcy laws, a few states also adopted or modified bankruptcy laws in this period.[225] The federal government also took steps to protect merchants who were defaulting on bonds posted to cover customs charges.[226]

Although most states did not adopt bankruptcy laws during the 1840's,[227] many did enact legislation protecting debtors and eliminating abuses in banking.[228] These enactments frequently included provisions requiring that property sold at the behest of creditors be appraised and bring a minimum price,[229] extending the types and value of property exempt from execution to pay debts,[230] exempting homesteads from attachment both during life and at death,[231] abolishing imprisonment for debt,[232] and, of course, insulating married women's property from the debts of their husbands.

The first wave of married women's acts meshes very nicely with this statutory reform movement. Laws exempting assets from attachment had existed in some form for decades and were simply extended in the 1840's. The married women's acts operated much like exemption laws. If the new model of family

223. S. REZNECK, *supra* note 216, at 96. In New York alone, 8000 debtors filed for relief under the federal act. P. COLEMAN, *supra* note 222, at 128-29.

224. P. COLEMAN, *supra* note 222, at 24.

225. Massachusetts, Connecticut, and Maryland passed such statutes. *See id.* at 50-51, 84, 171-75. Other states, such as New York and South Carolina, had long-standing insolvency relief systems. *Id.* at 105-29, 179-90.

226. S. REZNECK, *supra* note 216, at 91-92.

227. Part of the reason for the hesitancy of the states to enter the field was a fear that states could not constitutionally legislate on bankruptcy. A series of early 19th-century Supreme Court decisions had raised concern in this area. *See* P. COLEMAN, *supra* note 222, at 31-36.

228. R. MCGRANE, *supra* note 212, at 121-22; S. REZNECK, *supra* note 216, at 94-95.

229. J. MCMASTER, A HISTORY OF THE PEOPLE OF THE UNITED STATES FROM THE REVOLUTION TO THE CIVIL WAR 45-46 (1906). *See generally* P. COLEMAN, *supra* note 222 (discussing each state).

230. The vast number of bills enacted in this period makes short summaries difficult. Rather than try, it makes more sense to simply refer readers to a few sources in which this material is described. The best I have found is P. COLEMAN, *supra* note 222. The author provides a state-by-state survey of laws adopted in each jurisdiction during a period of more than 200 years. This survey describes in detail the content of bankruptcy laws, appraisal and minimum value laws, exemption statutes, and imprisonment for debt reforms. *See also* R. MCGRANE, *supra* note 212, at 91-144; S. REZNECK, *supra* note 216, at 85-96; 7 J. MCMASTER, *supra* note 229, at 45-49, 153, 183; H. FARNAM, CHAPTERS IN THE HISTORY OF SOCIAL LEGISLATION IN THE UNITED STATES TO 1860 150-52 (1938).

231. Homestead acts are thought to have appeared for the first time in this period. 2 A. CASNER, AMERICAN LAW OF PROPERTY 810-11 (1954), discusses the Texas act of 1839. Development after 1840 was quite widespread. *See* Dillon, *The Homestead Exemption*, 10 AM. L. REG. 641 (1862); Note, *State Homestead Exemption Laws*, 46 YALE L. J. 1023 (1937). P. COLEMAN, *supra* note 222, also reviews homestead laws.

232. The movement to abolish imprisonment for debt began long before the Panic of 1837. The final phase of this movement, however, occurred in the decade of the 1840's. A number of states abolished debtor imprisonment in this period. Among them were New Hampshire, Vermont, Connecticut, New York, New Jersey, Pennsylvania, Maryland, Delaware, North Carolina, and Georgia. P. COLEMAN, *supra* note 222, at 62, 68, 78, 119, 139, 149-51, 177, 210, 224, 235. The system of imprisonment no longer made sense in an era when commercial interests relied more and more on secured transactions, commercial paper, property attachments, and garnishment. *Id.* at 261-64.

finance appearing in the first half of the nineteenth century called for men to undertake financial risks for the benefit of their families, then setting aside wives' property simply provided another body of exempt assets when the risk taking went sour. The statutes themselves reflected this reality. Almost without exception, women's acts which insulated only slaves or land from attachment appeared in agricultural and Southern states, while the more urban areas adopted broader laws protecting property generally.[233] Since women generally had less property than their husbands, it was logical that legislators would see wives' property as a safe way of adding to the pool of assets insulated from attachment. While these acts may also be justified because they preserved inherited property from rapacious husbands[234] or provided married women with some independent means of support, they also provided some husbands and families with continued access to assets despite bad economic times.[235]

While the connection between the first wave of married women's acts and

---

233. The correlation between the degree of urbanization in 1850 and the content of the first wave of married women's acts is really quite remarkable. Below is a table presenting urbanization values derived from STATISTICAL HISTORY, *supra* note 6, at 24-37. Of those states adopting debt statutes protecting only slaves or real property, only Maryland was heavily urbanized. The Maryland legislation did, however, contain general statements regarding married women's separate equitable estates. Of the fourteen states passing more general legislation, only Alabama, Florida, Michigan, and Wisconsin had less than 10% of their population living in urban areas. Wisconsin was more urbanized than most of the states that passed limited statutes and Florida's act may be explained by Florida's civil law background. *See supra* note 200 (discussing Florida). *See also supra* notes 204-09 (listing state statutes).

	Type of Debt Statute			
State	Slave	Real Property	Property generally	% Urban in 1850
Alabama			x	4.5
Arkansas	x			0
Kentucky	x	x		7.5
Maryland	x	x		32.5
Mississippi	x			1.8
Iowa		x		5.2
Indiana		x		4.5
N. Carolina		x		2.4
Tennessee		x		5.2
Vermont		x		1.9
Connecticut			x	15.9
Florida			x	0
Maine			x	13.6
Massachusetts			x	50.7
Michigan			x	7.3
Missouri			x	11.9
New Hampshire			x	17.0
New Jersey			x	17.6
New York			x	28.2
Ohio			x	12.2
Pennsylvania			x	23.6
Rhode Island			x	55.8
Wisconsin			x	9.5

Alabama's first statute does not fit well into any particular model, since it dealt only with property held before marrige.

234. Such motivation was certainly part of the debate over some married women's acts passed later in the decade. *See* P. RABKIN, *supra* note 2, at 91-98.

235. The earliest statutes did not alter the husbands' management and control of property and a number of the later debt statutes were construed consistently with this view. *See supra* note 211 and accompanying text (describing limitations of acts).

the Panic of 1837 is impossible to dismiss,[236] other factors also must have been at work. The country had seen bad economic times before 1840, while married women's acts were a new legislative response. The fact that many of the acts had general statements adopting the notion of a separate estate for married women's property also suggests a broader purpose. The acts must therefore have been part of a larger evolution in the treatment of women by the law.[237]

2. Statutory Precursors to the Married Women's Acts

A very substantial body of legislation affecting women appeared before 1840. Probate laws were modified, abandoned wives gained greater economic protection, imprisonment of women for debt was largely abolished, and federal land grant policy displayed some desire to protect widows. By 1840 most of the obvious ways of increasing married women's access to property without altering the traditional coverture rules had been exhausted. If further reform was to occur, married women's acts would have to appear.

As previously mentioned, colonial and early territorial and state governments had dramatically simplified conveyancing law and had eliminated primogeniture.[238] Dower rules were swept up in this process, leading many jurisdictions to permit married women to waive dower by deed and separate examination and some jurisdictions to permit dower only in lands actually owned by the husband at death. One might hypothesize that as more women lost access to dower, inheritance rules would change to provide widows greater access to their deceased husbands' personal estates. Such a movement would still give first priority to creditors in distributing the assets of an estate, but it would also increase the likelihood that widows of solvent husbands would emerge with some assets. Probate codes adopted in many states in the first third of the nineteenth century extended the late eighteenth-century reforms in intestacy law. The new codes permitted widows to reject their husbands' wills in favor of the share of the estate mandated by law.[239] The well-known eight-

---

236. The connection has even been discussed in litigation. *See* Kleinert v. Lefkowitz, 271 Mich. 79, 259 N.W. 871 (1935). Some scholars have picked up the connection as well. *See* E. Warbasse, *supra* note 2, at 146-59, 202-05.

237. In fact, a good argument can be made that the 1840's was a decade of reform in a wide array of areas important to women. In addition to the emergence of married women's acts, changes appeared in divorce, child custody, and abortion laws. State statutes that significantly altered the English rule that abortions before quickening were lawful began to appear for the first time in the 1840's. *See generally* Zainaldin, *supra* note 2; J. MOHR, *supra* note 2. Both property reform and restrictions on abortion were consistent with the emerging special sphere of 19th-century women.

238. *See supra* notes 157-82 and accompanying text.

239. E. Warbasse, *supra* note 2, at 72, examines developments in New York, Pennsylvania, and Mississippi. But the changes were far more extensive than that. I have found a number of statutes that gave widows access to a share of their deceased husband's personal estate. Alabama: Act of Dec. 22, 1812, ch. 1, 1812 Ala. Acts 259; Indiana: Act of Jan. 29, 1831, ch. XXIX, 1830 Ind. Acts 209 (1831); Maine: Act of Mar. 23, 1835, ch. 180, 1835 Me. Acts 280; Maryland: Act of Jan. 20, 1798, ch. 13, 1798 Md. Laws (no page); Massachusetts: Act of Feb. 18, 1833, ch. XL, 1833 Mass. Act 547; Michigan: Act of Mar. 30, § 1, 1825 Mich. Terr. Acts 8 (statute providing for extension of debtor exemption statute to estates of husbands); Mississippi: Act of Feb. 9, 1839, ch. 24, 1839 Miss. Laws 33 (statute providing for extension of debtor exemption statute to estates of husbands); New Hampshire: Act of July 2, 1822, ch. XXXXI, 1822 N.H. Laws 30; Ohio: Act of Mar. 23, 1840, § 46, 1839 Ohio Laws 126 (1840); Pennsylvania: Act of Apr. 8, 1833, No. 143, 1832 Pa. Laws 316 (1833) (provides generally for widow's election of dower, but grants elective share of personal estate only when husband's will was drafted before marriage); Act of Apr. 11, 1848, No. 372, 1848 Pa. Laws 537 (full election); Vermont: Act of

eenth-century practice of permitting widows to reject their husbands' wills in favor of dower[240] was expanded to include access to a share of the personal estate. The entitlement was generally the same as the amount provided by intestate succession statutes. Many of these statutes also provided widows with some priority over creditors.[241] The new probate codes did not alter the traditional rules that gave a husband the right to manage his wife's real estate and the right to own outright the personal property the wife brought to the marriage. If all went well financially during the marriage, however, the probate reforms of the early nineteenth century entitled widows to receive a segment of their husbands' personal estates, perhaps regaining some of what they had lost upon marriage. Without directly attacking the coverture rules, probate reform was an avenue for altering slightly the economic impact of the common law.[242]

Early nineteenth-century legislation also eroded some of the other economic consequences of the coverture rules. Abandoned or deserted wives, left by the general content of the common law without either feme-sole status or property, were granted some relief by changes in the divorce statutes[243] or by acts specif-

---

Nov. 15, 1821, ch. 3, 1821 Vt. Acts 55. In addition, case law suggests that other states had long-standing practices of providing widows an elective share of the personal estate. *See* Illinois: McMurphy v. Boyles, 49 Ill. 110 (1868); Kentucky: Trigg's Adm'r v. Daniel, 5 Ky. (2 Bibb) 301 (1811); Tibbs v. Tibbs' Ex'r, 46 Ky. (7 B. Mon.) 112 (1846); Maine: Brown v. Hodgon, 31 Me. 65 (1849); Massachusetts: Crane v. Crane, 34 Mass. (17 Pick.) 422 (1835) (by a progression of statutes starting in 1783, with the final stages in 1816 and 1833); Missouri: Davis v. Davis, 5 Mo. 111 (1838) (by statute adopted in 1825). *See also* 2 C. SCRIBNER, *supra* note 162, at 257-60 (describing long-standing practice in South Carolina, and statutes in Missouri, Georgia, Pennsylvania, Massachusetts, and Vermont). Other material on this issue may be found in M. SALMON, *supra* note 2, at 264-73; 1 C. SCRIBNER, *supra* note 162, at 23-57; Cahn, *Restraints on Disinheritance*, 85 U. PA. L. REV. 139, 141 (1936); J. SCHOULER, DOMESTIC RELATIONS, *supra* note 44, at 279. Friedman erroneously writes that forced share statutes did not appear until the middle of the 19th century. Friedman, *The Law of the Living, The Law of the Dead: Property, Succession and Society*, 1966 WISC. L. REV. 340, 361.

240. *See* M. SALMON, *supra* note 2, at 257-63. Increased ability to gain access to personal property and to obtain cash in lieu of dower also appeared by 1800. *Id.* at 264-73, 298-319.

241. The statutes in Alabama provided priority only for real property, Indiana provided for a small amount of money ($100) to be free of debts, Massachusetts law provided priority to creditors, Michigan and Mississippi used the debtor exemption model as the bases for their statutes, and New Hampshire and Vermont gave the courts authority to make an allowance for a widow from an insolvent estate.

242. These statutes would obviously have limited impact where husbands disposed of their estates by gift before death, or dissipated the assets. But these problems could only be attacked by directly confronting the doctrines of coverture. In addition, there is some evidence that the statutes reflected fairly closely the habits of even the least generous husbands in writing their wills. There are few reported cases in which wives exercised their options to renounce the wills of their husbands. Studies of wills suggest that there was usually no reason to do so. Gundersen & Gampel, *supra* note 143, at 121-24. The wills of men in the Baltimore study generally confirm this, because wives were a frequent primary beneficiary. *See supra* Table 10. Nonetheless, the Dukes County wills also suggest the potential importance of the rules for widows who rejected estates. Petitions for widows' allowances that requested control over some or all of the personal estates were almost always granted. Eight out of the 10 petitions read were granted in *toto*, one in part, and the other result is not known. Though the requested amounts were usually small, they sometimes involved assets of great importance to a struggling widow. One case gave a widow furniture and both family cows; another all the furniture. Some of the decisions involved substantial amounts, such as over $1,200 in personal property in one case and a ship in another. The practice is discussed in Crane v. Crane, 34 Mass. (17 Pick.) 422 (1835).

243. There was a significant rise in the number of divorces in the first third of the 19th century. L. FRIEDMAN, *supra* note 22, at 181-84. While this did not necessarily indicate any increase in domestic dissatisfaction, *see* C. DEGLER, *supra* note 2, at 166, there is little doubt that significant changes occurred in divorce law and practice during the opening decades of the century. Desertion was among the grounds that began to find favor in this period. R. RIEGEL, AMERICAN WOMEN: A STORY OF SOCIAL CHANGE 127 (1970); N. BLAKE, *supra* note 2, at 48-63. A number of states shortened the period of desertion required to obtain a divorce. For example Alabama, which adopted a five year desertion

ically granting them some economic rights against their departed husbands.[244] This trend is demonstrated nicely by a string of Alabama private bills granting deserted wives feme-sole status.[245] The bills emerged in the mid-1820's and disappeared in the 1840's with the passage of general legislation for the benefit of deserted wives. Those husbands not fulfilling the expected obligation to provide their spouses with support began to find that the coverture rules no longer came to their aid. The reforms were not dramatic. They did little more than redefine the meaning of coverture to exclude some husbands who were not providing support for their families. But during the 1840's there was little room left for enhancing the economic status of mistreated wives unless the coverture rules themselves were altered.

The slow development of protections granted to abandoned, deserted, and divorced women in the first decades of the nineteenth century provides a context in which one would expect to find alterations in child custody and support obligations. Indeed, the case law suggests that women gained greater custodial rights during the first third of the century and that the modern "best interests of the child" test emerged more fully in the decade of the 1840's.[246] The change evident in the reported case law finds even more vivid confirmation in the records of one state, Maryland, in which private bill divorces providing for custody by women began to appear after 1820.[247]

Other statutes also singled women out for special treatment.[248] During the

---

statute on March 10, 1803, shortened the period to two years by legislation passed on December 21, 1820. Blake notes that by 1850, Pennsylvania, Connecticut, New Hampshire, Vermont, Rhode Island, Tennessee, Ohio, Kentucky, and Georgia had adopted legislation providing for divorce on the ground of desertion for a time shorter than the seven year presumptive death period. Numerous private divorce bills also were passed. N. BLAKE, *supra* note 2, at 48-56.

The development of Maryland divorce law is quite revealing. A student author discovered 535 private legislative divorces between 1790 and 1850. Three divorces occurred between 1790 and 1800, 30 between 1801 and 1810, 28 between 1811 and 1820, 95 between 1821 and 1830, 295 between 1831 and 1840, and 84 between 1841 and 1849. Maryland adopted a divorce statute on March 1, 1842, displacing much of the demand for private bills. Gilpatrick, Marital Infidelity in Nineteenth Century Maryland 10 n.61 (1982) (unpublished paper) (copy on file at *Georgetown Law Journal*).

244. Other than Alabama, a number of states adopted legislation protecting abandoned married women. Iowa: Act of Jan. 17, 1840, ch. 81, 1839 Iowa Terr. Laws 152 (1840); Kentucky: Act of Feb. 7, 1843, ch. 103, 1842 Ky. Laws 19 (1843); Maine: Act of Feb. 2, 1828, ch. 380, 1828 Me. Acts 1148; Massachusetts: Act of Mar. 16, 1833, ch. 127, 1833 Mass. Laws 693; New Hampshire: Act of Dec. 24, 1840, ch. 573, 1840 N.H. Laws 488; Act of July 2, 1841, ch. 607, 1841 N.H. Laws 533; North Carolina: Ch. 44, 1828 N.C. Laws 25; Ch. 28, 1829 N.C. Laws 27; Rhode Island: Act of June 2, 1841, 1841 R.I. Laws 43; Tennessee: Act of Oct. 18, 1825, ch. 10, 1825 Tenn. Laws 8; Vermont: Act of Nov. 2, 1846, No. 128, 1846 Vt. Pub. Acts 34. *See also* 1 J. BISHOP, *supra* note 27, at 11, 140-42; R. TYLER, *supra* note 204, at 484-86. The statutes were not all designed to adapt to new family roles. Enactments indicating antipathy to early 19th-century Christian communist celibate groups also appeared. *See* Ohio: Act of Jan. 11, 1811, ch. 8, 1810 Ohio Laws 13 (1811) (act provided that a court could grant a woman a share of the estate of a man who joined "himself to any sect whose rules and doctrines require a renunciation of the marriage covenant, or forbid a man and woman to dwell and cohabit together in the conjugal relation"). These trends apparently had their American roots in disputes arising over the legal rights of women deserted during the Revolutionary War. M. SALMON, *supra* note 2, at 132-43.

245. *See supra* note 46 (listing private bills).

246. Zainaldin, *supra* note 2, at 1052-74. This is one of the most interesting and important legal history articles on women and children before 1850.

247. Private bills for divorce in Maryland began awarding custody of children to wives in the 1820's. Between 1823 and 1846, 21% of private divorce bills granted mothers custody of their children. Gilpatrick, *supra* note 243, at 18.

248. The variety of statutes is amazing. Arkansas enacted a tax exemption statute for poor widows. Act of Nov. 21, 1829, 1829 Ark. Terr. Laws 102. Connecticut provided for the support of widows pending the resolution of probate. Act of May 21, 1825, ch. 10, 1825 Conn. Laws 72. This was a fairly

1820's a number of states prohibited the imprisonment of women debtors.[249] Abolition of the practice for men generally did not occur until later.[250] A number of reforms in debt imprisonment were adopted throughout the late eighteenth and early nineteenth centuries.[251] Use of debtor oaths, extension of prison bounds to include fairly large areas beyond the jail walls, prohibition of imprisonment for petty debts, and release of debtors when creditors declined to pay the cost of imprisonment had significantly reduced the importance of debtors' prisons by the 1820's.[252] Nonetheless some women continued to be imprisoned until the practice was prohibited.[253] All these reforms may have been only symbolic, because poorhouses were growing in popularity during the same period.[254] There are some indications, however, that the abolition of debt imprisonment for women may have been related to the early nineteenth-century tendency to provide protection for widows and abandoned women. Such women were more likely to be without means of support than young unmarried women and children. During the first third of the nineteenth century, abandoned and widowed women were more likely to be isolated from extended families or friends than in the previous century. The growth of industrial cities and the opening of the Western territories provided ample occasion for husbands to leave their families or for widows to find themselves without means of support. As the nineteenth century progressed, changes in poor laws dealt with these developments, at least in one jurisdiction, by pro-

---

common reform showing up in many state codes. Some states provided that wives of husbands under guardianship could join in suits for the partition of land. *See* Maine: Act of Feb. 1, 1831, ch. 485, 1831 Me. Acts 1269; Massachusetts: Act of Feb. 21, 1831, ch. 54, 1831 Mass. Laws 569. Many states adopted statutes permitting husbands to join suits previously being pursued by their wives when they were unmarried in order to avoid abatement of the action. *See* Michigan: Act of Mar. 27, 1835, 1834 Mich. Terr. Laws 180 (1835). A number of states also adopted acts permitting wives to insure the lives of their husbands. *See* Maryland: Act of Feb. 23, 1841, ch. 212, 1840 Md. Laws (no page) (1841). Other states provided that certain portions of a husband's estate would be exempt from creditors. *See* New York: Act of Feb. 16, 1824, ch. 44, 1824 N.Y. Laws 32.

249. Coleman provides a great mass of detail on changes in imprisonment for debt legislation. Women were freed of the possibility of debt imprisonment in Connecticut (1826), Georgia (1847), Maryland (1824), Massachusetts (1831), New Hampshire (1831), New Jersey (1818), New York (1828), North Carolina (1823), Pennsylvania (1819), and Vermont (1834). P. COLEMAN, *supra* note 222, at 77-78, 235, 177, 45, 62, 138, 119, 224, 149, 68 (respectively). Georgia was a bit late, but that state had adopted other reforms in the 1820's that virtually removed imprisonment from the list of available creditor remedies. *Id.* at 235.

250. Connecticut (1842), Delaware (1841), Georgia (1858), Maryland (1830), Massachusetts (1857), New Hampshire (1840), New Jersey (1842), New York (1831), North Carolina (1844), Pennsylvania (1842), and Vermont (1838). *See* P. COLEMAN, *supra* note 222, at 78, 210, 235, 177, 52, 62, 139, 119, 224, 151, 68 (respectively). The abolition movement was primarily a Northern enterprise, since Southern states had adopted very effective debtors' oath provisions earlier in the century. Available data suggests that by the time the reform movement got rolling, many more people were being imprisoned for debt in the North than in the South. *See* FIFTH ANNUAL REPORT OF THE BOSTON PRISON DISCIPLINE SOCIETY (1830) (2,742 debt imprisonments in the North and only 35 in the South in 1829).

251. *See* P. COLEMAN, *supra* note 222, at 9-15, 249-68.

252. Randall, *Imprisonment for Debt in America: Fact and Fiction*, 39 MISS. VALLEY HIST. REV. 89 (1952).

253. The SIXTH ANNUAL REPORT OF THE BOSTON PRISON DISCIPLINE SOCIETY 443-447 (1831) reports on a survey of jailers in Massachusetts. Although there were a number of women reported to have been jailed in Boston, a much smaller number had been jailed in other counties. The report's findings are logical as cities were likely to contain more "disconnected" women. These findings are comparable to the findings of a study of poor laws in Maryland. The Maryland study found that outpensions for widowed or deserted women were most common in Baltimore. *See infra* note 255.

254. L. FRIEDMAN, *supra* note 22, at 190-92.

viding outpensions to increasingly large numbers of such women.[255] This development is consistent with other legal developments occurring in the same period. Even in places where divorce for desertion was available, the imposition of substantial waiting periods meant long delays before women could obtain relief. Moreover, statutes like Alabama's, which provided feme-sole status to abandoned wives, would not take care of everyone. It is likely that some deserted women who were unable to work were given poor relief if their husbands left no property behind.

Finally, widows and women who headed families also appeared as something of a protected class in federal land grant policy. While some early land provisions explicitly provided benefits for white males only,[256] other legislation for the benefit of widows of deceased land claimants appeared in the early decades of the century.[257] By the 1840's land grant legislation routinely provided grants for heads of families[258] in addition to widows. Although federal land grant law never fully absorbed the married women's property move-

---

255. C. McKenna, Women, Welfare, and Work in Maryland: A Historical Survey of the First Two Hundred Years 25-29 (1982) (unpublished paper) (copy on file with author). McKenna found a significant increase in the number of women receiving outpensions in the first few decades of the 19th century, particularly in the cities. In addition, a number of private bills were also adopted. The pensions and private bills frequently benefitted women with children.

256. *See* Ordinance of 1785, 28 J. CONT. CONG. 375 (1785); An Act Authorizing the Grant and Conveyance of Certain Lands to the Ohio Company of Associates, 1 Stat. 257 (1792). Much early legislation was gender neutral in terminology, speaking only of "purchasers" or "settlers." It is not presently known whether women, even single women, were able to make use of such provisions. *See* An Act Providing for the Sale of the Lands of the United States, in the Territory Northwest of the River Ohio and Above the Mouth of Kentucky River, 1 Stat. 464 (1796); An Act Making Provision for the Disposal of the Public Lands in the Indiana Territory and for Other Purposes, 2 Stat. 277 (1804). This sort of legislation was sometimes amended to take care of widows and heads of families. *See* An Act to Grant Pre-emption Rights to Settlers on Public Lands, 5 Stat. 251 (1838) (amending earlier pre-emption act passed in 1830). The variety of terminology in the early land acts is staggering. It is fair to suggest that the notion of "family head" grew in prominence as the century unfolded and that early on women unaccompanied by living husbands became eligible to hold the status of "family head."

257. *See* An Act for the Relief of the Refugees From the British Provinces of Canada and Nova Scotia, 1 Stat. 547 (1798); An Act Making Provision for Certain Persons Claiming Lands Under the Several Acts for the Relief of the Refugees From the British Provinces of Canada and Nova Scotia, 2 Stat. 712 (1812) (private bill granting land to a widow and a remarried widow). By 1830 many states had statutes providing that widows would be heirs to their deceased husbands and federal land rode piggyback on these provisions. *See* An Act to Authorize the Investigation of Alleged Frauds Under the Pre-emption Laws and for Other Purposes, 5 Stat. 619 (1843); Johnson v. Collins, 12 Ala. 322 (1847). *See also* 2 J. GALES & W. SEATON, PUBLIC ACTS OF CONGRESS RESPECTING THE SALE AND DISPOSITION OF THE PUBLIC LANDS 548, 557 (1838) (discussing two Commissioner of General Land Office decisions issued in 1831 holding that Pre-emption Act of 1830, 4 Stat. 420, permits widow to act as a settler and to perfect her deceased husband's claim).

258. *See, e.g.,* An Act for Granting Lands to the Inhabitants and Settlers at Vincennes and the Illinois County, 1 Stat. 221 (1791); An Act Regulating the Grants of Land, and Providing for the Disposal of the Lands of the United States, South of the State of Tennessee, 2 Stat. 229 (1803); An Act Giving the Right of Pre-emption, in the Purchase of Lands, to Certain Settlers in the States of Alabama, Mississippi, and Territory of Florida, 4 Stat. 154 (1826); An Act to Grant Pre-emption Rights to Settlers on Public Lands, 5 Stat. 251 (1838). By the 1840's the term "head of family" was used in federal land laws. *See* An Act to Appropriate the Proceeds of the Sales of Public Lands and to Grant Pre-emption Rights, 5 Stat. 453 (1841). This Act was routinely administered to include female heads of families within its ambit. *See* 1 W. LESTER, LAND LAWS, REGULATIONS, AND DECISIONS 360-65 (1860) (Circular to Registers and Receivers of the United States Land Offices issued Sept. 15, 1841, construing Pre-emption Act of 1841 and making it clear that widows and female heads of families included within its terms). In the 1850's married women were still precluded from purchasing most federal lands unless state or territorial law permitted them to do so. *See id.* at 466.

ment,[259] it did reflect the early nineteenth-century trend to provide special treatment for female heads of families and widows.

3. Married Women's Acts, Separate Estate Trust Deeds, and a Glance at Later Developments

Legal developments between 1800 and 1840 tended to protect married women by adjusting the impacts of coverture without altering the central features of married women's status. By 1840 there was a somewhat greater likelihood that legal institutions would attempt to assist a married woman in distress because of death, abandonment, poverty, or divorce. The increase in such legal responses suggests a change in attitude toward those women who fell off the edge of the separate domestic sphere. Whether the cause of the fall was extrinsic to the marital relationship or a rupture of the marriage, recognition began to be given to the particular problems confronting some married women.

While these legislative changes were emerging, the separate equitable estate became more widely understood, and, if the Baltimore will and trust deed study reflects general trends, more widely used.[260] By 1850 the legal strands began to merge. The separate estate, even before it was converted from an equitable contrivance to a statutory entitlement, was often set aside as a special class of property immune from the husband's debts and thus available to sustain the family in troubled times. Because the documents creating separate estates had long been used to insulate property from creditors,[261] thus causing courts of equity to require that husbands in debt seeking access to their wives' separate estates set aside an equity to a settlement to protect a portion of their spouses' wealth.[262] Women had long been the subject of special legislative attention, so that the earliest of the married women's acts could hardly have been perceived as radical. But they were important. Like trust instruments, they generally did not give married women control over the disposition of their separate estates, but they did set the stage for later legislation and judicial decisions that loosened the dispositional constraints.[263]

---

259. The closest federal land law came to a married women's act was the Oregon Donation Act, 9 Stat. 496 (1850), which explicitly granted land to married women. This is the only such piece of legislation I have found. It is interesting to speculate on why federal land law did not reflect the developments on the state level after 1850. It is likely that once state law developed to permit married women to contract, there was little need for federal law to change. Even if married women could not purchase land directly, they could gain title by deed after the federal patent was issued. Many, if not most, of the purchases of land by persons moving to the frontier territories were not directly from the government but from others who had already obtained title to the land. By the time state law had fully developed to permit women to control their own earnings, most of the good federal lands open for private settlement had already been sold. For background and history of federal land sales, see generally Cole, *Cyclical and Sectional Variations in the Sale of Public Lands, 1816-1860*, 9 REV. ECON. STATISTICS 41 (1927); Danhof, *Farm-Making Costs and the "Safety Valve": 1850-1860*, 49 J. POL. ECON. 317 (1941); Gates, *The Role of the Land Speculator in Western Development*, 66 PA. MAG. HIST. & BIOG. 314 (1942).

260. *See supra* notes 59-92 and accompanying text (archival study).

261. L. FRIEDMAN, *supra* note 22, at 220-22. The trust deed study confirms the same fact. *See supra* Tables 12, 13, and 14 and accompanying text.

262. Equity to a settlement had a strong tradition in England in the 17th century. 5 W. HOLDSWORTH, *supra* note 106, at 314; 6 W. HOLDSWORTH, *supra* note 108, at 645. The tradition continued here. *See* N. BASCH, *supra* note 1, at 89-96; 1 J. BISHOP, *supra* note 27, at 449-516; 2 J. STORY, *supra* note 34, at 630-50.

263. Legislation creating a separate estate for married women appeared over a wide range of years beginning in the 1840's and ending after the Civil War. Most of this legislation was enacted before the

If in 1850 there was still debate over whether women could own property without the intervention of a trustee,[264] trustees became unnecessary by 1860 in the North and 1870 in the South. If equity was a changing and sometimes uncertain means for legitimizing married women's control of property, then a legal estate created by statute could substitute nicely. If previously only wealthy men and women could afford to create the documents needed to formalize a separate estate, permit women to retain title to their personal property, insulate married women's property from creditors, and provide for its disposition at death, there was eventually room for language in a simple deed or transfer agreement to automatically serve all these and other ends. Thus, the fact that the early married women's acts fit into a network of mild reforms from 1800 on should not blind us to the significance of their arrival. They were, after all, the earliest examples of a long stream of statutes focusing specifically on the economic consequences of women's property ownership during marriage. The fact that many of the statutes adopted after the mid-1840's contained provisions that may have been intended to do more than insulate married women's property from a husband's debts gave the blossoming feminist movement reason to hope that further reforms would occur.

Despite the well-known connection between legislative petitioning and lobbying by a few women in the late 1840's and the passage of a few of the married women's acts,[265] most of the early acts, modest and conservative in tone, were compatible with prior and contemporary legislation of the most ordinary sort. Even the New York act of 1848,[266] the best known of all the early statutes, was extremely narrow in scope. The first two sections of the act insulated a married woman's property from her husband's debts and also declared that the property "shall continue her sole and separate property, as if she were a single female."[267] The third section provided that property coming to married

---

war. Mississippi, Maryland, Arkansas, Alabama, Michigan, Maine, Massachusetts, Iowa, New York, and Pennsylvania each adopted debt statutes with separate estate provisions. *See supra* notes 207, 209. These acts were passed between 1839 and 1852. Another batch of separate estate statutes was adopted in the following decade in the newly burgeoning territories, and after the war in the Southern states. The states adopting such acts included Michigan: Act of Feb. 13, 1855, No. 168, 1855 Mich. Laws 420; Illinois: Act of Feb. 21, 1861, 1861 Ill. Laws 143; Ohio: Act of Apr. 3, 1861, 1861 Ohio Laws 54; Delaware: Act of Mar. 17, 1865, ch. 572, 1865 Del. Laws 663; Georgia: Act of Dec. 13, 1866, No. 204, 1866 Ga. Laws 146; Vermont: Act of Nov. 21, 1867, No. 21, 1867 Vt. Acts 29; Tennessee: Act of Mar. 2, 1870, ch. 99, 1869 Tenn. Laws 113. These statutes, especially the early ones, did not, on their face, remove the need for a trustee. Sometimes this was accomplished by later statutes, *see* Maryland: Act of May 24, 1853, ch. 245, 1853 Md. Laws 323; statutes cited *infra* note 361; and by court decision. Harris v. Harris, 42 N.C. (7 Ired. Eq.) 111 (1850); Gibson v. Walker, 20 N.Y. 476 (1859); Harding v. Cobb, 47 Miss. 599 (1873); Blood v. Humphrey, 17 Barb. 660 (N.Y. 1854); Burnett v. Hawpe's Ex'r, 25 Gratt. 481 (Va. 1874); Radford v. Carwile, 13 W. Va. 572 (1879); Maiben v. Bobe, 6 Fla. 381 (1855).

264. In New York, there was a 20-year debate over the relationship between equity and married women's estates. *See* P. RABKIN, *supra* note 2, at 61-105. Since equitable language was so often used in the statutes, it was reasonably common for courts to call upon equity precedent to construe the new statute. *See id.* at 125-38.

265. *See* E. Warbasse, *supra* note 2, at 205-36; P. RABKIN, *supra* note 2, at 106-17.

266. Act of Apr. 7, 1848, ch. 200, 1848 N.Y. Laws 307.

267. The act reads in full:

AN ACT for the more effectual protection of the property of married women.

Passed April 7, 1848.

The People of the State of New York, represented in Senate and Assembly do enact as follows:

§ 1. The real and personal property of any female who may hereafter marry, and which she

women in the future "from any persons other than her husband" shall be held "to her sole and separate use, as if she were a single female."[268] It is this "sole and separate use" phrase which later generations have pointed to as break-through language.[269]

The similarity of the statute's sale and separate use phraseology to typical language in equitable instruments and its presence in sections dealing with debt made narrow construction almost inevitable. Equity courts frequently had construed trust instruments containing sole and separate use language but lacking explicit grants of dispositional authority to deny married women the right to contract about or will separate estate assets. The statute only prohibited "disposal" of a separate estate by husbands, leaving intact the range of other restrictions, providing husbands with management authority, and preventing unilateral contractual or testamentary disposal by wives. The statute's primary effect was to create a new category of exempt assets for family use. The special sphere of married women was thus largely confirmed. Assets belonging to married women were to be set aside and insulated from the harsh realities of the commercial world. Married women's property, like married women themselves, was to be specially treated and protected. Indeed, the statute underscores the limited sphere of women by providing that assets received by a wife directly from her husband would not be free from her husband's debts.[270] A married woman was not easily going to become a device for insulating a husband's assets from commercial liability. These were the features of the early married women's act that finally persuaded conservative New York legislators to support the 1848 bill.[271] Neither substantial harm to creditors nor great risks of family divisiveness were likely to result from this sort of legislation.

The growing use of equitable separate estates confirms the same trends. Property management was a fairly new adventure for most married women.

---

shall own at the time of marriage, and the rents issues and profits thereof shall not be subject to the disposal of her husband, nor be liable for his debts, and shall continue her sole and separate property, as if she were a single female.

§ 2. The real and personal property, and the rents issues and profits therof of any female now married shall not be subject to the disposal of her husband; but shall be her sole and separate property as if she were a single female except so far as as the same may be liable for the debts of her husband heretofore contracted.

§ 3. It shall be lawful for any married female to receive, by gift, grant devise or bequest, from any person other than her husband and hold to her sole and separate use, as if she were a single female, real and personal property, and the rents, issues and profits thereof, and the same shall not be subject to the disposal of her husband, nor be liable for his debts.

§ 4. All contracts made between persons in contemplation of marriage shall remain in full force after such marriage takes place.

268. *Id.* § 3.

269. Other states used similar language before New York. *See supra* notes 204-09. Section 1 of Mississippi's 1839 act provided that married women become "seized and possessed of any property, real or personal, . . . in her own name, and as of her own property." Maine's 1844 statute mirrors the Mississippi language. Michigan's 1844 statute provides that after marriage, property shall be the "estate of such female after marriage to the same extent as before marriage." Despite the fact that Massachusetts was the scene of much early female agitation on both women's and slavery issues, its first married women's act was very narrow in content. It basically permitted the establishment of trusts through ante-nuptial agreements and limited the husband's control of the trust assests.

270. This provision in section 3 was judicially expanded to void conveyances made by wives directly to their husbands. White v. Wager, 25 N.Y. 328 (1862).

271. *See* E. Warbasse, *supra* note 2, at 218-29.

From receipt of inheritances in the eighteenth century, through development of income by unmarried women, to management of middle class family incomes by some married women by the middle of the century, the domestic sphere and the separate equitable estate were stretched to accommodate the presence of money and women's new role in the family. But the stretch was narrow. Independent commercial endeavors by married women were not included on the mid-century reform agenda. Married women were singled out for special treatment, their assets were subject to dispositional constraints established by others, and their property was largely controlled for the benefit of their families. The appearance of both married women's acts and separate estate instruments suggests that a married woman's property was largely viewed as a family resource or as a safeguard for a wife upon her husband's death or departure, not as mercantile or speculative wealth. Married women were still homemakers, and the gradual emergence of dispositional authority over separate property reflects women's greater activity in the home economy more than their widespread entry into the business world.

But the statutes and separate estates also reflect myriad contradictions. The very device used to confirm women's special sphere—the separate estate insulated from the husband's debts—created a wedge in the coverture bastion, and confirmed for women a small degree of independence from their marriage partners. Indeed, the contradictions go deeper. Despite the prohibition on debt exemption for property coming to a wife from her husband, the New York statute, and others as well, created an incentive for husbands to use their wives' new insulation from creditors to hide assets. While a conveyance to a third party was necessary to avoid the restrictions on intramarital exchanges, extramarial property coming to a married woman was not so constrained. Those with wealth were certainly going to take the bait[272] by using straw party exchanges or causing extramarital property to be held in their wives' names. The separate equitable estate was available for similar use. The statutes and separate estates themselves contained the sorts of contradictions that would lead later reformers to urge more similar treatment of men's and women's property by refining the definitions of property owned by husbands and wives and equalizing the availability of these assets to creditors.[273]

III. The Historical Blanket

In her address "The Wrongs of Woman" before the 1850 Salem, Ohio, Women's Convention, J. Elizabeth Jones, like speakers at earlier gatherings, spent much of her time on law and Blackstone.[274] Jones noted that many women had conflicting feelings about their position. Some, she said, do not know they

---

272. *See* P. Rabkin, *supra* note 2, at 126-37; S. Breed, Conflicts of Interest: The Evolution of Married Women's Property Rights in Nineteenth Century New Hampshire (1982) (unpublished paper) (copy on file with author).

273. Breed's paper on women's property rights in New Hampshire, *supra* note 272, lays out this story in wonderful detail. Disputes over use of the marital property exemption eventually led to more equitable treatment and creditor access. This was the pattern followed nationally as the century unfolded. For later married women's acts, *see infra* note 361.

274. The Salem, Ohio 1850 Women's Rights Convention Proceedings 52-62 (R. Audretsch ed. 1976) [hereinafter Ohio 1850 Women's Rights Convention].

are "robbed of [their] rights," others feel "weak and dependent."[275] Others fear "to expose their own situation" or "dread of seeming to be out of their sphere" and therefore masculine.[276] Still others "have no sense of injury" because "all their wants have been duly supplied" or "labor for a mere pittance because they are women."[277] After making a lengthy critique of the inequities of the common law and contending that women should obtain the right of suffrage at the impending Ohio Constitutional Convention, Jones concluded:

> We but ask that our equality in point of rights be acknowledged; we ask that none shall strive to obliterate or deface the image and superscription our Creator stamped upon our souls. I am aware that the great mass of women in this country have no sympathy with the views I have expressed. I wish it were otherwise. I wish they could be led to see their true position, and be made to understand that the gallantry and devotion of man is offered them in lieu of a recognition of their rights, and that it is only in a few rare cases he approaches and converses with them as equals, as being as fully rational, intelligent and morally accountable as himself, endowed with the same rights and clothed with the same duties.
>
> But I will not further extend my remarks. I have already said enough to secure the disapprobation which is always bestowed upon a woman who thinks and speaks for herself. I have said *more* than enough for those women who are contented with their rose-covered chains and gilded prison-bars; and I could hope that I have said something to encourage to earnest action those of my sex who feel that no length of legislation can sanction and sanctify the wrongs that have been inflicted upon them; that no social usages, however time-honored, can justify the oppressions they have been compelled to endure; that no religious creed, however sanctimonious its supporters, can find the least excuse for the inequality in the church.[278]

This statement is a remarkable indication of the social pressures felt by one of the more radical of mid-nineteenth-century women.[279] Why would a public

---

275. *Id.* at 54.
276. *Id.*
277. *Id.*
278. *Id.* at 62 (emphasis in original).
279. Jones' speech also roundly condemned slavery and applauded by name many of the prominent feminists of her time. After 1840 she consistently turned up at important gatherings of feminists and abolitionists. Jones lobbied for the adoption of the 1861 Ohio married women's property act, lectured on health and hygiene (common interests of the feminists of her era), and for a time edited the Anti-Slavery Bugle with her husband. 2 E. JAMES, NOTABLE AMERICAN WOMEN 1607-1950, at 285-86 (J. James & P. Boyer eds. 1971).

At one point in her speech, Jones noted that she may choose not to

> exercise my right so to [vote], after it is accorded to me; indeed all who know my sentiments in relation to Constitutions and government, and you, Madam President, may not, and all whom I address may not; but that is no reason why others should judge for us, of the propriety and expediency of our so doing; *that* is a right I insist upon exercising for myself, and these 'Daniels' who have 'come to judgment' have me-thinks, assumed an air of wisdom, as foreign to their own characters as it is derogatory to us.

OHIO 1850 WOMEN'S RIGHTS CONVENTION, *supra* note 274, at 58 (emphasis in original). At first blush, this seems to be a statement that Jones would not vote because of social constraints on the role of

woman of 1850 castigate limitations on her social role while confessing to the unwillingness of most women to follow her lead?

A brief examination of the historical literature on women in the first half of the nineteenth century reveals a series of changes relevant to the mid-century emergence of married women's acts. By 1800 the importance of married women as active participants in the family was more widely recognized. Symptoms of the changes surfaced in a number of ways. Women became more involved in religious and social service activities, more literate, and more deeply involved in raising and educating their children. At the same time that married women were assuming greater importance in the family and in family-related social organizations, single women were beginning to leave home for reasons other than apprenticeship or marriage. Employment opportunities beckoned in teaching, domestic service, and the mills. As the nineteenth century unfolded, these trends accelerated, creating very substantial differences in the roles of single and married women. For many women an active unmarried life was followed by marital domesticity. Married women's acts reflected this situation. The significant features of the acts did not reject married women's separate domestic sphere, but recognized the importance of women as caretakers of children and family resources.

A. THE POST-REVOLUTIONARY WAR ERA

J. Elizabeth Jones did not invent women's conflict over public and private spheres. Recent literature suggests such tension appeared at least as early as the Revolutionary War era. Both Norton and Kerber contend that the Revolutionary War was a catalyst for some redefinition of women's social position. They note that the pre-Revolutionary War domestic role of women took on a different content by the end of the eighteenth century[280] due to participation of women in the Revolutionary War political scene through economic boycotts,[281] home production,[282] and political correspondence and discussion.[283] By coping with the inevitable disruptions caused by conflict, political disagreements, and absent spouses, women sensed they were participating in important cultural developments.[284] Kerber finds that at the core of cultural values "a concensus developed around the idea that a mother, committed to the service of her family and to the state, might serve a political purpose."[285] Norton agrees, writing that the "war necessarily broke down the barrier which seemed to insulate women from the realm of politics, for they, no less than men, were caught up in the turmoil that enveloped the entire populace."[286] While Norton states that domesticity was no longer denigrated and the feminine sphere

---

women. It is probably, however, a statement typical of the radical Garrisonian wing of the Abolitionists, who perferred withdrawal from participation in a union with slavery to creation of an anti-slavery political party or to work with the existing parties. For a history of the Garrisonians, *see* W. WIECEK, SOURCES OF ANTISLAVERY CONSTITUTIONALISM IN AMERICA, 1760-1848 228-48 (1977).

280. M. NORTON, *supra* note 2, at 155-299; L. KERBER, *supra* note 2, at 157-288.
281. M. NORTON, *supra* note 2, at 157-63; L. KERBER, *supra* note 2, at 35-39.
282. M. NORTON, *supra* note 2, at 163-70; L. KERBER, *supra* note 2, at 41-45.
283. M. NORTON, *supra* note 2, at 170-77; L. KERBER, *supra* note 2, at 73-85.
284. M. NORTON, *supra* note 2, at 195-227; L. KERBER, *supra* note 2, at 455-67.
285. L. KERBER, *supra* note 2, at 283.
286. M. NORTON, *supra* note 2, at 297.

no longer subordinate,[287] Kerber prefers a less egalitarian portrayal of Republican Motherhood as a "concept that legitimized a minimum of political sophistication and interest, and only of a most generalized sort."[288] Both writers agree, however, that in contrast to the subservient role of women before 1770, the Revolutionary War era provided women with a new egalitarian vocabulary, a few well-known, if ridiculed, radical figures,[289] and a potential for limited participation in public events. The stage was set for a cultural redefinition of the married women's separate sphere.[290]

Evidence of conflict over the relationship between a married woman's public and private life appeared in a number of ways in the years just before 1800. Since public debate by women was still the extraordinary exception,[291] the evidence is largely confined to other areas. Kerber and Norton both investigated private correspondence and diaries in their efforts to sort out the effects of the Revolutionary War.[292] Just as women in the nineteenth-century tended to correspond with other women in intimate, supportive ways,[293] literate women of the eighteenth-century have left us a historical record of their friendships.[294] Female friendships and correspondence were symbolic of the larger possibilities for group female activity,[295] and consistent with the already noted tendency of women (and men) to will property to other women.[296]

Despite the basically private nature of the separate sphere, women began to participate in some worldly activities before the eighteenth-century was complete. Petitioning, particularly by widows, arose.[297] Female societies and auxiliaries to male voluntary groups appeared during the war to organize home production, nursing, and fund-drives.[298] These groups continued in a different guise after the war. Female religious, reform, and service societies proliferated in the last two decades of the century.[299] Although most female societies dealt with matters closely related to the domestic sphere[300] or religious concerns,[301] the societies inevitably led women to make public choices. The economic panics in the late eighteenth century[302] and the appearance of impoverished wo-

287. *Id.* at 298.

288. L. KERBER, *supra* note 2, at 285.

289. For a description of public reaction to Mary Wollstonecraft's VINDICATION OF THE RIGHTS OF WOMEN (1792), see L. KERBER, *supra* note 2, at 224-25, and M. NORTON, *supra* note 2, at 251-52.

290. *See* M. NORTON, *supra* note 2, at 228-55 (discussing emergence of the "reverance of self" during post-war period); L. KERBER, *supra* note 2, at 73-113 (discussing women's emerging role outside the home both during and after war). *See also* C. DEGLER, *supra* note 2, at 191-92 (attributing women's separate sphere in 18th century to society's new emphasis on freedom and individualism).

291. *But see* L. KERBER, *supra* note 2, at 99-110 (describing women's campaign to raise funds for troops during war, commonly referred to as "Philadelphia Project").

292. M. NORTON, *supra* note 2, at 309-14; L. KERBER, *supra* note 2, at 289-93.

293. C. DEGLER, *supra* note 2, at 144-50.

294. N. COTT, *supra* note 2, at 185-99.

295. M. NORTON, *supra* note 2, at 105-09.

296. *See supra* Tables 9 and 10.

297. L. KERBER, *supra* note 2, at 85-99 (petitions included requests to cross enemy lines to join husbands and claims for property left behind).

298. *Id.* at 99-105.

299. *Id.* at 111-13.

300. *Id.* at 111. Women and children in distress were of particular concern.

301. *Id.*

302. *See* P. COLEMAN, *supra* note 222, at 18-19 (economic problems even led to adoption of short-lived national bankruptcy act in 1800).

men and children, prostitution, town slums, and alcohol abuse created opportunities for many groups of middle and upper class women to become involved with social concerns.[303]

The subtle post-war changes in attitudes toward domesticity are also revealed by improvements in female literacy and education.[304] If, as both Kerber and Norton suggest, the post-war family was assigned a substantial new role in the education of children in appropriate civic virtues, then women themselves had to be literate.[305] There is no doubt that girls continued to receive lesser educations than boys long after 1800 and that expressions of support for gender equality in education met with strong disapproval.[306] Yet female academies emerged after the war and flourished with the growing public education movement after the turn of the century.[307] Literacy rates for women increased after 1780 until the first literacy census, taken in 1850, showed little difference between literacy rates for men and women.[308] Reading and writing by women exploded around the turn of the nineteenth century.[309] Ladies magazines, as well as fictional and religious reading and writing, became an important part of many women's lives, though histories and the like were

---

303. J. FURNAS, THE AMERICANS: A SOCIAL HISTORY OF THE UNITED STATES, 1587-1914 313-17 (1969).

304. L. KERBER, *supra* note 2, at 198-99.

305. *Id.* at 199-200; M. NORTON, *supra* note 2, at 256-57. Norton adds that the exigencies of the just-completed war also suggested the need for educated women on the homefront. M. NORTON, *supra* note 2, at 256.

306. L. KERBER, *supra* note 2, at 193-221; M. NORTON, *supra* note 2, at 263-72.

307. L. KERBER, *supra* note 2, at 198-205.

308. *Id.* at 193. School enrollment among whites age 5-19 also displayed little difference by gender in 1850. About 59% of boys and 53% of girls were in school. STATISTICAL HISTORY, *supra* note 6, at 369-70. Very little work on female literacy rates in the early 19th century has been done, but what has been done suggests that vast changes occurred between 1800 and 1850. While the proportion of women signing wills in the 18th century was fairly stable at about 40%, K. LOCKRIDGE, *supra* note 28, at 38-41, men's signature rates were substantially higher. Lockridge found some evidence for literacy increases among females in the decades just before 1800. *Id.* at 38. But by 1850 differences between men and women appear to have virtually vanished. L. SOLTOW & E. STEVENS, THE RISE OF LITERACY AND THE COMMON SCHOOL IN THE UNITED STATES 157-58 (1981). *See also* GOODSELL, PIONEERS OF WOMEN'S EDUCATION IN THE UNITED STATES 1-12 (1931); 1 T. WOODY, *supra* note 9, at 159-60 (during colonial period percentage of illiteracy was greater among women than men).

309. It is perhaps not accidental that women's wills began to appear in greater numbers after women became more literate. The will studies produced some additional data on literacy. The recorded Baltimore wills noted whether wills were signed or marked. Similar notations in the Dukes County recorded wills were found to be unreliable. All the wills were probated in 1810 or later, so one would expect fairly high signature rates. The small size of the sample makes hard conclusions difficult, but over 60% of women's wills were signed. Surprisingly, no significant change appeared over time.

Women's Will Literacy (Baltimore)

Probate Year	Signed	Marked	Not Known
1810	3	5	5
1825	14	5	0
1840	23	16	4
1846	34	13	1

If the 1810 and 1825 data are merged, 63% (17/27) of the wills where information was available were signed. Similarly, 66% (57/86) of the 1840 and 1846 wills were signed. The signature rate for males among the wills read from all four of the sample years was 83% (20/24) with nine unknown. These results are compatible with the very high (90%) literacy rates of an 1860 sample of married women. L. SOLTOW & E. STEVENS, *supra* note 308, at 156, and the lower literacy rates (less than 50%) found among female will writers in the late 18th century. K. LOCKRIDGE, *supra* note 28, at 38-39.

still thought of as men's fare.[310] The movement to literacy was not without opponents fearful of introducing worldly concerns into women's lives or causing impure desires among the ladies.[311] These concerns were particularly important in an era that witnessed a substantial increase in courting freedoms and premarital pregnancy rates.[312] But female novel reading also found philosophical support in the contemporaneous rise of romanticism.[313]

With all this activity in reading, writing, and education, women began to enter teaching in new ways. The jump from household tutoring of one's own offspring to the education by unmarried women of a group of children was made by some, opposed by others, but reasonably steady in its growth.[314] By the end of the century, a middle or upper class married woman was more likely than her mother to be literate, a participant in a voluntary society or religious group, and aware of a link between her own role and the larger political culture.[315] And her female offspring were more likely to be teachers.[316]

Another link between women's domestic role and larger social activities was found in religion. The domesticity of women was linked to morality and virtue long before the Revolutionary War.[317] Women outnumbered men in churches from very early colonial days, and this trend became very noticeable by the turn of the nineteenth century.[318] Although teaching and eventually mill work provided avenues for unmarried women to leave the home, religion provided that opportunity for their mothers. Some religious groups, particularly the Quakers, provided opportunities for substantial female participation and even for religious travel.[319] Nineteenth-century revivals and camp meetings, religious fervor, religiously-based social service groups, and the Second Great Awakening had their roots in the late eighteenth century.[320] The conflicts in women's domestic role that emerged in the nineteenth-century egalitarian religious and communal movements were largely defined by the stresses

---

310. *See* L. KERBER, *supra* note 2, at 235-64 (explaining importance of reading fiction to women in the early republic); N. COTT, *supra* note 2, at 64-74 (tracing common theme of domesticity in literary works appealing to women).

311. L. KERBER, *supra* note 2, at 239.

312. C. DEGLER, *supra* note 2, at 20; L. KERBER, *supra* note 2, at 245; M. NORTON, *supra* note 2, at 51-60; Smith, *Dating the American Sexual Revolution: Evidence and Interpretation*, in THE AMERICAN FAMILY IN SOCIAL-HISTORICAL PERSPECTIVE 321 (M. Gordon ed. 1973). Smith found that premarital pregnancy rates peaked in the later 18th century and troughed in the later 19th. *Id.* at 321-22.

313. *See* N. COTT, *supra* note 2, at 76-83 (romanticism conveyed in literature influenced women to wish for ideal mate); K. MELDER, *supra* note 2, at 34-47.

314. M. NORTON, *supra* note 2, at 290-94; C. KAESTLE & M. VINOVSKIS, EDUCATION AND SOCIAL CHANGE IN NINETEENTH CENTURY MASSACHUSETTS 26-27 (1980); W. BUTTS & S. CREMINS, A HISTORY OF EDUCATION IN AMERICAN CULTURE 246-47 (1953) [hereinafter BUTTS & CREMINS].

315. M. NORTON, *supra* note 2, at 289. Norton has compiled some fascinating data on education trends over time, suggesting that among notable women, the proportion with some advanced education jumped from 18% for those born before 1770 to 65% for those born after 1770. *Id.* at 288-90.

316. *Id.*

317. *See* C. DEGLER, *supra* note 2, at 289-303 (women organized as the Social Purist to control sexuality and became involved in religion and churches).

318. N. COTT, *supra* note 2, at 126-28.

319. C. DEGLER, *supra* note 2, at 302; K. MELDER, *supra* note 2, at 77-92; M. NORTON, *supra* note 2, at 126-32.

320. *See* C. DEGLER, *supra* note 2, at 298-305 (during second awakening most converts were women and women played active role in reform organizations, religious groups, and antislavery movement); J. FURNAS, *supra* note 303, at 327-32 (discussing tactics of the leaders of the Great Awakening and camp meetings); W. MCLOUGHLIN, REVIVALS, AWAKENINGS, AND REFORM 98-140 (1978).

of the post-war era. The use of special sphere ideology to permit movement of women into religious activities related to, but outside, the home suggested both the potential for larger change and the role limitations that undoubtedly guided most married women's lives.[321]

But for most married women the combination of agricultural stability and the late eighteenth century concern over teaching young children appropriate social behavior led to concentration on child rearing rather than on activities outside the home.[322] It is, in hindsight, not surprising that the turn of the nineteenth century would see the blossoming of the domestic sphere in all of its contradictions.[323] Even though modern notions of child rearing and new techniques of manufacturing were emerging, families were still confronted with a child-rearing experience vastly different from our own. Fertility rates were extraordinarily high, with live births numbering more than twenty-five percent of the child-rearing age population.[324] The rates peaked around the turn of the century and declined thereafter.[325] The average household size was over five and one-half persons, and did not fall below five until the end of the nineteenth century.[326] Despite the large households, infant mortality rates were

---

321. *See* C. DEGLER, *supra* note 2, at 298-327 (discussing emergence of "separate sphere" for women in 19th century; protection of home and preservation of its moral character justified women's active role in outside world).

322. N. COTT, *supra* note 2, at 84-98.

323. Cott's use of the title "Bonds of Womanhood," which she explains on the first page of her book, *supra* note 2, is an appropriate signal of the potential for domesticity to be both an uplifting and binding experience.

324. Miscarriages, still births, and abortions are excluded from this high figure. It is plausible to suggest that during 1800 over one-third of the white women ages 15-44 became pregnant. Birth rates declined throughout the 19th century, with substantial declines starting after 1810. Data from STATISTICAL HISTORY, *supra* note 6, at 49, fills this table:

Year	Birth Rate for White Women 15-44 (Live births/1000 population)
1800	278
1810	274
1820	260
1830	240
1840	222
1850	194
1860	184
1870	167
1880	155
1890	137
1900	130
1930	87.1
1960	113.2
1970	84.1

325. W. GRABILL, C. KISER & P. WHELPTON, THE FERTILITY OF WOMEN IN AMERICA 1-24 (1958).

326. Household size is now well under three. Putting together material from the STATISTICAL ABSTRACT, *supra* note 13, at 45, and STATISTICAL HISTORY, *supra* note 6, at 41, yields the following table:

high, perhaps averaging fifteen percent.[327] Maternal mortality was also high.[328] The high birth rate and its attendant risks made the occurrence of pregnancy, the completion of childbirth, and the process of child rearing the focus of an enormous amount of attention. These events caused awe and fear, delight and depression with much greater frequency than today. The possibilities for tragedy were remarkably greater than we can imagine. Cott put it mildly when she wrote that "the arrival of another child posed anxieties."[329]

B. THE EARLY NINETEENTH-CENTURY

Such anxieties produced a rich variety of responses as the nineteenth century unfolded. Reproductive rates declined more noticeably after the turn of the century.[330] There seems to be little doubt that some form of birth control operated to produce the substantial decline in fertility between 1800 and 1850.[331]

Year	Average Household Size
1790	5.79
1850	5.55
1860	5.28
1870	5.09
1880	5.04
1890	4.93
1900	4.76
1930	4.11
1970	3.14
1979	2.78

327. Data from Massachusetts suggests that from 1850 until after 1900, about 15% of newborns died. Earlier rates were presumably of a similar magnitude. The somewhat lower mortality rates for the 1850's, however, suggest the possibility that rates rose contemporaneously with the decline of midwifery. There is need to explore the relationship between death rates and male entry into the birth process. Were midwives more sanitary? STATISTICAL HISTORY, *supra* note 6, at 57:

Infant Mortality For Massachusetts 1851-1970
(per 1000 live births)

Time	Rate
1851-54	131.1
1855-59	122.9
1860-64	142.5
1865-69	146.3
1870-74	170.3
1875-79	156.3
1880-84	161.3
1885-89	158.5
1890-94	163.2
1895-99	153.2
1900-04	141.4
1905-09	134.3
1910-14	116.7
1915-19	100.2
1920-24	78.7
1925-29	67.6
1970	16.8

328. Even in 1915 the rate was over 60 per 10,000 live births. The rate did not begin to fall until after 1930. Presumably 19th-century death rates were at least as high. STATISTICAL HISTORY, *supra* note 6, at 57.

329. N. COTT, *supra* note 2, at 91.

330. *See supra* notes 324 and 325 and accompanying text.

331. C. DEGLER, *supra* note 2, at 181-96, 210-16. The decline in birth rates was also attributed to improving economic status, while the primary method of birth control was probably abstinence.

Abortion appears to have been a common practice of the middle class by the 1840's when the first antiabortion laws appeared.[332] The variety in early nineteenth-century communal groups probably mirrored the tensions over childbirth present in the larger community. Some sects were celibate,[333] others openly espoused birth control, and a number adopted communal living patterns and carefully controlled programs of sexual access to handle the problems of childbirth.[334] Some groups, like the Mormons, encouraged childbirth.[335] But whether the community chose celibacy, birth control, abstinence, communal child care, or high reproduction rates, control over family formation and fertility was central to each group's self-image.

Such control is a major theme in Degler's scholarship. He argues that the period from 1780 to 1830 witnessed the emergence of the modern American family characterized by marriage based on affection and respect, greater influence and autonomy for women in the home, child rearing and home maintenance as the wife's primary role, devotion of a larger amount of parental energy and resources to young children, treatment of young children as persons different from adults and needing special treatment, love, and solicitude, and smaller family size.[336] Degler and Cott suggest that the emergence of the modern family both created an opportunity for women to increase their influence within the family and established limitations on the ability of women to work in the public sphere.[337] As the separate domestic sphere grew to define middle class as well as wealthy women's roles,[338] it both legitimated domestically related activity outside the home and created a new standard for defining deviance.[339]

---

332. *See* J. MOHR, *supra* note 2, at 16-18, 86-118. Abortion probably gained in importance when mechanical means of terminating a pregnancy became preferred over taking of poisons. Abortion frequency apparently rose in the 1840's. *Id.* at 46-85. Use of instruments probably increased during the mid-19th century. *Id.* at 61, 65. In addition, infanticide probably fell off in importance around the turn of the 19th century. *See* Dellapenna, *The History of Abortion: Technology, Morality and Law*, 40 U. PITT. L. REV. 359, 392-400 (1978). It is also interesting to note that knowledge of fetal development was improving in this period. As early as the 1820's some were writing that quickening did not represent the beginning of vitality but the point where fetal growth permitted movement to be felt. W. BECK, ELEMENTS OF MEDICAL JURISPRUDENCE 199-203 (1823). Such knowledge was important to the development of the antiabortion laws. It permitted the emerging professional male doctors to argue that laws permitting abortion until quickening did not comport with either morality or medical knowledge.

333. The group best known to most 20th-century persons is the Shakers, but a number of other celibate groups existed. The most prominent during the 19th century may have been the Harmony Society. *See* K. ARNDT, GEORGE RAPP'S HARMONY SOCIETY, 1785-1847 (1971); 1 WOMEN AND RELIGION IN AMERICA 47-48, 60-66 (R. Ruether and R. Keller eds. 1981) [hereinafter RUETHER & KELLER].

334. RUETHER & KELLER, *supra* note 333, at 48-50. The Oneida Perfectionists led by John Humphrey Noyes also believed in birth control, and communal sexual access and child rearing. The Owenites, led by Robert Dale Owen and Fanny Wright were also involved in birth control and multiple partners. They were notorious in the 1830's. *Id.* at 49-50, 66-69.

335. *Id.* at 49, 69-70.

336. C. DEGLER, *supra* note 2, at 8-9.

337. *Id.* at 28; N. COTT, *supra* note 2, at 201.

338. Cott suggests that by 1830 many of the attributes of a modern family had affected middle class as well as upper class women. N. COTT, *supra* note 2, at 185. Degler goes further and argues that even lower class women were affected by the ideology of the separate sphere. C. DEGLER, *supra* note 2, at 111-43 (discussing role of Afro-American and immigrant women in 19th century).

339. *See* C. DEGLER, *supra* note 2, at 298-327 (discussing 19th century women's roles outside the home as justified by duty to act in world in order to protect morality). Degler finds that little opposition to female academies emerged while strong disapproval surfaced to women entering college. *Id.* at 309-11. Degler also describes the gradual evolution in patterns for selection of marriage partners from parental arrangements before the Revolutionary War to romantic selections with parental veto power

The rapidity of change in definitions of domesticity and deviance in the first decades of the nineteenth century is difficult to measure. But there is now little doubt that the definition of women's sphere was under greater strain in 1840 than it was at the turn of the century. The trends of the late eighteenth century in education and social services accelerated, with a large number of female academies opening after 1810.[340] Colleges open to women began to appear.[341] Social and moral reform groups emerged in great profusion, spurred by urban growth, agricultural efficiency, trade and commerce, and economic dislocations and panics.[342] Literary societies, religious charitable societies, missionary groups, associations to aid the poor, temperance societies, and societies for reform in education, prisons, and treatment of the insane emerged in greater numbers.[343] Many women found a moral foundation for their work in religion. Although some male religious leaders debated the appropriate scope of women's activities, women often found support among male religious colleagues for activities that neither challenged male leadership nor endangered appropriate feminine decorum.[344] The generally accepted notion that the virtue and morality of women was superior to that of men made religious groups a natural milieu in which to develop female leadership.

Many of the prominent women of the early nineteenth century found their power writing or speaking about issues of moral, religious, or ethical significance. Francis Wright came from Great Britain in 1824 with General LaFayette, met with many prominent Americans, helped establish the colony of Nashoba to aid in the emancipation of slaves, and participated with Robert Dale Owen in the New Harmony Community. In 1830 she openly advocated free thinking and infidelity, free public education for all persons, birth control, divorce, and married women's law reform.[345] She was a radical, outside the American mainstream of moral and social reform movements. When the abolitionist Grimke sisters[346] emerged from their Quaker background to speak in 1836 before women in New York and in 1837 before mixed audiences in Massachusetts, they could already point to Wright's prior speaking tours, as well as the actions of a number of other women, as the real groundbreaking. Harriet Martineau, another English woman, gave abolitionist lectures from 1834 to 1836.[347] Mixed prayer meetings occurred in the 1820's,[348] and female educators like Emma Willard, Mary Lyon, and Catherine Beecher established fe-

---

by the end of the 18th century. *Id.* at 9-25. Courtship became much less constrained, and perhaps 10% of women gave birth to children less than nine months after their marriage. *Id.* at 20. Women were acting with fewer constraints during courtship, but using marriage as the escape from social disapproval.

340. N. COTT, *supra* note 2, at 115-25. *See* BUTTS & CREMIN, *supra* note 314, at 239-51.

341. K. MELDER, *supra* note 2, at 115-18; C. DEGLER, *supra* note 2, at 310-15. After three years of separate treatment, Oberlin permitted women to enroll with men in 1837. C. DEGLER, *supra* note 2, at 310.

342. *See generally* B. BERG, *supra* note 2.

343. K. MELDER, *supra* note 2, at 77-92, 118-21.

344. *Id.* at 88-94; A. DOUGLAS, THE FEMINIZATION OF AMERICAN CULTURE 17-139 (1977).

345. K. MELDER, *supra* note 2, at 59-61.

346. Sarah Grimke migrated to Philadelphia from South Carolina in 1821 and her sister, Angelina, followed in 1829. K. MELDER, *supra* note 2, at 156, 192. *See also* G. LERNER, THE GRIMKE SISTERS FROM SOUTH CAROLINA: PIONEERS FOR WOMEN'S RIGHTS AND ABOLITION (1971).

347. K. MELDER, *supra* note 2, at 146.

348. *Id.* at 73-75.

male academies, raised funds, and lectured on women's education before 1835.[349]

The decades of work in female voluntary societies, moral reform groups, and religious activities blossomed into significant participation in the abolitionist movement in the early 1830's. Female antislavery societies emerged by the early 1830's, and women solicited signatures on antislavery petitions beginning in 1835.[350] The egalitarian rhetoric of the Revolution, the Enlightenment, and Jacksonian Democracy began to be used publicly by women. The expansion of suffrage opportunities for white men created an opportunity for radical abolitionists and feminists to focus America's attention on the appropriate role of women. Less than a decade after the Grimkes' controversial tour, discussion in mainstream newspapers on the similarity between slavery and the status of married women was possible.[351]

These developments were given added impetus by fairly constant economic developments. Economic historians generally argue that per capita wealth increased very moderately between 1800 and 1840, but none are willing to state that great increases in wealth occurred.[352] The incidence of economic contractions beginning in 1792, 1819, and 1839,[353] the fairly constant presence of debtor reform movements and legislative activity,[354] the lack of internal sources of capital,[355] the reliance on cotton as a major source of external trade,[356] and the enormous internal improvement debts of the 1830's suggest a growing but struggling economy, heavily reliant on the world economy for support. While certainty on these issues is not yet possible, it is logical that the collapse of European trade before the 1819 and 1839 panics, the stress of economic dislocations, and the changes in employment patterns, job descriptions, and family roles would occur side-by-side with reform movements, religious and moral revivals, radical agitation, and strong public debates.

It is tempting to conclude that the 1840's blossoming of public debates on slaves and women completely explains the arrival of married women's acts.

---

349. *Id.* at 107-15. Mary Lyon founded Mount Holyoke College in 1836. *Id.* at 111.

350. *Id.* at 176-82.

351. An anonymous article entitled *Wives and Slaves: A Bone For the Abolitionists to Pick* was published in 17 DEMOCRATIC REV. 264 (1845) and reprinted in other papers. *See* N. C. Standard, Oct. 22, 1845, at 8, col. 1.

352. For literature on the 19th-century economy see P. TEMIN, *supra* note 213: Gallman, *Gross National Product in the United States, 1834-1909*, in OUTPUT, EMPLOYMENT AND PRODUCTIVITY IN THE UNITED STATES AFTER 1800 3 (National Bureau of Economic Research ed. 1966); Lebergott, *Labor Force and Employment, 1800-1960*, in OUTPUT, EMPLOYMENT AND PRODUCTIVITY IN THE UNITED STATES AFTER 1800 117 (National Bureau of Economic Research ed. 1966); Parker & Whartenby, *supra* note 6; Goldsmith, *The Growth of Reproducible Wealth for the United States of America From 1805 to 1950*, in INCOME AND WEALTH OF THE UNITED STATES: TRENDS AND STRUCTURE 247 (S. Kuznets ed. 1952); Andreano, *Trends and Variations in Economic Welfare in the United States Before the Civil War*, in NEW VIEW ON AMERICAN ECONOMIC DEVELOPMENT 131 (Andreano ed. 1965); A. JONES, *supra* note 14.

353. P. COLEMAN, *supra* note 222, at 19; S. REZNECK, *supra* note 216, at 51-100; P. MCGRANE, *supra* note 212, at 1-42.

354. Coleman's book on debtors and creditors exhaustively catalogues the developments. *Supra* note 222.

355. Large captial inflows from overseas funded much of the 1830's boom. *See* North, *The United States Balance of Payments 1790-1860*, in TRENDS IN THE AMERICAN ECONOMY IN THE NINETEENTH CENTURY 573, 585-87 (National Bureau of Ecomonic Research ed. 1960).

356. *See* P. TEMIN, *supra* note 213, at 152.

Indeed, there is some truth in the causal link because women actively petitioned for the married women's acts adopted in New York and Pennsylvania during the later years of the decade.[357] But as we now know, the story of women's property acts is much more complex than a simple tale about progressive ideals winning out over blind forces of reaction. As Degler forcefully reminds us:

> [t]he women's movement throughout the 19th century left untouched the great mass of women, married and unmarried. At no time were more than a few thousand women actively involved in the feminist or suffrage causes. The great preponderance of women either had nothing to do with feminism, or actually scorned it as unnecessary and wrongheaded.[358]

The public exposure of contradictions in separate sphere ideology by communal groups, abolitionists, and feminists led many women to fight rather than accommodate change. The generally middle class nature of the reform movements[359] spoke peripherally to working class women, many of whom preferred the ideal image of a comfortable separate sphere at home to the potentially deviant life of a radical and frequently unmarried feminist. The tracing of reform movements therefore should not blind us to the obstacles the reformers confronted. Rather, one must hypothesize that shifts in the nation's economy, job map, family structure, agricultural productivity, banking practices, and trade structures would be mirrored by piecemeal, one step to the left, one step to the right, reforms in legal norms, and that changes would reflect generally held perceptions about women's appropriate sphere of influence.

CONCLUSION

And, of course, that is exactly what my archival and legal research suggests. Though by 1850 married women performed new legal roles within the family, property law still singled them out for special treatment and confirmed their primary role as family participants. Developments in non-property areas also confirm the patterns Degler and Cott describe. The culture's growing concentration on wifely domesticity suggests that family law reform should have been vigorous by mid-century. Indeed, by the 1840's divorce, custody, and adoption law were conforming to new notions of family and childhood development. Divorce was more prevalent and easier to obtain, women gained custody of children more frequently than in 1800, and adoption was becoming an accepted practice. Similarly, the arrival of the first antiabortion statutes in the 1840's signaled the importance attributed to married women's maternal

357. E. Warbasse, *supra* note 2, at 205-37. Later acts, such as those in Ohio and Massachusetts, were also supported by women. *Id.* at 265-71.

358. C. DEGLER, *supra* note 2, at 306. Degler provides an insightful chapter on why it took so long to gain women's suffrage. He discusses the reasons why suffrage was perceived as a radical step, including women's wide acceptance of the separate sphere, the perception that voting and politics threatened the family, and the substantial opposition to the amendment by women. *Id.* at 328-61. Cott also reminds us that the separate sphere was for many an acceptable level of accomplishment. N. COTT, *supra* note 2, at 197.

359. *See* C. DEGLER, *supra* note 2, at 341 (some radicals realized that giving women the vote would give middle-class women more influence but would do little to help lower class women).

role.[360] While the coexistence of married women's property acts and antiabortion laws seems strange to modern feminists, they were compatible developments in a reform era accepting domesticity as a primary ideology for rationalizing changes in legal norms.

Although organized women's groups certainly had more influence on property law after 1850, the domestic role model also gained additional authority by the Victorian era. The appearance of narrow married women's acts and abortion restrictions in the 1840's was mimicked in the 1870's by the virtually simultaneous adoption of legislation protecting married women's earnings[361] and imposing severe restrictions on the dissemination of birth control information and devices.[362] Even women's suffrage was not achievable without the aid of moral reformers, protective labor supporters, and an ideology lauding the capacity of women to make finer moral judgments than men.[363] Not until very recent times has the legal system taken seriously the notion that equality norms rather than special treatment norms should govern the outcomes of gender-based disputes. The basic thrust of Thomas Herttell's 1837 argument[364] in favor of an early version of the New York married women's act can be substituted for arguments made decades later in favor of protective labor legislation and women's suffrage:

> But have not women as much prudence and judgement to save and manage their property, after as before marriage? Has marriage deprived them of their senses and their wits, as well as of their rights of property which they possessed before marriage? With the additional incitement of maternal solicitude for the well-being of her children, has not a married woman even more inducement to the discreet appropriation of her property to their maintenance, than an unmarried woman, who has no such immediate motive for the prudent and due exercise of the right to possess and dispose of her property as she may please, and as by law she is authorized to do? And with such additional, natural, and maternal obligations, is not the discreet use of her property by a married woman, for the maintenance of her children,

360. *See supra* notes 330-35 and accompanying text (discussing abortion, birth control, and the maternal role).

361. The 1870's saw the arrival of statutes protecting earnings of married women in a number of states. Earnings statutes appeared first in the 1850's, but most of the acts were passed later. Among the states adopting earnings acts were Massachusetts: May 5, 1855; Kansas: Feb. 11, 1858 (Territorial Legislation); New York: Mar. 20, 1860; Alabama: Dec. 31, 1868 (free trader statute); Illinois: Mar. 24, 1869; Iowa: Apr. 14, 1870; Ohio: Mar. 30, 1871; Pennsylvania: Apr. 3, 1872; Delaware: Apr. 9, 1873; Kentucky: Apr. 11, 1873; Arkansas: Apr. 28, 1873; Indiana: Mar. 25, 1879. A few states also adopted limited earnings statutes, which only protected married women who were no longer living with their husbands. Pennsylvania: May 4, 1855; Minnesota: Ch. 49 (1860); Iowa: Mar. 12, 1866; Vermont: Nov. 19, 1866; Delaware: Mar. 28, 1871; New Jersey: Apr. 5, 1878. Bishop also discusses codes adopted in the 1860's and 1870's containing earnings provisions in California, Georgia, Illinois, Maine, Maryland, Massachusetts, and Mississippi. 2 J. Bishop, *supra* note 27, at 490-91, 507, 512, 520, 524, 530, 536-37.

362. *See generally* C. Dienes, *supra* note 2.

363. Indeed, moral reformers and supporters of special workplace legislation for women, not equality minded feminists, were the major backers of women's suffrage. *See* C. Degler, *supra* note 2, 328-61. After the Suffrage Amendment was adopted, the Women's Party quickly became a radical fringe, a model to be picked up later in the century. *See* E. Flexner, *supra* note 1, 271-345 (1959).

364. Thomas Herttell, along with John Neal and Elisha Hurlbutt, was among the major male figures urging reform of women's law in New York from 1835 on.

> as much more to be relied on, than that of her husband, as maternal is more strong, constant, and unconquerable, than paternal affection? Are not the cases rare in which unmarried women waste their property? And are not the instances numerous in which men spend their fortunes in riot, intemperance, extravagance, and every species of irregularity and dissipation? And when their pecuniary resources are exhausted or impaired, is it not a common practice for men to endeavour, by marriage, to obtain the property of young, inexperienced, unsuspecting, and credulous females, with a view to the means by which to gratify their avarice, or to continue their dissolute habits of life? Does not the existing law hold out inducements to mercenary marriages, by furnishing the means by which worthless fortune-hunters are enabled to effect their iniquitous purpose? Is not the alleged law, therefore, the source of the vicious and immoral practices to which it prompts; and the cause of all the injustice and misery to which married women become the devoted victims? And is not that law justly characterized by the vice, immorality, injustice, and misery consequent on its existence and operation?
>
> That the affirmative are the true answers to the above questions, is as certain as that such answers prove conclusively, that married women's property would be safer in their own hands, and more certainly applied to family maintenance, than it now is, when given indiscriminately to good and bad husbands, to be disposed of as they please, or as their good or bad habits may happen to direct.[365]

The property reforms of the 1840's should not be perceived as an attack on coverture law. Though the seeds of later reforms were planted by the first wave of married women's property acts, married women's separate domestic sphere was not seriously challenged by their adoption. The legal changes of the mid-nineteenth century recognized that the women's role within the family had changed to encompass greater control over the raising of children and the disposition of family wealth. But not until this century would such increased participation in the family lead to broad participation in the political and economic fortunes of the culture at large.

---

365. Herttell, Remarks Comprising in Substance Judge Herttell's Argument in the House of Assembly of the State of New York in the Session of 1837 in Support of the Bill to Restore to Married Women the Right of Property as Guaranteed by the Constitution of this State, at 57-58 (1839) (copy on file at *Georgetown Law Journal*).

Radical Reconstruction and the Property Rights of Southern Women

By Suzanne D. Lebsock

In the summer of 1870 the editors of the *Revolution*, the New York–based woman-suffrage weekly, printed a buoyant letter from an unidentified Georgia feminist. "The cause of Woman's Rights in our state has undergone a wonderful reform within the last few years," she reported, and she went on to detail the property rights secured to married women under Georgia's Reconstruction constitution. A married woman was empowered to own property in her own name, and her husband could not sell it without her consent.[1] For northern feminists this was good news, proof that the southern states were not incorrigible where the rights of women were concerned.

Revisionist historians have likewise taken approving notice of the women's-rights measures that appeared in the Reconstruction constitutions, for here is evidence of Radical Republican sensitivity to yet another enlightened reform of the day. The reforms were in fact something less than enlightened, enacted by men who were hardly feminists. But on the face of it the Radical record was impressive. From late 1867 to early 1869 Radical-dominated conventions created new constitutions for ten states; in nine of them the "wonderful reform," the guarantee of property rights to married women, was made part of the fundamental law.[2]

For all their prominence in the Reconstruction constitutions,

[1] *Revolution*, VI (July 7, 1870), 10.

[2] The other major constitutional provision pertaining to the status of women was South Carolina's first legal provision for divorce. The legislature passed the divorce law in 1872. That law was repealed by the Redeemers in 1878, and divorces were made unconstitutional in 1895. Divorce was not again legalized in South Carolina until 1948. See John R. Millar, Jr., "A Study of the Changes of Divorce Legislation in the State of South Carolina" (unpublished Ph.D. dissertation, Florida State University, 1954).

Ms. Lebsock is a graduate student in history at the University of Virginia.
She acknowledges with gratitude the comments of Lawrence D. Cress, Daniel J. Flanigan, Joseph F. Kett, Charles W. McCurdy, Willie Lee Rose, and Brent Tarter on successive versions of the essay.

however, the place of these provisions in Reconstruction histories has been confined to honorable mention on running lists of those "other significant reforms" instituted by the Radicals. The meaning assigned the married-women's clauses in particular has thus hinged very much on the historian's interpretation of Radical reform in general. To James S. Allen, a Marxist who read Reconstruction as a bourgeois revolution, the women's provisions were added testimony to "the thoroughgoing nature of the democratic overturn" in the postwar South. A more moderate appraisal was offered by Kenneth M. Stampp, who placed the expansion of women's rights among the "modest" and "long overdue" reforms that appeared in "essentially conservative" constitutions. For Jack B. Scroggs the women's-property sections were instances of carpetbagger constitutional reform in the Atlantic seaboard states.[3]

Of the three, Stampp is nearest the mark. For the South as a whole the reforms were indeed modest, if modest is the proper term for constitutional provisions that in most places amounted to very little but in others meant a great deal. It was only in three of the older, eastern states that the married-women's clauses of 1868 made a difference. The *Revolution*'s Georgia correspondent was justifiably enthusiastic, for in Georgia, and in North Carolina and South Carolina as well, the Reconstruction constitutional conventions launched the women of their states on the road toward legal equality with men, at least on the matter of property rights and obligations. Farther to the west, however, the Reconstruction conventions did very little, partly because there was less to be done. In six states, Alabama, Arkansas, Florida, Louisiana, Mississippi, and Texas, some rights had been granted married women well before the Civil War, and with the exception of a minor revision in Louisiana, the 1868 conventions merely gave constitutional status to principles already firmly established in the statutory law. The Montgomery *Daily Advertiser* gave an apt assessment of the Alabama convention's work; the section containing the women's-property provision presented "nothing particularly worthy of notice."[4] As of 1868 the property rights granted women varied greatly among these six states. What they had in common was that few additional powers

[3] Allen, *Reconstruction: The Battle for Democracy (1865–1876)* (New York, 1937), 118–19; Stampp, *The Era of Reconstruction, 1865–1877* (New York, 1965), 172–73; Scroggs, "Carpetbagger Constitutional Reform in the South Atlantic States, 1867–1868," *Journal of Southern History*, XXVII (November 1961), 484–85. See also Robert Cruden, *The Negro in Reconstruction* (Englewood Cliffs, N. J., 1969), 99, 108; Rembert W. Patrick, *The Reconstruction of the Nation* (New York, London, and Toronto, 1967), 148.

[4] Montgomery *Daily Advertiser*, December 13, 1867. The *Advertiser* was extremely hostile to the convention, however, and this statement should probably be read as "nothing inviting ridicule" or "something deserving of praise."

were granted women during the entire period of Republican rule.[5] Virginia, meanwhile, did not budge. A proposed women's-property section was tabled in the closing days of Virginia's 1868 convention, and nothing further was done until the General Assembly took action in 1877.[6]

The Reconstruction period, in other words, was but one phase of an ongoing process of reform that had begun in Mississippi in 1839 and continued by fits and starts in the southern states (and in the North as well, beginning in the 1840s) well into the present century.[7] The reforms enacted by the Radicals, significant as they were for the southeastern states, continued an established southern tradition of legislation, a tradition of progressive expansion of the property rights of married women for utterly nonfeminist purposes.

Feminists, not ones to quibble over the motivation behind the passage of the reforms, continued to hail each new property law as a victory for the cause. "Alabama has given married women equal property rights with their husbands," Kentuckian Mary B. Clay told the 1884 convention of the American Woman Suffrage Association. "I . . . recommend to the Southern women particularly the petitioning for property rights, because pecuniary independence is one of the most potent weapons for freedom, and because that claim has less prejudice [than woman suffrage] to overcome."[8] Southern feminists knew that property rights were far more easily secured than political rights, and they hoped to use economic equality as a stepping-stone to the more elusive right to vote.

Their optimism was ill-founded, however. Married-women's-property reforms stood a chance for the same reasons that woman suffrage did not—there was something in them for men, and they had nothing to do with feminism. While it was true that a sequence

[5] The exceptions are noted below.

[6] Virginia. *Debates and Proceedings of the Constitutional Convention . . . 1867* (Richmond. 1868), 58–59, 554–55; Richmond *Dispatch*, April 14, 1868; Virginia, *Acts and Joint Resolutions . . . 1877–78* (Richmond, 1878), 333–34.

[7] On the possible origins of the Mississippi law see Elizabeth G. Brown, "Husband and Wife—Memorandum on the Mississippi Woman's Law of 1839," *Michigan Law Review*, XLII (June 1944), 1110–21. Historical treatments of married-women's-property law are few. The best is Kay E. Thurman, "The Married Women's Property Acts" (unpublished LL.M. thesis, University of Wisconsin School of Law, 1966). See also Mary R. Beard, *Woman as Force in History: A Study in Traditions and Realities* (New York, 1946); John D. Johnston, Jr., "Sex and Property: The Common Law Tradition, the Law School Curriculum, and Developments Toward Equality," *New York University Law Review*, XLVII (December 1972), 1033–92; Peggy Rabkin, "The Origins of Law Reform: The Social Significance of the Nineteenth-Century Codification Movement and Its Contribution to the Passage of the Early Married Women's Property Acts," *Buffalo Law Review*, XXIV (Spring 1975), 683–760.

[8] Quoted in Elizabeth C. Stanton *et al.*, eds., *History of Woman Suffrage* (6 vols., New York and Rochester, 1881–1922), IV, 407–408. Alabama women, however, did not have equal property rights at that time.

of laws in any given state made wives the legal equals or near equals of their husbands, this equality was a by-product and not the intended object of reform. Southern women were granted property rights by virtue of chivalry, of familial self-interest, and of hard times. And this was as much the case in the Reconstruction constitutional conventions, carpetbaggers notwithstanding, as with any previous time and place.

South Carolina's 1868 constitutional convention was a showcase for chivalry. James M. Allen was the delegate who introduced the resolution calling for a married-women's-property clause, and as the measure's most vigorous spokesman, Allen set the terms of the debate: "I appeal to you who have lived here all your lives, and seen women suffer from the hands of the fortune hunters; the plausible villains, who, after securing the property of their wives, have squandered it in gambling and drinking; a class of men who are still going about the country boasting that they intend to marry a plantation, and take the woman as an incumbrance." Benjamin F. Randolph echoed Allen: "It is a common thing for men to talk about marrying rich wives, and to marry them for no other purpose than to squander their property." In the brief debate next to nothing was said about women. The discussion was rather a recital of the failings of men, a sequence of testimonials on the necessity of a law to prevent the "profligate," the "drunkard," the "villain," the "scoundrel," from raking off the fortunes of innocent women.[9]

Under the law as it then stood scoundrels had their opportunities. South Carolina, like most of the United States, had adopted the English common law as its basis for the legal relationships between husband and wife.[10] For single women the common law held no special restrictions on property ownership and control; a "feme sole" had the same rights as men. For married women it was a very different story. In theory marriage was a fair exchange in which the

[9] South Carolina, *Proceedings of the Constitutional Convention of South Carolina . . . 1868* (2 vols. in 1, Charleston, 1868), I, 64–65; II, 783–88; quotations on pp. 785–86.

[10] Texas, however, retained a few features of the Spanish civil law. Louisiana law, an adaptation of the Napoleonic Code, was entirely outside the common-law tradition. To reduce a very complex set of laws to a simple statement, in Louisiana the property inherited alone by either spouse remained her or his separate property, but any other property acquired during the marriage belonged to the community. The management of both the community property and the wife's property was assumed to be the husband's, although the wife could bring action to empower her to manage her separate estate. Louisiana law was known for the relative economic security it provided the wife. The 1868 constitutional provision outlawed the use of the "tacit mortgage," a loophole that had permitted the husband to evade creditors by claiming a prior, unrecorded debt to the wife. See Harriet S. Daggett, *The Community Property System of Louisiana, with Comparative Studies* (Baton Rouge, 1931).

woman relinquished her property and her autonomy and received in return protection and support from her husband. The wife at marriage surrendered the control of her real estate and the ownership of her personal property to her husband. The wife's services, and therefore her wages if she were gainfully employed, also belonged to the husband. Although the wife was empowered to act in her husband's stead under certain circumstances, she had no standing as an independent economic agent. She could make no contracts, she could not sue or be sued in her own name, and she could not execute a valid will. For his part, the husband was obliged to pay his wife's premarital debts, and he was instructed to support her and their minor children according to his means. Otherwise, the common law licensed the husband to do as he pleased with his wife's property. The law assumed that the husband would exercise his prerogatives for the couple's mutual benefit, but no legal remedy was available to the wife whose husband abused his power. A woman's property was at the mercy of her husband, and if he fell into debt her property was at the mercy of her husband's creditors.[11]

There were loopholes. Alongside the common law there had grown a second legal system, that of equity, which offered some relief to the cautious and wealthy few. By means of either a marriage contract or the establishment by will or deed of an estate in trust the property of a married woman could be freed from the control of her husband and from the claims of his creditors. If the terms of the settlement were liberal, the woman, acting through trustees, assumed all the powers ordinarily associated with property ownership. These equitable estates, however, required foresight and legal expertise, their administration was often complicated and expensive, and there was no absolute guarantee that the woman's rights would be upheld if her title were challenged in court. The vast majority of married women possessed no separate equitable estates; the minority who did lacked perfect security. Equity remained an uncertain escape route for the well-to-do.[12]

[11] For a detailed treatise on the legal status of women in the nineteenth century see Joel P. Bishop, *Commentaries on the Law of Married Women Under the Statutes of the Several States, and at Common Law and in Equity* (2 vols., Boston, 1873–1875).

[12] Mary Ritter Beard in *Woman as Force*, 131–33, asserted that equity effectively mitigated the harshness of common-law doctrine and that statutory reform in the law of married women's property was therefore virtually unnecessary. More research is needed, but the current work of Carol Elizabeth Jenson of the University of Wisconsin–La Crosse, "Equity Jurisdiction and Married Women's Property: The Situation in Ante-Bellum America" (paper presented at the Conference on the History of Women, St. Paul, Minnesota, October 1975), suggests that Beard gave equity far too much credit. My own survey of Virginia wills and deeds indicates that equitable settlements were extremely rare before 1820. Thereafter,

Most married women, therefore, took their chances under the common law. In the worst of circumstances the woman was the helpless victim of her husband's malevolence, incompetence, or plain bad luck in business. In the best of circumstances, at least as far as the law was concerned, she was economically passive. For some women this passivity was in itself exasperating. South Carolinian Mary Boykin Chesnut protested in a diary entry of 1862, "We had our share of my father's estate. It came into our possession not long after we were married, and it was spent for debts already contracted. . . . That being the case, why feel like a beggar, utterly humiliated and degraded, when I am forced to say I need money? . . . What a proud woman suffers under all this, who can tell?"[13]

The delegates to the South Carolina constitutional convention of 1868 were not, however, troubled by wounded female pride. They posed a simple problem—it was too easy for conniving men to exploit vulnerable women—and they proposed a simple solution: Permit the wife to retain title to her property; exempt that property from liability for the debts of her husband; let her sell her property should she need ready cash to support herself and her children; and let her bequeath it as she should see fit. Neither the problem nor the solution was that simple, as became apparent later, but the new married-women's-property provision did offer women some protection from fortune hunters and other varieties of unreliable manhood.

It also protected the blood relations of the woman, and this was no small matter. As long as women's hold on property was insecure delegates faced the prospect of having their own accumulations wasted or sold off to satisfy the claims of creditors. As Allen put it, "We are ourselves poor men now, but should we succeed in saving a little property, and leaving it to our wives, it is not a comfortable thought that when we are dead, some villain may marry our widows, and squander what we have saved for the care and comfort of those we love." Charleston representative Robert Carlos DeLarge

settlements were more commonplace, but they usually did not give the wife active control over her estate. Thurman, "Married Women's Property Acts," 12, suggests that the early statutory reforms were prompted in part by a Jacksonian desire to give poorer women the same kind of protection that had been available to wealthier women through equity. I have seen no direct evidence of this for the southern states, but British reformers frequently pointed out the class bias of equity. See for example "The Property of Married Women," *Westminster Review*, XC (October 1868), 179–80. For a discussion of connections between the merger of common law and equity and married-women's-property reform in New York see Rabkin, "Origins of Law Reform."

[13] Chesnut, *A Diary from Dixie*, edited by Ben Ames Williams (Boston, 1949), 186.

added, "We also propose to secure the hard earnings that may be bequeathed by a mother on her death bed to a child, so that it cannot be taken and squandered by the husband or father of the child."[14] Men wanted their property to remain in the family. The protection of widows and daughters and granddaughters increased the odds that legacies would pass intact from one generation to the next.

Few of the South Carolina delegates opposed so well intended a measure on principle, although there were some reservations on details. DeLarge was afraid that the married-women's provision as proposed left too much room for fraud. If some men were so unscrupulous as to marry women strictly for their money, some would no doubt be unashamed to use the new law to elude creditors. A debtor might make an eleventh-hour transfer of property to his wife in order to defraud his creditors of their just claims to that property. DeLarge suggested the loophole be closed by requiring women to register with the local officials all property that was legitimately their own. Once DeLarge and other doubters were persuaded that a registration system was unnecessary, the married-women's-property section was approved with only eight dissenting votes.[15]

Although there was nothing in the speeches of the South Carolinians to indicate it, it appears that the married-women's provisions of 1868 were as much a response to the critically widespread indebtedness of the postwar years as to the evil designs of fortune hunters. There was, after all, nothing new about fortune hunting or in the awareness that it was a problem. "The impression now seems to prevail to a very great extent in South Carolina," a state senator had told his colleagues in 1855, "that protection of the property of the wife is due her, because, forsooth, there is a class of fortune hunters over the country .... I have been rather inclined to the

[14] South Carolina, *Proceedings of the Constitutional Convention . . . 1868*, II, 786, 784.

[15] *Ibid.*, 783–88. The new provision read: "The real and personal property of a woman, held at the time of her marriage, or that which she may thereafter acquire, either by gift, grant, inheritance, devise, or otherwise, shall not be subject to levy and sale for her husband's debts: but shall be held as her separate property, and may be bequeathed, devised, or alienated by her the same as if she were unmarried: *Provided*, That no gift or grant from the husband to the wife shall be detrimental to the just claims of his creditors." South Carolina, Constitution of 1868, Art. XIV, Sec. 8, Francis N. Thorpe, comp., *The Federal and State Constitutions, Charters, and Other Organic Laws* . . . (7 vols., Washington, 1909), VI, 3304; cited hereinafter as Thorpe, comp., *Constitutions*. Clyde and Sally Griffen have found evidence that husbands did at times use married-women's-property laws to defraud creditors. See their "Family and Business in a Small City: Poughkeepsie, New York, 1850–1880," *Journal of Urban History*, I (May 1975), 328–30.

opinion that there is a good deal of this in our State."[16] The South Carolina legislature was not sufficiently moved, however, to pass the married-women's bill of 1855. What seems to have made the difference in 1868 was not that the Radicals were more tender-hearted than their predecessors (although they may have been) but rather that in hard times a married-women's-property act became a significant new form of debtor relief. It was no coincidence that the first southern laws to secure the property of married women were enacted, from Florida to Texas, during and in the wake of the panics of the late 1830s and the severe depression that followed.[17] In Georgia and North Carolina, and initially in South Carolina, the married-women's-property provisions of 1868 were packaged with homestead exemptions in articles designed to relieve distressed property owners of both sexes.[18]

Homestead exemptions and the married-women's laws were functionally similar, for both protected families from the economic disaster that might, in the absence of the laws, stem from a husband's indebtedness. While the married-women's laws exempted whatever property the wife brought to the marriage from liability for her husband's debts, homestead provisions protected part of the property belonging to the head of the household, male or female. No matter how deep his or her indebtedness, a portion of shelter, land, and implements, amounting to a stipulated maximum value, was set aside for the continued use of the family. A creditor could not touch it. The family's assets might be considerably reduced, but its members could not be thrown out of their home, and the head of the household would remain in possession of sufficient property to allow the making of at least a meager living.

In the postwar South unscrupulous husbands presented a lesser danger to the fortunes of women than did the general economic

[16] Columbia *South Carolina Legislative Times*, December 7, 1855.

[17] Act of February 15, 1839, Mississippi, *Laws of the State of Mississippi . . . 1839* (Jackson, 1839), 72–73; Texas, Constitution of 1845, Art. VII, Sec. 19, Thorpe, comp., *Constitutions*, VI, 3561; Act of March 6, 1845, Florida, *The Acts and Resolutions, Passed by the Legislative Council . . . 1845* (Tallahassee, 1845), 24–25; Act of December 8, 1846, Arkansas, *Acts and Resolutions . . . of the General Assembly . . . One Thousand Eight Hundred and Forty-Six* (Little Rock, 1846), 38–39; Act of March 1, 1848, Alabama, *Acts . . . of the General Assembly . . . 1847* (Montgomery, 1848), 79.

[18] Georgia, *Journal of the . . . Constitutional Convention . . . 1867 and . . . 1868* (Augusta, 1868), 356–57; Georgia, Constitution of 1868, Art. VII, Thorpe, comp., *Constitutions*, II, 838; North Carolina, *Journal of the Constitutional Convention . . . 1868* (Raleigh, 1868), 219–20, 249–50; North Carolina, Constitution of 1868, Art. X, Thorpe, comp., *Constitutions*, V, 2818–19; South Carolina, *Proceedings of the Constitutional Convention . . 1868*, I, 64–65. In South Carolina the married-women's section was separated from the homestead-exemption clauses in committee.

crisis that threatened women and men together. Under the common law, of course, the property of married women was particularly vulnerable, and convention speakers did not hesitate to use the peculiar plight of married women to arouse sympathy for general measures of debtor relief. No story had more potential for evoking compassion and an outraged sense of justice than that of the woman who was impoverished by virtue of debts that she herself had not contracted. William L. Goodwin worked the story for all it was worth in urging a stay law on the Georgia convention: Fatherless children were "turned houseless and homeless on the charities of this cold-hearted world, forced from a once happy fireside, to roam our country over in search of daily labor, that their few scanty earnings may yet render comfortable that poor old silvery-headed mother . . . . She now is reduced to abject poverty, suffering not only for the luxuries, but for the actual necessaries of life. All for what?" Goodwin demanded. "To satisfy liabilities not of her own contraction—liabilities in the hands of that class of men which now holds our unhappy people in its grasp."[19] Married women, at least those who were married to debtors, had everything to gain from any general law that protected the indebted.

At the same time, the general demand for debtor relief probably did much to promote the approval of laws specifically for the protection of the property of married women. A married-women's law shielded the husband while it shielded the wife; a man who was about to lose his own holdings could rest in the knowledge that in the future his wife's property would be secure. And if given retroactive force, the married-women's-property provisions could function in the manner of a stay law. The provisions as written were models of ambiguity. Did they apply to women who were already married? Did they apply to property acquired by the wife before the provisions took effect? If a court answered yes on both counts, then here was a major new form of emergency economic relief; any creditor who had relied on a woman's property to satisfy her husband's debts would be left in the lurch. It is not clear whether any of the conventions intended the provisions to be interpreted in this way.

The Georgia convention, in any case, lost no time. No sooner were the major debtor-relief measures approved—a section to abolish imprisonment for debt and one to suspend most debts contracted before June 1865 as well as the homestead–married-women's article—than they were hurried off to military governor

[19] Charleston (S. C.) *Daily Courier*, February 11, 1868.

George Gordon Meade with an urgent request that they be given immediate effect by the general's order. Meade complied.[20] Georgia Republicans evidently believed the homestead–married-women's article to be one of the most popular they had devised. As the day approached for the election to ratify the new constitution the front page of Atlanta's Republican *New Era* carried the text of the article, issue after issue. Political considerations, it appears, had their part in the bestowal of property rights on married women.

The only relevant question that was not considered was what the new property laws might mean for the status of women. The makers of the 1868 constitutions of Georgia and the Carolinas leaped to provide the kind of protection that suited the immediate crisis. They did not stipulate what women might do with their property once they gained title to it. Future courts and legislatures were left to sort out the implications of constitutional clauses that were designed not to free the woman but to restrain the husband's creditors.

Elsewhere in the South the Reconstruction constitutional conventions exhibited the same protective impulse. With the exception of Virginia the remaining southern states had long since exempted the property of the wife from liability for the husband's debts, and the Reconstruction conventions sealed the case by elevating the earlier laws to constitutional status. In addition, three states built safeguards for women into their homestead-exemption clauses. Men in Alabama, Florida, and Texas were forbidden from selling their homesteads without the wife's consent.[21] None of the conventions outside South Carolina, North Carolina, and Georgia granted married women any new powers over their property.

Indeed, few traces of feminism were evident in any of the conventions. James M. Allen, the chief sponsor of the married-women's-property provision in South Carolina, was asked point-blank whether he was also in favor of woman suffrage. "I am not," Allen declared, adding with some irrelevance, "nor do I believe in that class of persons who carry poodle dogs, and follow in the trail of mere fashion . . . ."[22] Allen demonstrated in that single sentence how simple it was for a delegate to be for women's property rights and against women's political rights, and in this he stood with the majority of delegates across the South. The treatment accorded

[20] Georgia, *Journal of the . . . Constitutional Convention*, 392–406, 603–605.

[21] Alabama, Constitution of 1868, Art. XIV, Sec. 2, Thorpe, comp., *Constitutions*, I, 152; Florida, Constitution of 1868, Art. X, Sec. 1, *ibid*., II, 717; Texas, Constitution of 1868, Art. XII, Sec. 15, *ibid*., VI, 3613.

[22] South Carolina, *Proceedings of the Constitutional Convention . . . 1868*, II, 785.

woman-suffrage proposals in the constitutional conventions showed just how far removed the advocacy of married-women's-property laws could be from any sympathies with feminism.

The Arkansas convention was already in progress when Radical delegate Miles L. Langley wrote Susan B. Anthony of his intention to propose a woman-suffrage amendment. For this, he announced, "I expect to suffer reproach and slander, if nothing worse." What Langley suffered, when his time came, was ridicule. Jesse N. Cypert greeted Langley's proposal with a tongue-in-cheek proviso that "no man who has a wife shall be allowed to vote when the right is exercised by his wife." Cypert explained, "I hold, sir, that I am a Union man; and that, not only so far as the government is concerned, but as regards the relations of families. I do not wish to assist in inaugurating any system that will be likely to give rise to secession in families." Robert S. Gantt then rose in support of Cypert's proviso: "There are, in all families, two articles, neither of which more than one member of the family ought to wear; the one is, the breeches; I will not mention the other. (Laughter)." Hilarity fast turned to acrimony as the issue of woman suffrage was lost amid accusations and counteraccusations of disloyalty and ungentlemanly behavior. The entire matter was eventually tabled, and the convention took up other business. Langley wrote again to Susan B. Anthony to report the disaster. "The Democrats are my enemies because I assisted in emancipating the slaves. The Republicans have now become my opponents, because I have made an effort to confer on the women their rights. And even the women themselves fail to sympathize with me."[23]

In South Carolina and Virginia woman-suffrage spokesmen took more expedient approaches, arming themselves against derision with brief and cautious statements of principle. When William J. Whipper moved to strike the word male from the suffrage section of South Carolina's new constitution, he made it clear that he expected no support from his colleagues: ". . . however lightly the subject may be treated; however frivolous you may think it, I tell you here that I know the time will come when every man and woman in this country will have the right to vote." The South Carolina delegates did not make light of Whipper's motion. Neither did they discuss it. The amendment was voted down without

[23] *Revolution*, I (February 12, 1868), 84 (first quotation); Arkansas, *Debates and Proceedings of the Convention . . . 1868* (Little Rock, 1868), 701–24 (second quotation on p. 708, third quotation on p. 710); Stanton *et al.*, eds., *History of Woman Suffrage*, III, 806 (last quotation). Cypert and Gantt, it should be noted, were Conservatives, but Langley received no help from members of his own party.

debate and without a roll call. Several weeks earlier John Curtiss Underwood had introduced a universal-suffrage resolution in the Virginia convention. Underwood spoke for nearly two hours in favor of enfranchising black men and the clergy before tacking on a final paragraph recommending woman suffrage. "But such is the prejudice of our people," he hedged, "and so little are we yet advanced beyond that savage state of society which makes conscientious and heaven-inspired woman the drudge or toy of her stronger and coarser companion, that I despair at this time of securing so desirable a progress . . . ." Underwood's speech provoked a lengthy rebuttal, but his adversary did not bother to address the issue of woman suffrage. In South Carolina, Virginia, and Louisiana woman suffrage got the silent treatment.[24]

Texas was the one state where the constitutional convention gave woman suffrage a hearing. A five-man majority of the Committee on State Affairs "earnestly" recommended the passage of a clause that would eliminate sex as a qualification for voters. This, the majority argued, would not only fulfill the principle of government by consent of the governed, but it would also give due recognition to woman's piety, her superior education, and her historic patriotism. The two authors of the minority report, meanwhile, took the classic "anti" position that woman in her proper sphere already exerted "an influence mightier, far, than that of the elective franchise." The report continued: ". . . we believe that the good sense of every true woman in the land teaches her that granting them the power to vote is a direct, open insult to their sex, by the complication [*sic*] that they are so unwomanly as to desire the privilege." When copies of both reports reached the desk of the *Revolution* in New York Elizabeth Cady Stanton pounced on the minority's prose as well as their reasoning. "We should think the men who penned the above bungling sentences had strayed out of their sphere," she noted acidly. Stanton went on: ". . . dearly beloved Texans, give your women at least a choice of *insults*, and rest assured they would prefer all these that flow from political equality to those they now enjoy in disfranchisement." It was not until several months later that the Texas convention made its final choice of insults. In January 1869 the woman-suffrage amendment failed by a vote of thirteen to fifty-two.[25] Stanton probably took the loss philosophically.

[24] South Carolina, *Proceedings of the Constitutional Convention* . . . *1868*, II, 836–38 (quotation on p. 838); Virginia, *Debates and Proceedings of the Constitutional Convention*, 458–68 (quotation on p. 467); Louisiana, *Official Journal of the* . . . *Convention for Framing a Constitution* . . . *1868* (New Orleans, 1868), 224.

[25] Texas, *Journal of the Reconstruction Convention* . . . (2 vols., Austin, 1870), I, 245–46,

No northern state had yet enfranchised women, and there was little reason to expect better from the South. "Say what you will about the rights of the conqueror and the duties of the conquered," she had written in 1868, "the safe and short way to reconstruction is for the North to lead in establishing a genuine republic in all her own borders. We cannot force on the South a higher civilization than we have ourselves."[26]

The conventions that so willingly gave married women constitutional rights to property ownership thus gave little serious consideration and less sympathy to woman suffrage. There was no paradox in this. The delegates regarded married-women's-property reform as a matter of debtors' rights rather than women's rights; apparently, no one worried that the granting of property ownership to wives would trigger "secession in families." Once the conventions of Georgia, North Carolina, and South Carolina had completed their work, however, subsequent lawmakers were obliged to decide just how much the legal status of women would be altered. The constitutional clauses were ambiguous. It was by no means clear whether the woman's new title to property carried with it any of the powers ordinarily associated with property ownership. Could a married woman mortgage her property? Could she enter into a business partnership? Could she bind her property as security for a loan acquired by some other person? By the default of the constitutional conventions the legislatures and the courts were given enormous interpretive latitude. They could, if they chose, remove in one stroke every disability the common law had imposed on married women. On the other hand, they could settle for minor repairs of the common law, giving the married woman the protection guaranteed her by the constitutions but leaving her as passive as ever.

No single approach was entirely satisfactory. Assuming that some husbands were incompetent, absent, or downright malicious, the wife would need some powers of disposal over her property in order to hold house and home together. But if she were given unqualified powers—meaning risks as well as rights—the protective function of the law would be lost; the husband and his creditors could no longer appropriate the wife's property, but she would be subject to exploitation by anyone with whom she had business dealings. The wife would have nothing to protect her but her own business wits, which at the time were held in no very great esteem. There was a

577–80 (first quotation on p. 579, second and third on p. 580); II, 413–14; *Revolution*, II (September 3, 1868), 137–38 (last quotation).

[26] *Revolution*, I (May 14, 1868), 294.

middle ground. The lawmakers could aim for the best of both worlds, granting women some powers and denying them others. This, too, could spell trouble, for the resulting confusion might befuddle creditors and hence retard the conduct of business.

The dilemmas were not new. Antebellum legislators in all three states had foreseen some of the complications, and this was in part responsible for their persistent refusal to pass the married-women's-property bills introduced in the 1840s and 1850s.[27] A Georgia newspaper, for example, endorsed the "ladies bill" of 1845 in principle but urged caution, "lest in attempting to remedy acknowledged evils, it should lead to others of still greater magnitude."[28] Legislators evidently regretted that the law as it stood made for perpetual open season on the property of married women, but they hesitated to trade the familiarity and the simplicity of the common law for the uncertainties of some new system. "But here you propose to take a little civil law and tack it upon the common law," objected a South Carolina state senator in 1855. "But when you have done it, you will find that the work does not fit at all."[29] After 1868 legislators and justices no longer had a choice; they had to make the work of the constitutional conventions fit as best they could. In each of the three states the results were different.

The most dramatic turnabout came in Georgia by virtue of an 1869 supreme court decision. Prior to the Civil War Georgia law was common law with a vengeance. "In this state," the code read, "the husband is the head of the family, and the wife is subject to him." Georgia statutes were harsher than the common law, for the wife's real estate as well as her personal property was made the absolute possession of her husband. The process of legal reform began during Reconstruction, but it did not originate with the Radicals. In 1866 the Georgia legislature enacted a terse protective statute that, like most initial married-women's-property acts, gave the wife title to her separate property, real and personal, and exempted that property from liability for the debts of the husband. When the Radicals wrote the new constitution two years later they added nothing to the 1866 law.[30] The 1868 constitutional provision

[27] The failure of the southeastern states to act at this time might also be attributed to the lesser severity of the depression or to the greater effectiveness of equity in the Southeast. Daniel J. Flanigan has noted a parallel east-west split on criminal procedure for slaves; see his "Criminal Procedure in Slave Trials in the Antebellum South," *Journal of Southern History*, XL (November 1974), 540 ff.

[28] Milledgeville *Federal Union*, November 25, 1845.

[29] Columbia *South Carolina Legislative Times*, December 8, 1855.

[30] Georgia, *The Code of the State of Georgia* (Atlanta, 1861), Secs. 1700, 1701, 1702. For a more detailed treatment of the legal status of Georgia women see Eleanor M. Boatwright,

was a condensed version of the act of 1866, and neither suggested that married women could do anything with their property other than possess it.

The state supreme court nonetheless granted sweeping new powers to women in the 1869 decision in *Huff* v. *Wright*. Defendant C. A. Wright argued that her property was not liable for a debt she had contracted in 1866; she had been married at the time and contended that the promissory note she had signed was consequently void. The court disagreed and took the opportunity to spell out the new law of married-women's property in Georgia. The constitutional provision of 1868 made of the husband and wife "two distinct persons, with separate and distinct rights. In a word," the court declared, "the common-law rule upon this subject no longer prevails in this state." The abrogation of the common-law doctrine meant an end to woman's enforced passivity. The woman who married after 1868 retained, in the language of the court, "power to purchase, hold and convey property, contract and be contracted with, sue and be sued, as a feme sole."[31]

The new law was not everything a champion of strictly equal rights might have desired. The wife was still, for example, restrained from binding her property solely for the benefit of another person. And while the wife could control her property, she was not made responsible for the support of her family. The entire legal burden of family support remained the husband's, a sign, perhaps, that Georgia lawmakers for better or worse trusted mothers to take care of their own. The most glaring inequality was on the ownership of the wife's wages, which remained the absolute property of the husband. It was a long time before the needs of working-class women would command the attention already given those of the propertied. Georgia wives were not granted legal control over their earnings until 1943.[32]

Georgia had nevertheless conferred major new powers on its women and, relative to other states, conferred them in record time. Progress was far slower in North Carolina, where the full potential of the 1868 constitutional provision was not realized until 1911. In the interim the guidelines for married-women's property ownership were laid down in an 1872 act of the legislature and a state supreme court ruling of 1876. The 1872 statute, enacted by a legislature that

---

"The Political and Civil Status of Women in Georgia, 1783–1860," *Georgia Historical Quarterly*, XXV (December 1941), 301–24.

[31] *Huff* v. *Wright*, 39 Ga. 41 (1869), at 43.

[32] Walter McElreath, *A Treatise on the Constitution of Georgia* (Atlanta, 1912), 166–68; Georgia, *Code of Georgia Annotated* (Atlanta, 1961), Sec. 53–512.

was no longer under Republican control, did permit married women to become free traders, otherwise called sole traders or free dealers. That is, a wife with her husband's consent (or without it, if she were deserted or divorced) could file for exemption from her common-law disabilities in order to carry on a trade or business on her own account. Otherwise, married women remained under the tutelage of their husbands, for no contract made by a wife was valid unless her husband joined in it.[33] In 1876 the court added further restrictions. A wife's contract was good only if it referred specifically to her separate estate and if it was of direct benefit to her separate estate. North Carolina law, the court explained, "by no means converts a married woman into a *femme sole* in respect to her separate property . . . ." Rather, the constitutional provision was a blanket substitute for the old system of estates in trust under equity and, like all equitable settlements, "must be construed . . . as conferring on married women no powers beyond those expressly given or implied."[34]

The North Carolina court was as cautious as the Georgia court had been bold, and the apparent consequence was that North Carolina women increasingly ignored the law. By 1905 the supreme court was finding the gap between law and practice intolerable. "Married women today are the owners of property, both real and personal, worth millions of dollars," wrote Associate Justice Henry Groves Connor. "They employ tenants and croppers and cultivate thousands of farms, engage in merchandise, conduct hotels, boarding houses and almost every kind of business suited and sometimes unsuited to their mental and physical capacity." Connor estimated that nine-tenths of women's contracts for all these enterprises were "not enforcible in the courts." The court had in recent years expanded married-women's powers but felt it was time the legislature clarified and settled the issue by giving married women full contractual powers. It was six years more before the legislature complied. Except for the unavoidable continuation of the constitutional requirement that the husband join the wife in the sale of her property the Martin Act of 1911 freed married women from their common-law disabilities.[35]

While Georgia hurried and North Carolina lagged, South Carolina seesawed. For more than a decade the law was liberal indeed,

[33] North Carolina, *Public Laws* . . . *1871–'72* (Raleigh, 1872), 334–36.

[34] *Pippen* v. *Wesson*, 74 N. C. 437 (1876), at 442–43, 445.

[35] *Ball* v. *Paquin*, 140 N. C. 83 (1905), at 90; North Carolina, *Consolidated Statutes* . . . *1919* (2 vols., Raleigh, 1919), Sec. 2507; see also Guion G. Johnson, *Ante-Bellum North Carolina: A Social History* (Chapel Hill, 1937), 238–45.

and this time feminism had an impact. In the heady reform atmosphere of Radical rule, feminism found a ready reception after 1868. Louisa Rollin broke the traditional public silence of South Carolina women in 1869 when she spoke for woman suffrage to a packed house of state representatives and senators. By late 1870 William Whipper was no longer the sole committed advocate of women's rights among Radical politicians. In December of that year Louisa Rollin's sister Charlotte Rollin presided at Columbia's first women's-rights convention. Those present organized an interracial woman-suffrage association, and among the officers were several high-ranking Republican officials and their wives.[36] Woman suffrage had become not only a debatable issue but, in Radical circles, a respectable one.

The General Assembly, meantime, had been at work on an enabling law to define with precision the property rights granted married women in the 1868 constitution. The debate was lengthy, the "Woman's Rights Question" was at its center, and the resulting legislation was powerful evidence of the new feminist face of South Carolina radicalism. The 1870 statute confirmed the powers stipulated in the constitution—to bequeath and convey property—and added a host of others. A married woman was empowered to make purchases, enter into contracts, and execute "all deeds, mortgages, and legal instruments of whatever kind" with the same force as a single woman. The wife would be solely responsible for the payment of her debts, although those contracted for her "necessary support" could still be charged to the husband.[37] With the act of 1870 the South Carolina General Assembly abandoned the protective posture that had prevailed just two years before.

The full implications of the new law were made clear some years later in the state supreme court's 1881 ruling in *Pelzer* v. *Campbell*. A married woman, Mary M. Campbell, had signed several notes as surety for her son's enterprises "without any advantage to herself or her estate." When her son's creditors sued the Campbells for

[36] Charleston *Daily Courier*, February 3, March 4, 1869; Stanton *et al.*, eds., *History of Woman Suffrage*, III, 828; Joel Williamson, *After Slavery: The Negro in South Carolina During Reconstruction, 1861–1877* (Chapel Hill, 1965), 338. The sources differ on whether it was Louisa Rollin or her sister Charlotte who addressed the legislature in 1869. The Rollin sisters, prominent in Charleston's free black society, were among Claude G. Bowers's favorite subjects, for an important part of the "tragic legend of Reconstruction" that Bowers did so much to popularize was, in his words, "the unprecedented prominence of women." A laudable insight, this, were it not for his leering approach. "Never," Bowers wrote, "had women lobbyists used their sex in securing legislative favors for selfish groups so brazenly—or so cleverly." *The Tragic Era: The Revolution After Lincoln* (Cambridge, Mass., 1929), vi.

[37] Charleston *Daily Courier*, December 9, 1869; South Carolina, *Acts and Joint Resolutions of the General Assembly . . . 1869–'70* (Columbia, 1870), Pt. 1, pp. 325–26.

payment Mrs. Campbell's attorneys argued that her property was not liable, as a married woman had no legal capacity to make any contract that endangered her separate property. The court held to the contrary that a married woman had such capacity under the statute of 1870 and that Mary Campbell's property was accordingly liable for the debt. The justices recognized that this ruling might be detrimental to some unwise women but reasoned that "When they take the right to control their separate estates they assume the risks of such control. . . . At first hardships may, in isolated instances, ensue from the inexperience of women in matters of business, but such hardships always arise upon any change in the rules of property or business."[38]

The South Carolina General Assembly, by then in Conservative hands, evidently did not look kindly on the court's interpretation. In 1882 the assembly trimmed the law of 1870, specifying that a married woman had no general power to contract. The court was thereafter an accomplice in the return to protectionism. In 1886 the court ruled that a married woman could not mortgage her property unless the mortgage was intended to benefit her directly. The year after, married women were deprived of the right to enter into business partnerships, for a partnership, the opinion read, "involves an obligation to contribute one's time and services, which a married woman has no right to control, and a personal liability for debts which she has no power to incur." Thus far no legal body had determined whether a wife's earnings were part of her separate estate. True to its policy of strict construction, the court ruled in 1887 that they were not. Until the legislature gave wives express power over their wages, the court insisted, husbands would retain their common-law possession of their wives' earnings. The decision had not yet gone to the printer when the General Assembly responded with an act that put married women in firm control of their wages. That much accomplished, the assembly made one final protective move in 1891, confirming by statute what the court had already established. The 1891 law prohibited married women from assuming responsibility for the debts of any other person and completed the legislature's attempt to take the risks out of property ownership for married women.[39]

Such a law would have rescued Mary Campbell in 1881, but in the 1890s it only seemed to compound the confusion over the

[38] *Pelzer* v. *Campbell*, 15 S. C. 581 (1881), at 582.

[39] *Aultman* v. *Rush*, 26 S. C. 517 (1887); *Gwynn* v. *Gwynn*, 27 S. C. 525 (1887), at 526; *Bridgers* v. *Howell*, 27 S. C. 425 (1887); South Carolina, *The Revised Statutes of South Carolina* (2 vols., Columbia, 1894). Secs 2165, 2167.

precise rights of married women. When delegates gathered for South Carolina's 1895 constitutional convention a married-women's-property resolution was among the first to be introduced. The resolution did not call for a revision of the law; it asked for clarification of the law.[40] The Charleston *News and Courier* reported one delegate's comments on "the now much tangled issue": "Mr. Sheppard said that the Acts of the Legislature tinkering with the laws relating to the property of married women had caused more litigation and expense to the people of the State than any other one thing. He then pointed out in detail the dreadful botches the Legislature had made until now a Philadelphia lawyer could not tell what the law in this State on the subject was."[41] One of the "botches" Sheppard no doubt listed was that it was often impossible to guess when a contract was signed whether it endangered the woman's estate. In these marginal instances no party to the contract was assured of its validity until it was litigated. By then, of course, it was too late.

It was this conviction that the law had become unintelligible that inspired a movement to simplify the whole matter by giving married women the same powers as men. Failing that, one delegate suggested, it would be better to reimpose all of women's common-law disabilities than to let their property remain in a legal twilight zone.[42] No one in the convention seriously proposed that the common law be restored, however. The choice was between the preservation of the clumsy protective structure that had been constructed during the previous thirteen years and the elimination of all restrictions on married-women's contracts. The decisive vote came on an amendment that would have maintained the exemption of a married woman's property from liability for the debts of other persons. The simplifiers prevailed over the protectionists, seventy-six to forty-two, and the convention went on to approve the provision that freed the property of married women once and for all. There would be no more strings on married-women's contracts, and as to her separate property, the wife would possess "all the rights . . . to which an unmarried woman or a man is entitled."[43]

The passage of the constitutional provision marked a return to the principles first articulated in the Radicals' statute of 1870. The

[40] South Carolina, *Journal of the Constitutional Convention of the State of South Carolina . . . Eighteen Hundred and Ninety-five* . . . (Columbia, 1895), 36.

[41] Charleston *News and Courier*, October 1, 1895.

[42] *Ibid.*

[43] South Carolina, *Journal of the Constitutional Convention* (1895), 147–48, 251–52, 287–89.

1895 delegates, however, were evidently not moved by any egalitarian theory. As a result of the simplification of the law married women were emancipated, but, more to the point, their assets were emancipated for investment in all kinds of enterprises, their husbands' included. Moreover, the property of married women was once again subjected to the same predictable rules of trade that governed men. South Carolina had experimented with protective legislation and found it more trouble than it was worth. The 1895 grant of equal property rights was less a vote of confidence in married women than it was a reaction against legislation that had clogged the courts and impeded the flow of capital.

The Radicals of Georgia, North Carolina, and South Carolina had left highly variable legacies when they gave the married women of their states constitutional rights to property ownership. In this, the three states behaved very much like other states, that is to say, according to no set pattern, once the initial bills to reduce women's common-law vulnerability were enacted. Mississippi, Alabama, and Texas, for example, all passed laws to protect the wife's property from husband and creditors by 1848; forty years later Mississippi, always ahead of the pack, abrogated women's common-law disabilities altogether, Alabama retained some, and Texas retained them all.[44] The hit-and-miss quality of married-women's-property reform was likewise visible in the performances of the Reconstruction legislatures of the younger southern states. There was progress in Mississippi, where wages were defined as part of the wife's separate estate in 1871; and Arkansas enlarged the powers of married women with a comprehensive new statute in 1873.[45] But Alabama resisted innovation. From 1865 to 1871 the Alabama legislature was flooded with petitions from married women who wished to be made free dealers. The legislature could have taken

[44] Mississippi, *The Revised Code . . . 1880* (Jackson, 1880), Sec. 1167. The Mississippi constitution of 1890, Art. IV, Sec. 94, however, reserved the right of the legislature to regulate contracts between husband and wife. Thorpe, comp., *Constitutions*, IV, 2100.

[45] Mississippi, *The Revised Code . . . 1871* (Jackson, 1871), Sec. 1778; Arkansas, *Acts of the General Assembly . . . 1873* (Little Rock, 1873), 382–85. The Arkansas law did not empower the wife to contract generally, but it did give her power to insure her husband's life for her benefit, to maintain her own savings account, to carry on a trade or business, to make transactions regarding her separate estate (provided a list of her property was duly registered), and to carry on litigation in her own name. The motives behind the passage of the act of 1873 are not discernible. It is clear, however, that the bill was not a party measure. In the Senate, where the bill originated, the Republicans split, ten in favor and eight against. The House approved the bill without debate in the closing hours of the session. Here party lines were more evident; the Republicans voted for the bill, thirty-three to five, the Democrats against, six to twelve. Little Rock *Daily Arkansas Gazette*, April 1, 25, 1873; Arkansas, "Journal of the House of Representatives, State of Arkansas, Session of 1873" (manuscript, 3 vols.), Vol. III, April 24, 1873.

the petitions as a mandate for a law that empowered all women to make business transactions. Instead, the petitions were regarded as a waste of precious legislative time, and power to grant free-dealer privileges was transferred to the local courts.[46] Major statutory changes in the law of married-women's property in Alabama, Mississippi, Florida, Louisiana, and Texas awaited the 1880s and beyond.

At century's end married-women's-property law in the South—and in the rest of the country, for that matter—was an odd assortment of powers, obligations, and disabilities, with the laws of each state different in detail, and sometimes in essentials, from those of any other. There were apparent inconsistencies within states as well. South Carolina in 1895, for example, had the dual distinction of having the most conservative divorce law in the United States (divorces were made unconstitutional in 1895), while its married-women's-property law ranked among the most progressive.[47] As an index to southern attitudes toward women, the law is completely unreliable.

There was, however, a kind of logic behind the diversity of the laws and the variable timing of their passage. Whatever status lawmakers might, in theory, have wished on women, some other consideration was always present to confuse—or to decide—the issue. All the initial married-women's-property acts were intended to insulate the wife from economic exploitation, but protection exacted its costs. For one thing, protective legislation often entailed a shift in the legal concept of marriage. The idealistic common-law assumption of a community of interests under the control of a benevolent husband was replaced by a rather cynical vision of masculine irresponsibility that made the interests of husband and wife separate and mutually antagonistic. This was clearest in the laws that prevented the wife from underwriting her husband's business ventures. Protection also required the maintenance of a legal system (or as the South Carolina case suggests, lack of system) that was more complicated and less certain than either the common

[46]At least twenty women were made free dealers by the legislature in the 1865–1866 session, thirty-eight in 1868, forty-one in 1869–1870, and eighty-four in 1870–1871. The 1868 free-dealer law eliminated the antebellum requirement that the husband be shown to be incompetent. The 1868 law required the husband's consent, and subsequent revisions prescribed remedies in cases in which the husband refused consent or the chancery court denied the woman's petition. Alabama, *Acts . . . of the General Assembly* : . . *1845* (Tuscaloosa, 1846), 23; *ibid.*, *1868* (Montgomery, 1868), 546–47; *ibid.*, *1872–73* (Montgomery, 1873), 93–94; *ibid.*, *1874–75* (Montgomery, 1875), 194–95.

[47] Given the belief that permitting divorce was a cause of marital conflict, there was a kind of consistency here; the outlawing of divorce and the emancipation of married-women's property both put the law on the side of cooperative marriages. On divorce in South Carolina see note 2 above.

law or the abrogation of the common law. And the more complex the law, the more inhibitions were placed on the mobilization of goods and services. The alternative, of course, was to abandon legal protection and let women fend for themselves.

Any significant change in the law of married-women's property thus amounted to a choice among evils, or among benefits, in the eyes of lawmakers. That being the case, it was no doubt possible for a small group of legislators with conviction to sway a much larger group of their ambivalent colleagues. The legal status of southern women hinged on the decisions of lawmakers for whom the status of women per se was rarely the paramount concern. The results, during Reconstruction and throughout the century, were correspondingly erratic.

Apart But Not Adrift: Wives, Divorce, and Independence in California, 1850–1890

Robert L. Griswold

The author is a member of the history department in the University of Oklahoma.

THE POPULAR IMAGE OF VICTORIAN housewives is not a flattering one: the tableau usually includes husbands commanding obedience from all members of the family and wives busying themselves in the front parlor or fluttering about the nursery. Women, according to this view, are sentimental, maternal, and above all dependent upon and submissive to their unemotional, rational, and austere husbands. This popular image is not without historical foundation. Nineteenth-century moralists urged upon women a set of values known collectively as the "cult of true womanhood" and with unremitting persistence they advised women to center their lives around piety, purity, submissiveness, and domesticity.[1] This cult, so historians and social

The author thanks Professors Carl Degler and Terrence McDonald for their helpful suggestions and criticisms and the Center for Research on Women at Stanford University for providing financial assistance during the early research on this project.

[1]On the cult of true womanhood, see Barbara Welter, "The Cult of True Womanhood: 1820–1860," *American Quarterly*, XVIII (1966), 151–174. The analysis of this domestic ideology has been refined by Nancy Cott, *The Bonds of Womanhood: "Woman's Sphere" in New England, 1780–1835* (New Haven, 1977), 8, 22, 63–100; and Kathryn Kish Sklar, *Catharine Beecher: A Study in American Domesticity* (New Haven, 1973), 158–167.

critics have argued, condemned women to the private world of home and family and cut them off from the social world inhabited by their husbands. Nineteenth-century wives were praised as angels, but treated like China dolls; cheered for their domesticity, but banned from public life; honored for their nurturing, but saddled with child care. The vacuous praise, the argument goes, merely covered the real oppression women experienced.

But did the cult of true womanhood strip wives of their independence and leave them captives in the home? The answer lies in finding evidence that reveals the actual marital situation of nineteenth-century women, evidence that goes beyond the exhortations of moralists and offers clues as to the real options open to women. This study draws upon such evidence—divorce records—to explore the family life of nineteenth-century wives in San Mateo and Santa Clara counties of California between 1850 and 1890.[2] An analysis of 401 cases offers both statistical evidence and personal testimony suggest-

[2]The divorce cases are from the Divorce Records of District and Superior Courts, 1864–1890, San Mateo County Hall of Justice and Records, Redwood City, California; and Divorce Records of District and Superior Courts, 1850–1890, Santa Clara County Superior Court House, San Jose, California. Throughout the period 1850 to 1890, these two San Francisco Bay Area counties were rural communities with an economy dominated by farms and small shops. Santa Clara had a population of slightly less than 50,000 by 1890 and San Mateo barely rose over 10,000. The divorce cases start with a Santa Clara case in December 1850 (San Mateo's first case came fourteen years later in 1864) and end with cases tried in December 1889 in both counties. The first date in the title is that of the earliest case on record and the second date marks that point where written testimony appeared infrequently and the cases provided less valuable evidence for historical analysis. The San Mateo evidence includes every case during these years, a total of 197 suits; in Santa Clara County, the larger population necessitated a systematic sample of every fifth case, a procedure that yielded 204 cases. Thus the total number in the study is 401 cases involving 276 female plaintiffs (68.8 percent) and 125 male plaintiffs (31.2 percent). Of these 401 cases, 272 (68 percent) ended in a divorce for one party or the other. All data unless otherwise noted are taken from this sample.

These 401 families represented part of a growing nationwide trend. For whatever reasons, Californians along with other Americans would not tolerate behavior that their parents and grandparents had accepted as a normal part of marriage. In the United States from 1870 to 1880, the population rose 30.1 percent but the divorce rate jumped by 79.4 percent; in the next decade the population increased by 25.5 percent and the divorce rate 70.2 percent. The rate of divorce increased even faster in the two California counties; for example, in the 1880s, the counties' population increased 33 percent but the divorce rate went up by 101 percent. For the national figures, see U. S. Bureau of the Census, *Special Reports: Marriage and Divorce, 1867–1906* (Washington, D.C., 1909), Part 1, 12.

ing that married women were not without options and that, through their own initiative or the help of friends and relatives, they could and did take action independent of their husbands.

* * *

Simply filing for a divorce is, of course, an independent action, and as Nancy Cott revealed in her study of the relationship between divorce and the status of women in eighteenth-century Massachusetts, an increasingly large number of women were exercising such an option. She also argued persuasively that the disproportionate growth in women's divorce petitions "suggests that they, even more than men, had rising expectations in marriage" and that women's increased success in gaining favorable decrees meant that the status of women improved during that century. Cott found that between 1692 and 1774, only 49 percent of the wives bringing suit received favorable decrees, but that between 1775 and 1786, 70 percent were successful petitioners; moreover, in that revolutionary decade, 62 percent of the petitioners were women, in contrast to earlier decades when the proportion of husbands bringing suit was either equal to or higher than that of wives.[3] The divorce evidence from California shows that this trend extended into the nineteenth century and that the divorce court had become an effective means by which wives could gain independence from their husbands. In the 1850s and 1860s, women brought 75 percent of the suits; in the 1870s, 74 percent; and in the 1880s, 65 percent. When the analysis shifts to actual decrees of divorce, the data reveal that women in approximately 90 percent of the cases either won the case or had it dismissed; thus, for all the emphasis placed on the sanctity of women's place in the nineteenth-century home, judges were by no means reluctant to grant divorces. Table 1 shows by decade the percentage of female plaintiffs who either received a divorce or dismissed their own complaints.

[3]Nancy Cott, "Divorce and the Changing Status of Women in Eighteenth-Century Massachusetts," *William and Mary Quarterly*, XXXIII (1976), 586–614; see also her article, "Eighteenth-Century Family and Social Life Revealed in Massachusetts Divorce Records," *Journal of Social History*, X (1976), 20–43.

TABLE 1
DIVORCE AWARDS AND DISMISSALS FOR WOMEN PLAINTIFFS BY DECADES

Decade of Complaint	I Plaintiffs Receiving Divorces		II Cases Dismissed by Plaintiff		I+II
	%	(N)	%	(N)	%
1850s and 1860s	73.1	(19)	11.5	(3)	84.6
1870s	89.2	(66)	9.5	(7)	98.7
1880s	80.6	(108)	16.4	(22)	97.0

Far from being hostile to women's desires, the divorce court, as the figures in Table 1 reveal, was an effective institution enabling women to start new lives. Community and family pressure certainly kept many women from filing for divorce, but when they finally summoned the courage to face economic uncertainty and social stigma, wives could expect a favorable disposition by the court.

But despite the increasing number of women in divorce court and the success they encountered there, many women chose a more direct and cheaper way to gain independence from their husbands. Perhaps the boldest display of independence from a wife came when she simply deserted her husband and made no attempt to obtain a divorce. Desertion was by far the most common complaint levied against women, and women were also more likely to be charged with and found guilty of desertion than were men; women were charged with desertion in 64 percent of the cases brought by men, but men were so charged in just 37.7 percent of the actions brought by women. The bases of divorce judgments showed a similar pattern; a finding of desertion appeared in 40 percent of the judgments against husbands and in 64 percent of the judgments against wives. The following two tables compare both the incidence of different legal complaints brought against men and women and the bases of divorce judgments by sex.[4]

[4]From the start, California law provided wide-ranging grounds for divorce. By an act of 1851, a man or woman who had established residence for six months could sue for divorce on the following grounds: natural impotency, adultery, extreme cruelty, willful desertion or neglect, habitual intemperance, fraud, and conviction for a felony. From 1851 to 1872, various legislative acts reduced the period required for a spouse to

TABLE 2
DIVORCE COMPLAINTS AGAINST MEN AND WOMEN

Type of Complaint	Brought by Husbands against Wives (total N=125) %	(N)	Brought by Wives against Husbands (total N=276) %	(N)
Desertion	64	(80)	37.7	(104)
Intemperance	9.6	(12)	21.4	(59)
Adultery	20.8	(26)	10.9	(30)
Nonsupport	0.0	(0)	48.2	(133)
Felony conviction	0.0	(0)	.4	(1)
Cruelty	20.8	(26)	45.7	(126)

TABLE 3
DIVORCE JUDGMENTS AGAINST MEN AND WOMEN

Basis of Divorce Judgment	Against Wives (total N=75) %	(N)	Against Husbands (total N=197) %	(N)
Desertion	64	(48)	40	(78)
Intemperance	5	(4)	20	(39)
Adultery	28	(21)	9	(18)
Nonsupport	1	(1)	45	(88)
Felony conviction	0	(0)	1	(1)
Cruelty	13	(10)	34	(66)

These tables suggest that desertion was the major way in which women escaped an intolerable situation in which husbands had the preponderance of physical and economic power. While husbands might turn to cruelty, drink, or general indolence to vent their frustrations, women more often simply abandoned the home when marriage soured.

demonstrate intemperance, desertion, and neglect from three years to a year; after 1872, the divorce statutes remained relatively unchanged, and the six grounds available to the plaintiff—adultery, cruelty, desertion, neglect, intemperance, and conviction for a felony—provided ample legal opportunity for unhappy California husbands and wives to escape from their bonds. See *Statutes of California: Second Session, 1851*, pp. 186–187; *Statutes of California: Eighteenth Session, 1869–1870*, p. 291; *West's Annotated California Codes: Civil Code, Sections 1 to 192* (St. Paul, 1954), 337. In Tables 2 and 3, the complaints are arranged according to several categories. Many individuals were sued on more than one ground, and rather than list the permutations, I have organized the complaints (and the grounds of judgment) as shown in the tables. For this reason, the numbers in the columns add up to more than the "total N" listed in the column headings.

Significantly, women from all class backgrounds were willing to incur the risks that came with desertion.[5] The percentage of women found guilty of desertion, as Table 4 reveals, showed no dramatic skewing at either end of the social scale. But one difference among classes and women's mobility appears when the location of the service of summons is examined by class: women from upper-class backgrounds were more likely to live far from their estranged husbands than were women from other classes. Table 5 compares by class the percentage of locally served summonses with summonses either published or served out of state.[6]

TABLE 4
DESERTION JUDGMENTS AGAINST WOMEN, BY CLASS

Social Class of Wife	% of Women in Each Class Found Guilty of Desertion	(Total N)
Upper Class	50.0	(16)
Middle Class	44.4	(9)
Farmers	37.5	(8)
High Trades	18.2	(11)
Low Trades	50.0	(6)
Laborers	40.0	(5)

[5]From the divorce records, county directories, manuscript censuses, and county histories, the occupations of more than half the sample were found, and these occupations were then grouped into six classes based roughly upon the same scheme employed by Michael Katz in his study of Hamilton, Ontario. (See Katz, *The People of Hamilton, Canada West: Family and Class in a Mid-Nineteenth Century City* [Cambridge, Mass., 1975], *passim*.) Those classes consist of the following: 1) the upper class—businessmen, merchants lawyers, and ranchers; 2) the middle class—bookkeepers, dentists, druggists, and storekeepers; 3) farmers; 4) high trades—such skilled tradesmen as bakers, carpenters, cooks, and tailors; 5) low trades—miners, teamsters, millworkers, and other unskilled tradesmen; and 6) laborers—those men who identified themselves as such or were so identified by others; their ranks included both town and rural laborers as well as men described as "unemployed" who were clearly not tradesmen, farmers, or members of the upper class. Of the 203 heads of families whose occupations were identified, 17 percent were classified as upper class, 17 percent as middle class, 14 percent as farmers, 19 percent as skilled workers, 9 percent as unskilled artisans, and 24 percent as laborers. Of course, unless the full occupational structure of the two counties is known, we cannot tell whether one class or another was over- or underrepresented. But even without this detailed analysis—an analysis that could be done with the manuscript census but is beyond the scope of this essay—the high number of working-class people is nevertheless surprising.

[6]Table 5 includes all women defendants whose class background was identified and for whom summons information was available; that is, this table includes women sued for divorce on all grounds, not just those sued for desertion.

TABLE 5
LOCATION OF THE SERVICE OF SUMMONS, BY CLASS

Social Class of Wife	(N)	I Served in Same County as Divorce Filing (%)	II Served in California But Outside County (%)	I+II (%)	Served Outside State or Published (%)
Upper Class	(13)	7.7	15.4	23.1	76.9
Middle Class	(7)	42.9	28.6	71.5	28.5
Farmers	(7)	57.1	14.3	71.4	28.6
High Trades	(8)	62.5	12.5	75.0	25.0
Low Trades	(6)	66.7	16.7	83.4	16.6
Laborers	(5)	60.0	20.0	80.0	20.0

Two explanations for this sharp contrast seem reasonable. First, upper-class women's access to money may have enabled them to leave California or to refuse to go there with their husbands, either action making them liable for a charge of desertion. Second, upper-class women, who were (in this study) for the most part the wives of lawyers, doctors, and merchants, may have felt particularly sensitive to social respectability and have fled the area rather than stay and face their neighbors once they were sued for divorce.

* * *

Women without their husbands encountered a hostile economic environment, but many women, nevertheless, were up to the challenge. The economic situation of wives who deserted their husbands is unknown—in these cases it is the husbands, not the wives, who appear in the divorce records—but the economic situation of wives deserted by their husbands or wives forced to leave cruel, intemperate, or financially nonsupporting husbands can be analyzed. Either situation required a woman to support herself or to turn to the community for help. The jobs held by the wives in this study are shown in Table 6.[7]

[7]Nationally, over 95 percent of white married women did not work outside the home in the nineteenth century. The sizeable percentage of working wives in this study stemmed from the fact that most of these California women worked because their

TABLE 6
OCCUPATION OF WIVES

Nonmenial	(N)	Menial	(N)
Actress	(1)	Domestic	(37)
Bookkeeper	(1)	Seamstress	(17)
Clerk	(1)	Prostitutes (alleged)	(7)
Hotelkeeper	(1)		
Doctor	(1)	Cooks/servants	(4)
Storekeeper	(2)		
Nurse	(2)		(65)
Teacher	(6)		
	(15)		

Menial occupations comprised 81 percent (65/80) of the work mentioned in the records, and nonmenial work made up the other 19 percent (15/80). The high percentage of women doing menial work paradoxically reveals both the narrowness of job opportunities for wives and the fact that jobs did exist that enabled them to use their domestic skills. The menial jobs clearly kept women in a domestic setting. Domestics, seamstresses, cooks, and servants spent their days not in the hurly-burly of the marketplace but in the protective confines of the home. Even among the nonmenial workers, the two nurses and six teachers worked in jobs thought particularly appropriate for women. For the great majority of these wives, then, self-support entailed no severe displacement from one sphere to another but merely a transfer of skills within a familiar setting. While such narrow job opportunities surely discouraged some wives from supporting themselves, the fact that women could use their domestic skills to earn an income must have encouraged others.

Specific cases reveal the determination and self-confidence of wives despite the economic obstacles they faced. J. W. Landon twice overheard William Hendrickson urge his wife to return home, but on both occasions she adamantly refused, telling him "to take care of himself and that she would look out for

husbands either refused to support them or because their husbands had deserted them. On the figures for working women, see Daniel Scott Smith, "Family Limitation, Sexual Control, and Domestic Feminism in Victorian America," *Feminist Studies*, I (Winter-Spring, 1973), 42–43.

herself."[8] Annie Parker showed similar determination and self-confidence. When her husband deserted her in Linden, California, Annie testified: "I came to San Francisco to find employment and better my condition." By her own labor and with the help of friends, she succeeded.[9] Susan Battey and Mary Gray did the same. When Battey discovered that her husband expected her to live in a decrepit flophouse, she became a laundress and secured decent quarters. Gray, who left her husband because of his cruelty, worked so profitably as a dress-maker that she bought property in Redwood City.[10] Elaika Mattson, a miner's wife, possessed similar determination. She endured a year of wifebeating and then, at the age of nineteen, escaped the cruelty and earned her own living. After five years on her own, she filed for divorce. When asked why she had waited so long to bring suit, she replied that she had to save enough money to bring a case. Her diligence was rewarded in 1881 when she received a divorce.[11]

An estranged wife's economic situation did not depend solely on her ability to support herself. Wives left in financial straits by indolent or departed husbands could turn to neighbors, friends, or relatives for help. Table 7 summarizes the sources of such aid for those women who provided this information in the divorce proceedings. (The total percentage is greater than 100 because women often received support from more than one source.) The table reveals that women depended primarily on themselves for support.[12] Despite the poor job opportunities, three-

[8] *William* v. *Sophia Hendrickson*, Case 382, San Mateo County, 1882 (testimony of J. W. Landon). This form of citation will be used throughout the essay. The date (1882) refers to the year in which the plaintiff's divorce complaint was filed. The information in parentheses refers to the specific source of the information. The cases are without pagination.

[9] *Annie* v. *Edwin Parker*, Case 403, San Mateo County, 1882 (testimony of Annie Parker).

[10] *Walter* v. *Susan Battey*, Case 1404, Santa Clara County, 1860 (defendant's answer); *Mary* v. *James Gray*, Case 635, San Mateo County, 1885 (formal complaint).

[11] *Elaika* v. *Marlin Mattson*, Case 214, San Mateo County, 1880 (testimony of Elaika Mattson).

[12] The records generally indicate that most women supported themselves and, in addition, received help from various people. The evidence does not, however, reveal the pattern of support. Thus, for example, it is impossible to determine whether women who supported themselves received steady additional aid from their parents or friends or received such help only in times of crisis. Nor can it be determined if children volunteered support or were requested to do so by their mother or her concerned

fourths of the wives earned at least part of their own livelihood. The other sources of help were split almost evenly between kin (parents, children, siblings, and other relatives) and friends or neighbors.

TABLE 7
SOURCES OF SUPPORT FOR WIVES

Source of Support	Women Who Mentioned Receiving Such Support (total N=172) %	(N)
Supported by Self	75.0	(129)
Supported by Friends/Neighbors	37.8	(65)
Supported by Parents	15.6	(27)
Supported by Relatives	15.1	(26)
Supported by Children	6.4	(11)
Supported by Siblings	5.2	(9)

Unfortunately, the records do not indicate the size of the contributions so the absolute numbers may be deceiving. Parental help, for example, was probably more substantial and of longer duration than neighborly aid. Nevertheless, the number of wives receiving community charity is striking. Women who "failed" in marriage were obviously not social pariahs avoided by their friends.

However, this community support was not automatic but usually came only after the wife's innocence or guilt had been established in the eyes of the community. When income sources for female plaintiffs (the innocent party) are compared with sources for female defendants (the accused party), sharp differences emerge, particularly in the support offered by friends and neighbors. Wives bringing suit received help from the community in 46.3 percent of the cases (total N = 134); but the same figure for women accused of destroying the marriage was a mere 7.9 percent (total N = 38). Community assistance was an accurate barometer of wifely morals; it was high when her actions were judged morally correct and almost nonexistent when her character was in question.[13]

friends. For 229 cases, there was no information whatsoever on the wive's economic situation.

[13]These figures came only from those cases which included information about the woman's source(s) of support, regardless of whether she was the plaintiff or the

For Victorian wives, life without a husband was hard but not impossible. Friends and relatives were willing to help, and their aid, coupled with the wife's own labor, meant that a husband's desertion or nonsupport was not catastrophic. Certainly the transition from domestic duties to work outside the home was eased by the domestic nature of much of the work, but the high percentage of women who supported themselves speaks well for their ability, when necessary, to move beyond dependence on their husbands.[14]

* * *

Economic support from relatives and friends was not the only kind of assistance wives received. Women also relied on other women for moral and sororal support. The "female world of love and ritual," so perceptively analyzed by Carroll Smith-Rosenberg, was a world of intense, life-long, and special friendships which could be called upon in times of crisis.[15] This is dramatically revealed in the case of Samantha Hughes, a farmer's wife, who was accused of desertion by her husband in 1863. Sometime earlier Elisha Hughes had written her a letter asking her to return and suggesting that she must be miserable now that they no longer lived together. Her reply appears in the divorce records. "You are very much mistaken," she told him. "I *am not* sad and lonely. I am only in bad health." She then thanked him for his offer of assistance but quickly added, "I do not neede [*sic*] anything. I am as happy as any one can be who is in bad health. I have a good home with Julia and plenty of good kinde [*sic*] friends." Samantha's language became even bolder and more resolute: "I would beg, starve, and die rather than live with you againe [*sic*]. I do not want a husband. All I want is a good home and that I have with Julia and will have as longe [*sic*]

defendant. Not surprisingly, most cases in which females were defendants contained no information about their economic situations, but these cases were not included in the comparison above.

[14]On the purposeful, instrumental nature of wives' domestic labor, see Cott, *The Bonds of Womanhood*, 42 ff., 54–58, 63–100; and Sklar, *Catharine Beecher*, 151–167. Also, see my "The Character of the Family in Rural California, 1850–1890" (Ph.D. dissertation, Stanford University, 1979), 61–69.

[15]Carroll Smith-Rosenberg, "The Female World of Love and Ritual," *Signs: A Journal of Women in Culture and Society*, I (1975), 1–30.

as she lives. . . . I never will live with you againe [*sic*]. Do you understand, never NEVER."[16]

Such sororal assistance threatened men who feared an independent wife. In 1882 Edwin Parker, an unemployed school teacher, was accused of cruelty and failure to support his wife. He attributed his wife's charges to her association with a group of women in San Francisco whom he disparaged as a "batch of low bred scandal loving women . . . who kneel at the shrine of a religion which teaches its devotees that they ought to leave their *undeveloped husbands* and seek their affinity elsewhere." Chief among the "low bred" and the woman responsible for convincing his wife to search for a rich husband (in contrast to an "undeveloped" one) was a "medium, Mrs. Wilson, No. 675 Mission Street, [who] received a communication from some one purporting to be her first husband that she ought to leave that undeveloped man." Edwin, often unemployed and anything but wealthy, saw a cabal of women—led by a mystic who communicated with her dead husband—luring his wife to the pursuit of a rich husband. He concluded a rather bizarre letter to his wife by revealing just how threatened he was by her new-found independence: "So you have secured the pound of flesh and . . . now as I assume the role of a mind reader for the time being, I can see you as you fly away on the wings of fancy to some drawing room, yourself the central figure reposing as a boudoir flower, all troubles at an end."[17] Certainly his wife's association with these women—whatever the merits of their beliefs—gave her a degree of support and independence that left her husband angry, threatened, and slightly dumbfounded.

If women drew strength and support from other women, they drew them as well from relatives. Disputes on moving to California offer evidence that wives were not powerless when husbands made unilateral decisions to head West. In the follow-

[16] *Elisha* v. *Samantha Hughes*, Case 1810, Santa Clara County, 1863 (letter of Samantha Hughes to Elisha Hughes). Emphasis in original. Samantha's friend, Arena Gardner, also testified that Samantha had no intention of living with her husband: "I have heard her say she never would live with him. Had heard her say so frequently. We had several conversations about it. She told me she would starve before she would live with him."

[17] *Annie* v. *Edwin Parker*, Case 403, San Mateo County, 1882 (letters of Edwin Parker to his wife and to the superior court judge). On the importance of mediums in many women's lives in the nineteenth century, see R. Laurence Moore, *In Search of White Crows: Spiritualism, Parapsychology and American Culture* (New York, 1977).

ing cases, the women either refused to leave or returned to the state in which they were married. If we assume marriage occurred at the bride's home, then these women chose their families of birth over their families of marriage. While this choice may seem like no great show of independence, it does suggest that women were not without options and that families were flexible and forgiving when daughters made choices that contravened the female role.

Jennie Denson, for example, refused to accompany her new husband to Galveston, Texas, soon after her marriage in 1876, but she did agree to move to New Orleans because it was closer to her home in Tennessee. To the detriment of his business, Richard Denson moved to Louisiana where his wife joined him, but in a few days she announced her refusal to live "in any other city or place in the world except at her home among her folks at or in the immediate neighborhood of Moscow, Tennessee." Denson refused to "sacrifice all his business affairs," and she refused to budge from Tennessee. The marriage ended with Jennie at home and Richard in California.[18]

Parental security also provided Zilpha Plumb with the confidence to remain apart from her husband when, after going bankrupt, he decided to recoup his fortunes in the West. She refused to follow him. "We had been living in Boston, Massachusetts and I failed in business," he explained to the divorce court. "My wife left and went to her mother's home in Orleans County, New York since which time we have never lived together." His wife's stubbornness—coupled with economic support from her mother—enabled her to defy her husband's intentions: "She refused to return then, and repeatedly since that time. . . . She has refused all and every offer I have made to her for reconciliation."[19] Addie Gray was another who refused to leave her relatives behind. Her stepdaughter overheard Addie tell her husband that she would not leave Illinois, and Addie personally informed her stepdaughter "that she would not under any consideration reside in the state of California."[20]

---

[18] *Richard* v. *Jennie Denson*, Case 1268, San Mateo County, 1878 (formal complaint).
[19] *Mills* v. *Zilpha Plumb*, Case 364, San Mateo County, 1882 (testimony of Mills Plumb).
[20] *William* v. *Addie Gray*, Case 480, San Mateo County, 1883 (testimony of Carrie Gray).

The experiences of other wives reveal that unilateral decisions by husbands to move were often fraught with danger when women had alternatives at their disposal. Park Henshaw convinced his wife to leave Missouri, but he failed to keep her in California after they reached Chico in 1877. Soon after arriving, she told a friend that she "did not like California," "regretted that she had come," "would not live in California and wanted to return to Missouri." When her two children died, Ella returned to her home in Missouri, later came back to California for one month, then returned again to Missouri, this time permanently, even though "Mr. Henshaw had gone to considerable expense in fitting up a house for them to live in."[21]

The love of kin and community also persuaded Emma Waterbury, Mary King, Jane Keith, and Emily Merrill to remain in their home state rather than make the trip to California. Like others, William Waterbury came to California in 1869 to "better my condition." A year later he sent for his wife because he "was anxious to have her with me." The feeling was far from reciprocated; she would neither leave her home in Virginia nor respond to his letters, and in 1883 William received a divorce on grounds of desertion.[22] Mary King and her husband married in Wisconsin and lived there for eight years before her husband was transferred to California. She refused to accompany him, an act of independence that resulted in a successful desertion suit against her.[23] For ten years, Jane Keith adamantly refused to leave Illinois to join her husband in California. Twice he sent his brother to Illinois to fetch her, and both times she refused to leave. Joseph Keith finally sued for divorce in 1865.[24] Brave words accompanied Emily Merrill's decision to stay in Maine when, five months after marriage, her husband announced they were moving to California. He could go where he pleased, she told him, but "she was capable of taking care of herself and

[21] *Park* v. *Ella Henshaw*, Case 837, San Mateo County, 1887 (testimony of Cora Kennedy). Ella was married in Missouri.

[22] *William* v. *Emma Waterbury*, Case 419, San Mateo County, 1882 (testimony of William Waterbury).

[23] *Will* v. *Mary King*, Case 375, San Mateo County, 1882 (formal complaint).

[24] *Joseph* v. *Jane Keith*, Case 385, San Mateo County, 1865 (testimony of Elisha Keith).

intended to do so. . . ." Three years later, Emily was still in Maine, reputedly living in bigamy with farmer James Miller.[25]

* * *

Another important area of female independence is virtually inaccessible to historical inquiry. Much to the dismay of their husbands, some wives refused to suppress their extramarital sexual desires, a refusal suggesting that the Victorian woman's alleged lack of interest in sex stemmed more from the fervent hopes of moralists than from reality. Women were not sexless, passionless creatures hopelessly locked in a suffocating domestic world. Nineteenth-century moralists might insist on sexual fidelity in marriage, they might insist that all women, regardless of social class, subscribe to the tenets of Victorian sexual morality, but dissatisfied women could establish a new sexual relationship if the opportunity arose and their sense of independence overcame the pull of contemporary morality.[26] Ann Stevens was such a woman.

Five years after marriage, Lew Stevens suspected his wife had committed adultery, and in late 1883, he brought a divorce suit against her. As part of the evidence, he included two letters his wife had written her lover, and though it was unclear how the letters made their way into court, they left no doubt that Ann was an independent woman enthusiastic about sexual activity. She was also quite clever. Ann wrote parts of the letters, specifically some of the sections dealing with sex, in an ingenious

[25] *Ruell* v. *Emily Merrill*, Case 895, San Mateo County, 1873 (formal complaint). For other cases of wives preferring to live in the state where they married, see *Joseph* v. *Helen Gilpatrick*, Case 633, San Mateo County, 1869 (formal complaint); *John* v. *Annie Bradbury*, Case 461, San Mateo County, 1883 (formal complaint); *Charles* v. *Kate Leszynsky*, Case 228, San Mateo County, 1881 (formal complaint).

[26] Although the cult of feminine purity is generally associated with middle-class women, Carl Degler is surely correct in arguing that middle-class women—and hence middle-class values—"undoubtedly set the tone and provided the models for most women." See Degler, "What Ought to Be and What Was: Women's Sexuality in the Nineteenth Century," *American Historical Review*, LXXIX (1974), 1469. The divorce records also reveal that women from all social classes were expected to follow middle-class ideas about sexual propriety. See my "The Character of the Family in Rural California, 1850–1890," 98–109.

code comprised of number substitutes for letters—the strange mix of "f38d th2 wly 5p y457 t94ws29s" became "find the way up your trowsers" when decoded. Moreover, she was not one to be put off by community pressure. When a friend disparagingly remarked that Ann apparently thought "a good deal" of Walter Knight, her lover, Ann defended her sentiments: "I told him I certainly did. I never should deny that at all. I told him I had a perfect right to think a good deal of you." Never mind she was a married woman living in a small California town. Ann also described to Walter how she planned to increase the friction within her marriage: "There is going to be a picnic here in Woodside next Sunday and I am going just to plague Lew. I am going everywhere I can [and] nothing will make him mad so quick as that." She hoped by such behavior to drive her husband away so that she and Walter could get togehter. "He thinks I do not care anything for him. That is just what I want—I hope I can act so that he will go to Colorado and if he once goes I will take good care he never comes back."[27]

Until Lew left, Ann could only fantasize about the future, but her letters gave her lover a vivid sense of the sexual enjoyments to come. Ann Stevens—and certainly many other Victorian women as well—bore little resemblance to the "typical" Victorian woman described by William Acton as "not very much troubled with sexual feelings of any kind."[28] After lamenting her loneliness, Ann excitedly wrote that she might soon visit Chico, Walter's town: "Then there would be some tall diddling done and a little hugging thrown in. . . . And when I see you again, perhaps I might find the way up your trowsers leg. At the same time, if I could see you a few minutes, I should sit down on you a few times."[29] In a letter written several weeks later, Ann even more directly stated her sexual desires: "I wish you was here tonight. I am upstairs in my room where you slept—and if you was here, I suppose we should do some tall fucking." Ann ended this second letter on a bittersweet note as she reaffirmed

[27] *Lew* v. *Ann Stevens*, Case 517, San Mateo County, 1883 (letter of May 4, 1882, from Ann Stevens to Walter Knight).

[28] Action is quoted in Degler, "What Ought to Be and What Was," 1467.

[29] *Lew* v. *Ann Stevens*, Case 517, San Mateo County, 1883 (letter of May 4, 1882, from Ann Stevens to Walter Knight).

her sexual desires yet bemoaned her separation from Walter: 'Oh how I wish you was round so I could get hold of you now and then. I just feel like having a racket with you once in awhile and there *you* are and *here* I am. I hope we won't always be so far apart. I can be near enough to them I care nothing for.'"[30]

The behavior of Julia Grosjean, like that of Ann Stevens, exhibited a lusty independence not generally associated with Victorian womanhood. Camille Grosjean, a successful grocer, described the disgrace he incurred due to his wife's behavior. "Whenever I took her into society she would act like a woman of loose character, and finally she was shunned by the best people in town." Her impropriety consisted of "flirting with everyone she met, and making love to married men with whom she was thrown into contact, until her name had become a byword for extreme levity of character if nothing worse. . . ." Camille worried that she would "ruin and disgrace me," a fear that suggests the close relationship between female sexual propriety and social standing among the middle class.[31] He then offered an explanation for her behavior that was restrained but firmly anchored in Victorian morality: "I can only say this. She could have no other reason than she could not be satisfied with the restraint of a virtuous life. She loved and coveted the admiration of other men, and in that respect she was unfit for the duties and responsibilities of wifehood and motherhood. I do not desire to speak stronger than this in regard to one that bears the station of wife to me." Grosjean had offered a classic Victorian indictment of his wife. She lacked restraint and virtue, her dedication to her husband was grossly suspect, and her general character meant she was ill-equipped for that most womanly of tasks—motherhood. Camille concluded by sadly noting the strength of the public's association of a husband with his wife, an association that gave Julia a negative but powerful influence over her husband: "After she left, I remained some time intending to brave it out, but the disgrace of her conduct made it impossible for me to continue business [any] longer in

[30] *Ibid.* (letter of May 23, 1882, from Ann Stevens to Walter Knight).

[31] *Camille* v. *Julia Grosjean*, Case 345, San Mateo County, 1882 (testimony of Camille Grosjean). "Making love" here apparently refers to flirting and not sexual intercourse; adultery was not charged against Julia.

Houston."[32] The moral weight of polite society was too great to bear; like others, Camille went West to get a fresh start.

While Lew Stevens and Camille Grosjean could not control their wives' extramarital affairs, Cornelius Paddock had a problem of a different sort. In 1877, the teamster complained that his wife repeatedly embarrassed him despite his patient efforts to curb her indelicacies. She sang lewd songs in front of friends and, on one occasion, had allegedly exposed herself to others at their home in Woodside by "lifting up her clothes and undergarments to her waist, having no drawers on and exposing her person." He also stated she caused him great anguish when she would tip back in her chair, "open her limbs, and indecently expose her person."[33] To prove his wife's intractableness, Cornelius obtained the testimony of a former lodger, Charles Peterson, who at one time had shared the same bedroom with Cornelius and his wife. "She sat down in a chair," recalled Peterson, "and told Ida, her daughter, to wash her feet and [then] she pulled her clothes up over her knees. She had drawers on as far as I noticed. She pulled her clothes up above her knees. . . . She lay back in the chair and screamed something. I went outside." The court asked if Peterson considered her exposure indecent: "Yes, if a man had a good view of her." On other occasions, the lodger "saw her sit down in chairs and pull her clothes up and put her feet upon the stove." He also remembered a lewd song that the irrepressible Ann Paddock had insisted on singing. "She sung a song in 1876. The song was beef steak, mutton chop and a little old hat. Mr. Paddock told her if she wanted to sing such a song to go outside and sing it." Peterson was slightly uncertain about the lyrics but quite sure that a true lady had no business singing them: "The meaning so far as I understand must be a fast house song. It means if you get hold of a woman, you want a little from her."[34] Peterson, it should be noted, was no sensitive shrinking violet.

[32] *Ibid.* (testimony of Camille Grosjean).

[33] *Cornelius* v. *Ann Paddock*, Case 1276, San Mateo County, 1877 (amended complaint). This case provides good evidence that middle-class ideas about sexual propriety infused working class values as well. The point of this testimony is to reveal that Ann—a teamster's wife—did not adhere to proper notions of female decorum despite social expectations that she do so.

[34] *Ibid.* (testimony of Charles Peterson).

At the time he testified, the laborer was a prisoner at San Quentin penitentiary.

The disposition of the Paddock case revealed a judge less concerned with household propriety than with a rising divorce rate. After Cornelius had presented his evidence, the judge dismissed the case: "The acts proven are only a little peevishness and some little jealousy," he declared, "but in my opinion are not such acts as are by the statutes considered good grounds for a divorce." They "do not endanger life or render matrimonial intercourse unsafe, and ought not even to render it unpleasant to a man of philosophic turn of mind."[35] Apparently Cornelius lacked—and the judge possessed—that turn of mind that might find something oddly refreshing in Ann's eccentric independence. Moreover, the judge believed that divorces "are becoming too common in this country and courts should in all cases require *full* statutory proof before dissolving so sacred a relation as that which should exist between husband and wife."[36] In light of the rising divorce rate, the judge reasoned that nineteenth-century marriage had ample room for female independence even if the wife's actions directly annoyed the husband's sensibilities.

* * *

If nineteenth-century American society restricted a wife's economic opportunities and the cult of true womanhood relegated her to the home, she nontheless could find alternatives to a life of constant submission and obedience. While many of the women in this study were perhaps more courageous than most in their willingness to test or break what people agreed was a sacred bond, the kinds of options and support available to them were open to other women as well. Self-support or assistance from friends and relatives helped wives overcome financial dependency on their husbands; a community of kin and friends protected wives against unilateral decisions made by husbands; and close friendships with other women provided emotional support in the difficult process of ending a marriage.

---

[35] *Ibid.* (judge's order dismissing the case).
[36] *Ibid.*

LAW, SEX, CRUELTY, AND DIVORCE IN VICTORIAN AMERICA, 1840-1900

ROBERT L. GRISWOLD
University of Oklahoma

IN 1874, JUSTICE JOHN M. SCOTT OF THE ILLINOIS SUPREME COURT DESCRIBED THE damage a husband inflicted upon his wife by his false allegations of infidelity: "Cruel treatment does not always consist of actual violence. There are words of false accusation that inflict deeper anguish than physical injuries to the person—more enduring and lacerating to the wounded spirit of a gentle woman, than actual violence to the person, though severe."[1] Sometime later the Oregon Supreme Court addressed the same issue and underscored the dire impact such accusations had on innocent wives: "To charge a woman, in the presence and hearing of others, with the commission of the crime of adultery, is to render her subject to the gross insults of lustful men who may hear and believe the rumor, which, whether true or false, tends to rob her of her good name, alienate her friends and acquaintances, and deprive her of their society and companionship."[2] Both justices then proceeded in each case to sunder the bonds of matrimony, the very foundation of Victorian social order.

Their decisions, while restrained and wedded to precedent, nevertheless directly or obliquely reflected contemporary debates over family stability, marital cruelty, conceptions of manhood, woman's place in nineteenth-century society, and Victorian attitudes about sexuality. The two judges were no more immune to these issues than anyone else and probably less so, for they held the responsibility of reconciling middle-class hopes for family cohesion with changing sex roles, marital expectations, and legal definitions of domestic cruelty.[3] These two appellate decisions, supplemented by about one hundred others dealing with sexual cruelty, thus provide a way to investigate the complicated connections among Victorian ideology, sexual behavior, and acceptable marital conduct. If the judges were not always consistent, if they sometimes favored marital indissolubility over freedom from objectionable marriage bonds and at other times preferred the reverse, their ambivalence or inconsistency surely reflected wider confusion over the competing claims of family life and personal autonomy.[4] Despite this ambivalence, judges during the nineteenth century nevertheless

The author would like to thank Professors Drew Kershen, David Levy, Robert Nye, and Robert Shalhope for their helpful criticisms and comments. Research for this essay was made possible in part by a 1983 National Endowment for the Humanities Summer Grant (FT-23334) and a 1984 University of Oklahoma Junior Faculty Summer Research Fellowship.

grew more sensitive to the issue of sexual cruelty and more willing to break a marriage when either spouse, but especially husbands, offended the sexual sensibilities of their mates.

The history of sexual cruelty and divorce is inextricably linked to the interrelated histories of the meaning of marriage in general and matrimonial cruelty in particular. In the century after 1750, middle-class family life increasingly became the realm of affection, mutuality, expression, and sentiment. While the economic aspects of marriage did not vanish—romantic marriages, in fact, obscured the fundamental economic dependence of wageless wives upon breadwinning husbands—the growing emphasis on companionate love shifted the balance of marital motivation away from instrumental concerns and toward matters of the heart. As part of this development, gender ideals changed: for women, the emergence of domestic ideology, the ideology of passionlessness, and the apotheosis of motherhood inflated women's moral and spiritual standing while simultaneously identifying them ever more closely with a separate female sphere centered in the home. For men, companionate family relations included the traditional requirement that husbands support their wives economically—now increasingly in a location removed from the home—and new demands that they respect their mates' moral superiority, control their sexual urges, and make a more profound psychological commitment to their wives and children.[5]

This shifting balance in the meaning of marriage brought more rather than less marital discord. Changes in sex roles and family life prompted thousands of Americans to demand more of their marriages than ever before: when expectations did not meet with reality, many of these same Americans sought relief in divorce court. By today's standards, the figures on divorce in the late nineteenth and early twentieth centuries are quite low, but they seemed alarmingly high to contemporaries. From 1867 to 1886, United States courts granted 328,716 divorces; in the next twenty years, the number jumped to 945,625, far outstripping the proportionate rise in population.

At the center of this increase was a giant rise in the number of cases brought on the grounds of cruelty. From 1867 to 1906, wives received 218,520 divorces because of cruelty and husbands 39,300. Next to nonsupport, cruelty cases rose more sharply than cases based on any other cause in these years. Comparing the years 1902-1906 with 1867-1871, divorces granted to wives on the ground of cruelty jumped 960 percent, and to husbands 1,610 percent. Between 1867 and 1871, 18 percent of divorces granted to wives were on the ground of cruelty; that figure for the years 1902-1906 was 29 percent. The same comparison for husbands reveals a jump from 4 percent to 12.5 percent.[6]

The surge in divorces brought on the ground of cruelty suggests a transforming marital relationship. Couples quite clearly expected more of marriage tnan ever before and showed an increasing willingness to use the courts for redress, a point especially true for women, who received over 80 percent of divorces on the ground of cruelty. Whether guilty of physical or more subtle forms of psychological abuse, almost a quarter of a million husbands found themselves successfully accused of matrimonial cruelty between 1867 and 1906. Pressed by these changing ideas about marriage, jurists after mid-century expanded the legal definition of marital cruelty to embrace behavior once considered endurable, albeit unfortunate. No longer did American courts insist on violence or threats of violence to prove cruelty sufficient for a divorce; inspired, in part, as we shall see, by a ew disposition toward sexual epithets and sexual excesses, jurists began to find mental torment sufficiently cruel to warrant the breakup of a marriage. Helped by vague statutes and equally vague but flexible appellate decisions, husbands, but especially wives, found in cruelty complaints a convenient repository for their marital discontents.

The transformation of the legal definition of marital cruelty was a slow process that took the better part of a century to accomplish. Until the 1840s, American interpretations of matrimonial cruelty remained closely aligned with English theories. All English libels for separation on the ground of cruelty included actual violence, and not until the landmark case of *Evans v. Evans* in 1790 were threats of violence and a "reasonable apprehension of bodily hurt" deemed sufficient to justify legal separation.[7] This narrow definition underlay the statutory laws that appeared in the new American states in the late eighteenth and early nineteenth centuries. Unlike England which technically had no absolute divorce, however, some American states granted absolute divorces on the ground of cruelty. For example, New Hampshire laws included cruelty as a ground for absolute divorce in 1791, Vermont and Rhode Island in 1798, Ohio in 1804, Kentucky in 1809 to the wife only, Pennsylvania in 1815 to the wife only and in 1854 to both the wife and husband, Delaware and Michigan in 1832, Iowa in 1839, Texas in 1841, and Kansas in 1855.[8] Other states, especially in the South, passed laws that permitted legal separations for cruel behavior but continued to limit grounds for absolute divorces to adultery or, in some cases, to incurable impotency, confinement in a penitentiary, premarital pregnancy by someone other than the groom, or desertion. By 1886, it is worth noting, only six states did not grant an absolute divorce on the ground of cruelty.[9]

Not until the 1840s did American judges draw away from the English insistence on violence or threats of violence as the basis for a partial or total divorce.[10] This reluctance stemmed from the belief that individual happiness was less important than social order and that instrumental aspects of marriage should take precedence over emotional matters. Certainly cruelty did not warrant a divorce simply because such behavior caused unhappiness or signified the absence of love.[11] The family unit was far too important to be dissolved for such capricious reasons: better to endure bickering, coldness, and insensitivity than to threaten the foundation of society.[12]

Yet, after 1850, faults and slippages developed within this traditional legal landscape. The granite of conservative doctrine began to crack, ever so slowly, as new views of family life, sexuality, the female psyche, and manhood emerged.[13] Although courts continued to insist that only "grave and weighty" reasons warranted legal dissolution of a marriage, the definition of "grave and weighty" expanded to include behavior that posed a serious threat to the health of the spouse yet offered no physical violence or even threat of such violence. By the late nineteenth century, even the emphasis on bodily health disappeared in some states as jurists began accepting mental cruelty as a justifiable ground for divorce.[14] One area that figured prominently in jurists' deliberations about cruelty was sexuality, specifically sexual epithets, sexual excesses, and sexual deprivation. The first two played key roles in prompting more expansive definitions of matrimonial cruelty that redounded to woman's benefit; the third revealed that jurists were as yet unwilling to see sexual satisfaction as essential to marriage. To jurists, companionate family relations did not necessarily include mutually satisfactory sexual relations: although a husband's sexual epithets or excessive carnal demands became divorceable offenses, sexual deprivation by either party did not.

Sexual Epithets, Social Change, and the Transformation of Matrimonial Cruelty

As the meaning of marriage in the nineteenth century shifted from a less instrumental to a more affective basis, and as the status of women within the home rose, the image of an uncontrollable, brutish husband falsely impeaching the sexual fidelity of his innocent, passionless wife troubled the Victorian conscience. While there is no direct evidence that the use of such epithets was increasing in frequency, husbands could not have been oblivious to the realization that such accusations could cause overwhelming pain. What better way to wound a wife than to challenge her fidelity to prevailing conceptions of sexual decorum.[15] If such accusations went unchallenged, a wife stood to lose not only her sexual reputation but any claim to respect whatsoever. While the risks for a woman seeking a divorce were great—after all, what a woman gained in peace of mind, she might lose due to social ostracism and economic vulnerability—thousands of women found the prospect of new dependencies less troubling than the prospect of remaining with a man who defiled all that gave meaning to nineteenth-century marriage. Against the backdrop of these moral and ideological changes in family life and womanhood, American courts began to acknowledge that a husband's false allegations of adultery justified a divorce. In short, legal leverage shifted in directions more favorable to women.[16]

Sexual epithets had not always possessed such power. Reflecting older English interpretations of cruelty and traditional views of marriage, an 1845 Connecticut decision deplored the husband's "vulgar, obscene, and harsh" epithets and his false allegations of adultery, but found them insufficient for divorce unaccompanied by acts of actual menace or violence. Though his jealousy caused her great sorrow and prompted pity, "the law furnishes no remedy for conduct like this. It may be intolerable, but [it] is not intolerable cruelty."[17] So, too, the Missouri Supreme Court in 1847 made a similar argument and worried that "too great a facility in obtaining divorces is exceedingly injurious to the good morals and happiness of domestic life." How, the court asked, could mere words qualify as cruelty without some scale or standard of refinement for estimating the degree of offense to female sensibilities?[18] (In fact, courts repeatedly stumbled over the difficulty of assessing the impact of cruel behavior on women of different social classes; however, most jurisdictions agreed that a refined, sensitive woman could endure less cruelty than a woman of "coarse" or "rough" background.)[19]

After the 1840s false allegations of adultery began to carry increasing weight in divorce suits. More traditionally inclined courts insisted that false adultery allegations must also create fears of bodily harm or actual damage to health to be sufficient for a divorce, but a divorce was at least possible; others suggested that such allegations, accompanied by even the slightest threat of personal violence, met statutory definitions of cruelty, for only a husband consumed by hatred—and hence a physical threat to his wife—would make such charges. A third group of interpretations emphasized that such accusations, if made publically, exposed wives to "the contempt of the world and the insults and assaults of the worst of mankind." The courts' fear that predatory, lascivious males might stalk and victimize the innocent, unjustly accused wife reveals Victorian suspicions, shared by conservatives and feminists alike, of male sexual aggression. Finally, some courts underscored the mental suffering caused by such accusations or, in states recognizing indignities as a ground for separation or divorce, the fact that false adultery accusations "make life burdensome" and the "discharge of marital obligations impossible."[20] These new perspectives on sexual epithets came about in large part because of changing judicial attitudes about the nature of family life.

Although statutory laws, the interpretation of such laws, and the analyses of precedent varied from state to state, judges in mid-century sexual cruelty cases began offering less traditional definitions of the family that reflected long-developing changes in courtship, romance, and child-rearing. In so doing they acknowledged that personal happiness and a woman's claim to sexual self-respect outweighed traditional commitments to marital stability. In 1854, the Indiana Supreme Court delineated this modern view of the family by noting that marriage was not simply a physical or sensual relation but a bond that ideally promoted "social happiness and mental enjoyments"; moreover, people's social, moral, and intellectual natures subjected them to both pain and pleasure, and "if they can be wounded and healed, as well as the physical part, with accompanying suffering and delight, then, we think, that conduct which produces perpetual sorrow, although physical food be not withheld, may well be classed as cruel, and entitle the sufferer to relief." The court added that cold neglect "has sent broken-hearted to the grave hundreds of wives, where the dagger, poison, and purposed starvation have sent one."[21] Likewise, the Kansas Supreme Court in 1883 criticized older interpretations for "taking too low and sensual a view of the marriage relation. . . . The tendency of modern thought," Justice Daniel M. Valentine added, "is to elevate the marriage relation and place it upon a higher plane, and to consider it as a mental and spiritual relation, as well as physical relation."[22]

Although state courts continued to struggle with the weight of traditional doctrine, and not all jurisdictions embraced such modern interpretations of the family and marital misconduct, enough did so by 1895 to inspire legal commentator William Nelson to concoct the following zoological metaphor to describe modern marriage:

> Marriage is not, in our time, regarded as the imprisonment of two beasts in a cage for the purpose of breeding, to be separated, if they quarrel, only when the weaker languishes in fear. It is an intellectual and spiritual union for the happiness and welfare of the parties, for nurturing and training of children under the most favorable circumstances, for the promotion of health, virtue, and morality of the parties and their children, and for the preservation of their homes.[23]

Emphasizing the companionate aspects of modern marriages, these decisions helped to heighten the emphasis on individual fulfillment within marriage and to make possible the shift to broader definitions of cruelty.

In addition, a more complex view of human emotion and physical health after mid-century promoted a more expansive view of cruelty. Concurring with doctors', domestic moralists', and popular writers' assertions that American women were by nature frail, sensitive, nervous, and subject to a host of "female complaints," judges increasingly recognized that physical well-being could be injured by behavior far more subtle than physical blows.[24] Such was the argument in an oft-cited case from Pennsylvania in 1849. After reviewing earlier English cases, the court reiterated the view that mere insults did not justify divorce, that marital stability was necessary for social order, and that couples must practice forbearance when problems arose. Judge Edward King followed these hoary truisms, however, by staking out new ground. Surely, he argued, violence or threats of violence were not the only behavior that threatened a spouse's health: "Again a husband may, by a course of humiliating insults and annoyances, practised in the various forms which ingenious malice could readily devise, eventually destroy the life or health of his wife, although such conduct may be unaccompanied by violence, positive or threatened." He added that the court's concern should be with the consequences of the cruel behavior, not its particular shape, and "that whatever form marital ill-treatment assumes, if a continuity of it involves the life or health of the wife, it is legal cruelty."[25]

The shape of cruelty, as jurists began to recognize, could take a myriad of forms, but what gave an especially sharp edge to sexual epithets was not only the redefinition of family life and female health underway in the nineteenth century but, more important, the contradiction between such calumnies and the image of female sexual passionlessness that had taken root in the late eighteenth and early nineteenth centuries. Inspired largely by the rise of evangelical religion and an oblique facet of the ideology of domesticity, passionlessness was both a prescription for women and a critique of male licentiousness. By inflating women's moral standing and downplaying their sexual characterization, the male and female architects of this ideology transformed sexual thought. Men were now the more carnal sex, women the more spiritual gender; men were the sexual predators, women the victims; men were in need of sexual reeducation, women in need of respect and protection.[26]

It was an ideology, as Nancy Cott has noted, that offered women a way to assert control in sexual matters, to inflate their moral stature, and to create homosocial solidarity among women; moreover, it was an ideology that legitimated female efforts to control the sexual behavior of men. Secure in the knowledge that females occupied the high moral ground, women found in the ideology of passionlessness a set of assumptions and a vocabulary to check traditional male prerogatives as well as justification for organized efforts to defend themselves against male transgressions of female purity. In prescriptive literature, domestic fiction, and temperance, religious, and sexual purity campaigns, women (and some men) set forth a new standard of manhood that asked of men greater psychological commitment to their wives and children. The new man—kind, affectionate, and attuned to his wife's sensitivity and refinement—respected and even deferred to her keener domestic, religious, and moral judgment. To do otherwise, to treat her as a menial or, worse, to impeach her sexual integrity and thereby expose her to the lascivious desires of undomesticated men, branded the husband a social deviant undeserving of the benefits of marital life.[27]

This interplay between the ideology of female passionlessness and the fear of male licentiousness gave rise in the years after 1830 to a variety of female reform groups and a blizzard of literature intent on controlling male sexual behavior. Although feminists after 1860 began to attack passionlessness—they decried both the medical community's efforts to establish a somatic rather than a spiritual basis for the ideology and the confusion of sexual passionlessness with prudery—the belief in Victorian women's sexual indifference only slowly receded, and not before American jurists had incorporated the assumptions of Victorian sexual ideology into legal interpretations of marital cruelty.

In conjunction with changing conceptions of family life and female health, such assumptions moved many courts after mid-century away from the insistence that marital stability take precedence over individual happiness. Writing in 1883, for example, the Texas Supreme Court left no doubt that malicious accusations of infidelity had the power to destroy a wife's life. After noting that some states did not accept the false charge of unchastity against the wife as a ground for divorce while others found it almost sufficient, the judge boldly stated that Texas courts found it not an *almost* but an *altogether* sufficient ground:

> And why should it not be so held? What are wounds to the person as compared with those that affect the mind? The former may be healed; the latter endure for a life-time. Of all the treasures cherished by a woman, her reputation for chastity is the dearest. "It is the immediate jewel of her soul"; and when an attempt is made by her husband, who should be her protector, to rob her of it; cruelty has reached its utmost limit.[28]

False accusations of adultery not only degraded wives and rendered happiness unobtainable but also heightened female vulnerability to lustful men, a vulnerability that obsessed those reformers who hoped to channel male sexual energy into more constructive pursuits. Men, viewed as predatory, needed control, and both social reformers and feminists hoped to furnish the institutions, the moral instruction, the social pressure, and the laws necessary to end male sexual aggressiveness and female sexual vulnerability. Reformers hung their hopes on "white life" campaigns in the WCTU, on antiprostitution, antipornography, and anticontraception campaigns, and on proper moral instruction of husbands and sons by mothers and wives. Feminists adopted some of these strategies and in the three decades after the Civil War also pursued a far-reaching effort to reduce the frequency of crimes against women: fornication, seduction, visits to prostitutes, adultery, connubial lust, rape, incest, these and other manifestations of aggressive male sexual behavior and the double standard came under attack as feminists tried to protect women victimized by men.[29]

The concern about false allegations of adultery should be seen in the context of these reform efforts: when a husband falsely accused his wife of adultery, he not only defiled her reputation but increased her vulnerability to sexually profligate, unreconstructed males. Such a husband became, in short, a deviant. In 1880 the Wisconsin high court, for example, chided a husband for failing to protect his wife's honor from the advances of a hired man; worse yet, when the husband found the hired man crying by the roadside because his attempt to have sex with his employer's wife had failed, the husband took the man home and paid him his back wages before dismissing him. Such perverse solicitousness did not go unnoticed: "for surely no husband with the feelings of a man, and who entertained for his wife proper love and affection," wrote the judge, "could but resent in some way such a deadly insult and indignity offered to his wife."[30]

The hired hand, despite his abject failure in this instance, represented the uncontrolled male lust that so troubled Victorians. The asymmetry of nineteenth-century sexuality meant that good husbands protected pure wives: deviant husbands exposed their good wives to the lascivious desires of untamed men. A decision in the Texas Supreme Court in 1884 illustrated this dynamic. The judge first argued that a husband must protect his wife's reputation from the "imputations and aspersions of others"; not to do so branded the husband "a poltroon," worthy of universal contempt. But when the husband went further, when he falsely disgraced and degraded his wife, cruelty reached its peak for she now stood exposed "to the contempt of the world and the insults and assaults of the worst of mankind."[31] When a husband impeached his wife's chastity, the protector became the assailant and she became "subject to the gross insults of lustful men who may hear and believe the rumor."[32] Judges, for their part, increasingly recognized the saliency of sexual complaints in cruelty suits, thereby expanding the range of legally unacceptable male behavior.

Despite the difficulty of defining marital cruelty, something of a rough consensus developed after the 1850s. Most American courts accepted some variant of the argument that cruelty could indeed occur without violence or threats of violence, but the behavior must somehow impair the health of the wronged spouse.[33] By the last quarter of the nineteenth century, an even more expansive interpretation of cruelty challenged this consensus as some judicial interpretations and even statutory laws began to recognize the reality of mental cruelty free from observable impact upon the body. It was, of course, a perilous step: physical cruelty or threats thereof were more tangible than the slipperiness of mental cruelty, for how could the courts, as the famous English jurist Lord Stowell asked in 1790, "gauge the quantum of injury done and felt" to women of different temperaments and social backgrounds? How could marital stability—so crucial to social order—be maintained if something so vague as mental cruelty was permitted? Nevertheless, several states explicitly included "mental cruelty" as a ground for divorce while other states passed laws permitting divorces when "indignities, excesses, or outrages" rendered living conditions intolerable or made "the discharge of marital obligations" impossible?[34] Still, the issue remained clouded, and most jurisdictions insisted that mental cruelty—like false allegations of adultery—be shown to cause physical harm before a divorce could be granted. Therefore the secure divorce ground continued to maintain some connection between verbal cruelty and the declining personal health of the wife.

Courts were far less certain about the status of men unfairly accused of adultery. Some states recognized no distinction: Nevada and Michigan shared the Oregon court's opinion that "if either party to the marriage contract falsely charge the other with the commission of the crime of adultery, such false accusation is a sufficient cause for divorce."[35] Other states, however, quite clearly discriminated against men. The reluctance to grant divorces in such cases likely stemmed in part from the judges' awareness of the devastating consequences for a woman if she were the unsuccessful defendant in a divorce suit.

Without hope of alimony, faced with the possibility of loss of child custody, and confronted by a job market that had little room for her, the guilty wife in such a case faced a perilous future indeed.

In addition to such paternalistic, protective considerations, there were other reasons why judges were reluctant to grant husbands a divorce when falsely accused of adultery. Despite increasing psychological demands made upon husbands over the course of the nineteenth century, despite the fact that restraint, sexual fidelity, and emotional commitment comprised elements of proper manhood as well as womanhood, some states maintained that the damage inflicted upon men by false adultery allegations paled compared to the harm done to women. The Texas Supreme Court, for example, found the male psyche far less vulnerable to malicious accusations of infidelity. In 1886 the court averred that a wife's false allegations did not endanger her husband's life, limb, or health, nor did it cause him mental anguish. Indeed, the court clearly supported a double standard: "But taking the gravity of the offense when made against the wife with the comparative levity of it when against the husband, we are of opinion that the mere charge of adultery on the part of the husband made by the wife, though the charge be often repeated and be false, is not, under our laws, a sufficient ground for divorce."[36]

No, this issue was peculiarly women's. Although changing family values prompted both husbands and wives to take advantage of less restrictive definitions of cruelty, women likely benefited more than men from these changes. Courts found the female psyche, not the male, especially vulnerable to false charges of sexual impurity and men, more than women, far more likely to make such charges. The burden of fidelity fell upon both women and men but more heavily upon women, a sexual asymmetry that increased women's power to break free of insensitive, hateful men.

The heightened legal significance given to sexual aspersions suggests a broader paradox: more companionate marital relations increased a wife's vulnerability to psychological abuse but simultaneously stimulated transformations in legal thinking especially helpful to women. Given changing definitions of gender and family relationships, women may well have expected more psychologically from their marriages than men. Unlike men who divided their time between home and work, nineteenth-century middle-class housewives invested almost all of their emotions and energies into their family relationships. When an insensitive husband cruelly assaulted his wife's sexual fidelity, her entire life might well be ruined unless she could end the marriage and start anew. Even if we acknowledge that many late nineteenth-century cruelty suits were actually consensual rather than adversarial in nature (a point made by legal historian Lawrence Friedman) wives likely gained more than husbands from this development.[37] As the patriarchal fiction of marital unity slowly gave way to the recognition that two individuals made up a marriage, wives no longer had to suffer at the hands of cruel, domineering husbands, and mutually miserable couples could now find legal redress by filing a "consensual" cruelty petition.

In addition to freeing wives from psychologically oppressive husbands, new definitions of cruelty signified a legal redefinition of family power relationships. The inflation of women's moral standing and the redefinition of family life brought women—bereft of most other forms of power—the leverage to expect and even demand higher standards of treatment from their husbands. A modicum of kindness and material support were no longer enough. Husbands now had to build relationships that were not only economically secure but morally, psychologically, and emotionally fulfilling.[38] Such, at least, was the message to the white middle class, a message that had special meaning for husbands. For the ideal to become a reality, husbands had to give up the traditional prerogatives of patriarchy, for no truly companionate marriage could take root in the soil of domestic oppression. Some husbands willingly gave up such prerogatives in return for a higher degree of emotional companionship; others were more reluctant, a reluctance reflected both in increasing divorce rates and in a variety of female reform groups that sought to change male behavior.

The changing significance of false allegations of adultery symbolized this transformation in a rather dramatic way: the legal meaning of what had always been a damning epithet clearly changed under the impact of new ideas about family life and gender ideals. Men, of course, could ignore these developments and castigate their wives unmercifully, but if they did so, they took the chance of encountering a judiciary increasingly disposed to more expansive definitions of matrimonial cruelty and a wife increasingly willing to file for a divorce. Wives, after all, received eighty-five percent of the burgeoning number of divorces granted on the ground of cruelty, a fact all the more remarkable in light of the difficulties unmarried women faced in the nineteenth century. With few economic opportunities available and alimony virtually nonexistent, an unmarried woman, especially if she had children, encountered an uninviting world once she left the home of her husband. Yet, the statistics suggest that thousands of women found the risks worth the trouble; a life of economic dependence or poverty may have been bad, but life with an abusive husband was worse.

Divorce Law and the Regulation of Sexual Behavior

Although false charges of adultery were the most common type of sexual abuse, they were by no means the only form. When spouses complained of too much or too little sex, jurists had to struggle not with character defamation but with the more complicated problem of regulating sex within marriage. They were not alone: moralists, ministers, physicians, feminists, free lovers, and utopians all offered contradictory ideas about regulating marital sex, but only judges had to decide exactly what constituted deviant sexual behavior sufficient to dissolve a marriage.

Conservative middle-class social thinkers and religious utopians might counsel abstinence while others advocated male control, but judges had to consider sexual behavior in light of legal precedent, their commitment to stable families, and their belief in personal autonomy.[39] Complicating the matter was the lack of consensus about sex in general: was it a drain on one's vital systems or an expression of intense, even spiritual affection between a husband and wife? Were sexual desires something that men could barely control and that women should scarcely recognize or were such desires for both genders healthy and natural?[40]

Answers to these questions varied, but almost all agreed that marriage properly disciplined, regulated, and channeled sexuality to a socially desirable end—procreation. While medical opinion remained divided on the question of female sexuality and some feminists insisted that women had sexual desires equal to men—health reformer Mary Gove Nichols claimed in 1854, for example, that "a healthy and loving woman is impelled to material union as surely, often as strongly, as man.... The apathy of the sexual instinct is caused by the enslaved and unhealthy condition in which she lives"—many American husbands and wives surely subscribed to the belief that the ideal woman had little interest in sex. This emphasis on passionlessness had become the reigning orthodoxy by 1850. The ideology was not necessarily antifemale, for wives, hopeful of inflating their moral standing, controlling male sexual aggression, and limiting their fertility, had their own reasons for supporting the ideal of female passionlessness. Even writers who recognized the importance of sexual expression to women underscored the necessity of restraining male lust and establishing sexual relations based on mutuality.[41]

This emphasis on sexual restraint did not bode well for husbands who had sex with their wives despite their wives' protestations. Just as nineteenth-century sexual ideology increased the legal impact of false allegations of adultery, the same ideas subjected husbands' sexual behavior to new standards of judgment. Sexual restraint within marriage became the goal, restraint that would, in the hopes of moralists like Henry Wright and William Alcott, direct marriage away from sensuality and toward spirituality.[42] Certainly no truly companionate relationship could develop if a husband disregarded his wife's sexual desires. Husbands did not have an unlimited right to their wives' bodies, a point made by conservative moralists, voluntary motherhood advocates, and progressive feminists: all agreed that husbands' sexual control would enhance women's autonomy, promote good health, and establish marriages based on mutuality, not coercion. Such ideas ultimately led to the formation of various organized efforts to control sexuality by increasing the age of sexual consent and eliminating prostitution and the double standard.

These campaigns converged with other efforts to control male aggression and violence within the family. In the 1860s feminists like Elizabeth Cady Stanton and Susan B. Anthony linked crimes against women—bigamy, seduction, wife-beating, rape, incest, and pornography—to male sexual privilege and aggression. Only when husbands stopped treating wives as property and adhered to a single standard of sexual morality, argued Stanton and Anthony, would such outrages end: in the short run, divorce must be made more accessible to women; in the long run, marriage must become a true spiritual, emotional, and physical partnership that guaranteed a wife's right to say "no" to her husband's sexual advances.[43] In the 1870s, conservative feminists like Lucy Stone and Henry Blackwell also turned attention to crimes against women and, like Stanton and Anthony, hoped social purity campaigns would foster male continence and end brutality toward women. Three times Stone proposed legislation to protect wives from husbands' assaults; three times her bill failed. Frustrated by these failures, Stone turned in the mid-1880s to supporting the establishment of a whipping post for wife beaters, and when that failed, to suffrage as the panacea for domestic violence.[44] Victoria Woodhull's bold declaration in 1873 that she "would rather be the labor slave of a master, with his whip cracking continually about my ears than the forced sexual slave of any man a single hour" expressed in extreme form the sentiments of less radical women as they joined the battle to tame male sexuality.[45]

Although jurists' personal reactions to these reform efforts cannot be gleaned from the case reports, their decisions reflected a growing belief that the control of male sexuality within marriage was within the regulatory powers of the state. At a time of unparalleled debate on male and female sexuality, fertility control, and the need for male sexual control, jurists after the Civil War had to decide what comprised acceptable marital sexual misconduct sufficient to justify a divorce. Legal confusion regarding the general definition of a cruelty compounded their problems as did changing conceptions of family life and gender roles. Finally, the fact that millions of American couples evidently cooperated on sexual matters—witness the dramatic decline in nineteenth-century fertility—likely intensified judges' difficulty in reconciling their desire to keep families together with their hope of protecting women's right to sexual self-possession.

Two important cases involving sexually abusive husbands reveal the resolution of this issue in favor of marital stability. In 1845 the Connecticut Supreme Court of Errors excused Daniel Shaw's sexual indulgence—not because his wife failed to tell him that his sexual demands endangered her health; she had done so—but because he supposedly did not know that his behavior actually harmed her health. (The court determined that it did so.) Not willing to stop with ignorance as an excuse, the court added words that later judges would reject and feminists and purity reformers would surely deplore: acknowledging that she had indeed informed her husband of the danger his behavior posed to her health, the court then asked, "But are we to allow nothing to the innocent opinions of a man mad with jealousy? Are we to allow nothing to the frailty of human nature, excited by passion? Are we to couple an act of this kind with an act where a violent blow was given, which must greatly injure or endanger, and which was so intended?"[46] No, the court inferred, such issues had to be taken into consideration, and in this case the judges decided that his jealousy, uncontrollable passion, and ignorance of his wife's real condition undercut her allegations of cruelty; therefore, they dismissed her suit.

The difficulties purity reformers and feminists faced in redefining and controlling male sexual behavior appeared even more tellingly in an 1876 New Jersey case. The wife, Abigail English, received a separation in chancery court on the basis of her husband's "gross abuse of marital rights." Despite her affliction with a uterine disease that made intercourse terribly painful, he insisted on having sex every night, sometimes two or three times, and used force when she resisted. Somehow enduring two years of such abuse, she finally left her husband and moved to her father's home. After considering the evidence, the lower court granted her a separation on the ground that his behavior rendered it "unsafe for her, under existing circumstances, to cohabit with him or to be under his dominion or control."[47]

Several months later the case appeared on appeal in the New Jersey Court of Errors and Appeals. The high court began by reaffirming the importance of family stability, then chipped away at her case by drawing on the testimony of a doctor who averred that although Abigail did, indeed, suffer pain during intercourse, "a large proportion of married women assent under exactly those circumstances." The judge followed this cheerless view of marital sex with a brief history of the couple's married life, emphasizing how they overcame class and religious differences to establish a marriage their friends and relatives characterized as "remarkably affectionate." But the deciding point was the judge's attitude. His wife's departure, wrote the judge, left John English miserable, remorseful, and "willing to make any reasonable concessions if she will return." Tender letters, entreaties to ministers, Christmas presents for the children, promises of self-denial and forbearance, all impressed the court with the husband's contrition and desire to reunite his family. Convinced that John posed no further threat to Abigail, the court dismissed her suit but warned her husband that a resumption of his past transgressions would bring a permanent separation.[48] Faced with a choice between preserving a marriage or chastising a husband for sexual incontinence, the New Jersey court chose the former on the ground that the husband, filled with guilt and properly repentant, no longer threatened his wife. This decision came despite the fact that he answered her protestations with the chilling reply, "You have stood it before and you will stand it again; you know I cannot help it."[49]

Such were the legal attitudes that purity reformers, feminists, and voluntary motherhood advocates strove to overcome in the late nineteenth century. For all of its traditionalism, however, the case involving Abigail and John English was less hostile to women than the Connecticut case of 1845. In the earlier case, the court excused the husband's actions because of his passion, jealousy, and ignorance; in the latter decision, the court emphasized the husband's ignorance but also his affection, contrition, and fervent desire to reunite his family. Despite the decision against Abigail English, the court hinted at the kind of reasoning that would prompt later American courts to grant divorces on such grounds. John English's behavior had run badly afoul of Victorian attitudes about male sexual control and female sexual vulnerability: he had also trampled upon mid-century attitudes about the importance of family relations built upon domestic morality and mutual respect. Given the enormity of these transgressions, the court in no way excused his sexual profligacy. What it did do, however, was to accept John's promises of reform. He had shown to the court's satisfaction his new allegiance to the companionate ideal: he was properly repentant; he loved his wife and children; he was broken-hearted without their company; and he would control his lust. At least in 1876, such promises prompted the New Jersey court to give the marriage one more chance. This adherence to the traditional reluctance to break up families, however, did not stop the court from warning John that a resumption of improper behavior would bring a permanent separation. In essence, the court placed John English on notice—curb his sexual aggression, control his passion, or face the consequences of state intervention in his family life.

Courts could not long sustain such reasoning in the face of widespread sentiment that men needed to control their sexual impulses. This sentiment developed largely as a corollary to the ideology of domesticity, and although not all women accepted some of the assumptions of domesticity—feminists, for example, criticized the identification of women with the home—most women, whatever their political persuasion, agreed that restraining male sexual aggression was a laudable goal. This consensus, in turn, prompted a reevaluation of cruelty cases involving sexual incontinence more favorable to reformers hoping to check male lust by redefining the nature of manhood.

The decision that best illustrates the shift in sentiment on this issue came in an 1891 Connecticut case. Emily Mayhew's successful lower court suit alleged that her husband insisted on sex despite his knowledge that such behavior undermined her health. In considering his appeal, the high court began by admitting that "what may or may not constitute intolerable cruelty by a husband towards his wife in the exercise of the marital rights is a difficult and delicate question." After this truism, the court moved well beyond the decision rendered by the same court almost fifty years earlier in *Shaw v. Shaw*. Now the court underscored not husbandly passion and jealousy as an explanation and excuse for uncontrolled sexuality but rather the importance of mutual rights and duties regarding sex. While not endorsing the feminist contention that wives alone decide when intercourse occurs, the court certainly emphasized that cooperation and reciprocity lay at the heart of sexual relationships. Marital sex, opined the court, required "the duty of forebearance on the part of the husband at the reasonable request of the wife, as well as the duty of submission on the part of the wife at the reasonable request of the husband."[50]

Despite the Victorian diction—husbands were the sexual aggressors, wives the submissive partners—the court emphasized that control, reasonable requests, and cooperation govern sexual relations. This emphasis on mutuality also appeared in the court's emphatic declaration that men's forbearance was as important as women's "reasonable" submission in regulating sexuality: "Any decision of what constitutes intolerable cruelty in these matters that should leave out of consideration the duty of the husband and look only to the duty of the wife, would be manifestly erroneous."[51] Wives had duties, but so, too, did husbands; past interpretations of cruelty, implied the court, had placed too much emphasis on wifely responsibilities and not enough on husbandly forbearance. That courts were moving, by the end of the nineteenth century, to correct this imbalance suggests that the efforts to promote female autonomy and to alter the meaning of manhood within the family were bearing fruit.

The regulation of excessive sexuality was one thing; sexual indifference was quite another. Husbands and wives who charged that their mates' refusal to have sexual relations justified a divorce received little sympathy and no legal redress in court. Time after time, judges insisted that the absence of sex constituted neither cruelty nor desertion: although such behavior was lamentable, it did not warrant the breakup of a family. The ideal Victorian family, after all, was built on moral and emotional commitment and sexual restraint. Gross, insensitive sexual indulgence clearly violated the tenets of Victorian sexual ideology, and justices responded by subsuming such behavior under the rubric of matrimonial cruelty. An unwillingness to have sex, on the contrary, was simply an overzealous extension of mainstream Victorian thought. Marriage involved love, affection, respect, economic support, child-rearing, and yes, carefully regulated sexual relations that led to procreation and, for a few progressives, to a spiritual union of husband and wife. The cultural meaning given to sexual control within the companionate family, therefore, worked against the interest of husbands and wives dissatisfied with their spouse's unwillingness to have sex.

While it is perhaps noteworthy that litigants considered sexual denial sufficiently grave to include in divorce suits, judges believed otherwise: to their minds, sex was an important part of the marriage relationship, but not essential for the perpetuation of the conjugal bond.[52] In 1891 the Illinois Supreme Court, for example, first alluded to legal commentator Joel Prentiss Bishop's claim that denial of sex for two years constituted desertion, then brusquely swept aside this view as one not "sustained by well considered authorities." Such a claim rested on the assumption that sexual intercourse was "the central element of marriage to which the rest is but ancillary," but the judges rejected such an emphasis: "We think that the willful desertion here referred to was intended to mean the abnegation of all the duties of the marital relation, and not one alone."[53]

The New Jersey Court of Chancery eloquently expressed the assumptions behind such findings in an 1894 decision dismissing a husband's desertion allegations. After twenty years of marriage, the wife in this case withdrew to the front room and insisted she would never sleep with her husband again; but she continued to care for their rooms and the couple continued to eat together and to consult about their two daughters away at school. This continued interaction typified to the court the many elements that made up the marital bond: "It would, I think, degrade the marriage relation," wrote the New Jersey judge, "to hold that it is abandoned when sexual intercourse ceases. The lawfulness of that intercourse is perhaps a prominent and distinguishing feature of married life, but it is not the sum and all of it." Marriage involved far more than a physical bond: it was a relationship that also satisfied emotional, psychological, and day-to-day needs and deserved to continue even in the absence of sexual relations:

> The higher sentiment and duty of unity of life, interest, sympathy, and companionship have an important place in it, and the thousand ministrations to the physical comforts of the twain by each in his or her own sphere, in consideration of the marriage obligation and without thought of pecuniary recompense, fill it up. These latter factors may possibly, to some extent, exist in other relations of life, but not in completeness. They are all necessary to the perfect marriage relation.[54]

This emphasis on the reciprocity, mutuality, and multifunctional character of marriage, in combination with the general interest in promoting marital stability and controlling sexuality, sorely circumscribed the power of divorce complaints based on sexual disinterest. In a culture obsessed with fear of sexual excess, cries of sexual deprivation received little sympathy.

Even the avoidance of sex to limit fertility did not constitute legal cruelty or desertion. Motherhood certainly comprised a key element of nineteenth-century womanhood but so, too, did women's growing right to control their fertility, a right that left husbands with little recourse when wives refused sex in order to avoid pregnancy. Surely, as scholars have suggested, the great fertility decline in the nineteenth century came not without considerable cooperation on the part of couples, but divorce evidence offers hints that marital tension may have accompanied this demographic earthquake as well. Against a husband's claims to the contrary, an 1866 Pennsylvania decision asserted that a wife's refusal to have sex and her simultaneous declaration that she would have no children did not comprise cruelty.[55] The next year the Supreme Court of Massachusetts likewise rejected Jonathan Southwick's claim that his wife deserted him when she withdrew from his bedroom in 1861 because he had permitted their eldest son to enlist in the Union Army. Despite her bold assertion that she "didn't intend to have any more boys for Mr. Southwick to send to the war," that she "had no love for him," and that she was now "nothing but a boarder," the court insisted that legal desertion was more encompassing than denial of sex and that it involved the cessation of cohabitation and abnegation of all the duties and obligations of marriage.[56] In short, refusing sex was wrong, but it was not a divorceable wrong: it was not cruelty because cruelty must threaten bodily health; it was not desertion because the marriage bond involved far more than sex.[57]

In fact, a mate's concern for his or her own health might well outweigh the duty to perform sexually. While Julia Disborough charged her husband with cruelty, she included among her allegations the fact that her sixty-seven-year-old husband refused to have sex with her. He defended himself by claiming that intercourse threatened his health, a point the New Jersey Court of Chancery evidently found convincing because it dismissed her cruelty suit in 1893. Although Victorian suspicions of sex made it difficult to prove that its absence caused bodily injury, these same suspicions, as this case reveals, meant that courts were ready to accept the idea that indulgence might threaten one's health. After all, how could courts chastise Isaiah Disborough for practicing, albeit perhaps to excess, the kind of sexual control that was the hope of feminists and purity reformers in the late nineteenth century?[58] If he carried it to extremes, they were extremes with which the court could live.

The decisions on sex and marital cruelty after mid-century reflected a wider nineteenth-century debate on the meaning of family and gender. Jurists in these years found themselves poised between two eras, forced to reconcile older, traditional views of marriage—a product of the patriarchal world of the common law—with newer assumptions about family life and sex roles so determinedly pressed by domestic moralists and reformers. Their resolution of this conflict in terms more favorable to divorce seekers—especially to female petitioners—reflects two important developments. First, it reflects the power of changing family and gender ideals to change traditional legal assumptions about the virtual indissolubility of marriage. The contradictions within domesticity—itself an ideology of social order—heightened the very breakdown in family stability so feared by domestic theorists: the celebration of women's moral stature, the valorizing of women's domestic contributions, the assertion that women had a right to control sexuality and fertility, the emphasis on female sexual purity, the insistence that men soften their patriarchal grip, all of these corollaries of domesticity increased the likelihood of marital dissolution.

Second, jurists' increasing willingness to grant divorces represents a facet of what historian Michael Grossberg has called nineteenth-century "judicial patriarchy."[59] No matter how much religious leaders agitated for uniform divorce laws and tougher legal restrictions on divorce, no matter how much conservative state legislators tinkered with statutory laws, jurists continued to grant divorces to the small army of petitioners who sought an end to their marital woes. In doing so, judges not only staked out new powers for the bench—they were the ones who gave legal meaning to vague statutory language—but expanded the powers of the state to protect weaker members of the family who were physically or psychologically harmed by stronger members. Most of the time, this meant legal intervention to protect wives, an intervention that eroded male patriarchy but simultaneously increased the discretionary powers of the judicial patriarchy.

Jurists gained such discretionary power by capitalizing on suspicions directed toward both the power of traditional patriarchs—now suspect within the context of nineteenth-century family and gender ideals—and the power of statutory regulation, power suspect because of wider suspicions about centralized government authority in general. As the "primary domestic-relations agents of the expanding republican state," trial and appellate judges in divorce trials (as in other areas of family law) were uniquely situated to examine domestic relations on a case-by-case basis. Only judges, not distant legislators, had the ability to assess a couple's situation, listen to the testimony, weigh the facts, and then grant or withhold a divorce. This power, "an expression of the nation's persistent localism," meant that jurists, pushed by changing cultural currents, interpreted and reinterpreted the meaning of unacceptable marital behavior, and they did so in a way that expanded the judiciary's protection of weaker family members.[60] Cruel treatment, once deemed merely unfortunate but insufficient for divorce, became acceptable as a basis for a divorce suit. Injury to the body and the psyche appeared possible without direct physical violence, and by the end of the century increasing numbers of jurisdictions even found "mental cruelty" sufficiently harmful to justify a divorce.

Sexual cruelty played a crucial role in legitimating this expanded conception of cruelty. Family life provided the terrain on which passionless, domesticated women encountered the insensitivity of carnal, undomesticated men, and out of this encounter between Victorian symbols of virtue and vice came a new definition of marital cruelty. What could be more cruel, judges asked, than for a husband to question falsely the fidelity of his wife or to insist on sex against her wishes? As an answer, judges moved to protect wronged women who had upheld their domestic responsibilities, and in so doing jurists substituted one form of patriarchal protection for another. Quite clearly divorce law had become a part of the domain of sexual politics, part of the multifaceted struggle over definitions of gender and the regulation of family life and sexuality.

This struggle not only broadened and redefined legal conceptions of marital cruelty but helped set the stage for the "divorce crisis" at the turn of the century. Confident that their cruelty petitions would receive sympathetic treatment in most American courts, thousands of late nineteenth- and early twentieth-century Americans petitioned for divorce. This upward trend continued until the Great Depression, fueled by changes in family life produced by urbanization, increased leisure and consumption, a cult of youth, and heightened marital sexual expectations. Paradoxically, the expanded conceptions of cruelty that owed so much to the assumptions of nineteenth-century domesticity were even more appropriate to the culture of the twentieth century as domesticity began to crumble and a heightened emphasis on personal autonomy and individual fulfillment began to take shape.[61]

From a late twentieth-century viewpoint, it is tempting to view the legal developments discussed in this essay in much the same way contemporary proponents did—that is, as the triumph of "advanced civilization" over the "barbarism of the past." And this perspective may have made sense to the husband who found himself legally yoked to a cruel, ill-tempered, insensitive wife or, more commonly, to the woman publicly humiliated by her husband or forced against her wishes to have sexual intercourse. Yet, we should not forget that divorce for women was still a perilous step: what a wife gained in peace of mind or physical well-being she may have lost because of social ostracism and economic vulnerability. In a society with so few economic options for women, divorce meant not general liberation but the advent of different dependencies: that thousands of women were willing to take such a step illustrates how powerfully new conceptions of family and gender resonated in the lives of late nineteenth-century Americans.

NOTES

[1]*Farnham v. Farnham*, 73 *Illinois Reports* 500 (1874).

[2]*Crow v. Crow*, 29 *Oregon Reports* 394 (1896).

[3]Although the historical literature on women and domestic violence is quite slim, three provocative articles by Elizabeth Pleck have begun to examine this issue: "Feminist Responses to 'Crimes Against Women,' 1868-1896," *Signs*, 8 (Spring 1983), 451-70; "The Whipping Post for Wife Beaters, 1876-1906," in Leslie P. Moch and Gary D. Stark, eds., *Essays on the Family and Historical Change* (College Station: Texas A & M Univ. Press, 1983), 127-49; and "Wife-beating in Nineteenth-Century America," *Victimology*, 4 (Fall 1979), 62-74. Jane T. Censer explores the expansion of legal definitions of marital cruelty in the antebellum South in "'Smiling through her Tears': Ante-Bellum Southern Women and Divorce," *The American Journal of Legal History*, 25 (January 1981), 24-47. On English reform efforts to punish wife beaters and to help their victims see Margaret May, "Violence in the Family: An Historical Perspective," in J. P. Martin, ed., *Violence and the Family* (Chichester, West Sussex: John Wiley & Sons, 1978), 135-67. Two works on late nineteenth- and early twentieth-century divorce use county court records to examine changing family values, rising marital dissolution, and changing conceptions of proper behavior—including changing perceptions of cruelty—among California couples: Elaine T. May, *Great Expectations: Marriage and Divorce in Post Victorian America* (Chicago: Univ. of Chicago Press, 1980) and Robert L. Griswold, *Family and Divorce in California, 1850-1890: Victorian Illusions and Everyday Realities* (Albany: State Univ. of New York Press, 1982). Lynne Halem examines divorce law and divorce reform in *Divorce Reform: Changing Legal and Social Perspectives* (New York: The Free Press, 1980); also see Michael S. Hindus and Lynne E. Withey, "The Law of Husband and Wife in Nineteenth-Century America: Changing Views of Divorce," in D. Kelly Weisberg, ed., *Women and the Law: The Social Historical Perspective* (Cambridge, Mass.: Schenkman Publishing Co., 1982), 2:133-53. An older survey is provided by Nelson Blake, *The Road to Reno: A History of Divorce in the United States* (New York: The Macmillan Co., 1962). William O'Neill examines the battle between liberals and conservatives over divorce in *Divorce in the Progressive Era* (New Haven: Yale Univ. Press, 1967) and Lawrence M. Friedman briefly discusses divorce law in *A History of American Law* (New York: Simon and Schuster, 1973), 179-84, 434-40. The most complete discussion of family law in the nineteenth century is Michael C. Grossberg's *Governing the Hearth: Law and the Family in Nineteenth-Century America* (Chapel Hill: Univ. of North Carolina Press, 1985).

[4]For an extended analysis of the competing claims of family life and personal autonomy as it affected women see Carl Degler, *At Odds: Women and the Family in America from the Revolution to the Present* (New York: Oxford Univ. Press, 1980). Most of the evidence in this essay is based on appellate decisions, and although such evidence is not without limitations—it may, for example, suggest a legal

clarity and consistency that did not actually exist at the local level—such cases can function as a kind of survey of legal thinking on important questions. The other major drawback with the use of appellate records is the tendency to treat the law as if it existed in a social vacuum, but my intention is to do precisely the opposite. Another methodological point also bears mention: although nineteenth-century divorce law was almost wholly a statutory creation, statutory law offers little insight into actual legal thinking about divorce. Most states, as Lawrence Friedman has noted, "compiled a hackneyed list of grounds: adultery, cruelty, impotence, desertion" (Friedman, *A History of American Law*, 440). What so vague a term as "cruelty" actually meant had to be determined by local and appellate courts. My own research in local California divorce records from 1850 to 1890 analyzes petitioners' complaints and witness testimony and confirms the general trends discussed in this essay: see Griswold, *Family and Divorce*, 72-75, 114-16. Whether using local or appellate level records, care must be taken to avoid confusing legal interpretations and constructs with actual behavior. Finally, with a few exceptions, the cases in this essay originated as cruelty complaints; however, a few cases involved desertion petitions. The category "sexual cruelty" is my own, a category that admittedly links both allegations about sexual activity (or the lack thereof) with allegations about verbal assaults concerning sexuality. On the use of appellate records see G. Edward White, "The Appellate Opinion as Historical Source Material," *Journal of Interdisciplinary History*, 1 (1971), 491-509.

[5]Among the many fine books on nineteenth-century family history, two of the best are Carl Degler, *At Odds* and Mary Ryan, *Cradle of the Middle Class: The Family in Oneida County, New York, 1790-1865* (Cambridge: Cambridge Univ. Press, 1981).

[6]These statistics are from Carroll D. Wright, *A Report on Marriage and Divorce in the United States, 1867-1886* (Washington, D.C.: Government Printing Office, 1889), 169; and United States Bureau of the Census, *Special Reports: Marriage and Divorce, 1867-1906* (Washington, D.C.: Government Printing Office, 1908-09), 1:11, 26-27.

[7]On the history of English legal definitions of matrimonial cruelty, the most helpful work is John M. Biggs, *The Concept of Matrimonial Cruelty* (London: Univ. of London/Athlone Press, 1962). Nineteenth-century legal commentaries are also useful in tracing the history of cruelty and indispensable for locating relevant cases in the state appellate reports; among the most complete are Joel Pretiss Bishop, *Commentaries on the Law of Marriage and Divorce*, 4th ed. (Boston: Little, Brown, and Company, 1864), 1:586-632; idem, *New Commentaries on Marriage, Divorce, and Separation as to the Law, Evidence, Pleading, Practice, Forms, and the Evidence of Marriage in All Issues on a New System of Legal Exposition* (Chicago: T. H. Hood & Co., 1891), 1:629-85; and William T. Nelson, *A Treatise on the Law of Divorce and Annulment of Marriage* (Chicago: Callaghan and Co., 1895), 260-318. Also helpful is Irving Brown, "Oral Cruelty as a Ground of Divorce," *Central Law Journal*, 46 (Jan.-June 1898), 81-86.

[8]George Elliot Howard, *A History of Matrimonial Institutions* (Chicago: Univ. of Chicago Press, 1904), 3:11, 14-15, 53, 71, 109, 111, 113, 120, 126-28.

[9]Ibid., 31-95 passim; Wright, *A Report on Marriage and Divorce*, 114.

[10]*Wright v. Wright*, 6 *Texas Reports* 6-7 (1851). Jurists repeatedly emphasized the importance of the family to social order; see, for example, *Gordon v. Gordon*, 48 *Pennsylvania Reports* 232-33 (1864); *Latham v. Latham*, 30 *Grattan* (Virginia) 329 (1878).

[11]Bishop, *New Commentaries*, 629-30.

[12]In the 1790 English case of *Evans v. Evans*, Sir William Scott (Lord Stowell) elegantly described what was and was not marital cruelty under the law. No case comes remotely close to being as often cited as this one. Lengthy excerpts appear in many case reports and Bishop includes much of the Evans text in his 1864 commentary (589-90), and in his 1891 commentary (632-33). On ill treatment that does not contitute cruelty see Bishop, *New Commentaries*, 668 and James Schouler and Arthur Blakesmore, *A Treatise on the Law of Marriage, Divorce, Separation and Domestic Relations*, 6th ed. (Albany, N.Y.: M. Bonder & Co., 1921), 2:1811-14, 1818-19. *Scott v. Scott*, 61 *Texas Reports* 121 (1884) discusses the importance of forbearance as does *Gordon v. Gordon*, 48 *Pennsylvania State Reports* 232-33: "But it is better that individual hardships should be borne by the party whose folly or passion has caused them," wrote the Pennsylvania Court, "than that the great interests of society should be periled by tampering with the marriage tie."

[13]The history of "mental cruelty" in American divorce law is analyzed in my essay, "The Evolution of the Doctrine of Mental Cruelty in Victorian American Divorce, 1790-1900," *Journal of Social History*, 19 (Fall 1986), 127-48.

[14]Such changes came at a time when conservative thinkers sought to arrest the trend toward more liberal divorce laws. From pulpits, newsrooms, and legislatures, post-Civil War moralists struggled to shore up family stability in the face of disorder inspired by immigration, industrialization, urbanization and, more directly, soaring divorce rates. Their efforts met with limited success: in the face of attempts by post-Civil War feminists to liberalize divorce laws, state legislatures actually began to limit the grounds of divorce, abolish open-ended omnibus clauses, restrict the right of remarriage, impose more stringent residency requirements, and establish stricter provisions for notice. Despite these conservative efforts at divorce reform, the late nineteenth- and early twentieth-century divorce rate continued to rise, in part as the statistics suggest, thanks to a great expansion in the number of cruelty suits. Clearly the cultural currents pushing the surge in divorce, especially divorce due to cruelty, were considerably more powerful than the currents pushing conservative efforts to strengthen family stability. On the conservative reforms, see Halem, *Divorce Reform*, 27-40.

[15]Conceivably some husbands made such accusations with the express purpose of gaining a divorce; however, the records do not yield such devious designs.

[16]The image of nineteenth-century women as sexually passionless is discussed in Nancy Cott, "Passionlessness: An Interpretation of Victorian Sexual Ideology, 1790-1850," *Signs*, 4 (Winter 1978), 219-36. On the effort to check predatory male sexuality, see Carroll Smith-Rosenberg, "Beauty, the Beast and the Militant Woman," *American Quarterly*, 23 (Fall 1971), 562-84.

[17]*Shaw v. Shaw*, 17 *Connecticut Reports* 194 (1845); also see *Poor v. Poor*, 8 *New Hampshire Reports* 308-09, 319 (1836).

[18]*Cheatham v. Cheatham*, 10 *Missouri Reports* 296-99 (1847). Several cases in the 1850s linked false accusations of adultery with other allegations of misbehavior to prove the defendant's cruelty. See *Sharp v. Sharp*, 34 *Tennessee Reports* 495-500 (1855); *Cook v. Cook*, *New Jersey Equity Reports* 195-201 (1856); *Cartwright v. Cartwright*, 18 *Texas Reports* 626-44 (1857). In the 1850s, however, courts began to move away from the tendency to combine malicious charges of infidelity with other evidence of cruelty to prove the husband's unworthiness. Words alone began to be sufficient.

[19]Social class and cruelty is discussed in Bishop, *New Commentaries*, 663-64; see, too, *Berry v. Berry*, 88 *North Western Reporter* 1076 (Iowa, 1902); *Cline v. Cline*, 10 *Oregon Reports* 476 (1882); *Bahn v. Bahn*, 62 *Texas Reports* 518 (1884); *Scoland v. Scoland*, 4 *Washington Reports* 122-23 (1892); *Whispell v. Whispell*, 4 *Barbour* (NY) 220 (1848).

[20]Nelson, *A Treatise on the Law*, 303; *Jones v. Jones*, 60 *Texas Reports* 460 (1883); *Crow v. Crow*, 29 *Oregon Reports* 394 (1896). In his study *A Report on Marriage and Divorce in the United States, 1867 to 1886* (Washington, D.C.: Government Printing Office, 1889), Commissioner of Labor Carroll D. Wright summarized divorce legislation, noting that Arkansas, Missouri, Oregon, Pennsylvania, Tennessee, Washington, and Wyoming all included "indignities rendering condition intolerable or life burdensome" as a ground for absolute divorce. Louisiana included "public defamation" as a ground for divorce (114-15). Wright's important document (77-122) and a later, even more comprehensive government report—United States Bureau of the Census, *Special Reports: Marriage and Divorce, 1867-1906*, 1:264-328—offer detailed compilations of divorce laws in the various states. Also see the compilation in *Hamaker v. Hamaker*, 65 *American Decisions* 708-25. Mental cruelty is discussed in note 34. Jane T. Censer found that several Southern states in the antebellum period included "indignities" as a ground for divorce and that women falsely accused of adultery secured divorces on this ground. With one exception from 1849, the case she cites to make this point all appeared in the 1850s, thus supporting the periodizations put forth in this essay: see Censer, "'Smiling though Her Tears,'" 27-33.

[21]*Rice v. Rice*, 6 *Indiana Reports* 85 (1854).

[22]*Carpenter v. Carpenter*, 30 *Kansas Reports* 744 (1883). This case is repeatedly cited among judges taking a more expansive view of marital cruelty than that suggested by English precedent. Also see *Elmes v. Elmes*, 9 *Pennsylvania State Reports* 167 (1848).

[23]Nelson, *A Treatise on the Law*, 262. On the law and "modern" family relations also see Schouler, *A Treatise on the Law*, 1805, and *Scoland v. Scoland*, 4 *Washington Reports* 118-24 (1892).

[24]The literature on women and health in the nineteenth century is sizeable, but a good starting point is Carroll Smith-Rosenberg and Charles Rosenberg, "The Female Animal: Medical and Biological Views of Woman and Her Role in Nineteenth-Century America," *Journal of American History*, 60 (Sept. 1973), 332-56. John S. Haller, Jr. and Robin M. Haller discuss neurasthenia in *The Physician and Sexuality in Victorian America* (1974; rpt. New York: W. W. Norton, 1977), chs. 1 and 2.

[25]*Butler v. Butler*, 1 *Parsons* (Pennsylvania) 337, 334-46 (1849). Another antebellum case in the 1850s put the issue even more bluntly: "And what to a virtuous woman can be more contumelious," asked the North Carolina Supreme Court in 1856, "than a charge made by her husband of infidelity to her marriage vow?" *Coble v. Coble*, 55 *North Carolina Reports* 395 (1856).

[26]Cott, "Passionlessness," 219-36. Passionlessness was an ideology that offered protection to vulnerable women and provided a powerful critique of male behavior. The behavioral reality of nineteenth-century female sexuality is another matter. In an important revisionist essay on Victorian sexuality, Carl Degler argues that prescriptive literature and sexual behavior were less uniform and more complex than commonly assumed. Many nineteenth-century doctors, for example, recognized the legitimacy of women's needs and desires; moreover, the only survey of nineteenth-century American sexual behavior suggests that women were far from uninterested in sex. Cott's data, however, is from the first half of the century, Degler's from the second half. What Degler may be finding is the unraveling of the ideology of passionlessness due to countervailing ideas and behavior; nevertheless, the legal records suggest that the ideology certainly retained sufficient power after 1850 to play an important role in reshaping interpretations of sexual cruelty. See Degler, "What Ought to Be and What Was: Women's Sexuality in the Nineteenth Century," *American Historical Review*, 79 (Dec. 1974), 1467-90.

[27]On organized efforts to reform men, see Smith-Rosenberg, "Beauty, the Beast and the Militant Women," passim, and David J. Pivar, *Purity Crusade: Sexual Morality and Social Control, 1868-1900* (Westport, Conn.: Greenwood Press, 1973), passim. On domestic fiction and its critique of aggressive men, see Mary Kelley, "The Sentimentalists: Promise and Betrayal in the Home," *American Studies*, 19 (Fall 1978), 23-40. Glenda Riley discusses the power of domestic ideology to rebuke and reform men in her analysis of nineteenth-century magazine editor Sarah Hale: "The Subtle Subversion: Changes in the Traditionalist Image of the American Woman," *The Historian*, 32 (1970), 210-27.

[28]*Jones v. Jones*, 60 *Texas Reports* 460 (1883). In this case the court added that "the law looks with much indulgence upon the conduct of a woman who is unjustly charged by her husband with the highest offense she can commit against his conjugal rights, and excuses any outbursts of resentment on her part under such accusation." Also see *Graft v. Graft*, 76 *Indiana Reports* 138 (1881).

[29]Pleck, "Feminist Responses to 'Crimes against Women,'" passim.

[30]*Beyer v. Beyer*, 50 *Wisconsin Reports* 255-56 (1880).

[31]*Bahn v. Bahn*, 62 *Texas Reports* 518-20 (1884).

[32]*Crow v. Crow*, 29 *Oregon Reports* 394 (1896). Husbands' duty to protect wives is discussed in *Straus v. Straus*, 22 *New York Supplement* 567-70 (1893).

[33]As of 1886, six states still did not allow an absolute divorce on the ground of cruelty: Maryland, New Jersey, New York, North Carolina, Virginia, and West Virginia. These states did permit legal separations due to cruelty. In Alabama, Kentucky, and Tennessee, only wives could receive a divorce on the ground of cruelty. See Wright, *A Report on Marriage and Divorce*, 114, 116.

[34]The key case in the development of the concept of "mental cruelty" is probably *Carpenter v. Carpenter*, 30 *Kansas Reports* 744 (1883); also see Justice McFarland's dissent in *Waldron v. Waldron*, 24 *Pacific Reporter* 754 (California, 1890) and *Barnes v. Barnes*, 30 *Pacific Reporter* 299 (California, 1892) wherein the California Supreme Court explicitly recognized mental cruelty in divorce suits. Also of interest are *Whitmore v. Whitmore*, 49 *Michigan Reports* 417-18 (1882); *Avery v. Avery*, 5 *Pacific Reporter* 418-22 (Washington, 1885); *Mason v. Mason*, 131 *Pennsylvania State Reports* 161-65 (1840). Irving Browne noted in 1898 the elasticity of the definition of marital cruelty as it appeared in divorce statutes: "ungovernable temper," "cruel treatment, outrages, or excesses," "such indignities as render life burdensome," "intolerable severity," "inability to live in peace and union," and "settled aversion which tends to destroy all peace and happiness" comprise just a few of the many statutory efforts to define cruelty. See Browne, "Oral Cruelty," 84.

[35]*Crowe v. Crowe*, 29 *Oregon Reports* 393 (1896); also, *Smith v. Smith*, 8 *Oregon Reports* 101 (1879); *Kelly v. Kelly*, 18 *Nevada Reports* 53 (1883); *Whitmore v. Whitmore*, 49 *Michigan Reports* 417-18 (1882).

[36]*McAlister v. McAlister*, 71 *Texas Reports* 696-97 (1886); also supporting a double standard, *Hart v. Hart*, 39 *Atlantic Reporter* 431 (New Hampshire, 1896).

[37]Lawrence M. Friedman, "Rights of Passage: Divorce Law in Historical Perspective," *Oregon Law Review*, 63:4 (1984), 649-69.

[38]Griswold, *Family and Divorce*, ch. 6.

[39]Linda Gordon's *Woman's Body, Woman's Right: A Social History of Birth Control in America* (New

York: Penguin Books, 1977) discusses efforts to regulate nineteenth-century sexuality in the interests of birth control. On utopians see Louis J. Kern, *An Ordered Love: Sex Roles and Sexuality in Victorian Utopias* (Chapel Hill: Univ. of North Carolina Press, 1981) and Lawrence Foster, *Religion and Sexuality: Three American Communal Experiments of the Nineteenth Century* (New York: Oxford Univ. Press, 1981).

[40]For a recent review of the literature on nineteenth-century sexuality see Estelle B. Freedman, "Sexuality in Nineteenth-Century America: Behavior, Ideology, and Politics," in Stanley Katz and Stanley Kutler, eds., *The Promise of American History: Progress and Prospects* (Baltimore: Johns Hopkins Univ. Press, 1982), 196-215.

[41]Nichols quoted in Cott, "Passionlessness," 236; Degler, *At Odds*, 249-78.

[42]Degler, *At Odds*, 270-71.

[43]Pleck, "'Crimes Against Women,'" 452, 454-55, 457.

[44]Ibid., 457, 459-62; also see Pleck's article, "The Whipping Post," 127-29. Stone's bill gave beaten wives the power to apply at the local police court for a legal separation, provided an order requiring the husband to support his estranged wife and children, and included a custody award to the wife. Opponents feared the bill would make marital separations too easy to obtain.

[45]Woodhull quoted in Degler, *At Odds*, 276.

[46]*Shaw v. Shaw*, 17 *Connecticut Reports* 196 (1845). The Western courts tended to be more flexible than those in the East, a point made by the Nebraska Supreme Court in 1898 when it criticized the Shaw decision for finding that false adultery allegations, husbandly tyranny, and excessive intercourse was "such cruelty as 'can be borne.'" Said the Nebraska court, "But we confidently say that no such a rule of law as announced by the court in the Shaw case exists west of the Alleghany Mountains." *Walton v. Walton*, 77 *Northwest Reporter* 398 (Nebraska, 1889).

[47]*English v. English*, 27 *New Jersey Equity Reports* 71-75 (1876). This action was for a legal separation, not an absolute divorce.

[48]*English v. English*, 27 *New Jersey Equity Reports* 580-86 (1876). The court divided nine to five on this decision. An earlier 1864 New Jersey case held that a "gross abuse of marital rights" may constitute cruelty, although the court found the wife's complaint unconvincing in this suit. The court suspected that she had fled her husband simply to avoid "the pains of childbearing," especially given the pain her last pregnancy had caused her. See *Moores v. Moores*, 16 *New Jersey Equity Reports* (1 C. E. Greene) 275-83 (1863).

[49]*English v. English*, 27 *New Jersey Equity Reports* 72 (1876). The complete text of these two decisions plus a brief introduction can be found in Robert L. Griswold, "Sexual Cruelty and the Case for Divorce in Victorian America," *Signs*, 11 (Spring 1986), 529-41.

[50]*Mayhew v. Mayhew*, 61 *Connecticut Reports* 235 (1891); also see *Melvin v. Melvin*, 58 *New Hampshire Reports* 571 (1879) and *Walsh v. Walsh*, 61 *Michigan Reports* 557 (1886). Nevertheless, traditional decisions continued to be voiced, most notably in Illinois where the court held that to constitute cruelty, excessive sexual indulgence must be against the will of the wife and, in addition, the husband must know that his actions harm her health: see *Young v. Young*, 33 *Illinois Appellate Reports* 225 (1889).

[51]*Mayhew v. Mayhew*, 61 *Connecticut Reports* 235 (1891). In *Grant v. Grant*, 53 *Minnesota Reports* 181-82 (1893), the court held that excessive sexual demands were legally cruel when they rendered it "unsafe and improper for her to cohabit with him. . . ." Bishop simply argued that sexual demands that endangered health comprised cruelty: see *New Commentaries*, 675.

[52]There were exceptions: in two New Hampshire cases, spouses who joined a Shaker community and thereafter renounced sex found successful divorce complaints lodged against them: *Dyer v. Dyer*, 5 *New Hampshire Reports* 271-74 (1830); *Fitts v. Fitts*, 46 *New Hampshire Reports* 184-85 (1865).

[53]*Fritz v. Fritz*, 138 *Illinois Reports* 438-40 (1891); also see *Stewart v. Stewart*, 78 *Maine Reports* 552 (1887). Bishop's claim that denial of sex for two years or more constituted desertion was implicitly supported by *Stein v. Stein*, 5 *Colorado* 55-57 (1879) and explicitly by *Steele v. Steele*, 8 *Washington, D.C. Reports* 505-08 (1874). Drawing on English precedents, the Pennsylvania Supreme Court in 1854 and again in 1864 maintained "that the fact that a husband sleeps in a different bed from that occupied by his wife and declines to exercise his marital privileges respecting the enjoyment of conjugal endearments, is not sufficient." *Eshback v. Eshback*, 23 *Pennsylvania State Reports* (11 Harris) 343 (1854); *Gordon v. Gordon*, 48 *Pennsylvania State Reports* 228 (1864). The English precedent is *D'Aquilar v. D'Aquilar*, 1 *Haggard* 776 (1794).

[54]*Watson v. Watson*, 52 *New Jersey Equity Reports* 350-51 (1894).

[55]*Magill v. Magill*, 3 *Pittsburgh Review* 25 (1866). This case is discussed in William H. Browne's *A Commentary on the Law of Divorce and Alimony* (Philadelphia: Kay & Brothers, 1890), 111.

[56]*Southwick v. Southwick*, 97 *Massachusetts Reports* 327-29 (1867). In an 1870 Massachusetts case, the court included denial of sex as part of its desertion findings, but in this case the husband had also physically left home, leaving his wife impoverished and thus forcing her to go to work: *Magrath v. Magrath*, 103 *Massachusetts Reports* 579 (1870).

[57]*Reid v. Reid*, 21 *New Jersey Equity Reports* 332-33 (1871); *Cowles v. Cowles*, 112 *Massachusetts Reports* 298 (1873); *Segelbaum v. Segelbaum*, 39 *Minnesota Reports* 258-62 (1888); *Latham v. Latham*, 30 *Grattan* (Virginia) 328 (1878); *Schoessow v. Schoessow*, 83 *Wisconsin Reports* 553 (1892). Although most argued the contrary, a few judges did suggest that the absence of sex constituted cruelty. The Maine Supreme Court in 1887 held that the refusal of sex did not contitute desertion while cohabitation continued, but it may amount to cruelty. To justify this positon, the opinion noted that impotence was a cause of divorce and then suggested that there was no meaningful difference between a spouse that cannot or will not assent to sex: *Stewart v. Stewart*, 78 *Maine Reports* 553 (1887). Bishop argued that the refusal of sex in conjunction with other facts may constitute cruelty, especially if the "health of the woman has suffered from her being obliged to sleep with a male person without any proper gratification of passions thereby excited." Bishop, *New Commentaries*, 660-61.

[58]*Disborough v. Disborough*, 26 *Atlantic Reporter* 853 (New Jersey, 1893).

[59]Grossberg, *Governing the Hearth*, 289-307.

[60]Ibid., 290, 295.

[61]In her book *Great Expectations*, Elaine T. May discusses how urban life created new expectations in marriage that often could not be met. See chs. 3-6.

WHO GETS THE CHILD? CUSTODY, GUARDIANSHIP, AND THE RISE OF A JUDICIAL PATRIARCHY IN NINETEENTH-CENTURY AMERICA

MICHAEL GROSSBERG

In the sprawling nineteenth-century American republic, law assumed a powerful role in defining status, rights, and appropriate behavior. A fundamental revision of the married woman's place in the legal order lay at the center of one of the law's branches, domestic relations.[1] Postrevolutionary changes in family life, ones which social historians label as "modern," such as child-centeredness, rigid age and sex divisions, companionate marital practices, and declining household production, required significant modifications in traditional gender-bound policies.[2] The state judiciary took the lead in determining the nature and extent of these changes. Their solutions institutionalized the era's gender beliefs and consequently were double-edged. Influenced by the society's growing glorification of motherhood and female domesticity, judges granted women new legal powers in family affairs; yet the courts used those same ideals to place severe limits on married women's overall legal rights. It was this critical distinction between dependent power based on judicial discretion and independent legal rights assertable by women themselves that proved crucial to feminine status in the emerging American law of domestic relations.[3]

The most telling example of these developments in the law comes from an area of nineteenth-century family life generally conceded to be the rightful domain of women—childrearing. Bourgeois, white married women mounted a campaign to attach superior legal rights to motherhood and thereby posed a direct challenge to traditional domestic governance. These family reformers used the domestic virtues newly ascribed to women as a wedge for extending the legal boundaries of the maternal

Feminist Studies 9, no. 2 (Summer 1983). © by Feminist Studies, Inc.

sphere. Their efforts engendered protracted and often bitter spousal, legislative, and judicial battles over child custody and guardianship, the unquestioned domain of fathers in previous legal practice. As a result of countless demands by women for their children, the traditional superiority given paternal custody and guardianship rights in England and colonial America became untenable. Significantly, however, instead of granting mothers those powers directly and independently, the courts usurped the role formerly held by fathers and claimed the authority to determine which parent would be granted custody. I will argue that this transfer of power from the male parent to the male jurist made judges a new kind of patriarch, one invested with a power over some families that came to rival their male predecessors.

Although patriarchy with its broad range of meanings must be carefully defined, it is the most accurate label for the new child placement powers of the nineteenth-century judiciary. As they did in so many areas of economic and social life, judges seized the power to determine what happened to children when one or both marital partners failed in their responsibilities. They did so first by wresting control of child placement from domestic patriarchs who presided over disrupted families, and then by using the broad discretionary authority sanctioned by equity law to reallocate custody and guardianship to mothers, fathers, and surrogate parents. In gaining control of child placement they created a distinctive set of doctrines and policies. Patriarchy identifies the content and context of those specific doctrines and policies. It describes the particular corpus of laws devised by nineteenth-century judges to decide which claimants triumphed in custody and guardianship contests.[4]

Courts acquired such authority because judicial power expanded greatly in postrevolutionary America. In the restructured republican polity, the judiciary aggressively assumed policy-making prerogatives. Judicial power increased as legislatures gradually conceded to the bench jurisdiction over matters as diverse as corporate charters and divorce, while professionally trained jurists ousted laypersons, and judges seized control of trials from juries. The judiciary also developed a more concrete conception of the common law as an instrument to shape and control society. As legal historian Mark DeWolfe Howe noted of the period, "it was clear to laymen as it was to lawyers, that the nature of American institutions, whether economic, social, or political, was largely to be determined by the judges. In such a period questions of private law were seen and considered as questions of social policy." Courts took the lead in devising policies to govern aspects of social and economic life ranging from railroads to families.[5]

Yet the sources of a judicial patriarchy extended beyond these institutional changes in the legal order. The assumption of patriarchal authority by the bench rested to a significant degree on the nineteenth century's increasingly rigid segregation of homebound female and worldly male functions. It represented a refined version of the distinction between the male authority to govern the home and the female responsibility to maintain it.[6] Indeed, the power of judges to define the legal abilities of married women helped perpetuate, albeit in altered form, patriarchal authority within republican society. Judges combined the traditional assumption that married women lacked economic and intellectual independence to act without male supervision (and thus needed special protection) with the new faith in separate and mutually exclusive sexual spheres so central to the organization of the modern family. The result was the double-edged character of married women's legal rights: judges remade the law to aid wives and mothers in performing their domestic chores while at the same time they used their powers to check radical alterations in the subordinate legal status of married women. Judicially inspired changes in custody and guardianship, as in most areas of domestic relations law, thus allowed for an expanded feminine presence in the legal order but in a way that ensured that women's domestic powers did not translate into extensive external political and economic authority.

The persistence of patriarchy in its new guise illustrates some of the basic changes and continuities in nineteenth-century family law. The rise of this potent judicial power must be clarified to reconstruct the changes in the relationship between married women and the state during the nineteenth century. However, the legal context of women's status has not received much attention.[7] Indeed, even the few historical studies of domestic relations law which touch on the topic have been marred by an uncritical reliance on modernization theory. Those works have been guided by implicit or explicit contentions that legal innovations such as adoption or married women's property acts reflected modern, and thus progressive, notions of family life. The changes are then classified more as parts of an onrushing, indeed inevitable, modernization of the entire society than as the products of distinctive historical situations. Such interpretations of legal change ignore or discount the complex character of new legal policies in which the family and gender acted as causal agents and where traditionalism not only persisted, but in some ways also gained new footholds in the law. Modernization theory, particularly the assumption that gender inequities must eventually disappear in modern society, unnecessarily reduces our understanding of the elements at work within nineteenth-century family law and offers an incomplete picture of the sources and results of this vital period in women's legal history.[8]

The following analysis will demonstrate that the legal rights of married women did not expand in a clear linear manner during the nineteenth century. Rather, alterations in child custody and guardianship took a distinctive course of legal development which blended innovation and traditionalism, and had their own chronology. Early in the century, judges took the lead in revamping traditional paternal rights and assumed control of child placement. Legislatures then began codifying the judicial creations. Around midcentury, under the press of increasingly insistent claims by mothers for custody and guardianship rights, the courts staked out the limits of the new maternal legal sphere. By the late nineteenth century, a distinctive American law of custody and guardianship had come to rest on the twin pillars of gender beliefs and a judicial patriarchy.

JUDGES TAKE CONTROL

Traditionally in Anglo-American law fathers had an almost unlimited right to the custody of their minor, legitimate children. The law assumed that the interests of children were best protected by making the father the natural guardian and by using a property-based standard of parental fitness. Custody law considered children to be dependent, subordinate beings. They were assets of estates in which fathers had a vested right. Their services, earnings, and so on became the property of their paternal masters in exchange for life and maintenance. This *quid pro quo* developed directly out of the settled conviction that fathers were best equipped to care for their offspring.[9]

The common law denied married women legal independence and relegated them to a status similar to that of children. Their lack of rights precluded them from maintaining custody and guardianship of their children. In the words of Sir William Blackstone, the great eighteenth-century compiler of the common law, a mother "was entitled to no power, but only to reverence and respect." Husbands not only had a paramount right to custody, but also the power to appoint a testamentary guardian and thus extend their authority beyond the grave. A man in a 1712 edition of *The Spectator,* an English journal with a wide provincial readership, described paternal domestic authority in stark terms, "in short, Sir, I look upon my family as a patriarchal sovereignty, in which I am both king and priest."[10]

Although equity jurisprudence often softened the harshness of the common law by expanding married women's right to legal redress, colonial law apparently made few inroads into the paternal bias of custody rules. Most likely many women gained the custody or guardianship of their children even though no specific legal justification for such legal deviations emerged. Rather, like much of colonial law, practices and customs that departed from English ways were not fully institutionalized until after the Revolution with the establishment of a formal and more self-consciously American legal culture.[11]

After the Revolution, state judges made a major contribution to that new legal culture by devising a new approach to child custody. They relied on two English legal innovations, the doctrine of *parens patriae* and the use of habeas corpus. In the seventeenth century, English chancery courts had assumed increasing jurisdiction over the welfare and property of minors by expanding the old doctrine of *parens patriae.* Under the doctrine, the courts claimed sovereign custodial power over children and other dependents. Although its sources are unclear, the development of judicial authority under the *parens patriae* rule accompanied changes in the legal standing of children and parental rights. Gradually the father's custody powers evolved from a property right to a trust tied to his responsibilities as a guardian. Armed with the authority of *parens patriae,* courts in England and America could, and did, dislodge the law's paternal bias.[12]

The eminent late-eighteenth-century English jurist Lord Mansfield provided the means. He issued a number of decisions authorizing the use of writs of habeas corpus to try custody controversies.[13] That procedure allowed judges to determine custody by examining a child's interests, rather than by merely assessing the legitimacy of parental claims. Judicial discretion, when linked to new attitudes toward the family and increasing demands by mothers for the custody of their children, enabled American judges to reshape the common law. In the first part of the nineteenth century they did so while resolving custody disputes triggered by separation, divorce, and death. At the center of their deliberations stood the issue of just how far to diminish domestic patriarchal authority.

In 1809 a South Carolina equity court heard Jennette Prather's demand for a marital separation and child custody. She charged her husband with living openly with another woman. The judges easily complied with her first request, but hesitated in granting the second. The chancellor, Henry Desaussure, was mindful, he said, of the father being the children's "natural guardian, invested by God and the law of the country with reasonable power over them. Unless his parental power has been monstrously and cruelly abused, this court would be very cautious in interfering with the execution of it." Even so, the court refused to let the adulterous man retain his full parental rights and ended up giving the custody of an infant daughter, though not the other older children, to Jennette. In doing so, the judges publicly acknowledged that they trod on new legal ground.[14]

The ambivalence of the South Carolina judges reveals the conflicting pressures custody cases placed on the early antebellum judiciary. Traditional male authority over the family remained a fundamental tenet of American family beliefs. Yet a new concern about child nurture and a rising conviction that women possessed special qualities for moral and religious leadership and for childrearing led to growing dissatisfaction over the primacy given paternal custody rights. The emergence of more clearly defined sexual spheres within antebellum society further reinforced that uneasiness. The Prather opinion illustrates how judicial discretion could be used to restrict paternal rights and make the law conform to new gender beliefs. Judges like those on the South Carolina court enlarged their authority to determine whether a father had so clearly abused his domestic authority that custody should be forfeited. These inquiries used the era's faith in the innate childrearing capacities of women as counterweights to paternal economic and political power and judicial policy-making prerogatives to counterbalance domestic patriarchy. Judicial innovations like *Prather v. Prather* gradually spread throughout the antebellum legal system by winning the support of more and more state judges. Custody rulings increasingly devalued paternally oriented, property-based welfare considerations and emphasized maternally biased child nurture ones.[15]

In his highly influential *Commentaries on American Law* published in the late 1820s, chancellor James Kent noted and accepted the changes under way in custody law. Maintaining that a "husband was the best judge of the wants of a family," he nevertheless cited Lord Mansfield and a number of American decisions to contend that paternal custody rights could be overruled when, as he put it, "the nature of the case appears to warrant it." The jurist took that position even though thirty years earlier he had revealed his own patriarchal sentiments by describing himself as "the independent. . .Lord of my own fireside." Justice Joseph Story reached similar conclusions in his equity treatise. Though he too genuflected to the traditional patriarchal ideal, Story urged judges to examine the fitness of each parent in selecting a custodian. He admitted an inclination to place a girl of "very tender years" with her mother.[16]

Legislators began to codify the judicial innovations as well. In an 1830s revision, New York formally recognized that husbands and wives were leaving one another without resort to the state's strict divorce laws. Apparently unwilling to leave child custody to informal arrangements, the new code authorized women to apply for writs of habeas corpus to let the courts settle child placement. In the first judicial test of the law, a vice-chancellor declared in 1840 that the legislature had "neutralized the rule of the common law," and placed parents "on an equality as to the future custody of the children, even if it does not create a presumption in favor of the wife." Massachusetts passed a similar statute in the same decade with an even more explicit charge to the courts that "the rights of the parents to their children, in the absence of misconduct, are equal and the happiness and welfare of the child are to determine its care and custody."[17]

Judges trimmed paternal custody rights not only by accepting maternal claims, but also by granting those of surrogate parents. The common law's allegiance to family integrity included a deep opposition to the informal relinquishment of custody. As a New Jersey chancery court phrased it in 1846, "the care and custody of minor children is a personal trust in the father, and he has no general power to dispose of them to another." Yet many antebellum fathers did just that. Judicial involvement commenced when a father changed his mind, demanded his children, and the surrogate parents refused.[18]

The inclination of antebellum judges to use child welfare as a means of monitoring such paternal claims appeared as early as 1796 in the Connecticut decision of *Nichols v. Giles.* The state supreme court dismissed a writ of habeas corpus issued on behalf of a man whose wife had left him and taken their three-year-old daughter to her family home. The judges concluded that because the child's "intemperate, propertyless father could not properly care for her" she should remain with her grandparents. They relied on the *parens patriae* doctrine which allowed courts to withhold custody from unfit fathers who had transferred or abandoned their children.[19]

But this negative power became a more positive and potent discretionary weapon under the influence of the newly developed standard of child welfare. In the first decades of the nineteenth century, judges broadened their custody authority by enlarging their definition of the child's interests. A New York court took a step along that path in 1816, when it was confronted with the case of a father attempting to regain his daughter after his financial setbacks had led the child and her mother to seek refuge with the woman's parents. Although at first the father visited his daughter frequently, he stopped doing so. The girl had been reared and educated by her grandparents after her mother had died. Chief Justice Smith Thompson seized upon rulings by Lord Mansfield and the Pennsylvania bench to decide the child's fate: "From the affidavits which have been laid before the court, little doubt can be entertained that it will be more for the benefit of the child to remain with her grandparents than to be put under the care of her father; and if this court has any discretion in such case, it will no doubt be discretely exercised by permitting the child to remain where she is."[20]

Eight years later Justice Story faced an almost identical case, except that before her death the wife extracted a promise from her husband to leave their daughter with her maternal grandparents. Denying his pledge, Elisha Williams had a writ issued to retrieve the girl. The paramount right of the father, Story insisted, "is not on account of any absolute right to the father, but for the benefit of the infant, the law presuming it to be for his interest to be under the nurture and care of his natural protector, both for maintenance and education." Story told Williams that courts settled custody disputes with regard to the "real, permanent interests of the infant." He added that Williams had no "absolute, vested right in the custody." Williams arrived at a private settlement with his father-in-law, spurred no doubt by a realization of the limits the courts imposed upon paternal rights.[21]

Contrasting Georgia and Ohio decisions illustrate the new standards of child nurture and parental fitness judges used to resolve custody disputes. The Georgia case involved the 1836 claim of a well-respected physician to his three-month-old child. The mother had died at childbirth and on her deathbed made her husband agree to let her parents raise the child. But the doctor soon disagreed with his in-laws' childrearing methods and demanded the baby. Superior Court Judge Robert M. Charlton issued the writ and summarized the bench's authority to settle custody disputes. "All legal rights, even those of personal security and liberty, may be forfeited by improper conduct," he maintained, "and so this legal right of the father to the possession of his child must be made subservient to the true interests and safety of the child, and to the duty of the State to protect its citizens of whatever age." Deciding that both parties appeared to be responsible custodians, Charlton deferred to the father's superior claim.[22]

The Cincinnati Superior Court treated Stephen Ball's assertion of paternal rights much less respectfully. Ball had abandoned his daughters and their mother when he and his father quit their carpentry trade to join the millennial Millerite movement. Without support, Balls' family had been taken in by his wife's parents. Ball's wife died, he joined the Shakers, and then sought custody in order to have the girls raised by the sect.

Ball's conduct and objective outraged the Cincinnati tribunal. Judge William Johnston argued that the right to custody flowed from the parental responsibility to clothe, feed, and educate a child. "Separate from the duty of providing," he lectured, "the right to custody does not exist." The Shaker's communal childrearing practices, which demanded that parental ties be broken and that all children be raised by caretakers, repelled the judge. Under such a system, he contended, the Shakers, not Ball, would actually receive custody, something which neither the grandmother nor the judge thought to be in their best interests. Johnston derided Ball's attempt to "sever them from the bosom of their grandmother and from his own bosom, and plant them in the cold ascetic bosoms of the 'female caretakers,' and transfer all his rights, title and interest in the child which God has given him, to total strangers." Such plans proved Ball's unfitness, Johnston decided, and could not counter the grandmother's "moral lien."[23]

By midcentury a distinctive judicial doctrine governed the

custodial rights of fathers who allowed their children to join other families. The judiciary used its newly assumed patriarchal authority to clothe these new family bonds with legitimacy. While paternal rights to custody remained superior, they became subject to much greater judicial supervision. Judges claimed the right to weigh assertions of paternal rights against their evaluation of the character and benefits of the new family ties.[24]

Judges and legislators began to alter guardianship much as they did custody. Fathers continued to be considered the proper legal guardian of children. Most states codified paternal guardianship with few alterations from the English tradition. Even Thomas Jefferson's liberal revision of Virginia statutes took paternal testamentary power for granted. Many men apparently appointed their wives as guardians, but the law's underlying premise remained: children should be distributed as men saw fit.[25]

Even when a mother secured the guardianship of her children, the law restricted her authority much more than it did a father's. Mothers had less claim to children's services, less control of their offspring's property, fewer defenses to removal from office, and inferior custody rights. The law made custody dependent on support, and the general assumption that widows lacked financial independence undermined their demands for guardianship as it did many other claims. Diminished guardianship echoed the social status in antebellum America of widows who, more often than not, were viewed as objects of pity and feared as potential drains on community resources. Consequently, widows, to an even greater extent than other middle-class women, were seen as persons in need of protection rather than as individuals with valid claims for legal rights.[26]

Yet the new approaches to child placement evident in custody disputes compelled judges and legislators to reformulate maternal guardianship. In 1835 when a New Jersey mother challenged the school selection her son's testamentary guardian had made, a chancery judge pointedly reminded the woman of her legal powerlessness. After a father appoints a testamentary guardian, he lectured, "the natural right of the mother must yield to the will of the father. It is paramount and [testamentary guardianship] is considered a continuation of the father's authority." But the jurists themselves no longer felt so constrained by paternal rights. The chancellor felt free to express his distrust of the paternal fiat and to use his discretion to assess the boy's best interests. Upon doing so, the court complied with the mother's wishes.[27]

The bench rewrote guardianship law not only by circumscribing paternal power, but also by enlarging maternal authority. For example, the traditional common law rule that remarriage extinguished maternal guardianship fell afoul of new judicial sentiments.[28] The bench's faith in women's innate childrearing instincts led jurists to question the old assumption that a woman became so dominated by her new husband that marital deference and affection overwhelmed maternal responsibility. In 1852, the Virginia Court of Appeals upheld the guardianship claim of a newly remarried woman against her ex-father-in-law. State law allowed a mother to request the guardianship of her children after her husband's death. The justices decided that the "right was not lost by her remarriage, there being no legal guardian to the child; and the facts and circumstances disclose nothing which would induce the court, in the exercise of its discretion, to deprive her of the custody." In issuing a similar ruling an Alabama judge explained the change: "it is safe to presume. . .that a mother. . .would be more careful of the moral, intellectual, and physical well-being of her children than any other person in the world." Such instances of judicial rule making narrowed the gulf between maternal and paternal guardianship, but did so by placing both firmly within the bench's domain.[29]

A widely publicized custody fight in the 1840s between the daughter of a wealthy Boston manufacturer and her husband, a Swiss nobleman, spelled out the implications of these legal changes. The pair parted because of the wife's dissatisfaction with her husband's filial dependence and his refusal to spend part of each year in America with her family. Fearing the baron might try to seize his heir, a son born in Boston, the distraught mother searched the East Coast for a maternal custody haven. Eventually she chose Philadelphia because of a series of appellate rulings by the state courts in favor of mothers. The judiciary vindicated her choice when it rebuffed her husband's challenge of its jurisdiction over the case and then refused his argument that paternal custody rights be considered paramount in the absence of clear proof of unfitness.

In a careful weaving of English and American decisions, the state supreme court argued "the reputation of a father may be stainless as crystal, he may not be afflicted with the slightest mental, moral, or physical disqualification from superintending the general welfare of the infant. . .and yet the interest of the child may imperatively demand the denial of the father's right, and its continuance with the mother." Such was the situation with the two-year-old boy before them, the judges asserted. They concluded by offering a paean to motherhood. "Not doubting that parental anxiety would seek for and obtain the best substitute which could be procured, every instinct of humanity unerringly proclaims that no substitute can supply the place of her, whose watchfulness over the sleeping cradle or waking moments of her offspring is prompted by deeper and holier feelings than the most liberal allowance of a nurse's wages could possibly stimulate." The court ordered the child to stay with his mother. John Cadwaller, the victorious mother's lawyer, added a coda to his argument that aptly summarized the growing gender orientation of custody law and its sources in the economic and social changes undermining earlier allocations of sexual responsibilities: "Everyone knows that a father is unfit to take care of an infant; physically unfit and unfit by reason of his avocations."[30]

The decision led a Massachusetts lawyer to publish an anonymous pamphlet in protest. He savagely attacked the contention that a wife could be granted custody without proving her husband had violated his spousal or fatherly duties. The unity of the husband and wife, he claimed, blocked such an outcome. Married women had no separate custody rights, just as they had none to sue or make a contract. Directly attacking the judiciary's growing patriarchal authority, the Bay State attorney charged that the Pennsylvania decision represented "nothing less than an *assumption of power by a court* . . . to determine the domestic arrangements of *a man's family*."[31]

The lawyer's tirade exposed the central tenets of an emerging American law of custody: each family member had distinct legal interests and the judiciary had the duty of resolving conflicts between them. This adversary view of the family and the patriarchal judicial powers it encouraged upset traditional family law. Legal rules had rested on a conception of the family as a community of interests governed by a patriarch. The displacement of that ideal initiated the major legal changes of the era. Among other things, by the 1860s it ensured that parental fitness not paternal rights would be the focus of custody disputes and that judges would assume the mantle of patriarchs.[32]

THE LIMITS OF CHANGE

Despite appearances, the judicially inspired changes in custody and guardianship shifted the locus of patriarchal authority much more than they challenged the subordinate status of women. They were symptomatic of the denial of full legal and political equality to wives and mothers in all areas of the law. Postrevolutionary egalitarianism, popular democracy, and capitalist individualism significantly enlarged the legal abilities of most white males. Relegation to a special sphere excluded women from those benefits. Married women acquired a distinct legal identity, but the greatest expansion of their legal capacities came in the form of familial privileges like the maternal custody preference. Exclusion from the polity and the economy thus helped women gain a foothold in the law in the form of protections for their domestic responsibilities. Yet that very homebound role imposed severe limitations on the extent of married women's overall legal rights and enhanced judicial power over family life. This double-edged character of antebellum family law is evident in the application of custody law by midcentury judges and in the persistent opposition to formal maternal rights.

In an 1858 self-help manual, *Every Woman Her Own Lawyer,* attorney George Bishop advised women that the law empowered courts to "give custody to the party that, in the court's judgment, is most competent to bring them up with advantage to the children themselves and benefit to society." As Bishop's statement indicates, the decline of paternal rights did not automatically increase maternal ones. On the contrary, the law reduced the rights of parenthood itself. Courts applied judicially created standards of child welfare and parental fitness to take the ultimate decision of child placement out of the hands of both parents. The standards paid heed to the child's best interest, tender years, and established ties, and gave priority to the innocent party in separation and divorce proceedings. Drawn from the bench's new commitment to nurture-based child welfare policies, they often biased custody determinations toward mothers. Yet they were so rooted in judicial sexual biases, that mothers could claim that preference only when they conformed to the bench's ideal of womanhood.[33]

The most sexually biased doctrine, the tender years rule, aptly illustrates the judicial approach. It decreed that infants, children below puberty, and youngsters afflicted with health ailments be placed in a mother's care unless she proved unworthy of the responsibility. The doctrine acted as a powerful leveler of paternal rights. Under it, mothers gained a presumptive claim to their young children, as an 1860 New Jersey codification of the rule reveals: "The mother is entitled to the custody of her children under the age of seven unless it affirmatively appears that, in her custody, they would be exposed to either neglect, cruelty, or the acquisition of immoral habits and principles." Nine years after the act's passage it won the hearty endorsement of the state court of errors and appeals. The justices declared that "it is not the dry, technical right of the father, but the welfare of the child which will form the substantial basis of judgment."[34]

The tender years doctrine thus institutionalized antebellum gender ideology. As courts began to refine their policies, they extended the doctrine by insisting that daughters of all ages were best cared for by mothers. An 1876 Alabama divorce decision explained the judicial rationale for broadening the rule. A woman, whose name the court refused to divulge, sued for divorce, charging cruelty. The court refused her petition, but accepted the fact that the pair would live apart. Agreeing that the woman had sufficient cause to do so, and to have custody of her daughter, the justices proclaimed: "All must feel, that no greater calamity can befall an infant daughter, than a deprivation of a mother's care, vigilant precept, and example. A mother's sympathy and culture exerts an influence on her life and character, perceptible only in its results. Therefore, courts are reluctant to deprive her of the custody of her infant daughter and but seldom if ever, do so, unless misconduct is imputable to her."[35]

Following Solomon-like logic, courts often used the tender years doctrine to split custody by giving fathers the custody of older sons and mothers that of girls and younger children. The Virginia Supreme Court considered such an action necessary in one case because, after the "tender nursing period has passed," it became time for the masculine duty of training a boy for life outside the home. Although the policy led to the separation of siblings, it relied on the antebellum insistence that specific gender skills and responsibilities be transferred from mother to daughter and father to son.[36]

Judges also used their authority to ensure that mothers who violated judicial expectations received no legal assistance. A Pennsylvania couple discovered the subtleties of judicial family governance early in the nineteenth century. Joseph Lee petitioned for the custody of his children after obtaining a divorce from his wife Barbara for adultery. He contended that her misdeeds and subsequent marriage to her paramour disqualified Barbara obtaining custody of the couple's daughters, ages seven and ten. Chief

Justice William Tilghman registered the court's "disapprobation of the mother's conduct," but noted that her care of the children had been faultless. "Our anxiety is principally directed," he asserted, "to the children. It appears to us, that considering their tender years, they stand in need of the kind of assistance which can be afforded by none so well as a mother." Consequently, "It is on their account . . . that exercising the discretion with which the law has invested us, we think it best at present not to take them from her."

But the court monitored the situation and three years later Joseph triumphed. Tilghman again based his decision on the needs of the children, now ruling that age had rendered them less in need of maternal nurture. Invoking his power to place children, the judge argued that Barbara's conduct disqualified her from continued custody because she had immoral ideas about "the obligation of the marriage contract." The court could not allow two potential wives to be reared by a mother who thought a marital vow could be so easily broken. "At the present they may not reflect upon it," he sagely concluded, "but soon they will, and when they inquire why it was that they were separated from their mother, they will be taught, as far as our opinion can teach them, that in good fortune or bad, sickness or in health, in happiness or in misery, the marriage contract, unless dissolved by the law of the country, is sacred and inviolable."[37]

The Supreme Court of Georgia issued an even more emphatic declaration on maternal fitness in 1854 when it refused the custody request of another adulterous mother. In response to her spouse's petition for a writ on habeas corpus, she claimed that his cruelty and lack of financial support had forced her to take her daughter and seek refuge with another man. The justices sustained a lower court ruling that the child's welfare would be best served by being placed with her father. They observed that "there may be no difference in the sins of the man and woman who violate the laws of chastity," but "in the opinion of society it is otherwise." Accordingly, when a man committed adultery, he did not automatically lose the respect of the community and his children would not necessarily be excluded from association with "decent people" and "may be educated to become good and useful members of society." Rigorously invoking the sexual double standard, the court reminded its listeners that with "the frail female" the outcome became quite different. Having violated the marriage contract, the wife inevitably found herself reduced to "utter and irredeemable ruin, where her associations are with the vulgar, the vile, and the depraved. If her children be with her, their characters must be, more or less, influenced and formed by the circumstances which surround them." In other words, the court decided that because the social stigma of adultery fell more heavily on women than men it negated maternal preferences.[38]

The Pennsylvania and Georgia verdicts illustrate a judicial tendency to use fault and gender-based social values to determine parental fitness. Although custom conceded a wife the right to sue for divorce or to file for separation, the ideological strictures of doctrines like the tender years policy and the fault principle ensured that the bench had the ultimate authority in determining the fate of a child when its parents parted. A firm belief in sexually endowed traits, the accepted division of the home from the world outside, and the priority accorded child nurture worked to replace paternal rights with maternal preferences in custody disputes. Crucially, however, the newly instituted maternal preference remained a discretionary policy, not a statutory prerogative. As a result, it could be easily revoked any time a mother did not meet the standards of maternal conduct decreed by judicial patriarchs.[39]

Frustration over the limited gains of the early antebellum period helped make equal custody and guardianship central goals of the women's rights movement that emerged in the 1840s. The "Declaration of Sentiments" issued at the first women's rights convention in 1848 assailed men for framing the law of custody after separations and of guardianship in disregard of the "happiness of women—the law in all such cases going upon the false supposition of the supremacy of man, and giving all powers into his hands."[40]

From the 1840s on, custody and guardianship figured prominently in every women's rights meeting and political campaign. An 1854 address to the New York legislature discloses the basic arguments advanced in support of equal rights, particularly the use of the same gender beliefs seized upon by judges to reformulate family law. The petition pleaded for the special nurturing qualities of women—"There is no human love so generous, strong, and steadfast as that of the mother for her child." It assailed the law for being "cruel and ruthless" because man "in his inordinante love of power" used it to defy nature's command to give children to women. Arguing from the worst possible case, and reflecting a widespread antebellum distrust of the domestic responsibility of worldly males, the address charged that gamblers and rum sellers had more secure legal rights to their children than did mothers. "By your laws," the petition concluded, "the child is the absolute property of the father, wholly at his disposal in life and at death." Its authors demanded that the legislature give mothers a superior right to their children.[41]

Unlike the incremental judicial adjustments in custody and guardianship, the mass campaign for maternal rights generated a mixed, often hostile response. Two examples reveal these divergent responses and suggest why judicial control won greater popular and professional support than did statutory reforms.

As women's rights campaigner Clarina I. Howard Nichols traveled from Vermont to Massachusetts on an 1852 lecture tour, an elderly man and a sheriff boarded her train a few miles from the Bay State border. The pair tried to seize the young children of a female passenger. Nichols immediately stood up and told the startled passengers: "It means my friends that a woman has no legal right to her own babies; that the law-givers of this Christian country (!) have given the custody of the babies to the father, drunken or sober, and he may send the sheriff . . . to arrest and rob her of her little ones! You have heard sneers at Women's Rights. This is one of the rights—a mother's right to the care and custody of her little ones." Learning that the husband had transferred his custody rights to his own father, Nichols quickly explained that a recent Massachusetts court decision held that only a father could take children away from their mother. The passengers then threw the pair out, and after the train crossed the border the mother got a favorable custody ruling from a local magistrate.[42]

Demands for formal custody rights, secured by statutes and not by judicial discretion, could receive a far different public response as was evident in an 1854 *New York Tribune* account of a women's rights rally. When a woman stood up and demanded custody and guardianship rights, the paper reported, male hecklers greeted her with cries of "Oh, Dry Up!" "Bow-Wow!" "Waugh!" "Hiss-s-s-s!" "Get Out!"[43] A perhaps more reasoned expression of the same sentiments came two decades later when lawyer and historian James Schouler published his 1870 *Treatise on Domestic Relations*. Discussing legislative changes in married women's legal status, he argued: "The danger to be apprehended from all legislation of this sort is that it will weaken the ties of marriage by forcing both sexes into an unnatural antagonism;

teaching them to be independent of one another, and to earn their own living apart; whereas God's law points to the family and the mutual intercourse of man and woman as among the strongest safeguards of human happiness." Given the choice of using the law for securing greater independence for women or for maintaining female subordination, Schouler declared that the best path would be to ensure that the law provided, as he put it, "honorably, faithfully, and generously against all possible misfortune," and taught a woman to "lean upon the stronger arm of her husband, and to look to man for guidance."[44]

Stubborn opposition to formal custody and guardianship rights for married women offers graphic evidence that many opponents of women's rights resisted all significant changes in the legal status of women, not just those, such as suffrage, which would clearly extend feminine authority outside the home. Opposition was intense even to changes within the home. The pleas for rights stirred up deep fears within turbulent mid-nineteenth-century America that legal reforms might upset a needed sexual balance of power within the home based on male sovereignty and thus contribute to the larger social dislocations of a society which considered the family its primary anchor. Critics of the women's rights movement pictured demands for domestic rights, such as child custody, as threats to the family. Massachusetts women's rights advocate Samuel Sewall identified these concerns in an 1869 tract: "The greatest difficulty to overcome is not that most men are unwilling to do complete justice to the sex, or that the majority of women care nothing for this object; but it is simply a superstitious dread lest a change so radical could unsettle all the foundations of society and bring down the whole fabric in ruins." In other words, aiding a defenseless mother on a train was one thing, giving her equal or superior statutory rights proved to be quite another.[45]

Popular resistance to women's rights reinforced the judicial assumption of power over the home and placed sturdy obstacles in the path of radical legislative changes in custody and guardianship. The fate of the few statutory victories of the women's movement indicates the lure of a judicial patriarchy. Most statutes merely granted women the right to petition the courts for custody of their children in the event of a separation or divorce. The most far-reaching acts provided for equal guardianship. In 1860, New York, the seat of the most organized women's rights effort, passed the first major act which enlarged married women's property rights and declared a wife to be the "joint guardian of her children along with her husband, with equal powers, rights, and duties in regard to them, with her husband." Even that was too much; in 1862 the lawmakers retreated and amended the act to dictate only that husbands obtain their wives' consent before appointing testamentary guardians or indenturing their children.[46]

Nevertheless, New York judges easily integrated the legislation into their custody determinations so as to preserve, indeed augment, their patriarchal powers. A state tribunal rejected a mother's contention that the 1860 act gave her independent custody rights. The justices held that her rights could only be exercised in conjunction with her husband unless she proved him an unfit father and spouse. "The common law," they declared, "remains, except as modified by the joining of the wife with him." By leaving her husband without a judicially acceptable cause, this mother lost her newly won custody rights. Two years later in *People v. Boice,* a widow challenged her husband's appointment of a testamentary guardian without her consent. The court construed the intent of the new legislation to be an enlargement of the "sphere of maternal authority" and ruled that unilateral paternal action nullified the appointment. Reverting back to the best interests of the child doctrine, they used their discretion to award custody to the widow.[47]

At the turn of the century, only the District of Columbia and nine states formally granted women equal custody and guardianship. The rest invested judges with the patriarchal power to place children.[48]

CONCLUSION

The reformation of custody and guardianship begun in antebellum America came to dominate the law after the Civil War. Legal consolidation and refinement occurred, but the basic principles and priorities of the earlier era remained in place. These included the use of child welfare custody standards, class and sexually biased rules, and especially a maternal preference. As a result, child custody and guardianship remained under the purview of judicial patriarchs. Their power represented, in part, a persistent refusal to place superior legal rights in the hands of women. It was as well a refusal issued by male institutions which excluded women as legislators, lawyers, judges, and jurors and granted them access only as spectators, witnesses, and supplicants. The law retained, in the words of the 1883 *American Legal Register,* "a sort of guardianship over the power and property of women."[49] Antebellum legal changes transferred that guardianship from domestic to judicial patriarchs.

The persistence of patriarchy underlines the importance of continuities in American domestic relations. The law's purpose, the traditional one of producing stable families, and male governance proved inseparable. That pairing and the feminist resistance it stirred are critical to an understanding of nineteenth-century family law. As an 1880 women's rights convention declared: "The theory of a masculine head to rule the family, the church, or the State is contrary to Republican principles and the fruitful source of rebellion and corruption."[50] Rebels remained on the sexual battlefield because women refused to mute their demands for maternal rights and accept the limitations sanctioned by law. These conflicts are better understood in their historical context as part of the nineteenth-century attempt to accommodate new family practices and sentiments than as examples of the modernization of the law. The character of legal change, such as alterations in custody and guardianship, can only be determined by locating their complex sources and actual impact on the lives of nineteenth-century families and not by trying to find a place for them on an ahistorical conveyor belt of Western social evolution.

The creation of a judicial patriarchy in the nineteenth century reveals part of that historical environment. A new relationship emerged between the family and the state; one described quite vividly by a lawyer in 1882. "While in ruder forms of government more power was left with the Family itself for its own protection, the State now has taken to itself most of the old *patria potestas* and other forms of family autonomy and assumed the maintenance of all rights pertaining to the family."[51] The assumption of patriarchal authority by the state, and its delegation to the courts, created an antagonistic relationship between the two. The liberal ideal of emancipating households from governmental supervision often clashed with the courts' growing insistence that families should perform their vital functions in a socially beneficial manner. The inherent tension between the two goals led to divergent legal policies. Family law placed restrictions on the right of the state to intervene in what the society considered normally functioning families; and yet, conversely, it augmented state power to intervene in homes labeled troubled or abnormal. Judges seized the power to make these determinations.

Perhaps the best way to summarize the new level of judicial responsibility for family governance produced by nineteenth-century family law is to let a judge describe his authority. Robert Grant served as a probate judge in Boston for over thirty years. Known in his time mainly for the popular romantic novels he penned, he is perhaps best remembered today as a member of the commission which upheld the conviction of Sacco and Vanzetti.

Grant learned the law in the 1870s when the changes of the antebellum era had become legal commonplaces. In 1919, at the end of his career, he published a volume on family law. In it the judge acknowledged the sexual biases of custody law: "The attitude of the courts where parents battle over children has inclined so steadily toward the mother that, unless she has shown herself wanton or exceptionally recreant or heartless, she is not likely to be separated from them." Yet Grant felt trapped by this judicial creation. He feared that the "pendulum has swung so far in the opposite direction and the theory of paternal ownership been so completely discredited that the boot is sometimes upon the other leg, and women are heard asserting that they own their children because they bore them, and ought under no circumstances to be deprived of them—a complete reversal of the original injustice." To let women know their place, Grant asserted the judicial ideal of child placement:

> Mother-love, though set upon a pinnacle in the conscience of modern courts, must yield to a higher consideration, the well-being of her offspring. Where the custody of children is concerned the only enemy which the modern woman has to fear is her own unfitness. This is more apt to be challenged by the social workers and charitable societies, who might be called liaison officers of the courts of domestic relations, than by masculine ill-will. The beneficent body-guards, who probe into and bring to the attention of the court the conditions which menace the child, serve as a buffer between it and maternal Bolshevism.[52]

Thirteen years earlier Grant had expressed similar sentiments a bit less ponderously, when he offered a local bar association his poetic description of the patriarchal powers he so confidently exercised.

A Probate Judge who outlives you
May break your will—yes tax it too.
. . . Concerning other things,
His power outrivals that of kings,
Your children, when you prove unfit,

Are whisked away by sovereign writ.
In short, it may truly be said,
He has you living, he has you dead.
The moral is, as on you trudge,
Propitiate the Probate Judge.[53]

NOTES

I would like to thank several colleagues for their comments on various drafts of this essay: Stephen Presser, Jamil Zainaldin, Peter Garlock, Bertram Wyatt-Brown, Carl Ubbelohde, Brian Gatton, Ann Warren, and Roberta Wollons. Earlier versions of this article were presented at the 1982 meeting of the American Society for the Study of Legal History, 23 October, 1982, Washington D.C., and the Interdisciplinary Faculty Seminar of the Charles Armington Foundation at Case Western Reserve University, Cleveland, Ohio, 17 February, 1983. Research for this article was made possible by Crown Fellowships from Brandeis University, Waltham, Massachusetts, a National Endowment for the Humanities Summer Stipend, and a grant from the Armington Foundation.

1. For a more detailed discussion of these issues see Michael Grossberg, "Law and the Family in Nineteenth-Century America" (Ph.D. diss., Brandeis University, 1979).
2. See, for example, Edward Shorter, *The Making of the Modern Family* (New York: Basic, 1975); Lawrence Stone, *The Family, Sex, and Marriage, 1500-1800* (New York: Harper & Row, 1977).
3. In *At Odds: Women and the Family in America, from the Revolution to the Present* (New York: Oxford University Press, 1980), Carl N. Degler argues that the changing status of women is the key issue in all areas of family history.
4. For discussions of patriarchy, see Gordon J. Schochet, *Patriarchalism in Political Thought* (New York, Basic Books, 1975); Janet Rifkin, "Toward a Theory of Law and Patriarchy," *Harvard Women's Law Journal* 3 (1980): 83-95.
5. Mark DeWolfe Howe, "The Creative Period in the Law of Massachusetts," *Proceedings of the Massachusetts Historical Society* 69 (1947-50): 237; and see Morton J. Horwitz, *The Transformation of American Law, 1780-1860* (Cambridge: Harvard University Press, 1977), esp. chap. 1; William E. Nelson, *The Americanization of the Common Law: The Impact of Legal Change in Massachusetts Society, 1780-1860* (Cambridge: Harvard University Press, 1975); Leonard W. Levy, *The Law of the Commonwealth and Chief Justice Shaw* (Cambridge: Harvard University Press, 1957).
6. See for example, Eleanor M. Boatright, "The Political and Civil Status of Women in Georgia, 1783-1860," *Georgia Historical Quarterly* 25 (1941): 301-24.
7. For descriptions of restrictive legal controls on women, see James C. Mohr, *Abortion in America: The Origins and Evolution of National Policy* (New York: Oxford University Press, 1978); Ellen C. Dubois, *Feminism and Suffrage: The Emergence of an Independent Women's Movement in America, 1848-1869* (Ithaca, N.Y.: Cornell University Press, 1978); Suzanne D. Lebsock, "Radical Reconstruction and the Property Rights of Southern Women," *Journal of Southern History* 43 (1977): 195-216. For a general discussion of the paternalistic orientation of antebellum law, see Linda Kerber, *Women*

of the Republic: Intellect and Ideology in Revolutionary America (Chapel Hill: University of North Carolina Press, 1980), chap. 5; Norma Basch, "Invisible Women: The Legal Fiction of Marital Unity in Nineteenth-Century America," *Feminist Studies* 5 (Summer 1979): 346-66; Albie Sachs and Joan Hoff Wilson, *Sexism and the Law: Male Beliefs and Legal Bias in Britain and the United States* (New York: Free Press, 1978).

8. See for example Maxwell Bloomfield, *American Lawyers in a Changing Society, 1776-1876* (Cambridge: Howard University Press, 1976), chap. 4; Jamil Zainaldin, "The Emergence of a Modern American Family Law: Child Custody, Adoption, and the Courts, 1796-1851," *Northwestern Law Review* 73 (1979): 1038, especially 1046-47; Stephen B. Presser, "The Historical Background of the American Law of Adoption," *Journal of Family Law* 11 (1971): 443-516; and for a full discussion of the problems and possibilities of modernization theory, see Raymond Grew, "Modernization and Its Discontents," *American Behavioral Scientist* 21 (1977): 289-312.

9. P.H. Pettit, "Parental Control and Guardianship," in *A Century of Family Law* ed. Ronald H. Graveson and F.R. Crane (Cambridge, England: Cambridge University Press, 1957), 56-70; Sir Frederick Pollack and Frederic W. Maitland, *The History of English Law*, 2 vols. (London, 1898), 1: 436-47; William Blackstone, *Commentaries on the Law of England*, 4 vols. (London, 1765-69), 1: 438, 456, 462.

10. William Blackstone, *Commentaries on the Laws of England: First American Edition, Philadelphia, 1771-1772*, ed. George Sharwood, (Philadelphia, 1860), 2: 452; Spectator quote in Julia C. Spruill, *Women's Life and Work in the Southern Colonies* (Chapel Hill, University of North Carolina Press, 1938), 44; and see Arthur Calhoun, *A Social History of the American Family* (Cleveland, 1917), 1: 77, 255; Mary S. Benson, *Women in Eighteenth-Century America: A Study of Opinion and Social Usage* (1935; reprint, Port Washington, N.Y.: Kenitkatt, 1966); Bloomfield, 97-99.

11. Lorena S. Walsh, "Child Custody in the Early Colonial Chesapeake: A Case Study" (Paper presented at the Berkshire Conference on Women's History, Vassar College, June 1981); Richard B. Morris, *Studies in the History of Early American Law* (New York: Columbia University Press, 1930), 126-200; Mary Beth Norton, *Liberty's Daughters: The Revolutionary Experience of American Women, 1750-1800* (Boston: Little, Brown & Co., 1980), 46-57.

12. Douglas T. Rendleman, "Parens Patriae: From Chancery to the Juvenile Court," *South Carolina Law Review* 23 (1971): 205-23; Howard Neil Cozen, "The English Background: Origins of Parens Patriae," *South Carolina Law Review* 22 (1970): 147-51.

13. Rex V. Delaval, 3 Burr. 1435 (K.B. 1763); and see Rollin C. Hurd, *A Treatise on the Right of Personal Liberty, and on the Writ of Habeas Corpus and the Practice Connected with It* (Albany, 1858), 453-72.

14. Prather v. Prather (S.C. 1809); 4 Desau. 33, 34, 44; and for the later acceptance of this power see *Ex Parte* Hewitt, 11 Rich. Law 326 (S.C. 1858); see also Anonymous, 4 Desau. 94 (S.C. 1820); Williams v. Williams, 4 Desau. 183 (S.C. 1811).

15. See for example, Commonwealth v. Nutt, 1 Browne 143 (Pa. 1810); Bedell v. Bedell, 1 Johns. Chan. 605 (N.Y. 1815); Richmond v. Richmond, 1 Green Chan. 90 (N.J. 1838); Clark v. Clark, Wright 226 (Ohio, 1833); and Grossberg, 262-68.,

16. James Kent, *Commentaries on America Law*, 4 vols. (New York, 1826-30), 2: 193, 194; Norton, 5; Joseph Story, *Commentaries on Equity Jurisprudence* (Boston, 1839), 2: 596-97; and see also Francis Hillard, *Elements of Law* (New York, 1835), 24.

17. Volume 2 Revised New York Statutes 562, art. 2; People v. Chegaray, 18 Wend. 637, 641 (N.Y. 1836); Ahrenfeldt v. Ahrenfeldt, 1 Hoffm. Chan. 497, 502 (N.Y. 1840); Bloomfield, 118-119; and see People v. Nickerson, 19 Wend. 16 (N.Y. 1837); State v. King, 1 Ga. Dec. 93 (1841).

18. For a general discussion of these issues see Grossberg, 281-85.

19. Nichols v. Giles, 2 Root 461 (Conn. 1796).

20. Matter of Waldron, 13 Johns. 417 (N.Y. 1816).

21. U.S. v. Green, 1 Mason 482 (U.S. C.C., R.I., 1824, Fed. Case #15,256).

22. In the Matter of Mitchell, 3 Charlton 489, 494-95 (Ga. 1836).

23. State v. Hand, 1 Ohio Dec. 238, 242, 244 (1848).

24. The American position was summarized in the New Hampshire decision of State v. Libby: "It is quite apparent that there may be cases where the father's conduct is such, as by permitting tacitly or by express agreement, another to assume and discharge for many years the duties of parent to his child, that he could not afterward attempt to reclaim his child in good faith, nor without subjecting to serious hazards its interests and happiness. In such a case the award of the custody of the child would not be consistent with the exercise of sound judicial discretion." State v. Libby, 44 Me. 469 (1858); and see *In Re* Kottman, 2 Hill 363 (S.C. 1834); Hutson v. Townsend, 6 Rich. Eq. 249 (S.C. 1854); People v. Cooper, 8 How. Pr. 288 (N.Y. 1853); *Ex parte* Williams, 11 Rich. 452 (S.C. 1838); *Ex parte* Schumpert, 6 Rich. 244 (S.C. 1953); Rollin C. Hurd, *A Treatise on the Right of Personal Liberty* (Albany, 1858), 540-48.

25. Tapping Reeve, *The Law of Baron and Femme* (New York, 1814), 295, 311-337; Kent, 2: 219-31; Hillard, *Elements*, 24-25; Boatright, 116; Grossberg, 274-75, 285-88.

26. Ibid.; and see Eldridge v. Lippincott, 1 Coxe's Law, 397 (N.J. 1795); Fields v. Law, 2 Root 320 (Conn. 1796); Kline v. Beebe, 6 Conn. 494 (1827).

27. In the Matter of Van Houten, 2 Green Chan. 220, 226 (N.J. 1835); and see Copp v. Copp, 20 N.H. 284 (1850); Williamson v. Jordan, Busb. Dq. 40 (N.C. 1852); Fullerton v. Jackson, 5 John. Chan. 277 (1821); Corrigan v. Kiernan, 1 Bradf. 203 (N.Y. 1850).

28. For invocations of the rule see, for example, Stenbrook v. McColm, 7 Halst. Law 97 (N.J. 1830); State v. Sheeseman, 2 South. 445 (N.J. 1819); Huie v. Nixon, 6 Porter 77 (Ala. 1837); Holley v. Chamberlain, 1 Redf. 333 (N.Y. 1860); Webb v. Webb, 5 La. An. (1850); Hovey v. Morris, 7 Blackf. 559 (Ind. 1812); Ransom Tyler, *The Law of Infancy* (Chicago, 1888), 253-54.

29. Armstrong v. Stone, 9 Gratt. 102, 107 (Va. 1852); Striplin v. Ware, 36 Ala. 87, 90 (1860); and see Lea v. Richardson, 8 La. An. 94 (1853); People v. Wilcox, 22 Barb. 178 (N.Y. 1854); Level v. Bettis, 3 Bush, 74 (Ky. 1867); Carlisle v. Tuttle, 30 Ala. 613 (1857); Porch v. Fries, 3 Green 204 (N.J. 1867).

30. *Report of the D'Hauteville Case* (Philadelphia, 1840), 292-93, 234, and see 47-50.

31. A Member of the Boston Bar, *Review of the D'Hauteville Case* (Boston, 1841), 25, 37, 41 (emphasis added).

32. An 1865 article by Vermont Chief Justice Isaac Redfield summarized the new judicial view. "The rule of the common law which recognizes the superior rights of the husband as to all matters pertaining to the control of the family, while the parents continue to live together, has not the same reasons of necessity of convenience in its favor after they become separated. The court may then fix the custody of the child as they think will most induce to their careful training, education, and comfort, without violation of any rule affecting quiet and good order in families; a right which is now generously secured in American states, either by custom or statute, but not in all, we are sorry to say." See "Recent Developments in English Jurisprudence," *American Law Register*, n.s., 4 (1865): 137; and see Grossberg, 597-612.

33. George Bishop, *Every Woman Her Own Lawyer* (New York, 1858), 181; Joel P. Bishop, *Commentaries on the Law of Marriage and Divorce* (Boston, 1852), 517-18,

525-26; Grossberg, 273-4, 598-612.

34. State v. Baird and Torrey, 21 N.J. Eq. 384, 388 (1869), and 18 N.J. Eq. 184 (1867); Landis v. Landis, 39 N.J. Law 274 (1877); State v. Kirkpatrick, 54 Ia. 373 (1880); Matter of Pray, 60 Howard Pr. 194 (1881); McKim v. McKim, 12 R.I. 462 (1879); Latham v. Latham, 30 Gratt. 364 (1878); Matter of Watson, 10 Abb. N.C. 215 (1882); Greenwood v. Greenwood, 84 Minn. 203 (1901).

35. Anonymous, 55 Ala. 428, 432-433 (1876).

36. Carr v. Carr, 22 Gratt. 168, 174 (Va. 1872); and see Bennett v. Bennett, 43 Conn. 313 (1876).

37. Commonwealth v. Addicks, 5 Binn. 520 (Pa. 1813); 2 Serge and Rawle, 174 (Pa. 1816).

38. Lindsey v. Lindsey, 14 Ga. 657 (1854); and see Matter of Viele, 44 How, Pr. 14 (1872).

39. People v. Olmstead, 27 Barb. 9, 31, 32; and see State v. Sitgall, 2 Zabr. 286 (N.J. 1849); Magee v. Holland, 3 Dutch. 86 (N.J. 1858); People v. Rhodes, 24 Barb. 521, (N.Y. 1857); Bryan v. Bryan, 34 Ala. 516 (1859); Lawrence M. Friedman and Robert V. Percival, "Who Sues for Divorce? From Fault through Fiction to Freedom," *Journal of Legal Studies* 5 (1976): 61-82.

40. Stanton et al., *History of Woman Suffrage,* 6 vols. (1881-1922), 1:71. This demand was repeated in women's rights platforms and addresses for the rest of the century, see 105, 194, 241, 254-55, 260-61, 562-63, 579-89, 776-79.

41. E.C. Strauder, *Address to the Legislature of New York* (Albany, 1854); Caroline H. Dall, *Woman's Rights under the Law* (Boston, 1861), 60; Caroline H. Dall, *Women, College, and Court* (Boston, 1878), 266-360.

42. Stanton et al., 1: 174-78.

43. Cited in Bell Squire, *The Woman Movement in America* (Chicago, 1911), 46.

44. James Schouler, *A Treatise on Domestic Relations* (Boston, 1870), 17, 18. For similar expressions of concern see Stanton et al., 3: 152.

45. Samuel Sewall, *The Legal Condition of Women* (Boston, 1869), 14-15; and for continued feminist agitation for custody rights see Stanton et al., 2: 102, 799, 3: 419; Dubois, 188; Rheta Childe Dorr, *What Eight Million Women Want* (Boston, 1910); Lucy Stone, "The Progress of Fifty Years," in *The Congress of Women,* ed. Mary K. Oldham Eagle (Chicago, 1894), 60; Alice Paul, *Outline of the Legal Position of Women in Pennsylvania* (Philadelphia, 1911), 31-32.

46. Stanton et al., 1: 686, 747-78 and see in general, chap. 14. For discussions of the property reforms that accompanied these custody changes, see Peggy A. Rabkin, *Fathers to Daughters: The Legal Foundations of Female Emancipation* (Westport, Conn.: Greenwood Press, 1980).

47. People v. Brooks, 35 Barb. 85, 91 (N.Y. 1861); People v. Boice, 39 Barb. 307, 309-10 (N.Y. 1862).

48. Stanton et al., 4: chaps. 24-72. For a complete assessment of the status of the law in turn-of-the-century America, see Jeannie C. Wilson, *The Legal Rights and Duties of Women* (New York, 1913); John Norton Pomeroy, *A Treatise on Equity Jurisprudence,* 2d. ed. (San Francisco, 1892), 3: 2012-14; Annie G. Porritt, *Laws Affecting Women and Children* (New York, National Woman Suffrage Publishing Co., 1916), 137; United States Bureau of Education, "The Legal Rights of Children" (Washington, D.C., 1880), 16-27; Roscoe Pound, "Individual Interests in the Domestic Relations," *Michigan Law Review* 14 (1916): 182-85.

49. Quoted in Morton Keller, *Affairs of State: Public Life in Late Nineteenth-Century America* (Cambridge: Howard University Press, 1977), 470. For a contemporary endorsement of this policy which reveals its paternalistic foundations, see Russell H. Conwell, *Women and the Law* (Boston, 1876), esp. 16-21, 28-29, 35-55.

50. Stanton et al., 2: 152. For an endorsement of judicial control of custody by a female attorney, see Mary A. Greene, "The American Mother's Right to Her Child," *American Law Review* 52 (1918): 371-82; George A.O. Ernst, *The Legal Status of Married Women in Massachusetts* (Boston, 1895), 24-31; Calhoun, 3: 108, 394.

51. M.H. Buckham, "Habeas Corpus: Custody of Infants," *Central Law Journal* 15 (1882): 384; and see Pound.

52. Robert Grant, *Law and the Family* (New York, 1919), 181-82, 183.

53. Ibid., v-vi.

Late Nineteenth Century Married Women's Property Law: Reception of the Early Married Women's Property Acts by Courts and Legislatures

by RICHARD H. CHUSED*

The reform of married women's property has been proceeding for more than a century.[1] Beginning around 1835, states began to alter the common law rules granting husbands management and control of their wives' real estate and ownership of their personal property. The initial wave of acts generally provided that married women's property was to be exempted from attachment by creditors of their husbands. Some of these acts also contained language permitting married women to own property in their own separate estates, although the statutory language gave almost no guidance as to the scope of management authority, if any, wives were to have over their assets. Frequently the statutes were construed narrowly. Subsequent legislation was necessary in all jurisdictions before the major tenets of common law coverture rules had been altered.[2]

That married women's property reform came in a slow piecemeal fashion suggests that those men dealing with the issue in legislatures and courts must have differed among themselves in their attitudes toward the changes being wrought. Such cultural ambiva-

* Associate Professor of Law, Georgetown University Law Center. I extend my thanks to David Zolensky, J.D. 1982, Georgetown University Law Center, and James H. Miller, J.D. 1982, Lewis & Clark Law School, each of whom helped gather valuable materials for this article. The staff at the Oregon Historical Society was very gracious in dealing with my requests for copies of documents from the opposite coast. Completion of this project would not have been possible without the financial support of Georgetown University Law Center, which has generously fulfilled my requests for research assistants and summer writer's grants.

1. Perhaps the final chapters in this long historical epic are now being written. The decline of male dominated marital property rules finally has constitutional impetus. *See* Kirchberg v. Feenstra, 450 U.S. 455 (1981). But there are other related issues left to resolve, particularly in the distribution of property at divorce and death.

2. *See* Chused, *Married Women's Property Law: 1800-1850*, 71 GEO. L.J. 1359 (1983). [Hereinafter cited as Chused, *Married Women's Acts*].

lence arose not only because of concern over the changing social roles of mid-nineteenth-century women, but also because of the alterations made in the operation of the family economy by the new statutes. Although scholarship in this area suggests that macroeconomic events, such as panics, were important to the adoption of some married women's acts,[3] close attention has not yet been given to the cumulative impact on married women's law of decades of disputes between husbands, wives, and family creditors. Throughout the period in which married women's property law was under revision, courts and legislatures were confronted with a variety of disputes raising issues about the appropriate definition of a married woman's separate estate. The vague language in many of the statutes left considerable room for argument and litigation. Disputes arose about the sort of property that could be owned by married women, the form of the documents necessary to establish a separate estate, the ability of women to invest in their own property or to dedicate their property to the payment of personal obligations, and the legitimacy of contracts dealing with separately held assets. While a number of influences in addition to family debtor-creditor issues were at work during the development of married women's property law, study of materials on legal issues in the family economy provides a useful window through which to analyze married women's property reform.

In this paper,[4] I trace the impact of family debtor-creditor problems on the development of married women's law in Oregon. The major provisions of Oregon's married women's law were adopted between 1850, when Congress adopted the Oregon Donation Act, and 1880, when the state legislature enacted a sweeping statute removing most differences in the treatment of property owned by men

---

3. It is now generally agreed that the first wave of married women's acts were adopted in part because of the dislocations caused by the Panic of 1837. Chused, *Married Women's Acts, supra* note 2, at 1400-04; N. Basch, In the Eyes of the Law: Women, Marriage and Property in Nineteenth Century New York, 39-40, 122-25 (1982); E. Warbasse, The Changing Legal Rights of Married Women: 1800-1861, at 146-59, 202-05 (Feb. 1960) (unpublished thesis). However, the continuing relationship between married women's property law and commercial law has not been thoroughly analyzed. The best paper on the subject that has come to my attention was written by a law student studying New Hampshire, Breed, Conflicts of Interest: The Evolution of Married Women's Property Rights in Nineteenth Century New Hampshire (1982) (unpublished paper, copy on file with author).

4. This is the second of two papers on the development of married women's law in Oregon. The first, Chused, *The Oregon Donation Act of 1850 and Nineteenth Century Federal Married Women's Property Law*, 2 L. & Hist. Rev. 44 (1984) [Hereinafter cited as Chused, *Federal Women's Law*], dealt with the treatment of women by the federal land grant system, the adoption of the Oregon Donation Act of 1850, and the role of Oregon's territorial delegate, Samuel R. Thurston, in gaining the passage of the donation bill.

and women. The Oregon Donation Act was the only federal land grant act permitting married women to obtain title to federal lands in their own right. During the thirty-year period following the adoption of the Donation Act, a confusing system of land regulations emerged as the fledgling territorial government passed and repealed land statutes, the General Land Office struggled to open offices in Oregon, and state and federal judges with dramatically different visions of the world battled over the meaning of the Donation Act and related provisions in the Oregon territorial and state codes. Through all the confusion a steady stream of disputes arose over the relationship between married women, husbands, and family creditors. From the territorial legislature's adoption in 1852 of an act exempting women's donation claims from the claims of husbands' creditors through the enactment of the last married women's acts in 1878 and 1880, debates over the rights of creditors played an important part in the development of married women's law.

One of the most interesting aspects of the developments in Oregon during the second half of the nineteenth century was the gradual development of a well understood asset holding device for married women. The taking of a fee simple by a man had long carried with it certain automatic appendages—rights of transfer, devise, and management. The need to increase creditor's security over the meaning of the new statutory married woman's separate estate meant that common understandings also had to be developed for women's property. Whether women were to be treated the same as men was not always as important to creditors as knowing precisely the status of married women's property. It is this process of developing common understandings on the meaning of the separate estate which ensued in Oregon after the Donation Act went into effect. As things turned out, married women slowly gained the transfer, management, and devising rights held by men for generations. The gradual entry of women into the workforce and the rising tide of women acting as the arbiters of family consumption habits guaranteed that the common understandings on the meaning of a married woman's separate estate would make it look very much like the male fee simple. Of necessity, these developments eventually led to a slow *loss* of special status for property owned by married women. The early Oregon legislation exempting married women's separately held property from the debts of husbands gave way to laws providing family creditors with equal access to the property of married men and women. Throughout this period, legislative and judicial resolution of disputes between married couples and their creditors displayed many contradictory and ambiguous strains of thought on married women. Telling this story sheds significant light on the development of married women's property law in the second half of the nineteenth century.

I. The Oregon Donation Act of 1850

The Oregon Donation Act provided that persons settling in Oregon by December 1, 1850, could claim ". . . the quantity of one half section, or three hundred and twenty acres, if a single man, and if a married man, or if he shall become married within one year from the first day of December, eighteen hundred and fifty, the quantity of one section, or six hundred and forty acres, one half to himself and the other half to his wife, to be held by her in her own right. . . ."[5] Although the act did not emerge from Congress with a provision exempting married women's donation lands from the claims of husbands' creditors, the issue was much debated.[6] Before finally adopting the Senate version of the bill,[7] the House had adopted an amendment proposed by Mr. Sackett providing that "no interest in the part so held by the wife in her own right, shall be liable for, or subject to sale upon the debts of the husband."[8] In addition, the original House committee version of the bill contained language which, if adopted, would have been a married women's act quite advanced for its time.[9]

It was certainly not surprising that the debtor-creditor status of married women's property would be of concern to those drafting the Donation Act. By 1850, most states had adopted acts exempting married women's property from attachment by husbands' creditors, a number had also passed homestead bills exempting residences and

---

5. An Act to Create the Office of Surveyor-General of the Public Lands in Oregon, and to Provide for the Survey, and to Make Donations to Settlers of the Said Public Lands, ch. 76, §§ 4-5, 9 Stat. 496, 497, 498 (1850).

6. The story of these debates may be found in Chused, *Federal Women's Law*, *supra* note 4 at 61-68.

7. The Act was adopted near the end of the Congressional session. If Samuel Thurston, Oregon's territorial delegate to Congress, had tried to alter the bill approved by the Senate he would certainly have run out of time to get the bill adopted. He, therefore, took what he could get. *See* his Letter to the Electors and People of the Territory of Oregon 7, (Nov. 15, 1850) (Thurston Papers, MSS 379, Oregon Historical Society).

8. Cong. Globe, 31st Cong., 1st Sess. 1094 (1850).

9. H.R. 250, 31st Cong., 1st Sess. (1850) (Record Group 233, United States Archives). The original bill contained the following crossed out language:

> and all lands herein provided for to be donated to females shall forever be the property of such females in their own right; to be by them held, used, aliened, and devised at their own will and pleasure, and not subject to the control of their husbands or be liable for their debts without the consent of such females first had in writing in such manner as may be provided for hereafter by the Legislative Assembly of Oregon Territory.

This language was replaced by the terminology "to be held by her in her own right", found in the adopted version of the bill. The crossed out language was never discussed on the floor of Congress. The reasons for its exclusion are not clear. *See*, Chused, *Federal Women's Law*, *supra* note 4, at 61-64.

surrounding land from seizure; and the free land, or homestead, movement urging the debt-exempt distribution of federal lands was becoming a powerful political force.[10] All of these issues were of concern to Samuel R. Thurston, the Oregon Territory's non-voting delegate to Congress from 1849 to 1851. Near the end of his term, Thurston wrote his constituents a lengthy reelection campaign letter.[11] His sentiments on the exemption of married women's assets from husbands' debts were clear:

> This land of the wife will serve as homestead exemption to the family, and it was with this view also, that I contended for this feature [the Sackett amendment] of the bill. While the wife has a home, the husband and children are sure to have one. If, then, the husband fails, or if misfortune overtakes him, he may return to the *sanctuary* of that guardian angel, his wife, who is ever watchful of his interest, and solicitous for his comfort, where he can rest from his troubles and be happy. I deem it highly important, and I care not how widely my doctrine is known, that Oregon should adopt the policy of legislating favorably for the masses at the earliest possible moment, and that she should throw around every one of her citizens a protection by way of *homestead exemption*, by which, with his ordinary industry, he can secure an honest and easy livelihood, and be protected against the hands of unfeeling oppression, and saved from the jaws of pinching want. In this way every man will be placed on an eminence, where *he can be a man, and his own man*; where he can be an independent suffragen, beyond the compelling grasp of the rich lord or politician, and where viewing all measures for himself, he can think, and speak, and vote as a well directed and untrammelled judgment shall direct. Hence, I favored the provision of the bill which passed the House, declaring this land of the wife not liable to the husband's debts or the grasp of his creditors, or subject to their control. That was stricken out in the Senate, to satisfy the scruples of some, that it was meddling too far with the domestic legislation of the Territory. It was said our assembly can pass such a law, which I hope they will do at their next session; and whenever we form a State, that this and the homestead exemption feature will find a place in our constitution.

The stage was thus set for three decades of judicial and legislative consideration of the relationship between wives, husbands, and family creditors. When, in 1852, the Oregon Territorial Legislature followed Thurston's advice and adopted an act exempting married

10. Chused, *Federal Women's Law*, *supra* note 4, at 55-56.

11. Thurston, Letter to the Electors and People of the Territory of Oregon, *supra* note 7.

women's donation claims from husbands' debts, a strong incentive was created to repose property in wives to protect it from creditors. To the degree that there was insecurity over which assets were protected by the exemption, it was also possible for married couples to use wives' property as enticement for deals, only to plead the debtor exemption provisions if trouble arose later. It was almost inevitable that these sorts of problems would require further deliberation, whether in courts, legislatures, or constitutional conventions.

II. The Oregon Donation Act from 1850 to 1857

Although Thurston died before the Oregon Donation Act was implemented,[12] the suggestion in his 1850 letter to his constituents that the new Oregon Territorial Legislature should protect wives' donation claims from husbands' creditors was taken up very shortly after Thurston's death. Perhaps his untimely death gave added impetus to the movement. In any case, on December 4, 1851, Matthew P. Deady, a member of the Council, one of the two houses in the territorial legislature, announced his intention to introduce exemption legislation.[13] The fact that Deady introduced the measure confirmed its uncontroversial content. By this time, of course, almost every state had adopted at least one married women's property act. In addition, Deady, who became an important lawyer and judge in Oregon, was a proslavery Democrat steeped in common law traditions. His later opinions in married women's cases displayed traditional, and unchanging, attitudes on coverture.[14] Six weeks after Deady's announcement appeared, an act was approved providing that a wife's donation claim was "secured to the sole and separate use and control of the wife" and that all legal and equitable interests

---

12. He died in 1851 on a boat off the shore of Mexico as he was returning to Oregon following his term in Congress.

13. Oregon Spectator, Dec. 9, 1851. This issue contained a summary of the activities of the Council. The entry for Thursday, December 4, contained this item:

> Mr. Deady gave notice that on Monday or some subsequent day of the session he would introduce a bill to exempt the wife's portion of the claim donated by the act of Congress approved Sept. 27, 1850, from the debts or liabilities of the husband.

14. Deady drafted many of the territorial and state statutes and codes and sat as a judge from 1853 until 1893, first on the Territorial Supreme Court, and then as a federal judge. For biographical material on Deady, see Platt, *Matthew P. Deady*, in Great American Lawyers 355-92 (W. Lewis ed. 1909); 2 H.H. Bancroft, Chronicles of the Builders of the Commonwealth 465-515 (1892); Teiser, *A Pioneer Judge of Oregon: Matthew P. Deady*, 44 Or. Hist. Q. 61 (1943); McBride, *The Oregon Constitutional Convention, 1857*, in Proceedings of the Oregon Historical Society Including the Quarterly Meetings of the Board of Directors and the Fourth Annual Meetings of the Members of the Society, Dec. 20, 1902, at 20, 23 (1906). Discussion of some of Deady's Donation Act decisions may be found *infra* in part IV of this paper.

in such claims "shall in no wise be made subject to or liable for the debts or liabilities of her husband, whether contracted before or after the passage of this act." [15] This act provided the sort of homestead exemption which Thurston wrote of in his letters to the members of the House and to his constituents, and which the Senate deleted during the debates on the Oregon Donation Act.

Like most of the married women's property laws adopted during the 1840's,[16] Deady's act was very narrow in its coverage. The common law rule that men gained title to their wives' personal property upon marriage was left untouched. Real estate other than donation land was not covered. Even the "sole and separate use and control" language of the statute did not guarantee that husbands lost their ability to manage wives' donation claims and control the profits. The language was probably borrowed from the equity tradition, where such words had to be used in trusts to guarantee the creation of a wife's separate estate. But even if the language in the trust succeeded in creating beneficial title to property in a married woman, control by her of the use, sale, or disposition at death did not necessarily follow. In many jurisdictions, the husband retained management authority unless the trust specifically guaranteed his wife the power to manage, sell, or will her real property.[17] Deady certainly knew about these cases, as his later decisions made clear.

In Oregon the most liberal meaning of the "sole and separate use" language was not accepted. At the time Deady's Exemption Act was adopted married women could not write wills except as provided by an antenuptial agreement.[18] Only after the Exemption

---

15. The act, found in General Laws Passed by the Legislative Assembly of the Territory of Oregon, 3d Sess., at Salem beginning Dec. 1, 1851, at 64 (1852), reads as follows:

> AN ACT to exempt the wife's portion of lands donated in Oregon Territory by act of Congress, approved September 27th, 1850, from the debts and liabilities of her husband.
>
> SECTION 1. Be it enacted by the Legislative Assembly of the Territory of Oregon, That all right and interest of the wife, both legal and equitable, in and to the land donated to settlers in Oregon Territory by an act of Congress, approved September 27th, 1850, both now and hereafter, be and hereby is secured to the sole and separate use and control of the wife, and such interests in said lands, both legal and equitable of the wife, and the rents and profits thereof, shall in no wise be made subject to or liable for the debts or liabilities of her husband, whether contracted before or after the passage of this act.
>
> SEC. 2. This act to take effect and be in force from and after its passage.
>
> Passed the Council, January 16th, 1852.
>
> Passed the House of Representatives, January 20th, 1852.

16. *See* Chused, *Married Women's Acts*, *supra* note 2, at 1398-1400, 1410-12.

17. *Id*. at 1365-72.

18. An Act Respecting Wills §3 (Sept. 26, 1849), in Statutes of a General Nature Passed by the Legislative Assembly of the Territory of Oregon, 2d Sess., Dec. 2, 1850, Oregon City, at 274 (1851).

Act was passed did the territorial legislature move to permit a married woman to write a will, but only for "real estate held in her own right, subject to any rights which her husband may have as tenant by the curtesy."[19] And tenancy by the curtesy, of course, provided the husband with management and control rights.[20] Oregon curtesy legislation went even further than usual by providing husbands with life estates in their wives' real estate regardless of whether children had been born of the marriage. More confusion was created when, in 1854, the territorial legislature adopted an act repealing all but a few statutes adopted before the fifth session of the territorial legislature.[21] This act, which arose because the chaotic politics of the territory produced arguments over where the legislature should sit and disputes over what laws were operative, had the effect of repealing the Exemption Act, but not the curtesy provisions.[22] Unless the language of the Donation Act itself was read to provide married women with the right to manage their claims, the exemption legislation, like the early married women's acts, acted only as a debtor protection measure.

But it was highly unlikely that the Donation Act provisions giving land to married women were intended to give them management authority over their assets. As already mentioned, Congress declined to insert either primitive or advanced married women's property provisions in the Donation Act. In addition, language in the act appeared to require depriving some married women of their claims if their husbands died before the family had occupied their land for the required four-year period. This was hardly the sort of

---

19. An Act Relating to Wills §3 (Dec. 15, 1853), in Statutes of Oregon, 5th Sess., Dec. 5, 1853, at 354 (1854).

20. An Act Relating to Estates in Dower, by Curtesy and General Provisions, Concerning Real Estates §30 (Jan. 16, 1854), in Statutes of Oregon, 5th Sess, Dec. 5, 1853, at 373 (1854).

21. An Act to Repeal All Acts Heretofore Passed, With Certain Exceptions (Jan. 30, 1854), in Statutes of Oregon, 5th Sess., Dec. 5, 1853, at 505 (1854).

22. *See* Kelly, *History of the Preparation of the First Code of Oregon*, 4 OR. HIST. SOC'Y Q. 185 (1903). At the first session of the territorial legislature acts were adopted which designated the location of a capital and transplanted the Iowa Code to Oregon. The validity of both of these acts was challenged on the ground that they contained material on more than one subject in violation of the federal act creating the Oregon Territory. Even the judges who were supposed to settle the matter fell into arguing over where to sit. Much of the dispute is described in Message From the President of the United States Inviting the Attention of Congress to the Condition of Things in the Territory of Oregon, H.R. EXEC. DOC. No. 94, 32nd Cong., 1st Sess. (1852). After Congress intervened to declare the capital to be Salem, A Joint Resolution Approving and Confirming an Act of the Legislative Assembly of the Territory of Oregon, entitled "An Act to Provide for the Selection of Places for Location and Erection of the Public Buildings of the Territory of Oregon," and for Other Purposes, Con. Res. 8, 10 Stat. 146 (1852), the mess was straightened out at the territorial level by a general repealer and adoption of a new code of laws.

provision one would expect if married women could manage their own estates. The Donation Act, which required the filing of a land claim by a "settler," appeared to permit the settler's wife to obtain her land only upon the successful completion of the claim process by her husband, the "settler."[23] Since one of the obstacles to perfecting a claim was four years of occupancy, there was a significant risk that death or marital discord would prevent some married women from obtaining land if their claims were derivative to their husbands' rights.

The problem was discussed in a Report of the Surveyor General of Oregon transmitted to Congress on the last day of 1852 by the Secretary of the Interior.[24] Among other things, the report discussed difficulties arising because widows and orphans of emigrants dying enroute to Oregon could not make claims under the Donation Act.[25] Very early in the administration of the Donation Act, the Oregon Surveyor General let it be known that women who had settled on land with their husbands before December 1, 1850, but whose husbands had died before four years of occupancy was complete, could file claims for the amount they would have been entitled to in their own right had their husbands survived.[26] But those portions of the act granting land to future emigrants provided for claims by single

---

23. Section 4 of the Oregon Donation Act provided that a grant of land would be made to a "settler or occupant" completing four years of residence and cultivation on the claim, and that "if a married man", his wife would get half of the claim in her own right. 9 Stat. 497. Section 5, though worded somewhat differently, also called for grants of land to "citizens" settling in Oregon, with the wife obtaining half of the citizen's claim. 9 Stat. 498. While the act certainly could have been read to make the claims of husbands and wives independent, the language of the statute, to say nothing of the tenor of the times, made it likely that married women's claims would be deemed to arise only after their husbands, as settlers, perfected their donation claims.

24. Reports of Surveyors General of California and Oregon, H.R. EXEC. DOC. No. 14, 32nd Cong., 2nd Sess. 12-30 (1853). The report, dated Oct. 23, 1852, did not reach Washington until late in the year. It was ordered to be printed on Jan. 14, 1853.

25. The Surveyor General wrote:

> I would earnestly suggest that the act of 27th September, 1850, be modified, or amended, to allow *widows* and *orphans*, made such by the death of the husband or mother on the route to Oregon, to hold a quarter section of land, the same as is now allowed to *white male* settlers under the fifth section.

26. In the May 8, 1851, issue of the Oregon Spectator, the following item appeared:

> We are authorized to state, by the Surveyor General of Oregon, that he has instructions to so construe the law making donations of land to the citizens of Oregon, as to include the widows of men immigrating to Oregon, whose husbands died upon the way or who shall have become such subsequent to their arrival in the Territory, that they will be entitled to all the benefits of the several provisions granted to white male citizens, or in such quantities as they would be entitled to, in their own right, provided their husbands were living; or in other words, as respects grants of land, they will be placed upon the same footing as male citizens: Provided that such widows were in this country before Dec. 1st., 1850, and are of American birth.

persons only if they were male, and widows newly arrived in Oregon lacked the joint occupancy with their husbands used by the Surveyor General to justify grants to widows of old settlers.[27] The territorial legislature followed with a resolution urging that the Donation Act be amended to confirm the Oregon Surveyor General's practices with respect to old settlers and to amend the act for new arrivals.[28]

The Oregon Surveyor General's Report was transmitted to Congress sometime after legislation amending the Donation Act had been introduced in Congress. H.R. 224, introduced on March 10, 1852,[29] provided that those settlers desiring to pay immediately for their donation claims or falling outside the terms of the Donation Act, could purchase their claim under the land sale system governing federal land disposition in other areas of the country. The bill passed the House on June 22, 1852[30] and was reported out of the Senate Public Lands Committee with amendments about two months later.[31] Very shortly after the Oregon Surveyor General's report appeared, Senator Felch asked the Senate to recommit the bill to committee for further work.[32] When the bill reappeared a short time later it contained new amendments to extend the Donation Act's operation until 1855 and to provide for women arriving in

---

This notice followed the general instructions sent by the General Land Office to those administering the Act in Oregon. These instructions were sent on Mar. 10, 1851. Letter to Surveyor General of Oregon from J. Butterfield, Commissioner of the General Land Office, in 1 Letters Sent to the Surveyor General of Oregon 6, 23 (Record Group No. 49, Division "E," National Archives) (Mar. 10, 1851). The instructions are in the same volume at 52-96, with the widow instructions at 92-93. For those who survived for the full four year period required by §4, but died before receiving a patent, rights under the Donation Act passed by will, or, in the absence of a will, to the surviving spouse and children in equal shares. §4, 9 Stat. 497, 498. Section 5 lacked a similar provision. *See* Davenport v. Lamb, 80 U.S. (13 Wall.) 418 (1871); Chambers v. Chambers, 4 Or. 153 (1871).

27. Section 8 of the Donation Act also provided that an actual settler's death before four years of occupancy meant that the deceased party's rights passed to the widow and children in equal shares. 9 Stat. 499. This suggests that a widow's claim under §4 should also have survived the husband's death, but the issue was certainly not clear. *See supra* notes 22-25 and accompanying text.

28. Joint Resolution (Dec. 18, 1851) (Item 4211, Provisional and Territorial Papers, MSS 1226, Oregon Historical Society).

29. CONG. GLOBE, 32nd Cong., 1st Sess. 710 (1852). The terms of the bill were described by Representative Hall during the brief floor discussion of the bill on May 22, 1852. *Id.* at 1447-48.

30. *Id.* at 1595.

31. Senator Felch reported for the Public Lands Committee on Aug. 18. *Id.* at 2238.

32. The Surveyor General's Report was ordered to be printed in the House on Jan. 14, 1853. CONG. GLOBE, 32nd Cong., 2nd Sess. (1853). H.R. 224 was recommitted to the Senate Public Lands Committee on Jan. 25. *Id.* at 390.

the territory as widows.[33] On February 1, 1853, the Senate passed the bill and the House concurred in the Senate amendments only a week later.[34]

As the act emerged from Congress it provided that settlers could purchase their claims after two years of occupancy, that emigrants could file claims through 1855; that the traditional land sale system would take over after 1855 as to all lands not claimed under the Donation Act; that all widows of settlers and emigrants could file claims for land they would have been entitled to but for the deaths of their husbands; and that the rights of wives dying before four years of occupancy passed to their heirs.[35] It was fortunate for Oregon's widows that this act was adopted, for the following year the Territorial Supreme Court decided that a wife's donation land claim was indeed derivative to that of her husband as the true "settler." In *Vandolf v. Otis*,[36] the wife's half of a Donation Act claim made by a white man was challenged because the wife was an Indian.[37] The court responded that the terms of the Donation Act limiting claims to white settlers or occupants applied only to the male family head, and that there was no racial limitation on the remaining members of the family. If this theory was correct, then widows of deceased claimants might also lose their claims,[38] since their title would depend upon their husband's continued settlement and occupancy.[39]

---

33. *Id.* at 413-14, 499.

34. *Id.* at 499, 538-40.

35. An Act to Amend an Act Entitled "An Act to Create the Office of Surveyor General of the Public Lands in Oregon, and to Provide for the Survey, and to Make Donations to the Settlers of the Said Public Lands." Approved September Twenty-seventh, Eighteen Hundred and Fifty, ch. 69, 10 Stat. 158 (1853). *See also* Notice to Settlers in Oregon Claiming the Benefits of the Donations Law of 27th September, 1850, in 1 Letters Sent to Surveyor General of Oregon 135-36 (copy of a public notice inserted between these pages while remaining unnumbered itself) (Record Group 49, Division "E," National Archives) (Apr. 30, 1853).

36. 1 Or. 153 (1854).

37. The court noted that a number of the early male settlers married Indian women. *Id.* at 157.

38. Section 8 of the original Donation Act permitted wives to inherit the settler's claim but was silent as to the continued validity of their own claim. 9 Stat. 499.

39. This later turned out to be true. *See* Fields v. Squires, 9 F. Cas. 29 (C.C.D. Or. 1868) (No. 4776); Vance v. Burbank, 101 U.S. 514 (1879); McSorley v. Hill, 2 Wash. 638, 27 P. 552 (1891). Although the Supreme Court eventually held that single women would be treated like single men for purposes of the Donation Act, Silver v. Ladd, 74 U.S. (7 Wall.) 219, 226 (1868), that only meant that widows had to start their claims over if their rights during marriage were derivative from their husbands. That may have led to loss of claims either to intervening contestants, or under the time limits of the Donation Act. Administrative materials confirm the problem. *See* Claim of Daniel F. Bradford, 10 Op. Att'y Gen. 380 (1862); Claim of David S. Maynard, Copp, Public Land Laws 751 (1873); Claims of Meek & Luelling, 2 Copp's Land Owner 21 (1874).

Of some interest is the possibility that the early administrative practice may have been more lenient than the later judicial decrees. Early administrative materials

The same year *Vandolf* was decided, Congress completed its review of the Surveyor General's recommendations for Oregon by extending the preemption system over Oregon and providing for grants to orphans of persons who would have been entitled to donations.[40] Perhaps more than any other event during the early 1850's, the passage of this act displayed the fleeting interest of Congress in the fate of female western land claimants. On April 4, 1854, the House Committee on Public Lands simultaneously reported three bills, one to establish a surveyor general and grant land donations in New Mexico, another to do the same in Utah, and a third to amend the Oregon Donation Act.[41] On May 2, the New Mexico bill was the first of the three to come up for debate in the House.[42] It had been drafted jointly by the two Public Lands Committees and the Land Commissioner and called for donations of 320 acres to single white males and 640 acres to married males.[43] During the floor debate, which was much more concerned with racial issues than gender roles, the House amended the bill to conform to homestead ideas then in vogue by restricting claims to 160 acres by white males.[44] Mr. Lane, Samuel Thurston's successor delegate from Oregon, noted his pleasure that discrimination between married and unmarried men

---

suggest that some effort was made to protect widows and divorced women. *E.g.*, in a Feb. 17, 1855 letter to Jos. A. Ebert, Esq. in Oregon City from John Wilson, Commissioner of the General Land Office, in 21 Letters Sent Relating to Private Land Claims 120-21 (Record Group No. 49, Division "D," National Archives) (Feb. 14, 1855), a divorced woman was permitted to protect her claims as if her husband was "in law" dead to her. This was said to be in accordance with a policy established the prior year. The Commissioner also tried to protect the entire 640 acre claim when a wife died before the enactment of the Donation Act by giving the wife's share to her heirs. Letter to Hon. Jos. A. Lane from Jos. S. Wilson, Acting Commissioner of the General Land Office, in 22 Letters Sent Relating to Private Land Claims 383 (Record Group No. 49, Division "D," National Archives) (Aug. 11, 1856). This practice was later reversed. *See* White v. Allen, 3 Or. 103 (1869).

40. An Act to Amend the Act Approved September Twenty-seven, Eighteen Hundred and Fifty, to Create the Office of Surveyor-General of the Public Lands in Oregon, etc., and the Act Amendatory Thereof, Approved February Nineteen [sic] Eighteen Hundred and Fifty-Three, ch. 84, 10 Stat. 305 (1854). One other fairly minor amendatory act extending time for filing notices of claims was passed in 1864. An Act to Amend the Act of Congress Making Donations to the Settlers on the Public Lands in Oregon, Approved September Twenty-Seven, Eighteen Hundred and Fifty, and the Acts Amendatory Thereto, ch. 154, 13 Stat. 184.

41. CONG. GLOBE, 33rd Cong., 1st Sess. 848 (1854).

42. *Id.* at 1054. This bill had already been passed with virtually no debate in the Senate. *Id.* at 956.

43. *Id.* at 956. The text of § 2 of the bill as adopted by the Senate and proposed by the House Public Lands Committee provided for grants to "every white male American citizen of the United States" in the territory before 1853 of "one half section, or three hundred and twenty acres of land, if single, but if married, one section, or six hundred and forty acres . . . ."

44. *Id.* at 1074.

had been eliminated from the bill.[45] After the House passed the New Mexico legislation, it took up the bill amending the Oregon Donation Act. During this debate, Lane remarked, somewhat tongue in cheek, that he didn't want married men to get more land than unmarried men, but that the grant in Oregon of half of a married couple's land to the wife was fair. "My wife is the better half," Lane said to his laughing colleagues. "She will not sell her claim, and I would be likely to give mine to any good man who will come and be my neighbor. Such a man will always be welcome to it. She would be, probably, more tenacious of hers."[46]

Thus, at the end of the Oregon Territory's first decade, its married women were in something of an anomalous position. Although the Donation Act had been amended to provide protections for widows of deceased male settlers and emigrants, and married women were coming to own substantial amounts of real estate,[47] the Donation Act had little immediate impact on the structure of coverture law in Oregon. The narrowly drawn married women's act exempting land from husbands' creditors was probably generated by the Donation Act debates, but it was lost in the repealer statute of 1854. Traditional curtesy rights of husbands continued to exist. Al-

---

45. *Id.*

46. *Id.* at 1076. This occurred during the debate on proposals to permit sales of land held under titles perfected but not patented because of surveying or other bureaucratic delays. The Utah bill met a fate similar to New Mexico's. It came from committee with larger grants for married men, but the provision was changed on the House floor. *Id.* at 1091-92. The Utah bill eventually failed to pass because of debates over polygamy. These debates are fascinating but a bit outside my topic. *See id.* at 1092-1102, 1109-14.

47. It is not clear if the Oregon Donation Act had an impact on the relative wealth of men and women in the state. What happened to all the land owned by women in Oregon as the nineteenth century progressed is not known. Until land title chains are studied in some detail, we are left with a hypothesis that some lasting cultural impact may have occurred as a result of the Donation Act. There is some indication that even this hypothesis may be false. Davenport, *An Object Lesson in Paternalism*, 4 OR. HIST. SOC'Y Q. 33 (1903). Davenport surveyed 100 square miles on the east side of the Willamette Valley in Marion County and found that:

> [S]ixty-six per cent of donation claims have passed out of the possession of the donees and their descendants, another fifteen per cent are mortgaged for all they are worth, and for practical purposes may be considered as lost to them. Not more than fifteen per cent of the whole have been ordinarily successful in holding and improving a part of their possessions and are now free from debt. Only five of all of them have increased their holdings and are thrifty.

Id. at 50-51. Davenport appears not to have studied how persons selling their land used the money received; nor did he focus on women's holdings. His study also reflects the late nineteenth-century biases against debt and fails to analyze the impact of the one third of the claims still held by the original donee families. But it is certainly possible that many of the claims obtained by women were transferred to men over the years.

though chancery actions were recognized in the territory,[48] and private bills in equity-like situations were adopted from time to time,[49] married women's separate estates were still subject to narrow rules of judicial construction. Furthermore, indications were strong that the language of the Donation Act was not intended to grant married women management of their donation lands. Not until the debates over the drafting of the state constitution did the Donation Act take on significance as a symbol, and perhaps even a contributing cause, to the development of a married women's law reform movement in Oregon.

III. Oregon State Constitution Debates

Oregon petitioned Congress for statehood as early as 1854.[50] A bill authorizing Oregon to frame a constitution passed the House of Representatives in 1856, but died in the Senate.[51] Nonetheless, the people of Oregon voted in June, 1857, to convene a constitutional convention. The delegates met at Salem in August, 1857, and elected Matthew Deady as President. The draft constitution emerged with a married women's property act among its provisions.[52] The debate on this provision took place on September 16, 1857. Complete reports

48. *See* An Act to Regulate Proceedings in Suits in Equity (Jan. 23, 1854) in Statutes of Oregon, 5th Sess., Dec. 5, 1853, at 173 (1854). *See also* Pittman v. Pittman, 4 Or. 298 (1872), where Emily Pittman was denied relief in a court of law for the use by her husband of a $1000 separate estate trust fund. She was told to seek a remedy in an equity court. *Id.* at 300. Chancery was important to the development of married women's property law. *See* Chused, *Married Women's Acts, supra* note 2, at 1365-72.

49. *See* An Act to Authorize Campbell E. Cristman and Lucinda Cristman to Make a Marriage Settlement of Their Property, (Jan. 15, 1857) in Special Laws of the Legislative Assembly of the Territory of Oregon, 8th Sess., Dec. 1, 1856, at 13 (1857) (permitted a postnuptial marriage settlement). Divorces were also granted, some of which reinstated property rights, permitted resumed use of maiden names, granted child custody to women, and confirmed divorce settlement agreements. *See* An Act to Divorce Dillard Martin and Miriam Martin (Jan. 17, 1859) in Laws of the Territory of Oregon, 10th Sess., Dec. 6, 1858, at 100 (1859); An Act to Divorce Nancy Judson and Lewis H. Judson (Jan. 19, 1859) *Id.* at 99; An Act to Divorce Susan Tary and William Tary (Jan. 19, 1859) *Id.*; An Act to Divorce Hessey Williams (Jan. 19, 1859) *Id.* at 92; An Act to Divorce Mary Culbertson From Her Husband, Wm. A. Culbertson (Jan. 20, 1859) *Id.* at 97; An Act to Divorce Sarah Torrence (Jan. 22, 1859) *Id.*

50. Memorial of the Legislative Assembly of Oregon Territory Asking Admission as a State into the Union, H.R. Misc. Doc. No. 61, 33rd Cong., 1st Sess. (1854).

51. For general background on Oregon statehood, see 2 H.H. Bancroft, History of Oregon 413-41 (1888). Reference to the failed statehood bill is at 419.

52. Article XV, §5, of what eventually became the Oregon Constitution of 1859, read as follows:

> The property and pecuniary rights of every married woman, at the time of marriage, or afterwards, acquired by gift, devise, or inheritance, shall not be subject to the debts or contracts of the husband; and laws shall be passed providing for the registration of the wife's separate property.

on the debates are not available, but extant newspaper accounts are quite revealing.[53] The debate was strikingly similar to the discussion preceding adoption of the New York married women's act almost ten years before.[54] Those opposing the Oregon constitutional provision argued that protection of married women's property would cause dissolution of families and lead to cheating of creditors. Others countered that love and affection, not money, were the roots of a good marriage, that families needed the economic protection afforded by married women's acts, and that contemporary women deserved the benefits of the proposed constitutional provision.

Among those arguing that the married women's provision should be removed from the proposed constitution was Matthew Deady, later to handle a number of Donation Act cases as a federal judge. Deady contended that married women's acts made "two persons of the husband and wife," causing "family alienation and jars."[55] Colleagues of Deady's argued that the provision would cause "much domestic trouble and many divorces."[56] Deady's fears of family discord implicitly assumed that the family was the core of American culture, that families needed a central male figure to survive, and that wives would vie for family leadership if they gained some economic independence from their husbands. These assumptions were made quite explicit by Mr. Kelsay, who argued that wives were amply provided for and expressed fear that a husband would become "simply a boarder at his wife's establishment," and by Mr. Williams who contended that the Donation Act's creation of distinct estates had caused "much domestic trouble."

Fear of marital discord was not the only focus of the opposition. Concern was also expressed that creditors would be cheated. Mr. Prim argued that the provision would become "a cloak for villiany [sic]," that debts would be contracted for the wife's benefit on the strength of what was thought to be a husband's property, and that "the honest creditor" would be cheated. As later experience in Oregon and elsewhere indicated, there was truth in Prim's argument

53. Reports on the proceedings in local newspapers have been pulled together in THE OREGON CONSTITUTION AND PROCEEDINGS AND DEBATES OF THE CONSTITUTIONAL CONVENTION OF 1857 (C.H. Carey ed. 1926) [Hereinafter cited as DEBATES]. The Sept. 16, 1857 discussions were reported in the Weekly Oregonian of Oct. 10, 1857, and the Oregon Statesman of Sept. 22, 1857. Only the latter reports are useful. All the references to the debates in the text that follows are taken from the Statesman report, found at DEBATES 367-69.

54. *See* E. Warbasse, *supra* note 3, at 205-29, for a nice summary of the debates on the New York Married Woman's Act of 1848. *See also* N. BASCH, *supra* note 3.

55. The quoted language represents the reporter's statements from the Oregon Statesman summary of the debates, not the mouth of Deady. Unfortunately, that will be true for all reports on these debates. Further cites to the Debates are not made, other than to reveal the names of speakers not mentioned in the text.

56. Mr. Williams. Mr. Kelsay also complained about divorces

that parties in economic distress might use married women's acts as a shield against honest creditors. Later legislation often corrected the imbalance in creditor access created by the early married women's acts.[57]

The proponents of the constitutional provision turned conservative sentiments very similar to those of Deady and Prim to somewhat different use. Mr. Smith, a proponent of the provision who was also concerned about family solidarity, argued that separate property rules did not cause divorce. Rather "it was the want of affection—the want of marriage of the heart," that created discord. The influence of early nineteenth-century changes in the family must have influenced Mr. Smith. Romantic notions of mate selection, companiate marriage, and greater participation by women in family decision making and child rearing,[58] could certainly have led him to see married women's acts as "an advance step, and only up to the provisions of many of the states."

Others noted the desirability of protecting wives' property from husbands' creditors, either because it carried on the spirit of the Donation Act,[59] adopted the doctrine of the civil law,[60] or protected women and daughters from spendthrift husbands.[61] These proponents focused on the misfortunes of honest women rather than the pitfalls for honest creditors. Mr. Logan cautiously observed that "If he [the husband] was prudent and thrifty she would give him control of her property. And if he was not, it was better that she should have the power to preserve her property to support herself and educate her children." And Mr. Waymire, said to be the prime supporter of the constitutional provision,[62] argued that, "He didn't want a man to marry a daughter of his, with a large band of cattle, and then skin the cattle, and skin her, and leave her. If men married for money they ought not to have control of it. Every day they lived together they lived in adultery, for he married the money and not the girl."

The proponents of the provision added one new element to the debates—a mild dose of language from the women's movement—not too much mind you, but enough to see the impact of the demo-

---

57. *See* Chused, *Married Women's Acts*, *supra* note 2, at 1409-10; discussion *infra* in Part IV.

58. *Id.* at 1412-23.

59. Mr. Dryer.

60. Mr. Boise. Compare Deady's attitudes towards the civil law, *infra* notes 80-81 and accompanying text.

61. Mr. Logan, Mr. Waymire.

62. 2 H.H. BANCROFT, HISTORY OF OREGON 426, n.23 (1888). Waymire, supposedly called the "old apostle of democracy" by his friends, was said to be "an energetic, firm, strong, rough man, and an uncompromising partisan." *Id.* at 142, n.8.

cratic, women's, and utilitarian movements of the mid-nineteenth century. Mr. Smith was "for woman's rights, and was not afraid of her having too many. She has been too long denied her just rights." And Mr. Waymire noted that, "If we should legislate for any class it should be the women of this [Oregon] country. They worked harder than anybody else in it." But this was still "equality" with a paternal cast; it was men urging protection of the special qualities of their female family members with "modern" language. For Smith "would protect her property from dissipated or mercenary wretches," and Waymire thought any delegate with "girls old enough to marry" would take his side of the question. Like Thurston earlier in the decade, these men saw a need to surround women with protections befitting their special family roles, not their public obligations.

The provision remained in the draft constitution by only a 27-22 vote. The debates between Deady, Waymire, and the rest set the stage for a remarkable series of court cases over the following several decades. For Deady was named to the federal court bench shortly after Oregon became a state in 1859.[63] And Waymire, though never a judge, found his views expressed by others named to sit on the Oregon Supreme Court.

IV. Judicial and Legislative Responses to the Oregon Donation Act and the Constitution of 1859

Important issues emerged in the judicial treatment of the Oregon Donation Act and related state statutes. Concerns expressed at the state constitutional convention about family harmony and the status of creditors were repeated in judicial opinions. Deady, as federal district judge, continued to note his disapproval of newer gender roles for women, while state court judges were more likely to take up Waymire's mantle. These differences in attitude certainly mirrored the currents of public debate then swirling around the courts. The *New Northwest*, a newspaper published by Oregon's leading suffragist, Abigail Scott Duniway, began publishing in May, 1871. Susan B. Anthony came to Oregon on a speaking tour shortly thereafter.[64] And as we shall see, family creditors, agitated over the difficulties caused them by early married women's legislation, obtained some legislative relief in both 1866 and 1872.

Different styles of judicial analysis also surfaced in the federal and state opinions. Deady paid lavish attention to English and American treatises and precedents, carefully analyzed old "legal

63. *See* An Act for the Admission of Oregon into the Union, ch. 33, 11 Stat. 383 (1859). For materials on Deady, see *supra* note 14.

64. A.S. Duniway, Path Breaking: An Autobiographical History of the Equal Suffrage Movement in Pacific Coast States 43-47 (1914, reprint 1971).

chestnuts" and painstakingly worked his way to decisions. He was highly critical of civil law and enamored of British common law as "the source and panoply of all those features of our system which distinguish us from the subjects of absolute governments."[65] State court judges on both sides of married women's issues were much more likely to insist that recent constitutional or statutory developments created a new legal milieu, to support results by referring to the will of the general public, to ignore old precedents and treatises, and to issue broad opinions with sweeping language. The fact that Oregon's judges were elected gave them some basis for assuming that they had a popular mandate. To the extent that such differences in judicial technique mirrored splits in public opinion, it is not surprising that intervention by the legislature was necessary to resolve many of the problems created or left open by the Oregon Donation Act, the debt exemption statute of 1852, and the state constitution of 1859.

The fears expressed by Mr. Prim during the Oregon constitutional debates that honest creditors might come a cropper if they relied on actions of husbands alone[66] were vindicated in the most important of the early Oregon Supreme Court donation land cases, *Brummet v. Weaver*.[67] In accordance with the mandate of the constitution of 1859, the state legislature had adopted a registration act for married women's separate property at its first session.[68] Sarah Brummet registered three horses as her property in 1861. She had purchased these horses with money received from the sale of her Donation Act claim. Later she divorced Banner Brummet, and, in 1864, remarried him. Upon her remarriage, however, she did not reregister her horses as separate property.[69] After her husband disposed of the horses to James Weaver, Sarah Brummet sued to recover possession of the horses. The Supreme Court reversed the trial court's verdict for Weaver and remanded for a new trial.

Weaver contended on appeal that the constitution and the registration act limited separate property to assets received by gift, devise, or inheritance, that divorce operated as a revocation of Brummet's registration, that registration only protected property

---

65. H.H. Bancroft, *supra* note 14, at 493.

66. *See supra* note 57 and accompanying text.

67. 2 Or. 168 (1866). One other case with import similar to *Brummet* was reported a few years earlier. Carter v. Chapman, 2 Or. 93 (1863). Significant cases did not arise earlier because of delays in setting up the new bureaucracy needed to implement the Donation Act.

68. An Act to Provide for the Registration of the Separate Property of Married Women, and to Declare the Effect Thereof (June 4, 1859), in Laws of the State of Oregon, 1st Extra Session of the Legislative Assembly, May 16, 1859, at 31 (1859).

69. By 1864, only two of the horses were the same as in 1861. The third had been exchanged for another animal.

described in the documents of record, and that he was, therefore, free to purchase the horses from Brummet's husband under the common law rule giving a married woman's personal property to her husband upon marriage. Brummet countered[70] that she had the right to dispose of registered assets, purchase new ones with the proceeds, and retain the new assets as separate property, and that registration was not the sole device by which persons could be put on notice of her claims.

The court, despite holding that divorce revoked registration, agreed that Sarah Brummet's claims had merit. The Constitution of 1859 effected a repeal of common law coverture rules, the court noted, adding:

> Under that instrument [the Constitution of 1859] no woman loses any pecuniary rights by marriage. Whatever property a woman has at the time of marriage, or afterwards acquired by gift, devise, or inheritance, remains hers, until, she, by her own consent, express or implied, parts with it. Without that consent she cannot be divested of her title to it, whether registered or not. No one having notice of her claim can acquire any title to her property by any contract of her husband to which she does not expressly or by implication assent. If she has duly registered her property, the registry is notice to the world, as to all property described in it. If she has not registered it, we think actual or constructive notice, as recognized in case of deeds and mortgages of land, would be sufficient to bind the party attempting to deal with the husband concerning her property. It seems that the registry act . . . has made no provision concerning property owned by the wife at the time of the marriage; but her title to such property after marriage is not less indefeasible. Whether, however, a purchaser of such property from the husband, acquires any title, or whether the wife has a right to repudiate a sale by the husband and recover the property, will depend, in every such case, upon the conduct of the wife in regard to the management of the property. . . .[71]

Sarah Brummet got a new trial on the issue of the property's management and control, the court also holding that the constitution:

> [M]ust be so construed as to allow a married woman not only to hold property as separate property, without the interference of a trustee, but also to exchange one species of her

70. Jurisdictions with low populations and few attorneys frequently provide surprises as to who shows up representing one or another party in a law suit. Sarah Brummet's counsel was Mr. Kelsay, who had argued against the adoption of Article XV, §5 of the state constitution. *See supra* note 56 and accompanying text.

71. 2 Or. at 173.

separate property for another, and to authorize her to sell any part of her separate property and retain the purchase money as her own; or with it buy other property to be held by her in the same manner and for the same purpose.[72]

The *Brummet* court took a number of significant steps to enlarge the nature and importance of the married women's separate estate. Though Sarah Brummet, and all other married women in Oregon, risked loss of unregistered property if its separate character was not maintained, she could hold property without use of trustees, transfer her donation claim assets, and retain the proceeds of any transfer as separate property. These results were similar to legislation adopted by a number of state legislatures during the 1860's.[73] Despite the importance of the *Brummet* decision, the broad language of the opinion was hardly justified by the constitutional debates of 1857 or the narrow language of the 1859 constitution.

Indeed, the court may have moved too far, too fast, since changes in Oregon's separate property registration scheme were adopted almost immediately after *Brummet* was decided.[74] The old registration statute was repealed and replaced by a new statute providing only for the registration of personal property. After *Brummet* the regular recording system was available to provide notice of married women's title to real estate. The legislature, therefore, narrowed their focus to personal property and tried to create incentives, via a prima facie evidence of title system, for women to register their assets. Registration became prima facie proof of title for *both* spouses. A wife registering her personal property gained presumptive title, but failure to register became prima facie evidence that the property belonged to the *husband*.[75] The preamble to the statute, in an apparent reference to *Brummet*, pointedly noted that while the constitution protected the rights of married women, "better protection" was needed for "purchasers and creditors of their husbands." Although the act ameliorated the common law rule that all personal property of a married woman belonged to her husband, it is apparent that the motivation for its adoption had more to do with protecting

72. 2 Or. at 171.

73. *See* Chused, *Married Women's Acts, supra* note 2, at 1409-10. Massachusetts adopted an advanced married women's act in 1855, New York in 1860. Most other states lagged behind.

74. An Act to Provide for the Registration of the Personal Property of Married Women (Oct. 20, 1866), in Acts and Resolutions of the Legislative Assembly of the State of Oregon, 4th Sess., at 6 (1866). *Brummet* was decided in Sept., 1866.

75. The provision adding this language to the bill was added by an amendment offered by Mr. Olney on the floor of the House of Representatives on Oct. 20, 1866. J. OF THE PROCEEDINGS OF THE HOUSE OF THE LEGISLATIVE ASSEMBLY OF OREGON FOR THE FOURTH REGULAR SESSION 397 (1866). The motivations of Mr. Olney for offering this change are not clear.

the claims of husbands' creditors than enlarging the role of married women.

Brummet is a fine example of the problems that surfaced after the adoption of the early debtor protection married women's acts. If, as these early statutes provided, married women's separate estates were not available to creditors of husbands, certain disputes were preordained to arise. First, insecurity over which assets were to be denominated as separate and which as subject to the traditional control of husbands, was inevitable under the new regime. Since the acts were imprecise as to whether trustees were required to hold separate property, the language necessary to establish the estate, the ability of married women to manage or dispose of their separate property, and whether third parties dealing with a married couple would be deemed constructively aware of the existence of separate estates, creditors of the family unit were subject to a significant amount of insecurity about the value of contracts, deeds, or security agreements involving separately held property. Second, the exemption of only married women's property created a strange set of incentives. The acts created a strong impulse to "bury" property in a wife to protect it from risk and creditors. To the degree that insecurity over the meaning of the new separate estate existed, it was possible for unscrupulous, or even well intentioned,[76] married couples to use a wife's property as enticement for a deal, only to plead the debtor exemption provisions if the deal later soured. It was predictable that these sorts of problems would require further legislative intervention. A variety of responses were possible, depending upon the degree of legislative sympathy with creditors or debtors. But in all such responses, one would expect the legislature to increase certainty as to which assets were available to creditors of the family.

The legislative response to *Brummet* is, therefore, perfectly understandable. The 1866 legislation attacked the insecurity problem frontally by establishing both a recording system and simple, though perhaps hard to enforce, rules on the impact of the system's use. The separate estate began to take on the appearance of a traditional property device. The need to increase creditor's security over the meaning of a separate estate meant that general rules about the transfer and management of the estate had to be developed. That, of course, is exactly what married women's acts did in the second half of the century. Women gained transfer, management, and devising rights, slowly obtaining parity, at least in legal theory, with male

76. Even an honest couple would be sorely tempted to plead coverture if a deal made using his wife's property fell apart. Certainly most lawyers would suggest to their clients that their good intentions did not legitimate an otherwise unlawful transfer.

property owners. The special debt exempt status of married women's property gave way to a family oriented pattern of exemptions. Women's property became more easily available to creditors of the family, unless the general exemption statutes applicable only to men were significantly modified. The movement from special status to equal treatment that marked the general content of married women's acts in the second half of the nineteenth century significantly increased the ability of creditors to rely upon married women's assets as viable security.[77]

Judge Deady, sitting on the federal bench, took a much more cautious approach than his state court brethren. Although Deady's decisions did not create direct conflicts with state law until the 1870's,[78] the overall tone of his early work was conservative. In a series of opinions, Deady confirmed the continued vitality of common law rules giving husbands management of wives' real estate and ownership of their personal property, and held that the state constitution did not retroactively alter these rules,[79] and that married women could not contract about their property.[80] Deady attached great importance to the study of the common law and the old treatises, criticized then prevalent trends to look to codes and civil

---

77. One of the more interesting phenomena in the history of women's private law status is the slow process by which regulation of women moved from special treatment towards equality. While there is still much debate about the extent to which this has occurred, particularly in areas related to childbirth and child rearing, *see, e.g.* Williams, *Firing the Woman to Protect the Fetus: The Reconciliation of Fetal Protection with Employment Opportunity Goals Under Title VII*, 69 GEO. L.J. 641, 653-65 (1981), there are a number of examples which suggest the validity of the notion. Protective labor legislation is a nice example, as is voting, ability to sue, access to damages for loss of consortium and a number of others. Some areas were equalized, at least in legal theory, before others. Women's property law happens to be one of the earliest to change, leaving women with access to the same sorts of property as men long before other aspects of society were prepared to let them fully use their economic rights. Perhaps this occurred because the debtor protection aspects of married women's property law created legislative coalitions that otherwise may not have existed.

78. *E.g.*, in Fields v. Squires, 9 F. Cas. 29 (C.C.D. Or. 1868) (No. 4776), Deady reaffirmed prior state court holdings that the widow of a person dying before the Donation Act was adopted took nothing under the act, *Id.* at 33, citing Ford v. Kennedy, 1 Or. 166 (1855), and that a husband could not contract to sell land without his wife's participation, 9 F. Cas. at 33, citing Carter v. Chapman, 2 Or. 93 (1863). But this opinion, like most others he wrote later, was highly detailed factually and analytically; his writing style was precise, technical, and hard to master.

79. Starr v. Hamilton, 22 F. Cas. 1107 (C.C.D. Or. 1867) (No. 13,314).

80. Dick v. Hamilton, 7 F. Cas. 660 (C.C.D. Or. 1867) (No. 3890). Deady had a tendency to rescue women at the last minute from the clutches of the common law. In addition to *Dick*, the tendency is evident in Chapelle v. Olney, 5 F. Cas. 503 (C.C.D. Or. 1870) (No. 2613), where he applied the old common law rule that a married woman's personal property belonged to the husband as soon as he reduced it to possession. *Id.* at 506. But he went on to find that the husband in *Chapelle* never reduced the property to possession. *Id.*

law as substitutes for common law, and revered common law's ability to provide every person with a right to sue, to limit the intervention of government, and to mold and shape morals, politics, and literature.

In a remarkable address, given in 1866 to the Portland Law Association, Deady described his attitudes toward the common law traditions. His linkage of Manifest Destiny, the inferiority of civil law tradition, and the superiority of a cautious precedent system was palpable:

> Nowadays, it is the fashion in some quarters to sneer at the common law as a relic of feudalism and barbarism, and to point to the civil law as the proper source from whence to draw the jurisprudence of highly civilized and refined people. But I caution you to beware of the spirit, and be not persuaded by it. . . . The laws of a people react upon them, and mould their character and opinions. The common law people—the English race, wherever they go, establish limited governments, with parliaments and juries; but the people of civil law—the Latin race, always come under some modification of the empire—in which the will of the prince, emperor, or chieftain is the supreme law.
>
> In so far then as we discard the fundamental principles of the common law, and adopt those of the civil, we are paving the way for the political and social condition of the Roman empire, in the age of the Caesars—both good and bad. Probably this is the innate tendency and inevitable result of our republic, with its diversified and aglomerated population and ever widening territory.
>
> But be this as it may, the common law is the source and panoply of all those features of our system which distinguish us from the subjects of absolute governments, ancient or modern,—either by monarchs or majorities. It was made by freemen for freemen, and so long as you think these distinctions between it and the civil law worth preserving, you should cherish it in private and exalt it in public.[81]

Deady's careful attention to the details of the common law surfaced in a number of opinions. Though he appeared to strive for fair outcomes, statutory modifications of old traditions in coverture law were routinely construed narrowly. A good example of his style was *Starr v. Hamilton*.[82] In this case, Christina Hamilton, prior to marrying Alexander in 1853, inherited land in Missouri from her mother.[83]

81. *See* H.H. BANCROFT, *supra* note 14, at 491, 493.

82. 22 F. Cas. 1107 (C.C.D. Or. 1867) (No. 13,314).

83. *Id.* at 1107-08. The receipt of inheritances by women was apparently common in the nineteenth century. *See* Chused, *Married Women's Acts*, *supra* note 2, at 1376-78.

In 1857, two years before the Oregon Constitution went into effect, she sold this land for $1200. The following year she used $500 of this money to purchase a parcel of land in the Portland area. She received a deed granting title to Christina Hamilton and her heirs by the body of her husband Alexander. In 1864 and 1865 Christina Hamilton bought additional land, this time titled in Christina Hamilton to "her own separate use, benefit and behoof forever, free from all control of her said husband." All this property was registered, but not until 1866, several years after Alexander fell into economic difficulties. Starr, who was the auction purchaser of the property of Alexander Hamilton, sued to gain possession of the property claimed by Christina.

Deady held that the real property owned by Christina when she married in 1853 was subject to Alexander's management and control upon marriage, that under the common law rule giving a husband ownership of his wife's personalty the $1200 received from the sale of Christina's property in 1857 became the property of the husband immediately upon his receipt of it, that the land purchased in 1858 was bought by Alexander as a gift for Christina, and that Alexander retained curtesy rights in the property. The creditor of Alexander was thus entitled to Alexander's curtesy, but not to Christina's title.[84] Deady then considered whether the constitution of 1859 altered these outcomes. He gave only a polite bow to *Brummet*, stating that if property was not subject to a husband's debts, then "he is thereby precluded from any control over it."[85] Deady went on to hold that vested curtesy rights of husbands predating the 1859 state constitution could not be altered by its provisions.[86] As to the rest of Christina Hamilton's property, Deady confessed he had doubts that land obtained by purchase could be included within the language of the 1859 state constitution, but saved Christina's assets by finding that they were purchased with money owned by Alexander, were gifts, and were, therefore, within the parameters of the state constitutional provisions.

The outcome of the case was somewhat Solomonic, with Alexander's creditors getting some of the property, and Christina the rest. But the clear implication of opinions like *Starr* was that Deady would strive to place the new fangled provisions of Oregon law into the old structure, rather than use the constitution as a device for largely ignoring the old law. The difficulties inherent in Deady's position were vividly revisited in *Dick v. Hamilton*.[87] This case in-

---

84. In Oregon, curtesy entitled Alexander to a life estate, even if the couple was childless. *See supra* note 20 and accompanying text.

85. 22 F. Cas. at 1108.

86. Deady cited New York cases which had held § 2 of the 1848 New York Married Women's Act invalid on similar grounds. *Id.* at 1110.

87. 7 F. Cas. 660 (C.C.D. Or. 1867) (No. 3890).

volved the same parcels as in the prior case. Dick, as another creditor of Alexander, was attempting to gain control of the remaining separate property of Christina—the postcurtesy rights in the 1857 parcel and the title to the other lands. He could not claim direct rights through Alexander since he had not purchased any rights at the sheriff's auction. But he could and did claim that any gifts or transfers between spouses were made in defraud of creditors.

Deady held fast to his prior decision on the 1857 parcel, noting again that Alexander made a gift to Christina and that the postcurtesy portion of this gift was unavailable to Dick since the transfer had been made before Alexander fell into economic difficulties and, therefore, had not been in defraud of creditors. As to the other land, however, Deady found himself in some difficulty. The transfers to Christina were made in 1864 and 1865 when Alexander was "notoriously insolvent."[88] If the property came to Christina by gift, as Deady held in *Starr*, then Dick could gain access to it. Rather than countenance this result, Deady confessed he erred in *Starr*, and held instead that the lands had been purchased by Christina as a settlement of dower rights in land of her husband claimed by creditors, and that if the settlement did not reduce the value of the assets available to Alexander's creditors, the sole and separate estate language in the deeds insulated Christina's property from Alexander's creditors. Some of this land was also encumbered by promissory notes and mortgages signed by Christina. As to these, Deady found the contractual promises in the notes void under common law coverture rules, and the mortgages valid as part of the operation of a married woman's equitable separate estate. When the dust settled, Christina retained the property left her after *Starr v. Hamilton*.[89] In the process, Deady was forced to recognize and accommodate himself to the inevitability that women holding property under deeds clearly creating married women's separate estates would bargain with others over its disposition.

Between 1866, when *Brummet* was decided, and 1871, four new members appeared on the five judge Oregon Supreme Court.[90]

---

88. *Id.* at 664.

89. Another interesting case from this time period is Lamb v. Starr, 14 F. Cas. 1030 (C.C.D. Or. 1868) (No. 8022), in which Deady construed the succession upon death provision of § 4 of the Donation Act, holding that successors to deceased claimants took as donees of the United States, not as heirs. *Id.* at 1032. *See also* on the same issue, Mizner v. Vaughn, 17 F. Cas. 543 (C.C.D. Or. 1872) (No. 9678).

90. In 1866, the judges were Stratton, Boise, Prim, Wilson, and Shattuck, the author of *Brummet*. In 1871, only Prim remained from the earlier court. He sat with Thayer, Bonham, Upton, and McArthur. *See* the judge lists at 2 Or. 8 (1869); 3 Or. vii (1872). It is difficult to know how significant these shifts were. Prim was continually conservative. His remarks during the debates on the state constitution, *see supra* note 57 and accompanying text, were consistent with the prejudices and peculiarities of a southern gentleman, according to Boise, *Bench and Bar of Early Oregon*, in PROCEEDINGS OF THE OREGON HISTORICAL SOCIETY INCLUDING THE QUARTERLY

Whether because of Democratic victories in the 1868 state elections, the influence of Deady, or a slowing of interest in women's issues after the Civil War,[91] the court began to issue much more conservative rulings. The most significant of these opinions was *Frarey v. Wheeler*.[92] Judge Bonham's opinion for the Oregon Supreme Court discussed two questions—the ability of a married woman to contract, and the role of equity in the resolution of a dispute between a married woman and the putative purchaser of her donation claim. Ignoring the broad language of *Brummet* permitting dealings in donation lands, and citing Kent's *Commentaries*, a celebrated but conservative classic, the court strongly, almost bitterly, declared its unwillingness to validate Jemima Wheeler's contract to sell her donation claim.

> Notwithstanding the doctrine which is so zealously promulgated by some (and which in some respects it is to be feared may be somewhat utopian in character), claiming an enlargement of the rights of women, yet it is the generally received opinion that the sphere of married women's duties, as they have been heretofore generally recognized and acquiesced in, precludes the means of acquiring by them that knowledge of law and commercial transactions necessary to enable them, as a rule, to safely and understandingly enter into covenants concerning real estate.[93]

MEETINGS OF THE BOARD OF DIRECTORS AND THE SIXTH ANNUAL MEETINGS OF THE MEMBERS OF THE SOCIETY, Dec. 17, 1904, at 17, 23 (1906). Boise also writes about all the other judges in this article, but rarely with any political content to his comments.

91. In 1872, the United States Supreme Court decided that reform of women's law was not to be included within the protective umbrella of the recently enacted privileges and immunities clause of the fourteenth amendment. Bradwell v. Illinois, 83 U.S. (16 Wall.) 130 (1872). Three years later, the Court held that the fourteenth amendment did not bestow the right of suffrage upon women. Minor v. Happersett, 88 U.S. (21 Wall.) 162 (1874).

92. 4 Or. 190 (1872). On Apr. 1, 1867, Jemima Wheeler and her husband Jacob agreed to sell Jemima's donation claim to D. W. Frarey. The contract provided that Frarey would pay $20 in gold coin at the signing of the agreement, that possession would immediately be given to Frarey, and that title would be transferred one year later upon the payment of another $380 in gold. *Id.* Frarey made improvements on the land, but had trouble raising the final payment. Not until Aug. 1, 1870, did he tender the money, along with accrued interest. The Wheelers declined the payment and refused to execute a deed. Frarey's suit for specific performance was dismissed by the trial court. *Id.* at 191.

93. *Id.* at 194-95. The court by way of analogy also noted that Oregon statutes voided married women's covenants in deeds, as opposed to contracts. *Id.* at 195. *See* An Act Relating to Alienation by Deed, and the Proof and Recording of Conveyances, and the Cancelling of Mortgages §2 (Jan. 13, 1854), in Statutes of Oregon, 5th Sess. Dec. 5, 1853, at 475 (1854). The court *could* have relied on this analogy and stopped. The gratuitous nature of the language quoted in the text is therefore all the more notable. It is much like the now famous concurring opinion of Justice Bradley in Bradwell v. Illinois, 83 U.S. (16 Wall.) 130, 139 (1872).

The court went on to construe narrowly the "in her own right" language in the Oregon Donation Act to refer only to the holding of property, not its disposition,[94] and to virtually overrule *Brummet*'s broad reading of the state constitution.

> We do not think it was the intention of the framers of our Constitution and laws on this subject, to entirely segregate the proprietary interests of husband and wife and make them to all intents and purposes *two* instead of *one* in law. But on the other hand, might it not be fairly inferred from the language of the law and its contemporaneous history, that the prime object and controlling purpose was, to secure to the wife the right to *hold* such property as the means of the support of herself and family in the event that her legal protector and provider might fail, through misfortune, improvidence or death, to do so?[95]

While Judge Bonham may have read the history of the state constitutional debates correctly, his studied ignoring of *Brummet*[96] led to some controversy. In 1872, the legislature appeared to respond to *Frarey* and the other creditor cases by confirming that a married woman's property was not subject to her husband's debts, and adding that property acquired "by her own labor" should "be subject to the same exemptions and liabilities as property owned at the time of her marriage or afterwards acquired by gift, devise or inheritance."[97] There probably was concern in the legislature over the redefinition of married women's property by the *Frarey* court and the resulting possibility that property assumed by creditors to be controlled by women would not be available in case of default. By 1872, in something of an ironic twist, the legislature had modified results of both a liberal and a conservative court in order to insure that those dealing with married persons could rely upon certain un-

94. 4 Or. at 195-96.

95. *Id.* at 196 (emphasis in the original).

96. Because of the narrow reading of the Donation Act and the state constitution, the court had to resolve a serious problem of fairness. Mr. Frarey had paid some money to the Wheelers and expended more on improvements. *Id.* at 191. Much as Deady had wrestled in *Starr v. Hamilton* and *Dick v. Hamilton* with the interplay between the rights of creditors and wives, *see supra* notes 87-89 and accompanying text, so Bonham had to resolve a dispute between wives and their partners in contract. "The law exempting a married woman from liability on her covenants to convey her real estate, was adopted for her better security and protection," the court noted. "[A]nd we do not think that it would be equitable, or in harmony with public policy and good morals, for courts of equity, in protecting the rights of persons, to encourage the perpetuation of actual fraud by them." *Id.* at 197. So Frarey got his accounting. Both the $20 and the value of the improvements were treated as a charge on the land until paid. *Id.*

97. An Act Relating to the Rights of Married Women (Oct 15, 1872), in Acts and Resolutions of the Legislative Assembly of the State of Oregon, 7th Sess., at 23 (1872). The act also created a process for women abandoned by their spouses to become free traders.

derstandings about the meaning of a married woman's separate estate. The act not only reversed the principal holdings of *Frarey*, but also slightly enlarged the potential extent of a married woman's estate by including property acquired by her own labors. This legislation marked the high-water mark for the exemption of married women's property from creditors of the husband.[98]

The state legislature's attempts to resolve disputes over creditor access to married women's property did not halt the flow of cases into the courts. In fact, the disputes became more serious. Some cases appeared in which men attempted to use the special status of their wives to defraud creditors.[99] In addition, many of the disputes began to involve old transactions dating back to the years just after the adoption of the Donation Act. In one such case, *Wythe v. Smith*,[100] Deady's undoing of long-settled titles set the stage for serious conflict with the Oregon Supreme Court.[101] In *Wythe*, Deady clearly, and for the first time, held that wives' donation claims were encumbered by the common law management rights of husbands as soon as the four year occupancy period required by the statute was complete, and that the 1852 territorial statute exempting wives' donation claims from husbands' debts was unconstitutional insofar as it voided vested marital rights of husbands.

The case apparently created something of a stir. By 1876 elections had again altered the makeup of the Oregon Supreme Court. Judges Boise and Shattuck, who both sat on the *Brummet* court,

98. Later legislation imposed the same status on the property of husbands and wives, making both liable for family debts and neither liable for the debts of the other spouse. *See infra* notes 116-18 and accompanying text. This development has a certain logic to it. To the extent that married women were entering the labor force in greater numbers towards the end of the nineteenth century, there is a significant likelihood that their property would eventually become important enough that it could no longer be ignored for purposes of insuring the ability of the family economy to use its assets as security for the purchase of property or the obtaining of general credit. It may well have been in the best interests of both women and creditors that married women's property lost its special status and became available for use in the purchase of family items, especially as the middle class grew in size and urbanization at the turn of the twentieth century.

99. *E.g.*, Elfelt v. Hinch, 5 Or. 255 (1874). In this case, A. W. Hinch supposedly sold land to his wife and then used the same land to obtain large credits for the purchase of merchandise. *Id.* at 255-56. The court made short shrift of such shenanigans, noting that the transfer was in defraud of creditors. *Id.* at 259. But it also noted that the state constitution did not abrogate the common law rules of coverture, and that A. W. presumptively owned any money used by his wife to purchase the property. *Id.* at 257.

100. 30 F. Cas. 771 (C.C.D. Or. 1876) (No. 18,122).

101. Wythe involved a long chain of transfers of a tract of land in Salem. The tract was part of the donation claim of Chloe Willson, wife of William Willson. William initiated the series of transfers and each transfer was allegedly accomplished with Chloe's permission, though not her signature. *Id.* at 722.

were again on the bench, and one other judge was new.[102] In *Linnville v. Smith*,[103] decided only a few months after *Wythe*, the court noted:

> In the argument of this case considerable discussion was had by counsel relative to the rights of a wife in her portion of a donation claim as to the matter of it being her separate property and it was claimed by counsel for plaintiff that by the operation of the donation law the wife's half of a donation claim is separate property, and also that it is such by the constitution of the state. These questions are of great interest to the people of the state, as they affect a large portion of the real estate of the country, and many important interests rest on the determination of these questions. The general understanding of the people has been that the wife's portion of a donation claim is separate property, and it has been generally treated as such. But the matter has not as yet been adjudicated by this court, and we do not feel called upon to determine it in this case.[104]

The court passed over Deady's holdings in *Wythe* because the donation claim in *Linnville* was transferred after rather than before 1852.[105] But, with Boise writing the opinion, it used equitable principles to designate the husband a constructive trustee for his wife of land purchased with proceeds from the sale of her donation claim and refused to permit the creditor of her husband to gain access to the newly purchased land.

The court quickly got another chance to review Deady's work. In *Rugh v. Ottenheimer*,[106] Judge Boise, again writing for the court, returned to the liberal sentiments of *Brummet*. While the court agreed with Deady that the marriage of William and Nancy Rugh during the territorial era gave rise to common law curtesy rights in William in the land of his wife, it went on to hold that the state

---

102. *See* judge lists at 2 Or. 8 (1869); 3 Or. vii (1872); 5 Or. iii (1876); 6 Or. iii (1878).

103. 6 Or. 202 (1876).

104. 6 Or. at 204-05.

105. William and Leah Linnville conveyed Leah's donation claim, and bought additional land on the understanding it would be titled in her name. Instead it was deeded to William and levied on by his creditors before the title could be corrected. *Id.* at 202-03.

106. 6 Or. 231 (1877). Nancy Rugh, in the year before her marriage to William Rugh, purchased a 160 acre farm with proceeds from the sale of her donation claim. *Id.* at 232-33. This was the claim of a single person, not that of a wife. Single women were apparently treated as single males within the meaning of the Donation Act. *See* Silver v. Ladd, 74 U.S. (7 Wall.) 219, 226 (1868). The deed was not delivered until after her marriage. Later she agreed to trade the land for some owned by Nelson Gardner, who promised to deed the new land to her. Instead he deeded it to William, who eventually abandoned Nancy and Oregon, and left behind disputes with his creditors.

constitution altered the old rules retroactively. All property owned by married women when the constitution went into effect was freed of common law rights of their husbands. Perhaps throwing a dagger Deady's way, Boise wrote:

> The simple natural construction of the words used in this section, read by scholars unrestrained by legal technicalities or rules of construction of statutes, would include the property and pecuniary rights of married women who were then married and owning property which could be made subject to this provision.[107]

The court argued that the "farmers" at the constitutional convention who had acquired donation claims enacted the married women's provision by a "large majority"[108] and hoped it would protect their wives' property from their debts and contracts. Despite the contrary cases decided in the prior decade, the court found that a broad view of the constitution had been the "almost uniform construction of this section by the people of the state."[109] If marriage rights of husbands could be retroactively terminated by divorce, the court held, then general provisions in the state constitution could perform the same task.[110]

Rugh was an unusual case. While some state courts retroactively applied married women's acts where a wife's personal property had not been reduced to possession[111] at the time a married women's act was adopted,[112] virtually none applied married wom-

---

107. 6 Or. at 234.

108. *Id.* at 235. A 27-22 majority can hardly be called large. *See supra* note 63 and accompanying text.

109. 6 Or. at 235. Although the court did not refer to it, there is some support in administrative materials for the proposition that the act had always operated to protect married women's claims from creditors. The General Land Office had a general practice of giving the more valuable half of the donation claims of married parties to wives, especially where there was an encumbrance on part of the property or a share had already been sold. Letters describing this practice during the period 1859-1865 are in Volumes 3 and 4, General Correspondence Including Surveyor General; Washington, Oregon and California, 436, 505-06 (Vol. 3); 147-48 (Vol. 4) (Record Group No. 49, Division "D," National Archives) (Apr. 18, Oct. 9, 1862). At times the Land Office went to some lengths to protect women's property from claims by creditors, inviting charges that couples chose to implement the General Land Office policies in a way that deprived creditors of valid claims.

110. 6 Or. at 236. As a result, Nancy Rugh's claim to the farm prevailed over her departed husband's creditors. Despite the presence of purchasers from her husband in the chain of title, Nancy was permitted to trace the proceeds from the sale of her original donation claim, and impose the equivalent of a constructive trust upon her husband to hold title for her to the exclusion of creditors or successors in interest.

111. The normal common law rule was that personal property of the wife belonged to the husband as soon as he reduced it to possession.

112. Clarke v. McCreary, 12 Miss. (1 S. & M.) 347 (1849); Deck v. Smith, 12 Neb. 389 (1882); Percy v. Cockrill, 53 F. 872 (8th Cir. 1893); Executor of Henry v. Dilley,

en's acts retroactively to alter rules governing real property held by women before the adoption of a married women's act.[113] Not until after *Rugh* was decided did the winds of change begin to affect real property retroactivity decisions in other states.[114] It is possible that Deady's consistently rigorous common law analysis of local law drove the state judges to render a more far-reaching judgment than otherwise might have occurred, or that the Oregon Donation Act heritage laid the groundwork for *Rugh*. In any case, Deady quickly let it be known that *Rugh* mattered little to him. In *Elliot v. Teal*,[115] Deady held that common law disabilities made both a wife's power of attorney and her separate deed invalid, and that her husband's deed purporting to convey her donation claim actually transferred only his life estate by curtesy in the land.

Only a year after the decision in *Rugh* and less than two months after that in *Elliot v. Teal*, the state legislature adopted a new married women's act.[116] While *Brummet* had been roughly received by the state legislature in 1866, *Teal* got the same treatment in 1878. The

---

25 N.J.L. 302 (1885). *Contra*, Stearns v. Weathers, 30 Ala. 712 (1857); Sperry & Niles v. Haslam, 57 Ga. 412 (1876); Dunn v. Sargent, 101 Mass. 336 (1869); Leete v. State Bank, 115 Mo. 184 (1893); O'Conner v. Harris, 81 N.C. 279 (1879); Cunningham v. Gray, 20 Mo. 170 (1854).

113. *Compare Rugh with* Darden v. Gerson, 91 Ala. 323 (1890); White v. Hilton, 13 D.C. (2 Mackey) 339 (1883); Nat'l Metropolitan Bank v. Hitz, 12 D.C. (1 Mackey) 111 (1881); Junction R.R. v. Harris, 9 Ind. 184 (1857); Day v. Bishop, 71 Me. 132 (1880); McLellan v. Nelson, 27 Me. 129 (1847); Meyers v. Gale, 45 Mo. 416 (1870); Prall v. Smith, 31 N.J.L. 244 (1865); Burson's Appeal, 22 Pa. 164 (1853). *See also* Nash, *The Constitutionality of Retrospective Statutes*, 2 W.L.J. 170, 197 (1845).

114. *See* Kirkpatrick v. Holmes, 108 N.C. 206 (1891); Hershizer v. Florence, 39 Ohio St. 516 (1883); Moninger v. Ritner, 104 Pa. 298 (1883). *See also*, Baker's Executors v. Kilgore, 145 U.S. 487 (1892).

115. 8 F. Cas. 545 (C.C.D. Or. 1878) (No. 4396). In this case, Violet and William Berry took a donation claim for which they received a patent in 1866, one year after their divorce. In 1854, Violet executed a power of attorney permitting William to sell the claim, which he did early in 1855 to Henry Fuller. Later, in an effort to insure Fuller's title, Violet also conveyed a deed to him. *Id.* at 545-46. After Deady's decision, rendered over 20 years after Fuller's purchase, Teal, who succeeded to Fuller's interest, was said to have purchased only a life estate for the life of William Berry (the curtesy interest), and Violet Elliot, nee Teal, who had remarried in the interim, owned the remainder. *Id.* at 546.

116. An Act Defining the Rights and Fixing the Liabilities of Married Women, and the Relation Between Husband and Wife (Oct. 21, 1878), in Laws of Oregon, 10th Sess., at 92 (1878). An omen of legislative sentiments appeared in the prior session when the civil procedure code was amended to permit married women to sue or be sued as to their separate property, wages, tort actions, or cases against their husbands. An Act to Amend § 30, in Title III; chapter 1 of Code of Civil Procedure, General Laws, as compiled by Matthew P. Deady and LaFayette Lane (Oct. 21, 1876), in General Laws of the State of Oregon, Enacted by the Legislative Assembly, 9th Sess., at 73 (1876). The 1878 act passed the Senate by only a 23-21 vote on Oct. 18, the final day of the Session. A very brief summary of the legislative debate on S.B. 23 may be found in the Morning Oregonian, Oct. 21, 1878, at 2.

new act legitimated transfers between spouses, permitted one spouse to designate the other spouse their attorney in fact, granted married women management, transfer, and will writing authority with respect to their property, designated a wife's wages as her property, and removed common law disabilities on the rights of married women to sue and be sued. In addition, the act stepped away from the extensive debtor exemption provisions protected by *Rugh*, providing instead that *neither* spouse was liable for the other's debts save for family and education expenses. And two years later a sweeping act was adopted providing that, "All laws which impose or recognize civil disabilities upon a wife which are not imposed or recognized as existing as to the husband, are hereby repealed." In addition, the act provided that the "rights and responsibilities of the parents, in the absence of misconduct, shall be equal" as to children's custody, earnings, and estate.[117]

These two statutes represent a watershed in the development of Oregon's married women's property law. For the first time, married women's property was to be treated the same as their husbands' assets. The dramatic difference in creditor access to husbands' and wives' property created by the 1852 exemption legislation and the early decisions under the 1859 state constitution was removed in favor of joint liability for family purchases and individual responsibility for other investments. Total exemption of married women's property from family creditors became untenable as more women entered the labor force, and women became the primary purchasers of family and consumer goods.[118] By 1878, the routine presence of women in the consumer market place made passé both Judge Deady's conservative notions of women's role and the highly protected status of married women's property under the 1872 exemption legislation.

V. Conclusion

The need to resolve conflicts among creditors, land buyers, and married women was a constant part of Oregon's jurisprudence from

117. An Act to Establish and Protect the Rights of Married Women (Oct. 21, 1880), in Laws of Oregon, 11th Sess., at 6 (1880).

118. By 1890, 17% of the labor force was female and 14% of the female labor force was married. U.S. Bureau of the Census, The Statistical History of the United States from Colonial Times to the Present 129-34 (1976). It is certainly likely that the number of married women working at some time during their marriage was significantly higher than the static number given in the census reports. In addition, there may have been an additional impact in Oregon if donation claims made women wealthier than in other states. There is the further interesting phenomenon that women were becoming the major purchasers of family consumer goods by the turn of the twentieth century. *See* S. Strasser, Never Done: A History of American Housework 242-62 (1982).

the 1850's through the adoption of the final married women's acts in 1878 and 1880. The need for rules providing reasonable certainty as to which assets were available in case of default and minimizing incentives to "hide" assets behind easily available special protective barriers led to temperizing actions by the state legislature whenever the courts drastically altered existing norms. The early married women's acts establishing a special status for married female debtors inevitably led to pressure to equalize the treatment of the spouses in order to simplify the rules and reduce incentives to hide assets in the secure grasp of married women. Although this pressure was certainly not the only reason for Oregon's adoption of the 1878 married women's act,[119] it made it easier for more conservative legislators to see the need for some equalization in the status of husband and wife. Most importantly, the pattern of disputes found in Oregon appears to have occurred in a number of other states. Statutes equalizing the availability to creditors of married women's and men's property were adopted in a number of jurisdictions after the Civil War.[120] Though the focus of this paper is limited to Oregon, its conclusions may be applicable on a much larger scale.

---

119. Pressure from suffragists, particularly Abigail Scott Duniway, was quite strong by 1878. Duniway appeared before the Oregon House of Representatives on Sept. 27, 1878, on behalf of the Women's Suffrage Committee, to argue for suffrage and coverture law reform. The Senate declined to hear her. Morning Oregonian, Sep. 28, 1878, reporting on the Senate session of Sept. 26. Her talk was reported in the same paper on Sept. 30, 1878. The married women's act was adopted on Oct. 18, just before the legislative session ended. The bill passed the Senate 27-1 on Oct. 5. Morning Oregonian, Oct. 7, 1878. The House approved the bill 23-21 on Oct. 18, 1878. Morning Oregonian, Oct. 21, 1878.

120. Some examples may be found in Connecticut: Act of July 9, 1869, ch. CXXIV, 1869 Conn. Pub. Acts 340; Act of Aug. 1, 1872, ch. XCIV, 1872 Conn. Pub. Acts 96; Act of July 3, 1873, ch. LXV, 1873 Conn. Pub. Acts 159; Act of Mar. 16, 1877, ch. CXIV, 1877 Conn. Pub. Acts 211; Indiana: Act of Mar. 25, 1879, ch. LXVII, 1879 Ind. Acts 160; Minnesota: Act of Mar. 10, 1860, Ch. XLIX, 1860 Minn. Laws 217; New Hampshire: Act of July 14, 1871, ch. XXVII, 1871 N.H. Acts 530; New Jersey: Act of Mar. 27, 1874, N. J. Rev. Stat. 468, 471 (1874); Ohio: Act of Mar. 30, 1874, 1874 Ohio Laws 48; Act of Mar. 20, 1884, 1884 Ohio Laws 65; Tennessee: Act of Mar. 2, 1870, ch. XCIX, 1869 Tenn. Pub. Acts 113. *See also* Bred, *supra* note 3. The uncertainties present in legal circles after the Civil War on the debtor-creditor issues is reflected in the major treatise of the day. *See* J.P. BISHOP, 2 COMMENTARIES ON THE LAW OF MARRIED WOMEN 270-73, 363-86 (1875).

REYNOLDS v. UNITED STATES: NINETEENTH-CENTURY FORMS OF MARRIAGE AND THE STATUS OF WOMEN

by Carol Weisbrod and Pamela Sheingorn***

INTRODUCTION

This article suggests a social context for the Supreme Court's late nineteenth-century anti-polygamy case, *Reynolds v. United States*,[1] in which the Court held that the first amendment's free exercise clause was not a defense to a prosecution for bigamy.[2] At the time the *Reynolds* case came down questions relating to the role and status of women were integral to the widespread debate over nonmonogamous domestic institutions. The *Reynolds* opinion was decisive legal reaction against certain elements in American society, Mormon polygamy —coexisting with woman suffrage in Utah[3]—and complex marriage at

---

* J.D., Columbia University (1961); Associate Professor of Law, University of Connecticut School of Law.

** Ph.D., University of Wisconsin (1974); Assistant Professor of Art, Baruch College, C.U.N.Y.

The authors are indebted to Jan Deutsch, Jane Isay, Dorothy Lipson, Leon Lipson, Ellen Peters, and Barbara Underwood for their assistance. Errors are our own. Carol Weisbrod's research was supported in part by a grant from the Johnson Fund of the American Philosophical Society.

1. Reynolds v. United States, 98 U.S. 145 (1878) [cited as 1878, although the decision was announced Jan. 6, 1879].

2. For recent discussions of the case, see Davis, *Plural Marriage and Religious Freedom: The Impact of Reynolds v. United States*, 15 ARIZ. L. REV. 287 (1973) [hereinafter cited as Davis, *Impact*]; Davis, *The Polygamous Prelude*, 6 AM. J. LEGAL HIST. (1962) [hereinafter cited as Davis, *Prelude*]; Linford, *The Mormons and the Law: The Polygamy Cases* (pts. 1-2), 9 UTAH L. REV. 308, 543 (1964, 1965). For an argument that the *Reynolds* case is "wrong" *see* Freeman, *A Remonstrance for Conscience*, 106 U. PA. L. REV. 806, 822-26 (1958). *Compare* Cleveland v. United States, 329 U.S. 14, 20 (1946) (Douglas, J.) (upholding conviction under the Mann Act of a Mormon polygamist), *with* Justice Douglas' opinion in Wisconsin v. Yoder, 406 U.S. 205, 247 (1972) (concurring and dissenting in part).

3. Kraditor has reviewed the early history of American woman suffrage:

> In 1838 Kentucky had given its women, under certain conditions, the right to vote in school elections, but it was not until 1861 that the second state, Kansas, adopted school suffrage. Michigan and Minnesota adopted a similar reform in 1875 . . . . [T]he territory of Wyoming decreed full political equality in 1869

Oneida,[4] which seemed at the time to threaten the stability of the family.[5] *Reynolds* did not rest solely on the proposition that polygamy and monogamy are alternate forms of marriage and that a multiplicity of forms need not be tolerated. The case was based on the idea that polygamy was a social evil. Plural marriage was viewed in the nineteenth century as an attack on traditional marital institutions and an affront, if not a threat, to the existing social structure. The opposition to the Mormons and the Oneida Perfectionists was rooted in part in the common belief that women were degraded in nonmonogamous systems.[6]

Some nineteenth-century concerns about the status of women

A. KRADITOR, THE IDEAS OF THE WOMAN SUFFRAGE MOVEMENT, 1890-1920, at 3 (Anchor ed. 1971).

Wyoming's enactment of woman suffrage, which included the right to hold office, was followed by the action of the Utah Territory (Feb. 12, 1870) giving women the franchise but not the right to hold office. One commentator has noted, however, that Utah women actually voted on two occasions prior to the vote of Wyoming women. Larson, *Woman Suffrage In Western America*, 38 UTAH HIST. Q. 7, 10 (1970). *See also* Alexander, *An Experiment In Progressive Legislation: The Granting of Woman Suffrage In Utah In 1870*, 38 UTAH HIST. Q. 20 (1970).

George Bernard Shaw saw Mormon polygamy as "[p]olygamy . . . under modern democratic conditions." G. SHAW, *The Revolutionist's Handbook*, in MAN AND SUPERMAN 254 (Penguin ed. 1946).

4. On complex marriage, see text accompanying notes 93 and 94 *infra*. *See generally* M. CARDEN, ONEIDA: UTOPIAN COMMUNITY TO MODERN CORPORATION (1969); R. MUNCY, SEX AND MARRIAGE IN UTOPIAN COMMUNITIES (Penguin ed. 1974); R. PARKER, A YANKEE SAINT (1935); C. ROBERTSON, ONEIDA COMMUNITY, AN AUTOBIOGRAPHY, 1851-1876 (1970) [hereinafter cited as C. ROBERTSON, AUTOBIOGRAPHY]; C. ROBERTSON, ONEIDA COMMUNITY: THE BREAKUP, 1876-1881 (1972); J. WHITWORTH, GOD'S BLUEPRINTS (1975).

5. T.W. Curtis in 1885 observed that it was "curious . . . that the principal objection made to woman suffrage is the same as the one made against the reform in Utah, that it will *destroy the home*!" T. CURTIS, THE MORMON PROBLEM 35 (1885) (emphasis in original) [hereinafter cited as T. CURTIS].

6. The Rev. John W. Mears, writing in *The* (New York) *Independent*, discussed the marital systems of Mormons and Oneida Perfectionists: "These two systems make loud boasts of their superiority over all other social arrangements," he said, "[b]ut the one fact which of itself would be sufficient to dispose of these extravagant claims is the manifest degradation of woman under both of the systems." Mears, *Utah and the Oneida Community*, The Independent, Apr. 10, 1879, at 1, col. 1.

A modern writer has summarized the charges frequently made against polygamy:

> [It] bred vice, incest, forced marriages, sexual slavery, degenerate children, and unbridled male lust. The situation of Mormon women was as bad as the position of female slaves under Southern planters. The morality of the Mormons was a fiction . . . . Polygamy was merely instituted to gratify the lechery and avarice of the Mormon leaders and to perpetuate their power. With the system of the harem came the vices of Turkey and Asia.

A. SINCLAIR, THE EMANCIPATION OF THE AMERICAN WOMAN [THE BETTER HALF] 214 (Harper ed. 1966).

seem odd today. It was thought that women might be injured through, for example, their exercise of the franchise. "If woman were to be admitted to an active participation in politics," said the nineteenth-century intellectual Francis Lieber, "she must do it at the price of her whole peculiar nature, her grace and her attraction." She would then "be distinguished from man by her greater weakness alone, and in consequence become greatly oppressed."[7] Lieber's support of the disenfranchisement of women in their own interest may be an illustration of Dicey's comment that "protection invariably involves disability,"[8] but it is more than that, since the system protected women for reasons beyond—though presumably including—their own welfare. The traditional family was seen as the basis of civilization, and a domestic role for women was considered essential to the stability of marriage. These were the propositions which underlay the nineteenth-century hostility to modification of women's roles.

The influence of the *Reynolds* case on the history of the Mormons is obvious. Less well recognized are the role of the case in the history of John Humphrey Noyes' Oneida Community and the relationship to *Reynolds* of the views of the two major centers of the woman suffrage movement, the more radical National Woman Suffrage Association (NWSA) and the more conservative American Woman Suffrage Association (AWSA).[9] Further, the case belongs in the discussion of the history of women's rights in America because women, who had voted in Utah since 1870,[10] were disenfranchised in 1887 as part of the federal antipolygamy campaign. The legitimacy of this campaign was established by the *Reynolds* decision.

A broader point, however, should be made about the *Reynolds* case. The Mormons, the Perfectionists at Oneida, and elements within the suffrage movement all criticized nineteenth-century domestic institutions. While some early feminists may have dreamed of radically restructuring marital institutions, the suffrage movement provided no models. The Mormons and the Perfectionists who lived in social structures completely at variance with those of mainstream

---

7. 2 F. LIEBER, POLITICAL ETHICS 126 (2d ed. rev. Woolsey 1875) (1st ed. Philadelphia 1838).

8. A. DICEY, LECTURES ON THE RELATION BETWEEN LAW AND PUBLIC OPINION IN ENGLAND 150 n.1 (1905).

9. *See generally* W. O'NEILL, THE WOMAN MOVEMENT 25 (Quadrangle ed. 1971) [hereinafter cited as W. O'NEILL]. *See also* Editorial, *Why There Are Two National Woman Suffrage Associations*, Woman's J., Dec. 3, 1870, at 380, col. 1.

10. *See* note 3 *supra*.

America did offer models, the Mormons arguing that in plural marriage Mormon women "enjoyed a higher social position"[11] than that enjoyed by the women of the outside world, the Oneida Perfectionists urging that Oneida's social principles contemplated a "glorious emancipation for man and woman."[12] These alternative marital structures were not accepted by the great majority of the American people, who stood firmly behind monogamous institutions. As one journalist commented at the time, "[t]he great support of monogamy, even among Gentiles, is, after all, not so much the law as social opinion."[13] The *Reynolds* decision, by giving the majority view the unambiguous force of law, made alternative forms of marriage difficult to sustain.[14]

THE REYNOLDS CASE

The *Reynolds* case arose on the following facts. In 1852, the Latter Day Saints in Salt Lake City announced publicly that they were practicing plural marriage.[15] By 1856, the Republican Party platform included a reference to polygamy as a twin relic of barbarism;[16] slavery was, of course, the other. In 1862 a federal statute, the Morrill Act,[17] was passed to deal with bigamy in the territories. The Act provided that "every person having a husband or wife living, who shall marry any other person, whether married or single, in a Territory of the United States, or other place over which the United States [has] jurisdiction, . . . shall . . . be adjudged guilty of bigamy . . . ." Sixteen years after the Morrill Act was passed, a test case[18] involving George Reynolds of Utah, secretary to Brigham Young, finally

---

11. Ivins, *Notes on Mormon Polygamy*, 35 UTAH HIST. Q. 309, 319 (1967) (originally published in 1956 in the *Western Humanities Review*).

12. Circular, June 27, 1852 (Oneida, N.Y.) (predecessor of American Socialist), *excerpted in* C. ROBERTSON, AUTOBIOGRAPHY, *supra* note 4, at 277.

13. 28 NATION 39 (1879).

14. There are occasional indications that the practice of polygamy, though denounced by church and state, nevertheless continues. *See* Comment, *Polygamy in Utah*, 5 UTAH L. REV. 381 (1957). On modern polygamy, see also *Polygamy, Growing in U.S. West, Is Encountering Little Opposition*, N.Y. Times, Oct. 9, 1977, at 1, col. 1.

15. T. O'DEA, THE MORMONS 104 (1957). Linford writes: "The Church of Jesus Christ of Latter-day Saints records the beginning of the practice of patriarchal marriage as July 12, 1843, the date assigned to the revelation which introduced the marriage system of the Church and permitted the Mormon brethren to have more than one wife." Linford, *supra* note 2, at 308-09.

16. Linford, *supra* note 2, at 312.

17. Morrill Act, Ch. 126, 12 Stat. 501 (1862).

18. Reynolds v. United States, 98 U.S. 145 (1878). On *Reynolds* as a test case, *see* Linford, *supra* note 2, at 331-34.

reached the Supreme Court.[19] Reynolds' central argument in the Supreme Court was that his conviction for bigamy could not stand because polygamy was an exercise of rights protected under the religious liberty guarantees of the first amendment, directly operative in the territories.

Reynolds requested the trial court to instruct the jury that if it found from the evidence that he was married "in pursuance of and in conformity with what he believed at the time to be a religious duty, that the verdict must be 'not guilty.' "[20] This request was refused.

Chief Justice Waite, writing for the Supreme Court, considered the jury instruction on the subsequent appeal.[21] The issue was whether religious belief could justify an act made criminal by federal statute.[22] The Court rejected Reynolds' claim that the religious practice of polygamy was constitutionally protected.

Congress, the Court said, could not pass a law for the territories which would prohibit the free exercise of religion, but the antibigamy act was not within the congressional prohibition. The Court found the Morrill Act within the legislative power of Congress, since Congress was "left free to reach actions which were in violation of social duties or subversive of good order."[23] The Court then asked whether those who made the practice of polygamy a part of their religious belief were excepted from the operation of the statute,[24] and concluded that they were not.[25]

---

19. It has been suggested that the delay in enforcement was due to the Civil War and Reconstruction. *See* Davis, *Prelude*, *supra* note 2, at 6.

20. 98 U.S. at 162.

21. The judge instructed the jury that:

> if the defendant, under the influence of a religious belief that it was right—under an inspiration, if you please, that it was right,—deliberately married a second time, having a first wife living, the want of consciousness of evil intent—the want of understanding on his part that he was committing a crime—did not excuse him; but the law inexorably in such case implies the criminal intent.

Id.

22. *Id.*

23. *Id.* at 164.

24. *Id.* at 166.

25. The court stated: "To permit this would be to make the professed doctrines of religious belief superior to the law of the land, and in effect to permit every citizen to become a law unto himself. Government could exist only in name under such circumstances." *Id.* at 167.

Reynolds served 19 months in jail. "Upon his release he was regarded by the Mormons as a 'living martyr' . . . . Ironically, in 1885 he was married a third time . . . ." Davis, *Impact*, *supra* note 2, at 291.

It is the Court's discussion of marriage as a foundation of society which is of interest here.

> Marriage, while from its very nature a sacred obligation, is nevertheless, in most civilized nations, a civil contract, and usually regulated by law. Upon it society may be said to be built, and out of its fruits spring social relations and social obligations and duties, with which government is necessarily required to deal. In fact, according as monogamous or polygamous marriages are allowed, do we find the principles on which the government of the people, to a greater or less extent, rests. Professor Lieber says, polygamy leads to the patriarchal principle, and [*sic*] which, when applied to large communities, fetters the people in stationary despotism, while that principle cannot long exist in connection with monogamy. . . .[26]

The decision in the *Reynolds* case has been read in the twentieth century as a statement which "found in polygamy the seed of destruction of a democratic society" and which viewed polygamy as "highly injurious to its female adherents."[27] *Reynolds* sustained a lower court instruction to the jury referring to "pure minded women," "innocent children," and "innocent victims of this delusion."[28] But while the decision refers to the odiousness of polygamy,[29] the *Reynolds* opinion does not detail the injuries to the innocent victims or other evils of the institution.

The evils of Mormon polygamy must, however, have been seen against the background of law and custom relating to the status of women in monogamous America. Contemporary observers were

---

26. 98 U.S. at 165-66. Chief Justice Waite quoted an edited version of Lieber's comments which appeared as a footnote in 2 J. KENT, COMMENTARIES ON AMERICAN LAW 95 *n.h.* (12th ed. O. Holmes 1873). Chancellor Kent cited Lieber to support his statement that "[p]olygamy may be regarded as exclusively the feature of Asiatic manners, and of half-civilized life, and to be incompatible with civilization, refinement, and domestic felicity." *Id.* at 94-95. For Lieber's original, see 2 F. LIEBER, POLITICAL ETHICS, *supra* note 7, at 9.

27. People v. Woody, 61 Cal. 2d 716, 724-25, 394 P.2d 813, 820, 40 Cal. Rptr. 69, 76 (1964).

28. 98 U.S. at 167-68.

29. "Polygamy has always been odious among the northern and western nations of Europe, and, until the establishment of the Mormon Church, was almost exclusively a feature of the life of Asiatic and of African People." *Id.* at 164. Chief Justice Waite referred to the opinion as his "sermon on the religion of polygamy." B. TRIMBLE, CHIEF JUSTICE WAITE 244 n.18 (1938).

aware of the relationship between the polygamy question and the debate over the status of women, and one observer summarized the relation this way: "We are mistaken in supposing the women of Utah are in any greater bondage than are the women of the United States."[30]

NINETEENTH-CENTURY CONVENTIONS OF HOME AND MARRIAGE

Francis Lieber on Monogamy

When Chief Justice Waite noted that the forms of marriage are basic to society and of critical significance to governmental institutions, he cited Professor Francis Lieber's thesis that polygamy leads to the patriarchal principle, and that this principle might fetter those people adhering to it in stationary despotism. Francis Lieber, a German emigré who achieved considerable distinction as a publicist in America,[31] was deeply interested in the forms of marriage. *Reynolds v. United States* constitutes an endorsement of Lieber's views on marriage.[32] It was an invocation of one of the serious intellectual names of the age[33] in connection with a cause he had long defended, and it is possible that Chief Justice Waite did not detail the dangers of polygamy because he assumed that in relying on the opinion of Professor Lieber he had done all that was required.

In *Political Ethics* Lieber had written: "The family cannot exist without marriage, nor can it develop its highest importance, it would seem, without monogamy."[34] In 1865, Lieber, still concerned with the protection of monogamy, had proposed a constitutional amendment declaring polygamy a crime.[35] Lieber set forth in detail his con-

---

30. T. CURTIS, *supra* note 5, at 35 (1885).

31. *See generally* F. FREIDEL, FRANCIS LIEBER: NINETEENTH CENTURY LIBERAL (1947). The citation to Francis Lieber has been described as "an early and unheralded use of social science findings." Galanter, *Religious Freedoms in the United States: A Turning Point?*, 1966 WIS. L. REV. 217, 232.

32. A posthumous endorsement. Lieber died in 1872.

33. A review in *Nation*, noting the "extraordinary favor" with which Lieber's ideas had been received in America, comments: "There must have been something in Dr. Lieber's mind and character remarkably in harmony with the spirit and tendencies of his adopted country to earn for him a reputation like this . . . ." 32 NATION 189 (1881).

34. 1 F. LIEBER, POLITICAL ETHICS, *supra* note 7, at 139.

35. F. LIEBER, *Amendments of the Constitution Submitted to the Consideration of the American People* in 2 MISCELLANEOUS WRITINGS 137, 173 (1881) (reprinting PAPER NO. 83 OF THE LOYAL PUBLICATION SOCIETY (1865)). Polyandry (more than one husband) should also be constitutionally forbidden, he said, for "what does not happen in our days!" *Id.*

ception of monogamy and its significance in an unsigned article published in *Putnam's Monthly* in 1855. Monogamy, he said,

> is one of the primordial elements out of which all law proceeds, or which the law steps in to recognize and protect. . . . Wedlock, or monogamic marriage, . . . is one of the frames of our thoughts, and moulds of our feelings; it is a psychological condition of our jural consciousness, of our liberty, of our literature, of our aspirations, of our religious convictions, and of our domestic being and family relation, the foundation of all that is called polity.[36]

This article specifically addressed the issue of whether Utah should be admitted to the Union and also considered more general questions of alternative forms of marriage. Among the forms cited in Lieber's article were Mormon polygamy and complex marriage as practiced by the Oneida Perfectionists.[37] Lieber's *Putnam's* article placed monogamy "beyond our religion," and "beyond Common Law," in the world of "primordial elements."[38] His arguments, however, would have established monogamy as the only marital system permitted under the law.

American Monogamy

Monogamous marriage in nineteenth-century American law was a relationship between the parties which was described by William Story in 1847 in terms of baron and serf, or hawk and dove.[39] Because the law was repressive to women, Lucy Stone and Henry Blackwell married "under protest" in 1855, writing into their mar-

---

36. [Lieber], *The Mormons. Shall Utah Be Admitted into the Union?*, 5 PUTNAM'S MONTHLY 225, 234 (1855). For attribution, *see* 2 F. LIEBER, MISCELLANEOUS WRITINGS 534 (1881); F. FREIDEL, *supra* note 31, at 262.

37. For another view on the forms of marriage, see Cleveland v. United States, 329 U.S. 14, 25-26 (1946) (Murphy, J., dissenting).

38. [Lieber], *The Mormons, supra* note 36, at 234.

39.
> In respect to the powers and rights of married women, the law is by no means abreast of the spirit of the age. Here are seen the old fossil foot-prints of Feudalism. The law relating to women tends to make every family a barony, or a monarchy, or a despotism, of which the husband is the baron, king or a despot, and the wife the dependent, serf or slave . . . . [I]f the husband choose, he has his wife as firmly in his grasp and dominion, as the hawk has the dove upon whom he has pounced. The age is ahead of the law. Public opinion is a check to legal rules on this subject . . . .

W. STORY, TREATISE ON THE LAW OF CONTRACTS NOT UNDER SEAL 74 (2d ed. Boston 1847).

riage contract a denunciation of the laws which gave the husband "custody of the wife's person," "the exclusive control and guardianship of their children," and "sole ownership of her personal, and use of her real estate," and finally, "the whole system by which 'the legal existence of the wife is suspended during marriage.' "[40] T. W. Higginson, the noted nineteenth-century reformer who officiated at the Stone-Blackwell marriage, quoted Story's remark many years later, and observed that while women's legal status had been greatly ameliorated since Story wrote, it was not clear "that the final and equitable fulfilment [sic]" had been reached.[41] For Higginson and many others, the issue became focused on suffrage.

While some of the nineteenth-century laws concerning women related exclusively to married women,[42] other laws incapacitated all women, married or single. In either case, the laws were rooted in a particular concept of the roles of men and women in monogamy. In nineteenth-century America the married state was seen as right and natural; the unmarried state was not the norm, and thus it was thought unnecessary to recognize the unmarried state in governmental action. In his concurring opinion in *Bradwell v. Illinois*,[43] Justice Bradley described the unmarried woman as unaffected by "the duties, complications, and incapacities arising out of the married state."[44] Unmarried women, in his opinion, were exceptions. "The paramount destiny and mission of women are to fulfill the noble and benign offices of wife and mother. This is the law of the Creator." The law of the Creator would also be the law of the state since the "rules of civil society must be adapted to the general constitution of things, and cannot be based on exceptional cases."[45]

Political Disabilities of Women

The principal political disability against which women fought in late nineteenth-century America was disenfranchisement. In 1874, in

---

40. The document is quoted in W. O'NEILL, *supra* note 9, at 112-13.

41. T. HIGGINSON, COMMON SENSE ABOUT WOMEN 98 (1882).

42. William Story specifically addressed the legal incapacities of married women. *See* W. STORY, *supra* note 39.

43. 83 U.S. 130 (1872) (fourteenth amendment does not prohibit state's refusal to admit women to the bar).

44. *Id.* at 141. Justice Bradley was joined by Justices Field and Swayne.

45. *Id.* at 141-42. Other explanations have been offered for the legal incapacities of women. John Stuart Mill wrote, "[Women's] disabilities elsewhere are only clung to in order to maintain their subordination in domestic life; because the generality of the male sex cannot yet tolerate the idea of living with an equal . . . ." J. MILL, THE SUBJECTION OF WOMEN 50 (M.I.T. ed. 1970).

the case of *Minor v. Happersett*,[46] the Court found that women's right to vote was not protected by the federal Constitution.

Some conservatives on the suffrage question did not oppose all changes relating to the status of women. A part of the antisuffrage movement was led by women,[47] and this group, of course, did not favor the "degradation" of women. Rather, antisuffrage women, like some antisuffrage men, were interested in achieving such emancipation as was consistent in their view with the laws of nature. Lieber had noted that the progress of civilization was accompanied by the acquisition of greater rights and privileges for women.[48] Some of these changes would be seen as good and humane by Lieber and also by Justice Bradley.[49] Other changes, other "emancipations" or "reforms," however, might lead to catastrophe. In particular, there remained a notable lack of agreement on the issue of the franchise for women. Lieber argued that there was no degradation of women in the refusal of the state to accept votes from women. On the contrary,

---

46. 88 U.S. (21 Wall.) 162 (1874). "If the law is wrong, it ought to be changed," Chief Justice Waite wrote for the Court, "but the power for that is not with us. . . . No argument as to woman's need of suffrage can be considered." *Id.* at 178.

47. *E.g.*, Mrs. Caroline Fairfield Corbin. In one of her later writings she said:

> For the loss of her rights and privileges as wife and mother, woman is to be compensated by equal work and equal wages with man, and the right to vote. With even a glimmering of a perception of the changes implied in the social order by the industrial and political equality of woman, is it any wonder that the overwhelming mass of women, as conceded on all hands, decline the specious bait of woman suffrage?

C. Corbin, The Position of Women in the Socialistic Utopia 10 (1901).

See also Petition to U.S. Senate Against Woman Suffrage (presented by Mrs. General Sherman and Mrs. Admiral Dahlgren), *quoted in* The History of Woman Suffrage 494 (E. Stanton, S. Anthony & M. Gage eds. 1889) [hereinafter cited as HWS]. The petition explained that: "Although we shrink from the notoriety of the public eye, yet we are too deeply and painfully impressed by the grave perils which threaten our peace and happiness in these proposed changes in our civil and political rights, longer to remain silent."

48. Lieber stated:

> [T]hat every step onward has assigned to woman some important element of civilization which, until then, was withheld from her as unfit or unnecessary for her—even education itself; nay, reading and writing not excluded. . . . [W]omen are freely admitted to occupations now which but a short time ago would have been withheld from them.

2 F. Lieber, Miscellaneous Writings, *supra* note 35, at 207. The underlying idea was that "the position which woman occupies in society is one of the gages [sic] by which we try to ascertain the civilization of that society in general." *Id.*

49. Justice Bradley noted: "The humane movements of modern society, which have for their object the multiplication of avenues for woman's advancement, and of occupations adapted to her condition and sex, have my heartiest concurrence." Bradwell v. Illinois, 83 U.S. (16 Wall.) at 142 (1872) (concurring opinion).

a nonpolitical role for women was considered an essential aspect of their nature.

> The nature and consequent duties of woman exclude her from public life; her timidity, bashfulness, delicacy, and inferior grasp of mind, as well as the necessity of acting out those sacred duties more especially assigned to her, require her being more retired than the other sex. A woman loses in the same degree her natural character, as a woman, as she enters into publicity.[50]

For the antisuffrage group, monogamy and the familial organization it ensured, sanctified by natural law and enforced by civil law, required the disenfranchisement of women.

If the issue of suffrage could involve questions greater than the franchise, reaching the questions of the home and civilization, it could also involve such lesser issues as the right to practice law. In his unsuccessful argument on behalf of Myra Bradwell's right to practice law, Matthew Carpenter pointed out to the Supreme Court that it "seems to be feared that doing justice to women's rights in any particular would probably be followed by the establishment of the right of female suffrage, which, it is assumed, would overthrow Christianity, defeat the ends of modern civilization, and upturn the world."[51] A majority of the Court found that the right of women to practice law was not the sort of claim which could be protected against state invasion by the fourteenth amendment.[52] The Bradley concurrence based its conclusion on the special characteristics, destiny, and mission of women.[53] Similarly, in 1876, Belva Lockwood was refused admission to the practice of law before the Supreme Court.[54]

---

50. 2 F. LIEBER, POLITICAL ETHICS, *supra* note 7, at 124-25. Lieber went on to say: "There are, of course, women whose extraordinary mental organization is such that they form exceptions; but whenever this fundamental principle is abandoned as a general rule, evil ensues, as in every other case of deviation from the laws of nature." *Id.* at 125.

51. Brief of the Plaintiff in Error at 2, Bradwell v. Illinois, 83 U.S. (16 Wall.) 130 (1872).

52. Bradwell v. Illinois, 83 U.S. (16 Wall.) 130, 139 (1872).

53. *See* text accompanying notes 44 & 45 *supra.*

54. Chief Justice Waite indicated:

> By the uniform practice of the Court . . . and by the fair construction of its rules, none but men are permitted to practice before it as attorneys and counsellors. . . . [The Court] dces not feel called upon to make a change until such a change is required by statute or a more extended practice in the higher courts of the States.

Thus the common notion that woman's calling was a higher, nobler sphere than career or politics, that woman's role essentially was domestic, and private, was paralleled by—if it was not reflected in—Supreme Court actions adverse to the cause of women's political rights. These rulings of the late nineteenth-century Supreme Court are a part of that history of American sex discrimination of which Justice Brennan spoke in *Frontiero v. Richardson*,[55] commenting that it was discrimination "rationalized by an attitude of 'romantic paternalism,' which, in practical effect, put women, not on a pedestal, but in a cage."[56]

SOME NINETEENTH-CENTURY DISSENTERS

The Suffrage Movement

Early feminists had met in Seneca Falls[57] in 1848, protesting a wide variety of injustices and disassociating themselves from nonfeminist women, who were viewed as unenlightened about the laws under which they lived because they declared themselves satisfied with their present situation.[58] The 1848 meeting ended with a close vote demanding the franchise.[59] As the women's movement concentrated increasingly on suffrage, the public debate on the issue of suffrage and its dangers to the home intensified.[60]

After the Civil War, the tension which had been growing for some time between two factions in the woman suffrage movement

---

Quoted in C. FAIRMAN, RECONSTRUCTION AND REUNION, 1864-1888, 6 OLIVER WENDELL HOLMES DEVISE HISTORY OF THE SUPREME COURT OF THE UNITED STATES 1366-67 (1971). Magrath writes: "[Still] Waite sympathized with the women's rights movement . . . and, with Justices Davis and Miller, unsuccesfully favored admitting women as members of the Supreme Court bar." C. MAGRATH, MORRISON R. WAITE: THE TRIUMPH OF CHARACTER 119 (1963).

A statute directing that women be admitted to practice before the Supreme Court was passed on Feb. 15, 1879. Mrs. Lockwood was admitted on Mar. 3, 1879. C. FAIRMAN, *supra*, at 1367.

55. 411 U.S. 677 (1973). *See* opinion of Justice Brennan, joined by Justices Douglas, White, and Marshall. The opinion goes on to quote the Bradley concurrence in *Bradwell*. *Id.* at 684-85.

56. *Id.* at 684.

57. "[A]n obscure village that happened to be the home of Elizabeth Cady Stanton . . . ." W. O'NEILL, *supra* note 9, at 22.

58. *See id.* at 110-11.

59. "It is," the feminists said, "the duty of the women of this country to secure to themselves their sacred right to the elective franchise." *Id.* at 111.

60. The movement was "constantly confronted by the antisuffragist argument that such a change would contradict the inherent nature of woman and would destroy the home." A. KRADITOR, *supra* note 3, at 82.

finally produced an open split in the movement. The Stanton/Anthony group, based in New York, organized the National Woman Suffrage Association[61] and, for a time, published *The Revolution*. The Stone/Blackwell group, organized as the American Woman Suffrage Association, worked out of Boston and published the *Woman's Journal*. Attempts to unite the two groups were frustrated by "differences in principle and tactics."[62] The Boston group was reluctant to be associated with the more radical ideas of the Stanton/Anthony wing and was particularly threatened by efforts of the NWSA to reform the institution of marriage.[63]

The important differences between the two suffrage groups were reflected in their positions on nonmonogamous marriage practices. The Stone/Blackwell group believed that "[m]onogamy is the rock upon which the church of Woman's Equality is founded,"[64] and that until polygamy was destroyed there could be no equality for women.[65] They denounced the Mormons, free lovers like Victoria Woodhull,[66] and the Oneida Perfectionists.[67] "Let the masculine half of humanity bear the blame," the *Woman's Journal* said, "when John H. Noyes proposes to substitute for the endearing ties of domestic life a system of 'scientific propagation' . . . founded expressly upon the cornerstones of polygamy and incest."[68] Monogamy was as central to the Stone/Blackwell position as it was to Lieber's.

The Stanton/Anthony wing developed a more complex stance.

---

61. This association is hereinafter cited as NWSA.

62. *See* W. O'NEILL, *supra* note 9, at 25.

63. *Id.*

64. *Woman's Rights Versus Polygamy*, Woman's J., June 21, 1879, at 196, col. 1.

65. *Id.* Polygamy "is social barbarism, and so long as it exists, the equality of Woman is impossible." *Id.*

66. On Victoria Woodhull's views, see R. RIEGEL, AMERICAN FEMINISTS 146-47 (1963). Kraditor writes:

> Victoria Woodhull and her sister, Tennessee Claflin, never for a moment represented suffragist thinking. Mrs. Stanton and Mrs. Anthony had defended Mrs. Woodhull in the 1870's only out of a sense of sex solidarity . . . . The very possibility of even such a temporary association with a Woodhull or a Claflin disappeared as soon as the suffrage movement became more than a radical demand by a few individuals.

A. KRADITOR, *supra* note 3, at 93.

67. For a relatively moderate account in the *Woman's Journal*, see Higginson, *The Oneida Community*, Woman's J., Mar. 2, 1872, at 65, col. 1. Although Higginson concluded that it would be a "calamity" for a child to be raised at Oneida, he also noted points to be admired. *See* text accompanying note 100 *infra*. For an account of an Oneida childhood, see P. NOYES, MY FATHER'S HOUSE (1937).

68. *Positivism Versus Woman Suffrage*, Woman's J., Oct. 1, 1870, at 308, col. 4.

The group never advocated polygamy and Mormon women themselves described the women of the National Woman Suffrage Association as "opposed in their feelings to plural marriage and without sympathy for our religious views."[69] But while rejecting the Mormon way of life, some members of the NWSA would occasionally view its evils as merely relative. There were three kinds of polygamy, Mrs. Stanton wrote—Mormon polygamy, bigamy based on fraud, and polygamy involving one wife and many mistresses, "everywhere practiced in the United States."[70] Another NWSA woman put it more succinctly: "The Mormons marry their mistresses, the congressmen don't."[71]

The root of the NWSA position was its dissatisfaction with American monogamy. The suffrage movement had always included a small group prepared to engage in a radical rethinking of the position of women.[72] Though this group could anticipate little success in overturning the traditional domestic system, it was open to the suggestion that the fundamental problem was not disenfranchisement, but rather marriage. "[W]e know that the ballot, when we get it, will achieve for woman no more than it has achieved for man,"[73] said a writer in Susan B. Anthony's *Revolution*. To drop all other demands in order to unite on a demand for the ballot was, she thought, only a very small part of the mission of the radical wing of the movement.[74] Mrs. Stanton argued that social roles and political rights were related, and publicly criticized both the conservatives for claiming that suffrage for women would destroy the family and the timid feminists for answer-

---

69. Woman's Exponent, Dec. 1, 1878, at 102 (resolution thanking the NWSA for its support, adopted Nov. 16, 1878).

70. Stanton, *Address at The Decade Meeting on Marriage and Divorce* in P. DAVIS, HISTORY OF THE NATIONAL WOMAN'S RIGHTS MOVEMENT 70 (1871).

71. Woman's Exponent, Feb. 1, 1879, at 187, *quoting* Sarah Spencer.

72. W. O'NEILL, *supra* note 9, at 29. O'Neill notes that "their minds were open to the possibility that the entire domestic system would have to be restructured as a precondition for sexual equality." *Id.*

73. Bullard, *What Flag Shall We Fly?*, Revolution, Oct. 27, 1870, at 264, *quoted in* W. O'NEILL, EVERYONE WAS BRAVE 19 (1969).

74. The ballot is not even half the loaf; it is only a crust—a crumb. The ballot touches only those interests, either of women or men, which take their root in political questions. But woman's chief discontent is not with her political, but with her social, and particularly her marital bondage. The solemn and profound question of marriage . . . is of more vital consequence to woman's welfare, reaches down to a deeper depth in woman's heart, and more thoroughly constitutes the core of the woman's movement, than any such superficial and fragmentary question as woman's suffrage.

W. O'NEILL, *supra* note 73, at 19-20.

ing that it would not.[75] In private, Mrs. Stanton was decidedly negative toward marriage,[76] and Susan B. Anthony seemed to grow more hostile toward marriage as she grew older.[77]

The statements of some of the Stanton/Anthony group, at least on occasion, indicated that their prime loyalty was to women, *qua* women, and not to domestic institutions at all. Susan B. Anthony, for example, emphasized the independence of women, whatever the domestic structure. Writing to *The Revolution* from Salt Lake City, Miss Anthony said:

> What we have tried to do is to show . . . that the principle of the subjection of woman to man is the point of attack; and that woman's work in monogamy and polygamy is one and the same—that of planting her feet on the ground of self-support. "Independent bread alone can redeem woman from her curse of subjection to man."[78]

---

75. "They are both wrong. It will entirely revolutionize it," said Elizabeth Cady Stanton, *Address at the Decade Meeting on Marriage and Divorce* in P. DAVIS, *supra* note 70, at 70.

76. W. O'NEILL, *supra* note 9, at 27. Mrs. Stanton, he said, "condemned [marriage] as 'opposed to all God's laws.' " *Id.*

77. R. RIEGEL, *supra* note 66, at 70 (1963).

78. 1 I. HARPER, SUSAN B. ANTHONY 389 (1899). S.B. Anthony's letters (1871) from Salt Lake City—one to *Revolution*, the other a letter home—are of interest in considering the response of the radical feminists to polygamy. In her letter to *Revolution* she described the pain involved in the change from polygamy to monogamy undertaken by a secessionist party in Utah.

> The transition of this people into the new life is complicated—is heartrending . . . . One man, a noble, loving, beautiful spirit—nothing of the tyrant, nothing of the sensualist—with four lovely wives, three of whom I have seen, and in the homes of two of whom I have broken bread, with thirteen loved and loving children—wakes up with a new idea. Four women's hearts breaking, three sets of children that must leave their father that the one-wife system may be realized!

Id.

But Susan B. Anthony's conclusion, as expressed in her private letter, was unquestionably antipolygamy. "The system of the subjection of woman here finds its limit, and she touches the lowest depths of her degradation." *Id.* at 390. The letter home concludes:

> The empire totters and Brigham feels the ground sliding from under his feet. These men will be very likely to try the 'variety' plan of Stephen Pearl Andrews, but the women will hate that even worse than polygamy. One man came to me relating a new vision, direct from Christ himself, to that effect, and I said: 'Away with your man visions! Women propose to reject them all, and begin to dream dreams for themselves.'

Id.

On Stephen Pearl Andrews and Victoria Woodhull, see W. O'NEILL, *supra* note 9, at 27-28.

Thus, the men and women in the suffrage movement approached the Mormon question from varying perspectives. For the more conservative wing, monogamy was intrinsically important. For the radicals, discussion of women's political disabilities would start with suffrage but end with a challenge to traditional domestic arrangements.

The Mormons

As a modern historian has said, the Church of Jesus Christ of Latter Day Saints, founded in New York by Joseph Smith, "has outlasted or outdistanced every other sect . . . brought into being in America."[79] The current position of the Mormon movement, another scholar has written, "is a far cry from that of the despised and persecuted minority whose existence was considered a national problem and which was driven across the continent to the wastes of Utah in the middle of the last century."[80] The early history of the Mormons reveals difficulties and persecutions in several states, culminating in the murder of Joseph Smith in 1844. It was Brigham Young who led the Mormons to Utah, where they established a "polygamous theocracy within a monogamous and democratic[81] nation."[82]

The *Reynolds* case, handed down on January 6, 1879, did not instantly destroy polygamy in Utah. The successful federal prosecution of a Mormon polygamist had little immediate impact on Mormon marriages, largely because of problems of proof.[83] Additional federal legislation was found necessary, and in 1882, the Edmunds Act was passed, making it a criminal act to cohabit with more than one woman.[84] This statute also disenfranchised polygamists, bigamists, and cohabitants. Still later, in 1887, the Edmunds-Tucker Act[85] disincorporated the Mormon Church and disenfranchised all the women of Utah—Mormon and gentile, polygamist and nonpolygamist. *Mormon Church v. United States*,[86] decided in 1890, reflects the intensity of the public reaction to polygamy. The practice of polygamy, the Supreme Court said, was "a return to barbarism . . . contrary to the spirit of Christianity and of the civilization which Christianity has

79. S. AHLSTROM, A RELIGIOUS HISTORY OF THE AMERICAN PEOPLE 501-02 (1972).
80. T. O'DEA, *supra* note 15, at 2.
81. For a suffragist gloss on "democratic," see the NWSA resolution of Jan. 9, 1879, quoted in text accompanying note 30 *supra*. *See also* note 148 *infra*.
82. S. MORISON, OXFORD HISTORY OF THE AMERICAN PEOPLE 548 (1965).
83. Davis, *Impact*, *supra* note 2, at 291.
84. Ch. 47, 22 Stat. 30 (1882).
85. Ch. 397, 24 Stat. 635 (1887).
86. 136 U.S. 1 (1890) (per Bradley, J.).

produced in the Western world."[87] The Mormons capitulated to the federal government and formally abandoned polygamy with a public statement solemnly placing the responsibility for the change upon the nation which had forced the renunciation.[88] In 1896 Utah gained admission to the Union.[89]

The Perfectionists at Oneida

Founded in Vermont by John Humphrey Noyes, and later reestablished in New York, the Oneida Community was well known, if not notorious, in its own time.[90] Noyes held these central religious ideas: That the second coming had already occurred at the time of the destruction of Jerusalem in 70 A.D. and that there was present salvation from sin.[91] The social system of Oneida derived from Noyes' theological propositions: "Jesus Christ offers to save men from all evil—from sin and death itself; but he always states it as a necessary condition of their accepting his help that they shall forsake all others; and particularly that they shall get rid of their private property."[92] The private property which Oneida disclaimed included both goods and persons. Oneida was committed both to community of goods and to a social system called complex marriage. Although complex marriage as practiced at Oneida was often denounced in the nineteenth

---

87. *Id.* at 49. *See also* Justice Field's comments in Davis v. Beason, 133 U.S. 333, 341 (1890) (upholding Idaho statute requiring voters to swear that they were not practitioners of polygamy and did not advocate or teach it). Justice Field stated that bigamy and polygamy are crimes, tending "to destroy the purity of the marriage relation, to disturb the peace of families, to degrade woman and to debase man."

88. *See* Declaration of Submission, *quoted in* L. PFEFFER, CHURCH, STATE & FREEDOM 533 (1953).

89. Utah's constitution contains a provision forever banning polygamy, as well as a provision for woman suffrage. *See* White, *Woman's Place Is in the Constitution: The Struggle for Equal Rights in Utah in 1895*, 42 UTAH HIST. Q. 344 (1974).

90. The Oneida Community has been described as the "most successful, most widely publicized and most ably defended example of evangelically inspired communitarianism in the United States." S. AHLSTROM, *supra* note 79, at 498.

91. Oneida's theology was sometimes expounded in advertisements in the community newspaper. For example:

> Legal Notice: Notice is hereby given that all claims issued by the old firm of Moses and Law were cancelled 1800 years ago. Any requirement, therefore, to observe as a means of righteousness legal enactments bearing date prior to A.D. 70, is pronounced by us, on the authority of the New Testament, a fraud and imposition.

Quoted in C. NORDHOFF, THE COMMUNISTIC SOCIETIES OF THE UNITED STATES 267 (Dover ed. 1966) (reprinting 1st ed. 1875).

92. *Quoted in id.* at 271.

century as polygamy or free love, the Perfectionists denied that complex marriage was free love, and, in fact, they did not think of the institution as marriage. The Oneida Communists considered themselves to be in this respect more like the celibate (no wife) Shakers than like the polygamous (many wife) Mormons.[93] But every man in Oneida was, in effect, married to every woman, in a system which first involved a form of birth control called male continence and later a form of human genetic experimentation called stirpiculture.[94]

The Perfectionists at Oneida were careful to say they were not advocates of women's rights[95] in the usual sense of that term. Yet within the context of Perfectionist thinking, they sought the fullest development of woman, "compatible with her taking her position as the helpmeet of man in the true order of the transmission of divine power as given by Paul—God the head of Christ, Christ the head of man, man the head of woman."[96] They followed the women's movement with interest,[97] and in their own social environment favored the "*mingling of the sexes* in labor."[98] The Perfectionists were highly critical of the role of women in monogamy, and as part of their 1852 theocratic platform advocated the abandonment of "the entire fashion of the world" particularly "marriage and involuntary propagation."[99]

While the Perfectionists may not have considered themselves advocates of women's rights, others, then and now, have perceived them as sexual egalitarians. In the nineteenth century T.W. Higginson admired the "fidelity" with which the Perfectionists maintained "the equality of the sexes."[100] A twentieth-century historian concluded

---

93. Am. Socialist, Feb. 20, 1879, at 59.

94. For further information on stirpiculture, see C. ROBERTSON, AUTOBIOGRAPHY, *supra* note 4, at 335-55. The word stirpiculture "invented and used by the Oneida Community, is a compound of two words, of which the first is *stirpes*, the Latin word for race, and *culture*, an English word meaning cultivation with a view to improvement." *Id.* at 335. *See also* Shaw's comments on Noyes, G. SHAW, *supra* note 3, at 222-25.

95. Am. Socialist, Jan. 16, 1879, at 21.

96. *Id.*

97. Thus, the Perfectionists said, we "read John Stuart Mill with pleasure; Mrs. Stanton and Miss Anthony and *The Women's Journal* [*sic*] with attention . . . ." Still, they said, "when it comes to doing anything for ourselves, we have to refuse to look at men and women as mutually independent and in a state of competition." Circular, Mar. 18, 1872 (Oneida, N.Y.), *quoted in* C. ROBERTSON, AUTOBIOGRAPHY, *supra* note 4, at 284.

98. Circular, Oct. 8, 1853, *quoted in* C. ROBERTSON, AUTOBIOGRAPHY, *supra* note 4, at 58.

99. Circular, Aug. 29, 1852 (Oneida, N.Y.), *quoted in* C. ROBERTSON, AUTOBIOGRAPHY, *supra* note 4, at 277. *See also* Am. Socialist, Feb. 20, 1879, at 63, "woman in the Oneida Community is made free."

100. Higginson, *The Oneida Community*, Woman's J., Mar. 2, 1872, at 65.

that John Humphrey Noyes had succeeded, "under unique and probably unduplicatable conditions, in abolishing marriage and raising women to a state of absolute equality with men."[101]

In the 1870's some of the clergy of central New York began to urge action against the Perfectionist group. Professor John W. Mears of Hamilton College, who led the anti-Perfectionist movement, called an anti-Oneida conference which was held at Syracuse University on the 14th of February, 1879.[102] The heightened national antipolygamy campaign seems to have affected the timing of the anti-Oneida conference and the *Reynolds* decision played a role by encouraging those opposed to any variation from traditional monogamy.[103]

Oneida's newspaper, *The American Socialist*, tried to defend the Community against these attacks on two levels. Their first argument was addressed to a legal issue: the antibigamy act related only to the territories and had no effect in New York.[104] Their second defense was political: the Perfectionist Community was completely unlike that of the Mormons.[105] But nothing the Perfectionists said or did pro-

---

101. W. O'NEILL, *supra* note 9, at 26.

102. Reports of this meeting appear in the *American Socialist* in early 1879.

103. The *New York Times* noted, "[t]he recent decision of the Supreme Court of the United States establishing the constitutionality of the laws against Utah polygamy gave heart to the movement to eradicate the community." N.Y. Times, Feb. 15, 1879, at 1, col. 7.

104. Am. Socialist, Feb. 20, 1879, at 59.

> Correspondent: Do you not think that the new Polygamy act of Congress [*sic*] has stimulated Dr. Mears and his *confreres* to renewed effort?
>
> Mr. Hinds: It has doubtless given life to this movement, but that act has no reference to Communities like ours, and only affects Territories under the jurisdiction of the United States government.

The Community also insisted more generally that its members were violating no existing laws. Adultery was not then a crime in New York as it had been in Vermont in 1847 when the original Perfectionist Community left Putney. Although prosecution for statutory rape was a possibility, the age of consent in New York in 1879 was ten. *See* D. PIVAR, PURITY CRUSADE: SEXUAL MORALITY AND SOCIAL CONTROL 1868-1900 at 142 (1973). (The age of consent was raised to sixteen in 1887.) Most of the girls at Oneida were older than ten at their sexual initiation. Compare discussion in M. CARDEN *supra* note 4, at 101; R. MUNCY, *supra* note 4, at 192. Clearly proof of any crime, for example, rape or incest, might in some instances have provided the basis for prosecution, but it seems not to have done so in fact. *See* R. PARKER, *supra* note 4, at 282; C. ROBERTSON, BREAKUP, *supra* note 4, at 272; J. WHITWORTH, *supra* note 4, at 161. Nothing ever came of the proposal discussed at the Syracuse conference that the disorderly conduct statute be amended to include persons living in adultery or concupiscence. *See* Am. Socialist, Feb. 20, 1879, at 62. *See also* Am. Socialist, Feb. 27, 1879, at [65] excerpting an article which appeared in *Nation* earlier in February 1879, at 128.

105. Am. Socialist, Feb. 20, 1879, at 59. *See also* J. WHITWORTH, *supra* note 4, at 157-58.

tected Oneida from having outsiders analogize its form of domestic arrangement to Mormon polygamy. A nineteenth-century work on Utah, for example, classified fanatics as sensualists or ascetics, and then remarked, "Of the former class are the Mormons, Noyesites of Oneida, the Antinomians[106] and the followers of St. John of Leyden . . . ."[107]

The link between Oneida and the Mormons had been made and denied from the very earliest days of the Community's history. The Perfectionists had insisted as early as 1852 that Oneida's system was really the opposite of polygamy.[108] Much later, the differences were spelled out in detail:

> The Mormons are supposed to be defiant of civil authority; the Oneida Community claim to be its peaceable subjects.
>
> The Mormons have their drilled soldiers; the Oneida Community are non-resistants.
>
> The Mormons send out evangelists and compass sea and land for proselytes; the Oneida Community use no such means to increase their numbers.
>
> The Mormons establish themselves in places remote from the centers of civilization; the Oneida Community seek those centers, and shun the wilderness and the desert.
>
> Mormonism is supposed to degrade woman; Oneida Communism elevates and ennobles her.
>
> The Mormons insist that every man has a right to as many wives as he can win and support; the Oneida Community insist that, in the highest form of society, rights in the sense of ownership and social bondage do not exist.
>
> The Mormons are supposed to recruit their numbers largely from the lower classes; the Oneida Community claim to represent the best classes in the churches and society.

---

106. Perry Miller provides a useful formulation of the substance of the antinomian concern. "If the elect are joined to Christ so that they move not of themselves but by the spirit within them, and if they are sure of their vocation, why need anyone study the commandments or fear condemnation for his sins?" P. MILLER, THE NEW ENGLAND MIND: THE SEVENTEENTH CENTURY 369 (Beacon ed. 1961). *See also Antinomianism*, 1 ENCYCLOPEDIA OF RELIGION AND ETHICS 581 (J. Hastings ed. 1908).

107. J. BEADLE, LIFE IN UTAH 333 (1870). On John of Leyden, the sixteenth-century radical Anabaptist, see note 120 *infra* and accompanying text.

108. Circular, Feb. 22, 1852, *quoted in* C. ROBERTSON, AUTOBIOGRAPHY, *supra* note 4, at 273.

> Mormonism is based on a new revelation, and has a new Bible; the Oneida Communists have no new Bible, and base their system on the teachings and examples of Christ and his Apostles.[109]

Nevertheless, the Oneida propagandists failed, and Mormonism and complex marriage continued to be discussed together. Professor Mears had the connection clearly in mind[110] when he commented that the Oneida Community was smaller than the Mormon settlement, but, if on the scale of Utah "would fill the public eye and create more profound and widespread indignation than Utah has ever done."[111] In the *Reynolds* decision itself, Chief Justice Waite may have associated polygamy and complex marriage, for the reference in his opinion to "an exceptional colony of polygamists under an exceptional leadership" is arguably an allusion to Oneida and John Humphrey Noyes.[112]

On August 26, 1879, soon after the *Reynolds* decision, the Oneida Community voted to give up complex marriage.[113] The

---

109. Am. Socialist, Mar. 13, 1879, at 84. The caution of the Perfectionists toward the degradation issue should be noted.

110. Rev. Mears wrote, "If polygamy is a great evil and immorality, the organized concubinage of the Oneida Community is still greater." The Independent, Apr. 10, 1879, at 1. Rev. Mears' article opens with a reference to the *Reynolds* case.

111. *Id.*

112. 98 U.S. at 166. The full text of the quotation reads:

> An exceptional colony of polygamists under an exceptional leadership may sometimes exist for a time without appearing to disturb the social condition of the people who surround it; but there cannot be a doubt that, unless restricted by some form of constitution, it is within the legitimate scope of the power of every civil government to determine whether polygamy or monogamy shall be the law of social life under its dominion.

See T. CURTIS, *supra* note 5, at 32, suggesting that the language referred to the Mormons themselves. This construction of Chief Justice Waite's words does not seem consonant with the concern over the political power of the Mormons. It is possible that Chief Justice Waite knew of Oneida through private as well as public channels. John Humphrey Noyes was a cousin of President Rutherford B. Hayes. R. PARKER, *supra* note 4, at 10; Am. Socialist, Feb. 6, 1879, at 42. *See also* C. MAGRATH, *supra* note 54, at 307, referring to the friendship between Chief Justice Waite and Rutherford B. Hayes in the years 1877 to 1881.

113. In September 1879, shortly after the Oneida Community abandoned complex marriage, there was a comment on the matter in the *Woman's Journal*. Lucy Stone wrote, "It is understood that it is not altogether outside pressure which has brought about this result. But when there has been a real wedded love among the members they naturally desired to be protected in their affection." Woman's J., Sept. 6, 1879, at 284. But while some at Oneida may have actively supported monogamist principles, the origin of the internal factionalism may have been elsewhere:

> The point of contention which brought into being two opposing parties was the

Community faced many difficulties, including internal factionalism, and the decision to abandon complex marriage had multiple causes. Still, at least one of these causes clearly was external.[114] A spokesman for the Perfectionists indicated that, in his opinion, the widespread tendency, "wholly without sense or justice," to link complex marriage and polygamy, contributed to their decision. The results of the *Reynolds* case had hastened the Community's action.[115] While the Perfectionists denied similarity between Perfectionism and Mormonism, they could not "be blind to the lessons which the Mormon conflict with the law affords."[116] In the future, Oneida would consist of the celibate and the monogamously married. This decision meant the end of Utopian Oneida. The structure of Oneida Community organization thereafter was fundamentally changed, and soon after, the former community became a joint stock company.[117]

The effect of the *Reynolds* decision on the Mormons had been to transform the antipolygamy campaign into a constitutionally legitimate rule of law. For Oneida, *Reynolds* was only one factor among others leading to the breakup of the Community.[118] Most significantly, *Reynolds* reinforced the general proposition that monogamy was the only acceptable form of marriage in America. In 1867 an English writer had observed that "Oneida Creek and Salt Lake City—communities founded by Vermont men—are practical replies to the one great question of our day—What shall be done to reform the abuses

---

> question of the initiation of virgins into the sexual realities of Community life. The initiation of young men posed no problem: sexual relations began routinely for them at puberty. The difficulty arose rather in connection with the young girls. By common consent Noyes had always assumed the responsibility for introducing them to sexual experience. . . . As he grew older, Noyes sometimes delegated the role of "first husband" to one of the several central men. Early in 1879, two of them questioned Noyes's right to decide who was to introduce the young women of the Community to sexual experience.

M. CARDEN, *supra* note 4, at 98-99.

114. The Perfectionists undertook their action "not as renouncing belief in the principles and prospective finality of that institution" but rather "in deference to the public sentiment which is evidently rising against it." Am. Socialist, Aug. 28, 1879, at 276.

115. The stubbornness "of the Mormons in Utah had arrayed the whole power of the law against them." Am. Socialist, Sept. 4, 1879, at 283.

116. *Id.*

117. For an examination of the post-Utopian Oneida, see M. CARDEN, *supra* note 4, at 113-212. "Without faith in Noyes's divine sanction, without a united belief in Perfectionism, and without complex marriage, Oneida lost its justification for existence." *Id.* at 104.

118. This may, however, be the factor imperfectly remembered in those accounts which suggest that Oneida was a victim of hostile state action. *See, e.g.*, W. MCWILLIAMS, THE IDEA OF FRATERNITY IN AMERICA 243 (1973).

of our social and domestic life?"[119] After *Reynolds*, those particular answers were unavailable. The elimination of the Perfectionist and Mormon alternatives strengthened conventional monogamy.

THE *REYNOLDS* CASE: ANOTHER PERSPECTIVE

There may be no certain or logical relation between political equality and any particular form of marriage. While some polygamous arrangements have been based on the subjugation of women,[120] it is possible to imagine forms of polygamy in which women would not be degraded. Thus, in 1903 the English writer, Edward Carpenter, suggested that polygamy arising in a society in which women were free and independent "in their relations to men would be completely different in character from the old-world polygamy, and would cease to act as a degrading influence on women."[121]

However, in any particular society at a given moment the relationship between the forms of marriage and the status of women is real. In America in the late nineteenth century several marriage patterns existed side by side and the variations on monogamy were well known. Were women better off in these institutions than in conventional monogamy? Did these institutions suggest possibilities for future family structures? The contemporary suffrage movement could not afford to ignore issues so central to women's rights in American society.[122]

The members of the suffrage movement could easily have viewed Chief Justice Waite's decision in *Reynolds* as another element in the pattern established by prior decisions.[123] The woman's suffrage

---

119. 2 W. DIXON, NEW AMERICA 54 (1867).

120. Polygamy did not, for example, operate in favor of women's rights in The New Jerusalem of John of Leyden. *See* N. COHN, THE PURSUIT OF THE MILLENNIUM 269-70 (rev. ed. 1970).

121. E. CARPENTER, LOVE'S COMING OF AGE 117 (1903), *quoted in* W. O'NEILL, DIVORCE IN THE PROGRESSIVE ERA 118 (1973).

122. Such questions are still discussed. *See* text note on *Communes, Group Marriage and Other Variant Family Styles* in K. DAVIDSON, R. GINSBURG, & H. KAY, SEX-BASED DISCRIMINATION 209 (1974), exploring an application of Wisconsin v. Yoder, 406 U.S. 205 (1972) to this problem. Kurland has noted that *Yoder* casts "deep shadows" on Reynolds v. United States. Kurland, *The Supreme Court, Compulsory Education, and the First Amendment's Religion Clauses*, 75 W. VA. L. REV. 213, 225 (1973). But *Reynolds* remains the basic statement on variant forms of marriage. *See also* Wilkinson & White, *Constitutional Protection for Personal Lifestyles*, 62 CORNELL L. REV. 563, 572-73 (1977).

123. In the decade preceding the *Reynolds* decision the United States Supreme Court had denied constitutional protection to women's right to practice law, Bradwell v. Illinois, 83 U.S. (16 Wall.) 130 (1872), and to women's right to vote, Minor v. Happer-

movement could not have been surprised that the Justices now condemned Mormon polygamy.[124] The behavior of the Supreme Court had been consistent with the most conservative and paternalistic of contemporary theories of women's rights. In his polygamy decision, Chief Justice Waite had failed to deal with woman suffrage in Utah,[125] a question arguably relevant to the link between polygamy and stationary despotism.

On a critical point Chief Justice Waite cited Professor Francis Lieber, whose anti-Mormon[126] and antisuffrage views rested on the linked propositions that monogamous marriage was the fundamental basis of civilized society and that a primarily domestic role for women was an essential component of monogamous marriage. This philosophy, applied to Utah after 1870 when women were allowed to vote, would result in condemnation of Mormon institutions on separate though related grounds. Polygamy and woman suffrage both were threats to the American home. From this perspective, woman suffrage in Utah would compound rather than cure the defects of Mormon polygamy. *Reynolds* was thus authored by a court whose orientation on the woman question would have made it difficult for even the most conservative and antipolygamy elements of the woman's movement to offer unrestrained endorsement of its decision.

---

sett, 88 U.S. (21 Wall.) 162 (1874). Years later, the NWSA was to recall by resolution (1889) the antifeminism of one judge, Ward Hunt, for his "infamous decision" in the voting trial of Susan B. Anthony. United States v. Anthony, 24 F. Cas. 829 (C.C.N.D.N.Y. 1873); 4 THE HISTORY OF WOMAN SUFFRAGE 155-56 (S. Anthony & I. Harper eds. 1902) [hereinafter cited as 4 HWS].

124. Reynolds v. United States, 98 U.S. 145 (1878).

125. Without suggesting the logical necessity of such a discussion, we may note that a treatment of the suffrage-polygamy issue might have taken a number of forms. The point might have been made, following Lieber, that polygamy in general is bad for women and for society, and so is woman suffrage; or that polygamy in general is bad, suffrage for women in general is good, but the situation of women in Mormon polygamy is so bad that suffrage in Utah is meaningless; or that polygamy in Utah is so bad that although suffrage in Utah is good, and women might have chosen their situation, the evils of polygamy are so great that women cannot be allowed to choose it. It is unlikely that the Court would have been able to agree on any approach to the suffrage question, and it is not impossible that this is one reason why the question was not discussed. On Chief Justice Waite's own position it should be noted that he, along with his predecessor, Chief Justice Chase, headed a list of "Eminent Advocates of Woman Suffrage" in *The History of Woman Suffrage*. 4 HWS, *supra* note 123, at 1076. *See also* C. MAGRATH, *supra* note 54, at 119 (1963). *See generally* note 54 *supra*. *Compare* 3 HWS, *supra* note 47, at 505.

126. Lieber described Mormonism as characterized by "vulgarity," "cheating," "jugglery," "knavery," "foulness," and as bearing "poisonous fruits." [Lieber], *The Mormons*, *supra* note 36, at 233.

The NWSA (Stanton/Anthony group) met in Washington on January 9 and 10, 1879, a few days after the *Reynolds* decision came down. This meeting would have provided the occasion for official applause for the *Reynolds* decision, if the suffragists had believed that approval was in order. But there was no public applause.[127] The Supreme Court's blow to Mormon polygamy, its liberation of the Mormon women of Utah from the yoke of barbarism[128] was not mentioned in the resolutions of the meeting. The NWSA meeting passed a resolution condemning the judges for denying Belva Lockwood admission to the Supreme Court Bar,[129] and then resolved:

> WHEREAS, The general government has refused to exercise federal power to protect women in their right to vote in the various States and territories; therefore,
>
> *Resolved*, That it should forbear to exercise federal power to disfranchise the women of Utah, who have had a more just and liberal spirit shown them by Mormon men than Gentile women in the States have yet perceived in their rulers.[130]

---

127. The point is not that the resolutions were a direct response to the *Reynolds* decision (the identical resolutions might well have been adopted if the decision had not come down at all), but that there is no resolution approving the decision. This is not likely to be a result of ignorance concerning the Court's decision or a lack of concern with the Court's activities. The suffrage movement was manifestly interested in decisions of the Court affecting women's rights. *See, e.g.*, the resolution on Minor v. Happersett, 88 U.S. (21 Wall.) 162 (1874), and discussions of the *Minor* decision in 2 HWS, *supra* note 47, at 584.

128. The image of Mormon women as bending under the yoke of polygamy was protested by George Tichnor Curtis when he argued on behalf of the Mormons before the Supreme Court. *See* argument in Snow v. United States, 118 U.S. 346 (1886), *reprinted in* G. CURTIS, A PLEA FOR RELIGIOUS LIBERTY 16 (1886).

129. 3 HWS, *supra* note 47, at 128, which introduces the resolutions of the meeting of 1879 by saying that "the resolutions give an idea of the status of the question, and the wide range of discussion covered by the speakers . . . ." *Id*. The *Woman's Exponent* reports the resolutions as adopted. Woman's Exponent, Feb. 15, 1879, at 196. The *Woman's Journal* says: "In the final action on the resolutions . . . [t]he eighth resolution, in opposition to the attempt to take from the women of Utah the elective franchise, was laid on the table for discussion. . . . The tenth, in relation to the Supreme Court of the United States, was adopted. . . ." Woman's J., Jan. 25, 1879, at 29.

130. 3 HWS, *supra* note 47, at 128. The motivation of the Mormons in granting woman suffrage has been variously described. One commentator notes, for example:

> To the Mormons . . . there could be no better way of proving that their system of polygamy was not degrading to women . . . than to declare woman suffrage in Utah, at the very time when Negro suffrage . . . was being offered to the former slaves to protect them from their former masters. . . . [Woman suffrage] would appear to have been a calculated move on the part of the Mormon hierarchy to forestall federal legislation on polygamy.

This resolution, as much as the presence of Mormon women on their platform,[131] reflected the solution of the Stanton/Anthony group to the problem of woman suffrage in a polygamous society.[132] They would support Utah on the question of suffrage, and maintain silence on "religious" questions.[133] In the case of Utah, support of suffrage meant opposition to disenfranchisement, for while it had originally been thought that the franchise for women in Utah might discourage polygamy,[134] it was now said that women would have to be disen-

---

A. GRIMES, THE PURITAN ETHIC AND WOMAN SUFFRAGE 33 (1967). Another historian has said:

> Mormon Utah was at that time threatened by the rapid settlement of the area by "gentiles"—non-Mormons—who came in the wake of the transcontinental railroad. In reaction to the pronounced distaste of the Federal Government and the rest of the nation for the Mormon practice of polygamy, the Utah government enacted woman suffrage to prove that Mormon women preferred polygamy and would vote to uphold it. This they did, and as expected, provided a counterbalance in voting strength to the—largely unmarried—non-Mormon population.

G. LERNER, THE WOMAN IN AMERICAN HISTORY 139 (1971). *But see* Alexander, *supra* note 3, at 29-30 (arguing that the Mormons were simply ahead of the rest of the nation in progressive spirit).

131. The Mormon women were Emmeline B. Wells, Editor of the *Woman's Exponent*, and Zina Young Williams. Mrs. Wells was a plural wife; she was born and raised in Massachusetts and had converted to the Mormon faith in 1842. *See* biographical entry in 3 NOTABLE AMERICAN WOMEN 561-62 (1971). As to Mrs. Williams, the *Washington Post* reports:

> A collection was taken, and the appearance of the baskets caused rather an energetic exodus on the part of the audience. But when it was announced that Mrs. Williams, of Utah, would speak, the popular curiosity concerning Mormon women arrested them, and when it was further stated that she was the fourth daughter of Brigham Young, they sat down. . . .

Wash. Post, Jan. 11, 1879, at 1, col. 3. The paper's account of this session was headed *The Females Subside*.

132. It was a serious problem, for involved was the issue of the meaning of the vote for the Mormon women, whether it was free, or controlled, and whether this mattered. In 1871, a history of the suffrage movement had concluded that woman suffrage was of less importance in Utah than in Wyoming because Utah's women were dominated by the church hierarchy. P. DAVIS, note 70, at 70. The *Woman's Journal* viewed the vote in Utah as problematic, pointing out that Brigham Young was "utterly opposed to Woman Suffrage." Woman's J., Feb. 24, 1872, at 61. The Stanton/Anthony group seems not to have addressed the question directly, apparently preferring not to go behind the fact of woman suffrage.

T. W. Curtis suggested at the time that, outside the suffrage movement, the linkage between polygamy and suffrage was largely ignored because suffrage did not fit with widely held views of polygamy. T. CURTIS, *supra* note 5, at 32.

133. One speaker commented that the NWSA had "nothing to do with the religious rights of women in Utah except insofar as they intermingle with and touch woman's political rights." Mrs. Gage, *quoted in* Women's Exponent, June 1, 1879, at 253.

134. This proposal was made in N.Y. Times, Dec. 17, 1867, at 4, col. 5. *See* Larson, *supra* note 3, at 9. Senator Julian introduced legislation under the title "A Bill to Dis-

franchised as part of the battle against polygamy.[135] The women of the Stanton/Anthony group believed that they could support woman suffrage in Utah[136] without taking a public stand on polygamy.[137]

But while the NWSA officially tried to make plain that they did not associate with the Mormons on any issues other than the suffrage question, these disavowals appeared inadequate to some in the suffrage movement. The *Woman's Journal* published a letter on the issue of Mormon women at the NWSA's convention under the title *Polygamy Degrades Womanhood.*[138] The attitude of the Stone/

---

courage Polygamy in Utah," to give the vote to the women of Utah in 1869. Alexander, *supra* note 3, at 24.

135. Disenfranchisement came with the Edmunds-Tucker Act of 1887, *supra* note 85 and accompanying text.

136. The response of the woman suffrage movement to the campaign for disenfranchisement in Utah deserves detailed study. This preliminary observation may be made, however: the evidence does not point in one direction, and observers in the nineteenth century drew somewhat different conclusions from the evidence they used. Thus, contemporary accounts may be used to support the proposition that the nineteenth-century woman suffrage movement worked to save the franchise for Utah's women. "The advocates of the rights of all women stood up boldly for those of Utah, notwithstanding the scoffs and obloquy cast upon them." 4 HWS, *supra* note 123, at 939. *See also* the *Anti-Polygamy Standard* (Salt Lake City) referring to "[o]ur Eastern friends, whose love for female suffrage exceeds their hatred of polygamy." These suffragists "allow their zeal to outrun their reason, when they insist that woman suffrage must be sustained here at all hazards." Anti-Polygamy Standard, Oct. 1882, at 1, col. 1. But T. W. Curtis suggested that the suffrage movement had not done well by the women of Utah. T. CURTIS, *supra* note 5, at 33. One suffrage woman, Lily Devereux-Blake, is quoted as having declared herself "reconciled" to the disenfranchisement, "because of the anomalous condition of local affairs." Daily Tribune, Aug. 11, 1888, *quoted in* R. DWYER, THE GENTILE COMES TO UTAH 202 (1941). A modern historian has concluded that the eastern suffragettes may have even joined other antipolygamy groups to work for disenfranchisement. T. O'DEA, *supra* note 15, at 249.

An inquiry into this question would have to take into account such psychological factors as the desire of Mormon women to believe that they had not been abandoned, and the desire of the radical feminists to believe that they had not betrayed their allies. One would also have to note the increasingly broadened base of the suffrage movement in 1887. When the NWSA protested the disenfranchisement in Utah it also noted as a hopeful sign of the times the endorsement of woman suffrage by the Knights of Labor and by the National Woman's Temperance Union. 4 HWS, *supra* note 123, at 122-23.

137. Privately, however, they might freely express themselves on the question. *See* note 78 *supra*.

138. Woman's J., Mar. 29, 1879, at 97. Amanda Dickinson of St. Louis conceded that "none who knew them would willingly suppose that the leaders of the recent convention of the National Woman Suffrage Association in Washington meant to endorse polygamy . . . ." Still "[s]uffragists everywhere must deeply regret any appearance of affiliation between the advocates of equal rights for Woman and those who advocate or apologize for a system which plunges her into the lowest depths of degradation. . . ." The movement could welcome people of all creeds and conditions of life and could even, "to a certain extent cooperate with free-lovers and polygamists for a good end, as,

Blackwell group prompted Mrs. Stanton to defend the NWSA's position on Utah representatives at the Washington meeting. In a letter quoted in the Mormon *Women's Exponent*, Mrs. Stanton pointed out that if the Mormon Congressman, George Q. Cannon,[139] could sit in the Congress of the United States without compromising the Congress on the question of polygamy, Mormon women could sit on the platform of the NWSA "without making us responsible for their religious faith."[140] From Omaha, on April 5, 1879, Mrs. Stanton wrote to Susan B. Anthony, referring again to Congressman Cannon, and suggesting that if "Congress can stand Cannon with four wives, we might stand the women with only the fourth part of a husband!"[141] Furthermore, she said, "When Congress proposes to disfranchise the women of a Territory, where should they go to plead their case but to the National Woman Suffrage Association?"[142]

A report of the January, 1879, NWSA program noted that Mrs. Stanton introduced "Mrs. Wells of Utah, wife of General Wells, the Mormon apostle and polygamist."[143] Mrs. Wells told the meeting that Congress should preserve the franchise held by the women of the territory.[144] Then Susan B. Anthony said that "disfranchisement [sic] is always political degradation to any class affected by it—disfranchisement [sic] and degradation being in politics synonymous terms . . . ."[145] The threatening perception of the NWSA leaders was this: if there was degradation in polygamy with woman suffrage, there was degradation in monogamy without it.

The suffrage movement as a whole may have approved, in private, the result in *Reynolds*, a case in which "polygamy, not Rey-

---

in this free country political parties and public conveyances are open to all." But the movement "must not make itself responsible for the various opinions and practices of its adherents." We can pity and try to understand and sympathize with our fanatical sisters among the Mormons, she concluded, "just as we do with the Hindoo widows who throw themselves on the funeral piles of their husband," but "the spectacle of women in this age and country accepting and defending polygamy is a phenomenon we are utterly unable to comprehend." *Id.*

139. On George Cannon, see 3 DICTIONARY OF AMERICAN BIOGRAPHY 474 (1929). Cannon served in Congress for 10 years. The operation of the Edmunds Act in 1882 caused his retirement by a vote of the House, 123 to 79. *Id.*

140. Elizabeth Cady Stanton, *quoted in* Woman's Exponent, May 15, 1879, at 240.

141. 2 E. STANTON, LETTERS 160 (T. Stanton & H. Blatch eds. 1922).

142. *Id.*

143. Woman's J., Jan. 25, 1879, at 29.

144. *Id.*

145. *Id.* The account of the session in Wash. Post, Jan. 10, 1879, at 1, col. 2, sharpens the Anthony comment: "[d]isfranchisement and degradation [are] synonymous terms."

nolds, . . . [was] on trial."[146] Members of this group may have approved of Oneida's decision to give up complex marriage for similar reasons. Nevertheless, even the most strongly antipolygamy factions of the suffrage movement must have felt ambivalent about a decision in support of monogamy by a court which had ruled against women's political rights.

This ambivalence is illustrated in the *Woman's Journal*. The rhetoric in one issue shows the deep antipolygamy feeling in the Stone/Blackwell group. Responding to an attempt to obtain a presidential pardon for Reynolds, and to Rutherford Hayes' refusal to grant it, the *Woman's Journal* said that if President Hayes would suppress this "relic of barbarism" he would "merit and receive the thanks of universal womanhood" and his name would go down in history with Lincoln's.[147] And again: "All honor to President Hayes! If he succeeds in extirpating this social cancer of polygamy, his name will be remembered in history as "[t]he friend of women."[148] But of the *Reynolds* decision itself, the *Woman's Journal* said very little. Hayes, they seemed to be saying, might be remembered as the friend of women. Suffragists could not be sure about the Court, no matter how strongly Chief Justice Waite denounced polygamy.

Elizabeth Cady Stanton years later addressed her diary in terms that suggest that the ambiguities of the polygamy struggle may never have been forgotten by the generation of feminists who witnessed it. "I still believe in Congress compelling every state to establish within its borders a true republican form of government," she said. "If Congress can forbid polygamy under the national flag, it can forbid disfranchisement."[149]

146. Woman's J., June 21, 1879, at 196.

147. *Id.*

148. *Id.* In private, Hayes expressed his approval of woman suffrage. 4 HWS *supra* note 123, at 1075. *But see* Resolution of January 9-10, 1879, on Hayes' public neglect of the suffrage issue in a presidential message in which "he makes a truly paternal review of the interests of this republic . . . yet forgets to mention twenty million women robbed of their social, civil and political rights." 3 HWS, *supra* note 47, at 128.

149. Aug. 1, 1892, diary entry of Elizabeth Cady Stanton. 2 E. STANTON, *supra* note 141, at 287. It may be noted that *Reynolds* involved a federal antipolygamy act operative in the territories. The question of whether a state might recognize polygamy was therefore technically left open. Lieber's proposed antibigamy amendment to the federal Constitution was not adopted—although federal protection of woman suffrage through a constitutional amendment did ultimately come about—and thus it remains possible to raise the issue of the status of a state law permitting polygamous marriages. *See* H. KRAUSE, FAMILY LAW 4 (1976).

CONCLUSION

The *Reynolds* case is cited in several fields of law. In the field of church and state, the "Supreme Court's concern with the religion clauses of the first amendment begins, for all practical purposes, with the case of *Reynolds v. United States*, where the Court first adopted the Jeffersonian statement that the amendment erected 'a wall of separation between church and State.' "[150] The concepts explored in *Reynolds* "were to cast the molds for subsequent interpretation of religious freedom."[151] In the area of private international law, *Reynolds* is relevant to discussions of *Hyde v. Hyde*, in which an English court refused to take jurisdiction of an action for divorce based on an 1853 Mormon marriage, the court concluding that the Mormon marriage (assumed to be legal in Utah) was not a marriage within the meaning of the English statute.[152] In the history of American federalism, the *Reynolds* case stands for the proposition that while states regulate their own domestic affairs, Congress has the power to regulate marriage in the territories.[153] *Reynolds* can be treated in relation to a general discussion of the nature of marriage and the role of the state in defining marriage as a civil status,[154] and

---

150. P. KURLAND, RELIGION AND THE LAW 21 (1962).

151. Davis, *Impact*, *supra* note 2, at 287.

152. Hyde v. Hyde, L.R.I.P. & D. 130 (1866) discussed marriage as "the voluntary union for life of one man and one woman, to the exclusion of all others." *Id.* at 133. "[T]he basic precept of *Hyde v. Hyde* has not been under direct attack since the unsuccessful attempt at polygamy in the United States in the late Nineteenth Century." Zabel, Hyde v. Hyde, *A Comparative Study of the Law of Marriage in the Sudan and Nigeria* (pt. 1), 1969 UTAH L. REV. 22.

Referring to the proof in *Hyde* that the "law of Utah, equally with the opinions and practices of the Mormon Church, sustained polygamy," J. P. Bishop added, "[b]ut however the law was then, it is not so now," citing the Morrill Act and *Reynolds*. 1 J. BISHOP, NEW COMMENTARIES ON MARRIAGE, DIVORCE, AND SEPARATION 128 (1891). A summary of *Hyde* as a "curious case" involving the validity of a Mormon marriage appears in an editor's footnote in 2 J. KENT, COMMENTARIES, *supra* note 26, at 94 n.1.

As to the recognition of Indian polygamous marriages, see Bartholomew, *Recognition of Polygamous Marriages in America*, 13 INT'L & COMP. L.Q. 1022, 1067-68 (1964). Indian polygamy provided no precedent for Mormon polygamy, perhaps in part for the reason suggested by John Stuart Mill. Polygamy, he said, "though permitted to Mohammedans, and Hindus, and Chinese, seems to excite unquenchable animosity when practised by persons who speak English and profess to be a kind of Christians." J. MILL, ON LIBERTY 112 (C. Shields ed. 1956).

153. 1 J. BISHOP, NEW COMMENTARIES, *supra* note 152, at 70-71.

154. *See, e.g.*, Drinan, *The Loving Decision and the Freedom to Marry*, 29 OHIO ST. L.J. 358, 360-61 (1968).

can, finally, be cited in the field of evidence.[155]

The case is also significant in social and historical terms. Interwoven with the story of the *Reynolds* case are the histories of the Mormons, the Utopian Community at Oneida, and the woman suffrage movement. The "triumph for believers in monogamy"[156] which the *Reynolds* case represented when seen in context was a vindication of a marital institution committed to a primarily domestic and nonpolitical role for women. Viewed in this light, the decision is of a piece with other pronouncements of the late nineteenth-century Supreme Court tending to protect a traditional conception of the monogamous home. The *Reynolds* case effectively ruled out experimentation with radically restructured marital institutions. The case helped define the direction which future reforms would take by establishing that nonmonogamous arrangements, even on a limited scale, were entirely unacceptable. For better or worse, options were available before *Reynolds* which were not available afterwards.[157]

---

155. "If, on the second trial of a cause, it is found that the accused kept away a witness, his evidence given on the first trial may be proved by the prosecution" (citing *Reynolds*). T. COOLEY, PRINCIPLES OF CONSTITUTIONAL LAW 295 n.2 (1880). *See also* MCCORMICK'S HANDBOOK OF THE LAW OF EVIDENCE 609 (E. Cleary 2d ed. 1972). In the *Reynolds* case, Mr. Justice Field concurred on the several points decided except one which related to the "admission of the testimony [of a plural wife] given on a former trial upon a different indictment." 98 U.S. at 168.

156. Wash. Post, Jan. 7, 1879, at 1, col. 1.

157. There has been no attempt here to connect the issues raised to the question of property, despite the view held, for example, by Francis Lieber, that "at all times property and marriage have stood or fallen together." [Lieber], *The Mormons*, *supra* note 36, at 234 n.†. In addition, there has been no effort to assess the value of any of the domestic institutions discussed.

WILLIAM L. O'NEILL
University of Colorado

Divorce in the Progressive Era

DURING THE PROGRESSIVE YEARS THE DIVORCE RATE, WHICH HAD BEEN RISING steadily since the Civil War, attained critical dimensions. Consequently, Americans of this period took a graver view of the problem than any subsequent generation. Their varied responses proved to be decisive as far as the future of divorce itself was concerned, and they illuminate aspects of the Progressive Era which have received little attention from historians.

The precipitate growth of the divorce rate can be easily demonstrated. In 1880 there was one divorce for every twenty-one marriages; in 1900 there was one divorce for every twelve marriages; in 1909 the ratio dropped to one in ten, and by 1916 it stood at one in nine.[1] Naturally this dramatic increase in the divorce rate stimulated public alarm.

In 1881 the New England Divorce Reform League was established to conduct research on family problems, educate the public and lobby for more effective legislative curbs on divorce.[2] Under the leadership of Samuel Dike, a Congregational minister, the league enjoyed a long and useful life, but Dike's reluctance to advance legislative solutions to the divorce problem failed to deter others from resorting to politics.

Efforts to arrest the spread of divorce by legal means took two forms. State campaigns were waged to amend local divorce laws, and repeated attempts were made to achieve uniform marriage and divorce laws either through a constitutional amendment or through the voluntary enactment of uniform codes by the several states.[3] Typical of the many local fights

1 The definitive statistical study is Paul H. Jacobson, *American Marriage and Divorce* (New York, 1959). Two great government reports contain the raw materials—they are U. S. Bureau of Labor, *Marriage and Divorce 1867-1887* (1889), and the later more comprehensive U. S. Bureau of the Census, *Marriage and Divorce 1867-1906* (1909). Interesting contemporary analyses are contained in E. A. Ross, *Changing America* (New York, 1912) and William B. Bailey, *Modern Social Conditions* (New York, 1906).

2 Its origins are described in an untitled autobiographical manuscript by Samuel Warren Dike in the Dike Papers, Library of Congress.

3 The legal and political history of divorce is described very fully in Nelson Manfred Blake, *The Road to Reno* (New York, 1962).

to alter state divorce laws was the successful battle in 1893 to end South Dakota's status as a divorce colony. After their admission to the Union in 1889 North and South Dakota retained Dakota Territory's generous ninety-day residence requirement. Sioux City, largest and most accessible town in the two states, soon developed a substantial divorce trade and gained national fame as a divorce colony. The resulting notoriety provoked local resentment which was mobilized by the return from Japan of the popular Episcopal Bishop William Hobart Hare, who in 1893 led Protestants, Catholics and Populists in an attack on the ninety-day residence requirement. The state legislature was successfully petitioned to extend the residence requirement to six months and the migratory divorce trade was diverted to North Dakota.[4]

The South Dakota campaign conformed to what was already an established pattern. It was led by conservative clergymen, supported by women's groups, and met little apparent opposition. Although these local campaigns did not succeed anywhere in abolishing divorce, they were part of a widespread tendency toward stricter divorce legislation.[5] When such local crusades failed, it was usually because of public apathy, sometimes coupled with undercover resistance from commercial and legal interests which profited from the divorce trade.

Serious attempts to secure uniform marriage and divorce legislation through a constitutional amendment began in 1892 when James Kyle, the Populist Senator from South Dakota, introduced a joint resolution which read in full: "The Congress shall have the exclusive power to regulate marriage and divorce in the several states, Territories, and the District of Columbia."[6] Senator Kyle's resolution died in committee as did all later resolutions, presumably because of a disinclination on the part of Congress to increase the power of the Federal government at the expense of the states.[7]

More popular, if equally unsuccessful, was the movement to secure voluntary uniformity through the drafting of model statutes which were to be enacted by the states. The most persistent of the organizations dedicated to this goal was the National Conference of Commissioners on

[4] See M. A. DeWolfe Howe, *The Life and Labors of Bishop Hare* (New York, 1912), *passim;* Blake, "Divorce in South Dakota," *Nation*, IX (January 26, 1893), 61.

[5] National League for the Preservation of the Family, *Some Fundamentals of the Divorce Question* (Boston, 1909). A pamphlet written by Samuel Dike and published by his organization, which had undergone two changes of name since its founding, deals with these changes at some length. They involved extending the time required to obtain divorces, and limiting the causes for which they could be granted.

[6] U. S. Congressional Record, 52 Cong., 1st Sess. (February 3, 1892), p. 791.

[7] See Senator Shortridge's candid remarks to this effect during hearings on a similar resolution years later. *Senate Judiciary Committee*, "Hearings on S. J. Res. 31" (November 1, 1921), *passim*.

Uniform State Laws, which met annually in connection with the American Bar Association. It was established by the Bar Association in 1889 to frame model codes on a wide range of subjects. The Commissioners were usually appointed by their state governors, and over the years drafted seven model statutes concerning marriage and divorce.[8] However, few of the states demonstrated an interest in these models, and by 1916 the Commissioners were forced to admit that their approach had been a failure.

If the experience of the National Conference of Commissioners on Uniform State Laws to 1906 had not been conclusive, the fate of the National Divorce Congress in that year was. A national meeting to draft uniform legislation had been talked about for years on the grounds that it would attract sufficient attention to succeed where the more diffident Commissioners had failed. In 1906 President Roosevelt was persuaded to request a new census study of marriage and divorce, and the interest aroused by this led Governor Pennypacker of Pennsylvania to call a national conference to draft model uniform legislation on these subjects. The Congress met twice, once in Washington to appoint committees, and again in Philadelphia to ratify the proposed statutes. The first meeting was attended by delegates from 42 of the 45 states and consisted largely of clergymen and lawyers, many of the latter having also been members of the NCCUSL. Despite the widespread approval which met their efforts, few states adopted their model statutes.[9]

The antidivorce forces were also active within the established Protestant churches. During the Progressive Era repeated efforts were made in almost all the great Protestant denominations to stiffen their positions on divorce. The Episcopal Church, traditionally more hostile to divorce than most Protestant bodies, was in the van of this movement, thanks principally to William Croswell Doane, Bishop of Albany, New York. Doane was perhaps the most vocal and consistent enemy of divorce in the whole country. He favored prohibiting divorce altogether, and his activities within the Episcopal Church were directed at the canon which allowed the innocent party in an adultery suit to remarry. This canon was only slightly less severe than the refusal of the Roman Catholic Church to allow any divorced person to remarry, but it seemed dangerously lax to Doane and he regularly introduced an amendment which would have denied the sacraments to all divorced persons without exception.

[8] "Secretary's Memorandum," *Proceedings of the 26th Annual Meeting of the NCCUSL* (1916).

[9] See Blake, 140-45, and *Proceedings of the Adjourned Meeting of the National Congress on Uniform Divorce Laws* (Harrisburg, Pa., 1907).

In 1898 the House of Bishops, usually more conservative than the lower House, which included laymen, at the policy-making Triennial Convention, rejected Doane's amendment 31 to 24.[10] In 1901 his amendment was defeated by a narrower margin, but in 1904 it passed the House of Bishops only to fail in the House of Deputies, whose members felt that it was too far removed from the spirit of the country.[11] Thereafter enthusiasm within the Episcopal church for the Doane amendment declined, and while it was re-introduced at later conventions, it failed to pass even in the House of Bishops. Similar efforts were made in the other Protestant denominations with what proved to be an equal lack of success.[12]

American attitudes toward marriage and divorce during the Progressive years must be seen in terms of the widespread fear of divorce demonstrated by these examples. It is not too much to say that there was a national crisis generated by divorce. It was a crisis to begin with because people believed it was. As Daniel Bell has demonstrated in his *The End of Ideology,* it is not necessary for activities seen to be antisocial actually to increase in order to create a crisis atmosphere—it is enough if people simply believe that such activities are increasing.[13]

An even better example perhaps was the white slave panic of 1912-13. If anything, prostitution was declining, but irrespective of the facts, widespread public alarm over this presumed social evil was triggered by local investigations and newspaper publicity.[14]

However, divorce actually was increasing by leaps and bounds. When one marriage in twelve ended in divorce, there were legitimate grounds for concern. These were crucial years for divorce, finally, because the Progressive period was the last time when public opinion could reasonably have been expected to support genuinely repressive action. With the 1920s and the advent of the revolution in morals the opportunity to abolish or seriously restrict divorce was lost forever. Some of the anti-divorce leaders sensed that time was running out for them, and this awareness gave their strictures an urgent tone which became more shrill with the years.

Although divorce had political, psychological and other dimensions,

10 "The Canon on Marriage and Divorce," *Public Opinion,* October 27, 1898.

11 "Remarriage After Divorce," *Outlook,* October 22, 1904.

12 The positions of the principal denominations on divorce and the efforts to change them are summarized in James P. Lichtenberger, *Divorce: A Study in Social Causation* (New York, 1909), chap. vii.

13 Daniel Bell, "The Myth of Crime Waves" (New York, 1961), pp. 151-74.

14 Roy Lubove, "The Progressives and the Prostitute," *The Historian,* XXIV (May 1962), 308-29.

the increase of divorce was usually seen as a moral and social problem.[15] It is difficult, if indeed not actually pointless, to try to determine which of these two aspects alarmed critics of divorce the most. The enemies of divorce invariably regarded it as both immoral and antisocial. Since most opponents of divorce were either clergymen or strongly religious people, it seems fair to assume that the moral side of the divorce question was what first engaged their attention, but having once declared divorce to be immoral, there is little more one can say in that direction, and most of the serious attacks on divorce emphasized its antisocial character.[16]

The attack on divorce hinged on the common belief that divorce destroyed the family, which was the foundation of society and civilization. Theodore Schmauk, editor of the *Lutheran Church Review*, President of the Lutheran General Council and a leading theologian, characterized the family as "the great and fundamental institution in social life." [17] *The Catholic World* in an attack on H. G. Wells' view of divorce felt that it had demolished his position when it observed that Wells failed to see that the family "was the cradle of civil society." [18] Lyman Abbott, an influential Progressive editor and associate of Theodore Roosevelt, once charged a prominent divorcee with being "the worst type of anarchist" because divorce, like anarchy, threatened to destroy society altogether.[19] President Roosevelt, in addressing Congress on the need for uniform legislation, described marriage as being "at the very foundation of our social organization. . . ." [20] Marriage and the family are, of course, quite different institutions, but the critics of divorce did not usually distinguish between them.

15 Generalizations of this sort which depend upon a close acquaintance with the popular literature are notoriously hard to document. My own conclusions are derived from an examination of almost everything dealing with marriage and divorce published either in book form or in more than thirty leading periodicals from 1889 through 1919. For details see my unpublished, "The Divorce Crisis of the Progressive Era" (Doctor's dissertation, Berkeley, Calif., 1963).

16 By dismissing the moral side of the opposition to divorce so casually I do not mean to imply that it was not important, but only that it was unremarkable and required no detailed analysis. Divorce was considered immoral because it was forbidden by the New Testament, and because it encouraged lust. Naturally the clergymen who opposed divorce supported themselves with Scriptural citations. One of the most elaborate efforts to relate divorce to licentiousness was Samuel Dike's first major address on the subject, reprinted in *Christ and Modern Thought: The Boston Monday Lectures 1880-81*, ed. Joseph Cook (Boston, 1882).

17 "The Right to Be Divorced," *Lutheran Church Review*, XXVIII (October 1909), 661.

18 W. E. Campbell, "Wells, the Family, and the Church," *Catholic World*, XCI (July 1910), 483.

19 "The Worst Anarchism," *Outlook*, August 11, 1906, p. 826.

20 Bureau of the Census, *Marriage and Divorce 1867-1906*, p. 4.

Felix Adler took this contention a step further when he insisted that divorce menaced "the physical and spiritual existence of the human race. . . ."[21] Adler was in some ways a surprising figure to find on this side of the divorce question. The founder of Ethical Culture and a leading advocate of liberal religion, he consistently attacked dogma and orthodoxy and supported a wide variety of social reforms.[22] He had earlier supported divorce, but by 1915 had changed his mind and accepted the point, usually advanced by the theologically orthodox, that divorce had to be suppressed as a matter of social survival. His conversion showed how this argument operated independently of its conservative religious base, and helps to explain why some enemies of divorce attached such importance to their campaign. One could hardly play for higher stakes.

A related theme which engaged the attention of divorce critics was the role of woman. It was generally believed that the family was woman's special responsibility and its protection her primary concern. Moreover women were thought to be more active than men in securing divorces (and they probably were since about two-thirds of all divorces were awarded to women). *The North American Review* reflected this point of view when it entitled one of its divorce symposiums, "Are Women to Blame?"[23] The *Review's* female panelists charged women with responsibility for the divorce rate, and accused them of being spoiled, romantic, impatient, jealous of men and usurpers of the male's time-honored functions. Many of these women were successful writers, as was Anna B. Rogers, a popular essayist, who repeated the same charges in her book, *Why American Marriages Fail,* nineteen years later.[24]

While the critics of divorce, especially the men, were inclined to argue that women were really happier when they stayed at home and held the family together, the more tough-minded accepted the fact that the woman's traditional role was often painful and difficult.[25] Few had a clearer picture of what was involved than the respected novelist Margaret Deland. Mrs. Deland was a warm supporter of many Progressive causes and a woman with courage enough to defend the rights of unwed mothers in Victorian Boston. But she believed that civilization "rests on the

21 *Marriage and Divorce* (New York, 1915), p. 15.

22 Henry Neumann, *Spokesmen for Ethical Religion* (Boston, 1951), deals with Adler's career at some length.

23 Rebecca Harding Davis, Rose Terry Cooke, Marion Harland, Catherine Owen, Amelia E. Barr, *North American Review*, CXLVIII (May 1889).

24 Boston, 1909.

25 Among the frequent male efforts to sentimentalize over the role and nature of woman were Lyman Abbott, *Christianity and Social Problems* (Boston, 1896), and Robert Lawton, *The Making of a Home* (Boston, 1914).

permanence of marriage."[26] For this reason women dared not turn to divorce, for it would mean the end of everything. "If we let the flame of idealism be quenched in the darkness of the senses," she cried, "our civilization must go upon the rocks."[27] Even adultery was no excuse for giving up the fight, she continued, because men were instinctively promiscuous and their lapses from grace had to be tolerated for the sake of the greater good.

Implicit in these arguments was the belief that the individual was less important than the group. Most opponents of divorce agreed that divorce was part of an unwholesome tendency toward a "dangerous individualism." Margaret Deland bewailed the absence of team-play among women and Professor Lawton called frankly for the "suppression of the individual in favor of the community."[28] Samuel Dike in his Cook Lecture attributed divorce to the rising tide of individualism menacing all progressive societies, while Felix Adler as early as 1890 was tracing the whole ugly business back to Rousseau's "false democratic ideals."[29] Although, as we shall see, most leading sociologists believed in divorce, Charles A. Ellwood did not. This future president of the American Sociological Society, despite his Progressive sympathies, also attributed divorce to excessive individualism.[30] Francis Peabody, an eminent theologian and student of the Higher Criticism, believed that the family's major enemies were scientific socialism and "the reactionary force of self-interested individualism. . . ."[31]

The opponents of divorce were more varied and had much more to say than I have been able to indicate, but the foregoing gives at least some idea of who they were and what they thought. The defenders of divorce, by way of contrast, were fewer in number and easier to locate. Opinion against divorce was so widespread and diffuse that it cannot be attributed to a handful of groups, but the sentiment favoring divorce was largely confined to sociologists, liberal clergymen and feminists. The defenders of divorce, like its enemies, viewed the problem primarily in moral and social terms. But unlike the critics of divorce, its supporters, who were with few exceptions liberals, were much more interested in the morality of divorce and more inclined to see its moral and social dimensions as too interrelated for separate discussion and analysis.

26 "The Change in the Feminine Ideal," *Atlantic Monthly*, CV (March 1910), 295; see also her interesting autobiography *Golden Yesterdays* (New York, 1940).

27 *Ibid.*, p. 297.

28 *The Making of a Home*, p. 594.

29 "The Ethics of Divorce," *Ethical Record*, II (April 1890), 207.

30 *Sociology and Modern Social Problems* (New York, 1913).

31 *Jesus Christ and the Social Question* (New York, 1903), p. 145.

The case for divorce gained initial momentum in the 1880s and 1890s when a trickle of protest against Victorian marriage began to make itself heard. The plays of Henrik Ibsen, especially *A Doll's House* (1879) and *Ghosts* (1881), were affecting English audiences in the late 1880s and American opinion somewhat later. By the 1890s a number of Englishmen were attacking marriage and the views of Mona Caird and Grant Allen became well known in the United States through their own writings, and through the publicity given their ideas by the American press. Mona Caird was a feminist whose essays appeared for the most part in high-quality limited circulation periodicals. Her most controversial proposal was an attempt to substitute for divorce short-term marriage contracts whose expiration would leave both parties free to separate or to negotiate a new contract.[32]

Grant Allen's best-known statement on the question was a sensational novel boosting feminism and free love entitled *The Woman Who Did*.[33] Allen was really calling for an end to marriage altogether, but his polemics against the institution supported divorce as much as free love. Within a few years the radical attack on marriage enlisted such big guns as H. G. Wells, who in a characteristically exuberant preview of the future in 1901 announced that monogamy was dissolving and sexual standards relaxing to the point where in a hundred years the present moral code "would remain nominally operative in sentiment and practice, while being practically disregarded. . . ."[34] Marriage was also under fire from the new moralists like the mystical Edward Carpenter, Havelock Ellis and his wife Edith, and the South African feminist Olive Schreiner, among others.[35]

The effect of this stream of marriage propaganda was to invigorate and inspire those Americans who believed in the right to divorce. Few respectable Americans were prepared to go as far as new moralists like Wells and Carpenter, but a substantial number of liberals were be-

32 *The Morality of Marriage and Other Essays on the Status and Destiny of Women*, London, 1897. A collection of articles which had previously appeared in the *North American Review*, the *Fortnightly Review*, the *Westminster Review* and the *Nineteenth Century*. Typical of the American press's treatment of her ideas are "The Millenium of Marriage—Mona Caird's Views," *Current Literature*, XVI (July 1894), reprinted from the *Boston Herald*. "The Practice of Marriage," *Current Literature*, XVIII (October 1895), reprinted from the *Saturday Review*.

33 Boston, 1895.

34 "Anticipations: An Experiment in Prophecy—II," *North American Review*, CLXXIII (July 1901), 73-74.

35 Carpenter, *Love's Coming of Age* (New York, 1911). *Little Essays of Love and Virtue* (New York, 1921), summarized the ideas Havelock Ellis had been advocating for years and the *New Horizon in Love and Life* (London, 1921), contains the thoughts of his wife, who died in 1916. Schreiner, *Woman and Labor* (New York, 1911).

ginning to feel that traditional marriage was needlessly tyrannical and repressive, that it discriminated against women, and that divorce was not only an escape hatch for abused women, but offered real opportunities for a reform of the whole marriage system. At the bottom of most, if not all, of this sentiment was the feminist impulse, for most divorce liberals were acutely conscious of the usefulness of divorce as an instrument for the emancipation of women.

Unlike the new moralists whose feminism was concerned with freeing women for a fuller sex life, the American feminist was inclined to defend divorce because it freed women from sex. Benjamin O. Flower, who edited the populistic *Arena*, called for easier divorce laws as a way of protecting women from the excessive sexual appetites of their husbands. He argued that the common prostitute was "far freer than the wife who is nightly the victim of the unholy passion of her master. . . ."[36] By 1914 this argument had become so familiar that it was thought fit for the respectable readers of the cautious *Good Housekeeping* magazine. In that year Jesse Lynch Williams, feminist and playwright, asked rhetorically, "is allowing herself to be owned body and soul by a man she loathes doing right?" before going on to delicately suggest "that seems rather like a dishonorable institution more ancient than marriage."[37]

Many feminists contended that not only did traditional marriage make women the sexual victims of their husbands, but it also exaggerated the importance of sex by denying women the chance to develop their other traits of character through work and education, and by forcing them to compete in the marriage market largely on the basis of their sexual attractions. The most desirable women had the best marital opportunities and so, through a kind of natural selection, sexuality prospered at the expense of other attributes. Divorce, along with expanded opportunities for education and employment, was a way of combatting this pernicious tendency.[38]

If the impulse to defend divorce came first from feminists who agreed with Elizabeth Cady Stanton on the need for a "larger freedom in the marriage relation," social scientists performed a crucial service in coping

[36] "Prostitution Within the Marriage Bond," *Arena*, XIII (June 1895), 68.

[37] "The New Marriage," *Good Housekeeping*, LII (February 1914), 184.

[38] Charlotte Perkins Gilman, *Women and Economics* (Boston, 1898), was an especially influential exposition of this point of view. For other information on this remarkable woman's life and work see Carl N. Degler's appreciative article, "Charlotte Perkins Gilman on the Theory and Practice of Feminism," *American Quarterly*, VIII (Spring 1956). See also Rheta Childe Dorr, *What Eight Million Women Want* (Boston, 1910), and C. Gasquoine Hartley, *The Truth About Women* (London, 1914).

with the public's fear of the social consequences of divorce.[39] The first man of stature to defend divorce was Carrol Wright, U.S. Commissioner of Labor Statistics and a self-trained social scientist, who at the national Unitarian convention in 1891 boldly declared himself for liberal divorce laws. A few years later he wrote:

> The pressure for divorce finds its impetus outside of laws, outside of our institutions, outside of our theology; it springs from the rebellion of the human heart against that slavery which binds in the cruelest bonds human beings who have by their haste, their want of wisdom, or the intervention of friends, missed the divine purpose as well as the civil purpose of marriage.[40]

But it was not until 1904 that a leading professionally trained social scientist joined the fight. In his massive *A History of Matrimonial Institutions* and subsequent writings George E. Howard, an eminent historian and sociologist, tried to show how the divorce rate was the product of forces which were dramatically improving American society.[41] He argued that industralization, urbanization and the other pressures which were breaking up the old patriarchal family produced not only more divorces, but a new kind of marriage marked by higher spiritual standards and greater freedom. Closing with the problem of individualism which so alarmed the enemies of divorce, he declared that the growing power of the state was tending to make the individual and not the family the functional unit of society and that this process not only freed the individual from familial authoritarianism but elevated the family by abolishing its coercive power and transforming it into a "spiritual and psychic association of parent and child based on persuasion."[42]

Within a few years Wright and Howard were joined by a host of social

[39] "Divorce vs. Domestic Warfare," *Arena*, I (April 1890), 56£. Alone of the great feminist leaders, Mrs. Stanton was a lifelong supporter of divorce, and in her later years it became one of her major interests. In this respect she was hardly a typical feminist, for while most divorce liberals were also feminists, they remained very much a minority within the women's movement.

[40] *Outline of Practical Sociology* (New York, 1900), p. 176.

[41] Chicago, 1904.

[42] "Social Control and the Function of the Family," Congress of Arts and Sciences, *Proceedings*, VII (St. Louis, 1904), 701. This abbreviated summary may not bring out the markedly utopian flavor which permeated discussions on the family by liberal sociologists and feminists during the Progressive period. Indeed, they entertained hopes for the future of the family which seem fantastically imaginative by the standards of our own more somberly clinical age. This visionary strain in Progressive social thought has been underestimated by historians in recent years, especially by Richard Hofstadter, whose influential *The Age of Reform* (New York, 1955), ignores the role played by feminism and the new morality in shaping the Progressive mood.

scientists including most of the leading men in the field.[43] The weight of sociological opinion was solidly on the side of divorce by 1908 when the American Sociological Society devoted its third annual meeting to the family.[44] President William G. Sumner, the crusty, aging president of the society who had done so much to establish sociology as an academic discipline, opened the proceedings by observing gloomily that "the family has to a great extent lost its position as a conservative institution and has become a field for social change."[45] The program of the convention confirmed Sumner's fears for virtually every paper described the changes affecting the family, called for more changes, or did both. Charlotte P. Gilman read a paper summarizing her *Women and Economics*, and a group of papers dealt with the damage inflicted on the family by urban, industrial life.[46]

The high point of the meeting was George Howard's, "Is the Freer Granting of Divorce an Evil?" Howard repeated his now familiar views and touched off a controversy which showed the drift of professional opinion.[47] He was attacked by Samuel Dike, who insisted that divorce was produced by a dangerous individualism and the decline of ideals, and by Walter George Smith. Smith was a prominent Catholic lawyer who had advocated stricter divorce laws for many years and was a leader in the campaign for uniform divorce legislation. His criticisms stressed divorce's incompatibility with orthodox religion and he accused Howard of condoning a social revolution that destroyed the divinely constituted order of things. Nothing, he declared, could alter the fact of feminine inferiority. Howard replied that marriage was a purely social institution "to be freely dealt with by men according to human needs."[48]

43 So many statements were made on marriage and divorce by sociologists during these years that I can list only a few of them here. Walter F. Willcox, *The Divorce Problem* (New York, 1891), was a seminal monograph that laid the statistical base for most later studies of divorce, but which was not well known outside of the profession and did not have the impact of other works which were more widely publicized. Elsie Clews Parsons, *The Family* (New York, 1906), caused a minor sensation by calling for trial marriages. Mrs. Parsons was a student of Franz Boas and the most radical of the academicians who dealt with the problem. Arthur W. Calhoun, *A Social History of the American Family, From the Civil War* (Cleveland, 1919), Vol. III, was written from an avowedly socialist point of view and is still the only comprehensive work on the history of the American family.

44 *Papers and Proceedings of the American Sociological Society*, III (Chicago, 1909).

45 *Ibid.*, p. 15.

46 "How Home Conditions React Upon the Family," *Papers . . . of American Sociological Society*, pp. 16-29. Margaret F. Byington, "The Family in a Typical Mill Town," pp. 73-84. Edward T. Devine, "Results of the Pittsburgh Survey," pp. 85-92; Charles R. Henderson, "Are Modern Industry and City Life Unfavorable to the Family?" pp. 93-105, among others.

47 *Papers . . . of American Sociological Society*, pp. 150-60.

48 *Ibid.*, p. 180.

Despite this unusually spirited clash, Smith and his friends were making an illusory show of strength. The moralistic flavor of their language, so different in tone from Howard's, revealed their professional isolation. Theirs was the faintly anachronistic rhetoric of a discredited tradition of social criticism. The opponents of Howard's position were, moreover, all laymen with the exception of President Sumner and Albion Small, while on his side were ranged most of the speakers, including E. A. Ross, James Lichtenberger and other leading scientists. As a profession then, sociology was committed to a positive view of divorce at a time when virtually every other organized group in the country was opposed to it. But although heavily outnumbered, the sociologists were the only people who could claim to speak on the problem with expert authority, and in the Progressive Era expertise was coming to be highly valued. As experts, the social scientists conferred respectability on the cause of free divorce at the same time as they did much to allay public anxiety over its effects.

A final problem that remained for the divorce liberals was finding some way to weaken the general conviction that divorce was forbidden by the Bible, and to diminish the impact of the clergy's opposition to divorce . It was here that the handful of liberal ministers who supported divorce performed a signal, and indeed indispensable, service. Simply by saying that divorce was a morally acceptable device, the liberal ministers endowed it with a certain degree of legitimacy. If supporting divorce with their moral prestige was the more important function performed by the liberal ministers, some went beyond this and effectively disputed the traditional charge that the Bible specifically prohibited divorce.

One of the most impressive statements of the liberal position was delivered by William G. Ballentine, classicist, Bible scholar, onetime president of Oberlin College and for twenty years editor of the *Bibliotheca Sacra*. Ballentine argued that "even if all thoughtful Christian men were today united in a resolute purpose of conformity to the letter of Scripture the path of duty would be far from plain." [49] He pointed out that a Biblical injunction against divorce cited by Bishop Doane in a recent magazine article appeared in the same passage as the admonition to resist evil. How, he asked, were Christians to know which commandment to obey and which to ignore? Ballentine described the life of Jesus as a struggle against Talmudic literalism:

> During His whole life, He fought against the tyranny of mere words, and for the lordship of the present living spiritual man. In his dis-

[49] "The Hyperbolic Teachings of Jesus," *North American Review*, CLXXIX (September 1904), 403.

course He suggested great truths by parables, by questions, by metaphors, by paradoxes, by hyperboles, by every device that could elude the semblance of fixed judicial formulas. It is the irony of history that such language should be seized upon for statute law.[50]

Other scholars, theologians and Higher Critics attacked the presumed Biblical sanctions against divorce in different ways, but the effect of their work was to undercut the general belief that the Bible clearly forbade divorce.[51]

On a more popular level the Rev. Minot J. Savage declared that as love was the essence of marriage two people who no longer loved each other had every reason to get divorced.[52] This same conviction informed the writings of John H. Holmes, a great civil libertarian and advocate of liberal Christianity, who believed that the passing of love destroyed marriage in fact if not in name.[53]

Gradually the climate of opinion began to change. As noted earlier there was a substantial organized opposition to divorce during the Progressive period, but despite local victories, the movement to retard divorce by legal and political means was resoundingly unsuccessful. There were other signs which demonstrated that attitudes were being modified. Samuel Dike died in 1913 and his League expired shortly thereafter. It was essentially a one-man operation, but it was supported by the enemies of divorce, whose financial contributions had declined sharply even before his death, to the point where receipts after 1910 were about half of what they had been in the 1890s.[54] The Committee on the Family which was routinely formed by the Federal Council of Churches in 1911 was singularly inactive, and in 1919 it was dropped altogether.[55]

At the same time the solid wall of opposition to divorce maintained by the nation's press was repeatedly breached. Before 1900 no important American magazine defended the right to divorce except the radical *Arena*. Articles favorable to divorce were very rare in the general press. After about 1900, however, a few bold magazines like the *Independent* endorsed the right of divorce editorially, and many more began to print

50 *Ibid.*, p. 447.

51 E.g., Ernest D. Burton, "The Biblical Teaching Concerning Divorce," *Biblical World*, XXIX (February and March 1907). Norman Jones, "Marriage and Divorce: The Letter of the Law," *North American Review*, CLXXXI (October 1905). Thomas S. Potwin, "Should Marriage Be Indissoluble?" *New Englander and Yale Review*, LVI (January 1892).

52 *Men and Women* (Boston, 1902).

53 *Marriage and Divorce* (New York, 1913).

54 *Annual Reports* of the National League for the Protection of the Family.

55 *Annual Reports* of the Executive Committee of the Federal Council of Churches of Christ in America.

occasional articles defending divorce. The *North American Review*, which was more interested in the problem than any other major periodical, began the new century with a rousing attack on the opponents of divorce by the aging but still magnificent Elizabeth Cady Stanton.[56] Other magazines, too numerous to mention, also began to print articles favoring divorce. Even the uncompromisingly hostile *Outlook* unbent to this extent, and in 1910 it conceded editorially that there were times when divorce was permissible.[57] This shift influenced popular as well as serious magazines. In 1910 the slick monthly *World's Work* announced that "The True View of Increasing Divorce" was that the divorce rate was not alarming, and that divorces should not be subject to excessive restrictions.[58]

Obviously the changes in public opinion which these articles represented did not constitute a general recognition of the desirability of divorce. Although a few journals accepted the liberal argument that divorce was a therapeutic social mechanism, most did not. In many cases nothing more was involved than the admission that there were probably two sides to the question. This of itself, however, was a form of moral relativism on the issue which would have been unthinkable in the 1890s. This new tolerance of divorce coincided with the eruption of a number of curious phenomena like the dance craze and the white slave panic which marked the onset of the revolution in morals.[59]

Divorce was a part of the complex transformation of moral values and sexual customs which was to help give the 1920s their bizarre flavor. It was not only the most visible result of this vast social upheaval, but in many ways it was the most compatible with traditional modes of thought. It was, on the whole, an orderly, public and institutionalized process which took due account of the formal difference between right and wrong, guilt and innocence. It had the blessings of the highest sociological authorities, and it was recommended by many feminists as a cure for the brutalizing sexual indignities known to occur in some marriages. Conservatives could, therefore, more easily resign themselves to divorce than to other, more extravagant, demonstrations of the changing moral order.

Although divorce has today assumed proportions undreamed of in the Progressive Era, the nature of the American response to mass divorce

[56] "Are Homogenous Divorce Laws in all the States Desirable?" *North American Review*, CLXX (March 1900).

[57] E. R. Stevens, "Divorce in America: The Problem," *Outlook*, June 1, 1907; "Just Grounds for Divorce," November 23, 1910.

[58] *World's Work*, XIX (January 1910).

[59] Henry F. May, *The End of American Innocence* (New York, 1959), II, Part IV, 333, 343-44.

was determined at that time. Between 1905, when the magnitude of divorce as a social problem had become fully apparent, and 1917, when the movement to limit or direct the spread of divorce had clearly failed, something of importance for American social history had occurred. This was the recognition by moral conservatives that they could not prevent the revolution in morals represented by mass divorce. Their failure of morale in the immediate prewar period paved the way for the spectacular changes which took place after the war.

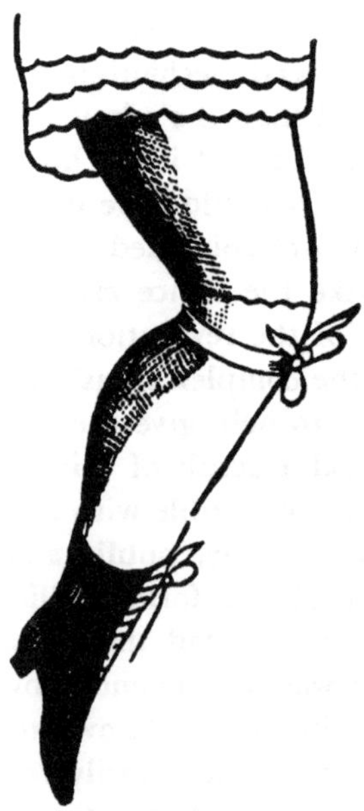

University of Minnesota Elaine Tyler May

THE PRESSURE TO PROVIDE: CLASS, CONSUMERISM, AND DIVORCE IN URBAN AMERICA, 1880-1920

In an era of massive production of consumer goods, what determines the normative standard of living, and what constitutes the necessities of life? These questions became increasingly difficult to answer during the decades surrounding the turn of the century, when profound economic changes ushered in corporate America. Scholars have documented a number of crucial developments, including standardized industrial technology, a mushrooming national bureaucracy, a shorter work week, and increased wages. Some observers hail these changes for providing security and material abundance to enhance the home and enrich private life. Others lament the loss of the craft tradition, and the intrinsic satisfactions that went with it. Still others claim that consumerism was a ploy to buy off workers and women, making them complacent while discouraging effective unionization and political action.[1] But, as yet, no study has used empirical data to probe the impact of these developments on American families, or determined how they affected individuals on different levels of the class order. This article examines and compares the effects of heightened material aspirations upon wealthy, white-collar, and blue-collar Americans. While the rising standard of living may well have enhanced family life for some among the comfortable classes, it often wreaked havoc in the homes of those who could not afford the fruits of abundance. It is no accident that the emergence of the affluent society paralleled the skyrocketing of the American divorce rate.

One way to explore the way in which prosperity took its toll is to examine the casualties themselves. I have used hundreds of divorce cases filed during these years to uncover some of the economic problems that plagued American marriages. The samples include 500 litigations from Los Angeles in the 1880s, and another 500 from 1920. A comparative sample includes 250 divorces filed throughout New Jersey in 1920. The proceedings cover a developing west-coast city with little manufacturing, and an eastern industrial state with a large rural population. Within the samples are individuals from virtually every ethnic group and occupational category. By comparing the accusations mentioned in the 1880s and in 1920, we can determine the effects of economic change over time, during these crucial transitional years. The testimonies of the litigants in these cases reveal the limits of abundance, and suggest that no class or locale was immune to the ill effects of rising material aspirations.[2]

Obviously, financial problems did not erupt in American homes with the onset of the corporate economy. In fact, money conflicts appeared in divorce cases well before the 20th century. Yet the turn-of-the-century decades did witness a profound change. In the first place, the number of divorces increased dramatically. Secondly, issues surrounding money — who should make it, how much is adequate, and how it should be spent — became increasingly prevalent. The divorce samples from Los Angeles and New Jersey reflect this trend.

Although the percentage of cases filed on the grounds of "neglect to provide" did not rise significantly between the two samples taken (see Table 1), these problems did become more complicated in the later decades. The Lynds found a similar development in Muncie, Indiana. In spite of the fairly constant rate of neglect complaints in divorce litigations from 1890 to the 1920s, "economic considerations figure possibly more drastically than formerly as factors in divorce."[3]

Table 1. Legal Grounds For Divorce as Originally Filed by Litigants in Samples, Los Angeles 1880s and 1920, New Jersey, 1920

	L.A., 1880s	Percent	L.A., 1920	Percent	N.J., 1920	Percent
Desertion	181	15	219	38	141	64
Extreme Cruelty	166	28	138	35		
Adultery	43	7	32	9	75	34
Neglect	47	11	51	10		
Intemperance	26	4	16	6		
Felony Conviction	3	1	3	1		
Valid Previous Marriage	2	3	13	1		
Fraud, Coercion	0	1	5	0	5	2

This table includes only the primary legal ground upon which the petition was originally filed. Other complaints were often included in the proceedings, and are included in tabulations elsewhere, as well as in the text.

Grounds for annulment.

Only two grounds for divorce were legal in New Jersey in 1920. The last category indicates annulment petitions.

At first glance, this appears rather perplexing. The nation was more prosperous in the later period than the earlier, and the standard of living was rising steadily for all classes. Moreover, women found greater opportunities to work, and both males and females experienced increasing wages and more free time off the job. During the same years, an unprecedented abundance of consumer goods became available on a mass level. Presumably, these developments would contribute to easing tensions between husbands and wives rather than creating them, while fostering a more pleasant, epressive, and comfortable existence. However, with the standard of living rising, and affluence filtering down to a greater proportion of the population, the "provider" was often expected to fulfill the increased demands sparked by widespread prosperity.

The evidence in the divorce proceedings suggests that this was not a major problem in the 1880s. Although financial conflicts appeared often, there was no controversy over what constituted the necessities of life. Either a husband supported his family, or he did not. Virtually all of the cases in the early sample that dealt with issues of neglect were clear-cut. If a man did not provide enough food, clothing, and shelter for his wife to live comfortably, she was entitled to a divorce. No husband questioned that; and no quarrels ensued over what his obligation entailed.

One typical case was that of Mary and Emmet Hickey. They were married in 1882, at Virginia City, Nevada. During their three-year marriage, they had one child, and Emmet worked as a teamster in Los Angeles. Their community property consisted of a small amount of household furniture worth $100. The basic problem in the marriage was Emmet's inability to fulfill his role as provider. When Mary requested money for "the necessities of life for herself and little child, her husband, disregarding his duties as a husband toward the wife, cruelly told her that he would not give her a dollar . . . if she did not like it, she could leave him and go elsewhere." To make matters worse, his behavior was hardly genteel; he swore often, calling her a "lying bitch" and a "bastard." As she was a "weak, frail woman," his behavior seriously impaired her health.[4] In a similar case, Christina Adams claimed that her husband, a miner, "never earned one cent," never provided for her, and told her, "You don't know enough to spend money. You don't know enough to buy your own clothes." To add to his other insults, when she requested two dollars for shopping, he replied, "I will shit you two dollars."[5]

In the 1880s, divorcing wives complained if their mates failed to provide for them. But they did not complain about how much their husbands provided. By 1920, however, it was no longer clear precisely what constituted adequate support on the part of a husband, and a number of bitter conflicts erupted over the issue. These difficulties were not limited to couples with inadequate resources. Money problems affected marriages of the wealthy as well as the poor (see Table 2).

Table 2. Total Number of Financial Conflicts That Appeared in Proceedings, According to Husband's Occupational Level, Divorce Samples, Los Angeles, 1880s and 1920, New Jersey, 1920 (In Numbers and Percentages)

Los Angeles, 1880s	Financial Complaints	Husbands in Sample	Percent
Upper White Collar	10	63	15.9
Lower White Collar	26	112	23.2
Blue Collar	43	136	31.6
Los Angeles, 1920			
Upper White Collar	8	28	28.5
Lower White Collar	54	122	44.2
Blue Collar	39	208	18.7
New Jersey, 1920			
Upper White Collar	4	17	23.5
Lower White Collar	25	53	47.1
Blue Collar	32	113	28.3

SOURCE: Divorce Proceedings.

The Keagys, for example, were an affluent Los Angeles couple who lived together only seven months. John Keagy was a dentist with a good deal of property, and his wife Zella was also fairly wealthy in her own right. According to John, Zella had a monthly income of $75 (although John did not say the source), plus six lots in Alabama, bank accounts, stocks, and diamonds. She had been married previously, and had a daughter. The evidence suggests that she was widowed, although that is not entirely clear. Apparently, John and Zella had a rather stormy relationship. Throughout their charges and countercharges of cruelty, humiliation, violence, and insult, they had a running debate over financial matters. Zella felt neglected. She complained to a friend that John "did not appreciate her enough, she didn't like the house he furnished her, that her house in Alabama was so fine, and that her first husband would have sacrificed anything for her." She requested a divorce, $500 in fees, and $75 per month alimony. Denying the charges, John filed a cross-complaint on the grounds of cruelty, claiming that Zella "proceeded to run bills against him, without justification, which were not for the necessities of life." Finally, Zella was granted a divorce, and the bitter financial conflict ended with a property agreement. In this case, money may not have been the primary issue, but it certainly aggravated an already bad marriage. In spite of their wealth, John and Zella Keagy could not agree on an appropriate level of expenditure.[6]

Another example suggests how a wife's material desires might put strains upon a marriage, if a husband's income was adequate but not enormous. Edward and Louise Atkinson were a middle-class couple who married in Brooklyn in 1910. During their ten-year marriage, they spent several years living apart, and had constant quarrels over money matters. Finally, Edward filed for a divorce. Aside from Louise's alleged adultery, her husband claimed that she "spent money freely and extravagantly and with utter disregard of his circumstances." Although they had no children, he gave her his $35 per week salary, keeping only $1 to buy tobacco and other small items for himself. From 1915 to 1917, she remained in New York, refusing to join him in California. At the same time, she corresponded with other men who gave her money.

One bone of contention between the two was Louise's fetish for pet dogs. Once she wrote to Edward, asking him for $75 for another dog, which she "would rather have than an evening gown." Complaining of the sacrifices she had made for her negligent husband, she bemoaned the loss of one of her animals: "I sold Peggy to buy you a suit." In another letter, she claimed that he owed her money, for "there is no Tom [reference unclear, perhaps her lover] here to take care of me, and I am not well enough to work."

Edward Atkinson considered his wife's material desires quite outrageous. But apparently she found a paramour who was more inclined to cater to her tastes for the trappings of elegance and high culture. He wrote her slick letters about fancy hotels where she could stay on New York's Fifth Avenue, learn painting "from a good teacher and meet artistic people," and frequent his luxurious new club house, which was "most comfortable in every way." At the same time, she wrote to her husband in California that she was in a dire situation: "Now, I am in need, do I have to make out an itemized bill, or do you have enough *manhood* to do the proper and decent thing towards me?" According to Louise, this meant "weekly payments until such time as you figure you have done your duty." She then told him to go ahead with the divorce, she will not object. The court apparently had no sympathy for her alleged difficulties, and granted Edward the divorce. Nevertheless, Louise's pleas are revealing. Not only did she consider herself "in need," but she equated her husband's ability to provide for her desires — however eccentric — with his very "manhood." For Louise Atkinson, manhood and duty meant taking care of women — and in the proper style.[7]

This equation reflected more than the demand of an outraged wife. It symbolized a much larger phenomenon that had evolved with the maturation of industrial society. Women who placed heavy demands upon their husbands were not merely selfish or lazy. Although these were the years of women's presumed "emancipation," females still faced limited options outside the home. Middle-class wives in particular may have felt restless as well as powerless. While their numbers in the work force increased, it was still considered undesirable for a married woman to work. If a wife did seek employment, she did not have access to the most lucrative, prestigious, and rewarding occupations. Most jobs available to women were routine and monotonous, with low pay and few chances for advancement.

What was left, then, to give these married females personal satisfaction? Even at home they may have felt a sense of uselessness. Childbearing and household responsibilities utilized less of a woman's creative energies as the birth rate declined and labor-saving devices proliferated. New avenues for self-expression had to be explored. The economy offered little in the way of jobs; yet it provided seemingly unlimited possibilities for consumerism. Indeed, female emancipation found its most immediate expression not in the work force, but in the realms of styles and leisure pursuits. These were purchasable, provided one had the means. If wives began spending to adorn their homes and themselves, it may have reflected their constraints elsewhere. It is no wonder that, for some women, this gave rise to an obsession with material goods and private indulgence. Thus, they turned the full force of their pent-up energies to these endeavors.[8]

With limited financial resources of their own, women often looked to men to provide the means for their consumption desires. This pressure was one of many new challenges facing 20th-century males. While public notice focused on new female activities, parallel shifts that affected men went virtually unnoticed. Males continued to work, their clothing styles remained practically unaltered, and their public behavior did not change dramatically. Yet they were experiencing a subtle transformation in sex-role expectations that, while not as obvious as the new status of women, was no less profound.

For white-collar men, the most far-reaching changes came with the maturation of the corporate system. The engulfing bureaucracies stabilized many uncertainties of the earlier era, and offered at least a modicum of security. The 20th-century businessman was less likely to enter business on his own, with the full burden of success or failure resting on his shoulders. If one followed the rules, he would advance up the hierarchy in a steady, predictable manner, and reach a moderate level of success and prosperity. There may have been few examples of men making a fortune overnight within the modern system; but, in fact, the Carnegies of the previous era served as little more than encouragement to fantasies. The top of the ladder was virtually closed then as well as later.[9] However, successful men had been models of 19th-century striving. In spite of new rewards, the corporations took away some of the unique triumphs of individual enterprise.

With the mechanization of industry, increasing production, the declining work week, and a rising standard of living, the benefits were obvious. In terms of purely material considerations, the corporate economy offered abundance and leisure. The tragedy, however, was that the aspiration for affluence was more widespread than the luxurious life itself. Even if an individual entered the white-collar ranks, he still faced enormous pressures to advance and succeed. Supplying increased demands necessitated continual striving. This was difficult enough for relatively successful businessmen, but infinitely more so for employees with modest salaries, or for petty proprietors without the cushion of corporate security.

We know from national statistics that the white-collar level of society shifted away from self-employed businessmen to corporate bureaucrats and clerical workers. Our Los Angeles samples reflect a similar trend (see Tables 3 and 4). These white-collar groups, possibly more than any other level in society, were striving for upward mobility, afraid of slipping down the socioeconomic ladder, and concerned with deriving the fruits of their labor in tangible material goods. Arno Mayer has suggested that, historically, the petite bourgeoisie was possibly the most insecure and status-conscious level in western nations. This group had its own unique aspirations and cultural forms geared toward emulating the more affluent groups above them. If this premise holds for 20th-century America, and I believe it does, then petty proprietors facing competition from large corporations, as well as rank and file white-collar workers, would be feeling these pressures most intensely.[10]

Table 3. Occupations of Husbands and Wives in Los Angeles, 1880s Divorce Sample, and Males and Females in Los Angeles Work Force, 1890

	Husbands		Male Work Force		Wives		Female Work Force	
	Number	Percent	Number	Percent	Number	Percent	Number	Percent
High White Collar	**63**	**21**	**1,795**	**11**	**6**	**8**	**468**	**14**
Professional	23	7	958	6	5	7	468	14
Major Proprietor	40	14	837	5	1	1		
Low White Collar	**112**	**36**	**5,181**	**33**	**21**	**29**	**695**	**21**
Clerks, Sales	24	8	2,369	15	0		315	9
Semi-Professional	2	1	169	1	3	4	188	6
Petty Proprietors	86	27	2,643	17	18	25	192	6
High Blue Collar	**71**	**22**	**3,095**	**20**	**15**	**21**	**781**	**23**
Skilled, Foremen	71	22	3,095	20	15	21	781	23
Low Blue Collar	**65**	**21**	**5,596**	**36**	**31**	**42**	**1,468**	**41**
Semi-Skilled	28	10	2,545	16	4	5	110	3
Unskilled	37	11	3,051	20	27	37	1,358	39
Total Given	311	100	15,667	100	73	100	3,412	100

SOURCES: Divorce proceedings, city directories, and census figures.

Totals given refer to occupations that were specified — unspecified occupations were deleted. Nearly every male worked, but only 311 indicated specific jobs. Of the female litigants, 167 held jobs, but only 73 were identified.

Table 4. Occupations of Husbands and Wives in Los Angeles, 1920 Divorce Sample, and Males and Females in Los Angeles Work Force, 1920

	Husbands		Male Work Force (total: 197,700)	Wives		Female Work Force (total: 68,400)
	Number	Percent	Percent	Number	Percent	Percent
High White Collar	**28**	**8**	**10**	**14**	**8**	**9**
Professional	13	4	6	13	8	8
Major Proprietor	15	4	4	1	0	1
Low White Collar	**122**	**35**	**27**	**87**	**51**	**43**
Clerks, Sales	59	17	20	62	36	33
Semi-Professionals	15	4	3	13	8	8
Petty Proprietors	48	14	4	12	7	2
High Blue Collar	**95**	**26**	**32**	**10**	**6**	**7**
Skilled, Foreman	95	26	32	10	6	7
Low Blue Collar	**113**	**31**	**31**	**62**	**35**	**41**
Semi-skilled	99	27	6	32	18	9
Unskilled	14	4	25	30	17	32
Total Given	358	100	100	173	100	100

SOURCES: Divorce proceedings, city directories, and census figures. 358 of the husbands indicated specific jobs; 173 of the 206 employed females indicated specific occupations.

Looking at the divorce samples from Los Angeles, we find that, by 1920, the low-white-collar level is overrepresented, compared to its proportion of the general population (see Tables 3 and 4). In the later sample, the proportion of divorces granted to the wealthy classes declined dramatically as the more bureaucratic clerical and sales categories mushroomed. At the same time, the percentage of petty proprietors in the work force shrank; but these small businessmen remained heavily overrepresented in the divorce samples. Those who remained among the entrepreneurial ranks may well have felt new pressures. As large chains and department stores began drawing local patrons and customers away from independent enterprises, owners of small shops and businesses may have faced increasing insecurity. To add to these burdens, many of them had to purchase goods from larger firms, making them dependent upon a national marketing system. Undersold by large competitors who often controlled production and supply as well as distribution, and bound by wholesale merchandise prices, they may have tried to cut costs by turning to family labor. This was not always a satisfactory solution, especially if proprietors of small concerns had to cope with diminishing returns as well as increasing consumer demands. It is perhaps no wonder that this group had more than its share of divorce.

Unfortunately, relatively few of the divorce litigants articulated how financial and status considerations affected their marriages and their lives. As with virtually every complex issue that eroded these relationships, we must glean insights from a handful of cases where evidence is rich and detailed. In terms of material considerations, we are able to discern a pattern of discontent for each of the major socioeconomic levels represented.[11] As we saw in the two cases cited above, affluence did not preclude the possibility of money squabbles. The leisured wife of a man with means might make a quasi-career out of purchasing goods and adorning herself and her abode. Even wealthy husbands may have reacted against frivolous or wasteful expenditures. But if a man's income was consistently a measure below his wife's aspirations for comfortable living, the tension could become chronic and destroy a marriage that otherwise might have survived.

In the divorce proceedings, conflicts over status and social mobility stand out in bold relief, particulary among white-collar families on the west coast. It is here that we can best perceive the intensified pressures placed upon men to supply heightened material desires. Norman Shinner, for example, admitted that he deserted his wife after five years of marriage because of his "inability to support her in the manner she desired on my salary, and on this account we could not live together in an amiable manner." Rather than struggling to meet up to his wife's aspirations, Norman Shinner simply left.[12]

Oscar Lishnog faced similar difficulties. He married Martha in Chicago in 1908, and had four children prior to their Los Angeles divorce. While the Lishnogs appeared to be a fairly comfortable suburban family, financial strain ultimately caused their union to collapse. Oscar was in the insurance and real estate business, working as an employee or salesman rather than executive or proprietor. His income was steady but modest. He spent some time living apart from his family while working in San Pedro; nevertheless, Oscar and Martha exchanged frequent loving, chatty, but slightly distant letters to each other. He sent her money, she tried to save, and they expressed affection for one another. Now and then Martha would tell Oscar to "mind the store and not waste time or money." Revealing her material aspirations, she wrote that many of her neighbors owned automobiles, for there was no street car line nearby. This suggests that their Los Angeles home was in a fairly new suburban development, removed from the downtown district and transportation network. Martha also reminded her husband that she was paying mortgage on the house, and the "kids want a hammock." She usually closed with affection, saying she was "waiting for him."

But in 1920, Martha filed for divorce on the grounds of willful neglect, saying that Oscar spent his $35 per week salary in "riotous living away from his family," squandering his money while depriving his wife and children. Claiming that she was not skilled in any vocation, Martha said she had to rely on the charity of friends. She asked for custody of the children. Oscar denied the charges, insisting that he earned only $21 per week and gave it all to his wife except a small amount for living expenses. He asked that the divorce be denied, and, assuming that they would remain living apart, requested joint custody of the children. Nevertheless, the court granted Martha the divorce, plus custody, $9 per week for the children, and $3 per month for her "personal recreation." This final item, though minimal in amount, suggests that courts were willing to designate some money for amusements and consumption within the category of necessities — which men were required to provide. Whatever other problems may be hidden from our view that contributed to this couple's woes, it is clear that money was a sore spot for a long time. Oscar's salary was hardly abundant, and he was finally unable to supply the demands of his wife and children to maintain their suburban lifestyle.[13]

Perhaps one of the most telling of these cases was the Los Angeles divorce of Margaret and Donald Wilton. She was a devout midwestern Protestant whose marriage to her clerk husband lasted two years. At one point, she wrote to her estranged spouse, hoping to be reconciled. She recommended that he read some bible passages relating to the duties of husbands and wives, and promised to be a "good Christian wife." In a revealing passage at the end, she wrote, "I heard something about you that made my heart sing with joy: you have climbed another rung on the ladder of success. I am proud to know it, dear. . . ." In spite of Donald's improved status, their marriage was beyond repair. After a rather bitter case, Margaret Wilton was granted a divorce.[14]

Families such as the ones mentioned above may not have suffered severe deprivation. But, like other 20th-century couples, they faced a greater potential for disappointment when a modicum of luxury became the anticipated norm. As the standard of living continued to climb, the golden age of affluence seemed imminent, and it was anticipated with almost religious fervor. For much of the American population, increasing prosperity appeared as a signal from the Divine that the culmination of progress was at hand. One observer perceived, "To most people a millenium implies spiritual overtones. So does the standard of living."[15] For a male provider, then, inability to keep up with this sanctified progress meant failure and damnation.

Although these pressures were particularly acute for the lower middle class, they were also severe for workers. Financial difficulties among working-class couples, however, were qualitatively different from those facing white-collar families. Laborers faced a double-edged problem. They may not have felt the same status anxieties as petty proprietors or rank and file bureaucrats, but it was often difficult for them to make ends meet. Blue-collar families lived with the uncertainties of a fluid labor market and usually lacked the cushion of corporate security. Weak or non-existent labor unions left them virtually unprotected. This is not to deny the fact that some of the abundance filtered down among the working classes. By 1900, their improved circumstances prompted Samuel Gompers, when asked if he thought the conditions of workers were worsening, to reply, "Oh, that is perfectly absurd."[16] In our samples, we find that financial conflicts among blue-collar families actually decreased somewhat between 1880 and 1920. However, their percentage of the total number of litigants increased markedly (see Table 2). This may reflect a number of factors. It is possible that in the 1880s, the very price of a divorce precluded legal action for many blue-collar couples. When they did come to court, nearly one-third of them included money conflicts among their complaints. By 1920, more workers may have been able to afford a divorce, and the wives might have been less likely to complain of financial desperation. Yet status and spending concerns might well have helped erode these unions as well. To add to the problem of meeting basic needs, working-class families also shared new consumer desires with their more affluent peers. But for those with meager incomes, luxuries were out of the question, and the affluence they saw everywhere around them only served to heighten frustrations.

Working-class couples, then, faced compounded difficulties. Often the breadwinner's earnings were inadequate and his job insecure. Moreover, he was subject to the same sorts of demands for mass-produced goods as his white-collar contemporaries. One of the crucial features of the consumer-oriented economy was the way it transcended class boundaries. On one level, this contributed to a certain superficial "classless" quality. But, on another level, it served to homogenize tastes in a society where wealth remained unequally distributed. Once self-esteem and validation came to rest upon supplying material goods, those on the bottom rungs would be considered less worthy. We have seen that Louise Atkinson, the middle-class woman in the case cited earlier, had tastes that outdistanced her husband's ability as well as willingness to provide. Yet her evaluation of his very "manhood" rested on this function of his income. For working-class women, the situation may have been less frivolous and more desperate. Nevertheless, the equation still held.

Alberta Raschke was a blue-collar wife in Los Angeles with a five-year-old daughter. She filed for a divorce on the grounds of desertion and neglect, claiming that her husband forced her to rely on her parents' charity. The couple married in Indiana in 1913, and separated four years later. At some point, Alberta came to California and William remained in Chicago. In a letter, she accused him of refusing to support her, and claimed that she was in a "weakened condition." "You have had ample time to *make a man of yourself* in all these six years, if you cared for your wife and baby, instead of driving a wagon for $12 a week. You would not take work offered you at $21 a week, so it is not because you could not find better. I stood for all the terrible abuse you gave me, and went without the very necessities of life to see if you would not come to your senses, but now I am tired of waiting and have decided to file suit for divorce . . . I am as ever Alberta."[17]

Although Alberta Raschke probably had a valid complaint, the pressure put upon William to "make a man" of himself may have been unfair. It is not clear why he did not take the job allegedly offered to him for more pay, but perhaps he simply enjoyed what he was doing. The conflict between working at a job one liked and working for money may have ultimately led to this divorce. Although William Raschke apparently found the lower paying job more satisfying, as far as his wife was concerned the primary purpose of his work was to make money. Undoubtedly, it was not easy for this woman to live on $12 a week with a five-year-old child. However, the equation of manhood with the ability to provide placed a particularly heavy burden on a working-class husband.

In general, working-class wives were less obsessed with status considerations and more concerned with bread and butter issues. Most blue-collar divorces that included money difficulties revolved around basic needs, similar to the conflicts that surfaced in the 1880s proceedings. These problems erupted frequently in New Jersey, where the majority of divorces were among blue-collar couples (see Table 5). It is important to keep in mind that New Jersey only permitted divorces on the grounds of adultery and desertion — not financial neglect. Nevertheless, money was at the heart of many New Jersey litigations. In fact, a number of these couples struggled, quite literally, just to keep a roof over their heads.

Table 5. Occupations of Male and Female Litigants in New Jersey Sample, 1920

	Husbands		Wives	
	Number	Percent	Number	Percent
High White Collar	**17**	**11**	**6**	**7**
Professional	8	5	5	6
Major Proprietor	9	6	1	1
Low White Collar	**53**	**29**	**30**	**31**
Clerks, Sales	30	16	25	26
Semi-Professional	7	4	3	3
Petty Proprietors	16	9	2	2
High Blue Collar	**40**	**21**	**10**	**11**
Skilled, Foremen	40	21	10	11
Low Blue Collar	**73**	**39**	**49**	**51**
Semi-Skilled	39	21	25	26
Unskilled	34	18	24	25
Total Given	183	100	95	100

NOTE: As the divorce statistics are from localities throughout the state, there is no available breakdown of the New Jersey state labor force for comparison.

A severe housing shortage in urban areas placed serious strains on several marriages. Providers with meager earnings often found themselves unable to provide a home. Numerous couples lived with parents or other relatives, or moved from one form of lodging to another. For these couples, the inability to acquire adequate housing was the fundamental issue that destroyed their marriages. The Shafers were one such family. "I want one thing," pleaded Anna Shafer to her husband. "Won't you please come back and make a home for me, I don't care if it is only two rooms, if you can afford to pay for two rooms." They had been married since 1910, when they ran away together to Hoboken, New Jersey. Anna claimed that William deserted her three years later. She said that her husband was "a drinking man who never made a home or provided for her and their child," although he worked for an insurance company. Anna was granted a divorce and restored to her maiden name. the same problems ended the marriage of Harris and Catherine Martin, two blue-collar workers in Newark. "I told him I would go anyplace with him as long as he could furnish me with a home," explained Catherine. "I didn't care where it was, even if it was only one room and I was alone." But after three months they separated, and Catherine was granted a divorce plus the return of her maiden name.[18]

Lack of housing and insecure work also disrupted the marriage of a Jewish couple in New Jersey. Sarah and Morris Dubin, who married in 1910, and had one child that died. Morris was a tailor by trade, but was unable to practice his craft. Instead, he worked for the railroad, and as a cook in a sanitarium. It appears that this duo had a rather stormy marriage, with Morris deserting now and then and Sarah continually begging him to make a home for her. Whenever she asked, "Why won't you make me a home and support me?" he replied, "I won't and can't live in Newark with you." Newark was particularly plagued by the housing shortage atthis time, which aggravated the situation for Morris, who was unable to find work that utilized his tailoring skills. But the court had little mercy. The interviewer concluded that Morris was "apparently one of those people who find it difficult to settle down and perform his obligations for any length of time." Sarah won her suit and the return of her maiden name.[19]

Although a chronic shortage of basic needs eroded most of these blue-collar marriages, a number of working-class couples quarreled over consumer spending and status concerns as well. A few cases illustrate how squabbles might ensue over how money should be spent. Emma Totsworth was 19 when she married David totsworth, a 22-year-old machinist, in Jersey City. Five years later she deserted. When asked about their difficulties, David said they argued "over different things, like going out and clothes, no clean clothes and all around jealousy. Simple meanness. She spent money on clothes that should have gone for eating." It appears that David Totsworth preferred to see his hard-earned income used for less frivolous items.[20]

Charles and Ada Davis were plagued by similar problems. They were married in New Jersey in 1902 and had one child. After nine years, Ada deserted and went to New York. Apparently Charles, a railroad brakeman, never managed to provide for her in the style that she wanted. According to the interviewer, Ada became "dissatisfied with her surroundings and complained of the style of life her husband afforded her. She wouldn't speak or recognize her husband sometimes for days at a time. Finally she left, saying she wanted to live where she wanted to, and also wanted him to support her." Charles' brother stood up for the aggrieved husband, saying the he "always worked steadily and was a good provider for his home and did everything he could for his wife and family that a man could do under his circumstances." But apparently it was not enough. Charles testified that Ada "insisted upon telling me how much more the neighbors had than she had, and what the neighbor's husband did, and what they didn't do. I told her that if she would stop listening to outsiders and live for me and our little girl as she had done up to that time, everything could be very nice and we could get along." But Ada's dissatisfaction increased until she finally left, and Charles was granted a New Jersey divorce on the grounds of desertion.[21]

These blue-collar couples were plagued by status anxieties. Both Emma Totsworth and Ada Davis had aspirations for material goods beyond the reach of their husbands' pay checks. Some wives not only held their spouses' incomes in disdain, they also looked down upon the work itself. Olivia Garside was a New Jersey housekeeper bent on feverish social climbing. After 26 years of marriage and three children, she finally left her husband Frederick, a machinist, who could not supply the lifestyle she craved. According to Frederick,

> My wife never considered me her equal. She told me this shortly after her marriage, and she was never satisifed with anything I might undertake to do and that I was not as neat appearing as a professional man. She would say my conversation wasn't as it should be and she felt I was socially beneath her. I have always turned over every cent I made to my wife outside of my travelling expenses. I have never been intoxicated in my life. I would very often work overtime and on Sundays around the neighborhood to earn a few dollars more. My wife always complained I wasn't making enough money.

This husband took pride in his hard work, his efforts to support his wife, his sobriety and discipline. But to his wife, he lacked polish and grace — and the ample income to go with it. The court granted Frederick a divorce on the grounds of desertion.[22]

The evidence in these cases suggests that mass consumption was not necessarily a positive outgrowth of the society's industrial development, even though it held the potential for increased financial security and a more comfortable lifestyle. Rather, these marital conflicts represent a failure or inability to come to terms with the changing economic order. For affluent couples, tensions emerged over how the family's resources should be spent. For those among the lower-white-collar ranks, status considerations clashed with limited incomes, creating enormous pressures upon the family breadwinner. For many working-class couples, mass consumption remained virtually out of reach, contributing to a greater sense of economic insecurity and heightened frustrations.

The testimonies of divorce litigants reflect the discrepancy between material desires and reality, for it was difficult to meet the soaring demands put before every consumer's eyes. Perhaps many Americans did indeed benefit from new opportunities created by the mature industrial system. But among those whose marriages fell apart during these years, and undoubtedly among thousands more whose thoughts and feelings are beyond the reach of scholars, there was a great deal of disappointment, disillusion, and despair that the good life they had hoped for could not be grasped.

University of Minnesota Elaine Tyler May

FOOTNOTES

1. See, for example, C. Wright Mills, *White Collar* (New York, 1956); Robert S. and Helen Merrell Lynd, *Middletown* (New York, 1956), Chapters IV through VIII; Stuart Ewen, *Captains of Consciousness: Advertising and the Social Roots of the Consumer Culture* (New York, 1977); Edward Kirkland, *Dream and Thought in the Business Community, 1860-1900* (New York, 1956); Daniel Miller and Guy Swanson, *The Changing American Parent* (New York, 1958). For a discussion of the scholarly debate, see Donald Meyer, "Churches and Families," in William McLaughlin, ed., *Religion in America* (Boston, 1968).

2. This is part of a larger study in progress tentatively entitled "The Pursuit of Happiness: Marriage and Divorce in America, 1880-1920."

3. In 1870, there were 1.5 divorces for every 1,000 marriages. By 1920, the figure had increased to 7.7 divorces per every 1,000 marriages. See Paul H. Jacobson, *American Marriage and Divorce* (New York, 1959), 21, 90; Lynd and Lynd, *Middletown*, 80-81, 126. Nationally, the percentage of divorces granted for "neglect to provide" rose steadily from 1870 to 1930, and then declined up to 1950. See Jacobson, *American Marriage and Divorce*, 126.

4. Case 4191, Los Angeles County Archives, 1885. Names have been changed in all of the cases cited.

5. Case 2773, Los Angeles, 1883.

6. Case D251, Los Angeles, 1920.

7. Case D127, Los Angeles, 1920.

8. This is more fully elaborated in my study in progress, "The Pursuit of Happiness."

9. For discussions of social mobility in America, see, for example, Stephan Thernstrom, *Poverty and Progress* (Cambridge, Mass., 1964), and *The Other Bostonians* (Cambridge, Mass., 1973); William Miller, ed., *Men in Business: Essays on the Historical Role of the Entrepreneur* (New York, 1962), esp. articles by Miller, Frances Gregory, and Irene Neu; Reinhard Bendix and Seymour M. Lipset, eds., *Social Mobility in Industrial Society* (Berkeley, 1959), esp. article by Bendix and Frank Howton. An intriguing exception is reported by Herbert G. Gutman in "The Reality of the Rags to Riches Myth: the Case of the Paterson, New Jersey Locomotive, Iron and Machinery Manufacturers, 1830-1880," in Stephan Thernstrom and Richard Sennett, eds., *Nineteenth Century Cities* (New Haven, 1969).

10. Arno Mayer, "The Lower Middle Class As Historical Problem," *Journal of Modern History* 47, No. 3 (September, 1975), 409 to 436.

11. Table 2 gives the total number of cases from which these patterns were drawn. Although few in number, these cases show striking variations.

12. Case D385, Los Angeles, 1920.

13. Case D177, Los Angeles, 1920.

14. Case D386, Los Angeles, 1920.

15. Edward Chase Kirkland, *Industry Comes of Age* (New York, 1961), 403.

16. Testimony of Samuel Gompers, *Report of the Industrial Commission* VII, 645, in Kirkland, *Industry*, 402.

17. Case D258, Los Angeles, 1920, emphasis added.

18. Case C-60-402, New Jersey, 1920; Case H-60-193, New Jersey, 1920.

19. Case C-60-75, New Jersey, 1920.

20. Case H-60-186, New Jersey, 1920.

21. Case Z-60-202, New Jersey, 1920.

22. Case H-60-215, New Jersey, 1920.

Copyright Information

Salmon, Marylynn. "Women and Property in South Carolina: The Evidence from Marriage Settlements, 1730 to 1830." *William and Mary Quarterly* 39 (October 1982): 655-685. ©Professor Marylynn Salmon, Smith College, Northampton, MA, USA.

Censer, Jane Turner. "'Smiling Through Her Tears': Ante-Bellum Southern Women and Divorce. "*American Journal of Legal History* 25 (January 1981): 24-47. ©*American Journal of Legal History*, Temple University School of Law, Philadelphia, Pennsylvania, USA.

Boatwright, Eleanor M. "The Political and Civil Status of Women in Georgia, 1783-1860." *The Georgia Historical Quarterly* 25:4 (December 1941): 301-324. ©*The Georgia Historical Quarterly*, The University of Georgia, Athens, Georgia, USA.

Goodheart, Lawrence B., Neil Hanks, and Elizabeth Johnson."'An Act for the Relief of Females . . .': Divorce and the Changing Legal Status of Women in Tennessee, 1796-1860." *Tennessee Historical Quarterly* 44 (Fall and Winter 1985) Part I: 318-39 and Part II: 402-416. ©Tennessee Historical Society, Nashville, Tennessee, USA.

Moncrief, Sandra. "The Mississippi Married Women's Property Act of 1839." *Journal of Mississippi History* 47:2 (May 1985): 110-125. "Reprinted with the permission of the Mississippi Department of Archives and History, the Mississippi Historical Society," Jackson, Mississippi, USA, and the author.

Basch, Norma. "Invisible Women: The Legal Fiction of Marital Unity in Nineteenth-Century America." *Feminist Studies* 5:2 (Summer 1979): 346-66. ©by Feminist Studies, Inc., Women's Studies Program, University of Maryland, College Park, Maryland, USA.

Chused, Richard H. "Married Women's Property Law, 1800-1850." *The Georgetown Law Journal* 71:5 (June 1983): 1359-1425. ©Richard H. Chused, Georgetown University Law Center, Washington, District of Columbia, USA.

Lebsock, Suzanne D. "Radical Reconstruction and the Property Rights of Southern Women." *Journal of Southern History* 43:2 (May 1977): 195-216. ©*Journal of Southern History*, Southern Historical Association, Athens, Georgia, USA.

Griswold, Robert L. "Apart but not Adrift: Wives, Divorce, and Independence in California, 1850-1890." *Pacific Historical Review* 49:2 (May 1980): 265-283. "©1980 by The Pacific Coast Branch, American Historical Association. Reprinted from Pacific Historical Review, Vol. 49, No. 2 (May 1980), pp. 265-283 by permission" of the Association and the author.

Griswold, Robert L. "Law, Sex, Cruelty, and Divorce in Victorian America, 1840-1900." *American Quarterly* 38 (Winter 1986): 721-45. "© 1973, 1985, 1986, 1965, 1966, 1981, 1982, 1980, 1979, 1967, 1974, American Studies Association, Washington, D.C., USA." Reprinted with permission of the Association and the author.

Grossberg, Michael. "Who Gets the Child? Custody, Guardianship, and the Rise of a Judicial Patriarchy in Nineteenth-Century America." *Feminist Studies* 9:2 (Summer 1983): 235-260. ©by Feminist Studies, Inc.,Women's Studies Program, University of Maryland, College Park, Maryland, USA.

Chused, Richard H. "Late Nineteenth-Century Married Women's Property Law: Reception of the Early Married Women's Property Acts by Courts and Legislatures." *American Journal of Legal History* 29 (January 1985): 3-35. ©*American Journal of Legal History*, Temple University School of Law, Philadelphia, Pennsylvania, USA.

Weisbrod, Carol, and Pamela Sheingorn. "Reynolds v. United States: Nineteenth-Century Forms of Marriage and the Status of Women." *Connecticut Law Review* 10:4 (Summer 1978): 828-858. ©*Connecticut Law Review*, University of Connecticut School of Law, Hartford, Connecticut, USA. Reprinted with permission of the Review and the authors.

O'Neill, William L. "Divorce in the Progressive Era. "*American Quarterly* 17:2, Part 1 (Summer 1965): 203-217. "© 1973, 1985, 1986, 1965, 1966, 1981, 1982, 1980, 1979, 1967, 1974, American Studies Association, Washington, D.C., USA." Reprinted with permission of the Association and the author.

May, Elaine Tyler. "The Pressure to Provide: Class, Consumerism, and Divorce in Urban America, 1880-1920." *Journal of Social History* 12:2 (Winter

1978): 180-193. ©*Journal of Social History*, Carnegie-Mellon University Press, Pittsburgh, Pennsylvania, USA.

Index

Bei Fragen zur Produktsicherheit wenden Sie sich bitte an:
If you have any questions regarding product safety,
please contact:

Walter de Gruyter GmbH
Genthiner Straße 13
10785 Berlin
productsafety@degruyterbrill.com